Boxing in New M
1868–1940

Boxing in New Mexico, 1868–1940

CHRIS COZZONE *and* JIM BOGGIO

Foreword by BRUCE TRAMPLER

McFarland & Company, Inc., Publishers

Jefferson, North Carolina, and London

All photographs are from the collection
of Chris Cozzone unless indicated otherwise.

LIBRARY OF CONGRESS CATALOGUING-IN-PUBLICATION DATA

Boxing in New Mexico, 1868–1940 / Chris Cozzone and
Jim Boggio ; foreword by Bruce Trampler.
p.   cm.
Includes bibliographical references and index.

ISBN 978-0-7864-6828-7
softcover : acid free paper ∞

1. Boxing — New Mexico — History.   2. Boxers
(Sports) — New Mexico — History.   3. New Mexico —
Social life and customs.   I. Title.
GV1125.C69 2013   796.8309789 — dc23   2012049774

BRITISH LIBRARY CATALOGUING DATA ARE AVAILABLE

On the cover: the Feb. 17, 1894, battle between Southwest star "Australian"
Billy Smith (center) and Dave Flaherty (left) went 32 rounds before Smith
knocked out the lighter Flaherty (Chris Cozzone Collection)

Manufactured in the United States of America

*McFarland & Company, Inc., Publishers
Box 611, Jefferson, North Carolina 28640
www.mcfarlandpub.com*

For the late Jim Boggio.
And the hundreds of named and nameless boxing
scribes who captured the action.

— Chris Cozzone

Table of Contents

Foreword
by Bruce Trampler

To appreciate the fighting men and women of New Mexico, one has to first have a sense of the state itself. New Mexico is a rugged land, ranking fifth in geographic size but only thirty-sixth in population. It is hard, lonely country, with more than 120,000 square miles of desert, mountains, and grasslands stretching from the Mexico border north to the Colorado state line, bounded on the west by Arizona and to the east by Texas.

Albuquerque, the largest city, sits one mile above sea level, where interstate highways 40 and 25 intersect. It is home to the University of New Mexico and boasts the state's only international airport. Santa Fe, the state capital of New Mexico, lies an hour to the north. In the southern part of the state, Las Cruces and New Mexico State University are less than an hour's drive from El Paso, on the western edge of Texas.

New Mexico has been inhabited for more than 10,000 years. Native American warriors from several tribes occupied its lands for eons until 1540, when the first non–Indian explorers ventured into the region searching for gold. Half the state's population — more than two million people — is Hispanic.

New Mexico's frontier wilderness was home to many of the Western characters in the writings of Louis L'Amour. In reality, it is the birthplace of gunfighter Billy the Kid and explorer Kit Carson. New Mexico is also home to racecar drivers Al and Bobby Unser, as well as champion prizefighters Johnny Tapia, Danny Romero, and Hall of Fame boxing king Bob Foster.

Much of the state is rural and devoid of people. The Rio Grande river flows south from Colorado through the length of New Mexico until it turns east near Las Cruces and enters Texas. Indeed, the entire territory was considered part of Mexico until the end of the Mexican-American War in 1848, after General Stephen Kearny captured the pueblo of Santa Fe in 1846 without firing a shot and declared New Mexico to be part of the United States.

Statehood did not follow until 1912, but even then, trouble flared. Pancho Villa raided Columbus, N.M., in 1916, during the Great War. U.S. troops not deployed in Europe were sent to New Mexico to contain the invading force.

The world's first atomic bomb was detonated at a nuclear test site near Alamogordo in 1945, shortly before the U.S. launched its nuclear attack on Japanese cities in an effort to bring World War II to a halt. Since then, New Mexico has prospered as industries and small businesses found their way into the Land of Enchantment. Tourism, with the fabled Carlsbad Caverns and the White Sands desert monument, along with the purported UFO landing in Roswell and New Mexico's ruggedly beautiful geography, has brought millions of visitors to the state.

There remains a strong fighting spirit in New Mexico that manifested itself inside box-ing rings in dozens of towns for a century and a half. Beginning with bareknuckle matches in 1868, Chris Cozzone (a Chicago native whose inner muse answered the allure of New Mexico) spent countless hours that turned into months, and then into years, researching anonymous and unheralded gladiators who answered the bell in previously unrecorded and undocumented fights that never made it into boxing's record books.

New Mexico's prizefighters battled for a dozen decades under hot suns, wearing worn-out boxing gloves and fighting in rings with little or no padding on the floor. Medical supervision was often non-existent. It is only in the last 50 years or so that the fight game in Cozzone's adopted state has caught up with civilization. That world champions Foster, Tapia, and Romero called New Mexico home is a claim which neighboring states such as Nevada, Arizona, Colorado, or Utah can't match.

A good man named Jim Boggio, once an Albuquerque TV sportscaster, began this book. Before he was cruelly taken by cancer, Jim handed off his passion project to one of the most qualified historians in the country. Cozzone was there to carry on after Boggio was forced to stop.

Their book recounts the history of New Mexico's boxers, many of whom would be unknown to fight fans today. Cozzone and Boggio give proper recognition to thousands of prizefights never before listed, and, in the process, unearth fascinating facts about New Mexico's storied history. Dozens of towns hosted bouts, and the men who fought them are brought to life by world champion authors Cozzone and Boggio.

It's a knockout of a book, and the winners are we, the readers.

Bruce Trampler has been involved in boxing as an amateur fighter, trainer, manager, publicist, promoter, ring announcer and matchmaker since the late 1960s. Working under the Top Rank banner since 1981, Trampler has orchestrated the careers of some of the modern era's greatest, including Floyd Mayweather, Jr., Oscar De La Hoya and Michael Carbajal. He is a 2010 inductee into the International Boxing Hall of Fame.

Preface
by Chris Cozzone

The book's gotten bigger than I originally intended.
—Jim Boggio, 1994[1]

Got to admit, if I had a time machine, I'd squander its use on prizefighting.

I've been lucky enough to get a spot on the apron in some of the biggest fights in the last decade, but to be at the ring for Zale-Graziano, Ali-Frazier, Gans-Nelson or Dempsey-Willard ... how can you beat *that*?

If my time machine was limited to New Mexico, my first stop would be the first known prize fight in 1868. I'd watch Jim Flynn headbutt his way to a loss against Jack Johnson in Las Vegas in 1912, then spend the year at the Alvarado in Albuquerque to witness the arrival of Benny Chavez at the Elks'. I'd come back a decade later to see Eddie Mack battle Jose Rivers at the Rialto in Santa Fe. I'd watch Billy Firpo batter Lew Jenkins at Silver City, then Benny Cordova and Bobby Waugh smack each other senseless in the sleeting rain at the Smelter Arena.... I probably wouldn't come back, for there are far too many fights, too many decades, to choose from.

But I *do* now where I'd make my final stop. The year would be 1997, and, no, it wouldn't be to see Johnny Tapia and Danny Romero in their long-awaited showdown, but to drink a beer and talk boxing all night with an old friend I'd never had the honor of meeting. The same year that saw Tapia-Romero saw the passing away of Jim Boggio. Ironically, it was also the first year I covered my first prizefight. It's entirely fitting that the year Jim departed would be one in which I'd arrived.

My subject matter has always been gritty — gangbangers, prisons and junkies — so it's no surprise to most that I gravitated toward a sport that can only be described as representing a dichotomy of everything that is ugly, and everything that is beautiful. While living in New York City, I covered my first fight in 1997 at the famous Blue Horizon in Philadelphia. It was purely a part-time endeavor, at least until I moved back to New Mexico, just one month before 2000. It's been full-time since then — about 40 shows a year, if not more.

I've been lucky enough to sit ringside at the biggest fights of the past 12 years. I've been spit on (accidentally) by Oscar De La Hoya and bled on by Manny Pacquiao. I've written about and photographed over 500 shows, as of 2011.

I've been even more fortunate in having covered over a full decade of New Mexico boxing, which is the reason for this book. In between the mega-fights in Las Vegas — Nevada, that is — I've captured the images and chronicled the ups and downs of an entire era. It's been quite a ride ... and quite an obsession.

Once you get immersed into a region of boxing, there's nothing like watching its champions and youngsters rise in the ranks — and nothing quite as heartbreaking as seeing one fail. I started the website NewMexicoBoxing.com to give the sport a home. After a year or two, I started to wonder. Who came before Tapia? Romero? I knew about Bob Foster, the former light-heavyweight champion of the world, one of the greatest in his division ever — but who was there before *that*?

I started to dig. I went to the library to dig up old articles on microfilm. What I found was enough to start thinking about a book project. I talked to the old-timers, like Stan Gallup, now deceased, who told me what others were telling me: "Jim was writing a book on New Mexico boxing."

Jim? Jim who?

I hadn't been in the New Mexico boxing scene long enough to know Jim Boggio. But word was that he'd been working on a book, off and on, for at least a decade. Jim had died before he could finish. Like myself, Jim had been an out-of-state transplant with a background in journalism, who fell in love with the sport in New Mexico. In his final years, before losing his battle with cancer at the young age of 54, Jim had been the chairman for the New Mexico Athletic Commission. It's very doubtful that Johnny Tapia would've ever been able to get a license after his fall from grace in the early '90s, if it wasn't for Jim.

I could keep digging around on my own, or, as advised, I could track down Jim's widow, Mary Ann, which I did. After a couple of meetings, I had "inherited" Jim's project, which included boxes and boxes of books and a manuscript.

The plan was to finish up Jim's book. It seemed easy enough. My predecessor had logged in 423 fight cards that had taken place between 1868 and 1997. I figured I'd sift through the boxes, the notes, the manuscript, and, in six or 12 months, crank out a crisp version ready for publication.

That was seven years ago.

Jim's "fight log" that had numbered 423, now numbers over 2,400 shows, 1868 to the present.

Though Jim had the key players right, there'd been a lot missing — through no fault of his own. It goes back to something Jim told the *Albuquerque Journal*'s Toby Smith when he was being interviewed, in 1994, about the book getting bigger than he'd meant it to be.

Jim had spent more than 10 years compiling information; I added seven more, cranking through just about every existing roll of microfilm that exists for New Mexico newspapers, not to mention those from El Paso, Colorado and others areas that are relevant. In hindsight, a lot of it was overkill, but the road was every bit as important as the destination, which you hold in your mitts.

I'm confident that Jim and I, working as tag-team boxing scribes, have accomplished what we set out to do. This has always been about setting the record straight, digging up the past, and celebrating what's been forgotten — the people, the places, the land, of New Mexico.

Oftentimes the underdog in its cyclical battles with the law, public opinion and racial tension, boxing in New Mexico has paralleled the state's struggles and glories through the Wild West, statehood, the Depression, world war and economic growth. The forgotten history of boxing in New Mexico is less about a sport than it is about boomtowns and ghost towns, the railroad and mines, race and politics and casinos. It's a story that includes every city, town and pueblo of the state, from Tucumcari to Gallup, Columbus to Raton, Albuquerque to Acoma.

And it's about people. Individuals.

This tome you have in your hand, for that's what it is, has been crammed tight with the generations of barrio-bred homeboys, cowboys, laborers and miners who laced on a pair of Sol Levinsons — or fought bareknuckle — through the decades for, or in, New Mexico.

Just as I hope to honor the best boxing buddy I've never had — Jim, of course — the two of us, in turn, honor the hundreds of writers who came before us. Without the scribes, those hunched over typewriters or pads of paper at ringside in the smoke-filled opera houses, or outside in the ghastly gales of wind at the open-air Smelter Arena, there would be *nada*.

There are also those who enabled the work to be completed. The Office of the State Historian was a tremendous resource, as was the staff at the State Records Center and Archives in Santa Fe. Fellow boxing historians — namely, Hall-of-Famer Bruce Trampler, with his parallel research in Nevada and Arizona — kept me motivated. Colleague Colleen Aycock gets a big thanks for including my piece on early New Mexican black fighters in her anthology.

The biggest motivators, as I'm sure Jim would agree, have always been the fighters. The guts and gusto, the triumphs and the heartbreakers, I've seen over the years, watching "kids" grow up in the ring, turning into champs or warhorses, have rubbed off.

This one's for all of you.

Keep the gloves up.

1. Bareknuckle, 1868

Strange we never heard of the big prize fight recorded here.
—*Santa Fe New Mexican*, 1868[1]

No one knew about it.

No one *would* have known about it, either, had not a loudmouth reporter come upon the scene on his way north through New Mexico, on the fateful day of June 26, 1868.

Charles Johnson, a reporter with the *Denver News*, was traveling back home when, 35 miles north of Albuquerque, most likely in the vicinity of La Bojada Hill, he spotted a large group of men alongside the road. Johnson slowed down his horse and, recognizing one of the men, approached.

"What's going on?" he asked.

"Prize fight," was the answer. The group—in London, such a gathering of fight fans would've been called "The Fancy"—were awaiting the arrival of one of the fighters. "Jack" was already on the scene, sitting in a horse-drawn ambulance while the gathering awaited the arrival of "Duffey," his opponent, later discovered to be well-known Colorado pugilist *Barney* Duffey.

Bets were high, Johnson was told, in total around $5,000. Piqued by curiosity, Johnson decided to watch. If he hadn't, what just might have been New Mexico's first official prize fight never would have made it to print.

Johnson wrote: "They fought 185 rounds, occupying six hours and 19 minutes. The left side of Duffey's head was fearfully swollen, his left eye closed, his right eye nearly so, two ribs broken, and his left arm useless. Jack's head was all cut to pieces. He was totally blind the last two rounds, his nose knocked on the left side of his face, three teeth knocked out, two ribs broken and his left arm useless. He presented a horrible appearance. He died 10 minutes after the fight was over."[2]

The apparent winner, Duffey, was also carried from the scene while Johnson was asked to keep quiet about the "strictly private fight," at least until the surviving prizefighter was able to travel.[3] "I should not have written about this," wrote Johnson, adding that he was only doing so due to the "fatal termination" of one of the pugilists.[4]

New Mexico had entered the prizefighting business.

Barney Duffey

Barney maintained an appearance of great meekness, and said he would never fight again, and would even never again put on the gloves to spar.
—*Cleveland Plain Dealer*, 1867[5]

7

It was a tough time to be a pugilist.

Though the Queensberry Rules had already been penned, by the ninth Marquess of Queensberry in England, calling for gloves, three-minute rounds and the 10-count, while banning wrestling moves, spiked shoes and hugging, it would be a couple more decades before the rules were accepted by pugdom.

In the meantime, bouts were bareknuckle fights to the finish under the London Prize Rules of 1743. Under the long-running London rules, a round ended when a man hit the ground, be it by punch or throw. A downed fighter had 30 seconds to "come to scratch," that is, return to the center of the ring where a line had been etched into the ground. The match would continue until a fighter could no longer perform, whether it happened in one round or a hundred, and whether the fight was over in one minute or six hours and 19 — as in the case of Duffey vs. Jack.

The official record, actually, for the longest bareknuckle fight is a six hour and 15-minute match fought in Melbourne, Australia, on Oct. 19, 1856, between James Kelly and Jack Smith. If Charles Johnson's account is accurate, the 1868 prize fight between Duffey and Jack in New Mexico has that beat by four minutes. It's only the obscurity and single source of the New Mexico fight that keeps it out of the record books.

Duffey vs. Jack also did not get the attention that a higher caliber fight like Kelly-Smith received; in the Wild West, it would never have been known at all if it weren't for Johnson. As it was, it was neatly swept under the rug of history.

Given the enormous amount of damage a fighter could sustain fighting under the London Prize Rules, it wasn't surprising to hear of a death in the ring. Unlike the boxers of the sport's Golden Age, decades later, prizefighters fought infrequently, spending most of the time recovering between fights. Ten to 20 bouts marked a war-horse veteran — as did a relatively low life expectancy, most fighters becoming shambling hulks in their 30s.

Barney Duffey was a fluke, however. By the time he fought "Jack," he was 39 years old and the veteran of 20-something fights. His tale, pieced together through fight accounts before and after the Civil War, in which he fought for the Union, tells the tale of the era's prizefighters.

For the two decades prior to 1868, America had been invaded by a multitude of pugilists from across the Pond, namely English and Irish toughs who were seeking a fresh market, only to find an American audience less-than-accepting and local law enforcement less-than-friendly. Fights were continually broken up and fighters arrested, calling for matches to be made in hard-to-get-to places, such as islands and barges where local jurisdiction would not impose.

While foreign pugs and prizefighting, in general, gained attention, it wasn't until Americans battled their way to prominence that the sport began to take off in the U.S. The 1849 battle for the heavyweight championship of America, between Yankee Sullivan, of Ireland, and Tom "Young American" Hyer, of New York, in which Hyer stopped Sullivan after 16 rounds and 17-plus minutes, pushed the sport to a new level. After Hyer retired and Sullivan took it upon himself to reclaim the championship, along came John "Old Smoke" Morrissey. In 1853, Morrissey won a controversial decision over Sullivan when, after 37 rounds and 55 minutes, he was awarded the fight on a foul.

Morrissey became one of the most famous men in America, until 1858, when John C. Heenan, nicknamed the "Benecia Boy" from his hometown in California, met the champ in Canada for $10,000 a side. He was knocked out in 10 rounds, but the loss — and his performance — skyrocketed Heenan to stardom when Morrissey refused the rematch and retired.

Taking up the mantle of American champion, Heenan went to England and fought the British champ, Tom Sayers, in what was the first international championship — for all practical purposes, the first *world* championship — in 1860. The fight was called a draw, when, after 42 rounds and over two hours of brutality, a near-riot brought the bout to sudden end. There was no rematch. Both Sayers and Heenan were awarded championship belts and were celebrated as heroes by their respective countries.

Hyer, Morrissey and Heenan were big names, big news of the era, but England's ban on boxing caught on as the sport grew. Staging fights became a game of evading the law and finding safe havens on the East Coast — that is, until the Civil War brought an end to big name fights.

As disrupting as war can be for what was considered a pastime, the Civil War actually helped package prizefighting due to a series of informal matches staged in camps. When the war ended, the sport picked up where it had left off, though fighters — in the form of veterans, settlers, immigrants and gold miners — trekked westward.

Before New Mexico added its name to the list, for a very brief time in 1868, mining towns in Colorado, the Dakotas, Idaho, Montana and Nevada became informal fight centers.

In the Southwest, Colorado could boast the first territorial champion, the self-proclaimed "Champion of the West," John Condle Orem, known in the fight game as "Con Orem."

Though an Englishman from Ohio, Orem found his way west as a miner, blacksmith, saloonkeeper and pugilist, fighting as early as 1863 and still doing exhibitions 20 years later. His most famous fight was a 185-round fight in 1865 against Hugh O'Neill in the gold-mining town of Virginia City, Montana, for the supposed middleweight championship of America. Thirty years old, standing but 5'6" and weighing 138 pounds, Orem gave up an astounding 52 pounds to O'Neill, as the two fought for three hours and five minutes, over 185 rounds, before the fight was declared a draw due to darkness. Orem was the stuff of legends.

Barney Duffey was not.

Strictly club level, though a recognizable name in sporting circles through the states and territories, Duffey, originally a trunk maker, fought before, during and after the Civil War, from the East Coast to the Midwest, landing in the Colorado Territory after dashing out of Detroit on a burglary and larceny charge in 1865.

In 1867, Duffey had two notable fights, one in August, the second in December — but it's the former that has significance to New Mexico. In June, Duffey agreed to fight John H. Shanssey of Baltimore, for $1,000 a side, the place to be determined (somewhere in Colorado) and the date tentatively set for the Fourth of July. After much wrangling, the fight took place on August 5, somewhere near the intersection of Arapahoe and Jefferson counties.

The *Rocky Mountain News* called both pugilists "modest professionals," with Duffey a veteran of several encounters (actually it was closer to 20) and Shanssey a newcomer, having had one previous fight — a 28-round stoppage over Johnny Martin in Baltimore two years before. While Duffey had the experience, Shanssey had youth and weight: 140 pounds to Duffey's 135, and 21 years of age to Duffey's 38. Both were Civil War veterans, Shanssey having fought for the Confederacy and Duffey for the Union. It was also a classic match-up for the era for another reason: Duffey was an Englishman and Shanssey, an Irishman.[6]

In front of several hundred spectators, the two threw their hats into the ring around 4 P.M. Shanssey scored first blood when he "levied a paister on Barney's potato trap" though

Duffey scored the first knockdown with a body shot. The fight went back and forth for several rounds, the two punishing one another severely. By the 20th round, it was apparent that Duffey's experience was getting the best of Shanssey — that is, until Duffey dislocated his left shoulder in the 22nd round. Shanssey remained competitive until the 26th frame, when, after 44 minutes of fighting, Duffey's corner "threw the sponge aloft," giving the Baltimore kid his second win.[7]

Despite the injury, Duffey could not have suffered too much additional damage for he was back in the ring in November, having agreed to fight Michael (Jack) Ryan, a local painter by trade, in, or near, Cleveland. On Nov. 25, the two met at the Berea train station (14 miles from Cleveland) where they trekked a half-mile away to further elude any law officials on their trail.

Ryan appeared on his way to a victory when, after 77 rounds lasting an hour and 15 minutes, a Cleveland police squad, summoned by telegraph from the desperate mayor of Berea, broke up the party. Ryan, unmarked from the battle, fled in his fighting togs and Duffey, "dreadfully punished," was arrested.[8]

Wire reports ran across the country, but it was the follow-up stories printed in the *Cleveland Plain Dealer* that were the most interesting. The day after the fight, the *Plain Dealer* not only ran a round-by-round account of the battle, but a story with the headline "A Disgusted Pugilist's Wife," in which Duffey's wife, sickened by her husband's behavior, paid him a visit in the local slammer.[9]

> Barney stood before her, with his gashed and battered face, hanging his head, and looking as sheepish as possible. Mrs. Duffy eyed him contemptuously for a time and then, walking around him, and eying him from head to foot exclaimed: "Who are you? Is this Barney Duffy? Nice looking man ain't you? A disgrace to your family and children. You ought to be arrested; and you ought to be made an example of. Presume you'll do the same thing again. I see your name now, around town, on those nasty sparring posters." Barney maintained an appearance of great meekness, and said he would never fight again, and would even never again put on the gloves to spar.[10]

Two months later, Duffey was back in the ring, losing to Teddy Smith in Virginia City, Montana, after 62 rounds in a fight that might've been fixed — a "frame-up" in the era's sporting vernacular. This time, Duffey took more time off before he returned to the ring — at least, as far as anyone knows — when he found himself in New Mexico fighting the fight of his life.

Ironically, the one fight that would have guaranteed Duffey a place in the annals of prizefighting would've been his fight to the death with Jack — a fighter whose identity went to the grave with him, wherever that grave might be, somewhere between New Mexico and Colorado, no doubt.

Surprisingly, the fight received very little attention, and though it had taken place on June 26, it wasn't until July 16 that the *Santa Fe New Mexican* printed word. By then, both, the *Denver News* (June 28) and *Rocky Mountain News* (July 9) had already published accounts, by way of *News* reporter Johnson. Under the bold headline "A Man Killed in Prize Fight," the editor of the *New Mexican* wrote:

> Strange we never heard of the big prize fight here recorded, especially if the "thirty-five miles from Albuquerque" extended in this direction, which would place the scene of the battle within about ten leagues of Santa Fe. A friend tells me that traveling along the road the other day Albuquerque-wards he noticed "about thirty-five miles" this side of there, a spot on the roadside very muchly torn up, the grassy prairie having been very roughly used and some blood and hairs and coat tails and shoe heels and so forth scattered around. This was doubtless the scene of the conflict. We

know Charles Johnson to be the son of old Mr. and Mrs. Johnson and therefore consider his account perfectly reliable, though we don't endorse it at all at all.[11]

The *Rocky Mountain News* took offense at the *New Mexican's* editorial slur, retaliated by assuring those "incredulous cusses" that their news was, indeed, correct and that they "may take one at the [Hotel] Fonda on our account."[12]

Not another word appeared about the fight.

But, just a week later, on July 31, there was another fight on New Mexico soil to report.

Elizabethtown and Shanssey

> *After the twenty-sixth round and forty-four minutes fighting, Duffy's second sent the sponge aloft, and Shanssey seized the colors. But, pshaw! You or I, outside the ropes, can tell nothing as to results, on the turf or in the prize ring. And well for us both that it is so. The chances and contests in horse-flesh and humanity, gaming or getting office, is a matter to which mortal science is a stranger.*
> — *Rocky Mountain News*, 1867[13]

Long before New Mexico was a big, dry, windy state, it was a big, dry, windy *territory*. In 1868, the territory boasted just over 90,000 people and 57,000 head of cattle. Like most of the country, New Mexico was recovering from the effects of the Civil War and it would be another 10 or more years before the railroads would reach the territory, bringing with them jobs and settlers. In the meantime, settlers struggled with Indians and New Mexico remained the Wild West.

One town that was prospering was Elizabethtown in northern New Mexico. In 1866, traces of gold were found in the area by a party of copper prospectors. Quickly, Elizabethtown became the center of the area's mining district, and the Moreno Mines became the most prosperous.

On July 26, just one month after Duffey and Jack pummeled each other in a fight to the death, Shanssey — the Baltimore youngster who'd beaten Duffey one year before — threw his hat into a ring staged near the Moreno Mines. Word reached the *New Mexican*:

A prize fight for $500 a side took place to-day between Shaugnessy [*sic*] and James, in which the former was victorious. Twenty-five rounds were fought in about thirty minutes, at the end of which time James "caved" and threw up the sponge. Considerable interest was manifested, and a large crowd gathered from the mines to witness the encounter, which, however, proved to be quite uninteresting, as Shaugnessy had the best of it from the start, and won his victory with but little effort. Neither of the men were badly injured, and the day wound up with a few rough and tumble fights, a dance, a tight rope performance, and equally innocent and refreshing Sunday afternoon recreations.[14]

No doubt, there were other prize fights that never made it to print; or those that did, disappearing with newspapers that never made it to microfilm. In fact, there is, virtually, *no* mention of local prizefighting during the next 12 years in New Mexico.

For a time, at least in Colorado papers, there was talk of a rematch between Duffey and Shanssey, but there is no reason to believe it was pulled off. As for Duffey and Shanssey? One fighter followed a downward spiral, resulting in a violent death, one year later, while the other became a living legend of the Wild West.

By November 1868, Duffey was back in trouble, getting arrested for arson in Pittsburgh, where he relocated, apparently separated from his family. There is one mention of a match Duffey was involved in, during 1869, in Virginia City, but, on Sept. 11, Duffey fought his last fight.

In a Pittsburgh saloon, Duffey met with Thomas Sullivan, also a prizefighter of local repute who'd nearly killed a previous opponent in the ring two years before. When an argument broke out, Sullivan pulled out a knife and stabbed Duffey, who, clutching his injury, ran to the streets in order to escape. Sullivan pursued, knocking Duffey down outside. After pounding him in the face with a rock several times, Sullivan finished the job with his blade, before making his escape. He was arrested later that day but was able to escape, at least for another day or so, during which time Duffey died from his wounds.

In stark contrast, Shanssey's story isn't quite as tragic, probably because his prizefighting career soon came to a close. Just a couple months before his former nemesis was brutally murdered, Shanssey stepped into the ring for the last time, against one of the best fighters of the era, Mike Donovan.

Donovan had turned to boxing after marching with General Sherman through Georgia during the Civil War. His lengthy career in the prize ring — from 1866 to 1896 — made him an American legend. Not only did Donovan fight for the American middleweight championship, losing to W. C. McClellan, but he stepped into the ring twice against the great John L. Sullivan and, afterward, became the long-running boxing instructor of the prestigious New York Athletic Club.

Donovan had an easy time with Shanssey when the two fought on July 4, 1869, in a bout refereed by legendary lawman Wyatt Earp before 3,000 people. Shanssey received such a beating that he never fought again.

Instead, Shanssey went into the saloon business, retaining a friendship with Wyatt Earp. In fact, it was at Shanssey's Bee Hive Saloon, in Fort Griffin, Texas, that the former prizefighter introduced Earp to another Wild West legend, Doc Holliday, ten years after Shanssey's fight in Elizabethtown, in 1878. What followed Earp's introduction to Holliday is legendary, and depicted in dozens of movies and books released on the so-called "Gunfight at the O.K. Corral"— Shanssey's character plays a noticeable part in film and fiction.

Shanssey's tale does not end there. He went on to operate a succession of saloons throughout Texas until settling down in Yuma, Arizona, in 1899. There, Shanssey was elected mayor, serving several terms before retiring in 1910. Thereafter, he became the Yuma County supervisor, holding that post until he passed away in a Los Angeles hospital in 1917.

2. Prizefighting Arrives, 1880s

Albuquerque is to have a prize fight for a purse of $200. The affair is to come off in about a week, within ten miles of the city.... And still we are told that Albuquerque is a city of culture, etc.

— *Santa Fe New Mexican,* 1882[1]

As quick as it had arrived in 1868, prizefighting left.

While there was a "free sparring match" on the Plaza in Santa Fe, on July 30, 1872, between a couple of local aspirants named "Nunez" and "Abe,"[2] there was, virtually, no action throughout the territory for an entire decade — as far as was reported on, that is. Albuquerque had occasional foot races, Santa Fe had regular cock fights and Las Vegas even tried its hand at bull fights, but the only printed references to the squared circle were those that took place *outside* New Mexico.

Nationwide, it was a transitional time for prizefighting. The barbaric accounts of bareknuckle matches had kept the sport from reaching its potential with the general American public. "Gypsy" Jem Mace had arrived from overseas in 1869, becoming a big name in the early part of the decade before returning to England. In 1876, when he returned to America, it was as a gloved fighter.

By the 1880s, Queensberry rules were becoming the norm and all the sport needed was a champion. John L. Sullivan, "The Boston Strong Boy," became just that, dominating the decade and transitioning the sport from bareknuckle into the era of gloved champions.

It was a combination of both the more palatable Queensberry version of prizefighting and the railroads that would forever cement the manly art of self defense to New Mexico.

By 1881, railways had zipped across the territory, bringing with them a wave of immigrants, miners, cattlemen and entrepreneurs. Albuquerque and Las Vegas became railway centers and mining towns sprang up across the state, from Raton to Gallup to Silver City. Where there were boomtowns and developing cities, there were saloons, gamblers, gunmen, prostitutes, and, of course, prizefighters.

Because New Mexico was a territory, there were no formal laws prohibiting prizefighting. That did not stop territorial law officials, citing a disturbance of the peace, from stopping a prize fight, however.

On the other hand, even when prize fights *were* deemed illegal, they still continued. Case in point: Colorado. Before 1876, when Colorado was a territory and prize fights were, *technically* legal, fights were staged whether the police hounded the sporting fraternity or not. When Colorado became a state, on Aug. 1, 1876, very little changed, other than the law. In 1877, a law was passed prohibiting prize fights in the state of Colorado and anyone engaging in such, promoters included, was subject to a year in prison and a $1,000 fine. Despite the edict, prize fights continued to be staged regularly.

Sometimes, New Mexico, destined for a rough start in prizefighting, was used as a decoy.

Beginning in 1880, newspapers throughout Colorado, and as far west as San Francisco, started to print word about an upcoming match to be arranged between Colorado fighters John Murphy, of Leadville, and Irishman Bryan Campbell, now of Denver, a ten-bout veteran launching a comeback after an inactive decade. (Campbell was best known for his brutal, 99-round, one-and-a-half hour win by disqualification over "Bendless" Dave Lewis, in 1870 in Pennsylvania.[3]) The location went from "some point in New Mexico"[4] to "the little station of Raton, formerly Willow Springs, New Mexico," with a fight date of Sept. 21, 1880.[5]

Unfortunately, Raton, a railroad point and thriving mining town, became the laughingstock of the prize fight community when, despite the $1,000 purse and the championship of Colorado at stake, Campbell refused to come to scratch due to weight differences — Campbell weighed 129 and Murphy 131. Although the agreement was to come in under 132, the two-pound "disadvantage" was too much for Campbell, who "sported with whisky in a jug" while making his objections. "Such foolishness is rarely witnessed," wrote the reporter at hand.[6]

The fight received the criticism of well-respected Frank Queen, editor of the *New York Clipper,* a paper known for its advocacy of prizefighting. "The articles of agreement should have designated a certain time and place for the principals to weigh, on the same scales and in the presence of each other, which would have obviated all difficulty," wrote Queen. "Under the circumstances the proper course to pursue is to arrange for another meeting, taking measures to prevent the recurrence of the former fiasco."[7]

The fight never did occur, in New Mexico or anywhere else, for that matter.

It would be another two years before the territory could organize another fight that attracted notice in the press.

Prizefighting Fever

> The latest "crank" in pugilism is "Hen" Smith, the heavyweight colored champion of New Mexico, who stands 5 feet 11¾ inches, and weighs 210 pounds. He has challenged Peter Jackson to fight in a 30 foot ring for $5,000 within 120 days. He says Jackson may name the place provided it is in America. Smith declares he has his money ready, and will deposit it in the First national bank of Albuquerque. A 30 foot ring and 120 days are novelties in championship fistic affairs.
>
> — *Cleveland Plain Dealer,* 1889[8]

Though the railroad boom might've paved the way for prizefighting in New Mexico, ultimately, it was John L. Sullivan who should really be credited. On Feb. 7, 1882, "The Boston Strong Boy" became, for all practical purposes, the world heavyweight champion when he defeated Paddy Ryan at Mississippi City, Mississippi, with a ninth-round knockout.

Prizefighting fever swept across America — and throughout New Mexico.

On Feb. 28, 1882, Albuquerque, destined to become the fight capital of New Mexico, landed its first fight. "The prize fight between Sullivan and Ryan has caused a pugilistic mania to spring up all over the country and Albuquerque has her share of aspirants for honors in the ring," reported the *Albuquerque Daily Journal*. "The first fight took place near this city last night between Tom Sullivan and C. Weidner. Sullivan, unlike his namesake, threw up the sponge after the second round. He however, claims that his defeat was not fair, and has challenged the victor for another bout to take place to-night in the hall over Enright & Fahey's saloon. The fight will doubtless be stopped as proceedings of that kind will not be tolerated by the authorities."[9]

The writer was only partially correct. Rumors of prize fights found their way into local print, and in opinionated comments by disapproving editors. The *Santa Fe New Mexican* scoffed at hearing of a planned prize fight to occur in the Albuquerque area, in early May 1882: "And still we are told that Albuquerque is a city of culture, etc.," the paper wrote.[10]

There were also challengers — brazen ones like "Jerry the Slugger," whose challenge to none other than the great John L. was printed in the *Daily Journal*, perhaps for comic effect: "A challenge has been forwarded here by the friends of 'Jerry the Slugger' to John L. Sullivan, the champion, for a fight, to take place in the vicinity of Albuquerque, within three weeks after signing articles. That Jerry is a good man there is no question and a large amount of money is ready in this territory that he is a better man than the present champion...."[11]

The Slugger's next challenge made a reprint as far away as Dallas. Jerry was a bit more realistic, this time, but there is no record of the fight ever coming off anywhere in New Mexico:

> Jerry, the slugger, authorizes this paper to state that he accepts the challenge of Charles Gallagher to fight, according to the rules of the prize-ring, the fight to come off within three weeks from to-morrow, within twenty miles of this city, and has deposited $250 at Messrs. Connor & Walney's, which Mr. Gallagher will please cover to close match. This fight will no doubt come off, both men think they have muscle and skill; and are backed by numerous friends. If the "mill" takes place, it will no doubt be in the vicinity of Isleta, south of this city, and excursion trains will be run to accommodate those who delight in seeing affairs of this kind. Bets are even, at this date, between the men, and if the fight takes place, it will be a hard one.[12]

Big fights — even overblown regional matches — continued to evade small-time New Mexico.

Astonishingly, the reluctant, whiskey-drinking Bryan Campbell, once again, made news when it was announced, on March 6, 1882, that the Irishman would face Thomas Walling, of Oak Creek, Colorado, for $500 a side, to take place in New Mexico — that is, "if the New Mexican authorities do not prevent."[13] This time, the money was in the hands of the stakeholder, the famous Richard K. Fox, editor of the *National Police Gazette*, *The Ring* magazine of its time.

Ironically, for this match, Campbell, who'd squawked about giving up two pounds in the 1880 fiasco, was now giving up 15 against Walling, an 11-bout veteran, whose first ten had reportedly occurred across the Atlantic. In his one U.S. fight, Walling had defeated Dick Mullenger at Denver in 1877, after a punishing 57 rounds lasting two hours and 45 minutes.

The date of the fight was set for May 6, 1882, but the location was changed to Coal Creek, in Colorado, between Pueblo and Denver. But when the two met, they could not agree to the referee and the bout was again postponed for another month until the *Gazette's* Fox could name the place and referee. Once again, New Mexico was named as the site.

When the fight finally came off, several things had changed. No longer intending a bareknuckle fight, the two had now agreed to go at it wearing "hard kid gloves, skin fit,"[14] though London Prize Rules would govern the fight rather than the Queensberry rules that were starting to become fashionable. Now, the site was named as Pueblo, but when it finally happened, on June 28, the site would leapfrog across the country, from the Southwest to Pittsburgh to West Virginia, before the fighters boarded a midnight steamer headed for Greensboro, Pennsylvania. Campbell won the fight, by the way, defeating Walling after 30 rounds and 31 minutes. (Two years later, they rematched, this time in Denver, where Campbell won again, this time after 18 rounds.) Losing out on Campbell vs. Walling might've been a *good* thing for a territory hoping to score on prize-fight action, for the fight received national attention and public outrage.

Meanwhile, back in New Mexico, the fight scene was quietly on the rise. The town of Deming, which was growing as a railway center, reported a nondescript account of a 96-round prize fight lasting an hour, 25 minutes, in May 1882 in which "both fighters were badly battered."[15]

Back in Albuquerque, Charles Gallagher and Z. Hogan were noted as preparing for a fight that might or might not have ever happened and, in October, "an African and a Mexican did a pugilistic act in Jake Miller's saloon."[16]

Colorado enjoyed steady action, almost all fights requiring a chase game by local authorities. At least one fight named New Mexico as neutral-ground territory to stage a fight, but, once again, it was called off long before a date could be named.[17]

The following year, 1883, lacked any action, but at least two newspaper blurbs — one in Las Vegas, the other in Las Cruces — were hinting that *some* sort of action was taking place. In Las Vegas, there was an attempt to pair up two newspaper employees — Colonel Bartow of the *New Mexican* and the "colored engineer" of the *Albuquerque Journal*. "The *Gazette* stands ready to back Colonel Bartow for $100. Any person wishing to accept this bet will address the sporting editor Las Vegas *Gazette*."[18] Once again, there was no mention beyond the challenge, or "defi," as they were called.

In a letter printed in the *Rio Grande Republican*, a Rincon reader shared, "The pugilistic colored gent, mention of whom has been frequently made before, has quitted the town, and I am told is slinging the festive hash-dish in your city. Deal with him gently, for he was raised a pet, and is a shoulder-hitter besides."[19]

In 1884, however, New Mexico would have its most active fighting year of the decade, forever cementing the sport to the area.

Vegas Sparks a New Era

> *Two darkies had a mill with soft gloves on Centre street last night. One of them said, "Now don't hit hard," and was given a blow on the nose that brought a gush of claret. The nosey man staggered out determined to fight no more duels with boxing gloves.*
> — Las Vegas Daily Gazette, 1884[20]

Not exactly opening up the year with a bang, the above account of a prize fight, though slightly comical and somewhat racist, was typical of the era. It also heralded a sport that was no longer possible to ignore. No longer hiding from local police, the fight had been openly staged in downtown Las Vegas. It would be one of at least four bouts that took place there — and one of the known 15 staged across the territory during 1884.

Clearly showing a disdain for the sport, the *Gazette* continued to hurl editorial blows at the sport — whether fights were staged in Las Vegas, Raton or Silver City. In February, a fight between Tom Fields and John Hogan was summed up with one line: "Both were negroes and the fight was devoid of interest."[21] A few days later, again, not bothering to mention the principals in yet another Raton prize fight, the *Gazette's* editor wrote, "Another prize fight took place at Raton yesterday evening for $100 a side. 'How long, O, Lord, how long?'"[22] Four days later, when a fight was held in Silver City, the *Gazette* wrote: "When will such beastly conduct cease to be tolerated?"[23] Eventually, the editor caved in to public demand and, by May, the *Gazette* was diligently reporting the local prize fight scene.

Las Vegas had a good run in 1884, though fights were regularly staged in Raton, as well. Albuquerque, Carlisle, Deming, Lake Valley, Lordsburg, Silver City and Socorro also got in on the action. A new era had arrived in New Mexico.

"I can lick any man in the house," had been the boast of larger-than-life world champ John L. Sullivan. Two years before, Sullivan had become the face of prizefighting when he'd KO'd Paddy Ryan for the world championship. Considered by most historians to be not only the first boxing star, but the first sports hero of America, Sullivan had transformed the sport, bridging the bareknuckle era and the gloved era under the Queensberry rules.

During 1883 and continuing into 1884, Sullivan did a 136-city, coast-to-coast tour of the country, giving 195 performances. Though most of the "John L. Sullivan Combination" shows resulted in exhibitions, to help promote the tour, the champ announced he would fight anyone, at any time, four rounds under the Queensberry rules, for $250. A total of 11 men took him up on his offer — all of 'em were KO'd.

Hoping to gain the champion's attention, the *Las Vegas Daily Gazette*, in early 1884, wrote, "When Sullivan comes to Las Vegas he will be confronted in a contest with soft gloves by a young Hercules named George Fuller, employed at present by G. P. Conklin. Fuller has gained a local reputation back east, and thinks that if he can stand before Sullivan for three rounds it will be an easy way to earn $1,000, the sum which comprises the great slugger's standing offer. 'Clear the ring.'"[24]

It might've been wishful thinking that the great John L. had added Las Vegas to his tour. Had he done so, the obscure "young Hercules" would've probably been the twelfth man to be knocked out by "The Boston Strong Boy" during his travels. As it was, Sullivan skipped Vegas, the territory capital of Santa Fe, as well as Albuquerque — but he *did* make it to southern New Mexico.

That Sullivan had added points in New Mexico to his tour was virtually unknown, but those in the prize-fight business would've known there was a valid reason why a man named W. Hugh Coyle was in Silver City on Feb. 29. Fighting for the championship of Silver City (the "Silver Cup"), Coyle, a seasoned professional, was matched up with local amateur Andy Mills in a one-sided affair that was hotly criticized afterward:

> The contest should not have been a knock-out, but a four-round Marquis of Queensbury [*sic*] bout, with judges to decide as to winner. Had the match been such it should have been declared in Mills' favor, and the cup retained here instead of being carried off by a man incapable of winning it except in a one-sided match.... The great difficulty in a contest of this character is to decide who was entitled to compete for the prize — who as professionals are to be excluded, and who as amateurs are to be admitted.[25]

Coyle was more than an out-of-town prizefighter, no doubt tempted to bring back home a pretty silver trophy in an easy fight; he was also a scout for the John L. Sullivan tour, arranging dates and locations for the traveling band of pugs.

It's no big surprise that Silver City was crossed off his list — perhaps to avoid a confrontation with the local miners seething about the win over Mills. Instead, Deming was picked up as the only New Mexico site, to the consternation of the Silver City fight fans. In hindsight, the fight-friendly mining town would have been a better choice, for only 100 people showed up at the Deming Opera House on March 24, 1884, to see the world heavy-weight champion's exhibition. In fact, a good percentage of those hundred in attendance were probably *from* Silver City.

The Deming Herald and *Lake Valley Herald's* account of Sullivan's performance was extraordinarily brief: "The Sullivan Sluggers passed through here on Monday, and in the evening appeared at the Opera House to a crowd of about one hundred, half dead-heads. Evidently our people don't go wild over this kind of talent."[26] More words were used in taking a shot at Sullivan:

> As the great bruiser, John L. passed out of the Cabinet saloon on Monday evening, he accidentally stepped upon the foot of a small Demingite at the door. "See here," said the little man, "If you do that again I'll paste you one on the ear." The giant looked down on the small man and replied good humouredly [*sic*]: "Oh, no, young fellow, not me." The Deming man says he knew it was the Slugger at the time he spoke, but we doubt that.[27]

Snubbed for choosing Deming over their city, the *Enterprise* opined that "had Sullivan given an entertainment at Silver City he would have had a good house, while the attendance at Deming was very small."[28]

The territory of New Mexico would get two more memorable visits from the legendary Sullivan before he passed away in 1918.

The first of which was on Sullivan's return from his coast-to-coast tour, in the winter of 1884. The account was written by none other than Anton Mazzanovich, a Croatian settler who became a well-known character of the Wild West. Mazzanovich enlisted in the U.S. Sixth Cavalry in 1881, taking part in the hunt and capture of Apache chief Geronimo, the details of which would go into his still-in-print book *Trailing Geronimo*, first published in 1926. In 1885, Mazzanovich joined the New Mexico Rangers to fight Indians — but one year before, during the Sullivan Tour, he ran a saloon in the mining town of Shakespeare, New Mexico, about three miles from Lordsburg. Not only was Mazzanovich a writer, saloonkeeper, settler and Indian hunter, but he was also a big fight fan who claimed to have been the area's champion. Though there has been nothing found to support this, there is probably no reason to think otherwise, when you consider what Mazzanovich achieved on the frontier.

Mazzanovich's story, "A Wild and Wooly Reception Committee," resides in the Special Collections Library at the University of Arizona, but another version was printed in a 1931 edition of the *Lordsburg Liberal* in which Sullivan travels from Los Angeles to Tucson, and then to Lordsburg, where Mazzanovich, as "champion boxer of New Mexico,"[29] led a reception to greet the champ. Sullivan's train was derailed, after crashing through a horde of cattle, and by the time the champ arrived in Lordsburg, Mazzanovich and crew had made the rounds to every bar in town. What had intended to be a "good natured reception committee," instead, became a band of drunk, reckless cowboys — especially when they were told by the champ's manager, Pete McCoy, that Mr. Sullivan would rather doze than arise and greet his admirers.

> McCoy's remark was just like waving a red flag in front of a Texas longhorn. Harry Williams was standing close to Sullivan, who was apparently in deep slumber. Williams slapped him on the knee and said he would not give an Arizona horned toad to see Sullivan in a glass case. Nichols invited McCoy to step on the platform and fight, and the rest, who had crowded in the coach, were not behaving as a reception committee should. Everyone had a chip on his shoulder, and wanted to scrap. The conductor grasped the situation.... When I hopped off the train the boys

fired a parting salute as the train moved out of sight. All our good intentions went sky-high just because a bunch of cattle took a notion to cross the track. Had McCoy acted like a gentleman instead of a bowery tough, all would have come out O.K.

The committee continued to celebrate until morning, and then the famous reception committee to welcome and congratulate the great John L. disbanded. We sure wasted much ammunition shooting, and the most remarkable thing about it was that no one got hit with a lead slug.

It was my good fortune in the late nineties to met John L. Sullivan in New York City. One evening my friend, Bob Fitzsimmons and I strolled in the Metropole Bar at 42nd and Broadway, and who should be there but John L. with a party of admirers. Bob introduced me. I recalled the time when the reception committee met the train at Lordsburg, New Mexico, and offered my apology in behalf of that bunch of wild men whose good intentions were upset by Pete McCoy's sassy remark. Everybody was introduced all around and Sullivan had me repeat the story to his friends, which was heartily enjoyed by all. Sullivan said that sure was a wild bunch of men. They had everyone on the train, as well as himself, scared stiff.[30]

Territorial Champions

> *Mike Conway and Rocky Mountain Jim, two Santa Fe sluggers, recently had a mill for the championship of New Mexico. Three rounds were fought, when Mike knocked his antagonist "out of time," and now proudly wears the championship belt.*
> — *Rio Grande Republican*, 1886[31]

With or without John L. Sullivan's visits, New Mexico was doing just fine during 1884. Not only did the year usher in the concept of active fight promotion, but New Mexico got its first name fighters and territorial champions.

"Professor" M. Cathcart — named so for the lessons of gloved sparring he conducted, though every fighter and instructor professing skill, rather than slugging ability, was a so-called "professor"— became the first name promoter of New Mexico, hyping up a successful series of shows, first in Las Vegas. Cathcart advertised "slugging matches," then "athletic exhibitions," hoping to entice the locals, but after his primary box-office draw, John Hogan, had a falling out with him, Cathcart moved to Albuquerque for two shows at the Palace Theatre, before hanging up the gloves for less-controversial forms of entertainment.

Though not all of his fights are accounted for, Las Vegas' Hogan became one of the first fighters known throughout the territory, along with John Smith, also of Las Vegas, Tom Fields, of Raton, and Harry Bennie, of Lake Valley. Out-of-town fighters making a presence in New Mexico included "Professor" Harry Morgan and Jack Healy, both seasoned professionals from Colorado.

Hogan, Smith and Fields, all black fighters, fought one another in Las Vegas and Raton. During their five-month run of fights, most of their blows were of the verbal variety. Promoter Cathcart was part of the mudslinging, almost all of which was printed in Las Vegas's papers, the *Gazette* and *Optic*.

Reportedly 10–0 in the local arena and the region's fleetest foot-racer, Hogan, clearly the best of the three, defeated Fields in February, though the pair were rematched in May in a fight billed as the "championship of Colorado and New Mexico."[32] Admission was 75 cents to get into the Opera House. The fight, however, did not come off, and Hogan blamed Cathcart for the cancellation. Unable to secure Hogan in another card, the following week Cathcart staged back-to-back shows, one at the Opera House, the other at the local fairgrounds, billing exhibitions with soft gloves, and finish fights with hard gloves.

When Hogan's name found its way onto Cathcart's posters, the short-tempered pug was furious. "I have nothing to do with Cathcart's business and don't intend to have," he told the local paper, "as I am not an exhibition man. He should let the men do the talking instead of talking himself. I am ready for [any fighter] at the Windsor hotel or Tararue's saloon. Put up or shut up."[33] Cathcart wasted no time responding: "The great cause of Hogan's kicking is, that he thinks I had something to do with breaking up his fight with Fields last week and he is now trying to break up my slugging matches at the opera house to-night. Bluffing don't go, Hogan. I do all I do on the square. Enough said at present."[34]

Meanwhile, John Smith, self-proclaimed "Champion Colored Pugilist of New Mexico," was hoping to get a shot at the undefeated Hogan. His defi appeared two days after Catchcart's letter. "For the last three weeks John Hogan, the foot-racer, has been challenging me on the street," wrote Smith. "His friends have been urging him on to fight me, and because I had no money I had to grin and bear it, but now I have the stuff and I challenge Mr. John Hogan for all the money he can raise assisted by his friends. Now come up, Mr. Hogan and put up or shut up. I am sick of this blowing."[35]

Hogan vs. Smith was made a day later, for a $50 wager, Marquess of Queensberry rules to govern one night later, at Ward and Tamme's Opera House. Though both had talked a good talk, the fight turned out to be a mismatch in Hogan's favor. Outweighing his foe by 20 pounds, "the little coon knocked his burly opponent right and left."[36]

Prof. Harry Morgan, reportedly Colorado's lightweight champion and veteran of 50 battles, served as both referee and ring announcer. "Not much science was displayed, but there were some powerful blows struck," reported the *Optic*. "Smith proved himself to be a gamey little fellow and received the sledge hammer blows from his big antagonist without flinching [and] it was apparent after the fourth round that Smith would lose the battle. He was very groggy in the fifth round, and in the middle of the sixth, Hogan planted a blow under the chin which lifted Smith clean off his pins and sent him sprawling on the stage. He quivered for an instant like a poisoned dog in the throes of death, and when time was called was unable to come up to the scratch."[37]

Four days later, Hogan was finally rematched with Fields, in a soft-glove fight to the finish, Queensberry rules, for $100 a side and a 60/40 split of the gate. Prof. Morgan took to the task of training Hogan while Fields prepared in Raton. The men were given ten days to prepare, which was reduced to five by the time the fight came off, on May 31, 1884, at the Opera House. Neither one had a problem accepting the fight on shorter notice, Hogan saying "that he can beat his man as good one time as another" and Fields coming up with, "Let him come any minute he wants to and I'll whip the life out of him."[38]

The fight was the talk of the town and, during the week, exhibitions of "scientific boxing" were staged by Leadville's Healy, who was hoping to get a shot at the winner. In the end, however, Hogan vs. Fields II did not live up to a "real stand-up and knockdown prize fight."[39]

By now, it was obvious that prizefighting was reaching its level of tolerance in Las Vegas. "If there is one thing above another, which we love above another, it is a real genuine prize fight where two men get up and bust each other's noses," wrote the editor of the *Optic*. "It is a delightful pastime and should be encouraged by the better class of our people. There is no better way to encourage this class of men to kill themselves."[40]

On the day of the fight, the *Optic* wrote, "The opera house will be crowded to-night to witness the prize fight between Hogan and Fields," followed by "Too much loud-mouthed rowdyism on the streets last night and no one to suppress it."[41]

On the Monday *after* the fight, there was minimal reportage of Hogan's second victory over Fields: "Hogan, the coon slugger, was enjoying himself on Saturday night by firing a gun on the streets and yelling at the top of his voice all manner of vulgar and profane epithets against our people. We think Mr. Hogan should be pointed out to other fields. We have had quite enough of him and his kind in Las Vegas."[42]

One day later, the final nail in the coffin was printed: "The coon sluggers might as well leave town. The people have had quite enough."[43]

It would be eight years before prizefighting returned to Las Vegas.

Las Vegas might've had the most colorful fights of 1884, but there was action throughout the state—though not all of it was welcome. The last known prize fight of the year took place in "one of the saloons opposite the depot" in Deming, when the town's deputy sheriff, Doc Gilpin, took on a "railroad bruiser of some note."[44]

> The railroader fought as though he were broke and the $10 wager was just what he needed in his business, for in the first round he knocked Gilpin stiff and in the second he almost paralyzed him. Gilpin squealed enough before the young fellow had got fairly in work. It is reported that he was badly used up and not presentable to the people whom he is supposed to represent as a peace officer. Before he entered the fight he laid aside his revolver and official badge. Nice officers we have in this county.[45]

While Socorro, the fourth largest town in the territory at the time, opened up a boxing school and Silver City staged occasional bouts and exhibitions, Lake Valley's Harry C. Bennie, proclaiming himself the middleweight champion of the territory, modeled John L. Sullivan to form the "Bennie Sparring Combination," which toured through New Mexico and Arizona. Unlike his contemporaries, Bennie targeted fighters from outside New Mexico, and one of his defis was printed in the *National Police Gazette*:

> I, the undersigned, do hereby challenge Billy Lynn, the present holder of the championship and "Police Gazette" medal for Arizona, to fight me a stand-up fight from $200 to $2,000, the winner to take all the gate receipts. The fight to take place either in Lake Valley or Silver City, New Mexico, six weeks from signing articles. Rules new "Police Gazette." Man and money to be found at Lake Valley, at any time.[46]

Bennie didn't get Lynn, but he *did* get the so-called Arizona middleweight champion, Frank White. On June 15, in Bennie's hometown of Lake Valley, the two fought a four-round draw under Queensberry rules, soft gloves, for a purse of $200. Weighing 159 to White's 168, Bennie was floored in rounds three and four while White went down in rounds one and two. It remains the one and only fight recorded in Lake Valley, a silver-mining town that, at its peak, in 1893, had a population of 4,000, 12 saloons and two newspapers. Since 1994, Lake Valley has been a ghost town.

Bennie remained in the news throughout 1885, as did Fields, while Hogan and Smith, Las Vegas' early name fighters, disappeared from print. By March 1885, Bennie had relocated to Gordon, Texas, and, on Feb. 25, at Fort Worth, he was outgunned in a four-rounder with Colorado champion John Moore. Sometime before May, Bennie lost again, this time to top-notch middleweight John P. Clow, losing by a knockout in two rounds, again, at Fort Worth.

It is Bennie's last known fight.

Ebb and Flow

> *A number of our athletically inclined young men have been going in vigorously for boxing of late. And give and take hard knocks and bloody noses with the greatest good humor and pleasure. There seems to be some pretty good boxing material in town.*
> —*Mesilla Valley Democrat*, 1888[47]

The years 1885 and 1886 were slow ones for New Mexico.

Top Irish middleweight Mike Cleary passed through Santa Fe, where he might or might not have given a sparring exhibition; Two Mexicans — "Nachez" and "Lonzera"[48] fought in Los Lunas in April 1885; and, in November, the silver mining town of Georgetown had its sole prize fight, between two miners, with hometowner W. A. Smith knocking out Rodney O'Hara.

The following year was even worse, with just one fight on record, between Santa Fe sluggers, Mike Conway and "Rocky Mountain Jim," who fought for the unofficial "championship of New Mexico" in April. "Three rounds were fought, when Mike knocked his antagonist 'out of time,' and now proudly wears the championship belt."[49]

Mid-summer, there was talk of a fight in Santa Fe coming off, between a local boxing instructor, "Professor" Christol, and, either "Big Bill," a wrestler from Kansas City,[50] or "the gruff, stalwart ranchman,"[51] who was probably Harry Pierson, but there was no follow-up report.

Santa Fe did carry the scene, however, but only for a short time during the month of February 1887 when another "professor"— Paul J. Pitzlin — arrived from Galveston, Tex., for a series of fights. Pitzlin, an immigrant from Prussia and billed as the Texas champion, was booked at Mottley's Opera House on Feb. 3 to fight Arizona's W. J. Clifford. Pitzlin KO'd the "gentleman from Arizona in such short order" that he "decided to sojourn in Santa Fe for a time."[52]

Nine days later, Pitzlin headlined Mottley's again, this time taking on local brawler Harry Pierson, a.k.a. "The Ranchman," who was definitely the underdog, "though he does not appear to be a pugilist" and "is as handy with his fists as any man that has ever come to New Mexico."[53] Five hundred people, including "members of the legislature and several women"[54] showed up to watch Pitzlin and Pierson duke it out for $250 a side with three-ounce gloves:

> Pierson showed himself very game and possessed all the scientific tricks of the manly art, but he was too light for his steady antagonist. Up to the fourth round, Pitzlin got the worst of it, Pierson striking him in the face many times with ease. In the last three rounds, however, Pitzlin forced the little fellow to his utmost, knocking him down three times, crowding him near his corner and injuring him by falling on him with his knees, once knocking him through the window. At the end of the seventh round, Pierson had to be picked up and carried to his corner. The victory was awarded Pitzlin. There is talk of a bare-knuckle set-to between the pair.[55]

A bareknuckle rematch *was* tentatively arranged, for $500 a side, to come off within six weeks and five miles from Santa Fe, but the next card at Motley's Opera House, six days after the Pitzlin-Pierson fracas, brought the burgeoning prize fight scene to its knees.

At first, the man identified as "Ladow," who was knocked out cold by local scrapper Joe Cuff in round two, was declared dead by the house physician. Fifteen minutes later, however, he was miraculously revived. Despite the near death, another match between two more local pugilists was arranged to take place within ten days, but public opinion won out, pulling the plug on prizefighting, at least for another year, in Santa Fe. The fresh round of defis that had been printed after Cuff-Ladow went unanswered.

Pitzlin moved on, going to Flagstaff for a fight, then returning to Galveston where, in 1890 and 1891, he fought two significant fights with Arthur O. Upham, winning the first in the tenth and losing the second, by KO, in round 23. Soon after, Pitzlin retired, becoming a physical culture advocate and setting up classes and gymnasiums throughout the Midwest. His fights with Upham, lauded as the area's gamest battles of the era, continued to be mentioned as late as 1940 in Galveston newspapers.

Meanwhile, in New Mexico, the scene suffered, though there was no lack of challenges during the latter half of 1887. Well-known Texas prizefighter Jack Gallagher, who was in Santa Fe assisting Pitzlin in February, issued challenges to locals Joe Cuff, "Professor" Sicotte and John G. Karl — nothing materialized, though that could've been due to his arrest in March, when it was discovered that he was a deserter from the U.S. Army three years prior. Jimmie Nichols, of Kingston, New Mexico, calling himself the Southwest lightweight champion, also put up defis in the summer and fall, but failed to drum up interest in an actual match.

The biggest challenge, one that never materialized for the territory, came from the world middleweight champion, future Hall-of-Famer Jack "Nonpareil" Dempsey:

> [Jack] Dempsey, the middle-weight champion pugilist, being indignant at some remarks of [John L.] Sullivan, has the following to say: Sullivan says that my arms are like pipe-stems and that while in San Francisco he offered to go to New Mexico and fight me. That is not a true statement. Sullivan nor no other man ever offered to fight that I would not fight, and if Sullivan had ever made such a proposition I should quickly have accepted, no matter whether he could whip me or not. Sullivan nor no living man can whip me in six rounds, bar accidents. Sullivan clams I can conquer Burke and whip Mitchell. Why, then, doesn't he give me a chance of boxing him? I know he is not able to box at present, but when his arm is well I will meet him at any time, and my backers will put up any amount from $1,000 to $5,000.[56]

Sullivan vs. Dempsey never happened, though if had, and in New Mexico, the fight would have turned the territory into a Southwest boxing mecca overnight. Though Dempsey — second only to Sullivan as the 1880s' pound-for-pound great — never got a shot at the heavyweight champion, he did get to step into the ring in 1891 against Bob Fitzsimmons, Sullivan's eventual successor, who took Dempsey's middleweight crown by a 13th-round stoppage. Dempsey proved his greatness by losing only five times in 13 years and 66 fights.

Prizefighting faltered in New Mexico until the spring of 1888, when a "local colored celebrity"[57] arrived in Santa Fe.

It would be years before Frank Childs made a splash on the big scene, becoming a threat to middleweight and heavyweight champs alike. But, in 1888, before he was known as a Chicago fighter, with the alias "The Crafty Texan," Childs landed in Santa Fe. A hundred years later, Childs would be regarded as one of the most overlooked fighters of his era, having defeated greats like George LaBlanche, "Australian" Billy Smith and Joe Walcott, while going the distance with Jack Johnson (twice) and Joe Choynski.

Though little is known of Childs' early fights in Texas, his reputation preceded him when he arrived in Santa Fe. After an afternoon sparring session at John Conway's Hall, Childs and sparring partner B. W. Harris, a Leadville, Colorado, pug, were matched to a hard-glove fight to the finish on the following evening, the winner to get 75 percent of the gate, the house 25 percent, and the loser *nada*.

In what turned out to be "an old fashioned negro slugging match," Harris scored first blood and first knockdown in the first but "fell apart after that." Childs floored Harris in the third, punished him severely through the sixth, nearly knocking him out. "Time was called and [Harris] failed to come, but the referee, judges and timekeepers seemed to enjoy the fun too much to declare him knocked out. When the seventh round was called Harris responded rather unwillingly and only tried to defend himself by dodging and dropping to the floor. A light blow on the temple brought him to the floor. Long time was given him, but he never attempted to come back to the scratch."[58]

The fight, lasting an hour and 20 minutes, was good enough to warrant a rematch, which was set up for May 7. This time, the "Leadville man weakened at the last moment and refused to stand before Childs, the Santa Fean, in hard gloves, hence the bout took place with soft gloves and was little better than a sparring match."[59] With only 150 people showing up, the small purse compelled Childs to head west, to Los Angeles.

In New Mexico, the action continued to dwindle.

The railroad and coal-mining town of Gallup received its first fight card on Thanksgiving Day 1888, at Capt. P. Smith's Saloon, between middleweight Tom Hennessey and "The Coolidge Kid," reportedly, New Mexico's lightweight champion, from the now-ghost town best known for an 1882 shooting and hanging.

Other mining towns staged shows throughout 1889, with all of the bouts between local prizefighters whose names were not mentioned again. San Pedro, known for its grapes and coal, staged a 16-round Queensberry bout for the territorial championship in February, between E. M. Cunningham and E. J. Carmody, the results of which have been lost. There were also fights at Rincon, a shipping center for the railroad; Pinos Altos, where gold was discovered in the 1860s; and Las Cruces, where a boxing match was part of "The Mexican Tournament," an outdoor festival that featured bullfights and horse racing.

In 1889, Deming staged two shows headlining Texas lightweight champion Tom Monaghan, of Galveston, Tex., who took out an unknown named Ed Kurnell in ten, and Philadelphia's Jack Hanlon in 27 rounds. Albuquerque returned to action, as well, staging at least two bouts between local sluggers. A bareknuckle three-rounder between a barber and a doctor got the greatest mention, however. When the barber, E. E. Betzler, refused to pay his doctor's bill, the physician had him arrested. After paying up his $10 bill, upon release, a three-rounder was arranged, with "the barber winning first blood, first knock down and the fight."[60]

The most press regarding boxing went to a little-known prizefighter named Fred Rogers, who went insane shortly after he helped local authorities capture the murderer of a local railroad worker: "At times in his worst moods [he] would discuss the boys at the ranch of endeavoring to poison him. He had all kinds of delusions, and when he left he was thoroughly a deranged man. He is now wandering over the prairie along the road in a crazed condition. His whereabouts are unknown."[61]

Outside the state, 1889 marked an historic fight that would forever change prizefighting. Fighting for the first time since winning the championship in 1882, John L. Sullivan, now as well-known for being a drunkard as he was for fighting, took on contender Jake Kilrain in what would go down as the last bareknuckle championship. Before a crowd of 3,000, at Richburg, Miss., and fighting for $20,000, Sullivan and Kilrain fought a grueling 75-round battle under the hot sun that resulted in Kilrain's corner throwing up the sponge after two hours and 16 minutes.

Sullivan would remain champion until 1892 — the same year that prizefighting entered its first successful period in New Mexico.

3. The Rise of Prizefighting, 1890–1895

Dashaway — Strange things happened. The other night at the Academy they had a prize fight and the next night a Wagner concert. Cleverton — What incongruity. I suppose they were both crowded, too? Dashaway — I don't know. I didn't go to the concert.

—Santa Fe New Mexican, 1891[1]

If the scene had gone unchecked in the 1890s, New Mexico would surely have established itself as an early mecca for prizefighting in the Southwest. Not only was the territory beginning to develop local fighters, but the waning-but-still-wild West was attracting well-known pugs from all over the country. When New Mexico made an attempt to play host to no less than the World Heavyweight Championship, midway through the decade, the territory had a chance to put itself on the fistic map.

When New Mexico lost that fight — thanks to politics — three years of momentum were knocked out with one punch, clanging shut the door for a fight-friendly environment that would not change until the territory achieved statehood in 1912.

The first two years of the 1890s were slow, but in 1892 the scene exploded. There are 37 known prize fights in the 1880s (possibly double that, when you factor in unreported fights and defunct newspapers); the 1890s had nearly twice that, with 70 known fights (you can probably double that number, as well). Almost all of those fights occurred between '92 and '96.

During the early 1890s, prizefighting was on the rise on the national scene, as well, since bareknuckle bouts were being fazed out for the less barbaric, gloved contests under the Queensberry rules.

Though he had embodied the transition from bareknuckle to glove, World Heavyweight Champion John L. Sullivan was about to end his reign. Sporting a pompadour and representing the sport's science over the slugging that "Sully" brought to the ring, "Gentleman Jim" James J. Corbett met the champ on Sept. 7, 1892, before a crowd of 10,000 in New Orleans. Though outweighed by 34 pounds, Corbett avoided the wild swings of a paunchy and past-his-prime champion, knocking him out after 21 rounds lasting one hour, 20 minutes.

Prizefighting entered a new era, the effects of which were felt in the territory of New Mexico.

McSparron

Flahrity, the pugilist, struck town the first of the week and is anxious to meet the prize fighters of Gallup in a body. He offers to knock out Harry Conway, Jack Bruce and John James in eighteen rounds and smoke a cigarette in the mean time. The town was

*crowded with pugilists of all kinds a short time ago, and in all probability, the woods
in the vicinity contain several of them at present.*

— *Santa Fe New Mexican,* 1894[2]

Before Gallup could be coined the "Indian Capital," in the 1890s and through the first half of the twentieth century, it was "Carbon City," for its lucrative coal-mining. During those same years, it was also known for prizefighting.

The town would become one of New Mexico's greatest fight towns, developing some of the scrappiest talent over the next half a century. In the 1890s, Gallup gave the territory one of its first name fighters in Hugh McSparron, the recognized lightweight champion of New Mexico.

Hugh was the seventh born of a dozen children to William McSparron. Born in 1858 in Glasgow, Scotland, Hugh was working alongside his father in the coal mines of Backworth, England, by the time he was 12 years old. Hoping for more opportunity, the McSparrons landed in the U.S. between 1879 and 1880, making their way from Georgia to Pennsylvania (where Hugh was married) and, finally, to Gallup, by 1888, the year of Hugh's first known fight. As early as '85, however, and while in Pennsylvania, Hugh was immersed in the fight game as a second, if he wasn't already fighting:

> A desperate bare-knuckle fight on roller-skates took place, March 16, in Lawrenceville Pennsylvania, for $150 a side and the affections of a female skater. The principals were J. M. McDonald and G. M. Kauffman. Bilson Jack and Hugh McSparron handled the men, who came together in a 12 × 8 room containing sixteen persons. Seven rounds were fought, both men being covered with cuts and blood. McDonald was almost helpless when, in an unguarded moment, Kauffman hit him when down and lost the fight on a foul.[3]

While Hugh was busy raising a family and working in the mines, he also fought, albeit sporadically. Upon his arrival, he won the lightweight championship of New Mexico from the Coolidge Kid. One year later, he was in Barstow, California, fighting hometown railroad bruiser C. H. McKinney in a fight to the finish with skin-tight gloves and a purse of $1,000, in front of 300. After "ten desperate rounds" that were "fought in 39 minutes ... McKinney knocked McSparron out by a right hand blow on the jugular, and it was nearly four minutes before he recovered."[4]

In the first half of the 1890s, McSparron was a regular mention in prizefight items and challenges. After his loss to McKinney, he fought a glove fight in Gallup against Arizona's middleweight champion Jimmy Edwards. Before a lively crowd of 400, at Captain Smith's Saloon — a regular spot for fights in Gallup — McSparron gave up 20 pounds, 137 to 157, to fight as an underdog. Though the favorite, Edwards "from the very first, he had the worst of the argument, receiving severe punishment, principally about the face. He fought with desperation to turn the tide of battle, but unavailingly, and in the sixth round a crusher on the point of the jaw settled the business for him, and McSparron got the money."[5] After 23 minutes and six rounds, McSparron picked up a $1,000 purse.

No doubt, $1,000 went a long way back then for it was nearly a year later when McSparron decided to fight again. In March 1891, McSparron made his return, against San Francisco's Bob Love, for $200 and gate receipts, the results of which are unknown. The following month, he was in Albuquerque to watch the highly publicized Reddy Welsch-John Stock mill, and to challenge the winner: "There has been much said in regard to the abilities of Reddy Welsch, your local slugger, that I wish to state right here that if Welsch has any friends with money all they have to do is to write me and I will find a man what will give him a fight, Queensberry rules, for any amount he can name. The man I mean is no greater in height than himself. He is right here in this locality, and if Welsch means business as a pugilist let him answer."[6]

Welsch responded immediately, posting a forfeit deposit of $25: "There is plenty of money, apparently, behind Welsch; let anybody come and get it, providing they can, is the way his backers talk."[7] McSparron, in turn, posted his forfeit but the fight, for whatever unpublished reason, never happened.

McSparron might not have fought the remainder of the year, but his brother, Peter, began to build a reputation fighting as "The Spider of Gallup," from featherweight to lightweight. Popular San Francisco fighter Jim McCoy, residing in Albuquerque in 1892, hoping to get a shot at El Paso's "Slim" Jim Lewis, called out both Peter and Hugh in February, to no avail.

Hugh McSparron might not have fought again, but he fulfilled other roles in the ring, from bottle-holder to timekeeper to cornerman. By 1894, he'd built up his reputation as a foot-racer, as well, with a 13-race winning streak and a claim to have run a mile in 49.8 seconds, attracting notice as far away as Nebraska.

McSparron's battles were limited to the courtroom by 1898, when his wife filed for divorce "on the grounds of abandonment and habitual drunkenness."[8] A month later, the McSparrons were in court, with Gallup judge Edward Hart "appointed referee."[9] Losing the case, McSparron abandoned his family to go off prospecting in Arizona.

According to John McSparron, Hugh's grand-nephew, family lore has McSparron buried in the infamous Boot Hill Graveyard in Tombstone, Ariz., though John doesn't believe it's the case, as most people buried there died in the 1880s. McSparron did, however, spend the remainder of his days near Tombstone; a death certificate has a "Hugh McSperrin" dying of pneumonia on Jan. 30, 1902.

The name lived on. One of Hugh's sons, Leon Hugh "Cozy" McSparron, became a famous trading-post owner and an Indian trader who had a significant impact on Navajo weavers. He also boxed in Denver as an amateur, winning at least one state tournament. In fact, "Cozy" later said he'd taken his first trading-post job because the owner wanted to be taught how to box.[10] John McSparron also says that his father, William, boxed while living in Australia during the 1930s.

The Carbon City

> *The town has been flooded with hopeful pugilists who claim science the past week, but they have generally proved to be hams.*
> —*Albuquerque Morning Democrat*, 1891[11]

Gallup had no shortage of miners, from which came willing scrappers. There were guys like Jack Bruce, Harry Conway and Jack Grady. Others had much more colorful *noms de guerre*, like the previously mentioned "Spider." Teddy "The Mick" Costello and John "The Terrible Dutchman" Butler, both local barbers, were one-hit wonders in New Mexico's boxing annals, but they hold the distinction of having fought one of the longest fights in the region, going 78 rounds in the summer of 1894 for a purse of $250, with "The Mick" winning by knockout.

Even longer was the 84-round knockout suffered by Irish-born John (Jack) Kennedy at the hands of Teddy O'Neill. Small heavyweights by modern standards, Kennedy at 194 and O'Neill at 187, the two fought before a crowd of 700—not bad, when you consider that the population was around 2,000—paying $2 apiece.

Kennedy fought another marathon session six months later when he took on another local, Thomas Dwyer, in a bareknuckle fight that nearly killed him. "The scrap lasted an hour and forty-five minutes, at the end of which time they had to be separated, being too weak to continue. The men fought like bulldogs, biting, scratching and gouging. Both are now in the hands of a physician, and it is believed that Kennedy cannot possibly recover."[12] The updated wire report added "it is thought Kennedy may die,"[13] but he didn't, though he never fought again.

The prize ring in Gallup was not limited to locals, or those brought in to fight a hometown favorite. In May 1892, Ohio middleweight Billy Groves knocked out Coloradoan William R. Johnson, better known as "The Terrible Swede," an infamous sponge for punishment. Johnson was knocked out in six, in a "revised" Queensberry rules bout fought outside Gallup's city limits. Earlier in the month, Johnson had been in Albuquerque, calling out local pugs while en route to the West Coast. "The birds have flown," said Johnson, who scoffed at the city's "reputation for first-class fighters."[14]

In his fight with Groves, Johnson was sent "to the grass" five times before the sixth-round knockout, suffering "one rib broke and both thumbs knocked up, and it will be several weeks before he will be able to do any more fighting."[15] Two-and-a-half months later, apparently healed from his war with The Terrible Swede, Groves fought in Pueblo, where he was knocked out by Colorado's heavyweight champion, Billy Woods, in two rounds. The Swede, on the other hand, continued to win some, lose some, until he was sentenced to a year in prison for prizefighting in Kansas, in 1895.

Gallup also holds the distinction of staging the first female fight in New Mexico history:

> There was a fistic and hair pulling contest to a finish one night recently between two of the "girls." The ring selected was a room about 14x14 and the fight held out for about half an hour, during which time three rounds were fought, and the fight was declared a draw at the end of the third round. The seconds were two of the carbon city young bloods and they state that there was hair and such scattered all around the room, and that the fight was a fierce one during one of the three rounds.[16]

Luckily, for New Mexico, the catfight between unnamed females, buried in the small print of the *Gallup Gleaner*, went undetected by wire services—another fight swept under the desert rug of New Mexico.

The biggest prize fight of the era to land in Gallup was on the Fourth of July 1895, shortly before the sport was knocked out by politicians. The fight goes down in the record books as a milestone fight for New Mexico for several reasons. It would be the last (known) fight staged in Gallup for, possibly, 15 years, marking an end to the town's seven-year string of battles that began with McSparron in 1888.

Not only was the match, between New Mexico's most popular fighter of the decade, James Flynn, and top Southwest slugger Billy Lewis, one of the most significant fights of the decade, but it was also the first ever held at Kitchen's Opera House. The long-running venue ultimately staged more boxing cards than any other venue in the state, a number estimated at 130 to 160.

"Gentleman James" Flynn

> *Jack Bruce, of Gallup, writes the Citizen that he can whip any man in New Mexico, but he does except one man and he is Jim Flynn, of Cerillos.*
> —*Santa Fe New Mexican*, 1894[17]

Long before there was "Fireman" Jim Flynn, there was *James* Flynn, though he was sometimes "Jim," once in a while "Jimmy," and once or twice "Jack." In New Mexico, he was "*Gentleman*" James, and if there was a local star during the first half of the 1890s, he was it. "The Cerillos fighter is a pleasant gentleman," the *Albuquerque Daily Citizen* printed in 1894. "And although he follows a profession not at all admired, still he has the instincts of a gentleman, [and] is not a braggart."[18]

Flynn's tale tells the story of the era, from his chosen occupations of miner and prizefighter to his fleeting hometown of Cerrillos. Fighting throughout the Southwest, James might've confused Coloradoans who were starting to take notice of Pueblo's Jim, who was starting his career when the other was finishing up. Unlike the next Flynn, though, this one did not become a full-time prizefighter or world title challenger.

James rode the rails west in search of mining jobs, not ring valor. Born in Piedmont, W.V., on Aug. 7, 1869,

"Gentleman" James Flynn, not to be confused with "Fireman" Jim Flynn, who started his career about the time the first Flynn was ending his, was the biggest name in boxing in the New Mexico territory during the early 1890s.

Flynn's first fight was, most likely, in 1891— a knockout over Jack Fisher. A nine-round win over Jack Hoffman in Cumberland, Md., and a 49-round knockout over Pat Malone, in Monroe City, Mich., followed, before Flynn settled in Creede, Colorado, during the mining town's heyday, in 1892. It's also likely that Flynn's early bouts were bareknuckle.

In Creede, Flynn fought at least five times during the year, losing one bout, to Charlie Johnson, of St. Paul, Minn. Though it was later reported that, after 80 minutes, Flynn lost by a foul, local papers describe a clear stoppage, with Flynn "blinded in the left eye and bleeding all over the face and in the nose like a stuck hog."[19]

There was no shame losing to a guy like Johnson. At the time he was, reportedly, undefeated, with an estimated 30 or more fights. He would go on to fight legends like Bobby Dobbs, "Mysterious" Billy Smith, Joe Walcott and Mike Donovan — an equal number of wins, losses and draws — and, along the way, challenge Tommy Ryan for the World Middleweight Championship in 1899, losing by KO in eight.

Despite the loss to Johnson, that year, Flynn picked up three wins, defeating respected veterans Billy Kennedy and Jack Lawrence. There was also a six-round draw with The Terrible Swede.

Sometime during 1893, no doubt, when the Silver Panic hit all of Colorado's mining towns, Flynn relocated to New Mexico's mining and railroad town of Cerrillos, which was just entering its peak period. By the time Flynn arrived, Cerrillos had a population estimated at 2,000, four hotels, five brothels and 20 saloons. It also had Hurt's Hall, an opera house named after one of the early property owners, William C. Hurt, and not for the pain inflicted in the many prize fights staged there.

Before Flynn became a regular attraction at Hurt's, though, he landed a fight in nearby Santa Fe, against W. F. Roberts, at the Old Aztec store, breaking his opponent's nose and knocking him out in round four. The win, and published challenges to take on any welterweight in the territory, piqued interest. The *National Police Gazette* printed defis, as well, with Flynn calling out "any man in America at 140 pounds for $1,000 or $1,500 a side."[20]

Cerrillos began a series of fights at Hurt's, beginning in December 1893. The first pitted Flynn, who was now the recognized territorial welterweight champion and touting, reportedly, a record of 17–1, more or less, against Arthur Edmunds (or Edwards), from Las Vegas. The agreement was for Flynn to score a stoppage in eight rounds, but the fight was stopped by the referee in the fourth, due to a foul committed by Edmonds, who "pursued the Mitchell tactics,[21] going down on every possible occasion."[22]

Next, Flynn rematched Kennedy, now, reportedly, Colorado's middleweight champion, for $250 a side and 75 percent of the gate. Once again, Kennedy was KO'd in four.

The much heavier Dave Flaherty, from Portland, Ore., was lined up next, promising to knock out Flynn, 20 pounds lighter, in ten rounds, on March 13, 1894. Shortly before the scheduled date, however, Flynn was forced to pull out after his foot was run over while working at Cerrillos' White Ash mine. "It is said by some that Flynn was really glad he met with the accident, and by others that he was really sorry,"[23] wrote the *Albuquerque Citizen*, for, the month before, Flaherty had been game enough to stand up to world class contender "Australian" Billy Smith for 32 rounds in what had been a milestone fight for the New Mexico territory.

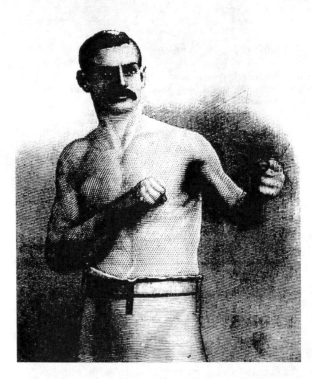

After fighting to a draw with "Australian" Billy Smith, of El Paso, Colorado veteran Herman Frazier became a threat to any New Mexican fighter during the 1890s — including the territory's biggest name, James Flynn.

When Flynn returned to action on April 21, it wasn't to give up 40 pounds by taking on a heavyweight like Flaherty, but to take on the lighter but game Colorado veteran Herman Frazier. Originally from Illinois, Frazier's most notable win in the area was a draw with Australian Billy. In fact, the *Police Gazette* named Frazier a favorite over Flynn in their finish fight under the Queensberry edicts. The fight received big coverage in Albuquerque. The *Morning Democrat* reported that at least 18 fight fans were on the passenger train bound for Cerrillos the night before, and that there were at least 40 "pleasure-seekers" on the 9:30 train arriving from points north.[24]

"FLYNN WON" read the *Citizen*'s front-page headlines Monday morning.[25]

Seconded by Hugh McSparron, also apparently mining at Cerrillos during this time, Flynn, 145 pounds, entered the house at 11 P.M. Twenty minutes later, Frazier, 143, followed. Both climbed into the ring shortly after 11:30, lacing up the gloves at quarter to midnight.

> Flynn knocked his opponent down three times in the first round and thereafter not a round passed without Frazer going down at least once. In the ninth round Flynn broke his left hand by a terrific left hand swing which landed upon the back of Frazer's head and knocked him down. After two and a half hours of extremely hard fighting and in the seventeenth round, Flynn knocked Frazer out by a vicious right hand upper cut that landed on Frazer's jugular."[26]

With the win, Flynn made $900—$250 from the side bet and $650 from the gate — becoming the recognized New Mexico welterweight champ, if not the Colorado and Arizona one, as well. Flynn then set his sights on Billy Lewis.

If Frazier was Flynn's coming-out party, Lewis was supposed to be his crowning achievement to date, solidifying a claim for the Southwest championship. Lewis, of Butte City, Montana, had not only stood up to Australian Billy for 14 rounds in El Paso earlier in the year, but was well known in the territory, having headlined several New Mexican fights. Flynn trained in Las Vegas, where the fight would be staged under the auspices of the Las Vegas Athletic Club, at Rosenthal's Opera House.

After the fiascos of the 1880s, Las Vegas had taken nearly eight years to return to prizefighting. In 1892, two shows had been staged, one of which matched up Flynn's foe, Lewis, with a local pug named "Happy" Jack Ryan. Lewis had little trouble with the overmatched Happy Jack, so much so that in the fourth, Lewis arose from his corner and remarked, "This is too slow, I'll knock him out." Lewis "tapped the Las Vegas man on the jaw with his right, intending to finish 'Jack' with a left-hand upper-cut, but it wasn't necessary — the coon was done for."[27]

Both Las Vegas shows of 1892 failed to draw more than small, dissatisfied crowds. This time around, the Las Vegas Athletic Club assured the fans that the headliner was not only well-matched but, unlike past shows, on the up and up:

> All tickets of admission to the contest of the Las Vegas Athletic club will have coupons attached. The coupons will be kept by the holder and in case of any discovery by the club officials leading them to think there is a fake or job put up on the part of the men in the contest, or if the referee decides there is no match, the coupon entitles the holder to admission to the next contest. This protects the patrons who attend the exhibitions and is a guarantee that all contests are strictly on their merits.[28]

By far the year's biggest fight in New Mexico, Flynn-Lewis was staged during the three-day celebration of the annual Firemen's Convention and Tournament. The winner, fighting for a purse of $500 and a $350 side bet, would be recognized as the Southwest champion. A crowd between 500 and 1,000 was expected, but, shortly before the fight, a local railroad strike isolated the city from surrounding towns. On fight night, only 175 people showed up.

The attendance wasn't the only disaster — at least for Flynn, who'd been named, for the second straight time, as the underdog by the *Police Gazette*. This time around, the *Gazette's* editor, Richard K. Fox, was right. Though apparently ahead on the scorecards, Flynn lost the bout in the 13th round.

Weighing 148 to Lewis' 144½, Flynn, donned in red, white and blue, shook hands with his opponent at 10:02 P.M., when the bell for round one clanged. Flynn was off to a strong start, and was slightly ahead after six stanzas. In the seventh, Flynn was floored, but he came back in the eighth. The ninth was even and Lewis took the tenth. In round 11, Flynn scored two knockdowns, and appeared on the verge of winning, but Lewis retaliated in what would be the 12th and final round. Flynn went down a second time and, this time, Lewis hit him while he was on his knees.

Referee Arthur Jilson gave Flynn time to recover but, when he was unable to continue, the victory was ruled in favor of Lewis. Flynn later claimed he'd been robbed — that Jilson had been unfamiliar with the rules. The *Optic* reported that "Flynn would make the better exhibition ... Lewis, the better prize fighter," who had the edge in ring generalship.[29]

Flynn told the *Citizen* that both, the referee, and having "green seconds," on account of the railroad shutdown, had worked against him. "He offered to fight Lewis again within a few weeks, but Lewis point blank refused to accept his proposition. He says he had Lewis whipped several times before he went out himself, but the crowd requested him to prolong the mill, so all could get their money's worth."[30]

Unable to secure a rematch, Flynn moved on. A fight in Creede, Colorado, was announced between Flynn and veteran "Mexican" Pete Everett, though it is unlikely to have occurred for, soon after, Flynn was trying to land a bout against an unnamed "California professional" on August 11 in Albuquerque. The West Coaster turned out to be Harry Morgan, and, for one reason or another, that bout, too, was nixed, most likely due to anti-prizefight politics brewing in Albuquerque. It was reported, however, that Flynn was training in Algodones and Morgan, at Isleta Pueblo. "The gentleman of this city, who had charge of the business, now states that he thinks the pugs have decamped,"[31] was the final newsflash.

Flynn dropped off the pugilistic map, though it was briefly mentioned that he was now back in the mines, this time in Gallup. The *El Paso Times*, on the other hand, reported that Billy Lewis had now changed his mind about a rematch and was on his way to Albuquerque to arrange it. Nothing surfaced and Flynn remained below ground — literally — over the winter. By April 1895, however, Flynn's name crept back into print. Once again, a Flynn-Lewis rematch was talked about, but, before anything could be signed, Flynn nearly died in a coal-mining accident. When one of the Crescent Coal Company mines caught fire, a number of mules were killed and 15 men nearly suffocated. Flynn was carried out unconscious.

Flynn recovered but the Lewis fight was, again, postponed. In the meantime, Flynn shook off the rust by taking on black Arizona fighter Abe "Swifty" Dinwiddie, on May 27, 1895, in Williams, Ariz. It would be the first of three fights, the initial match being a tune-up for Flynn, who KO'd his foe in five.

In June, the rematch with Lewis was finally secured, and set for the Fourth of July in Gallup, one year and one day from the original bout. With holiday fight cards staged in both Santa Fe and Las Vegas, Gallup was still able to draw a capacity crowd at what would be the initial boxing show to be staged at the Kitchen's Opera House on Main Street.

> The large hall was packed when time was called at 6:40. Some trouble was had to get a referee, but finally a gentleman, who thoroughly understood his business, stepped on the stage and made a few remarks appropriate to the occasion and he was duly chosen to umpire the fight. Both men were in splendid condition, and when they stepped on the platform the cheers from the large audience was deafening. At first it looked as though there was some mistake, and instead of witnessing a fight, the audience were to see a walk for a prize cake or some points. In the second round a little sparring was done, and some blood drawn. From the 12th to the 15th round Jim Flynn, who was the aggressor throughout, forced Lewis to the ropes, landing hard. Flynn slipped and Lewis struck out as Flynn fell, but missed. In the 19th round Lewis forced the fight and knocked Flynn down the first time. In the 19th round Lewis fouled Flynn and the referee gave the fight to Flynn on the foul. It was a square fight and all the sports and those interested seemed

to be satisfied. Considerable money changed hands. After this event the hall was cleaned and a grand ball concluded the day's festivities.[32]

It was a bittersweet victory for Flynn, for, while evening the score, Lewis was still considered the better fighter. The *Democrat* reported that Lewis "had the best of the fighting, but the decision was given in favor of Flynn on a foul."[33]

Flynn had better offers, but chose to return to Arizona instead for another fight against Swifty in September. It was probably Swifty's insults about Flynn's assumed yellow streak in the *Arizona Journal-Miner* that motivated him. Flynn responded: "I wish it properly understood that I will fight any man in the two territories, regardless of weight or color. First come, first served, but 'Swifty' preferred."[34]

When the two clashed for the second time, this time around, Swifty — and not Flynn — came prepared: "It was of short duration as in the second round 'Swifty' succeeding in getting in a swinging blow on Flynn's neck which sent him to the earth limp as a rag, and where he remained until medical assistance was called. Parties who were present at the fight state that a physician worked with him nearly three hours before he succeeded in restoring him to consciousness."[35]

Eager to erase the knockout loss, and ignoring the many challenges coming from New Mexican fighters, an immediate rematch was arranged for Nov. 2, for $500 a side, in Prescott. Before a crowd of 250, Flynn punished Swifty, who "failed to get up in the sixth round."[36] Swifty proved a sore sport, claiming "he was jobbed and that the referee gave him the worst of it,"[37] though the blow-by-blow in the local paper reported otherwise. Before a fourth fight could be arranged, Flynn disappeared again.

There was talk of fighting Billy Gallagher, but nothing came of it. In July 1896, Flynn, working now in Williams, Ariz., called out top contender Tom Sharkey but, again, nothing materialized. So he disappeared.

The last known mention of a Jim Flynn — and not the future title challenger, Jim, from Pueblo, who began his career in 1899 — was in 1898 when the *Arizona Republic* mentioned that Flynn, "the pugilist who achieved considerable fame,"[38] was working in the Gallup coal mines. There were no comebacks, and no further mention of Flynn.

Flynn's foes Swifty and Lewis continued to fight. Swifty's battles, however, were against drugs. Some time after achieving his local fame as a pugilist, Swifty became a morphine and cocaine addict. By 1899, he was walking "the streets aimlessly, a human wreck."[39] One year later, he was found guilty of murder, after having injected a local barber in Flagstaff with cocaine. Lewis, on the other hand, built up a respectable record fighting all over the country, drawing with Dick Case in 1896, losing to Dummy Rowan by DQ in 1897, going ten rounds on a moment's notice with legend Young Griffo in 1898, and drawing with Rowan in a rematch in 1899. In 1900, though, Lewis passed away from injuries sustained in the ring.

Dona Ana, the Texas Trump

> *If we furnish the place for a fight absolutely safe from police interference some club in the east or north will not hesitate to back the enterprise with the necessary purse. The greatest trouble now is finding a place where those actively interested will be secure from arrest. It is well known that such place can be found near El Paso.*
> —*El Paso Daily Times*, 1894[40]

The biggest adversary of prizefighting in New Mexico history has proven to be politicians hell bent on outlawing the sport. Some of the biggest benefactors, however, have been *Texas* politicos with the same agenda.

Because Texas had been annexed into statehood in 1845, territorial laws on prizefighting did not apply. This made legalities a gray area until the Act of 1889, which gave would-be pugilists and promoters the official thumbs up, provided they pay an occupation tax of $500 and obtain a license. "For every fight between man and man," read the statute, "or between men and bulls, or between bears and dogs, or between bulls and other animals, or between dogs and dogs, or between dogs and bulls, five hundred dollars for each performance."[41]

Two years later, however, in March 1891, a statute was added to the Texas penal code outlawing prizefighting, punishable by a $500 to $1,000 fine and a county jail sentence between 60 days and one year. The only problem was that the original 1889 act remained, contradicting the new statute. In other words, how could the State of Texas arrest and fine a prizefighter when, at the same time, the law clearly stated that, for a $500 tax fee, one could *stage* such a contest?

Well, El Paso pugs and promoters had that worked out — both the tax *and* the contradictory laws.

Enter Dona Ana County, New Mexico.

Over the next 50 years, a patch of land just over the Rio Grande, five miles west of downtown El Paso across what would later be called the Courchesne Bridge, would become the most infamous site for New Mexico prize fights. On one side of the Rio Grande, it's El Paso; on the other side of the bridge, it's what is now east Sunland Park, New Mexico — magically free of all Texas jurisdiction *and* the hefty $500 tax.

In order to circumvent the law, the legalese and the tax, not to mention the edict that Texas religious factions had persuaded politicians to pass laws forbidding saloons and opera houses to open on Sundays, promoter James McDermott worked out a deal with the Southern Pacific Railroad to run a chartered train from downtown El Paso across the bridge and river onto New Mexico soil.

Leaving at 4:30 in the morning on June 1, 1890, three coaches carrying an estimated 300 spectators and the two principals, Charles Herald, of St. Paul, Minn., and local colored fighter Tom Standard, left the downtown station.

> The ring was quickly made and Chas. Dowd was chosen referee at ring side. Time was called at 5:15. Standard led with a righthander on Herald's side, made two clever ducks, when Herald caught him in the neck with a swinging right hand blow and knocked him silly. Standard failed to respond at the call of time. The fight was given to Herald. The battle lasted two minutes, and ten seconds. Standard weighed 143, Herald 138½, a perfect piece of manhood.[42]

There was little said throughout Texas, but at least one editor in New Mexico voiced his outrage, writing, "The authorities should take matter in hand and show these El Paso toughs that this is a law abiding land even if Texas is behind the times on the matter."[43]

For the next several years, there was no need for fight fans to creep across the bridge into Dona Ana County — not until 1894, for that's when Australian Billy Smith moved to the border town of El Paso.

New Mexico might've had James Flynn for a time, during the flurry of prizefighting that occurred between 1892 and 1894, but the *real* star of the Southwest, south of Denver, that is, was Billy Smith. Smith, whose real name was Charles E. Matthews, was not only the pioneer of prizefighting for El Paso, but, having fought everyone from then-champ

James J. Corbett to future champ Bob Fitzsimmons, the Australian-born veteran was the closest thing to a world contender the area would see for another decade. Smith's 32-round knockout in a fight-to-the-finish heavyweight bout over Portland's Dave Flaherty was, arguably, the biggest fight of the year in 1894, for both New Mexico and El Paso.

What most historians haven't quite established is exactly where the fight took place. Unfamiliar to the patch of turf across the Courchesne Bridge, historians have dubbed the fight as having taken place in El Paso, but accounts clearly describe the "special train" that transported fans from the border town into Dona Ana County. At 9:30 A.M. on Feb. 17, 1894, a chartered train left the Southern Pacific depot with 300 passengers, crossing over the Rio Grande into New Mexico territory where a 24-foot ring was quickly erected.

> The men entered the ring at 10:40, and after the usual ceremonies were called to shake hands, and a minute afterwards the fight began. Smith stepped to the center of the ring and offered to bet that he would win the fight, but there was no Flahrity [sic] money in sight. Smith, although the smallest and lightest of the two men, was the cleverest, and he forced the fighting all the way through. Flarity acted entirely on the defensive and it took some what longer for Smith to find the right place than was expected. In the 32nd round Smith jabbed Flarity with the left twice in rapid succession in the mouth, knocking him down. He was unable to respond in ten seconds and Referee Merrill declared Smith the winner. Flarity's friends soon had him on board and the train started for El Paso. Mr. Theo Eggers passed the hat around for a slight contribution for the loser and a fair sized amount was raised. It was a good fight from beginning to end and everyone who attended was well pleased. Flarity's face showed very plainly the terrible punishment he had received. Smith was as fresh looking as when he first entered the ring.[44]

For his trouble, Smith picked up $500.

There were several notables in attendance. In fact, "a committee of five leading citizens"[45] from El Paso, carefully unnamed by the *El Paso Daily Times*, had organized the prize fight. Indignation was shared by Las Cruces; four days after the bout, the *Las Cruces Democrat* ran a headline that read "Thirty Cents Reward, in Chips," noting a reward would "be paid for the return of two unsophisticated 'Judges' who followed the Band wagon [sic] to El Paso, Saturday night, and lost their way in the crowd at the prize fight Sunday morning."[46]

News of the Smith-Flaherty bout hit the telegraph wires from coast to coast, but it wasn't so much because the fight, in and of itself, had been so important. What *was* important, however, was that the secretive New Mexico site was now being considered for the site of World Heavyweight Champion James Corbett's title defense against Peter Jackson.

Unlike his predecessor, John L. Sullivan, Corbett had not drawn the color line, at least not in 1891 when he took on Jackson, a black contender nobody else was willing to fight, and the two fought a 61-round draw. Three years later, after Corbett had defended his crown by knocking out England's Charley Mitchell in Jacksonville, Florida, a rematch with Jackson was now being considered, hopefully for Texas — or the secret New Mexico site.

By February 1894, the state of Texas was still up in arms as to whether prize fights were legal. Smaller inconsequential fights were often overlooked — fights involving the world heavyweight champion, on the other hand, were not. So, if New Mexico were to host the fight, on a patch of land no one had paid an iota of attention to, much less cared about, that would be fine, as far as nearby Texas politicos were concerned.

Editors of New Mexico papers were not so enthusiastic. "We can forgive the El Paso people for stealing a match on the sheriff of Dona Ana county and running their prize-fight

The Feb. 17, 1894, battle between Southwest star "Australian" Billy Smith (the mustachioed fellow on the right) and Dave Flaherty (left) was always assumed to have taken place in El Paso but in actuality took place in New Mexico across the Rio Grande. Due to Texas laws prohibiting prize fights, a special train was commissioned to bring spectators across a bridge into New Mexico to escape the law. The fight went 32 rounds before Smith knocked out the lighter Flaherty.

special train over into New Mexico for the Smith-Flaherty contest," wrote the *New Mexican's* editor, "but we want to warn them that they can never hope to secure the Corbett-Jackson fight."[47]

  The argument was moot, for Corbett-Jackson II never did get worked out. It would be another two years before anyone could drag the dapper dan of a champion into the ring. In the meantime, the local scene continued to cook.

Billy Lewis, fighting in Butte, Montana, and who was on a collision course with James Flynn, several months away, wanted a shot at Smith. With all the excitement brewing with the possibility of a championship fight, local sports arranged another mouth-watering local match, between Smith and Lewis, for a $500 purse. Lewis telegraphed an eager response: "Send two tickets."[48]

In the meantime, Flaherty, battered down in 32 rounds by Smith, wasn't quite as battered as anyone thought, for, one day after his fight with Smith, he was in good enough shape to get into a bar fight with another local pug, Lew Gassier. Both men were arrested and released on bond, presenting another potential grudge match while, at the same time, coloring local opinion on pugs' thug behavior. (Despite the flogging received by Smith, Flaherty would fight again one month later in Cerrillos, defeating Herman Frazier, who'd stepped in for an injured James Flynn.)

While Smith vs. Lewis was anticipated, local sports started pooling resources to make Corbett vs. Jackson a reality, raising nearly $10,000. Twice that amount would be needed for the bout that was destined for cancellation. Meanwhile, Smith-Lewis was the biggest local fight yet. Lewis, "who cannot be knocked out with anything less than death," wrote the sports editor of the *Times*, is the "best fighter that had ever been seen in El Paso before the coming of Smith."[49]

"The El Paso prize fight seems to be the only topic of conversation in the City of the Pass at present, which is about the only sporting town in the southwest, all other cities being too much occupied with their mercantile and mining pursuits; as for instance, Albuquerqueans," wrote the *Albuquerque Morning Democrat*. "We have no time to waste on pugilistic entertainments."[50]

The *Democrat's* competitor, the *Citizen*, a much more fight-friendly paper, did. Two days before the fight, the paper reported the bad news: New Mexico was ruled out as the fight site for Smith-Lewis. "The authorities on this side are watching the movements of the ringleaders in the contest, and declare that they will prevent, at all hazards, any attempt at prize fighting.... It is therefore a certainty that the contest will occur on Mexican soil."[51]

Mexican soil was where Smith-Lewis was fought. To ensure the fight would not land in the no-longer-secretive-anymore site in Dona Ana, county officers were stationed at the bridge connecting New Mexico and Texas, on the lookout for a Southern Pacific train rumored to be carrying the pugilists and spectators.

That much the New Mexico authorities got right. But instead of a train running from El Paso to *New* Mexico, the train in question dumped off a crowd of 500 in *Old* Mexico, 50 yards from the northern boundary, hardly a distance requiring the use of rails. But doing so, and keeping the site top secret, not only prevented Mexican and Texan authorities from getting involved, but kept "people from riding out in their buggies and seeing the fight for nothing."[52]

The day before their fight, the two contestants could not agree on weight.

Lewis, a welterweight, refused to fight Smith should he tip the beam a pound heavier than 150 and Smith wanted 154. In the end, Smith won out, forcing Lewis to give up eight pounds when the two met on March 18, 1894.

The fight was a hummer: "Lewis, who could not be knocked out, was knocked out after 14 punishing rounds. After four competitive rounds, Smith took over, the difference in weight and height too much for Lewis. Lewis was badly punished in the body and on returning to the city passed a large amount of blood from the kidneys."[53]

Though victorious, Smith was at the tail-end of his career, having fought 60 or more times since 1888. After hanging up the gloves in 1898, Smith remained a resident of El Paso, becoming a city detective, a deputy sheriff and a deputy U.S. marshal. He would also remain in local sports, becoming a well-known referee through the decades before passing away in 1948 at the age of 79.

Smith's career would not only draw attention to New Mexico's Dona Ana County,

Above and opposite: **Over 120 years later, these images are still mistakenly captioned as being the Feb. 21, 1896, heavyweight championship between Peter Maher and Bob Fitzsimmons. In actuality, they depict the March 17, 1894, battle between "Australian" Billy Smith and Billy Lewis, who was knocked out in 14 rounds. The fight took place on Mexican soil, across from El Paso — and would have taken place in *New* Mexico had local lawmen looked the other way as they had done one month before when Smith had battled Flaherty. To ensure the fight would not land in the not-so-secretive-anymore site in Dona Ana, county officers were stationed at the bridge connecting New Mexico and Texas, on the lookout for a Southern Pacific train rumored to be carrying the pugilists and spectators.**

however. There would be another region Smith would prove instrumental in helping to develop.

Phenix Rising

Our instincts are finer than they were and we are not so coarse and brutal as our ancestors. But is this quite true? We no longer bait bears and badgers; and we read

with a shudder of the Spanish bull fight, though the American abroad always wants to see one at least. But how is it about that brutal form of sport, the pugilistic encounter? Within the memory of those who are still less than middle-aged the prize fight was an essentially low and brutalizing exhibition. In the days of Tom Hyer and Yankee Sullivan, Country McCluskey and John Morrissey, no decent citizen dared to go openly to a prize fight. Those who pretended to decency did sometimes go; but they paid their tribute to decency by going in secret and lying to their wives and their pastors just as the man converted from Sabbath breaking paid his tribute by hiding his rod under his cost when he went fishing on the first day of the week. How is it to-day?
— *Rio Grande Republican*, 1893[54]

Arizona might've had Phoenix, but New Mexico, for a brief time in the 1890s, had *Phenix*. Actually, it was *Carlsbad* that had Phenix — before Carlsbad knew it had caverns, that is, and when it was known as Eddy.

Before a local cowboy discovered the caverns for which Carlsbad is now known, and before the name was even *un*officially changed, the town was Eddy, after cattle baron and teetotaler Charles B. Eddy. In 1891, the railroad had reached Eddy, and the town grew quickly, so quickly, in fact, that it became a haven for gamblers, outlaws and prostitutes. In an effort to control the indecency, the teetotaling town officials developed the suburb of Phenix, which became less of a suburb and more of a tumor for the community that shunned its saloons and whorehouses. And, prizefighting, of course.

If there was a rowdiest saloon in Phenix, it was the Silver King Theatre, home of the first-known prize fight in Phenix — a six-round glove contest on June 1, 1893:

> The glove contest for ten dollars to the winner at Phenix, came off last night as previously announced in this paper. The leading participants were C. F. Welch better known as "Dallas Painter" and Wm. Davis, better known as "The Kid." Dallas knocked the kid down the first round. The kid drew first blood in the second round by giving Dallas a tap on the nose. The fourth round, the kid hit Dallas while he was on the ground and it was declared a foul. The first four rounds, it is said the kid got the best of it. The last two rounds it is stated Dallas got a little the best of it. The timekeeper, J. C. Marrow, better known as "Craps" time keeper and M. Lasswell referee decided Dallas won on a foul. The contest closed at about twelve o'clock after which time the Kid and Dallas bowled up considerable the final outcome of which was an old fashioned scrapping match. The Kid claims the time keeper was unfair to his position and a dispute easily arose. The Kid was "hot" and did not care to conceal it. Dallas it is said when set upon hit the Kid on top of the head with a rock in a handkerchief, and "Craps," the time-keeper, was also drawn into the row. Deputy Williamson arrested all hands and they were before Justice Staleup this afternoon.[55]

Welch won the purse — all of $10, which was the exact amount he was fined for his charge.

Three weeks later, the Silver King hosted a second show, this one "crowded to suffocation," with 300 to 400 spectators who showed up to watch a fight at midnight, along with "an extra police force ... all of whom patrolled the place fully armed."[56]

"Kelly" was the local favorite, a welterweight from Pecos, who was matched up against Jim Jeter, of San Antonio (Texas, not New Mexico), in a finish fight. Outweighed by 21 pounds, Kelly fought a defensive fight, dodging and clinching, coming up short of wind and suffering the first knockdown and first blood. In the eighth, however, "with more force than was supposed to remain in him, dodged a terrific blow and let loose with his right over Jeter's left rib and at the same time gave an upper cut with his left, taking Jeter in the neck near the jugular vein. Jeter fell back on one hand and his knees, slowly sinking to the floor.... It is said Kelly believed himself whipped, but Holohan (his second) called him an

Irish mick and told him to fight."[57] Not quite showing the enthusiasm as its competitor *Eddy Current*, the *Eddy County Citizen*, headlining "That Prize Fight," referred to it as "that moral, elevating, intelligent, gentlemanly — disgusting — physical encounter" in which "not very much blood was spilt except in a figurative sense."[58]

Needless to say, an immediate rematch was arranged for the following week, with four-ounce gloves in a 21-round fight for a purse of $300. This time, showing better wind, Kelly nearly needed the entire distance to win, knocking out Jeter in the 21st and final round. This time, the *Santa Fe New Mexican* joined in on the criticism, noting "We are getting civilized."[59] (A month later, however, James Flynn was headlining the snooty territorial capital.)

Kelly was reported to have had 20 battles, "having met and defeated everyone who has ever strayed this way, regardless of size and weight,"[60] but the Phenix fancy could not talk him into staging a comeback a year-and-a-half later, in 1895, even when it came down to fighting unknown Jim Thompson, a printer from Phoenix, Ariz., who was not only an amateur but was 15 pounds lighter. Turned out, the rank amateur Kelly had refused to fight wasn't such a rank amateur after all — and no doubt, the local favorite had gotten wind of this. "Thompson" was none other than James Davis, self-proclaimed lightweight champion of the Southwest, reportedly, a 26-bout veteran with but two losses, one of them being to Jack Everhardt, the English lightweight champ, who'd kayoed him in 28 rounds, in 1893.

Kelly remained retired, but when Australian Billy Smith came to town, two months later, the fight scene rose from the ashes — pardon the pun — like a Phoenix. This time, Phenix took a more refined approach to reintroducing the sport, staging exhibitions and short bouts under the Queensberry rules rather than slugging matches in a finish fight. The shows were staged under local promoter Ed Piontowsky, who charged patrons 75 cents or $1 for a reserved seat.

Smith, a local celebrity who'd gone the distance with the big boys, would give an exhibition of his skill against Davis, who'd, by then, been exposed as a veteran, on a comeback card on March 14, 1895. The show was such a success that Piontowsky staged a second show two nights later, then he took the show on the road to nearby Roswell, four nights later.

In 1895, Roswell, with a population of around 500, was known for its artesian water. The railroads had linked Roswell with Eddy and Pecos City, Texas, and it was fast becoming a shipping point for cattle. Roswell received its first taste of prizefighting, and the community that was, at first, skeptical, embraced the sport. "As this was the pioneer exhibition of the kind the croaker was largely in evidence beforehand with the cry of 'fake,'" wrote the *Roswell Record*. "Many who would otherwise have attended stayed away. Those who ran the gauntlet of the croaker were richly paid for their faith."[61]

In one of the first well-rounded fight cards, shorter bouts preceding the main go, two four-rounders between young local pugs warmed up the crowd, before the eight-round exhibition between Smith and Davis.

"They are both men of rare ability in the fistic arena as was clearly demonstrated throughout the entire contest," the Roswell reporter gave his thumbs-up and clamored for another card. "This is the first fistic exhibition that we have witnessed in many years and we are compelled to confess that there has been a great deal of improvement in the art of giving and avoiding blows that was in vogue a score of years ago."[62] Encouraging the scene even more, the *Record* noted that Jim Jeter, the now local heavyweight who'd been KO'd twice in 1893 to Eddy's pug, Kelly, would like a shot at Smith in a comeback bout. That fight came off five nights later, March 25, 1895, back in Phenix.

As expected, the fight wasn't much of one, Smith knocking out Jeter in one round.

Unable to get a rise out of Kelly, who was "steering shy of all-around professionals,"[71] Smith, $200 richer for his easy win, along with Davis and promoter Piontowsky, departed Eddy to ply their trade back in El Paso.

Sometime later that year, the exact date is unknown, Smith returned to Phenix for a bigger fight against Louis Jester, of Wilkes-Barre, Pennsylvania, though an account of the fight was printed in newspapers never making it to microfilm. Most likely, the fight took place in April.

It wasn't long after — by October of 1895 — however, that prizefighters were among the number of undesirables booted out of the vicinity when Eddy do-gooders had had enough.

The Smith-Jester fight closed the book on Eddy's prize fight scene, though it would return full force in 1912 under the renamed town of Carlsbad.

Duke City

> *The individual who had the gall to come into* THE DEMOCRAT *office yesterday, and walk off with all the latest Denver dailies is invited to come again today. We have a club in waiting for him, and it will be used regardless of Marquis of Queensbury* [sic] *rules.*
>
> —*Albuquerque Morning Democrat,* 1892[64]

> *The prize fight really to the dogs is going*
> *As everybody knows,*
> *For though the pugilists are always blowing,*
> *They never come to blows.*
>
> —*Santa Fe New Mexican,* 1892[65]

By the turn of the century, Albuquerque would forever establish itself as New Mexico's leading city, its population expanding from six thousand to eight, thanks to the railroad. By 1895, there were seven churches, five hotels, three schools, several streetcars and a brewery. And still no homegrown prizefighters.

Local talent was scarce, when it came to native New Mexicans. It wouldn't be until well after 1900 that Albuquerque could produce a New Mexico born-and-bred pugilist. In the meantime, at least in the 1890s, the division of labor in the prize ring looked no different than the miners, railroad workers, businessmen and other imports who were populating the area.

Out-of-towners who called Albuquerque home came from a variety of professions, from miners like James Flynn to railroad men and businessmen looking for a fresh start on the frontier. As the prize ring scene grew, it attracted professional fighters who found both easy prey and easy money to be made from the territory's weekend warriors calling themselves local champions.

As it had done in the 1880s, Albuquerque, officially incorporated in 1891, quickly established itself as the headquarters in New Mexico for professional fighting.

Technically, it was Old Town, the village adjacent to Albuquerque that allowed the fight scene to prosper. When the Atchison, Topeka and Santa Fe Railroad arrived in 1880, the railyards and passenger depot had been built two miles away from Old Town, from which Albuquerque (originally "New Town") sprang. Due to the city's growth, Old Town was absorbed, becoming an official part of Albuquerque in the 1920s. In the 1890s, if you wanted liquor, gambling or women, Old Town was the place to go — ditto prizefighting.

It was in Old Town where Albuquerque's version of The Fancy gathered to watch area prizefighters in a makeshift ring — guys like Reddy Welsch, a local bricklayer, and J. Edward Priest, who not only fought but served as promoter, referee and local saloon owner.

As a pug, Priest was less than spectacular. In his initial bout of 1891, he defeated even-less-renowned Louis Meyers in a finish fight called "the most laughable glove contest of the age":

> Both men tip the scales beyond the 200 point and when they appeared it was the signal for tremendous cheering. Ed. Parker first came forward and deposited in the ring ... four of the largest mittens ever manufactured, then came Mr. Priest, who was followed a second later by Mr. Meyers. Both gentleman were recorded the most enthusiastic applause. So ... they went at it, but when Meyers made one of his celebrated rushes his feet left the floor and his posterior struck with a mighty force. The building shook as if the entire place had met the atmosphere, carrying devastation in its path, and it was at best five seconds before the referee, time keepers, battle doctors and the audience could gain their equilibrium for the contest to continue. Louis' employees in the balcony and the jar was so great that she fell from his chair and disappeared through a crack in the floor. This round ended in favor of Mr. Priest, who for a large man, is a lively one on his feet. One more round of fun ended the circus.[66]

Despite the hilarity, a rematch, for the unofficial New Mexico heavyweight championship, no less, was set for the following month, during the eleventh annual Territorial Fair, once again, before 300 people who were crammed outside Post's Exchange in Old Town, a popular hotel where you could stay for a $1.50 a night.

Though Old Town had been chosen because it was outside the corporate limits of Albuquerque, where officials had naysayed prizefighting, there was still quite a bit of resistance. So, when the "Albuquerque Athletic Club" quickly formed, they assured officials that any staged bouts weren't so much *prize fights*, "in the strictest sense of the word,"[67] but a friendly boxing bout between club members.

ARMORY HALL.
SATURDAY, AUGUST 15,
BENEFIT OF
REDDY WELSCH
The Albuquerque Champion
SPARRING CONTEST,

Three good events will be given, in which the art of self defense will be demonstrated by
TWO HEAVY WEIGHTS
234 and 230 respectively
who will spar for four rounds for points
BILLY PICKETT
—AND—
TOM SMITH

Two Colored boys will then wear the mittens for four rounds, after which

REDDY WELSCH
—AND—
TEDDY FOLEY
Will Spar six rounds.
Admission 50c.

Fight poster and advertisement for the Aug. 15, 1891, card at Armory Hall in Albuquerque. Reddy Welsch was the top fighter in the Duke city, though the main event featured local heavyweights Ed Priest and Louis Meyers in what was described as the "most laughable glove contest of the age" by the *Albuquerque Morning Journal*.

Prize fight or club exhibition, Meyers lasted two rounds, quitting "in a manner that was surprising to everybody" when Priest "sent him to the grass and out of the battle"[68] in an easy victory. Priest took home $100 and 60 percent of the gate—probably about $90. As bad as the fight was, it received the unwanted attention of the governor.

Originally from Queens, New York, Governor LeBaron Bradford Prince held office from 1889 to 1893. Though part of the controversial "Santa Fe Ring," a group of politically corrupt attorneys and land grabbers, Prince was primarily known for his attempts at campaigning for New Mexico statehood. Prince might also have been the first governor — though he was certainly not the last — to shun prize fights.

"I should have thought some of those interested in the fair would have had influence enough to stop that proposed prize fight," Gov. Prince told the *Santa Fe Sun.* "It is hurting the good name of the town more than a good many other things can make up for."[69] Unlike the *Sun,* the editor of its competitor, the *New Mexican,* countered with, "And we would

Originally from San Francisco, Jim McCoy was the first known New Mexico middleweight champion. He was Albuquerque's top fighter during 1892 but after ducking a showdown with El Paso's Billy Lewis and an embarrassing loss to Joe Cotton on a card in Barelas, he moved on.

like to know in what way the holding of a boxing match in old Albuquerque is going to hurt the territorial fair? We fail to see where the two are connected. Has not the governor become so addicted to finding fault with the fair that he has become a chronic kicker?"[70]

Meyers, by the way, soon after gave the sport another black eye when he was arrested for stealing a stack of silver dollars from a roulette table at a local gambling establishment. Neither Meyers nor Priest fought again. Priest went on seconding fighters, promoting cards and matchmaking.

Bigger than Priest was another Albuquerque fighter — lightweight "Reddy" Welsch, a brickmaker who headlined shows between 1891 and 1893 before unsuccessfully taking his career on the road. Before fights were, generally, kicked to Old Town, Welsch headlined the first big show of the decade for Albuquerque when he took on Chicago's John Stock in a finish fight at Grant's Opera House, on Aug. 6, 1891. Despite his underdog status and a tough fight, Welsch was able to come out ahead, knocking out Stock in round four. Welsch became an overnight celebrity. His light winnings had local promoters throwing a benefit show for him, challengers for whom were being encouraged to show their skill:

The boy showed up so well in his battle with Stock that the light gate receipts, owing to the feeling that it was a "fake" makes lovers of the honest sport feel that something is due the Albuquerque champion. A bout of four rounds will be sparred between two heavy weights — 224 and 281 respectively — for points. The two bantams will give an exhibition of the manly art for four rounds, and after that if anybody can be found who is anything nearly equally matched with Welsch there will be a setto between them. The town has been flooded with hopeful pugilists who claim science the past week, but they have generally proved to be hams. On Tuesday, an individual walked into the sporting editor of THE DEMOCRAT and after claiming all sorts of science, was invited to try a round or so with Red to see if there was anything in him. Not seeing any good way out of it, he went up to the rooms of the Athletic association and lasted, in as kind a set-to as Welsch can make, a fraction under two minutes. Of course no thought of such a parrot and monkey play could be thought of in public. Good men will be well treated here, but the gentlemen who are intending to form an athletic association have no time to spend on plugs, and the man who hopes to get an exhibition without first showing his ability, will save car fare by staying away.[71]

Challenges did arrive, from reputable fighters like Gallup's McSparron, but Welsch could not be induced to return to the ring, preferring the less dangerous work of brickmaking. When he did return, two years later, in a fight against Las Vegas' Harry Slater for the New Mexico middleweight championship, he was knocked out in a single round. When a rematch was talked about, for a $50 side bet, Slater told the *New Mexican* that "if Welsh [*sic*] would talk less and fight more, he would please the community better."[72]

The offended Welsch then agreed to a rematch on Nov. 9, 1893, but, before it could come off, Welsch "tired of waiting for the slow arrangements of a fight within the ropes" and walked into a local saloon, where he challenged Slater to a fist fight, "that he might wipe up the earth with him. Slater at once answered. A ring of bystanders was formed and they went at it, hammer and tongs. Welsh [*sic*] was not in it from the first. Slater knocked him down six times in succession, always waiting for Welsh to get up and come at him. The last time Welsh could not rise. He was badly punished, while Slater did not show a scratch."[73]

Welsch was finished and, unheeding the challenges of rising local star Flynn, disappeared from the headlines in New Mexico, though he did step into the ring again one year later in Dallas. Proclaiming himself the middleweight champion of New Mexico (the *Dallas Morning News* got it wrong, omitting the "New" portion of Welsch's imaginary title), Welsch took on the great Jack Everhardt, the English lightweight champion who was being groomed for a shot at World Lightweight Champion Jack McAuliffe. Welsch lasted four minutes.

San Francisco's Jim McCoy ruled Albuquerque for a time, in 1892, gathering more steam in the Duke City than had Priest, Welsch or even Flynn. Claiming a long list of victories on the West Coast (he was, at best, a mediocre fighter in San Francisco), McCoy built up a strong following in prize-fight-ignorant Albuquerque. He also found easier pickings in New Mexico than the experienced fighters he'd been matched against on the West Coast.

On Jan. 20, 1892, he was paired up with John Marshall, "a colored waiter at the Armijo house," with promoters assuring that there "is no hippodrome business about it, that both men mean a genuine fight."[74] The fight was set for the Post's Exchange at 3 P.M. Before a crowd of 250, McCoy vs. Marshall made front-page headlines in the *Daily Citizen* with a lengthy round-by-round report. Equal in length, the *Morning Democrat* ran their story inside. The fight was "decidedly hot and swift, with scientific boxing from the winner."[75] Marshall, later reported to be from Denver, took punishment for 14 rounds before yielding to the more scientific McCoy, who laid him out with a right on the jaw. By the time the story hit the wires, McCoy's $100 had blown up to $1,000 and the fight was being called "the first square fight that has ever taken place in New Mexico."[76]

McCoy was here to stay, at least for a while, and he wasted no time in setting up a boxing school and gymnasium over the Miner's Exchange in Old Town. He also started calling out Southwest middleweights, from the experienced Omaha's Jimmy Lindsay to less-known-but-local black fighter L. Talbott. Many responded, but McCoy conceded to local promoters who insisted on running any challengers through exhibitions to ensure a good fight, before signing any articles.

Of course, Billy Lewis and Gallup's McSparron were touted as naturals to take on McCoy. Lewis, really a welterweight who would be giving up 20 to 30 pounds, responded, "I will not fight in Albuquerque for the simple reason that an El Pasoan is barred in winning anything there."[77] McCoy responded, saying he would be willing to fight at a weight between 150 and 160, if Lewis entered the ring between 140 and 160, for a $250 purse. Promoters changed the demands, calling for a 150-pound limit for both fighters, a $250 purse or for a $500 stakes, with both fighters agreeing to train in Albuquerque.

Before a big main event could be arranged, in April, several smaller shows were staged, including a bantamweight matchup that soured the scene when overmatched local Louis Wilson picked up the win when he was struck while down by Kansas City's George "Kid" Thompson. Five hundred people gathered outside the Post's Exchange. The "attendance was as large as the placita could hold and give spectators a chance to see the ring" while "from the roof of a house a block away a few ladies witnessed the encounter" that ended in a near-riot—"altogether too much excitement for a Sunday afternoon."[78]

The disappointing outcome only encouraged local pugs to throw out challenges. Hugh McSparron's brother Peter, a.k.a. "The Gallup Spider," challenged both Thompson and Wilson; A Salt Lake City pug named W. "Slim" Henry, who was backed by his railroad co-workers, called out anyone near 185 pounds; while future mayor of Cerrillos, Austin Goodall, owner of the Miner's Exchange, over which Welsch had set up his boxing school, immediately called for a rematch, offering up $200 to any takers caring to bet that Thompson could whip Wilson in less than ten rounds, next time around.

There was no rematch, for the bigger fight demanded by local railbirds was a showdown between McCoy and Lewis. Two days after the Thompson-Wilson fiasco, the *Citizen* ran a front-page story, titled "Now Let McCoy Accept," with Lewis agreeing to a fight on slightly modified terms from their previous agreement. After fighting Louis Golding (a.k.a. "Sparrow Golden) on Feb. 21, Lewis, win, lose or draw, would head to Albuquerque for a March 11 fight with McCoy, 150-pound limit four hours before first bell, the purse to be split $175 winner/$75 loser with an optional side bet from $250 to $1,000. "In all fairness, let the terms of the El Paso sparer [*sic*], which are as fair as any aspirant of the ring could ask, be at once accepted, so the men can begin placing themselves in first class condition,"[79] wrote the *Citizen's* editor.

After knocking out Golding in five, Lewis, as good as his word, arrived in Albuquerque on the 24th, along with his brother "Slim" Jim Lewis, who offered to take on anyone at 120 pounds. Met by "sporting inclined citizens" at the depot, "Mr. Lewis appears to be a born fighter, and although following an occupation not all looked upon as strictly proper, he nevertheless talks and acts like he is a gentleman. He has none of the sickening braggadocio, so characteristic of a majority of those who make a living by pouching the wind out of each other, and has already made friends here in the city."[80]

With little choice, the somewhat reluctant McCoy agreed to fight Lewis, though the original date of March 11 was moved to March 23 to give both fighters enough time to drop their weight down to 150.

McCoy-Lewis became the most hyped fight seen yet in New Mexico. Near-daily updates ran in the local papers, posters of the upcoming match were posted as far as 50 miles away, and the four-ounce gloves to be used in the fight were on display at the Miner's Exchange.

Noted by reporters and watched by throngs of spectators, Lewis and McCoy prepared for one another. McCoy's daily regiment began with a 10- or 12-mile run on the track in Old Town, followed by a rubdown. In the afternoon, McCoy could be found at Goodall's on First Street, working the "clubs, dumb bells and sandbag." Lewis, on the other hand, was "training altogether for his wind. In the morning he takes cross country runs in and the afternoon he takes the customary exercises in his quarters over the Branch saloon."[81]

Three weeks out, the only apparent problems were McCoy's problem in making weight, securing a site that would not raise the eyebrows of local officials, and finding a so-called "neutral" referee.

The coming mill attracted attention in surrounding states. Several notable sporting men were, reportedly, on their way from Colorado, Las Vegas and El Paso, as were fighters. San Francisco's Joe Cotton made his way to New Mexico and Paul Pitzlin, who'd fought in Albuquerque in the late 1880s, offered $1,000 a side for a go at Lewis, a favorite over McCoy.

As an appetizer, Lewis' brother Slim Jim and Jim Daley, a St. Louis pug, fought on March 7 at Post's Exchange, though the small crowd and outcome didn't exactly help the Lewis-McCoy promotion. After repeated fouls, Daley lost the fight by disqualification. Worse, after the referee had rendered his decision, Daley sucker-punched him and was immediately taken down by several spectators and Jim McCoy, who was, for some reason, working his soon-to-be opponent's brother's corner. (Slim Jim Lewis and Daley rematched in El Paso a month later and, this time, Lewis punished Daley, who was unable to answer the ninth-round bell. After the fight, however, the two were arrested and had to spend ten days on the chain gang.)

Nine days before the fight, the location of the big fight was announced as top secret, for fear that the local authorities would find a reason to upset plans. Meanwhile, Lewis announced he was on target, nearing 160 pounds on his way to 150. Neither the Slim Jim Lewis-Daley fight, nor a mention in the *National Police Gazette* that Lewis' last opponent in El Paso was not really Sparron Golding but an imposter, soured the upcoming Lewis-McCoy fight.

What *did* was McCoy's alleged illness.

A warning first appeared on March 13, when McCoy told the press he had to break from training due to a severe cold, though he would have plenty of time to get into top shape by fight night. When the papers reacted negatively, suggesting a possible yellow streak, McCoy turned to his physician, a Dr. Pearce, who assured the media that "he is in no way afraid of Lewis, and is only too anxious to meet him, but can not do it at present."[82] McCoy's condition quickly elevated from holding off a mere cold to "suffering from a disease that renders him unable to engage in the contest."[83]

Just like that, the fight was off.

In its place, a benefit card with several exhibitions was arranged for the 23rd. Talk turned to bringing to town New Orleans fighter Jack Burke to fight Lewis. Sick of waiting and not wanting to waste his peak condition, Lewis went to Las Vegas to headline a show there against their local favorite, Happy Jack Ryan, whom he defeated with ease on the night of March 20, 1892. The next day, Lewis returned to Albuquerque for the exhibition show at the Grant's Opera House, fighting a five-round no-decision contest with Jack Lawrence.

A Detroit lightweight fighting since 1885, Lawrence had gone eight rounds with Harry Gilmore in 1886, before Gilmore had challenged Jack McAuliffe for the world lightweight championship the following year. From the Midwest, Lawrence found his way to New

Orleans, where he'd gone 19 rounds with the dangerous Charlie Johnson (whom would defeat James Flynn in Creede shortly thereafter), then to Texas and, ultimately to New Mexico. Considered past his prime, the 34-year-old Lawrence found easier prey in New Mexico than anywhere else. On March 20, just a few days before his exhibition with Lewis in Albuquerque, Lawrence knocked out the virtually unknown Ynez Ivaris, "the Mexican who lives on Whisky creek,"[84] in ten minutes at the one-and-only prize fight known to occur in Pinos Altos. Soon after, Lawrence arrived in Albuquerque, hoping for a fight, or to second Lewis against McCoy. With the fight cancelled, Lawrence settled for an exhibition with Lewis — the two had, reportedly, fought a 19-round draw in El Paso some time before.

That same card also featured a four-round draw between McCoy, now miraculously recovered, and Joe Cotton, who was itching for a finish fight with any takers. The black San Bernadino fighter — no doubt seen by McCoy as easier prey than Lewis — got his wish.

McCoy had told the press that he'd still been sick during his exhibition with Cotton ("but in order to please his admirers appeared in the benefit"),[85] but since Lewis had left the city, his health miraculously improved. After Lewis graciously thanked the town for their hospitality, leaving for bigger, better fight opportunities (he'd return in 1894 for James Flynn), McCoy called out Cotton for a finish fight to come off within 15 days for a $500 purse. Cotton accepted and, on April 10, the two met outside the then Albuquerque limits, in Barelas. The fight did little to bolster the prizefight scene, and even less for McCoy's sagging reputation.

A good crowd assembled Sunday afternoon to witness the glove contest between Jim McCoy and Joe Cotton, lately of California. The local officers objected to holding the fight in the old town, and the managers selected a spacious corral in Barelas for the sport. Buggies, carriages, wagons and Trimble's big omnibuses brought the spectators to the ground. Admission was $2.50. The crowd expected a fight to the finish, but were doomed to disappointment. Four rounds of good hard work, with some splendid in-fighting, led the attendance to believe that there was nothing in the rumors that the "fight would be a fake." It was good fighting, and the lovers of the sport were delighted. However, several opportunities for stunning licks were intentionally passed, and thereafter the crowd was not much disappointed when in the fifth round McCoy was sent to the ground by a fore-arm swing of Cotton and staid there. At this juncture the roof of the adobe house adjoining in which Cotton had his quarters, went down with a crash, and with it the over-weight of humanity that had crowded it. The incident caused considerable excitement, and it is charitable to suppose that this very excitement nerved McCoy to spring from his prostrate condition on the floor and leap the ropes with as much agility as he could before receiving the "stunning" blow that "knocked him out." Nobody was seriously hurt by the falling of the roof, and neither was McCoy by the blow that knocked him out. The majority went away disappointed. Cotton won the fight but lost his clothes under the fallen roof. Of the 40 or 50 people who went down with the roof only a few were slightly scratched.[86]

"The next time that Albuquerque people pay $2.50 for admission it will be to see a prize fight,"[87] wrote the *Democrat*. The latest debacle gave the sport another black eye, but in May, prizefighting returned with a 20-round Queensberry bout between two new headliners, Sailor Jack Frazier and George "Kid" Thompson, of Kansas City, while McCoy, fighting two days later, had to settle for an even less-hyped bout well outside city limits and Old Town.

The Frazier-Thompson bout received rave reviews by the papers that barely mentioned it was even happening. "The contest proved a fight for blood and was considered one of the best scrap matches Albuquerque ever saw," told the *Democrat*. "The crowded condition of our columns forbid the details by rounds. Twenty-one were fought and Thompson went to his corner and ordered off his gloves, claiming he was not getting justice."[88]

McCoy's fight, a win over little-known Edward Blakeley, of Las Vegas, received but a mention: "There is fighting and fighting, there are exponents of the manly art and there are sluggers, who not only give rank exhibitions, but are rank in themselves, simply beats, who dodge this way and that for a living. Such sport, if it can be called sport, is too low for respectable people to be engaged in. But there is a plane upon which these sports and exhibitions can be run. If it must be done, boys, get on that level."[89]

Having worn out his stay, McCoy left town and was last mentioned in Albuquerque as on the lam, having escaped officers in El Paso, who'd arrested him for fighting in the courthouse on yet another charge, connected to Pecos City, Texas. Ironically, as late as December 1892, a portrait of Jim McCoy appeared in the *National Police Gazette,* challenging anyone in the country for $1,000 and proclaiming himself to be the New Mexico middleweight champion. McCoy headed east, resurfacing in 1895 by losing to English pugilist Dick Collyer in a fight that "was for blood, and would have been fierce, but for the faintheartedness of McCoy, who proved himself a quitter in the fourth round."[90]

With McCoy no longer touted in New Mexico, the next big fight during 1892 landed 50 miles north in Santa Fe on May 24 — whether they wanted it or not. In what was another case of an out-of-towner with experience beating up a less-than-ready local, the fight took place on the narrow-gauge road, where the Denver & Rio Grande Western Railroad was laying the last rails of the "Chili Line," which would ultimately stretch from Santa Fe to Antonito, Colorado.

> A prize fight on the quiet took place last night when about 100 admirers of the manly art, having received the tip, were on hand to see the sport. A special train carried the party ten miles out on the narrow gauge road. The contestants were two colored men, "Kid" Robinson, of San Francisco, and a local slugger named John Marshall. They fought with skin tight gloves for a purse of $100. Robinson weighed 137 pounds and his opponent 172. From start to finish the combat was an interesting one. Robinson, though much the smaller of the two, was far ahead in ring practice and at the close of the eleventh round he had his man whipped, not however, until Marshal had scored two square knockdowns against the kid. There is a talk of arranging another similar contest at an early date.[91]

With the disappointment, decline and departure of McCoy, prize fights in and around Albuquerque came to a sudden stop for nearly a year, though the city did tolerate an exhibition in December by well-known George La Blanche. Nicknamed "The Marine," LaBlanche was best known for his "pivot punch" used against World Middleweight Champion Jack "The Nonpareil" Dempsey in 1889. LaBlanche was on the brink of beating Dempsey in round 32, but his knockout punch was declared illegal and the champ kept his crown.

En route to New Orleans, where a rematch with Dempsey or Stephen "Reddy" Gallagher was in the works (neither one happened), LaBlanche and sparring partner C. H. Davis arranged for an exhibition at the Armory Hall where he'd demonstrate the punch that had floored the great Dempsey. LaBlanche received a fair attendance, but, in Santa Fe, dual shows were held at Gray's Hall on New Year's Eve and Jan. 2. The LaBlanche tour stopped at Raton before leaving New Mexico.

While Albuquerque shunned prizefighting for much of 1893, Eddy's ill-reputed suburb of Phenix, Las Vegas and, surprising all, Santa Fe, picked up the slack, staging a few shows during the year.

Meanwhile, in Raton, the prize-fight scene was well and alive until its mayor, J. J. Kelly, outlawed the sport in 1893. Up until that time, there might not have been any fights on record, but the mining and railroad community was evidently fight crazy from 1892 to 1893, evidenced from the diary that has been archived of Nebraska-born railroad worker E. Meeks.

For an eight-month period, May 1892 to early 1893, Meek chronicled daily life in Raton, covering local crimes, gambling, entertainment — and the interest there in prizefighting. Though there are no chronicled local fights, Meek's entries include local bulletins on big-name fights, like the world featherweight championship, in which champion George Dixon, "this (nigger) knocked Skelly out," Jack McAuliffe's KO of Billy Myers and Jim Corbett's defeat of John L. Sullivan (he "had him all over ring during really whole of fight. Sullivan's not in it. Could have made big money if he'd had cared to bet.")[92] Of greater importance is Meek's experience in the local gym, sparring with fellow railroad workers and miners Gillette ("He got to striking hard & I quit him"), Young Sowers, Benson ("got in a pivot blow, bringing the red from his nose, swelling my fist up some"),[93] and several others. Meek also mentions seeing LaBlanche and Davis spar while in Raton.

While Raton eventually outlawed prize fights, Santa Fe went against the grain of its leading paper, the *New Mexican*, when local enthusiasts formed the so-called Sage Brush Prize Ring Association.

Under cover of a private club, bouts were allowed to be staged for members only without local law enforcement screaming a public disturbance. Later promoters and "athletic clubs" would fine-tune this operation, not selling "tickets" to the general public, but *memberships*. After a handful of mentions and even fewer shows, the association disappeared, while prizefighting impetus moved to Cerrillos during 1894.

By the end of the year, however, the momentum swung back to Albuquerque with the arrival of a Kansas City bantamweight named Kid Dovey. The bigger battle for prizefighting would ensue.

The Real Battle Begins

> H. S. No. 15, Mr. Carr's prize fighting bill, adversely reported by the committee on militia, was read in full.
> Mr. Pino moved to table the bill indefinitely.
> Mr. Carr spoke in favor of the bill, stating that it embodied ideas that should become law. He thought the territory should take this forward step toward preventing the brutality of the prize ring and that the interests of advancing civilization demanded action by the legislature. He said that the provision of the bill making a killing, in a prize fight, murder in the first degree was most wise in view of recent events in the prize rings of the east.
> Mr. Martin said that the bill made murder out of manslaughter.
> Mr. Carr said that if it was Mr. Martin's only objection on it might be obviated by striking out the obnoxious clause.
> Mr. Christy opposed the law on the ground, not that the bill was bad, but that it was unnecessary, as there had never been a prize fight in New Mexico.
> Mr. Carr asked if the gentleman had never read of the recent fight at Cerillos.[sic]
> Mr. Christy said he never had.
> A voice in the rear interrupted: "That was only a little amateur performance."
> Speaker Dame: "I saw that fight myself and it was a pretty good one."
> The motion to postpone the consideration of the bill indefinitely was carried by a vote of 18 to 10.
>
> —Santa Fe New Mexican, 1895[94]

Kansas City bantamweight Kid Dovey fought a handful of fights, from the Midwest to Colorado, before he arrived in Raton in the fall or early winter of 1894 to defeat local slugger Jerry Haley. Raton was just a stopover for Dovey, who was headed for Albuquerque where he challenged "any and all comers in the territory of New Mexico and Arizona."[95] One day later, his defi was answered, by another out-of-towner of equal experience, Jack Gibson, of Omaha, Neb., who replied, "Dear Sir — I will accept your challenge for a finish fight, date and time to be hereafter named."[96]

For the first time since McCoy's rise and sudden fall, the Duke City became excited about a prize fight, which was set up for Old Town, on December 11. On the day of the fight, however, Dovey, Gibson, 800 spectators and a handful of local policemen crammed into Exhibition Hall for a disappointment:

> Information was received that owing to the opinion of Judge Collier the sheriff forbade the contest. The crowd was unwilling to believe Sheriff Yrsarri's interpretation of the Sunday law was the proper thing under the circumstances, and delegated the local builder of the Citizen, who it was said was managing the affair, to plead with Judge Collier, to consent to permit the law to be violated. Of course the judge refused to be moved by such importunings, even in behalf of entertaining an event as a slugging match, and the reporter sadly returned from his unsuccessful mission. Charles Yondorf, a republican who desires to serve the territory as justice of the peace of this precinct, was delegated to argue with the sheriff about the matter. "My honor would not permit it," replied the official. "No sir, I would not let the fight go on for a million of dollars." As Mr. Yondorff did not happen to have a million dollars about his clothes or person at the time he had no effective way of meeting the sheriff's objections. It was remarked, however, that Sheriff Yrsarri's honor has grown surprisingly sensitive since he erected a bull pen in Old Town. The fight was not pulled off and the pugs and sport returned to Albuquerque.[97]

Despite the reporter's pessimism that the fight would be pulled off on another date, Dovey-Gibson was rescheduled for Dec. 14 at Old Town's Floral Hall. Instead of a finish fight, though, the crowd would have to be to be content with a scheduled ten-rounder. Unfortunately, once again, the bout did not live up to the hype:

> Dovey against Gibson. Been in town a week. Worked a basketful of sports. Also hotel men. Dovey wore a sweater. Also thrummed guitar in front of his Windsor hotel. Gibson was exclusive. Had a record. Both men were anxious to get at each other. Given permission to fight last night. In Floral hall in Old Town. Admission one dollar. Manager reported box office delinquent. Gibson did not want to put up his mits. Nothing in it. Dovey made a play, said he would scrap for fun. Crowd wanted a fight. Forced management to bring the men together. Dovey jabbed Gibson in the mouth and the MAN WHO HAS MET THE BEST FEATHER WEIGHTS IN THE COUNTRY took off his gloves after the ninth round. Rank Fake. Case of must fight or be pulled. Pass Gibson up. Also Dovey. The sporting editor of the MORNING DEMOCRAT who witnessed the fiasco last night wishes to know what sort of a reception a square boxer would receive in Albuquerque.[98]

Though maybe he should have, Dovey did not give up trying to make an impression in New Mexico. He fought a little-publicized, on-the-sly fight with a man named Frazier sometime during February in Old Town, KO'd little-known Jimmy Love in Las Vegas in the early months of 1895, then was part of a renewed effort in Albuquerque to rejuvenate prizefighting in a finish fight for the featherweight championship of the Southwest on March 2.

Though the prize-fight scene was about to explode again, there was also reason to think it might *im*plode, for the anti-prizefight sentiment was building across the country. The sporting fraternity was clamoring for James J. Corbett to defend the heavyweight championship against rising star Bob Fitzsimmons, who'd knocked out World Middleweight

Champion Jack Dempsey in 1891, before giving up the title to campaign as a heavyweight. With his sights set on the champion, Corbett, "Lanky Bob," really a middleweight, became the public's No. 1 Contender.

The only thing promoter Dan Stuart needed was a fight site.

A hastily-formed "Albuquerque Athletic Association" submitted an offer of $30,000 to the managers of the champion and challenger, stating that since prizefighting with gloves was tolerated in the territory of New Mexico, more or less, why not stage it here?

Of course, a town that saw a minor fight like Dovey vs. Gibson nixed on the spot, whose to-the-finish fight was reduced to an unmotivated ten-round sparring session, had little hopes of receiving a fight of championship caliber. Anti-prizefight politicians sought to quickly squash the thought and a bill was introduced to the New Mexico legislature in January 1895 that would make the sport definitely illegal. The bill "developed quite a following," wrote the *New Mexican*, "but not enough to save it from indefinite postponement. Mr. Carr says that the trouble is, some of his bills are a little ahead of the times."[99]

Seemingly free of any legal static, the fights went on. While Albuquerque prepared for Dovey's March 1895 fight, Santa Fe promoters, encouraged by the killing of the Carr bill, staged a fight to the finish at Motley's Hall, between the little known "traveling lightweight" Cockney Sterling (a.k.a. Jockney Stirling — the combinations and spellings of his name proved numerous) and local blacksmith Jim Williams, who "was pretty badly punished"[100] before losing by KO in round 15, before a crowd of 100.

Meanwhile, lightweight Charles Rochette, of San Francisco, emerged on the scene, destroying unknown Jack LeMoin on Feb. 4, in Deming. Rochette, a solid veteran since 1888, had draws with top fighter Dal Hawkins and had gone ten rounds with George "Kid" Lavigne in 1892. Midstride his career, he was taking a southwestern tour, having also fought in Denver and Arizona.

While Wilson got Rochette, Dovey was assisted by a local pug named Charles Allinson, who would, later in the year, attempt to initiate his own career in the Duke City.

Adding to the buzz astir in Albuquerque, Rochette offered to train Dovey's foe, Charlie Wilson. Dubbed "The English Kid," an England import recently of New Orleans but now fighting out of Denver, he "made the bantams fly before him."[101] His challenge had been printed under the headline "Now For a Fight," when he stated, "I hereby challenge any 118 pound man. Dovey preferred."[102]

"The fight will be a wicked one,"[103] wrote the *Morning Democrat*, after the two principals agreed to fight for a purse of $75 and a side bet of $500, in a finish fight at 118. It was the first time a big local fight had been arranged at a lower weight. By the 26th of February, a makeshift arena at the Albuquerque Street Car's company "auditorium" became the site while the promoters promised not only an evenly matched finish fight between scientific fighters, but "no fake ... no delays ... no collections on the side taken up."[104] A day before the fight, Wilson was at 117 ("after he had done a five-mile spin over the mesa"[105]) and Dovey 116, both certifiably in the pink of condition.

Despite all the pre-fight hype, there was little written on the fight itself, only that Dovey won easily over Wilson, who gave a lively fight but refused "to stand up and receive punishment any longer,"[106] after four rounds, authorizing his seconds to throw up the sponge.

In a less-hyped bout, Rochette headlined the next Albuquerque card, knocking out Las Vegas' Happy Jack, then was himself knocked out in El Paso by Lew Gassier (some record books erroneously list otherwise), before bouncing back in Raton (so much for Mayor

Kelly's 1893 edict against prizefighting) by stopping Young Dugan in 17 hard-fought rounds.

In April 1895, Rochette returned to the Duke City to headline another card at the Albuquerque Street Car's "auditorium" against Gallup's Jack Grady for the lightweight territorial championship. Compared to the veterans and topnotchers Rochette had faced in the ring, Grady should've been easy pickings, but the Gallup miner was hardy enough to last 23 rounds before he was knocked out. After beating Grady, Rochette left for San Francisco where, a year later, he went up against the great Joe Gans, losing by a 12-round knockout.

Meanwhile, in Albuquerque, Young Dovey had not been forgotten, and a suitable foe was being sought for a May date. The unfamiliar "Missouri Spider" was brought in and, on May 25, the two met in Old Town in front of 150 spectators. There was a delay before the two were allowed to mix, and when the first-round gong clanged, the fans witnessed yet another fiasco of a fight when a local lawman, Deputy Sheriff Hubbell, leapt into the ring after the eighth round when the Missouri Spider claimed Dovey had fouled him. Hubbell declared the bout over but when Dovey came forward to fight when the bell rang for round nine, the fighter was arrested. "The crowd then displeased, and the talk now among the sports is that those who backed 'The Spider' had a very narrow escape from losing their money."[107]

Dovey was released on a $400 bond, with the order to appear before the Old Town police magistrate. Although there was controversy whether Dovey's blow had been foul or not, the bigger debate was why the lawman had soured the fight — many believed Hubbell had wagered on the Missouri Spider.

"Matters seemed likely for a little while to turn into a free fight," editorialized the *Las Vegas Daily Optic*, "and there would have probably been trouble, but for the presence of the minions of the law. These so-called prize fights are becoming a nuisance which eventually will have to be abated by the strong arm of the law."[108]

Tired of New Mexico, Dovey moved on to Arizona, in search of an easier place to fight.

Albuquerque's back-and-forth acceptance of the sport dissuaded other towns from staging bouts. Santa Fe flirted with prizefighting for a time, announcing for its 1895 Fourth of July celebration a 20-rounder at Motley's Opera House between known pugilists Kid Gallagher of Helena, Mont., and Jim La Chapelle, of Kansas City.

But when the local churches protested, denouncing the contest as "unlawful, unchristian and barbaric,"[109] the city fathers submitted to the pressure, despite having already authorized the glove contests under city ordinance with a special license for the celebration. "Owing to the numerous other attractions last night, the proposed glove contest was postponed," the *New Mexican* reported on the fourth. "Possibly it will take place in a day or so."[110] Well, it didn't.

By July 25, when there was still no action for the Helena pug, Gallagher was run out of town after an incident at a local saloon resulted in his suffering seven stitches on his wrist made by a lemon-cutting barkeep who was trying to prevent the desperate out-of-work prizefighter from breaking into a nickel slot machine.

Las Vegas had no problem, meanwhile, throwing a fast contest for its own, nor did Gallup, with the aforementioned Billy Lewis-James Flynn rematch fight at the opening of Kitchen's Opera House.

In Vegas, local black fighter Happy Jack Ryan headlined a card at Rosenthal Hall, against the much more experienced San Francisco import Vic Legay in what just might be the first blatant hometown decision in New Mexico history. "Las Vegas will be a sporting town, one of these days," the *Optic's* fight report began, noting that "the exhibitions of the manly art of self-defense in the city of Las Vegas have been very much on the bum." While the contest itself was no snoozer, Legay clearly won the fight — but the referee raised the hometown kid's hand, setting off a chorus of boos. "Legay made a host of friends by his square work, but lost several of them when he tried to slug [referee] Manning for giving 'Ryan' the decision, Legay claiming that while 'Billy' got the decision, he did not win the fight."[111]

Despite the several failures in attempting to stage a high caliber local fight, Albuquerque refused to be counted out just yet and, in August, the local papers not only carried coverage of the ongoing saga of just where Corbett vs. Fitzsimmons was going to land, but hinted that since it was not likely to be pulled off in Dallas, where the governor was dead set against it, why not consider Albuquerque where it was, technically, legal to do so? The pro-prizefight articles enraged local churchmen and, on Aug. 3, Reverend Thomas Harwood wrote a lengthy letter that was printed in the *Morning Journal*.

"I believe I voice the sentiment, 75 per cent of the men and 90 per cent of the women of this city, when I say that the city and territory in general, instead of inviting such sport, or rather, brutality, to our city or territory, we ought to utter our most earnest protest against it,"[112] Harwood began. In part, the letter read:

> As a citizen of twenty-six years standing in New Mexico I am not willing to sit still and see the fair name of our territory soiled by accepting that which Texas and every other state and territory in the union reject. Because there is no territorial law opposing prize fights, therefore bring the disgraceful affair, namely, the Corbett-Fitzsimmons fight in New Mexico.... In brief, I oppose the prize fight because it is wrong. I oppose it because it is a violation of law, civil and moral, in spirit and in word. I oppose it in New Mexico because it makes our territory the dumping ground for a nuisance that is too obnoxious to be tolerated in Texas or almost any other state or territory. I oppose it because its dependency, like the bull fight or any other division which inflicts animal suffering, is debasing, demoralizing and blunts the finer feelings of those who witness it. I oppose it because it will stand in the way of law loving and law abiding men coming to our territory, bringing their families with them.[113]

In the end, it was a futile argument for New Mexico had never seriously been in the running for Corbett-Fitzsimmons — all the fuss did was make it harder to establish a local scene. Yet, at the end of August 1895, yet another attempt was made.

The latest hopeful was Albuquerque's Charles Allinson, a foot-racer hoping to break into prizefighting, and, on Sept. 20, he was matched to fight Charles Burke, of New Orleans, or, at least, go ten rounds with him for 80 percent of the gate. Two days before Allinson-Burke, El Paso middleweight Charles Morgan and Albuquerque's Claude E. Silvers were matched for a finish fight, but when only a handful of spectators showed up, the show was cancelled and money refunded. Allinson's match with Burke was nixed soon after.

While the Corbett-Fitzsimmons debate was heating up, Allinson did receive his chance to headline a card, on Nov. 24 in Old Town, when he netted $75 by knocking out New Orleans' Jack Kelly in three rounds before a crowd of 100 at Post's Exchange. Allinson headlined one more fight card in Albuquerque, fighting a safe four-round exhibition with San Francisco's Vic Legay in what was the grand opening of the Turf Exchange. It would be his last chance to shine, for in 1896 the prize-fight business in New Mexico came to a grinding halt.

4. The Fall of Prizefighting, 1895–1896

Corbett and Fitzsimmons must find another place other than Texas in which to have their fight for the championship of the world. The Legislature to-day, by a vote that was practically unanimous in the Senate and only a little less in the House, passed the bill prohibiting prize fighting.

— The New York Times, 1895[1]

The idea of "Don't mess with Texas" might have originated with Governor Charles Culberson and the biggest debate during his reign — prizefighting.

Prizefighting was what the governor's old political foe, promoter Dan Stuart, was all about. When a site was needed to host the world heavyweight championship, between James J. Corbett and challenger, former middleweight champion Robert Fitzsimmons, Stuart had the perfect place: his hometown of Dallas. He was sure enough that any political static could be smoothed over, that by September 1895 he'd already invested more than $18,000 for 600,000 feet of lumber to build an outdoor arena for the big fight. Texas' version of Madison Square Garden would hold 52,000 ... or it *would have*, if the venue, and the fight, had been allowed to happen.

But, unprecedented in Texas history, Governor Culberson called for a special session of the state legislature on Sept. 26. The session would convene Oct. 1 with one purpose: "To denounce prize fighting and kindred practices in clear and unambiguous terms, and prohibit the same by appropriate pains and penalties, putting the law into immediate operation and making necessary provisions for its enforcement."[2]

Hoping to test the validity of the existing law prior to sudden legislative session, promoter Stuart, under guise of the Dallas Athletic Club, proceeded to stage a welterweight fight to the finish between Thomas Cavanaugh and Jess Clark, but the fight had been stopped by interfering police in the 23rd round and the principals arrested. On advice from the promoter, the pugilists Cavanaugh and Clark refused to put up the $1,000 bond and spent two weeks in jail. But when the case went to court, the judge ruled in favor of the defendants, declaring the penal law against prizefighting as "dead and inoperative."[3]

The pugs had won round one — but *not* the war.

Even more remarkable than Gov. Culberson's quick call to session was the passing of the bill. On Oct. 3, in the record time of 180 minutes, both the Senate and House stamped their approval on a bill to make prizefighting a felony in Texas. The state was suddenly out of the picture for the world championship fight.

Other countries, states and territories began their campaign to snag the championship fight.

Within days, several new possibilities were in the works. Hot Springs, Arkansas, was at the forefront, but locations ranged from Old Mexico to *New* Mexico. When a representative of Stuart met with interested parties in Santa Fe, Governor William Thornton immediately made it clear that the promoters would have a Texas-like war on their hands if they tried to stage the fight on his turf. "No law breaker will find asylum in New Mexico as long as I'm governor," he told the *New Mexican*.[4]

Stuart knew, however, that legally, there was nothing preventing such a fight from coming off in the territory. He also knew that the legislature would not meet again until January 1897, and there was little to no chance of Thornton pulling off Culberson's Texan trump.

Stuart's team left for El Paso where they assumed they'd find a more sympathetic ear across the river in Juarez. Meanwhile, Hot Springs, Arkansas, was crossed off the list of hopeful sites, when Gov. James P. Clarke of Arkansas threatened military action should the promoters get any wise ideas about a fight. El Paso — rather, Juarez — was looking better and better for Stuart, who moved his base of operations to the border town, snubbing Gov. Culberson by remaining in Texas.

Stuart had several options. He could pull off the fight in Juarez, where the Plaza de los Toros could seat 4,000, saving him the cost of building an outdoor arena. Or he could find a place in the New Mexico territory.

When investors began to raise funds for the fight, New Mexico papers were quick to criticize. "El Paso hasn't been able to raise that bonus for the White Oaks railroad, but she had no difficulty in putting up $15,000 to get the prize fight," editorialized the *New Mexican*. "Good deal of a sporting town that, if El Paso succeeds this time it will attract national attention to her advantages for becoming the Monte Carlo of America."[5]

Before promoter Stuart could improve upon his plans, he was hit with another near-knockout blow.

The Champ Bails

"I have retired from the ring. I'm tired of the championship. You can have it."— James J. Corbett to Peter Maher

—New York World, 1895[6]

The heavyweight champion of the world had had enough. Sick of the on-then-off-again fight with Fitzsimmons and more interested in his burgeoning acting career, James J. Corbett not only stunned the sporting community by announcing his retirement, but shocked and outraged the world when he decided to pass on the championship to Irish contender Peter Maher.

"What guff! ... As well might I bequeath the treasures of the Portland mine to the Cuban patriots!"[7] became the general sentiment of sports scribes, who argued that world championship honors couldn't be merely passed on, like an old hat or sweater. Titles had always been *fought* for — and earned — in the ring. Equally insulting, rather than face the man likely to beat him, Corbett was taking the easy way out by retiring.

Without skipping a beat, Stuart, after efforts to induce Corbett to *un*announce his retirement, ran with the next best thing: top Irish contender Peter Maher would fight Fitzsimmons for the now-vacant, or borrowed, title.

On Dec. 17, he announced to the world that the two would fight on Feb. 14, 1896, "near El Paso, Texas," for a purse of $10,000. The vagueness of a site — "near El Paso" — was intentional, of course, for both New and Old Mexico were at the top of his list ... that is, until General Miguel Ahumada, governor of Chihuahua, threw his hat into the political ring, announcing that his country would forgo a financial profit to stand ground with Texas.

That left New Mexico.

Little was said, or printed, about the big fight coming off in New Mexico, until the end of the year when the *Albuquerque Citizen* alleged that Governor Thornton was in on a secret deal that would allow the fight to be staged in Dona Ana County, just over the Rio Grande in New Mexico territory, where Australian Billy Smith had knocked out Dave Flaherty in 1894.

Thornton denied the allegations — hadn't he introduced a bill to the New Mexico legislature to outlaw fights in his territory? Thornton's attempt to ensure order in the territory had been in vain, for the bill presented before a fight-friendly legislature earlier in the year had failed to pass, 14 votes to ten. Regardless of his failure, Gov. Thornton announced he would fight Stuart's fistic carnival, stating that "all the power of the territorial administration would be used to prevent such a fight on New Mexico soil."[8]

The fight — the one *outside* the ring, that is — was on.

Political battle in New Mexico

> *It appears to be definitely settled that the Maher-Fitzsimmons prize fight, on St. Valentine's day will take place on the dividing line between New Mexico and the Republic of Mexico, three miles west of El Paso, on the line of the Southern Pacific railroad. Seats in the arena to witness the fight will cost $20 each.*
> *—Silver City Enterprise, 1896*[9]

Governor William Taylor Thornton, born in Calhoun, Missouri, in 1843, was a veteran confederate of the Civil War. Before taking office in 1893, he'd served for two years as mayor of Santa Fe. Miguel Otero, who succeeded Thornton in 1897, described Thornton as a no-nonsense politician who took "particular pains to suppress crime and disorder"[10] during a period of outlaws, train robbers and desperadoes.

Otero had less favorable things to say about one Thomas B. Catron, a congressional delegate who would later become one of New Mexico's first senators, in 1912. Also a former confederate during the Civil War, Catron would be one of the most controversial politicians in New Mexico history. He would be credited for the growth of the Republican Party in New Mexico, *dis*credited for his controversial involvement in land grant issues, and later praised for becoming the territory's leading advocate for statehood. Otero, however, alleged that Catron was behind a covert assassination attempt to poison him while he was in office.

In 1896, however, it was Catron's dislike of prizefighting that gave him national recognition, and his dislike of Thornton, that made him a household name.

Ironically, Thornton and Catron had much in common, their lack of love for prizefighting being at the top of the list, making them likely allies in the political battle to come. But their like-minded viewpoint that pugilism was barbaric, somehow, only made them bitter enemies.

If Gov. Thornton had it his way, any attempt to toss leather in the prize ring would be a felony, with a death in the ring bringing a charge of murder in the first degree. Legally, the only action Gov. Thornton could bring against those involved in a prizefight — world heavyweight championship or not — was that it could, under common law, be prevented if deemed a disturbance of the peace.

"Had public sentiment been aroused last winter as it has been since the fate of the bill in the legislature of this territory would have been a different one," Thornton told the press in January 1896. "At the next session adequate punishment for the human brutes who make public exhibition of their brutality for gain will be provided by statute and New Mexico will not thereafter be disgraced by alleged sport, which even in Texas is a felony."[11]

In the meantime, with no laws prohibiting the sport, it looked as if Fitzsimmons and Maher could very well be duking it out for the world title on New Mexico soil.

While rumors began to spread that Thornton was secretly in collusion with promoter Stuart, the New Mexico governor became increasingly outspoken about the big fight. Thornton, however, was unaware at the time that his political battle would be less against the boxing promoter and more against Delegate Catron.

Fitzsimmons, Maher Set Up Camp

> *Tuesday Maher got down to actual work to fit himself in condition to give the lanky monstrosity from Australia a lesson in astronomy, and the manner in which Peter took to his task bespeaks for him the best of condition on the day of the fight.... Maher is a big, whole-souled Irishman, good natured at his work, and it is laughable, indeed, to see him and Jerry Marshall, the colored boy, put on the gloves for a bout.*
> — Rio Grande Republic, 1896[12]

> *A big, burly, uncouth, unregenerate prize fighter came to the city recently from east Texas where he had not been winning souls for Christ, to labor in this branch of the Devil's vineyard. Did the citizens turn out to receive him? You may be sure they did. The entire sporting fraternity of El Paso and Juarez, the Mexican city over the river, broke their record by rising early, very early and with a band of music marched up to the Southern Pacific depot with what imaginative reporters would call a "vast concourse of citizens," and every hack in town, to welcome the big bruiser.... So this bruiser, Bob Fitzsimmons, "Lanky Bob" they called him as a term of endearment, was given a royal welcome.*
>
> — The Independent, 1896[13]

The combatants arrived. Fitzsimmons set up training camp in El Paso while Maher settled in Las Cruces, ironically, where Catron made his home.

Las Cruces, chosen over El Paso ("Very sorry for the Pass City, but she's too slow. Not enough ginger, boys, not enough ginger"[14]), was hardly what one would consider a fight town. With national attention, however, the city rolled out the red carpet for the Irish champion, with the *Rio Grande Republican* running a stream of consistent fight-camp reports with each issue. "Las Cruces will unquestionably receive much good advertising throughout the country," wrote the *Republican*. "If nothing else people will certainly appreciate the energy displayed by the business men of our little city in the oft wrongfully termed 'desert' of New Mexico."[15]

As Fitzsimmons and Maher wowed daily crowds of fight fans, giving exhibitions of skill at opera houses in the two respective cities, optimistic scribes wrote that success was guaranteed in the upcoming fistic carnival.

As would be expected by hosting one of the principals, Las Cruces favored Maher. Though he had suffered a large boil during his stay in New Mexico, the Irish lad was in the pink of condition. He stood ready "to make Fitz feel his oats ... his muscles stand out like whipcords and are as hard as iron.... No trouble in the least has been experienced in keeping him at his work and this shows that Peter is going in to win and will be through no fault of his own if he doesn't."[16]

The two had met before.

In 1892, Maher had lost to Fitzsimmons in the 12th round of a finish fight held in New Orleans. In the second round, Maher nearly had his man knocked out when someone in Fitzsimmons' corner "accidentally" kicked the bell, prematurely signaling the end of the round. Fitz recovered and went on to knock out Maher ten rounds later.

The controversial ending spiced up the rematch.

As an added bonus on the card, Jerry Marshall, of Maher's camp, was slated to fight World Featherweight Champion George Dixon while Maher's sparring partner and trainer, Peter Burns, would do a lead-up fight against local favorite Australian Billy Smith, for $500 a side. To ensure fairness in all bouts, George Siler, sporting editor of the *Chicago Tribune*, had been selected as referee.

Excitement brewed between Las Cruces and the border.

To hype the fight, Maher's camp gave a show of exhibitions, on Jan. 31, at the local skating rink in Las Cruces. Maher sparred with Burns while Marshall took on both Fred Ross, of Denver, and Maher, giving "the 'big un' an opportunity to display his wonderful agility." Against Maher, Burns "accidentally stopped a right-hand blow from the champion that wound him up in sure enough style. The administration of restoratives was necessary before Burns would realize 'where he was at.'"[17]

Souvenir coins for the 1896 world heavyweight fight between Peter Maher and Bob Fitzsimmons. The locale of the fight was top secret until the last minute — though El Paso, as noted on the coins, was printed. The date, too, is wrong, for the fight was moved from the 14th to the 21st when Maher suffered inflammation to his eyes after running through a dust storm outside Las Cruces, New Mexico.

Though Maher was referred to as "champion" by the locals, having been "given" the belt by Corbett, Maher's manager, John J. Quinn, clarified to the local paper that the Irish contender had declined the championship belt "on the grounds that he had not won it by fighting, and that he would not take it any other way.... He will not be the recipient of any gifts."[18] Furthermore, Quinn stated that although Corbett had handed over the belt to Maher, a win over Fitzsimmons would not deter the would-be champ from fighting the retired champ, or anyone else, for that matter, for a side bet of $5,000, of course.

While the press hyped the fighters, the site remained a mystery with just two weeks to go. Stuart had his reasons. The last time he'd named the site, he'd been blindsided by politicians, costing the promoter nearly $20,000. This time around, Stuart was playing it safe. While spreading rumors that the fight could be moved to Arizona (sending *those* politicians up in arms) or Hot Springs (politicians had already answered with an adamant "no"), he was busy securing a top-secret site most assumed was in New Mexico.

Whether or not a world title fight in New Mexico was good for tourism, Gov. Thornton remained steadfast, threatening to patrol the state lines with deputy marshals if that's what it took to prevent the prize fight. But he was also throwing up his hands, blaming the territorial legislature for not passing his bill some months before, and contradicting himself by saying that only a public disturbance could stop the fight as there was no specific law outlawing fights. Meanwhile railroads were advertising tickets, starting at $13.40 from Santa Fe or $20 from Silver City, to the mysterious site-to-be-announced.

Popularity dictated reportage, on both front pages and sports sections of national newspapers, though opposition was also on the rise. Mexico's General Ahumada assigned 500 troops from Mexico City to prevent the fight landing in Juarez while ministers at the border preached about "brutal bruisers"[19] and lost souls who were destroying their beloved town:

> If there were any arrests to be made, why, the bruisers could be fined nominal sums for disturbing the peace, or for a light form of assault and battery. But the Governor of New Mexico is to be put on to this dodge, and no stone will be left unturned to break up the proposed Fitzsimmons-Maher prize fight. El Paso is already suffering from the effects of the bad reputation given by the advent of the prize fighter and his unholy combination; for the town is filling up with tramps and vagabonds, and the great army of toughdom is yet to come.[20]

On February 4, less than two weeks from the fight, the governor, appearing increasingly toothless as the fight approached, and without a means of prevention, assured the public that he was doing everything within his power under current law. But outside of arresting the promoters and fighters for a minor violation, should they, in fact, be caught in time, there was very little that could be done.

It appeared as if promoter Dan Stuart was going to have the last word, for he was telling the media: "There is nothing that can stop the prize fights."

He was both right —*and* wrong.

Blindsided

> *Dan Stuart says: "There is nothing that can stop the prize fights. They are coming off just as advertised. You can say for me that so sure as the principals are alive and in condition to get into the ring on the day for the contests so sure will they fight to the finish. If there is anybody who evinces any sort of doubt as to this I will lay them four to one for any part of $50,000."*
>
> *—Santa Fe New Mexican, 1896[21]*

Two days after Thornton's latest assurances, the news broke from Washington, D.C., about a new bill being presented before Congress that would not only outlaw prizefighting (and bullfighting) in the Territories and District of Columbia, but make it a felony with a sentence of one to five years of imprisonment. The bill originated from New Mexico, and was being lobbied at record speed by one Thomas B. Catron.

Shrugging off the new threat, promoter Stuart not only insisted the fight would still come off, but said that he was willing to lay a bet up to $50,000 with 4-to-1 odds if there were any takers. Had Stuart bet on the anti-prizefight bill floundering in Congress, or failing to pass, he would have lost, for in 24 hours' time, on Feb. 7, 1896, the bill, which would forevermore be known as the Catron Law, passed. As long as New Mexico remained a territory, prizefighting would, forevermore, be illegal.

Denied in Texas, Mexico and, now, New Mexico, threatened with federal law, promoter Stuart put on a brave front and continued to shrug, his quote making national headlines: "'THE FIGHT IS A SURE THING' Locality Still a Mystery."[22]

In New Mexico, the battle had less to do with the promoter. It was a political war.

When the Irish champ, Maher, left Las Cruces for El Paso on the 7th, fearing that the fight might be staged earlier than announced, Gov. Thornton took up watch at the border with a number of Dona Ana County deputy sheriffs, giving, if nothing else, the appearance of having the situation under control. On the 8th of February, after receiving word of the new federal law that bore his political rival's name, Thornton packed up for Santa Fe.

"The governor got in from Las Cruces on the train that brought Peter Maher to town last night and, curiously enough, the pair took the same train out of here this morning," reported the *El Paso Times*. "Sheriff Acarate, who accompanied the fighter to El Paso, returned to Las Cruces this morning and was advised by the governor that his vigilance was unnecessary, as the federal government has relieved him of all responsibility in the matter."[23]

Catron continued to make waves from D.C., telling national media that he was displeased at the impression given by Gov. Thornton. "Mr. Catron not only denies that he has received the governor's co-operation," ran the wire, "but makes the direct charge that Gov. Thornton has abetted Dan Stuart in his efforts to bring off the fights."[24] Catron's statement the next day was expanded to set himself apart from Thornton and erase any belief that he'd been acting under the governor's orders:

> The statement that has been published substantially that action was taken by me on the prizefighting bill was on the advice and at the request of Gov. Thornton. Gov. Thornton never consulted with me, never advised me, nor requested me to do anything in regard to the subject. From information which I have received from New Mexico, I do believe that Gov. Thornton, while pretending that he would like to stop the fight, was actually acting in collusion with Dan Stuart in order to have the prize fight come off, and has advised Stuart that there was no law in New Mexico which would enable them or the authorities to stop the fight, and substantially informed Stuart that the fight might go on, although he would not openly consent. As soon as the bill had been signed last night the officials here telegraphed the United States Attorney in New Mexico to see that the law was enforced.[25]

While the politicians traded barbs, Stuart continued to insist the fight was a go and the arrival of several notables—including Bat Masterson, Judge Roy Bean, notable boxers and top prizefight authorities—supported his plans. "That all this commotion has been stirred up because the two men are going to box with five ounce gloves, it seems to me to be utterly ridiculous," Stuart told the *Albuquerque Morning Journal*. "When the senate and the house of representatives of this great country can find nothing better to do than to make laws prohibiting boxing contest in territories, it is high time that something was done."[26]

Never mind the threat of arrest in two countries, there were other matters at hand, like how sporting fans would receive word in time to hop aboard a train headed for a top secret destination only Stuart seemed to know. Watched like a hawk by local officials in two cities, the two principals continued preparation, but the fight was postponed after Maher suffered near-blindness when his eyes became inflamed after coming home from a run in the desert during a dust storm.

"Maher came in here this morning with a badly inflamed eye, which he offers as an excuse for not fighting until next Monday," quipped a scribe for *The New York Times*. "He claims that both eyes are very sore as the result of getting some dirt in them while training. The Fitzsimmons party claims the black eye is due to the fact that he was hit with a pillow in a pillow fight. Vassar College rules, with his trainer and backer."[27]

As for Fitzsimmons? The *Times* reported that "finding no chance for a fight, [he] went out and got a job at making horseshoes at Noake's blacksmith shop. He made a half dozen shoes, and remarked at the conclusion that it was the first honest day's work he had done in several years."[28]

The fight was postponed, at least a week, and an estimated 1,500 would-be attendees left the area.

By the 20th, Maher's eyes were reported to be in fair condition and the fight was, once again, declared on, for a secret site-to-be-announced, on the following day. The same day, Gov. Thornton responded to Catron's allegations of acting in collusion with fight promoter Stuart. Declaring himself indignant at Catron's charges, he stated that the congressional delegate was merely trying to glorify himself.

Thornton stated that he "had left no stone unturned to prevent the fight coming off in New Mexico,"[29] citing a laundry list of preventative measures that included asking Washington for federal troops to aid civil authorities, and countless correspondence, from authorities in D.C. to adjacent counties in southern New Mexico. The back-and-forth accusations were best summed up by a writer with the *Rocky Mountain News*:

> If this wrangle was not disgusting, it would be amusing. The worst that can be said of either Delegate Catron or Governor Thornton is that they are politicians, although in this regard truth compels the admission that Catron holds the belt. Both are lawyers, both are gentlemen of education and culture, and both are equally interested as good citizens in stopping a prize fight. To assume that Thornton was willing to become a bottle-holder for either one of the pugs, as some New Mexican papers are trying to make out, is simply ridiculous. It is idiotic.[30]

Later that year, relations between Thornton and Catron would degrade to such a state that "mutual friends between the two parties fear a personal encounter between them."[31] Thornton served until 1897. Catron, despite his success as a congressional delegate and the passing of the anti-prizefight law, failed to be re-elected in 1896. Some surmised that there were more fight fans than haters in New Mexico; others said it was the sum result of countless other controversies stacked against Catron.

The Fight

> *A great deal of talk is indulged in about the departments here to-day over the prospective fight. The department of justice has information that it is the plan of the prize fighting*

*party to go by rail from El Paso, Tex., into New Mexico along the southern border and
to disembark upon the territorial soil. From there it is the plan of the party to walk
over into Old Mexico and hold the contest there. The United States marshal will be
ready to catch the crowd as soon as it disembarks from the train, and even if there is
no intention of fighting on United States ground there may be some trouble in getting
the combatants and the accompanying crowd onto Mexican soil.*

— Santa Fe New Mexican, 1896[32]

In the end, promoter Dan Stuart proved smarter than 'em all.

But, believe it or not, less than a day before the fight, Stuart had more to worry about
than the latest anti-prizefighting bill.

Like Peter Maher's eyes. While Maher recovered, six Texas rangers kept guard on
Maher's room. In El Paso, Fitzsimmons, also under ranger watch, had crossed over from
his training camp in Juarez to attend the theater and, there, was arrested but let go when
there was no reason to detain him.

For his world championship fight against Peter Maher,
Robert Fitzsimmons trained in El Paso. Fitzsimmons
was the sport's first three-division world champion and
considered, pound for pound, one of the greatest ever
(Library of Congress, Prints & Photographs Division
[LC-USZ62-78655]).

The fight was on, the fight was
off— no one was sure whom to believe.

While Texas rangers watched the
principals, promoter and trains for
signs of activity, a squadron of Mexican
cavalry from Chihuahua patrolled the
river to the north and westward of the
boundary line. Likewise, a squad of
deputies set up headquarters in the
southern portion of Dona Ana County.

Undisturbed, Stuart announced
that a local fight — between Texas pug
Scott "Bright Eyes" Collins, a lightweight, and Joe Walcott — would come
off before the big fight, most likely as
a diversion and as reassurance that
Maher-Fitzsimmons was still a go. The
other prelims — the Dixon fight and
Burns-Smith — had already been
nixed. News that there was an abnor-
mal amount of Southern Pacific trains
being assembled for Arizona (suspected
now as the secret locale) and that the
fight would now be filmed with a kine-
toscope failed to keep interest in the
bout from taking a nosedive.

Even *The New York Times* was
running sarcastic comments. "A pleasing little episode last night was a
shooting match in which 'Joe'
Copeland, a dealer in Stuart's bank
at Dallas, was shot in the shoulder
by 'Bill' Quaries of Greenville, this

State. A dozen shots were fired, but unfortunately none of the sports were killed, and not a prizefighter was even injured."[33]

With the uncertainty, those cheering for the fight to happen were even having a change of heart. A northbound train returning from the border was "crowded with disgusted sports returning from the prize fight fiasco."[34] In El Paso, fight headquarters appeared deserted, needing "only a streamer of crape on the door to complete the funeral aspect. The feeling is that something will again happen to keep the men from meeting at the ringside."[35]

While there was no word what was going on in the Maher camp, Fitzsimmons continued his training, calling his would-be opponent a yellow dog who had no intention of fighting him. Meanwhile, Corbett, who chose this moment in time to re-enter the picture, made a public statement to Fitzsimmons, promising to make him take it back for calling *him* a cur. Fitz's camp, in turn, promised to put Corbett "out of existence the day he puts Maher among the 'has-beens.'"[36] It was the first real bit of news in some time, having to do with the fighters and not politicians, the promoter or the new law.

There was nothing to worry about, assured Stuart, who released a statement two days before the fight that not only would Maher-Fitzsimmons take place, but since all the lesser fights on the all-star card had been declared off, the main go was in an even better position to happen. The site of the occasion was set, said Stuart, and there was no need to fear interference from any state, territory or country.

One day before the scheduled fight, Maher's condition was reported as improved and he was on his way to El Paso, having returned to Las Cruces to tend to his eye injury. "The big Irishman, despite the stories of his not being in condition to fight a hard battle, never looked better in his life," wrote a scribe with the *National Police Gazette*. "With his mustache shaved off, his face looked much better, and his skin was as brown as a berry. His eyes showed no trace of the affliction which had compelled a postponement, though he and the strong rays of the sun still made him wink and occasionally wince. He said he never felt better, and expressed supreme confidence in his ability to whip Fitzsimmons on the morrow."[37] Taking the day off from training, Fitzsimmons entertained a crowd of sightseers and made horseshoes before several military officers (U.S. Marshall Hall of New Mexico included).

That afternoon, a notice was posted at Stuart's fight headquarters on North Oregon Street, in downtown El Paso: "Those intending to witness the fight will have to be at this office at half-past nine tonight. The railway tickets will not cost over $12 for the round trip."[38]

Finally, activity!

At 9 P.M., 250 men made up of ticketholders, cornermen, officials, writers and Stuart's promotion team boarded a 10 P.M. train headed for who-knew-where. "As each man received his ticket the rendezvous for the departure was given him in an undertone,"[39] wrote *The New York Times* correspondent. Among the notables seen boarding the train were Bat Masterson, who was designated both master of ceremonies and chief sergeant-at-arms, and George Siler, chosen referee, who was given a bag of cash — $10,000 in hundred dollar bills from two local banks. Siler was to produce the pile of cash at ringside, wherever that would be.

By 10 P.M., the train departed El Paso headed for Langtry, Texas, a small town on the Mexican border, where it arrived two hours past its expected arrival, around 3:30 P.M. the next afternoon, Feb. 21, 1896. Most expected the fight to be held off until the morning, but there was no time to be wasted. "Fitz and Maher were instructed an hour before their arrival here to be ready to enter the ring at a moment's notice after Langtry was reached," wrote a reporter for the *New Mexican*. "Both were stripped, rubbed and prepared for the fight."[40]

A cold, drizzling rain awaited the principals and spectators — and a troop of Texas rangers under command of distinguished Brigadier General Woodford Mabry, no less. Ignoring the troops drawn up to one side of the train, Stuart and his party walked by, headed for the Mexican side of the border, well within walking distance. There, before Mexican troops could crash the party, let alone receive word that the fight was on their soil, Peter Maher and Robert Fitzsimmons would fight for the world heavyweight championship.

Braving brambles, muddy banks and a slapdash pontoon bridge that spanned the Rio Grande, the visitors walked in double and single file down a seldom-used path to a canvas enclosure at the bottom of a slope on the Mexican side of the river. Two tents were erected, yards apart, for the principals and their cornermen. At 4:25 P.M., time was called.

The New York Times ran the most complete coverage, with blow-by-blow detail. Both Fitzsimmons and Maher landed telling punches early, between clinches, until "Fitz side-stepped and, swinging his left, landed full on the point of Maher's chin. Maher measured his length on the floor, his head striking the canvas with great force. He vainly attempted to rise, but could not do more than raise his head. His second called on him to get up, but he failed to respond, and sank back to the canvas." After one minute and 35 seconds of "rather lively fighting," Maher was counted out.[41]

The *Santa Fe New Mexican* skipped the details and summed up the months of drama and controversy with one line: "Fitzsimmons knocked Maher out in the first round with a right hand lick on the jaw."[42]

5. Outlawed, 1896–1911

It took congress about three days to pass an anti-prize fight law; but it has been hammering away for nearly two months on a law to relieve the United States treasury of the unnatural necessity for engaging in the banging business, and still there is no prospect of its accomplishing anything.

— Roswell Record, 1896[1]

Oh, no, we can't allow a prize fight in New Mexico, it is too brutal. But not a week goes by that does not witness a cold-blooded murder at some point in the territory. Why don't the preachers band together and cry aloud against the awful truth? It would be more in keeping with the eternal fitness of things.

— Lincoln News, 1896[2]

Eighteen-ninety-six.

In 1896, Athens, Greece, was preparing for the first modern Olympics, the "horseless carriage" was being test-driven in Detroit and Utah transformed from territory to state. In New Mexico, Butch Cassidy and his Hole-in-the-Wall gang was hiding out in the Frisco Valley near Silver City. Up north, near Raton, a posse was on the look-out for notorious outlaw "Black Jack" Ketchum. Belle La Mar, a.k.a. "Madam Varnish," was running a booming casino business at White Oaks, near Carrizozo; and mask-wearing Hispanics were making things uncomfortable for *gringo* land grabbers throughout the state, one of the most notorious of whom, Thomas B. Catron, had just been responsible for adding prizefighting to the list of punishable crimes in the territory.

In what was left of New Mexico's Wild, Wild West, prizefighters were now as criminal as bank robbers.

Hoping to ride the wave of prizefight mania generated by the Fitzsimmons-Maher world heavyweight fight, Albuquerque hopeful Charles Allinson had been scheduled to headline an Old Town card in Albuquerque on Feb. 9, 1896. But, "owing to the passage of the anti-prize fight law," his mill with a man named Walsh was cancelled. "Now that prize fights can no longer be permitted pugilists will be invited by the police to give this town the go by,"[3] wrote the editor of the *Morning Journal*.

Left with little choice, Allinson hung up his gloves. Other local pugilists were more stubborn. Two minor shows were staged in Old Town within two weeks of the new prizefight law, under cover that each bout was a "purely scientific exhibition."[4] Local officials looked the other way, allowing owners of Old Town's Turf Exchange to stage the two free shows featuring Frenchy Hurst, reportedly the Texas welterweight champion, who continued on his way to the West Coast afterward.

No further risk was taken as officials began standing by the law. The sport, given increasingly less attention in local papers, started to die. After an even-less mentioned four-round bout between unknowns took place in Old Town during October 1896, Albuquerque was finished, at least for the next four years.

Las Cruces, on the other hand, was unexpectedly brash, at first, with a card in April at Amador Hall. Under the guise of a benefit "for gymnasium funds," several "exhibitions" were staged and all were encouraged to see "how the boys have profited by Maher, having trained there."[5] Not too many "physical culture shows" with so-called exhibitions, however, finish up with a "hot stuff"[6] 25-round draw between seasoned fighters like El Paso's John "The Black Diamond" Mandell and "Minnesota Cyclone," Price Houston.

After one more show of exhibitions, no names participating this time, Las Cruces was through. Silver City got away with a prize fight some time in 1896 (it might even have occurred before the prizefight law passed) between little known fighters Kid Lorraine and Jack Lorenz. In April or early May, the short-lived gold mining town of Red River, near Taos, also staged a show, adding "a little spice to the monotony of mining life by pulling off a prize fight of a lively character."[7] But name fighters cleared out of the now-hopeless-area, from the border through New Mexico, and the boxing buzz faded from print as the sport's momentum crashed.

Within a year of Fitzsimmons–Maher and the sudden prizefight law, the boxing scene was dead. For the first time, a sudden burst of interest in world-caliber championship fights did little to kindle a resurgence — not even the return of James J. Corbett against not-quite-fully-recognized champion Robert Fitzsimmons.

Fitzsimmons vs. Corbett was staged on St. Patrick's Day, March 17, 1897, in Carson City, Nevada, with promoter Dan Stuart finally finding a home free of legal interference. Just as quickly as Texas and New Mexico had passed laws outlawing the sport, Nevada approved laws legalizing the sport. Solidifying his claim to the heavyweight throne, in front of 6,000 fans, Fitzsimmons KO'd Corbett in the 14th round. Rejuvenating the sport, Fitzsimmons reigned supreme while heavyweight James J. Jeffries made his climb toward a title shot.

But while the rest of the world experienced sudden growth, New Mexico remained stagnant.

Pugilism at Bay

> *A fellow who owns a projectoscope which reproduces a very wicked prize fight is trying hard to get the committee to let him exhibit it at the territorial fair. Albuquerque's high moral tone is generally known, that it seems awful to think that such a proposition would be entertained for a moment, but the reporter is ashamed to confess that some of the members of the committee seem to have "fallen by the wayside" and talk as though they really wanted to see the brutal exhibition.*
>
> *—Albuquerque Democrat, 1897[8]*

> *The people of the west, in their anxiety to win the good opinion of the east, pass stringent laws against prize-fighting, and rally troops to chase pugilists off the earth if they appoint a meeting place. New York looks on and smiles, and when the men get through talking and mean business, gives them all the privileges desired, and the chief of police of the great city attends to see that nobody interferes with the fun.*
>
> *—Santa Fe New Mexican, 1899[9]*

The turn of the twentieth century ushered in an era of growth, development and prosperity for New Mexico. In less than a decade, the territorial railway had more than doubled, enabling dozens of towns to serve as trading points for railway workers and farms. Older towns, particularly Albuquerque, served as major distribution centers. By 1912, the territorial population would increase by 70 percent, with Anglo-Americans comprising half the total for the first time.

By 1900, New Mexico's fight game was starting to show signs of life again.

Outside the territory, the sport was bigger than ever. It wasn't only about a heavyweight champion any more — though James J. Jeffries' knockout of Fitzsimmons in 1899 had ushered in a new era. The lighter weights now captured the attention of the fans, names like Tommy Ryan, Frank Erne, George Dixon, Joe Gans and "Terrible" Terry McGovern making headlines across the country.

New Mexico slowly started to stir.

In 1899, the New Mexico Military Institute in Roswell, called "The West Point of the West," started what would develop into a long-standing tradition of amateur boxing. Meanwhile, at the Territorial Fair in Albuquerque, "burlesque-style" boxing bouts staged a mock-up of the Jeffries-Fitzsimmons heavyweight fight. Retired pugs Hugh Coyle and E. Cunningham also put on sparring exhibitions at the fair, which was attended by Governor Miguel Otero.

In 1900, there was a glimmer of hope that things would restart, when Albuquerque, Las Cruces, Santa Fe and Taos all staged shows with glorified sparring exhibitions. "The sporting fraternity may not know that there is a United States law prohibiting prize fighting and boxing matches in the territories, and providing severe penalties for infringement,"[10] the *Albuquerque Citizen* reminded its readers after a brief recap of the Feb. 14 show at Orchestrion Hall.

When organizers of the San Geronimo carnival in Taos decided to match a pair of out-of-town lightweights, New York's Harold Cobb and Ohio's Louis Meyers, it was strictly as a "five-round glove contest under Marquis of Queensbury rules" and "not a prize fight,"[11] as if there was a difference.

The short-lived Las Cruces Athletic Club was less concerned about attracting heat when they staged a show of sparring exhibitions to raise funds for a gymnasium — probably because the headline bout featured Dona Ana County sheriff Pat Garrett, who sparred with a local physician. Garrett, a local legend, was, of course, the man who'd shot and killed notorious outlaw Billy the Kid in Fort Sumner, 19 years before. From 1896 to 1902, he was the Dona Ana County sheriff.

With prizefighting restricted in the territory, other sports excelled, particularly baseball. Though championship fights staged on either coast continued to receive mention, fighters who'd previously headlined in New Mexico were overlooked. When prizefighter Billy Lewis died, on Aug. 12, 1900, from a brain hemorrhage (details were unclear whether a recent bout, horse-riding injury, street fight, or a combination of the three was the cause of brain trauma), the death received no mention, despite Lewis having made quite a hit with the local fight scene just five years before.

Just because prizefights were not reported on, and were outlawed, did not mean they did not happen; only that they were kept on the sly, either local newspapermen, politicians and lawmen were in on the action, or they were just plain unaware.

For nearly three years, the sport remained repressed and underground.

Then, in 1903, a Southwest fighter, George Griffith, taking up the name of legend Young Griffo, who was nearing the completion of his own career, fought at least twice in New Mexico, once in Clayton, beating unknown Jimmy Dorn, and once in Las Vegas, where he KO'd Colorado veteran Jack Haley. Both fights managed to escape attention in the press.

But, the following year, sometime in February or March, Old Town promoters managed to pull off a finish fight between Colorado's Otis Bolt and Willard "Kid" Bean, of Kansas City, who was knocked out in 14 rounds. The principals and promoter eluded authorities and newspapermen leading up to the fight, and immediately afterward, but the fighters were indicted by a United States grand jury in late March. Warrants were issued for their arrest but the matter was not pursued.

The message was clear enough, however, to keep pugilism at bay, or further underground, for two more years. By mid–1906, though, not even the law could keep boxing away.

Athletic Clubs Pave Return

> The Geronimo Club, the recently organized social and athletic organization which has rapidly become one of the leading societies of the city will give an entertainment next Saturday night to its friends at the finely equipped gymnasium from nine to eleven o'clock. There will be some interesting exhibition games of hand ball and boxing exhibitions.
>
> —Albuquerque Morning Journal, 1907[12]

> Last Friday evening the young men called a meeting in Aztec hall for the purpose of organizing an athletic club in Cimarron ... the entertainment committee to arrange for a big dance and other entertainment on the night of March 16th. Prior to the dance there will be wrestling and boxing matches. So bear in mind, the date, March 16, for that is the gala day. Get out your new buggies, boys and your fast horses, and get here early and don't miss a minute of good time.
>
> —Cimarron News & Press, 1907[13]

Laws or no laws, boxing returned to New Mexico in earnest midway through the first decade of the twentieth century. Under the umbrella of private clubs —athletic clubs — exhibitions ("entertainment") for members at club get-togethers were "friendly, scientific" matches for points or no decisions. It silenced the alarm that prizefighting was back. From Albuquerque's Geronimo Club to the Cimarron Athletic Club, the local organizations took the lead, and the sport was able to worm its way back into public favor, evading the prizefight laws that, technically, still applied.

There were hints, however, that something more than was being reported was happening. The Police Gazette mentioned an active Las Vegas boxer, D. B. Mathias, in 1905, and the Morning Journal, a local by the name of "Kid Stephens," who'd sparred with Joe Gans, fighting to a draw in Winslow and hoping to get a shot at Jim Flynn in Pueblo. There was also a surprise visit by Mexican pugilist Aurelio Herrera in Las Vegas, in mid–July 1905, who showed up to watch a local theatrical performance of "The Girl in Red."

The fighting scene was maintained on the sly.

A good, old-fashioned Wild West scrap in Las Cruces between anonymous fighters opened up the action in early 1906. "A very unexpected boxing bout in which two of our citizens were participants, took place on Main street last Friday night,"[15] began the report in the Rio Grande Republican. The round-by-round follows, with the first-round description of a give-and-take bout. In the second, the action between "Roe" and "Doe" heats up:

Roe leads off for a terrific blow to the heart, and follows it up with one to the jaw. Doe is seen to weaken and leans against the ba — we mean the ropes — for support, all the while Roe making vicious attacks at the head and body. Suddenly Doe seems to receive a new state of vitality, and, with the spring of a panther, hits his opponent squarely in the right optic [applause]. The burst of fireworks is magnificent, and the astronomical view of the heavens is grand. Mars is there and also is Jupiter with their constellations. Roe goes down on one knee. Getting up, he procures a six-shooter, and disregarding all Queensbury [sic] rules, gives Doe a 16-inch-stitch cut on the head with the butt. The pall of death settles on the crowd; the clock could be heard in the back of the room; the referee did not dare interfere and the spectators are in suspense as to the next move. Doe, with blood flowing down his face, grapples with Roe and succeeds in getting the revolver, minus the cylinder of cartridges, which had dropped out unnoticed by either during the scuffle. Roe, seeing that he had displayed his best, and lost, ran out through the doorway, closely followed by the triumphant Doe, carrying the cylinders and gun. Both are convalescent.[15]

The limited action in Albuquerque did not attain a serious level until later in the decade, as seen at the 1906 Annual Territorial Fair with its, reportedly, "first Indian boxing match ever seen in New Mexico."[16]

Most people have never heard of a Navajo boxing contest and those who have seemed to be skeptical but a few people have seen them and these few people declare the exhibition the richest thing on top of the earth. One man who is solicitous about the welfare of the association has write [sic] to know if it wouldn't be against the law to pull off prize fights in front of the grand stand, but he has been gently informed that they will not be real prize fights. The Indians will wear gloves so big that damage to each others [sic] is entirely impossible and anyway, the Indians have learned the places where it hurts to get hit, and they are learning lots about the points in the game. One boxing match will take place each day. But Arrington's Indians are going to do a lot more than box. They are bringing a lot of wild ponies with them, and there will be roping of ponies on foot and on horseback. The roping of ponies by the unmounted Indian is about the funniest sight imaginable. It never fails to bring the grand stand to its collective feet.[17]

Serious fighting — not burlesque, not sparring — would make its return in the farther reaches of New Mexico, in the unlikely town of Clayton. Boasting a population around 800, the town, tucked away in the northeast corner of the territory, was known for two things in the 1900s: livestock and a hanging. In 1901, infamous train robber Thomas "Black Jack" Ketchum told his executioner, "Hurry up, I'm due in hell for dinner," before he was hanged on Main Street.

But, in 1906, the town started to pick up a reputation for prizefights, thanks to New Mexico's first born-and-bred hometown pugilist, Serapio Lucero. Fighting under the alias "Serapio Romero," Lucero became the first Hispanic-name fighter to attract attention.

Most of the era's newspapers during that time are missing, but at least one account remains in Clayton's weekly *Fenix* from 1906 in which the hometown favorite defeated "Wilson, " by weathering body blows in the first to come back like "*un toro anejo*"[18] to score a third-round knockout.

Clayton's Lucero would appear off and on in the local prizefight arena over the next five years, never rising above the level of a sound local fighter. But both Lucero and Clayton gave the sport a much-needed push through the next several years. While other towns flirted with the sport and skirted the authorities, Clayton leapt into promotion, staging fights without pretending to be a membership-driven club or claiming the bouts were purely of a scientific nature.

There may have been as many as a dozen fights between 1906 and 1908, but the spotty remains of newspaper archives account for just a few. By 1909, however, the prizefight purist could be found 110 miles west of Clayton, in Cimarron.

An occasional prize fight or two might have escaped the attention of politicians, but the formation of an organization promoting an ongoing series of shows could not be ignored. Though Clayton was the inspiration, Cimarron provided the blueprint on resurrecting the illegal sport with so-called "athletic clubs." It was the formation of several clubs around the state that began the anti-*anti*-prizefight war, inspiring bigger towns, like Las Vegas, to brazenly defy the federal laws that governed the territory.

The village of Cimarron became a watering hole for ranchers, miners and outlaws. During its heyday, in the 1860s, everyone, from Kit Carson to Buffalo Bill Cody, had the inclination to visit the town. By the time the railroad arrived, Cimarron's Wild West reputation had declined, though the town had another period of prosperity around 1905 due to mining and lumbering.

The sudden influx of development provided the perfect setting for prizefighting.

Launching a three-year run of an estimated 12 to 15 shows, beginning in March 1907, the town formed its own athletic club for the purpose of staging dances and entertainment — prize fights, of course, in the most demand — between Cimarron and surrounding villages.

The first show was held March 16, 1907, at Cimarron's Aztec Hall, with wrestling and boxing bouts between unknown fighters on a "smoker" — a term originating during the era to mean an informal (usually illegal) fight card. Though the details are unclear, the smoker must have been successful for, two nights later, at the nearby coal-mining town of Dawson, a crowd of 200 (10 percent of the town's population) showed up to watch a scheduled 20-rounder between Dawson hopeful Kid Mallet and Jimmy Garvey, of Trinidad, Colorado. Though giving up 10 pounds to fight the local favorite, Garvey, a lightweight with more experience, had little trouble with the Dawson welterweight, picking up the $150 side bet and gate, with a third-round knockout. Three preliminaries were staged.

Hoping to outdo the Dawson card, the Cimarron Athletic Club staged its full-fledged show two months later at Aztec Hall, pitting Wyoming featherweight Kid Butler, who'd been fighting for at least six years, with their hometown hopeful, Kid Joy. Once again, the hometowner was outclassed, though he nearly staged an upset in round three before the fateful fourth when Butler "placed a right and a left to the jaw in quick succession," dropping Joy, where he lay for "some time before he regained consciousness."[19]

It was nearly a year before Cimarron staged another smoker. This time, the main go was a total fiasco and a suspected frame-up that had the town running both fighters out of town. One fighter was heavyweight George R. Fitzgerald, of St. Louis; he was matched against a middleweight named Delaney, from Rock Springs, Wyoming.

Fitzgerald's record dated back to at least 1895, but his recent ring exploits in Las Vegas should've given Cimarron citizens the heads-up. Reports of Fitzgerald pulling out of fights and "boozing hard ever since he has been in the city"[20] appeared regularly in the *Optic*. There was also suspicion that Fitzgerald's August 1907 fight with Vegas' Charlie Williams had been a fake.

Much less is known of Delaney, but if he'd come from fight-friendly Rock Springs, he was probably a seasoned veteran. "But clever as he was, Delaney could not guard his face and side of the neck from the seemingly light and easily given love taps of the big man, and this led to his knockout in the fifth round, by a short arm punch over the heart and a left back hand tap on the jaw," ran the report in the *Cimarron Citizen*. "The blows were so seemingly light and easily given that cries of 'Fake' were at once raised. And to this day Cimarron is divided between the 'Twas Fake' and the 'Twasn't Fake' factions."[21]

Right after the fight, the local deputy sheriff arrested Fitzgerald, but not for his alleged frame-up; Fitzgerald had not paid his boarding bill while residing in Las Vegas. His winnings in the ring were sent to the widow of the boarding house.

The sporting editor of the *Citizen* admitted he'd been satisfied with the fight, though he could not resist running a poem that the "office 'devil,' while sweeping out the morning after the contest, found ... tied to the tail of the office cat"[22]:

> We, the undersigned citizens of Cimarron, here agree
> To pay the amount set opposite each and respective name,
> To these two combatants (take 'em away) as a fee.
> To carry out successfully their little skin game.
> With this provision and it is willingly so agreed,
> That the money we give and so cheerfully spend,
> Shall go to apply on the past dues feed
> Of Fitzgerald, our pugilistic, and mutual friend
> "Gollie" may have been a "go-getter" and a prize fight prompter,
> A circus man, a "brakey" and a "cute cut up" before,
> But in the land of the "square deal" and the "pistol toter"
> People are fooled once, mayhap twice, but no more.
> Little Delaney was a shifty chap, full of vim and grit,
> When Fitz swung his left out, he'd side step and "duck-er"
> He would have whipped the brawny Fitz we think — "nit"
> So each hereunto subscribes his name — a "sucker."[23]

On their next show, on the Fourth of July 1908, the Cimarron Athletic Club decided to downgrade the scheduled 10-round main event to a five-round prelim, in order to spotlight a completely *un*professional contest between two locals with a grudge:

> Some fertile brain conceived it would be a good plan to pay the fines imposed if the two men would fight it out with the gloves for the edification of the lovers of the manly art of self defense.... The last and main event of the evening was between the afternoon's combatants, Jose Pablo Derera, and Jose Armijo, and this contest did not lack in interest of fastness at any stage of the game. The two men were given instructions and were told that in breaking, neither one was to strike at the other, but in the contest, each forgot instructions, and fouls were landed thick and fast. When the gong sounded time, the two boxers had to be pulled off to their corners. Of science, there was none, and each man's idea seemed to be to get to the other and land on him hard. They had an old standing grudge to settle and they went after each other like wild men. At last in the fifth round, Armijo landed a swift left followed up with a hard right on Derea's already badly battered face, and the heavier man of the men gave up the contest, beaten to a standstill. With characteristic tender heartedness, the victor having demonstrated that he was the best man, felt sorry for his opponent and immediately went over to his corner with brotherly love in his heart and kind words on his lips. An apology was extended and accepted, and the once enemies, but now fast friends, literally fell on one another's necks and wept. A most fitting climax for the evening of strife.[24]

Under tighter scrutiny than their Cimarron colleagues, Albuquerque promoters were working out their own methods to bring back the sport. In December 1906, 25 Albuquerque socialites organized the "Geronimo Club," an athletic organization that would stage smokers with live entertainment and dances, all the while maintaining a gymnasium and equipping a local baseball club under its name. Athletic entertainment would, of course, include sparring — and whatever they could get away with, or what could be overlooked, by local law enforcement.

On Feb. 9, 1906, a smoker was thrown at their local club, with three boxing exhibitions, four rounds apiece, between club members, with "no decisions being rendered."[25] On Apr. 20, another one was held, four bouts taking place between members, in addition to an evening's entertainment that included guitar and piccolo duets, "good refreshments" and "an exciting badger fight."[26]

The Geronimo club did not last too much longer, but, by April 1908, a new club — the Albuquerque Athletic Club — had formed. This one, with 100 original charter members, took a while to get started, waiting until the end of the year to stage smokers.

Meanwhile, during the Territorial Fair of 1908, a boxing bout was permitted to take place in the Duke City, between Chicago's Bob Walker and a local soldier, though the promoter, a man named Kelly, took advantage of the situation to withhold Walker's purse. "Bobbie Walker doesn't think Albuquerque the finest place he ever visited," reported the *Las Vegas Daily Optic*. "He has no objection to the city itself, but he says the way he was treated by the management of an event which he believed to be first class was, in the language of the country, 'something little short of scandalous.'" Walker told the *Optic* that after he defeated his opponent, the promoter, Kelly, refused to pay him, telling him, "It is against the law of this territory to pay for anything in connection with a boxing match, and that is all there is to it." The *Optic* added, "Bob says he was too much of a gentleman to collect satisfaction with his fists."[27]

By the time the Albuquerque Athletic Club was brave enough to advertise boxing as part of its entertainment (for members only, of course), several other factors had developed to encourage the club, mainly, to replicate the brazen fight cards being thrown in Las Vegas and Cimarron.

District Attorney F. W. Clancy, meanwhile, was stirring things up, providing the *Morning Journal* with a copy of the 1896 anti-prizefighting law that everyone had seemed to have forgotten — especially those in Las Vegas.

What Happens in Vegas....

"Meet me at the ringside!" That is what the fight fans are saying.
— *Las Vegas Daily Optic*, 1908[28]

Fight promoters of Las Vegas are seeking other worlds to conquer. They now plan an invasion of Albuquerque.
— *Las Vegas Daily Optic*, 1908[29]

Albuquerque might claim "Fight Capital of New Mexico" during the 140-plus years of fighting, but Las Vegas has, time and again, been the town responsible for pushing the envelope. As prizefighting made its return in the first decade of the twentieth century, it was Las Vegas that showed the most disregard for territorial laws. Prizefighting illegal? Tell that to a town that staged four shows in 1907 and a dozen in 1908.

Las Vegas (Spanish for "The Meadows") was established by a Spanish land grant in 1835, but it wasn't until the arrival of the railroad, in 1879, when the town split into east and west, much as Albuquerque had done with New and Old Town, that Vegas established itself as the territorial mercantile center. By the turn of the century, the Meadow City was on its way to becoming one of the largest cities in the Southwest. By the time Las Vegas returned to boxing, in 1907, however, the expansion of the railroad in other parts of the state had reduced the town's productivity.

Barber's Hall on the west side of Las Vegas opened up the action on March 15, 1907, with Bill Russell of Pueblo, Colorado, going ten rounds and drawing with New Yorker Henry James.

One night later, a second show took place, participating fighters unknown.

It wasn't until August when another ten-rounder was scheduled in Vegas, this time at Mackel's Hall, between St. Louis' George Fitzgerald, the fighter who would cause such a fiasco the following year in Cimarron, and Charles Williams, of Rawlins, Wyo.

Seats were 50 cents for general admission, or $1 reserved, but the crowd of 300 that attended did not leave satisfied.

"Fake! Fake!" the crowd yelled, "Another California fight!" referencing the May 8, 1907, world heavyweight title fight between champion Tommy Burns and Philadelphia Jack O'Brien in Los Angeles. Burns had agreed to avoid using his in-fighting tactics in order to get O'Brien to sign the contract, then double-crossed his reluctant foe, resulting in a less-than-pleasing decision win for Burns, who had to literally chase O'Brien for 20 rounds.

"The big fight that was to be, was no fight at all," wrote the *Optic* reporter. "It was not even a graceful laydown." Johnson, the "colored pugilist who was to uphold the honors of Las Vegas, got cold feet when he saw the burley 185 pounds of G. R. Fitzgerald ... loom up in the ring." Johnson went down for the count upon Fitzgerald's first swing, being careful "not to make any false motions 'til the full ten had been doled out."[30] Even after the count, when Williams sat up, referee Frank Stewart offered to overlook his own count and give Williams a second chance but it was refused. Williams, who'd been outweighed by 25 pounds, left the hall unpaid by promoter C.A. Tooley.

Local prelim fighters helped pacify the angry crowd, most notable of whom was a 16-year-old flyweight named Louis Newman, who doubled as a press feeder for the local paper, and the Berry brothers, Ovie and Teddy (a.k.a. "Over Bear" and "Teddy Bear"; there was also "Black Bear," whose real name is unknown), who'd warmed up the crowd with an exhibition. Of all local hopefuls, Newman was the one destined for success in the ring. The Las Vegas-born fighter would not only get his start in New Mexico, but would also become the first Southwest star from the territory.

Several more fight cards were staged, though promotions changed hands, from "Professor" C. A. Tooley to the East Las Vegas Athletic Club.

Tooley, a local dancing and boxing instructor, skipped town with the cash box after a card, leaving the fighters unpaid for their efforts. Tooley was dismissed lightly and his actions did little to tarnish a developing fight town's taste for boxing. "The late unsportsmanlike fluke of one Professor Tooley so disgusted the fight fans of Las Vegas that a few prominent ones have formed a club to encourage the devotees of the manly art of self-defense, and to put the public exhibitions on a higher plane."[31]

Not even two boxing-related deaths halted the action.

On Sept. 15, 1907, eight-year-old Melano Valdez, of Las Vegas, begged his older brother Benito to show him how to box. During their sparring, Benito struck blows "which he intended to be harmless," knocking Melano down with a blow over the heart. "The blow was purely accidental and as the boy was soon able to be up and around, little was thought of the incident at the time."[32] But, later that night, Melano complained of chest pains and was unable to neither sit up nor move his left arm. His condition worsened and on Sept. 17 Melano died.

Ten days later, Barber's Hall threw a fight card.

Less than seven months later, this time in Santa Fe, another non-professional died from sparring injuries. This time, the victim was 21-year-old Joseph T. Lacome, whose father owned the Claire Hotel. While sparring in a "friendly boxing contest" with Joe Clenfuegos, Lacome received a blow on his nasal bone "causing an internal rupture of a blood vessel."[33] Bleeding heavily, Lacome was taken to his parents' home, where he died three days later. On that same day, the Albuquerque Athletic Club formed, with plans to build a gymnasium for boxing instruction.

The second death might've served to temporarily reduce fights in the territory, but there were few roadblocks in Las Vegas.

Following the Fitzgerald-Williams disappointment, and promising no "'funny' business"[34] the newly-formed Eagle Athletic Club pitted Teddy Bear against Fitzgerald. After the St. Louis pug, who'd been boozing in the saloons since his arrival, suddenly "developed a case of cold feet,"[35] Fitzgerald's name was further muddied a couple days after his pullout when one of his teammates was arrested and brought back to Chicago where, it was believed, he was wanted for the brutal murder of a schoolteacher.

English pugilist C. Fitzgerald — no relation to George — who'd been training in Romeroville for Over Bear, stepped up to fight his foe's brother instead, Teddy Bear. The fight proved a bust when Berry was "dropped and it was fully thirty minutes before he was able to raise up and ask, 'What's the matter?'"[36]

Whether because of the Fitzgerald fiascos or the two boxing-related deaths, Las Vegas kept low key a string of shows in the first half of 1908. Then, near the end of June, hometowner Louie Newman, not quite 17 and undefeated in eight fights, was deemed ready to headline Mackel's Opera House with the town's return to boxing.

Newman's opponent was black featherweight Charles Williams, also of Las Vegas, who would come in ten pounds heavier. The two agreed to fight 15 rounds at catchweights on June 27 — in a fight "that is not to be a prize-fight, but will be a scientific boxing match, which will be decided at the end of the fifteen rounds strictly on the merits of the two principals."[37] Despite the weight difference, Williams was outboxed, quitting in round two.

When Newman left for Trinidad, for a fight that never materialized, Las Vegas moved on, borrowing Clayton favorite, lightweight Serapio Romero, to go 15 on July 31, 1908, with Jim Murphy of Oklahoma City. Near-daily reminders were printed in the *Optic*, stating "the greatest mill that has ever been seen in this town" (a staple for fight reports for the next 30 years), that the fighters were in perfect condition and that the Las Vegas Military Band would furnish music, playing the Plaza before the fight and while the crowd gathered in the hall.

Though lacking experience against seasoned professionals, Romero was named as a slight favorite by the *Optic*, which provided front-page reportage leading up and following the fight — a rarity. Another rarity? Not only did the fight come off as announced, but it was fiasco- and frame-up-free. With the only drawback a missing gong, the *Optic's* outcome was: "A win, a quit and a draw, plenty of steam and a crowd that howled its head off every time the willing fighters mixed it up."[38] The report, in part:

The superior speed of Murphy gave him decided advantage. He landed repeatedly with both hands and chug-chugged like a triphammer on Romero's head and face, but his engine was too weak to produce the desired effect. Romero was worried and his wind went away about the eighth round, but Murphy's jabs were too weak to finish what his faster work would otherwise have made possible. When the two shook hands it looked like a contest between a mosquito and a grasshopper. Much is to be said for the Romero side of the war. At long range he was the superior of Murphy, lashing him repeatedly in the face and keeping the blood flowing after the end of the second round.

His swings were slow, but he has a reach like a giraffe and hogged a lot of punishment without batting an eye. He weighed fully twenty pounds more than little Murphy, as things looked from the ringside. This was an advantage, or would have been were it not for the fact that he maneuvered like an anchored battleship with a broken propeller, his principal occupation being standing still in the center of the ring and making faces while Murphy circled around him. Round seven was the only one that was distinctively the property of Romero. In that paragraph of the main event, he sent home a full-arm punch into Murphy's pie tank that had he been fast enough on his feet to follow it in close, might have ended the battle. But he did not grab his advantage and Murphy stalled off and covered up till he got the wind back into his refrigerator.[39]

For all his colorful writing, the reporter, Edwin R. Collins, could not help but conclude that, "Personally, I'd rather see a dogfight in the street than all the prizefights on earth — for the dogs don't know any better while men ought to. But that's their business! Anyhow they gave me a free ticket so I haven't any right to knock the game."[40]

Two days later, it was announced that Vegas' Newman was coming back home to headline a show, most likely in September. In the meantime, one promoter, Harry Oakes, moved to Albuquerque with the hopes of putting on a show there (he had no luck), and James Tolle formed the East Las Vegas Sporting Club, which took over the local scene.

For September, Newman was matched up with 115-pounder Teddy Mapleson, known only in Raton, though the fight would, of course, "be in no sense a prize fight. It will be a boxing match pure and simple,"[41] set for Labor Day at Rosenthal Hall. Though the explanations that prize fights were scientific exhibitions were now beginning to escalate, Newman-Mapleson would be the first New Mexico championship fight since the 1896 legal ban.

It was about this time, that a goat-herding prizefighter made a splash on the Meadow City's scene.

Harry "Kid" Wallace, a black fighter originally from Leavenworth, Kansas, had been a moderately successful pug on the West Coast before joining up with former Nebraska cowboy, Spanish-American War veteran Captain Edwards "and his famous team of Angora goats."[42] Edwards, a crippled 52-year-old, endeavored to walk across the country from San Diego to New York while herding a team of goats with his two assistants, another veteran and the prizefighter Wallace. The task of promotion was, apparently, Wallace's task, for newspapers at points along the route mapped out by his boss were given the heads-up that Edwards and his famous goats were on the way.

Wallace also made it clear that, being such a successful prizefighter, he was more than ready to meet anyone in his class, at any location, for any agreed-upon purse. According to his letters, Wallace claimed to be anywhere from 24–2-2 to 27–2, and boasted quite a resume, including a 20-round draw with the respected Jim Tremble, a six-round distance loss with newly-crowned World Middleweight Champion Stanley Ketchel, a draw with well-known Philly lightweight Gus Gardner, a win over Tommy Reilly in 20 and knockouts over West Coast pugs Kid Kane and Kid Williams. Just how exaggerated Wallace's claims were is unknown, for most of the bouts listed above have not been recorded anywhere; and his 20-round "draw" with Tremble was a distance loss for the goat-herding pug.

Within a month of his heralding letter to the *Optic*, Wallace, Edwards and the prize Angora goats hit Vegas. The goats received a casual mention, but the "colored pugilist who has fought and won many ring battles,"[43] judged to be the "strong healthy-looking specimen of the mulatto,"[44] became an instant attraction to the fight-friendly town. Upon his arrival, Wallace agreed to box an exhibition on the Newman bill — if he could headline the next show. Local promoters agreed.

Keen to Wallace's arrival and challenges, the Vegas papers had already been solicited by the likes of Chicago's Bob Walker and Pittsburgh's Jack Graham, who'd been fighting in El Paso. Walker had, to his credit, a ten-round draw with Colorado middleweight champion Johnny O'Keefe, and had lost to Dick Fitzpatrick, also from Chicago, in a 17-round war. Graham, on the other hand, claimed to have nearly 80 bouts in his nine-year career, and had faced (and lost) to world class fighters "Fireman" Jim Flynn, Charles "Kid" McCoy, Tommy Ryan and Jack Everhardt.

Vegas fans, however, cared less about experienced out-of-towners when there was a local kid to rally behind — like Newman. For his bout against Mapleson, Newman arrived six days before the contest to train with Wallace, despite the 30-pound difference between them. The fight itself was one-sided, Newman breezing through Mapleson in eight out of ten rounds to win the territorial featherweight title. The 17-year-old then returned to Denver, setting a precedent for New Mexicans with potential: Get outta town, if you want to make it in prizefighting.

Losing their one and only hometown hopeful, Las Vegas moved on, headlining Wallace against Bob Walker. The goats and Edwards left, too, moving on to Raton without their marketing prizefighter (news clippings on the goat team also stopped about this time.)

Little is known of Walker, though he claimed to be a veteran of over 100 battles, winning the majority of them. With Walker locked in to a fight, Wallace saw his opportunity to call out New Mexico's top middleweight, Bill Pettus, sending an "ambitious defi" to the *Morning Journal*. The paper reported, "Wallace writes in red ink and goes at it as if he means business."[45]

Though, for the most part, the *Morning Journal* frowned upon prize fights, the editors could not resist stirring the pot by printing defis. On behalf of Newman, manager A. C. de Baca challenged anyone from feather to lightweight; Wallace wanted Pettus; Pettus wanted Wallace; and Jack Graham wanted *both* Wallace and Pettus. The challenges did not escape the notice of District Attorney Clancy, who made a complaint, "in view of numerous recent pugilistic [defis] issued by various New Mexico aspirants to ring honors and looking for a mill in this city,"[46] sending newspapers copies of the federal law outlawing fights.

Ninety miles away in Las Vegas, the threat was taken lightly, though promoter Tolle increased his explanations that his prize fights were not *really* prize fights but scientific exhibitions for points. Tolle assumed his shows would continue as long as he kept the rounds down to ten, and as long as any mention of a purse or the price of tickets were kept out of print. Without a dollar amount attributed to any fight, there was no way, really, to prove any fight was anything other than an exhibition.

On Sept. 16, Walker arrived in Las Vegas for his bout with Wallace. By now, the winner was being touted as a challenger to no less than Pueblo's rising star "Fireman" Jim Flynn. The fight itself was a letdown, with Walker proving "no nearer a match for Harry Wallace than mud is ice cream."[47] Though the Chicago veteran did fight gamely, he was outclassed, going down twice to the goat-herding prizefighter. Touted as an instant threat to Flynn and any middleweight in the country, Wallace enjoyed the spotlight in Vegas while the next victim, Jack Graham, was lined up for October.

Vegas was getting greedy and careless now. "Why limit the boxing exhibitions to ten rounds?" wrote the *Optic's* editor. If Flynn could be enticed to fight in Vegas, ten rounds would not be enough to determine a winner. The *Optic* argued against the 1896 statute: "They point to the fact that any prize fight is against the law, but that boxing exhibitions of a strictly scientific nature are not mentioned in the statute and there could as well, be for sixty rounds as six.... Purely scientific exhibitions were never intended to be prevented and there is no reference to them in the laws."[48]

Wallace, meanwhile, enjoyed his local celebrity status in Las Vegas, where former black fighters had been walloped by the press. "He does not drink or smoke," printed the *Optic*. "He is hard as nails and always in training.... Watch him go!"[49] Graham proved the opposite of Walker, in respect to smack talking, making his match with Wallace an easy sell. "It will be nice for me when I whip him,"[50] bragged the Pittsburgh pug.

Once again, however, the actual battle did not live up to expectations, with Graham losing by disqualification in round four for throwing low blows. There was nothing accidental about the blows; the press and fans believed Graham was trying to save face by avoiding a knockout. Graham had further soured the show by sitting in the audience and refusing to enter the ring before the promoter agreed to a purse of $50 whether Graham won, lost or drew.

Graham's escapades gave the sport a black eye, for the audience at the next show went from fair to "a crowd that one could load into a one-seated buggy and not especially overcrowd it."[51]

Wallace was getting other offers now beyond Vegas, from his hometown of Leavenworth, to a fight against Bill Pettus, a natural for the territory. When Albuquerque turned it down, the town of Madrid offered up the fight, for a $400 purse.

"[Madrid] is a mining camp and there are more than 200 men regularly employed in the mines," promoter Tolle told the *Optic*. "Each of these will give up $2 for a ticket to the fight and probably will bet his month's wages on the result of the game.... Those people have made us a good offer down there, and we have accepted it."[52] For one reason or another, though, the Madrid fight did not come off.

In Las Vegas, another attempt was made to erase the Graham-Wallace bout from the fans' mind, by matching up Walker with Clayton's Serapio Romero. In a supporting bout, someone named "The Mexican Kid" was billed but neither he nor Romero showed up. Instead, Wallace was enticed to step in for a six-rounder, to play "with Walker like a cat does a mouse," waltzing around his foe and having him nearly knocked out before backing off, "like a bull dog fighting a rabbit with Walker on the hare end."[53]

The *Optic* wrote, "By the attendance it would look that prize fighting has as much of a voge [*sic*] here as ping-pong has. Walker is going to the coast. He is sorely disappointed at the gate receipts. They were so small that it took an opera glass to find them. 'I'm on my way,' he said this morning. 'Good-a-bye, kid.'"[54]

Las Vegas' love affair with the gloves had come to an end–for now.

Law? What law?

> The number of pugilists who are wasting their muscle on the desert air of New Mexico is surprising. The Morning Journal *received still another challenge yesterday as follows.*
>
> —*Albuquerque Journal, 1908*[55]

By the end of 1908, Jack Johnson had knocked out Tommy Burns to become the first black world heavyweight champion. Burns had defeated Marvin Hart in 1905, after James Jeffries — defeating Bob Fitzsimmons in 1899 — had given up the belt the year before.

By the end of 1908, boxing had also returned to Albuquerque under guise of the Albuquerque Athletic Club, which was comprised of "professors" and out-of-town pugilists hoping to make a buck in the Duke City. Their first show was lined up for Nov. 30 in what would also be the inaugural boxing card at downtown's National Guard Armory. Over the decades, the Armory would play host to more than 130 fight cards.

The Nov. 30 card began as a "membership drive." For just $2 a month, sports-hungry fans in the Duke City could be a member of the new club managed by "Professor" Harry Kennedy. Though suddenly a "professor" in New Mexico, in his hometown of Kansas City, the club's athletic instructor went by the name of "Spike" Kennedy, a minor-league prizefighter whose claim to fame had been a six-round knockout loss to "Denver" Ed Martin. According to the *Morning Journal*, however, Kennedy was also a former wrestler and Notre Dame football player. Whether that was true or not, or whether his exaggerated ring career had any merit, the professor proved more than enough to wow the locals when he battered down Albuquerque's "Kid" Lavigne in four, in their scheduled 15-rounder. Kennedy became the latest and greatest — and an instant target for visiting pugilists.

"After scouring the southwest for almost two weeks,"[56] Kennedy was matched up next with Bob Walker, who'd been hanging out in Las Vegas until the boxing scene had dried up a couple months before. Testing local law enforcement, another 15-rounder was set for Dec. 19, and the fight proved to be a mismatch. No match for Kennedy, Walker was floored ten times before a solar plexus punch sent him to the count at 1:30 of the sixth. Now touted as the best in the Southwest, Kennedy enjoyed his time in the limelight until he was matched with Bill Pettus.

As Las Vegans had tried to do by offering up Harry Wallace, you could not call yourself the No. 1 middleweight in New Mexico without going up against Pettus. In between baseball gigs and prize fights, Pettus was working in Madrid as a coal miner when the offer came to fight Kennedy. Albuquerque's professor was expected to "give the colored boy a big long run for his money."[57] The two agreed to go 15 rounds, winner take all, for $400 on Jan. 19 — admission, of course, confined to members ($2 monthly membership or $15 annual).

Announcement of the fight brought resistance to the anti-prizefight lobbyists, who argued that private club or no private club, prizefighting was still illegal. The Armory withdrew its support, just as the Elks' Theater offered hosting the "private function." Hoping to appease the sudden resistance, the Albuquerque Athletic Club proclaimed that all future matches between pros and non-pros would be eliminated from their "exhibitions." Of course, Pettus-Kennedy was on.

The Jan. 19 show would be Albuquerque's one-and-only card for 1909 — and would prove a mismatch. Clearly not in Pettus' class, Kennedy "apparently had no show from the start,"[58] and lasted less than three rounds when his second threw up the sponge.

Possibly, because he was disgraced, but, more likely, because he'd gotten wind of a warrant being served against him, Kennedy, dropping the *nom de ring* of "Professor" for his original alias "Spike," left town to lose a wrestling match in El Paso in February. But one month later, he was, along with former foe Walker, indicted by the United States Grand Jury for participating in a "pugilistic encounter" for a purse.

"Both men left for parts unknown some time ago and the warrants issued for them will probably be pigeon-holed for all time,"[59] wrote the *Morning Journal*. Kennedy escaped prosecution but Walker wasn't so lucky. He went south, becoming a temporary hit with Las Cruces' version of an athletic club (what else? The Las Cruces Athletic Association) by calling himself the "Cactus Kid of the Rio Grande," defeating Kid Lee of Kansas City in February and drawing with Jimmie Considine of San Francisco in March. Walker was matched up against Kid Herold of El Paso in April when he was arrested with the outstanding warrant. That was the last New Mexico was to see of Walker — and also the last fight in Las Cruces while boxing was illegal.

No action was taken against the popular Pettus, who resumed his career in northern New Mexico. Pettus was one of several fighters who'd learned his craft on New Mexico home turf. Pettus was from Albuquerque; Newman was developed in Las Vegas. There was also Everett Winters in Raton and Al Smaulding, from Clayton. Once Newman moved to Denver and opportunities dried up, Winters and Smaulding became the primary home-towners in northern New Mexico.

In 1909, the primary spot for fights remained Cimarron. After two cards in '08, Cimarron promoters returned full force with seven shows in '09, all built around Winters, Smaulding and, finally, the long-awaited showdown between Pettus and Wallace.

During one four-week period in 1909, a visitor in Cimarron could have attended three fight cards, each one headlining three of the four top names of the era. In February, Raton's Winters, fighting with a broken hand, no less, KO'd Cimarron's Jimmie Burns in 11 rounds. A few weeks later, New Mexico's answer to middleweight, heavyweight and everything in between, Pettus, outclassed the Las Vegas-hyped Wallace, busting up his ribs in the fourth round as a parting gift on his way out of the territory. A few days later, "The Clayton Blacksmith," black middleweight Smaulding, made his debut in the ring over Oklahoma veteran W. E. Moon.

Having defeated someone like Wallace, Pettus became the instant attraction in Cimarron. After notable Denver pug John Geyer (who would eventually become well-known "Denver" Jack Geyer) hit town in April 1909, to defeat an unnamed Mexican, he was pitted against Pettus in June. Before its biggest crowd to date, estimated at 400, Pettus toyed with Geyer, flooring the man who would soon be a popular great white hope, three times en route to an eighth-round finish. Pettus was declared ready for the big leagues.

In between the Smaulding and Winters headliners, Cimarron, meanwhile, continued to bring in seasoned out-of-towners, most of whom were fighting the Colorado circuit. Frankie Harris of Milwaukee defeated Muggsy School of Cheyenne in July, then drew with Denver's Young Erlenborn in August. The action continued to spread, and Clayton returned to staging shows, featuring their new hopeful, Smaulding.

The largest reported attendance of any fight to date did not take place in Cimarron, Clayton nor the larger cities of Albuquerque or Las Vegas, but rather in unlikely Taos, known for its ancient pueblo and a developing mecca for artists. The *Cimarron Citizen* reported that 2,000 spectators showed up in Taos during the early winter (exact date unknown) to watch a 58-year-old prizefight veteran return to take on local barber "Sledge Hammer" Tommy Vest. The veteran — Elisha Levi Spickelmier — had been promising, or threatening, to return to the squared circle since the beginning of 1909, when a host of New Mexico newspapers printed his humorous defi:

> I have followed the ring for the past twenty-two years, and was known as the '4 D Kid.' I have been in training here in Cimarron for the past seven or eight weeks and am expecting a tour of the coast next spring, and again enter the ring. I am the oldest man to re-enter the ring to my knowledge, being now past fifty-eight years of age. I feel young and in the best of condition. You can say for me that I will meet any local heavyweight in the territory for any sort of a bout he may wish under the usual ring conditions and $500 on the side. I will bar none, but, of course I do not pretend that I could make good against Johnson, Burns, Jeffries and those fellows, although there was a time when I would like to have done so. For these reasons, I limit the

challenge to the territory, although I will take on Colorado fighters, who think they know something about the ring troubles.[60]

The *Cimarron Citizen* spoke familiarly of the old-timer, noting, "Those who followed the ring for the past twenty years will no doubt remember that nifty heavyweight fighter known as 4 D Kid."[61] No accounts of his previous fights are known, but the Iowa-born Spickelmier's age is questionable. Though he claimed to be 58, U.S. Census reports in 1910 and 1920 have conflicting data, the former listing 1850 as his birth year, the latter showing 1867. Descendants of Spickelmier support the later year, listing Oct. 15, 1867, as his birthdate.

Whether 58 or 41, Spickelmier was serious about a comeback in 1909. That is, until "a sunny-faced, breezy, good-natured chap" by the name of "Red" Mike Flannery arrived at the Cimarron depot in search of the wily pug. Local fight promoters sprang into action and Spickelmier was summoned. But "alas and alack, the man who would far rather fight a buzz saw than eat, wanted six weeks to train and this after a steady training of over eight weeks under the care of some of the best trainers in the country, who had entered Cimarron in disguise." Promising to return, the 4-D

Fighting out of Cimarron, New Mexico, and in at least his 40s, Elisha Levi Spickelmier, a.k.a. the "4D Kid," was an old-timer staging a comeback in 1908–1909. He threatened to take on any younger man in the territory or Colorado who "think they know something about the ring troubles." Barber Tommy Vest of Taos took up the challenge and defeated ol' Elisha (courtesy of Shyla Blair).

Kid "took the next train out of town, accompanied by his ever-loving spouse who stated that the Kid had never fought in the ring in his life."[62]

After the papers had humored their readers about Spickelmier's comedic return, in the fall, the 4-D Kid *did* enter the ring while living in Taos and working in construction. "If he can hammer nails as fast and furious as he can hammer his opponents,"[63] wrote the *Citizen*, Spickelmier would have little trouble dispatching local barber Tommy Vest.

By this time, fight promoters in Cimarron had caved in not to territorial politicians but to local anti-prizefight pressure. "It is not thought that the principals will pull the go off in Cimarron," wrote the *Citizen*, "because of the antagonism here to prize fights, which the Cimarron people have recently shown, in declaring the fights in Cimarron a thing of the past."[64]

Sometime in late October or early November, the fight came off in Taos, where Spickelmier "met his Waterloo":

The contest was one of two short exhibitions which were pulled off for the purpose of having a little outside amusement other than the aboriginal sports and dances of the Taos Indians. The old time favorite and veteran of many a hard fought battle, though out-weighing his opponent, by about twenty pounds, was clearly out-classed from the start. He at first waded into his lighter man intending to put him to the hay by mere weight. but Sledge-Hammer Vest side-stepped handily and sent in crushing blow after blow to the stomach and face, and before the third round was ended, the battle was easily the younger man's. The 4 D Kid seemed bewildered and dazed and seemed unable to protect himself or to cover up at all. He was unable to land on his opponent with any degree of certainty, and clearly showed that his balmy days had passed. He has stated that his age being nearly sixty years old, did not affect his ability and strength, but it is evident that he over-estimated himself, and under-estimated the effects of having been so long out of the ring. It is highly probable that this will be the last appearance of the 4 D Kid in the ring. Those who saw the contest state that the Kid must have been an extraordinary man in his prime.[65]

The colorful Spickelmier, by the way, never did fight again. Some time after his time in Taos, Spickelmier, his wife, and four children moved to Grand Junction, Colorado. Then, on August 5, 1923, Spickelmier was struck down by Chicago tourists on a state highway near Provo, Utah, while examining his car. Two days later he died from brain trauma. Spickelmier and his family had been camping nearby and had planned to move on to California in the coming weeks. At the time of his death, Spickelmier's age was given as 60 — which would have made him closer to 46, not 58, at the time of his 1909 ring return.

Fight of the Century

> You can stop a prize fight, but you can't kill the public interest in it.
> —*Albuquerque Morning Journal*, 1910[66]

White America had a black champion and it was determined to do something about it. World Heavyweight Champion Jack Johnson never would have been given the chance to fight for the title in the U.S. But in Australia, on Dec. 26, 1908, the opportunity arose to meet champion Tommy Burns. After 14 rounds of punishment, Johnson was crowned champ, giving birth to a new era — and a new term.

After writer Jack London coined the phrase "Great White Hope," the search was on for someone of lighter color to dethrone Johnson. Philadelphia Jack O'Brien, Tony Ross, Al Kaufman and World Middleweight Champion Stanley Ketchel all failed to appease the demand in 1909. But White America was clamoring for a challenger. Unable to find one, they decided to resurrect former champion James J. Jeffries, who was cajoled into making a reluctant comeback, reportedly telling the press, "I feel obligated to the sporting public at least to make an effort to reclaim the heavyweight championship for the white race.... I should step into the ring again and demonstrate that a white man is king of them all."[67]

Billed as "Fight of the Century," the bout landed in the fight-friendly railroad town of Reno, Nevada — but not before Clovis, New Mexico, made an unrealistic bid for the fight: "Clovis is out with a proposition to land the big Jeffries-Johnson scrap within eight miles of town. Dr. J. Foster Scott, president of the chamber of commerce, and Cash Ramey, a local capitalist, have wired Tex Rickard, inviting him to stage the battle on the unsurveyed strip of land on the Texas-Mexico border, eight miles east of Clovis. It is said that no authority can interfere with the fight if held on this piece of ground, as both New Mexico and Texas claim jurisdiction."[68] There is no record that Rickard even acknowledged the fight proposal. Then again, there was no need, for after San Francisco was ruled out, thanks to anti-prizefight Governor James Gillett, Nevada welcomed the chance to be the center of the world on July 4, 1910.

"Give the people what they want" became the new creed of the *Morning Journal,* their writers not hiding their disgust for the sport: "It may be all a deep dyed disgrace. Probably it is. But what are you going to do with the people that want it? And no matter how deep the disgrace, it is a disgrace that is going to keep millions of people at fever heat of excitement until the last blow is struck."[69]

On the day of the fight, in Albuquerque and Las Vegas, Johnson-Jeffries became the center of attention when crowds gathered at the *Morning Journal* and *Optic* to hear returns of the fight. Members of Albuquerque's Elks Club listened to the fight in style, with a wire extended to the club's exclusive rooms. In a vacant lot adjacent to the *Journal*'s office, an immense crowd gathered for several hours to listen to the "clarion tones of Announcer R. E. Sherman"[70] announce the returns:

> It was the next thing to seeing the real fight in the Nevada town and the intent and patient crowd was a striking proof of the intense interest taken by Albuquerque people in the result of the great battle. There were several thousand people in the audience and no public speaker ever held more rapt attention than Mr. Sherman. It was mostly a Jeffries crowd. Whenever Jeffries got a shade the best of it, wild cheers arose from the crowd in multitude. Johnson, however, was not without his noisy supporters in the crowd, who made a respectable racket when the black man landed.[71]

The fight itself proved to be a mismatch. In front of a crowd of 20,000, Johnson made a statement by humiliating Jeffries, flooring the former champ twice before he quit in round 15. Johnson's victory triggered race riots across the country.

In Santa Fe, Johnson-Jeffries inspired at least two fist fights, one of which was reported in the daily arrest record, turning into an impromptu prize fight: "The two combatants fought two rounds before George Stark, a well known painter who is in the city acted as referee and called a halt."[72]

The crushed hopes of those praying Jeffries would put the black man in his place inspired mixed reaction throughout New Mexico. "Today there is a feeling of depression everywhere among followers of the white fighter,"[73] editorialized the *Optic*. In Roswell, Mayor G. T. Veal issued a statement that he'd "do everything in his power to prevent the showing of the Johnson-Jeffries fight pictures."[74] The *Alamogordo Advertiser* wrote, "Fighting belongs to the back and dark ages — not to civilization."[75]

But there was no stopping prizefighting — *especially* in New Mexico during the year 1910.

Military Aid

> *If a battle is arranged, it will in all probability be fought at Fort Wingate, where the civil authorities cannot interfere with a boxing contest held under the auspices of the soldiers.*
>
> —*Albuquerque Morning Journal,* 1910[76]

The first consistent boxing among the troops in New Mexico occurred in 1910, with both Fort Wingate and Fort Bayard staging several shows for the soldiers' entertainment. As would prove true over the next two decades, boxing at army camps in New Mexico received little or no resistance from law enforcement.

Both forts had been built to control the Indians. Established in 1866 to keep a check on roving Apache bands, Fort Bayard was located near the gold and silver mining towns of Silver City and Pinos Altos. With the surrender of Geronimo in 1886, the threat was reduced and, by 1899, the fort was nearly depopulated. Instead, Fort Bayard became a medical center for the treatment and research of tuberculosis.

The first known fight card held at Fort Bayard, in May 1910, would be one of 30 shows held there during the next decade-and-a-half. The one show during 1910 pitted soldiers against locals, and debuted a Silver City miner named Gus Flores, who would be a local favorite during the next decade.

Established near Gallup in 1862, Fort Wingate's purpose was to control the Navajo population to the north until 1870, when the soldiers switched their attention to the Apaches in the south. From 1911 to 1914, the garrison was depopulated. Fort Wingate staged at least two shows in 1910. In the initial card there, on Feb. 3, 1910, with a cow bell substituted for the typical gong at ringside, soldier "Chinless" Smith decisioned "Humpty" Sydney for the fort's welterweight championship. Later that month, cavalryman Louis "Cotton" Hilton KO'd civilian prizefighter Frank Spears for the Southwest featherweight championship.

A native of Paterson, N.J., Spears was a veteran of a dozen battles in Nevada and throughout the Southwest. Shortly before arriving at Wingate, Spears fought at the town of San Marcial, near Socorro, against Kid Philbaum of Colorado (outcome unknown). Soon after, Spears was in Albuquerque, proclaiming himself the New Mexico featherweight champ by virtue of defeating local Jimmy McCaffrey on a show thrown by the Knights of Columbus, which marked the Duke City's return to the sport.

It hadn't even been a year since the Albuquerque Athletic Club had pulled the plug on pugilism, when boxing returned. This time around, the focus of the reformed club was wrestling for, unlike boxing, there was nothing prohibiting mat artists from plying their trade. Under cover of grappling and amateur athletics, in general, both professional and non-professionals were free to join the reformed club. Members could, therefore, participate in smokers or attend entertainment functions under the umbrella of the Knights of Columbus.

On Jan. 20, with an initial membership of 200, the club, with the backing of the National Guard's Col. Manuel Stern (who would soon be a professional boxer), staged a show that headlined a wrestling match. Preceding the main go was a six-round boxing bout between Spears and a local who was "pretty much out of Spear's [sic] class, but still managed to put up a game scrap."[77] Spears headed for the two cards at Fort Wingate and, after his defeat at the hands of soldier Hilton, left for Denver and, ultimately, for San Francisco.

Meanwhile, boxing was back on in Albuquerque.

Before it became illegal for fight films starring Jack Johnson to be circulated, Albuquerque's Pastime Theater showed the Johnson-Stanley Ketchel fight in early 1910 for a 20-cent admission. As on paper reported, "Pictures are so perfect that one fight fan, who was evidently a strong backer of Ketchel jumped from his chair as the seventh round was drawing to a close and shouted, 'Fifty dollars on Ketchel!' He had no takers."[78]

Tucked neatly within several grappling shows under the Knights of Columbus, boxing bouts continued to be staged. The fight fever spread to other towns.

The village of Costilla, near Taos, staged a show in March 1910 while the farming community of Colfax, during its heyday, headlined Henry Perry from nearby Dawson, one month later. Perry KO'd a man named Blosfield, then, sometime in the fall, headed north to Raton, where he fought a 20-round draw with Kid Davis.

In northeast New Mexico, Clayton staged several shows headlining their blacksmith,

Al Smaulding, San Francisco featherweight Spider Moffatt and Oklahoma heavyweight Louis "Thunderbolt" Fink. In July, Fink KO'd Clayton negro Joe Sutton in the ninth for the territorial heavyweight championship — Fink's claim to fame would be a disqualification win over future champ Jess Willard in 1911.

In the south, promoters in Silver City, encouraged by Fort Bayard's success, staged an all-soldier show while, out of the ring, well-known West Coast prizefighter Johnny Murphy, who'd arrived in the city to combat tuberculosis, quietly passed away on April 14.

In August, Gallup returned to boxing for the first time in 15 years, borrowing veteran Spider Moffatt, who won a 15-round decision over little-known Billy Leonard. In December, Gallup was the scene of another fight, between hometown youngster Dick Givens and Fort Wingate's John Kaiser. Entertainment staged at fairs held in Taos and Tucumcari included informal bouts of boxing while Spring Lake, close to Artesia, in the only known card to be held there, staged a late July show.

Also staging its first show in 15 years, and able to attach itself to local military influence, was the town of Roswell. In March 1910, the New Mexico Military Institute held a seemingly professional show by matching up its cadets. Though most considered the bouts to be amateur, a local middleweight, Alfred Higgins, son of local Captain Fred Higgins of the New Mexico Mounted Police, easily defeated Alamogordo's Walter Baird with a first round knockout. Following the example set by Albuquerque, Roswell's sporting fraternity formed the Roswell Athletic Club and, in June, again headlined Higgins who fought six rounds with Albuquerque's Robert Ross. "There were no decisions and it was planned to discourage betting and develop only the spirit and sport of athletics,"[79] assured the local *Daily Record* and *Morning Journal.*

"Pecos Town's" love affair with the gloved sport was brief, this time around. Though the town hailed Higgins as a future "star artist with the gloves"[80] in June, by November, Roswell had changed its tune:

> Enraged at paying their money to see what they believed was a fake fight, local sports broke up a boxing exhibition this afternoon by running onto the stage and causing a general row. Alfred Higgins of this city was boxing Kid Clark, who claimed the welterweight championship of Texas. Clark proved to have a guard and nothing else. He was merely taking six rounds of punishment for half the receipts, the crowd thought. Higgins was giving a good show. About fifty men and boys ran onto the stage. Clark was knocked down and kicked in the stomach and face, a long gash being cut in his face. The sheriff of the county, a deputy and a policeman were present and stopped the row as speedily as possible, and before any one was seriously hurt. Fire Chief Whiteman dispersed the crowd by bringing in the hose and threatening to turn on the water. Two arrests of citizens were made. Sheriff Ballard and Marshal Woofter announce [*sic*] that there will be no more mills in Roswell.[81]

The animosity to fighting in Roswell would disappear by 1912.

Bat Nelson Raises the O-bar

> *Obar has to be a strenuous place. You see that is where Battling Nelson lives between battles.*
> — *Albuquerque Morning Journal,* 1910[82]

> *Nelson was dressed in an easy up-to-date cut of clothes, and wore a bright red necktie, with a diamond sparkler in it that dazzled the eyes. His face showed the result of the terrific battles that he has engaged in, but although it is badly scarred in many places,*

*it still retains that aspect of confidence and bull-dog determination which has char-
acterized his entire pugilistic career.*

                                       —*Albuquerque Morning Journal,* 1910[83]

How many prizefighters can brag to be an original settler of a town?

Enter Oscar Nielson, known to the prize-fight world as Battling Nelson.

As 1908 began, the fight community was already beginning to write about "The Durable Dane" as if he'd already seen his best days. Nelson won the world lightweight championship in 1905 with an 18-round knockout of Jimmy Britt, then lost the title in 42 rounds a year later to Joe Gans in one of the most epic battles of all time.

BAT. NELSON

Oscar Nielson, a.k.a. "Battling Nelson," was one of the greatest lightweights of all time — he was also significant to the sudden popularity of the short-lived town of O-bar (Library of Congress, Prints & Photographs Division [LC-B22-361-15]).

Proving everyone wrong, Nelson weathered a rough start in '08 by losing a newspaper decision to tough Rudy Unholz (who would fight in New Mexico several years later), then bouncing back to championship form and gaining the newspaper nod over former champ Britt, drawing with Abe Attell in 15 and knocking out the unbeatable Gans in 17 rounds to reclaim the lightweight championship in July. Taking a much-needed vacation, Bat Nelson went to New Mexico.

Nelson's New Mexico connection was a former trainer from early in his career. Bill Brenner, who'd invited the Chicago-based champ for a few weeks of rest at his ranch in Perry. The town, little more than a clump of buildings and ranches at the time, was located five miles from west Texas and ten miles north of Tucumcari in Quay County. Though formed in 1906, the development of the railroad had formed a "new town" community on the other side of the tracks. This new community became "O-bar," named after its ranching brand, a circle with a bar under it.

When reports of Nelson leaving for the Southwest hit the wire, the *Optic* was the first New Mexican paper to publicize his expected arrival. "Local fight fans will ascertain that what day Mr. Nelsn [*sic*] will be passing through Las Vegas and will make an effort to get him to stop over and referee a match which it is hoped can be got up for the occasion."[84]

Vegas had no luck, however, for Nelson arrived in Albuquerque shortly after his stopover in the Meadow City, where his stay sparked several articles, the first of which dealt with the champ's difficulty in finding out the location of his destination. "There was no one who could give him the information," wrote the *Morning Journal*. "When he arrived here he was still up a tree, as far as the location of the destination was concerned. Finally, after much inquiry among hotel clerks, mail clerks, baggagemasters and ticket agents, he elicited the information that Perry was in the eastern part of New Mexico and that he could reach there over the Belen cutoff and Rock Island railway."[85]

While in the Duke City, Nelson stayed at the Alvarado Hotel, where he made headlines the following day after he was proclaimed a hero for saving a woman who found herself at the mercy of a frenzied, runaway horse: "There was nothing to it," said the Battler afterwards, "those other guys standing around were too slow, and I couldn't stand there and see the woman killed. Of course I took a big chance, as I might have been so badly hurt myself that I wouldn't be able to fight Gans on the 9th of next month."[86]

The journey to New Mexico lasted nearly as long as Nelson's stay, for, after four days of hunting and fishing with his old pal Brenner, the champ was off to San Francisco for Gans, vowing to "whip Gans so badly that he will retire from the ring."[87] Nelson nearly made good on his words, for Gans was knocked out in the 21st round of a scheduled 45-rounder. The 175-fight veteran, future Hall-of-Famer fought just once more, six months later, while Nelson fought on for nine more years, holding the lightweight title until 1910.

Nelson also returned to New Mexico after the September fight with Gans. In fact, by December, Nelson was not only buying property, but talking about starting a town named after himself. Since "Battling Nelson" never became a town, the battler settled for part-time residency, after Brenner convinced the champ to put up $1,000 for a "chunk of ranch property."[88] On Feb. 13, 1909, while putting on an exhibition at the Bush Temple in Dallas, Nelson told reporters that he had to skedaddle back to O-bar to finalize a real estate deal there.

While Dallas promoters were able to secure the services of Nelson, Las Vegas and Albuquerque had no luck getting the champ to stage an exhibition. Not only did Nelson prove elusive to New Mexico promoters, but also to his own manager. Four days after Nelson's Dallas exhibition, the champ's manager, Willus Britt, stopped over in Albuquerque in search of his fighter, hoping to line up a fight between Nelson and the World Middleweight Champion "Philadelphia" Jack O'Brien. While local promoters worked on Britt, trying to get him to commit his fighter to an exhibition, the frustrated manager told the press that he was having a hard enough time trying to find Nelson and O-bar, and left the next day.

Though O'Brien-Nelson did not happen, Nelson returned to action in May, defending the lightweight championship against Dick Hyland (who was KO'd in round 23 of yet another 45-rounder). After knocking out Jack Clifford in June, then losing a 10-round newspaper decision in July, to rising star Ad Wolgast, the Durable Dane returned to O-bar, where, it is believed, he worked on his autobiography.

Around the country, Nelson was now being described as a "cattle baron" and "owner of a big ranch in the southwest territory, for he has a few thousand acres in New Mexico surrounding the town of Obar, which he named after his cow brand which is an 'O Bar.'"[89] The reports were, of course, exaggerations, for even in his own autobiography, Nelson never claimed to own more than "some of the best corner lots in town"[90] (in addition to 80 acres of vineyard near San Francisco, property in the Midwest, and mining property in Nevada).

The following year, Nelson lost the lightweight championship when he was TKO'd in the 40th round in a rematch with Wolgast. He returned to his O-bar ranch to rest and plot his comeback. "There are fight fans, however, who believe that the Battler's best days are over and that he is a 'has been,'" reported the *Morning Journal*. "Repeated smashes on his battered ear have caused him to become partially deaf and continued hard training and the strain and excitement incident to his big fights have resulted in his becoming affected."[91]

Though unable to win another world championship, the "man who made O-bar, New Mexico famous"[92] was far from finished. Seven more years of fighting would follow, before ending his career with a final, unsuccessful shot at the lightweight title against champ Freddie Welsh.

In 1912, Nelson came close to fighting several New Mexicans. In Pueblo, Colorado, that year, he challenged the winner of the Eddie Johnson-Louis Newman fight, though it did not materialize. One month after that, there was talk of Raton's Ev Winters fighting Nelson, if local promoters in Clovis could put up $1000 (they didn't). Albuquerque's Benny Cordova also came close to fighting Nelson, but lost his chance by losing to uber-nemesis Bobby Waugh in an elimination bout held in Silver City.

Nelson never did get the chance to fight or even give an exhibition in New Mexico, though, in 1912, there was talk of staging Nelson-Waugh across the Courchesne Bridge in Dona Ana County, New Mexico. Negotiations failed, but three years later, Nelson-Waugh landed in Juarez; their 20-round war, won by Waugh, was talked about for the next five decades by sports scribes at the border.

During that epic fight, Nelson trained in Juarez, though there was mention of Bat's brother Harry living at the former champion's O-bar ranch. After 1915, there was no further mention of Nelson's ranch, though, in the end, the Durable Dane proved more durable the town of O-bar. By the time Nelson returned to O-bar, for the last time in 1915, the town that once held two dozen buildings and a hotel was nearly deserted.

Nothing in O-bar remains today the foundations of a brick building alongside the highway and a plaque marking where the town once stood, with a list of founding fathers — and no, the name "Battling Nelson" is not on the list.

A Fight to the Finish Line

One hour in the county jail was the unique sentence pronounced upon "Brownie" Buckley, self-confessed prize fighter, this morning by Judge Clarence J. Roberts in the United States district court.
— *Albuquerque Morning Journal*, 1911[93]

We beg to enter an emphatic protest against prize-fighting in Gallup on Thanksgiving Day, and respectfully ask the City Council to take such action as will prevent the occurrence of any bouts during the day or the night.
—Local ministers of Gallup to the *McKinley Republican*[94]

It took the territory of New Mexico more than half a century to become a state. When President William H. Taft signed the Enabling Act on June 20, 1910, it was only a matter of time. Statehood was one step closer on Jan. 21, 1911, when the state constitution was approved by territorial voters. The territory had only to wait for President Taft to sign off on the paperwork.

Statehood would breathe new life into New Mexico, especially when it came to boxing. Statehood would render territorial laws null and void — including the 1896 statute prohibiting prizefights. All New Mexico pugs and promoters had to do was to sit back and wait for the inevitable day — expected early in 1912.

With the sport on a sudden rise from 1908, however, it was obvious that most fighters and athletic clubs weren't going to wait it out. Fight cards were definitely on the rise. The year 1906 had seen but three shows in the territory. By 1908 the number rose to 17, with 13 in 1909, 25 in 1910 and 21 in 1911.

Those involved in the sport weren't the only ones getting busy, however. Anti-prizefight factions renewed their efforts in the final year of territorial New Mexico. An end to the prizefight ban would mean an explosion of a subculture that was kept under wraps for decades. The underground sport was already front-page reportage in several towns: Cimarron in the north, Gallup to the west, and Silver City to the south.

Cimarron opened up its final season of illegal prizefights on Jan. 14, 1911, with a 20-rounder headlining Al Smaulding against Dawson coal miner Henry Perry. Special trains were leased to accommodate crowds from surrounding towns to watch the 18-year-old middleweight outbox Perry.

When promoters tried to match up another local fighter, Cimarron's Eddie Rhodes, with Gallup's latest star, former East Coast veteran Dick Givens, there was sudden resistance, "owing to the fact that the conditions up there were such that it would not do to pull off a contest between the white and colored man."[95]

What they should've been concerned about was not drawing the color line, but pairing up a relative novice with an experienced fighter like Givens. The Gallup fighter, originally from Pittsburgh, had been fighting since 1903 and had, reportedly, half a hundred bouts. Gallup, however, had no qualms about a mixed bout or a mismatch, and on Feb. 18, the two were matched at Kitchen's Opera House, which staged its first boxing event since its 1895 inception of Flynn-Lewis II. Rhodes lasted but three rounds with Givens, his corner throwing up the sponge.

With the Kitchen's Opera House's second show, a new chapter had begun in New Mexico boxing history. "The sports crowd was being sought and this meant a different type of clientele," writes historian Roger M. Zimmerman in his book *Stories from Kitchen's Opera*

House. "Gambling and heavier drinking would be the feature during fight nights and it is assumed that patrons of the saloon and café would more or less reflect this change. Gallup wasn't going to grow into a sophisticated cultural center that was known for the performing arts. Gallup was going to be a sports center and the headquarters was going to be at Kitchen's Opera House."[96]

The opera house pulled off a string of smokers during the year, headlining at least five known shows, more than anywhere else in New Mexico. Kitchen's also holds the distinction of pulling off the last fight card ever held in the *territory* of New Mexico when, on Thanksgiving Day, Nov. 30, Gibson featherweight Fidel Silva won a 15-round decision over local lightweight Joe Corretto. It was a fight that had been adamantly protested by Gallup ministers, to no avail.

One of two fight cards held in Cimarron in 1911 had also been protested enough to catch the attention of the law. In one of the most hyped fights of the year, Raton lightweight Ev Winters took on Brownie Buckley of Pueblo, Colorado, on March 24 in a 15-round "boxing exhibition." In the third, Winters landed a right on the jaw, "putting Buckley in the land of dreams."[97]

It was the last fight in Cimarron that year. For reasons that are unclear, the community pulled the plug on prizefighting until 1914, causing a previously-announced rematch between Smaulding and Perry to move north to fight-happy Trinidad, Colorado, while both Winters and Buckley ended up indicted by a federal grand jury. Winters was able to evade officials but, in June, Buckley was arrested and indicted on a charge of violating the federal statute prohibiting prizefighting in a territory. The law caught up to Winters in November when both fighters were arraigned.

Buckley pleaded guilty, asking the court for mercy, while Winters told the judge he was not guilty. On Nov. 15, 1911, Buckley, having been imprisoned since June when initially arrested, was sentenced. The "self-confessed prize fighter" Buckley was sentenced by Judge Clarence J. Roberts, and ordered to serve one hour in the local slammer. "Buckley's return to the jail was only a matter of form, for the purpose of creating a little diversion in the gloomy old jail," printed the *Morning Journal.* "Buckley secured permission from the deputy sheriffs to enter one door and come out through another, making a round trip."[98]

It was expected that Winters, on the lam since June, would get the equivalent of a legal knockout, at least several months in jail. But the jury hearing his case was unable to reach an agreement. "The jury was discharged and Winters' case continued until the next term of court."[99] Most likely, Winters had friends — or fans — in high places, for he continued to fight. His case was swept under the rug, and eventually forgotten.

Impending statehood and the political changing of the guard might also have been factors in Winters avoiding jail time. Fighters and promoters were getting braver as statehood neared.

In Albuquerque, boxing made a sly return in June 1911.

First, a smoker was thrown by the Knights of Columbus, who staged several boxing (and wrestling) exhibitions. The *Morning Journal*— or the Albuquerque Building Trades Council that hosted the event — were careful to note that the athletes were amateurs of local labor organizations and "the only reward for the winners was the applause of the audience," though "they strove as mightily as though $50,000 purses had been hung up on the events."[100]

On June 7, the latest version of the Albuquerque Athletic Club, under the latest "professor," this one bearing the name "McDonald," reopened at the once-again fight-friendly Armory, with a six-round "exhibition" between Eddie Rhodes, who'd now made the rounds from Cimarron to Gallup to Albuquerque, and the Cherokee Kid. Though it was an exhibition, Rhodes "was no match for the Indian." Other entertainment included wrestling, barrel jumping and "showing the development of the human form."[101]

In order to ease boxing into public favor, to "give the patrons in this city an opportunity of seeing a couple of top notch professional boxers in action," and where "ladies can see sparring bouts as physical culture lessons,"[102] four-round sparring exhibitions by Rhodes and the Cherokee Kid were staged nightly at the Airdome Theatre, following a vaudeville musical comedy.

The promotional attempt did not catch on, for it wasn't until October that a full boxing card was attempted, this time at Redman's Hall under the local post of the American Federation of Labor in a smoker held to "discuss" political issues. Amid the "various stunts of an athletic nature put on to relive [*sic*] and balance out the other portions of the program,"[103] a thinly-disguised account of a prize fight, between two black lightweights John "Lefty" Floyd and Clarence "Soldier" Hunt, was described by the morning paper:

> Lefty and "Soldier" Hunt then argued the high cost of living. Lefty declared in favor of free chicken and more possum in four warm paragraphs, but "Soldier" Hunt told the audience that there are other things beside a chicken upon the bill of fare of life, the most important of which is to get the money to buy bread. The argument was so close that Judge Tony Ortiz declared the argument a draw, to which both the contestants acceded and shook hands.[104]

That was Albuquerque's last attempt to stage, cloak, or conceal boxing. Those hoping to elevate the sport were not to make another attempt until statehood, three months away.

The real core action during New Mexico's final year as a territory was in the southern half of the state, in and around the mining town of Silver City.

By 1911, Silver City had grown from a boomtown mining community to a mecca for tuberculosis sufferers. The mines around Silver City kept prizefighting alive for the next decade in the surrounding hills. Though dates are unknown and fight accounts rare, between Central, Silver City and Fort Bayard, from six to 12 shows took place, most headlining local miner Luis Gonzales.

Clovis had the most interesting show of the year, when 400 soldiers found themselves in the eastern town in July:

> Four hundred dusky United States soldiers, bronzed and rugged from their bloodless, but strenuous campaign on the Mexican border, took possession of Clovis this afternoon. No lives were lost, the town surrendered gracefully, and the citizens saw to it that the boys in khaki had the time of their lives. A feature of the entertainment was a boxing bout staged at the H. M. C. Athletic club, between Kid Mathis of Clovis and Edward Connelly of Company B, Eighteenth infantry. The contest lasted four rounds and was fast and furious from start to finish. At the beginning of the fifth it appearing that a knockout was imminent, the referee stopped the bout and both men agreed to call it a draw. The fight attracted many fans from the city and the soldier boys were present almost in a body. The train carrying the soldiers, who comprised over a battalion of the Eighteenth infantry was held here over ten hours on account of soft track to the westward. The men got away about 9 o'clock tonight cheering for Clovis as the train pulled out. They are bound for Fort Whipple, Arizona.[105]

Though there were certainly bigger fights, the most significant card of 1911 went unnoticed when Benny Chavez made his return to New Mexico. Though born in Wagon Mound, the aspiring bantamweight had taken up boxing the year before after his family had relocated to Trinidad, Colorado. Now 6–0 as a professional, Chavez was matched up with Canadian Eddie "Kid" Leach at Clayton. Though he might've made a splash in Clayton, smashing

Leach to the canvas in nine rounds, the native New Mexican who was being hailed in Colorado as a contender was, for the most part, unknown in the territory. That would soon change. By the end of 1912, Chavez would be the most-talked-about fighter in New Mexico.

The other big topic of conversation in the sporting fraternity throughout New Mexico — and everywhere else, for that matter — was who would take the heavyweight championship from Jack Johnson. Though New Mexico had no answer — it might've have been completely different had Bill Pettus been a *gringo* — but in the Southwest, the likely aspirants for a great white hope were "Fireman" Jim Flynn of Pueblo, Colorado, and Carl Morris, of Sapulpa, Oklahoma.

Throughout the spring and summer of 1911, a Flynn-Morris clash became the talk of the country; the winner of the bout was likely to meet Johnson in 1912. At first Tulsa and Oklahoma City were named as possible sites, but after Oklahoma Governor Lee Cruce called the fight a "brutal contest" that would put a "blot on the state,"[106] Flynn-Morris landed in New York City's Madison Square Garden on Sept. 15, 1911. Morris was battered beyond recognition and Flynn easily gained the ten-round newspaper nod.

On his way to New York, however, Flynn made a stop in New Mexico that went entirely unnoticed by the national — and local — media. On Aug. 11, Flynn was in Lordsburg, where he knocked out unknown fighter George Haley. One month later, six days before meeting Morris at the Garden, Flynn scored another mismatch knockout win in Tulsa, Okla., the victim another relative unknown.

Flynn liked to keep busy, for after beating Morris, he was back on the road, from Fort Smith, Ark., to Salt Lake City, Toronto and Milwaukee. Flynn's busy-ness kept his name in the papers for, by the early part of 1912, the biggest fight on the table was a match-up between the Pueblo contender and World Heavyweight Champion Jack Johnson. The talk, build-up and eventual showdown between Johnson and Flynn would forever impact New Mexico, ushering in a golden era of boxing for the newly-minted 47th state of the U.S.

6. Hometown Pioneers Pre–1912

Local followers of the Mexican boy declare that a few more bouts giving him experience, he will be the equal of the man who put him out tonight.
— *Rocky Mountain News,* 1911[1]

A blacksmith, baseball player, cadet, railroad worker, two miners, a press boy and a youngster from Wagon Mound hold the distinction of becoming the first New Mexico–produced hometown pugilists.

The eight homegrown hopefuls ran the gamut in weight, color and origin. Fighting middleweight to light heavy were Albuquerque baseball player Bill Pettus and Al "The Clayton Blacksmith" Smaulding. In Roswell, military cadet Alfred Higgins took up the sport as a rising middleweight, while in Silver City, lightweights Luis Gonzales and Gus Flores spent their days in the mines, their nights in the ring. In Las Vegas, there was featherweight Louis Newman, who would join a Wagon Mound-born bantamweight — Benny Chavez — in Colorado to forge their respective reputations.

For the first time, New Mexico was in the business of developing hometown fighters. There were others who'd begin careers during the territorial years, continuing on when boxing was legal in 1912, but none of the others would make it past the club level. As early as 1906, Clayton's Serapio Romero had etched out a local reputation as a willing prizefighter. Romero was joined by Dawson's Henry Perry and a host of lightweights across the state — John "Lefty" Floyd, Eddie "Kid" Rhodes, Clarence "Soldier" Hunt, Fidel "Young" Silva and Eddie Gregory — who became regular names at local shows. Unlike the aforementioned eight, however, these locals did not have a shot at something bigger.

All eight fighters began their careers when it was illegal to fight in New Mexico. Knowing the limitations of fighting in politically hostile land, three were able to further their legacy by stepping into the ring elsewhere. All eight continued to fight on when the laws changed in 1912 — but only one would make an impact in the ring beyond the Southwest.

The Ballplayer

Pettus is also a first class ball player and it is a question as to which career he will shine in the most.
— *Albuquerque Morning Journal,* 1910[2]

Texas-born William Thomas Pettus might have developed into a real contender, if he hadn't been plagued with several problems. One was skin color. Pettus had the misfortune of being black in a country obsessed in unearthing great white hopes and limiting some of the sport's greatest fighters — guys like Sam Langford, Joe Jeanette and Sam McVey — from ever getting a title shot.

Which brings us to the second, third, and fourth problems Pettus faced: location, location, location. As fighters developed locally would find out over the next 140-something years, building a fighter in New Mexico was not easy. This was especially so in the early 1900s. In Pettus' case, fighting at middleweight to heavyweight was rare enough in the Southwest. But being a good black fighter in the era of great white hopes, even mediocre ones, afforded little opportunity.

Pettus tried, however, and his curse became a blessing when, unable to make it in the leather tossing game, he returned to the sport in which he'd started — baseball. In doing so, Pettus became a well-known pioneer in the Negro Leagues, though finding himself just as limited in one sport as he'd been in the other, as this was a full 50 years before Jackie Robinson broke the baseball color barrier. James A. Riley, author of *The Biographical Encyclopedia of the Negro Baseball Leagues*, wrote of Pettus, "This big, left-handed power hitter was one of the best batsmen of the deadball era and is one of the most underrated players from black baseball."[3]

Born in Goliad, Texas, on Aug. 13, 1884, Pettus, 18 at the time, moved to Albuquerque to play ball in 1902, narrowly escaping a tornado that ripped through his hometown that destroyed more than 100 buildings and killed 115 people — it was tied for the deadliest tornado in Texas history and was rated tenth most devastating in the nation. With more opportunity in California, Pettus became the top player for San Francisco and Oakland teams. In 1904, he returned to New Mexico as a manager, catcher and big hitter on teams in Albuquerque, Santa Fe and Madrid. Pettus' athletic abilities as a baseball player were unparalleled in the territory, but his desire to show his skills in the squared circle went unnoticed until 1908 when he sent a defi to the *Morning Journal*:

> Sir: I noticed in the columns of your paper, where Mr. Graham of El Paso, is looking for a fight. I've never knocked out Jack Johnson, Langford nor Jeffries, nor do I make my living at fighting, but I will entertain this Graham from one round to the finish, and if I do not win I will give the Albuquerque sports a good run for their money. All I ask is to get permission to box the last of fair week, because I expect to play baseball fair week and I don't want to take any chances with my hand until the last of the week. If we get permission from the law to box, I will give Mr. Graham a jolly good time.[4]

Graham did not bite, though seasoned veteran Harry Wallace did. The Kansas prizefighter who was residing in Las Vegas was itching to fight any locals he considered easy targets. "I would like to fight Will Pettus or any other man from 150 to 160 pounds any number of rounds or any time," Wallace told the *Morning Journal*. "Will fight for percentage or purse of $500. Winner to take all. Would like to hear from someone anxious to pull off a bout."[5]

Whether anyone thought Pettus had a chance against an experienced fighter like Wallace is unknown. But Pettus had star power in a sport bigger than boxing at the time. What was the worst that could happen? Whether Pettus scored the upset or was KO'd mattered little when a killing was guaranteed at the gate.

Pettus' ring debut was a scheduled 20-rounder set for Nov. 16 in Las Vegas, with a weight limit of 165. But when "the little town of Madrid, New Mexico, having a population of less than 500 souls,"[6] most of them miners, offered up a $400 purse on Oct. 29, the fight changed locales, then was dropped altogether, for reasons that are unclear.

Pettus went back to managing the Madrid baseball team, until December 22 when the

Albuquerque Athletic Club's Harry "Spike" Kennedy decided to take advantage of Pettus' inexperience. Kennedy announced that he would "give the colored boy a big long run for his money,"[7] and the two were matched for Jan. 19, 1909, at the Elks Theater for a purse of $400.

Easy pickings, Pettus was not; Kennedy found out the hard way after his corner threw in the towel after but three rounds. "Kennedy has done some pretty ring work in this city and is no cinch for the ordinary fighter," wrote the *Morning Journal.* "But didn't get a smell last night and is clearly not in Pettus' class."[8]

Wallace was next. Having cleaned out the local scene during the last several months while residing in Las Vegas, the veteran who claimed he'd gone six rounds with World Middleweight Champion Stanley Ketchel was spanked through 15 rounds with Pettus, on a bout staged in Cimarron, on March 6, 1909.

With two big purses in two straight months, Pettus returned to Albuquerque, calling out Jimmy McDonald of Denver, Jim Barry of New Orleans and "Fireman" Jim Flynn, of Pueblo, Colorado, who offered the biggest opportunity.

"Looks like a comer," the *Morning Journal* described of Pettus. "While he lacks the experience that other fighters possess he is there with many other qualifications which are overlooked by other boxers. Local lovers of the fighting game are enthusiastic about Pettus' prospects and declare that he will be one of the best heavyweights or middleweights in the country within a few years."[9]

"Denver" Jack Geyer, a young fighter out of Colorado who was on the rise, was next. After Geyer headlined an April show in Cimarron, the two were matched for June 5. The man who would soon be touted as a great white hope, fighting notables Carl Morris, Frank Moran and Gunboat Smith, crumpled beneath Pettus' fists.

> In a fourteen round bout here last night between John T. Grier [*sic*], white, of Denver, and Bill Pettus, colored, of Albuquerque, Pettus won by a knockout in the eighth round after the two men had been at it hammer and tongs from the start. The first, fifth and seventh rounds belonged to Grier, Pettus becoming groggy, but coming back fresh at the beginning of each new round. Pettus had the advantage in the second, third and eighth rounds, the fourth and sixth being practically an even break between the two men. Pettus scored a knockdown at the sound of the gong. Pettus also scored two clean knockdowns in the eighth, Grier taking the full count on the first down and being counted out the second time the heavy swing of the Albuquerque lad laid him out. Grier plainly showed that he was weakening from the beginning of the eighth and it was at once seen that it was Pettus' round whether Grier lasted through it or not. Both fighters took to aggressive mixing from the start, were well matched and gave splendid exhibition.[10]

"Pettus is a wonder," said Geyer after the contest. "I did my best. I'd like another match but I am not attempting to take any credit from him. He is one of the fairest fighters I have ever boxed and he's as game as they make him."[11]

"Some Denver writers stated that the match would be a joke for Geyer and that Pettus would be a lemon for him," wrote the *Optic.* "They ridiculed Pettus' fighting ability and tried to put the kazoo on him good and hard."[12]

There were no more takers for Pettus after that — except for baseball scouts, who called on him in August. Pettus left his gloves, and New Mexico, behind to join the Kansas City Giants. Against the Leland Giants for the mythical Negro League championships, Pettus led the Giants to victory, batting .417 in the three-game series. The Giants reportedly won 54 games that year against semi-pro teams but also fought a well-publicized series against the Cuban Stars in Chicago, winning eight of 12 games.

Despite his success on the diamond, Pettus, once again, put baseball on the backburner when he received a fight offer he could not refuse — against Jim Flynn in Pueblo, Colorado, who'd turned down previous bouts because Pettus "was dead easy and wouldn't be worth while boxing."[13] Though changing his tune in order to promote the fights, the scribes were less kind, calling it a mismatch. Pettus was just 3–0, going up against a veteran with more than 50 hard fights — someone who'd knocked out the great Langford the year before, and who'd gone 11 rounds with the current world heavyweight champion in 1907 (before Jack Johnson was champion).

A ten-round go was set for Sept. 22, on Flynn's home turf of Pueblo. Pettus, "who many believe will develop into Jack Johnson,"[14] left Kansas City for Colorado where he was trained by Bob Watkins, well-known black middleweight in Denver, and assisted by none other than former foe Wallace. Four weeks to train and with just three bouts under his belt would prove insufficient enough time and experience to take on someone like the Pueblo Fireman, who'd been fighting often since 1899 against the biggest names in the sport. Flynn left Los Angeles, where he'd been training, for home, "where he is matched to fight a comparatively unknown middleweight," reported the *Los Angeles Herald*. "Jim expects to trim him easily."[15]

Though a big underdog, Pettus showed confidence, telling reporters, "I know I will have to go faster than I ever did before to even hold Flynn, but despite his cleverness and aggressiveness, I feel confident I can get the decision. I will try at any rate, if I fail it will only be after every ounce of effort in me is exhausted. I can only say that I will be the most surprised boxer in the game if I lose."[16]

Pettus received more publicity than ever before. In New Mexico, the Albuquerque-based fighter was on the verge of overnight contention, should he somehow find the means to score the upset. "Just tell [my supporters] to get down on me, hook and sinker," Pettus told the *Morning Journal*. "Those who have backed me in all my previous mills have never lost a cent so far as I know and this will be no exception."[17]

As the date of the fight neared, the choice of referee became a point of contention. Flynn's people wanted Denver's E. W. Dickerson (who would ultimately get the fight) but Robert Cochrane, a Pueblo newspaperman who was looking after Pettus' interests (a rare enough occurrence for an out-of-towner fighting on Flynn's turf), went to bat for the ballplayer-fighter, suggesting Otto Floto of Denver, the Damon Runyan of the Southwest and a well-respected referee.

Winning over Pueblo's smelter workers by sparring with the local boxers, Pettus trained, for once, in a real camp to get into the pink of condition — really, just two, three weeks at most. So ready for Flynn was Pettus, assured trainer Cochrane, that four days before the fight, he eased off the work on his fighter to avoid overtraining.

Roy Corhan, a local sporting man from Albuquerque, visited the camp, proclaiming Pettus to be "fast as lightning and strong as a bull and even though he is a colored man." "He's from Albuquerque and I'll be at the ringside Tuesday night," he wired the *Morning Journal*, "pulling for him as hard as I can."[18]

While training for Flynn, Pettus made plans to return to baseball as a catcher for the Albuquerque Grays, immediately after his mill with Flynn, win or lose. Word of his return to baseball was taken two ways — that he'd either resigned himself to losing, or that he was so confident he would come out unscathed with Flynn that he was looking ahead.

In the end, Flynn's experience proved too much for Pettus: "In the first three rounds the battle was a fierce one, but after that Flynn was the aggressor, almost continuously, and

Pettus seemed only to be trying to stay the limit. Flynn punished his opponent badly, and in the fourth round closed the colored man's left eye and he kept adding to the injury in almost every one of the following rounds."[19]

Back in Albuquerque, Pettus, "not much the worse for the grueling he received at the hands of the husky fireman," attributed the loss and sudden decline in round four to an eye injury. "After Flynn jabbed Pettus in the left lamp, however, he fought at a disadvantage, and had all he could to do to fight Flynn off," said trainer Fat Shearn. "Before he received the injury to his eye Pettus was the aggressor and forced the fighting."[20]

Pettus returned to baseball. Just a month after losing to Flynn, Pettus was lauded as one of baseball's best catchers by Pittsburgh Pirates pitcher Babe Adams. Pettus remained persistent about prizefighting, though, and became the first New Mexican fighter to make the move to the West Coast in order to make it in the ring. Over the next 100 years, some of New Mexico's top fighters — from Benny Chavez to Art Aragon — would be making the trek west, hoping to get better opportunities than New Mexico could offer. Pettus, however, could not secure a single bout.

Pettus joined the camp of Joe Willis in Los Angeles, who was training for Geyer, whom Pettus had already defeated. At least noticed by the press as a live sparring partner, he told the *Los Angeles Herald* that he wanted a second shot at Flynn. Instead, Willis got the shot on Dec. 31, 1909, losing by a six-round KO.

Next, Pettus found himself in Langford's camp, with whom he remained a regular sparring partner through February 1910. Langford was next for Flynn, who beat the "Boston Tar Baby" a second time on Feb. 8, with a disputable newspaper decision win. On Mar. 17, though, Langford avenged his two previous losses with an eighth-round knockout in Vernon, California.

"Providing he can get the recognition he believes is due him," ran the *Morning Journal*, "Pettus will remain in the fighting game permanently. If he decides, however, that his career is not to be a prize fighting one, he will abandon the pills and go back to baseball."[21]

Unable to land a single bout, Pettus left Langford's camp. By now, Pettus was receiving several offers to return to baseball, the most notable of which was with the Kansas City Giants. "Pettus tried hard to get a fight in California, but was unable to do so," reported the *Morning Journal*. "His greatest handicap being the lack of reputation as a fighter."[22] "[Sam] Langford and Flynn both refused to fight me under my conditions," said Pettus. "I know their greatest reason is that they didn't care to take a chance with me."[23]

In March, Pettus announced his return to baseball, passing up offers from Kansas City to play with the Chicago Leland Giants. He left for the Giants' camp in Fort Worth, Tex.

Pettus said he would play ball until the fall, then try one more time to land a boxing match. The odds were stacked against Pettus, who excelled every time he returned to the sport that clamored for him. By September 1910, it was reported that the "reformed prizefighter" was "leading the world in batting" and "hitting the ball as regular as clock work and thus far his batting averages better than any of the big leaguers, his name being ahead of Lajoie, Wagner or Cobb."[24] Returning to prizefighting made little sense, financially or otherwise, for Pettus. In January 1911, the *Chicago Record Herald* reported that Pettus was in the top spot for the Giants in hitting, with an average of .347. One year later, Pettus was playing with the Giants in Cuba, where his batting average was a remarkable .500.

After Cuba, however, in October 1912, with a lull between baseball offers, Pettus returned to boxing, now legal in New Mexico. Down to a lean 169 pounds, Pettus was matched up on Nov. 25 against respected Chicago journeyman Tony Caponi, who'd faced (and lost to) Flynn, Langford and Stanley Ketchel. It was Pettus' first fight in front of his hometown of Albuquerque, and if he wins, Clayton's Al Smaulding Pettus was punishing during public workouts the week leading up to the fight next.

The return to the ring — and the fight itself — was a flop. The Morning Journal the win at Clayton with Pettus "wild and nervous, falling repeatedly missing with a right, never one to go long without a fight opportunity, showed 'coolness and ring generalship, coupled with clever defensive work" that made Pettus "appear like a pro."

Despite the loss, Pettus returned to Los Angeles where he joined the camp of McCarty who was KO'd by Pettus' old nemesis, Flynn, on May 10. On his way to the Coast, where he would ultimately rematch McCarty, Flynn stopped over in Albuquerque where he was asked about Pettus. "He wasn't anything that I know of," said Flynn. "I think he intends to play ball."[26]

Play ball is what Pettus did. In 1913, Pettus left prizefighting and New Mexico for good, and was well on his way to solidifying his legacy as a top-notch Negro League ballplayer. He played until 1923, but got sick in 1934 with other illness. Pettus was confined to the Sea View Hospital on Staten Island. After an appeal for help went out in the local dailies, baseball fans and James Keenan, owner of the New York Lincoln Giants, contributed $230.50 to send Pettus to Phoenix. It was too late, however, for two weeks after turning 40, on August 1, 1934, in New York, Pettus passed away.

Though his prizefighting was a side attraction, at best, for someone who is considered one of the pioneer greats of the Negro Leagues, Pettus remains not only possibly one of the top heavyweights in New Mexico annals, but also one of the state's greatest and most overlooked athletes.

Tanky Lou

All my friends that I will make Las Vegas famous.
— Louis Newman, in the *Las Vegas Daily Optic,* 1908[27]

After Louis Ignace Newman died, on Nov. 24, 1955, at the age of 64, he was recognized for his 30 years of managing fighters, matchmaking and promoting fight cards in the Detroit area. What the boxing world had forgotten were Newman's roots — and his own boxing career that had started in 1907 in his hometown of Las Vegas, New Mexico.

Though he would later say Denver was the place of his birth, while fighting out of the Mile-High City, early records tell a different tale. His father and mother were native New Mexicans — father David L. born in Villiamiera, New Mexico, in 1891 and his mother, Elena Aragon, born in Las Vegas. Census reports from 1900 give Newman's date of birth as July 31, 1891, and his city of birth as Las Vegas.

Also downplayed, if not virtually ignored, in Newman's career was his Hispanic roots. Unlike the Chavez's and Romeros and Gonzalez's of his time, Newman was primarily marketed as a *gringo* fighter, though his blood was at least half Spanish. Not only was Newman's mother's maiden name Aragon, but the family names listed in a 1900 census report give the name *Luis*, not Louis, and his siblings Elliott and Grace as "Ecolastica" and "Altagracia."

Vegas or Denver, *gringo* or Chicano, Newman remains a forgotten pioneer in New Mexico annals. Not only does he hold the distinction of becoming the first New Mexican

Albuquerque Athletic Club's Harry "Spike" Kennedy decided to take advantage of Pettus' inexperience. Kennedy announced that he would "give the colored boy a big long run for his money,"[7] and the two were matched for Jan. 19, 1909, at the Elks Theater for a purse of $400.

Easy pickings, Pettus was not; Kennedy found out the hard way after his corner threw in the towel after but three rounds. "Kennedy has done some pretty ring work in this city and is no cinch for the ordinary fighter," wrote the *Morning Journal*. "But didn't get a smell last night and is clearly not in Pettus' class."[8]

Wallace was next. Having cleaned out the local scene during the last several months while residing in Las Vegas, the veteran who claimed he'd gone six rounds with World Middleweight Champion Stanley Ketchel was spanked through 15 rounds with Pettus, on a bout staged in Cimarron, on March 6, 1909.

With two big purses in two straight months, Pettus returned to Albuquerque, calling out Jimmy McDonald of Denver, Jim Barry of New Orleans and "Fireman" Jim Flynn, of Pueblo, Colorado, who offered the biggest opportunity.

"Looks like a comer," the *Morning Journal* described of Pettus. "While he lacks the experience that other fighters possess he is there with many other qualifications which are overlooked by other boxers. Local lovers of the fighting game are enthusiastic about Pettus' prospects and declare that he will be one of the best heavyweights or middleweights in the country within a few years."[9]

"Denver" Jack Geyer, a young fighter out of Colorado who was on the rise, was next. After Geyer headlined an April show in Cimarron, the two were matched for June 5. The man who would soon be touted as a great white hope, fighting notables Carl Morris, Frank Moran and Gunboat Smith, crumpled beneath Pettus' fists.

> In a fourteen round bout here last night between John T. Grier [*sic*], white, of Denver, and Bill Pettus, colored, of Albuquerque, Pettus won by a knockout in the eighth round after the two men had been at it hammer and tongs from the start. The first, fifth and seventh rounds belonged to Grier, Pettus becoming groggy, but coming back fresh at the beginning of each new round. Pettus had the advantage in the second, third and eighth rounds, the fourth and sixth being practically an even break between the two men. Pettus scored a knockdown at the sound of the gong. Pettus also scored two clean knockdowns in the eighth, Grier taking the full count on the first down and being counted out the second time the heavy swing of the Albuquerque lad laid him out. Grier plainly showed that he was weakening from the beginning of the eighth and it was at once seen that it was Pettus' round whether Grier lasted through it or not. Both fighters took to aggressive mixing from the start, were well matched and gave splendid exhibition.[10]

"Pettus is a wonder," said Geyer after the contest. "I did my best. I'd like another match but I am not attempting to take any credit from him. He is one of the fairest fighters I have ever boxed and he's as game as they make him."[11]

"Some Denver writers stated that the match would be a joke for Geyer and that Pettus would be a lemon for him," wrote the *Optic*. "They ridiculed Pettus' fighting ability and tried to put the kazoo on him good and hard."[12]

There were no more takers for Pettus after that — except for baseball scouts, who called on him in August. Pettus left his gloves, and New Mexico, behind to join the Kansas City Giants. Against the Leland Giants for the mythical Negro League championships, Pettus led the Giants to victory, batting .417 in the three-game series. The Giants reportedly won 54 games that year against semi-pro teams but also fought a well-publicized series against the Cuban Stars in Chicago, winning eight of 12 games.

Despite his success on the diamond, Pettus, once again, put baseball on the backburner when he received a fight offer he could not refuse — against Jim Flynn in Pueblo, Colorado, who'd turned down previous bouts because Pettus "was dead easy and wouldn't be worth while boxing."[13] Though changing his tune in order to promote the fights, the scribes were less kind, calling it a mismatch. Pettus was just 3–0, going up against a veteran with more than 50 hard fights — someone who'd knocked out the great Langford the year before, and who'd gone 11 rounds with the current world heavyweight champion in 1907 (before Jack Johnson was champion).

A ten-round go was set for Sept. 22, on Flynn's home turf of Pueblo. Pettus, "who many believe will develop into Jack Johnson,"[14] left Kansas City for Colorado where he was trained by Bob Watkins, well-known black middleweight in Denver, and assisted by none other than former foe Wallace. Four weeks to train and with just three bouts under his belt would prove insufficient enough time and experience to take on someone like the Pueblo Fireman, who'd been fighting often since 1899 against the biggest names in the sport. Flynn left Los Angeles, where he'd been training, for home, "where he is matched to fight a comparatively unknown middleweight," reported the *Los Angeles Herald*. "Jim expects to trim him easily."[15]

Though a big underdog, Pettus showed confidence, telling reporters, "I know I will have to go faster than I ever did before to even hold Flynn, but despite his cleverness and aggressiveness, I feel confident I can get the decision. I will try at any rate, if I fail it will only be after every ounce of effort in me is exhausted. I can only say that I will be the most surprised boxer in the game if I lose."[16]

Pettus received more publicity than ever before. In New Mexico, the Albuquerque-based fighter was on the verge of overnight contention, should he somehow find the means to score the upset. "Just tell [my supporters] to get down on me, hook and sinker," Pettus told the *Morning Journal*. "Those who have backed me in all my previous mills have never lost a cent so far as I know and this will be no exception."[17]

As the date of the fight neared, the choice of referee became a point of contention. Flynn's people wanted Denver's E. W. Dickerson (who would ultimately get the fight) but Robert Cochrane, a Pueblo newspaperman who was looking after Pettus' interests (a rare enough occurrence for an out-of-towner fighting on Flynn's turf), went to bat for the ballplayer-fighter, suggesting Otto Floto of Denver, the Damon Runyan of the Southwest and a well-respected referee.

Winning over Pueblo's smelter workers by sparring with the local boxers, Pettus trained, for once, in a real camp to get into the pink of condition — really, just two, three weeks at most. So ready for Flynn was Pettus, assured trainer Cochrane, that four days before the fight, he eased off the work on his fighter to avoid overtraining.

Roy Corhan, a local sporting man from Albuquerque, visited the camp, proclaiming Pettus to be "fast as lightning and strong as a bull and even though he is a colored man." "He's from Albuquerque and I'll be at the ringside Tuesday night," he wired the *Morning Journal*, "pulling for him as hard as I can."[18]

While training for Flynn, Pettus made plans to return to baseball as a catcher for the Albuquerque Grays, immediately after his mill with Flynn, win or lose. Word of his return to baseball was taken two ways — that he'd either resigned himself to losing, or that he was so confident he would come out unscathed with Flynn that he was looking ahead.

In the end, Flynn's experience proved too much for Pettus: "In the first three rounds the battle was a fierce one, but after that Flynn was the aggressor, almost continuously, and

Pettus seemed only to be trying to stay the limit. Flynn punished his opponent badly, and in the fourth round closed the colored man's left eye and he kept adding to the injury in almost every one of the following rounds."[19]

Back in Albuquerque, Pettus, "not much the worse for the grueling he received at the hands of the husky fireman," attributed the loss and sudden decline in round four to an eye injury. "After Flynn jabbed Pettus in the left lamp, however, he fought at a disadvantage, and had all he could to do to fight Flynn off," said trainer Fat Shearn. "Before he received the injury to his eye Pettus was the aggressor and forced the fighting."[20]

Pettus returned to baseball. Just a month after losing to Flynn, Pettus was lauded as one of baseball's best catchers by Pittsburgh Pirates pitcher Babe Adams. Pettus remained persistent about prizefighting, though, and became the first New Mexican fighter to make the move to the West Coast in order to make it in the ring. Over the next 100 years, some of New Mexico's top fighters — from Benny Chavez to Art Aragon — would be making the trek west, hoping to get better opportunities than New Mexico could offer. Pettus, however, could not secure a single bout.

Pettus joined the camp of Joe Willis in Los Angeles, who was training for Geyer, whom Pettus had already defeated. At least noticed by the press as a live sparring partner, he told the *Los Angeles Herald* that he wanted a second shot at Flynn. Instead, Willis got the shot on Dec. 31, 1909, losing by a six-round KO.

Next, Pettus found himself in Langford's camp, with whom he remained a regular sparring partner through February 1910. Langford was next for Flynn, who beat the "Boston Tar Baby" a second time on Feb. 8, with a disputable newspaper decision win. On Mar. 17, though, Langford avenged his two previous losses with an eighth-round knockout in Vernon, California.

"Providing he can get the recognition he believes is due him," ran the *Morning Journal*, "Pettus will remain in the fighting game permanently. If he decides, however, that his career is not to be a prize fighting one, he will abandon the pills and go back to baseball."[21]

Unable to land a single bout, Pettus left Langford's camp. By now, Pettus was receiving several offers to return to baseball, the most notable of which was with the Kansas City Giants. "Pettus tried hard to get a fight in California, but was unable to do so," reported the *Morning Journal*. "His greatest handicap being the lack of reputation as a fighter."[22] "[Sam] Langford and Flynn both refused to fight me under my conditions," said Pettus. "I know their greatest reason is that they didn't care to take a chance with me."[23]

In March, Pettus announced his return to baseball, passing up offers from Kansas City to play with the Chicago Leland Giants. He left for the Giants' camp in Fort Worth, Tex.

Pettus said he would play ball until the fall, then try one more time to land a boxing match. The odds were stacked against Pettus, who excelled every time he returned to the sport that clamored for him. By September 1910, it was reported that the "reformed prizefighter" was "leading the world in batting" and "hitting the ball as regular as clock work and thus far his batting averages better than any of the big leaguers, his name being ahead of Lajoie, Wagner or Cobb."[24] Returning to prizefighting made little sense, financially or otherwise, for Pettus. In January 1911, the *Chicago Record Herald* reported that Pettus was in the top spot for the Giants in hitting, with an average of .347. One year later, Pettus was playing with the Giants in Cuba, where his batting average was a remarkable .500.

After Cuba, however, in October 1912, with a lull between baseball offers, Pettus returned to boxing, now legal in New Mexico. Down to a lean 169 pounds, Pettus was matched up on Nov. 25 against respected Chicago journeyman Tony Caponi, who'd faced (and lost to) Flynn, Langford and Stanley Ketchel. It was Pettus' first (and only) fight in front of his hometown of Albuquerque, and if he won, Clayton's Al Smaulding, whom Pettus was punishing during public workouts the week leading up to the fight, would be next.

The return to the ring—and the fight itself—was a flop. The *Morning Journal* gave the win to Caponi, with Pettus "wild and nervous, falling repeatedly, missing wild swings." Caponi, never one to go long without a fight opportunity, showed "coolness and ring generalship, coupled with clever defensive work" that made Pettus "appear like a novice."[25]

Despite the loss, Pettus returned to Los Angeles, where he joined the camp of Luther McCarty, who was KO'd by Pettus' old nemesis, Flynn, on Dec. 10. On his way to the East Coast, where he would ultimately rematch McCarty, Flynn stopped over in Albuquerque where he was asked about Pettus. "He wasn't anything that I know of," said Flynn. "I think he intends to play ball."[26]

Play ball is what Pettus did. In 1913, Pettus left prizefighting and New Mexico for good, and was well on his way to solidifying his legacy as a top-notch Negro League ballplayer. He played until 1923, but got sick in 1924 with tuberculosis. Pettus was confined to the Sea View Hospital on Staten Island. After an appeal for help went out in the local dailies, baseball fans and James Keenan, owner of the New York Lincoln Giants, contributed $230.50 to send Pettus to Phoenix. It was too late, however, for two weeks after turning 40, on August 25, 1924, in New York, Pettus passed away.

Though his prizefighting was a side attraction, at best, for someone who is considered one of the pioneer greats of the Negro Leagues, Pettus remains not only potentially one of the top heavyweights in New Mexico annals, but also one of the state's greatest and most overlooked athletes.

Lanky Lou

> *Tell my friends that I will make Las Vegas famous.*
> —Louis Newman, in the *Las Vegas Daily Optic*, 1908[27]

After Louis Ignace Newman died, on Nov. 24, 1955, at the age of 64, he was recognized for his 30 years of managing fighters, matchmaking and promoting fight cards in the Detroit area. What the boxing world had forgotten were Newman's roots—and his own boxing career that had started in 1907 in his hometown of Las Vegas, New Mexico.

Though he would later say Denver was the place of his birth, while fighting out of the Mile-High City, early records tell a different tale. His father and mother were native New Mexicans—father David L. born in Villiamiera, New Mexico, in 1891 and his mother, Elena Aragon, born in Las Vegas. Census reports from 1900 give Newman's date of birth as July 31, 1891, and his city of birth as Las Vegas.

Also downplayed, if not virtually ignored, in Newman's career was his Hispanic roots. Unlike the Chavez's and Romeros and Gonzalez's of his time, Newman was primarily marketed as a *gringo* fighter, though his blood was at least half Spanish. Not only was Newman's mother's maiden name Aragon, but the family names listed in a 1900 census report give the name *Luis*, not Louis, and his siblings Elliott and Grace as "Ecolastica" and "Altagracia."

Vegas or Denver, *gringo* or Chicano, Newman remains a forgotten pioneer in New Mexico annals. Not only does he hold the distinction of becoming the first New Mexican to become a regional contender, he's the first one smart enough to realize he had to leave home turf for greener pastures, if he wanted to make it as a prizefighter. Several years before Pettus left for Los Angeles, Newman trekked north to active Denver to reach the next level. The move would leave a blueprint for others to follow: go north, go west or go east — but just go.

But even after leaving, Newman did not forget his hometown. Not only would he return as a southwestern contender, but after hanging up the gloves, Newman managed New Mexico's top prospects for many years before relocating to the Midwest.

Newman's early career, unlike many others in the territory, did not go unchronicled, due to his connection to the local paper of his hometown, the *Las Vegas Daily Optic*, where he worked as an office boy, press feeder and gopher.

At 16, "a lean Mexican youth,"[28] Newman was considering a career as a linotype operator — before he discovered boxing, that is, almost entirely by accident. Sometime before the summer of 1907, Newman got into a street fight. After he knocked down his adversary, a cop came upon the scene and gave chase. To evade arrest, Newman ducked into a doorway, which happened to be the one for the local YMCA, that had opened the year before in East Las Vegas, where "Louis looked around and saw a ring, a few people around it and a couple of young fellows boxing with big gloves."[29]

Curious, Newman returned to the gym and, soon after, the 110-pounder had signed up to fight on a local fight card, on Aug. 23, 1907, going four rounds to a draw with 126-pound Fred Logan in a prelim bout. Newman floored his foe in the third, and "had his dusky antagonist on the go from that time on,"[30] but continual clinching kept Newman from a knockout win. After the fight, Newman issued a defi to anyone his weight in the section.

A month later, he appeared on another show, winning a decision over Harry Barnes, of Chicago. Newman tired quickly and the scheduled six-rounder was stopped in the fourth, with the win going to the hometown kid at the insistence of an impatient crowd who'd grown bored with the bout. Newman improved his wind over the winter and, in March 1908, returned, rising from prelim to main event by the summer. The five wins in Vegas — and two in Colorado, where his father was working — set him up for a fight with Charley Williams, in the summer.[31]

Newman, barely a bantamweight now at 115, agreed to give up ten pounds to fight the black featherweight, in a scheduled 15-rounder, on June 27 at Mackel's Opera House. A week before the bout, the two met on the Plaza, nearly getting into a street fight during a band concert when a fellow fighter, Leo Trujillo, offered to make a side bet with Williams that he couldn't go six with his friend, Louis. "I'll stop him — I don't need to wait six rounds. I can do it right now,"[32] Williams said. He and Newman nearly came to blows.

When they met in the ring, the fight lasted less than two rounds, with the *Optic* reporting: "Never since the time that Ham discovered the strange animals that inhabited Africa has there been a more surprised negro than the one who had his face beaten to a jelly by Louis Newman.... Williams, for that is the patent-leather person's name, made two discoveries — and he made them quick. One was that he couldn't fight, and the other was that he didn't want to." Williams "took off the gloves and quit. The smile was gone from his face and in its place was slopping blood, while about his ribs and under his arms the hide had been peeled away in great red spots."[33]

After breezing through Williams, Newman was in a hurry. Newman returned to Colorado for a series of fights, knocking out Leo Padeo and Kid Hardy in Denver, decisioning Young Texas in Central City, then knocking out Young Baldy, again, in the Mile-High City, before returning to Vegas in what would be his last hometown fight for years.

During his Colorado ventures, Newman, working now at Denver's Twentieth Century Press as a typesetter, continued to keep his hometown informed by writing regular letters to the *Optic*. He wrote that he was making the right connections for his career in Colorado, having met sportswriter Otto Floto, champion Battling Nelson (who told him "to always fight my opponent's game and I would make good"[34]), promoter Jockey Maynard and other local movers and shakers. Newman also penned that he expected to soon get a shot at the 115-pound Rocky Mountain champion, Mickey McAllister, since he'd defeated Young Texas. "I can lick him right now,"[35] he told the *Optic*.

Vegas promoter Jimmy Tolle arranged for Newman to make his homecoming on Labor Day, against Canadian Teddy Mapleson, now of Raton, for the featherweight championship of New Mexico. Tolle poured on the hype, telling anyone who'd listen that Newman, the "Pride of Las Vegas," was "never so fast as now, has developed a punch that stings and is light on his pins as a pneumatic tire" while Mapleson was "built like an ox and not lacking confidence or backers."[36]

In the end, the 17-year-old kid from Vegas would win not once, but twice that night, securing his place as the territorial featherweight champ. In the first fight, Mapleson was disqualified for hitting Newman, who went down from slipping on the loose canvas. "Let's forget the foul!" Newman demanded, walking over to Mapleson's corner. "Come on, you, and fight!"[37] The fight was on again. This time, it went the distance, Newman clearly out-pointing the Raton hopeful, though the *Optic*'s scribe, Collins, ended his front-page report by stating his "unvarnished and triple-plated opinion ... that Lanky Lou Newman, who is only seventeen years old, ought to be in school or at home with his mother — and leave prizefighting to people who are old enough to know better. But Newman knew my opinion on this matter long ago and he didn't care, so I guess nobody else does either."[38]

Newman returned to Denver and his job while his manager, A. C. de Baca, went to work sending out defis which, in New Mexico, only generated more anti-prizefight static. Newman would not return to New Mexico for three years, but he kept busy in Colorado, launching a six-bout win streak, beginning the first of the year in 1909. When he was unable to find enough willing featherweights, Newman targeted the many lightweights.

Having to give up weight, Newman fought several Southwest-significant fighters over the next two years. In April 1909, he fought a four-round draw with Peter Jensen, "The Battling Dane," who would go on to compile a record of more than 100 bouts over the next 15 years. On July 30, Newman suffered his first loss — a second round knockout — to Monte Dale, who would later fight Battling Nelson. Newman finished out the year with an estimated record of 16-1-3, two no-decisions and 11 KOs. By the end of 1910, he'd added two knockout wins and three draws to his record, all against regional fighters from Denver to Trinidad. At the beginning of 1911, Newman was a seasoned pro, and, at 19, though still fighting barely past today's featherweight limit of 126, was ready for anyone in the region at 133.

On his way to finally fighting for a Southwestern championship, Newman lost a six-round decision in April to former sparring partner Young Erlenborn, though "with his Jeffries crouch, wicked upper-cut and nice cover, was at least entitled to a draw."[39] A 15-round draw with Frankie White, of Chicago, followed. Newman's toughest test to date, White had twice the experience, and had met everyone from World Featherweight Champion Abe Attell (twice, once going the distance) to contenders Frankie Conley and Jack Britton. A Labor Day bout against Muggsy Schoel in Leadville, Colorado, was next, in another 15-rounder.

The veteran from Cheyenne, Wyo., was a slight favorite but Newman upset the odds, showing a tight defense and working "like lightning in the clinches" to win a decision.[40]

Newman was suddenly in big demand and a clever pick for Southwestern championship honors. He got the chance, too, in his next bout, against Perry Lewis, of Walsenburg, Colorado, on Sept. 28, 1911, in Trinidad, Colorado. Lewis would later earn a solid reputation fighting in Nevada after World War I, but in the early part of the decade he was favored to oust Newman for Rocky Mountain honors. Though Newman proved a faster, more clever fighter, Lewis evened the score with endurance and a bigger punch, as the fight was ruled a draw.

Two more bouts rounded out 1911: A loss to veteran Willie Canole, a 50-bout veteran from New York who'd campaigned recently in California, and a KO-in-one over less-regarded Jimmy Finley. By the time 1912 rolled around, Newman was ready for another shot at the Southwestern title and a second push for national contention. He was also planning a return to New Mexico.

Ev Winters

Winters has not had much experience in the ring, but the record he has made shows, that with good trainers and advisers, he will land the lightweight championship.
— *Cimarron News*, 1911[41]

Everett "Ev" Winters may not go down in history as a contender in the annals of New Mexico, but he *will* get credit for a few things: He's the first New Mexican to beat a top-notch fighter; the first fighter heaped in controversy; and the best-known pug from Raton in a century-and-a-half of prizefighting.

Winters fought from 1909 to 1915, though he was competitive earlier on as a foot-racer. The first mention of a Winters prize fight is in February 1909, when he fought a scheduled 15-rounder against hometowner Jimmie Burns at Matkin Hall in Cimarron. It was Winters' coming-out party.

Though it's likely that Winters had fought before the Burns fight — and probably after, as well — his next known fight wasn't until September 1910, when he went rode ten miles north to fight in Trinidad. There, Winters defeated Kid West by a third-round disqualification on a card headlined by Young Togo, a jiu-jitsu expert who was pitting his martial arts against Eddie Lennan in an early mixed martial artist vs. boxer bout (Togo won, forcing Lennan to quit in the sixth). Las Vegas' Newman was also on the card, defeating Harry West, who might've been a relative to *Kid* West.

On Thanksgiving day 1910, Winters was scheduled for a 15-rounder in Raton with Young Erlenborn, but the results are unknown. Then, sometime between the Erlenborn bout and March 1911, Winters fought a draw with well-respected Kid Texas.

The Raton lightweight had his busiest year yet in 1911. In March, Winters was pitted against San Francisco's Brownie Buckley in Cimarron. The fight itself might not have been a noteworthy one — Winters outclassing his opponent and knocking Buckley out in the third round with a hard right — but the delayed aftermath would haunt both fighters for months.

After defeating Buckley, Winters returned to Raton to take up his old position with the Santa Fe railroad. He did not fight again until the end of May when he returned to Trinidad to take on his toughest foe yet, "The Battling Dane" Pete Jensen, in a 15-round lightweight bout. Despite Winters' half a dozen bouts up against Jensen's 40-to-50 fight career, the Raton lightweight was favored to win in his hometown. Believing "it is impossible for their man to lose" on the basis that "He has never been knocked out and has always completely outclassed his opponents,"[42] a heavy New Mexico crowd was in attendance to see "The Boxing Event of the Year," a 15-rounder that would be declared a draw should both men remain on their feet at the final bell.[43]

> For fifteen long, hard rounds, Winters battled, and wore himself out in a vain effort to administer punishment to the stoical Dane. The tow-headed Battler was like so much granite and Winter's fiercest swings fell harmless upon his broad back, head and shoulders and always safely removed from the vital spot. In the ninth round and also in the tenth, eleventh, and twelfth, the Raton man held his own, but at no time after the third was it a question of who would win, but whether the New Mexican would stay on his feet.[44]

Finishing exhausted and on the verge of losing by knockout, Winters survived, pulling off the draw. Going 15 with Jensen gave Winters' resume enough mileage to secure bigger fights over the following years.

Winters went from one near-knockout to another one — this one outside the squared circle. On June 17, 1911, it was announced that both Winters and Brownie Buckley had been indicted by a federal grand jury in Las Vegas for their 15-round prize fight in March. Buckley was arrested in Colorado in early June and taken to Las Vegas. Not so Winters; not only did he manage to evade federal authorities, keeping a low profile in June and July, but Winters returned to action on Aug. 4, when he took on Chicago's Frankie White in a 15-rounder staged in Alamosa, Colorado. It was the first of four encounters.

Taking the fight on 10 days' notice, Winters left for Alamosa on July 29, seeing a win as a chance at bigger game and bigger purses. Before 500 fans at Alamosa's Oliver Opera House, Winters proved his mettle by fighting White to a 15-round draw — the official decision should both men remain standing. Though both men were still fighting strong at the finish, White's early lead gave him a newspaper decision with at least two local Colorado newspapers. Eddie Gregory, Winters' manager, however, told New Mexico press that his charge had the best of it, never mind White's veteran record. "With good trainers and advisors, he will land the lightweight championship," Gregory boasted.[45]

Winters' scrap with White was the last fight on record through 1911—unless you count the hit-and-run bout he had with federal officials. By November, the feds had caught up with the elusive Winters who was, along with Buckley, indicted and brought to trial in Las Vegas. Winters, the winner in their 1910 fight, pleaded innocence and a judgment was postponed.

Winters waited out the year until New Mexico became a state in 1912, when he could resume his career and shake off the indictment, which was eventually forgotten. When Winters arrived in Clovis in February 1912 for his next bout, not a word was printed about Winters' crime. With nothing standing in the way, Winters stood ready to face the biggest lightweights in a new era of boxing.

The Clayton Blacksmith

> *Arising from obscurity he is fast attaining fame. The skill displayed by him in his training quarters marks him as a coming champion.*
>
> — *Cimarron News,* 1911[46]

Owen "Sonora" Smaulding is one of the greatest athletes ever produced by New Mexico. Before he graduated from Albuquerque High School, in 1919, Smaulding had broken eight state records in track. Not only was he an outstanding track-and-field state athlete, but, in 1915, Smaulding was named the most outstanding high school athlete in the U.S. After leaving New Mexico, Smaulding, like Pettus had done 10 years earlier, went on to make a name for himself playing baseball in the Negro Leagues, but not before earning a scholarship at the University of Idaho. Upon graduation, Smaulding went on to play with the Kansas City Monarchs with legendary Satchel Paige. Afterward, Smaulding was with the Chicago's American Giants and the St. Louis Blues.

As late as 1980, Smaulding's accomplishments of the 1910s were still being talked about. Nowadays, no one knows much about "Sonora"—and even less about the *other* Smaulding who preceded him, Owen's older brother Al "The Clayton Blacksmith" Smaulding.

Alfred T. Smaulding was the oldest of seven children born to Bazz and Paulina Smaulding, the third-born of which was Owen. Born on March 29, 1892, Al grew up in Wichita Falls, Texas, before the family relocated to northeast New Mexico's Clayton, sometime between 1900 and 1908, where Bazz found work in the sawmills and herding sheep. In 1910, the Smaulding family relocated to Albuquerque—but not before Al brought a bit of local fame to his hometown as a prizefighter.

Matching his younger brother's physique, 5'11" and 170 pounds, Al might have been the one breaking records had he been able to attend high school rather than help his father provide for his family as a cowhand and blacksmith. As it was, though, Owen's older brother was able to carve out a formidable reputation as a middleweight and looked like a promising comer in the first half of his career.

"The Clayton Blacksmith," as he was known early on, did not have an easy career. Black fighters, in general, were not exactly groomed nor given golden opportunities. Promising athletes like Pettus, who was known through the region as an ace ballplayer, had to leave the area to find fights—and were unsuccessful, at that. Smaulding stayed put, but, between 1909 and 1911, fought close to a dozen times, losing but one decision.

At the age of 17, Smaulding was talked into trying on the gloves when he was brought in to serve as a sparring partner for local attraction Serapio Romero. Smaulding proved effective enough to take a stab at it himself and on March 11, 1909, fought his debut in Cimarron, defeating veteran fighter W. E. "Battling" Moon, of Kenton, Oklahoma, by a third round foul in a scheduled ten-rounder. "I was surprised at the canvas on the ring,"[47] Smaulding would recall, nearly half a century later. Before his fight with Moon, Smaulding had never been inside the ropes and had sparred only on gymnasium floors.

Smaulding had to wait until December for his second fight, which was a six-round decision over Billy Lynch in Clayton. Two fights are known in 1910, both in Clayton: a ninth round knockout over Tug Wilson in April and a six-round decision over Perry Miller in September. At 4–0, Smaulding was ready for his first big showdown—a 20-rounder against Henry Perry of Dawson, in a showdown between the two biggest names in northern New Mexico, barring lightweight Ev Winters.

The fight was set up for Jan. 14, 1911, at the Athletic Hall in Cimarron. On paper, it was an even match. Perry had an estimated half-dozen fights during the previous year and Smaulding had four. Both were 150 pounds and Perry was just one year older, at 19. Stylewise, it was a different story. Smaulding, still learning the craft, was a slugger, while Perry, "a hard one to tap," had a "peculiar style of boxing that is hard to get into."[48]

After training in Cimarron, Smaulding convinced local sports that he would defeat Perry; actually he said that he would "bring home the chicken,"[49] a play on Joe Gans' famous line, "Bring home the bacon." Smaulding showed fast footwork and a sleep-producing punch, everything a so-called aspirant needed to set his sights on the middleweight championship, barring color, that is.

Special trains ran from Raton, Dawson, Koehler, French and other points in New Mexico and southern Colorado to Cimarron to see Smaulding defeat Perry, who brought a big crowd from the coal camps. "It was clear from the close of the third round that he had Perry out-classed in every way and the Dawson man never had any show to win the decision.... Smaulding was too quick on his feet and his guard was too perfect that there was no chance to land a knockout of him."[50]

A rematch was set up for Apr. 26 in Cimarron, but it was moved to Trinidad, three days later, when the two met in another 20-rounder. This time, Perry walked away with the decision.

Smaulding would make up for the loss by netting four more wins during the year, the most notable of which was a six-round knockout over well-known Chicago middleweight Tony Caponi, who'd built up a 50-bout record fighting (though losing to) the likes of Jack Blackburn, Stanley Ketchel, Jim Flynn, Billy Papke and Tommy Burns. Smaulding also gained kayo wins over Herman Grant (twice) and Louie Miller.

With just the one mark against him — the loss to Perry — Smaulding remained New Mexico's foremost middleweight by the time 1912 rolled around when the Smaulding family moved to Albuquerque. Plenty of opportunities awaited the former blacksmith.

Silver City's Luis Gonzales and Gus Flores

> *Monday night at the Elks' Opera House the sport fans of Silver City will be served*
> *with a program that will be worth seeing and will make you feel ten years younger.*
> *— Silver City Enterprise, 1913*[51]

Fort Bayard had been established in 1866 to protect the nearby mining communities of Pinos Altos and Silver City from Apaches. Following the capture of Geronimo, in 1886, the Apaches were no longer a threat, though the fort continued to operate, mainly as an Army tuberculosis hospital and research center.

It was on Fort Bayard's inaugural fight card, on May 11, 1910, that two local miners, Luis Gonzales and Rafael (Gus) Flores, would make their debut in the ring fighting prelim bouts. Both Flores and Gonzales would ultimately become the area's main attractions during the next several years.

On that night in Fort Bayard, before a paltry crowd of 50, Flores, age 17, battered soldier Frank Gaddi for two rounds, until "the small Filipino refused to box anymore,"[52] while Gonzales, age 19, would box an exhibition with Frank Marquez, also of Silver City.

Fighting as a featherweight through most of his career, Raphael Garcia Flores was born in Chihuahua, Mexico, on Oct. 7, 1892. Fighting under "Young Flores" and later merely as "Gus," Flores' fight record immediately following his debut in Bayard is unknown, but by 1913 he was a regular in the Silver City ring. It's entirely possible that his 1910 bout was his one and only until 1913, for when he started to fight consistently he'd also migrated from the mines to a local drug store where he worked as a makeshift pharmacologist.

Gonzales' parents, Antonio and Higinio, from Santiago, Mexico, had crossed the border in 1866 to settle in Silver City. Luis was one of several brothers, two of whom, Jose and Benny, would also become prizefighters, for a time. In fact, Luis' older brother Joe had also debuted on that fateful Bayard card, losing a decision.

Though the newspapers are no longer available, Gonzales was undefeated between 1910 and 1912, fighting at least seven times in cards staged around the area. Only one opponent had gone the distance with Gonzales — Dick Casidine — whom Gonzales had demolished in five rounds in a return match. Two wins had been by DQ, the rest by knockout. By the time 1912 rolled around, Gonzales, nicknamed "Native Citizen" for his New Mexico birth or "The Stanley Ketchel of New Mexico," was seen as the southern threat to the regional middleweight title, and to Al Smaulding.

With New Mexico poised to enter its first golden age in 1912, Gonzales and Flores were among the handful of fighters expected to put the new state on the pugilistic map.

A Cadet from Roswell

> *Higgins needs no introduction here as he was practically raised in this county. One thing we all know for him, he possesses those requisites of a good fighter, strength, nerve and a cool head.*
>
> — *Clovis News*, 1912[53]

Half a century before the New Mexico Military Institute in Roswell became a breeding ground for some of the state's top amateur boxers, it spawned two locals who put the town on the map. One of these fighters — Johnny Connolly — would emerge after statehood. The path taken by the more successful of the pair of Roswell pugs, Connolly, would be paved by a middleweight who preceded him by a couple years.

Alfred Liberty Higgins, born in 1891 in Weatherford, Texas, arrived in Roswell with his family some time before 1900, his father, Frederick, marrying into the local Rainbolt family. At 18, he was enrolled at the Institute where he took up boxing with his brother Irving, another fighter everyone knew as "Babe."

In the earliest known fight card at the Institute, Higgins made his initial ring appearance with a second round destruction of Alamogordo's Walter Baird. Due to his father's position as captain of the New Mexico mounted police, Higgins was given special attention in "Pecos Town." By June 1910, he was the "champion boxer" of the school, and headlines around the state were noting that "Fight Fans Have Taken Roswell."[54] By the end of the year, the short-lived scene hit a roadblock when enraged fans rioted at a card headlined by Higgins (see Chapter Five).

There were no more mills in Roswell, at least not until they were fully legal, which made it difficult for Higgins to improve his skills. With just a couple fights under his belt, Higgins kept his bouts either secretive or in the school gymnasium, until 1912 when the scene allowed his re-emergence.

Not long into 1912, Higgins would earn his reputation as the "Duke of the Pecos."

Benny

> *Chavez has a legion of supporters in this city who claim he is a world beater, judging from the showing he has made in his recent battles here.*
>
> —*The Trinidad Chronicle*, 1911[55]

New Mexico has produced a world-beater boxer once every decade or so, beginning with Epimenio Benjamin Gonzales Chavez, known to most as Benny Chavez.

Chavez was born on Aug. 23, 1893, just two years after Wagon Mound had been incorporated. Originally named Santa Clara, from a nearby spring of the same name, the town was renamed after a local butte landmark on the Santa Fe Trail resembling a covered wagon. After the railroad arrived, the town became an important wool and stock shipping point. Nowadays, the population is around 350, but during its heyday as many as 5,000 inhabited the town.

Chavez may be not just the greatest fighter to come out of Mora County, but one of the greatest to come out of New Mexico. If he'd fought in the modern ring, with double the number of weight classes, quadruple the available "world titles," and groomed ("protected" is another modern term) by the very few top boxing promoters running today's sport, there's no doubt he would've collected at least the number of belts earned by modern champions Johnny Tapia and Danny Romero.

As it stood, Chavez would score a number of firsts for New Mexico, becoming a bona fide contender. Along with early Mexican greats Aurelio Herrera and Joe Rivers, he helped pave the way for Mexican and Mexican-American fighters nationwide.

Benny was one of four sons raised by Antonio Chavez and Agapita Gonzales Chavez, of Chihuahua, Mexico, who'd crossed the border prior to Benny's birth in 1893. Sometime between 1910 and 1911, the Chavez family moved from Wagon Mound to the coal mining town of Trinidad, Colorado, just over the Colorado-New Mexico state line. When Benny departed his hometown, Wagon Mound had no idea he was a diamond in the rough, but Trinidad soon caught on when Chavez started to make regular appearances at a local boxing gym.

There would be no amateur bouts for Benny. No four-rounders, no grooming, no coddling. On May 14, Chavez jumped into deep water for a ten-round fight against another local fighter, hoping to impress the locals. The headliners were heavyweights Louis Fink, of Sapulpa, Oklahoma, and Charles Lucha, from nearby Aguilar, Colorado, and they only merit mention because the winner was slated to fight Pueblo's Jim Flynn — which wouldn't happen anyway. The local paper hyped the 20-round heavyweight bout for the Southwestern light-heavyweight championship, while two "rattling good preliminary bouts" were arranged between "local boxers, well-known, clever boys"[56] who would "add zest to the main event of the evening" and insure that fans would get a good show for their pricey $2 and $3 tickets. While suffering rainy weather at Trinidad's Central Park, Chavez knocked out local opponent George Waldon in the ninth round.

Chavez fought two more preliminaries after that, with the local papers hardly bothering to mention his name, but when he KO'd Lone "Money" Malone in four rounds, on May 30, 1911, Chicago featherweight Patsy McKenna, a recent import to Colorado, was in the crowd to challenge Chavez. The aspiring bantam from Wagon Mound was beginning to attract attention. After his next fight — another knockout of Waldon — the rest of Colorado's banties were calling out the 5'4" fighting machine.

McKenna got his wish on June 19, and instead of fighting a prelim, Benny, now referred to as "The Trinidad Whirlwind" by the press that had warmed to him, had graduated to main event status. They signed to go 20 rounds at 122 pounds on June 12. McKenna was a step-up in opposition. Having fought since 1902 from one coast to the other, his experience overshadowed Chavez' three bouts. "Chavez has demonstrated what he can do by his recent fights,"[57] reasoned the *Trinidad Chronicle*, and they were right, for Chavez knocked out McKenna in round one.

Now that he was 4–0, all by the short route, local fight fans clamored for an opponent who would give Chavez a test. Harry Riede, a.k.a. "The Aspen Whirlwind," was just the man. Barely 16 years of age to Chavez's 18, Riede had fought several times as an amateur in Denver, carving out a solid reputation at the Denver Athletic Club's tournaments earlier in the year. Since fighting as a bona fide pro, Riede was undefeated in several fights. The two were matched for Aug. 20 in nearby Walsenburg, for a 15-rounder.

Proclaiming a campaign outside of Colorado next, Riede promised to stop Chavez in less than six rounds. If nothing else, Riede did provide a challenge, for Chavez was forced to go the distance for the first time, though the result was the same — a win: "Although he failed to administer a knockout, it was clear that Chavez was a boxer of a different class than his adversary. The decision in favor of Chavez was a popular one."[58]

Chavez was back in Walsenburg in September, knocking out Denver's Tommy Cody in five rounds in what was an unofficial fight for the bantamweight championship of Colorado. Wire reports ran nationwide about the "little Mexican, who was ever willing to accept punishment for an opportunity to use his right." [59] Then, in October, Chavez fought for the first time in New Mexico, stopping Canadian Eddie "Kid" Leach in the ninth on a card in Raton.

Pegged as Colorado's bantam and featherweight champion, in overzealous Trinidad Chavez was proclaimed a likely aspirant to fight World Bantamweight Champion Johnny Coulon (who had at least 40 bouts at this stage). "Local admirers of Chavez are encouraged in the belief that he can defeat any fighter of his weight in the country," cheered his hometown paper. "After a few more matches expect to see him ripe to go up against Coulon."[60]

Next up for Chavez was Pueblo's Kid Mex, a 20-bout veteran with, reportedly, no losses. The two were matched to go 15 rounds for the Colorado bantamweight championship on Nov. 3 that saw Benny's return to Trinidad. Mex was an expected test, but the fight lasted less than two minutes, during which time Benny's opponent was sent to the floor four times, "rising the last time with a stream of blood flowing from his nose, dazed and staggering."[61]

An elimination tournament to determine a Rocky Mountain bantamweight champion was also being discussed, with Chavez at the top of the list, followed by former foes Riede, Olaf Shonskey of Walsenburg and Kid Mex. Riede was demanding a rematch with Chavez and Harry Lub, another Colorado bantam, was calling out the Trinidad Whirlwind as well. Realizing they had a champion in the making, a contender at the very least, local talk turned to whether it was time to up the opposition, or continue weeding out the locals, and whether the "little wonder" had outgrown Trinidad and was ready for the coast.

Chavez chose to stick close to home for the rest of the year. On Nov. 23, he headlined another Walsenburg card, taking on Salt Lake City pug Harry Lub, whose real name was Kiskus Loeb. "It was the shortest fight ever seen in this part of the state," wrote the *Chronicle News*. "When the Utah boy climbed over the ropes to go to his dressing room the spectators were referring to him as not Lub, but Dub."[62]

After the fight, Pete Alvarado, Chavez's manager at the time, accepted a challenge to meet Patsy Brannigan of Cleveland, Ohio, for a side bet of $500 — this to come after a Dec. 7 bout against Young Abe Attell. Attell, whose real name was Willie Clar, of New York, had gotten his start in California working as a peanut vendor at a boxing venue when he stepped out of the crowd as a last-minute substitute. Both fights — Attell on Dec. 7 and Brannigan on Dec. 25 — would prove near disastrous for the aspiring contender.

Named after the former featherweight champion, Young Abe had been fighting for two years out of Denver. Though a solid bantam, he was not assumed to be a threat to

Chavez — which made a ten-round draw all the more surprising, when the two fought at Central Park in Benny's backyard at Trinidad. Chavez landed the hardest blows but Attell proved a better boxer. Attell attested to Benny's punching power — "He hit me several times last night so hard that my eyebrows fell asleep and my teeth rocked"[63] — and no one thought too much about it, until the next day when rumors of a possible frame-up became fact.

Protecting manager Alvarado, who claimed he was out of the loop, and the local chapter of the Elks, who'd sanctioned the fight card, the *Chronicle News* reported that Chavez had been paid off to let Attell go the distance. The Elks immediately pulled the funding for the Brannigan fight set for Christmas Day and Chavez' reputation took a hit. "Everybody with a drop of sporting blood in his veins wanted to see the Trinidad boy make good and conquer," the paper claimed. But "after investigating the facts and being convinced, the *Chronicle-News* declares the act of Benny Chavez and whoever inspired it an exhibition of shortsightedness and ingratitude, that cannot be tempered by mercy."[64]

Anti-Chavez stories faded rather quickly, however, when less than a week later, a 20-round battle between the local hopeful and Brannigan was on, once again, for Christmas evening, for a $1,000 purse and a $500 side bet, both fighters to weigh in at 115 at the ringside. Talk of frame-ups and easy local opponents disappeared promptly when the Brannigan bout was made official.

Brannigan was no joke. With over 50 bouts behind him (Chavez had but 11) Brannigan had been fighting since 1903 — eight years longer. The Pittsburgh bantam was at the peak of his career, fully developed at the age of 25 while Benny, 18, was barely beginning. Brannigan had faced the best fighters in the world — men who would become legends. He'd fought the bantam champ, Johnny Coulon, to a

After less than a year of fighting, on Dec. 25, 1911, young Benny Chavez made the mistake of fighting solid contender Patsy Brannigan, of the East Coast, in his hometown of Trinidad, Colorado. After a good showing in the early rounds, Chavez was KO'd in the sixth. Chavez schooled Brannigan in the rematch, a year-and-a-half later.

draw in 1909; faced former bantam champ Montel Attell three times, winning twice, losing once, between 1910 and 1911; and taken on the future featherweight champ (*very* near future) Johnny Kilbane three times, drawing twice and dropping a decision. It was, at best, a long shot.

Having smoothed things over with the local press, who were once again back on the Chavez bandwagon, manager Alvarado was already looking past Brannigan to line up a rematch with Attell for January. When Attell declined the offer of a $1,000 purse, Alvarado kept the local papers hopping with reports from fight camp that Chavez would make good with a victory over Brannigan.

It worked. By fight week, there was but a brief mention of the Chavez-Attell fiasco: "He has defeated every man of his weight in the state except Attel [*sic*] who Benny generously but foolishly permitted to stay ten rounds instead of going after him and adding another laurel."[65] Beyond that, everyone from Trinidad to Denver was talking about Chavez's chances with a world class contender.

Despite his lack of experience, Chavez was given a fighting chance on account of endurance, having already gone 15 rounds twice. In half a hundred bouts, Brannigan had never been past 12 rounds, at least as far as anyone in Trinidad knew (Brannigan had, in fact, gone 20 rounds twice, 15 rounds twice, and scored a 13th-round knockout, all during 1911). On the other hand, losing to Brannigan would not be the end of the world for Chavez. It was a different era than today's version of the sport, when a loss can destroy a fighter's marketability. In the 1910s, a loss could be forgotten in a few fights. "If Chavez loses to the Pittsburg boy he will not be disgraced by any means," wrote the sports scribe of the *Chronicle News*. "If he wins he will be champion in less than one year."[66]

The press in Pueblo, where Brannigan trained for a week before the fight, set up a less forgiving scenario for Chavez, printing "Puebloans cannot figure how a scrapper who has come to the front in less than a year, and never has engaged in a dozen battles, can successfully come with a veteran of nearly 300 ring encounters, during the course of which he has never even lost a decision.... If the Trinidad Mexican falls before the blows of the red headed easterner then there will be reason to believe that another phenom has been exploded and that the people down there have been backing a second rater all the time."[67]

Training "as if the championship of the world depended upon the outcome of the approaching hostilities,"[68] Chavez attracted hordes of fans at the gym. Top fighter Spike Sullivan was brought in to help local trainers get Chavez ready. Thirty miles away in Pueblo, however, Brannigan was looking unbeatable. "He is a finished scrapper in the full sense of the word, and from his record all he needs to make him a champion is a sturdier wallop."[69]

On Christmas Day, special trains brought in the biggest crowd Trinidad had ever seen for a prize fight. In town, the local streetcar company doubled their traffic to accommodate a crowd hoping to watch their local whirlwind break into contention with a victory over Brannigan. It wouldn't happen, at least not on Dec. 25, 1911.

For the first five rounds, Chavez gave as good as he got. "The Pittsburg boy showed no great superiority as a boxer. Up to the fatal sixth round the outcome of the bout was doubtful. Chavez landed as often and as hard on the anatomy of his opponent as the easterner landed on him ... But experience and ring generalship was his advantage. Chavez was the aggressor and wore himself out while Brannigan was calm and fresh and taking it easy. Then after he had Chavez unnerved he took advantage of the opening and planted a mitt on the point of the chin."[70]

Chavez went down for the first time. "Admirers of the clever local lad stood speechless amidst the uproar and saw only the figure of Referee Jerry Mahoney, standing over the prostrate form counting off the seconds. Chavez on his face with arms outstretched was lifted up and taken to his corner while friends of the Pittsburg boy at the ringside carried the victor off on their shoulders."[71]

There was no disgrace in the defeat, reasoned local press. The *Chronicle News* wrote, "Chavez lacked what the Pittsburg boy had after five years of fighting and the best of training. The local boy was not ripe for the Irishman."[72] The *Pueblo Star-Journal* was equally forgiving of Chavez, but not of his handlers: "Chavez's defeat was to be expected when it is taken into consideration that he is but a novice in the ring, while his opponent of yesterday is recognized as one of the best boys in the country. As we have stated several times, a great mistake was made by the handlers of Chavez in making this match. It might be the means of spoiling an otherwise brilliant career in the ring."[73]

Many changes would have to be made in 1912 if Chavez was going to make the climb to contention and a shot at the title.

7. The Boxing Explosion of 1912

No loyal citizen of New Mexico can avoid feeling great anxiety about the everlasting shame and disgrace that now threatens our State by permitting, encouraging, and legalizing the prize-fight within her borders. He must feel surprised that men can have such tastes and feelings as to delight in the brutality and wickedness connected with it.
— *Las Cruces Citizen*, 1912[1]

It took New Mexico 50 years to go from territory to state. There were many reasons, from racial to religious, political to economical, preventing statehood, but whatever was holding back New Mexico ceased to be an issue on June 20, 1910, when President William H. Taft signed the Enabling Act. On Jan. 21, 1911, delegates across the territory convened in Santa Fe to draft a constitution that was signed by Taft at 1:35 P.M., Jan. 6, 1912.

With New Mexico now a state, the territorial law prohibiting boxing was, legally, null and void. Four hours after New Mexico became the 47th state of the United States, Kitchen's Opera House in Gallup ushered in the new era with the state's first legal card of the twentieth century, between two local heavyweights no one would ever hear about again. A tough fight was expected between local sluggers Frank Pantalone and Emmett Kadletz, but "those who so thought or expected, were quickly undeceived when Kadletz assumed a recumbent position as the result of a well directed punch from his opponent. A repetition or two, and Kadletz was not in the game."[2]

New Mexico's first legal main event of the new era lasted but two minutes; if not for its place in history, the show would not otherwise merit attention. Gallup would go on to stage five more bouts during 1912 — exactly the same number as thrown the year before, when boxing had been outlawed. Legality may not have made much difference to the Carbon City, but it did throughout the rest of the state. Through the previous two years, the territory had staged more than 20 fight cards. Year 1912 racked up three times the number — 65 legal shows — New Mexico's biggest year yet.

In the north, Raton staged five bills, Santa Fe four, Las Vegas five and Ute Park, once a thriving point on the railway, had its one and only show. To the east, Clovis fight bugs had nine shows and Tucumcari staged two. Southeast New Mexico racked up seven: one in Carlsbad and the other six in Roswell. Three fight cards were held in southern towns: two in Las Cruces and one in Cutter, in its heyday as a mining town. Called "Hub City" at the time, due to railway traffic, Belen staged their initial two cards. The remaining 20 were all held 20 miles north in Albuquerque.

Because very few newspapers paid attention to fistic matters in Gallup, the obscure Pantalone-Kadletz fight made no rumblings beyond the area. Instead, it was the inaugural fight in Albuquerque and, more importantly, its promoter, who would set the standard for decades to come, that made the most noise.

On Jan. 21, 1912, the formation of the New Mexico Athletic Club was announced and its debut card occurred the following Friday, praising the efforts of promoter Mark Levy. The year before, Levy, as president of the Fraternal Order of Eagles, had managed to circumvent the law by slipping several boxing matches into club meetings held at the Elks Opera House. But now, there was no need to masquerade the fight game by calling them "debates" or "athletic stunts." No longer able to "deny those who followed the trend of things athletic," Levy promised a "real ripe luscious pippin."[3]

The fights were not without flaws. Former Fort Wingate soldier Clarence "Soldier" Hunt was no match for New Mexico's "Native Son," Luis Gonzales, going down 18 rounds short in their scheduled 20-rounder. One fighter quit with an injured wrist, while promoter Levy himself stopped another featured bout, leaping into the ring and declaring a no-contest after hearing that West Coast import Kid Boyd was going to take a dive against John "Lefty" Floyd.

Flawed as the matches might have been, the town of Albuquerque was hooked — the rest of the state would quickly follow.

Champion of the World and the 47th State of the Union

No loyal citizen of New Mexico can avoid feeling great anxiety about the everlasting shame and disgrace that now threatens our State by permitting, encouraging, and legalizing the prize-fight within her borders. He must feel surprised that men can have such tastes and feelings as to delight in the brutality and wickedness connected with it. It is not almost incredible that men with the enlightenment of twenty centuries of Christian civilization will either enjoy or tolerate such brutality? That they do so is strong confirmation of the theory that men in ages past had a very close relationship with the savage beast of the jungle. Surely some are not removed far from such yet.
— *Las Cruces Citizen*, 1912[4]

Ex-champion or not, there was little hope in James Jeffries reclaiming the heavyweight throne from Jack Johnson. And chances were equally slim that a black world champion like Johnson could score a big payday. Going on two years since he'd destroyed the hopes of White America by obliterating Jeffries, on July 4, 1910, in Reno, Johnson, offered few opportunities to fight, was forced to hit the vaudeville circuit. There, he collected rust, while the desperate search for a great white hope gathered momentum.

The best of these was Carl Morris, a 6' 4", 240-pound giant from Sapulpa, Okla., and when he started knocking out second- and third-raters in his backyard, he was prodded to step-up the opposition. "Fireman" James Flynn, of Pueblo, Colorado, a proven heavyweight who'd already lost to Johnson in 1907, was the logical choice in the battle of mighty whiteys. Since losing to Johnson, Flynn found himself on the rise again, unbeaten since 1910 when Sam Langford had knocked him out.

Flynn and Morris were scheduled to meet during the summer of 1911, with hometown advantage going to Oklahoman, until the governor there shut down the fight. The fight was moved to New York's Madison Square Garden on Sept. 15, 1911, where Morris was completely outclassed and punished through ten bloody rounds. With Morris out of the picture, there was a renewed interest in Flynn — and renewed hype on the part of his manager, Jack Curley.

Hoping to milk Flynn for another run, Curley approached Johnson to fight his man, who demanded the same purse his predecessor had received fighting *him* in 1908: $30,000 plus expenses. Curley agreed, and announced the Garden as his first choice for the site, until New York State Boxing Commissioner Frank O'Neill shook his head. Though black fighters like Joe Jeannette and Langford were free to fight there, a black heavyweight champion was an entirely different matter.

Curley looked for an alternative site while Flynn kept busy with tune-ups. Nevada and Utah were named as initial possibilities — that is, until Jan. 16, when New Mexico made even bigger headlines than it had ten days prior when it had achieved statehood.

"LAS VEGAS SEEKING FAME BY BIDDING FOR PRIZE FIGHT" hit the papers and wires after the *Las Vegas Daily Optic* ran a story about local electrician Charles O'Malley. Leading a select group of businessmen and politicians, "arousing the enthusiasm of the fight fans of the fair Meadow City, but incurring the wrath of the church people and that element that frowns on prize fighting as a brutal sport,"[5] O'Malley wired promoter Curley about staging the fight in Las Vegas. O'Malley was convinced that hosting the world's heavyweight championship would boost the local economy and restore Las Vegas to its former glory as New Mexico's premier city. With an offer of $100,000, Curley was hooked.

Before there was Don King or Bob Arum — before there was even "Tex" Rickard — there was Curley. The July 4, 1910, "Fight of the Century" between Johnson and Jeffries had been masterminded by Curley, who also managed several fighters and promoted wrestling.

On the New Mexico level, there was O'Malley, who knew a little something about the fight game. While in the Navy, O'Malley had boxed, but it was his skills as a pitcher that had him excel in sports, playing minor league baseball for the St. Louis Browns from 1897 to 1899. In 1900, he answered an ad in the *Optic* for an experienced telephone lineman and moved to Vegas. There, O'Malley started up an electrical appliance store which he operated until retiring, in 1967.

"King" O'Malley — as he would later be known — might not have been destined to become the influential promoter that Mark Levy would be, but teaming up with Curley and persuading the town of Las Vegas to cough up the money to stage the World Heavyweight Championship might be the single greatest feat to boost the fight scene in New Mexico boxing.

O'Malley was able to cajole the city fathers to make a run at hosting the fight, though not everyone agreed. The grumblings against now-legal prizefighting had been relatively minor, but when word hit that nothing less than the biggest fight on the planet could land in the new state, opposition grew. Still, with Curley talking about Nevada, Utah or Mexico, no one quite believed it would land in the Middle of Nowhere, i.e., New Mexico, but that didn't stop them from protesting.

Hiram Hadley, founder of the New Mexico State University and deemed the "Father of Education" in his state, stood on his soapbox preaching the evils of prizefighting and trying to nudge the new governor, William C. McDonald, to take action. Not only would prizefighting debase the "enlightened people" of New Mexico, but it would "greatly retard the immigration of desirable people" and, generally, stink the place up for generations to come.[6]

Editors of the *Las Cruces Citizen* agreed with Hadley, but for different reasons. They were not against the sport, but against what they deemed a mismatch. "Let us steer clear of such a shady fight, which might be a frame-up or at best could be nothing more than out and out FIASCO," they editorialized. "Let's bid our time and perhaps we can get a real fight, one between [Ad] Wolgast and [Packey] McFarland, for instance."[7]

Curley was in no hurry deciding on a venue, and he bounced back and forth from Nevada to Salt Lake City. On Jan. 29, he told the media that, in addition to Las Vegas, Albuquerque was now in the running.

Meanwhile, with New Mexico a very real possibility to host Johnson-Flynn, Gov. McDonald launched his campaign to derail not just the fight, but the sport itself.

New York-born William Calhoun McDonald had ventured west to White Oaks, New Mexico, hoping to make his fortunes in mining. Instead, he became one of the territory's largest cattle ranchers in Carrizozo, earning a no-nonsense reputation by weeding out rustlers. After serving as a territorial legislator, McDonald campaigned with a vow to break the current corrupt New Mexico political machine. His first big battle would be boxing. When word broke that the new state would be tarnished with the world championship fight, McDonald quietly introduced a bill to the state legislature. As quickly as he could move, however, the boxing promoters could — and did — move faster.

The legislature would not convene until April. In the meantime, local promoter Levy staged show after show while the talks with Curley continued in finding a home for Johnson-Flynn. On Feb. 8, Curley arrived in Albuquerque, declaring the city his choice for the big fight; due to the railroad's direct passage to the West Coast and Levy's bolstering, the local scene was on the rise. All he wanted was $25,000 to $40,000 as insurance. When told that the governor had plans to derail boxing in the state, Curley scoffed. "You have no law against prize fighting now, have you?"[8] he asked. The answer, of course, was no, and Curley remarked that even *if* Gov. McDonald were somehow able to convince the legislature to pass such a law, it could not *possibly* pass in time to prevent his July 4 target date for the world's heavyweight championship.

Curley moved on to Las Vegas to meet with O'Malley, Las Vegas Mayor R. J. Taupert and businessman E. T. Plowman. While there, he crashed the reception held for the newly-appointed governor. According to Plowman, Curley "donned his glad rags and a stiff hat and we took him to the reception and ball which followed. Curley was a big man there that night, met the best people in the state and Las Vegas won him right over then. Later we made all the arrangements."[9]

Instead of praising Las Vegas as a town that had won him over, however, Curley continued to tease the press by adding two Nevada sites — Jawbridge and Wendover — to the list of cities in the running. Encouraged by Levy's success in Albuquerque and hoping to benefit from the attention drawn by Johnson-Flynn, other towns jumped on the boxing bandwagon, while other groups started to protest.

After a bloody, brutal bout in Clovis with Ev Winters, in early February, the local Christian community, "humiliated" and "shocked," launched an anti-boxing campaign, appealing to Gov. McDonald for a statewide ban on the sport, in "the good sense for the manhood and womanhood of this city."[10] Anti-prizefight newspapers — most notably, the *Santa Fe New Mexican* — piled on the pressure for the governor to make an official stand against boxing. New Mexico's "wild and wooly" reputation would be further tarnished by extending a "clamorous welcome to the plug-uglies," wrote the editor of the *New Mexican*. If the governor, who unofficially was already frowning upon the fight, along with the district attorney and district judge, would only publicly declare that they were "against the prize fight and would recommend a law to prohibit it and other exhibitions of like character ... they will not need to stretch existing laws until they creak, to find a statute that will enable them to prevent the nasty exhibition of brutality."[11]

Three days later, an unofficial announcement leaked from Las Vegas: "JOHNSON AND

FLYNN WILL FIGHT IN LAS VEGAS" ran as headlines across New Mexico. According to O'Malley, the fight was as good as done, though contracts were not yet signed by either fighter. O'Malley and lead promoter Curley had committed to posting forfeits of $10,000 to guarantee the match that would take place on the Fourth of July.

Though Curley continued to shrug, neither confirming nor denying, the unofficial declaration prodded Gov. McDonald into publicly launching his battle. The day after the announcement, he declared that he was not only "bitterly opposed" to the fight, but that he would, if necessary, use state rangers and militia to prevent it. No, there was no law preventing it, McDonald admitted, but he would see to *that* during the next legislative session. The governor went on to say that even if prizefighting was legal—which it, technically, *was*—he would do everything in his power to prevent a fight between a white and black man.

The newly appointed governor had obviously been paying little attention to the local scene, for fights between whites and blacks were fairly common. In fact, just a couple days after the governor made his declaration, promoter Levy staged a show at the Elks' Opera House in Albuquerque pitting black Gallup pug Eddie Gregory with white Denver fighter Johnny Murphy, who fought to a 20-round draw.

Back in Chicago, Curley was telling reporters that an official site would not be named until after May 1. "I positively will not select the spot for some time," Curley teased. "But I do feel partial to Las Vegas."[12] In New Mexico there was no holding back the local press. On Feb. 20, the *Optic* revealed that Curley was on his way back to solidify arrangements to make Las Vegas the bona fide battleground for the championship fight.

The main bill might have had Jack Johnson's world championship on the line, but the real prize at stake was the survival of the sweet science in New Mexico.

Dual Battles

> We recommend the willingness of Governor McDonald to do all the law permits to prevent it, we condemn the prize fight as out of keeping with this age: we call upon the legislature to provide means of keeping this stain off the name of New Mexico.
> —Melrose Mothers Club in *Albuquerque Morning Journal*, 1912[13]

> We, the Indians of the Laguna pueblo, Valencia county, New Mexico, in meeting assembled, express our disapproval of all kinds of fighting, prizefighting or fighting for money included. What is not good for Indian boys and men is not good for white boys and men.... We believe fighting to be bad and is a sin. Sin is bad, whether it is big or little. Sin does not care who it hurts. Fighting will be bad for Indians and all. We believe it will disgrace our state, and we want our law-makers and governor to stop it. White men tell us not to fight and then fight themselves and set us a bad example.
> —*Albuquerque Morning Journal*, 1912[14]

While the rest of the world began to criticize the Johnson-Flynn fight as a mismatch—"Flynn will be a child in the big black's hands,"[15] wrote one reporter—in New Mexico, the protest mounted for an entirely different reason.

In Clovis, ministers banded together to praise the governor, derailing—albeit temporarily—the budding fight scene in that town. "The eyes of the nation are upon us!" they declared. "We appeal to our legislature to act immediately in such way as spare the good citizenship of the state this disgrace."[16]

Long-time heavyweight contender "Fireman" Jim Flynn is significant to New Mexico for more than his 1912 title fight with Jack Johnson. Flynn headlined Lordsburg in a little-publicized card in 1911. He'd also defeated Albuquerque hopeful Bill Pettus in 1909 in Pueblo, Colorado (Library of Congress, Prints & Photographs Division [LC-B2-2266–9]).

Similar meetings were held by social and Christian clubs around the state. Petitions were organized and the paperwork sent to the state capital for the marathon legislative session that convened throughout April and May. During that time, petitions came from Alamogordo, Albuquerque, Amistad, Artesia, Belen, Canode, Carlsbad, Clovis, Cottonwood, Dayton, Dixon, East and West Las Vegas, Eddy County, Embudo, Estancia, Forest, Fort Sumner, Gallup, Grady, Grant County, Hagerman, Hudson, Jemez Springs, Laguna Pueblo, Las Cruces, Lordsburg, Maxwell, Mesilla Park, Mountainair, Orchard Park, Pinos Altos, Portales, Raton, Rincon, Rio Arriba County, Roswell, Springer, Stonehaven, Trementina, Tucumcari, Tularosa, and Valencia County; and from religious clubs, social organizations and churches around and out of the state, from as far away as Providence, Rhode Island — giving the appearance that boxing, let alone the world's heavyweight championship, couldn't *possibly* be allowed.

Newspaper reports on the session, however, often included the audible laughter when yet another anti-boxing petition was presented. Gov. McDonald had plenty of opposition from the New Mexico Republican ring that was still smarting from the Democrat's upset win for office, and from influential Las Vegas businessmen. Though petitions supporting the sport came from Albuquerque, Belen, Folsom, Fort Sumner, Las Cruces, Mogollon and Santa Fe, totaling nearly 3,000 names, the biggest counterpunch came from a bill introduced by Representative George Tripp of San Miguel County. "The opponents of the fight game entered a punch in the solar plexus yesterday in the senate," wrote the *Albuquerque Morning Journal* on April 10. "Today the house countered with a wallop to the jaw."[17]

House Bill No. 48, which became known as the Tripp Bill, did not seek to legalize the sport — why bother, since it was, technically, legal, anyway? Instead, the bill proposed to *regulate* boxing — the first of its kind in New Mexico. Under the bill, boxing contests under the Marquess of Queensberry rules would call for five-ounce (or heavier) gloves, physical examinations for fighters prior to contests, the ban of alcohol at fight venues, and a state tax: for bouts over 20 rounds, a $1,000 license fee; for under 20, five percent of the gate's gross receipts, with a $25 minimum. Further rankling or, possibly, an attempt to pacify Gov. McDonald, fees received from boxing matches would go into improving roads around the state, which was a pet project of the governor.

On April 16, the Tripp Bill passed, 29 votes to 17. After both Johnson and Flynn voiced no objection to fighting in the desert climate, the only remaining hurdle would be the governor and his anti-prizefight bill, which still had a chance to upset.

With the passing of the Tripp Bill, promoter Curley, passing on new offers from Juarez, El Paso and Roswell (businessmen there offered up a collective $50,000), saw no need to wait until May 1 to officially declare Las Vegas as the fight site. On April 18, the wire buzzed with the official news, with Curley bragging about a bonus received from Las Vegas businessmen that would be used to construct an open-air arena. Architect E. W. Hart, who'd relocated to Las Vegas from Columbus, Ohio, for health reasons, drafted the plans for the arena, to be built two-and-a-half miles from downtown at what is now a residential area adjacent to Robertson High School on the north end of Sixth St. (Later, he would have to threaten Curley and O'Malley with a lawsuit in order to get paid.) "Curley's Arena," with a $15,000 price tag, would seat 17,950 and measure 350 feet in diameter, with a height of 45 feet at the outer edge.

On Tuesday, May 28, on the 79th day of the legislative session, the governor made his last attempt to hijack the big fight. Hoping to sway the vote his way, McDonald said that while it was not his purpose to interfere with the legislation, allowing Johnson-Flynn would have the rest of the country "judging us adversely" while "causing serious injury to every good cause and proper interest in New Mexico."[18] While papers speculated about a complete cancellation, when the legislature adjourned on Saturday, June 8, it voted against the anti-prizefight bill.

The fight was on.

Fight Town, New Mexico, U.S.A.

> *The Meadow City is fight crazy these days. The Johnson–Flynn fight is all one hears. Father talks it over at the breakfast table, with mother and the kids; father brings home the latest dope at noon which he has heard while down town, and at supper time, the papers are read by father to the family, who gather closely to hear what the sport writers have to say on the forthcoming battle. Then the family, collectively and separately, express their opinions. If anything should happen to prevent the big fistic encounter taking place, it would be necessary to hold a gigantic funeral and bury this town, as the city would actually pass away.*
>
> — *Albuquerque Morning Journal*, 1912[19]

With the world's heavyweight championship apparently finalized, the city was burning up with boxing — but it was also due in part to Mark Levy's New Mexico Athletic Club who brought back New Mexico's rising star Benny Chavez. The southwestern bantamweight champion headlined three shows in May, two in Albuquerque and one in Las Vegas.

While Chavez gathered steam, the talk that made the town the "Hub of the World"[20] was, of course, Johnson vs. Flynn. Stamped fight headquarters, the entire lower floor of La Pension Hotel, on the corner of Sixth and Lincoln, accommodated Curley, O'Malley and the "small army of sporting writers from the big newspapers of the country"[21] expected to arrive for the fight. There, the media machine cranked out a wave of pro–Flynn press that might not have convinced the rest of the country, but New Mexicans fell for it.

Before a crowd of 500 and a blaring brass band, Flynn, his apparel "decidedly it," stepped off the train platform in Vegas on May 9, "displaying diamonds which must have weighed as many carets as the 220 pounds he claimed he weighed."[22]

Curley set Flynn up at the cushy Montezuma Hotel, located five miles north of the city and surrounded by hot springs, on the north side of the Gallinas River. Before opening up camp under the direction of former middleweight champion Tommy Ryan, Flynn expected to begin his stay in New Mexico with a week of relaxation and fishing. He assured the press, however, that "Johnson will not face a fisherman on the 4th, but a well-trained athlete backed by a strong heart." With yet more fishing analogies, Flynn explained that his 1907 loss to Johnson was "due more to the reel and hook game than to the punches that came from Johnson's long arms."[23]

"Something about Flynn's confidence is positively infectious," ran the *Morning Journal*.[24]

"Fireman" Jim Flynn upon his arrival in Santa Fe for his July 4, 1912, world heavyweight showdown with champion Jack Johnson. Though most of those pictured are unknown, Flynn is in the center, his brother Joe to the left, and Las Vegas promoter Charles O'Malley in the dark hat next to Joe. The grinning man to the right with the floppy hat is Jack Curley, who was the lead promoter for the event (photograph courtesy of O'Malley Family/Annie Leonard).

The great Jack Johnson during his stay in Santa Fe, New Mexico. Johnson's 1912 title fight in New Mexico would be the last time he fought in the U.S.— as a champion (photograph courtesy of O'Malley Family/Annie Leonard).

By the end of the week, an estimated $10,000 had been wagered on Flynn in New Mexico, with the 3 to 1 odds expected to drop to 5–4 by the day of the fight (which did not happen.)

Hoping "Flynn Fever" caught on in Albuquerque, Curley arranged with promoter Levy for the "Pueblo Fireman" to headline a show at the Elks' Opera House held in honor of the Firemen's Convention. On May 22, Flynn arrived before a "bigger crowd than has often assembled in New Mexico to greet Taft or Teddy."[25] On a card that saw lightweight scrapper Stanley Yoakum defeating Lee Brazos, "The Cheyenne Kid," Flynn went four rounds with his sparring partner, Al Williams. It was enough to convince Albuquerque fans that he had, at least, a chance to defeat the long-limbed Johnson, whom they'd never seen in action.

"Flynn does not pretend to be a boxer," surmised the *Journal's* scribe. "He is a slugger, and does all his telling work at close range. He works both arms with the rapidity and precision of a trip hammer."[26] It didn't take a genius to figure out that the only way Flynn could win was to fight in the proverbial phone booth — or "pickle barrel," as Flynn put it.

It was a longshot, at best, and at least one New Mexican refused to buy into the hype. Wealthy sheep breeder William McIntosh became the subject of an article when he approached Flynn after his exhibition. "I've got a thousand dollars bet on you — and I think I'm goin' to lose," he said. Flynn responded, "Well, I'll take your bet, take it right now, and pay you $20 for it beside."[27] With money to spare, McIntosh took the bet.

Two nights later, Flynn showed his wares in Las Vegas with an exhibition that played second fiddle to the Benny Chavez-Kid Williams headliner at the Duncan Opera House. Flynn went two rounds with his sparring partners. It was supposed to be his last appearance before going into hard training, and it wasn't as well received as his showing in Albuquerque. After knocking down [Jack] Skelly, he "went after him in vicious fashion, punishing him severely." The crowd booed Flynn for beating on his sparring partner and someone yelled,

Jack Johnson (center, in robe) and his training camp in Santa Fe, New Mexico. While Jim Flynn enjoyed the cushy Montezuma Castle outside Las Vegas for his camp, Johnson had to be content with a modest adobe house in Old Town, Santa Fe. He was joined by Marty Cutler (who would fight Carl Morris in Clovis the following year), pictured to Jack's right (photograph courtesy of O'Malley Family/Annie Leonard).

"That's the way Johnson is going to do to you on the Fourth!" "This aroused Flynn's anger and he threatened to 'take on' the man who made the remark."[28]

Flynn trained away at the Montezuma. The champion, meanwhile, upon his arrival on May 26, was expected to train eight miles away at the Forsyth Ranch or 64 miles west of Las Vegas at Jemez Springs, at best, a six-hour round trip, depending upon the conditions of the road. Johnson shipped his automobile ahead of his arrival, but opted out of Jemez for the ranch, at which he stayed but a single night.

Showing Vegas fans that "the world's heavyweight champion has a mind of his own," Johnson packed up for the city, declaring, "No lonesome ranch life for me, where the coyotes keep you awake all night howling their heads off. I'll train right here in town, where I can see people and where they can see me. Then there will be no stories told of me fooling away my time, things that are no good for fighters. Why, there's no trees out there on that ranch, water is scarce and the roads are dusty."[29]

Ignoring the Albuquerque press' plea to relocate there, Johnson toured Las Vegas and settled in at a modest two-story adobe house in Old Town owned by Francisco Baca[30]—a stark contrast to Flynn's digs at Montezuma Castle. Makeshift bleachers and a crude platform on which to train were hastily erected. With Johnson came trainer Tom Flannigan, sparring partners Marty Cutler and Ray Perkins, the champion's white wife, Etta, and mother, who would see to it that "Johnson's table is supplied with the best of eatables, prepared as only a southern mammy can cook them."[31]

With both principals now in New Mexico, it was full speed ahead for Curley to hype the fight.

On June 1, the champion told local reporters that he expected the hyped-up great white hope to grab and clinch his way through the fight on the Fourth of July. "Mistah Flynn will touch me but twice in our coming battle," Johnson laughed. "The first time will be when he shakes hands at the beginning of the fight, and the other will be when he tries to hold on to keep from being knocked out when I put over the anesthetic punch."[32]

With three weeks already in Las Vegas, Flynn had had more than enough time to warm up to locals by attending local baseball games and coming into town on weekends for dances, where it was written, he was a "regular dream" to the girls and nightmare to the local boys.[33] Though weeks before Flynn had been praised for his fancy threads and glittering diamonds, it was a different story for the black champion, who was causing unease walking about town with his white wife. Johnson did not entice warm words from reporters, who wrote, "He continues to dress up in his dandy togs every time he comes down town. He looks like a Rah! Rah! Kid from some Ethiopian college with his fancy duds and loud hosiery."[34]

Both fighters were threatened on at least one occasion. Johnson received an anonymous note to "Lie down or we'll string you up," signed by the "K.K.K." Flynn's threats were of a comical nature. One morning while doing roadwork, he was chased by security at the New Mexico Hospital for the Insane when they mistook him for a runaway patient. He told the press he was only "crazy" on one subject—his fight with Johnson. "I have it so strongly implanted in my bean that I am going to win," said Flynn. "Jack Johnson will have to give me some tough pounding to beat it out of me. I am just crazy enough or just wise enough to believe that he can't do it and that I will be champion about the fourth of next month."[35]

Public workouts were staged to entice the local fans, and, on June 7, Johnson went to Santa Fe where Levy, in the running to referee the big fight at the demand of New Mexico fans and press, staged a show at the Elks' Theatre before a capacity crowd. Johnson boxed several rounds with sparing partners "who were fine physical specimens but seemed pygmies beside the black champion who punched them about at will," negating the rumors that "Big Smoke" was out of shape for his defense.[36]

Though very well spoken, Johnson's words were often reduced to stereotypical dialect. When asked about fighting Sam Langford, his reply in the local *Optic* was: "Ah's willin' tu fight a man a day frum now tel' Labuh Day. Ah's made up my min' to retiah aftuh Labuh Day an' Ah wants tu have all de fights Ah kain befo' dat time.... Ef dat Langford want to fight me, he and his manager, Joe Woodman, has got to put up de coin. Ah ain't doin' any fightin' dese days widout gettin' paid fo' it."[37]

The *Santa Fe New Mexican*, to its credit, noted the champion's articulate speech and his insinuation "that he is able to handle boxing gloves and words with equal facilities," especially after telling the crowd who showed up to watch him spar that "I wish to show the people of Santa Fe that a boxer can be a gentleman."[38]

When the two fighters met for the first time in Las Vegas, entirely by accident, on June 7, both Johnson and Flynn were perfect gentleman. "It was, 'Howdy, Mr. Flynn,' and 'Hello, Jack,' when their autos meeting on the road, were stopped for a brief conversation."[39]

In the camps, neither one lived up to the cordiality. The hundreds who showed up to pay a dime to watch Johnson train in the afternoons called the champion a clown or a show-man, noting how he'd winked at spectators or sang while sparring. Flynn, on the other hand, was said to be abusing his sparring partners in his efforts to get in shape.

"How can I lose when I'm in such shape?" Flynn told the *Optic*. "If I don't win this fight, I want to die before they carry me out of the arena. What I want is to make Curley have a gun trained on me during the fight and if I am not declared the winner, I want him to touch it off right at my head."[40]

Things were not quite as dramatic in the champ's camp. They were also not what they appeared to be, at least to the casual observer. "There is a great deal of complacency," wrote Ed Smith for the *Chicago Examiner,* with reprints running in the *Optic*. "Indeed this feeling borders to the casual onlooker upon actual carelessness and indifference. The champion himself loafs along through his idle hours and some of the sharps near here are complaining that he is not displaying the snap and ginger he should three weeks in advance of such an important fight."[41]

But beneath the laughing and kidding around, Johnson was putting in real work. "He gets a whole lot out of what he does," noted Smith. "He never makes work look like work.... When one digs deep one sees that Johnson is training as hard for this contest as he ever did for any, and is slowly and surely getting results."[42]

Not that it mattered — outside New Mexico, Flynn's chances were hardly worth spec-ulating. *The New York Times* headlined "Johnson-Flynn Bout Regarded as a Joke," panning it as a failure that would probably implode before its scheduled date due to lack of interest. Real fight fans, knowing Flynn "has not even a ghost of a chance," would "refuse to flock to Las Vegas for such a lemon."[43]

When Flynn's trainer, former champ Tommy Ryan, left Las Vegas halfway through June, his legitimacy took another blow. "Am disgusted with Flynn," he telegraphed the *Morning Journal.* "He is hog fat and has no chance whatever with Johnson. I refuse to have my name used any further in connection with this affair and am leaving camp tonight."[44]

Squelching both the "hog fat" rumor and one about the governor still hoping to use state militia to interfere with the fight, promoter Curley went to Albuquerque where he told the press that he'd been reassured by the other politicians that the fight was untouchable,

Outside the camp of Jim Flynn in Las Vegas, New Mexico, in June 1912. Front row, from left to right: Al Williams, A. M. Balke, Flynn, C. Colman, promoter Jack Curley, Jim's brother Joe, Las Vegas boxing promoter Charles O'Malley. In back: M. M. Padge, H. Elfeld (Library of Congress, Prints & Photographs Division [LC-DIG-ggbain-12201]).

and that Flynn had not only acclimated himself for the fight of his life, on July 4, but that Johnson's two-year "spell of idleness"[45] at his age would prove fatal. In trying to round "himself into fit shape," Johnson was "trying to make up for lost time."[46] Furthermore, Ryan's departure was explained as a conflict of personalities.

When *Los Angeles Times* reporter Bert Smith visited Flynn's camp, he made damning observations that unless the fight was a fix — and he doubted Johnson would hawk his legacy and title — that Flynn was not *only* hog fat, but doomed. Dispelling the myths and rumors that Johnson's "high life and wine dinners" had made the champion a lesser fighter, Smith wrote that the champion "could lick Flynn in five rounds if they were to enter the ring today" and that "Flynn has been unmasked for just who he is — a pretender, who had absolutely no chance to win unless things are fixed."[47]

Countering one Smith was the other Smith — Ed Smith, of Chicago — who'd now been chosen to referee the Johnson-Flynn fight after Jack Welch passed on the assignment for the Ad Wolgast-Joe Rivers lightweight title held on the same day in California. Angering Albuquerque fans who figured their local promoter, Levy, was a sure thing for the job, Smith arrived two weeks ahead of the fight to serve as a sort of press agent for Curley. Right after the *Los Angeles Times* report broke, Smith penned an article for the *Optic*, giving four reasons why Flynn had a chance of scoring the upset: He was bigger and better; hitting straighter;

had the right style to neutralize Johnson; and he was fit to go 100 rounds. "I'm as tough as a wedge from head to heels," Flynn was quoted to say. "I rushed before and was harpooned. You won't notice me rushing this time."[48]

Flynn was not alone in his fight against Johnson. Not only was he backed up by the promoter, who was also his manager, but the United States government had an unfriendly interest in Johnson. It would be another year before the government cooked up charges of Johnson violating the Mann Act, but in 1912, politicians and law enforcers were finding other ways to harass the black champion, who dared flaunt his wealth and white women before White America.

On June 11, a federal grand jury announced it would indict the champion for "smuggling" jewelry into the country. According to the government, Johnson had failed to declare a $3,000 necklace that was "set with diamonds which glitter like a row of electric lights,"[49] upon re-entering the U.S. from a tour in Europe. The unpaid duty and penalties now amounted to $6,000. No, officials would not interrupt Johnson's training for Flynn, but he was forced to pay a $5,000 bond in Las Vegas and would be required to immediately return to Chicago once the fight was over.

The feds weren't the only ones trying to put one over on Johnson — he was up against Curley, as well. On June 22 the champ told the *Optic* that the ring constructed for the July 4 battle would have to be rebuilt if he was to step into it. Regulation called for a 24-foot ring, not the 17½-foot ring it was expected to be when finished, the smaller ring, of course, favoring Flynn. "It looks to me as if they built that thing, or intended to have the ring to suit Flynn's style of boxing, or fighting or whatever you may call it," Johnson told Ed Smith. "From the looks of things you're the only one that gave me a thought in the matter for I wasn't consulted at all.... It won't do."[50]

In the end, Johnson conceded to a 20-foot ring.

Unwilling to risk disgrace, Johnson cancelled an exhibition in Albuquerque on a Levy card. Though Johnson had signed a contract that guaranteed him $600, he pulled out, saying, "I don't want to be humiliated by being refused first class hotel accommodations."[51]

In the meantime, Johnson put up with a house that flooded when it rained, with insufficient training quarters and a pro–Flynn town. Despite Flynn dropping down in weight and beating up sparring partners who had to be replaced, Johnson remained a 2 to 1 favorite not too many were willing to bet on.

Letterhead from fight headquarters in Las Vegas, New Mexico, for the 1912 world heavyweight fight between champion Jack Johnson and challenger Jim Flynn. As noted in the upper right hand corner, Las Vegas became the "Hub of the World," for a time. The event remains the single biggest fight show ever staged in Las Vegas, New Mexico.

Gambling became Gov. McDonald's final sally against the prize fight. Still making waves as the fight neared, the governor promised he would not interfere with the fight — as long as the gambling laws were obeyed.

"It's going to be a clean town, all right," ran the *Optic*. "Not a wheel is turning in the gambling line. Mayor Taupert's order that even the more or less innocent P.O. be squelched have been observed strictly to the letter and the card players are standing about wondering what is to be the next move. But rooms are tightly closed and not even a lonesome game of solitaire is tolerated."[52]

Yet despite the governor's insistence of a clean town, even *The New York Times* reported betting houses where you could get three-to-one rates on the underdog Flynn, a two-to-one payoff on Johnson, or bet on the round of stoppage for Johnson — the 11th being the most favored.

Two days before the fight, Johnson and Flynn tapered down training, doing light road work and gym exercises to keep limber. Referee Smith went over rules with the two camps, stressing mainly that there would be no hitting and holding, and should the police interfere with the contest, the referee would designate a winner.

Las Vegas braced itself for the 17,000 people promoter Curley had promised. Special trains from all points were arranged though Curley warned the town to expect flocks of people, "an army of machines" from the north and south, "a detachment from the cattle country ... on horseback," even a "dog team guided into town by a desert traveler."[53]

The town was ill-prepared for even a fraction of the much-promised 17,000. "Every private house anywhere within hailing distance of the town's center was placarded with signs announcing that beds might be obtained inside. Glimpses through the windows showed lines of cots set up in best parlors and more cots poked into hall corners. From lawns arose impromptu lunch counters and the town generally assumed a fiesta appearance ... 'Where are we going to sleep?' was a question to be heard on all sides."[54]

In hopes of enticing an earlier crowd as well as testing the auditorium, a warm-up show was arranged for the evening of July 3. With Johnson watching at ringside, the 20-round draw between lightweights Stanley Yoakum and Rudolph "Boer" Unholz drew a crowd of 3,000 at 9 P.M., but failed to rev up any excitement.[55]

With an apparent lack of concern for his fight the following day, Johnson "sat in silence," then "drove his training staff back to his camp in his automobile and went straight in bed." Flynn, on the other hand, visited town for the first time in several days, dressed in a "brilliant red sweater which showed to advantage the lines of his huge chest and powerful shoulders. As he marched about the hotel porch his ruddy, sun-burned face and springy step indicating perfect health, he was followed by a mob of fight fans. His stay was short, however, and before dark he was back in his quarters, six miles away, and visitors were discouraged."[56]

The Fight

> From the beginning the Journal was opposed to the fight. First, because forty-five round slugging matches are not elevating spectacles, and usually brings [sic] with them a horde of bad characters, tin horn gamblers, sure thing bettors, sneak thieves and prostitutes. They come into the state and it takes the state a long time to get rid of them. It was a bad advertisement for New Mexico, and it will require a long time for the state to live it down.
>
> — *Albuquerque Morning Journal,* 1912[57]

World Heavyweight Champion Jack Johnson and challenger "Fireman" Jim Flynn meet in the center of the ring for instructions for their July 4, 1912, title fight in Las Vegas, New Mexico (Library of Congress, Prints & Photographs Division [LC-USZ62–28931]).

New Mexico's first world championship fight has been described as a fizzle, fiasco, foul-fest and a financial failure. Instead of 17,000 spectators, Las Vegas received but 4,000. Instead of a fight, the fans saw a flop that had Flynn flailing his head about like a human goat with the hopes of head-butting the champion. And instead of an event that would put Las Vegas back on the map, the town saw little but negative press for its $100,000 investment.

Headlines ran the gamut, from "POLICE STOP BIG FIZZLE AT VEGAS"[58] to "FLYNN PROVES A MISERABLE MATCH FOR JOHNSON"[59] to "FANS UNANIMOUS IN CONDEMNING VEGAS FIASCO."[60]

In the end, the governor got the last word in, and the critics were right on the money in calling Flynn a great white *hype,* rather than a hope.

The turnout might've been disappointing, but for a town that could boast no more than 7,000 residents, there was an air to the town that has probably not been seen since. "The crowds, the Fourth of July bunting here and there and the cries of the newsboys and hucksters lent an air of excitement and anticipation," went the wire report. "But the feeling of uncertainty and eager interest in the outcome which marked the Fourth of July morning at Reno was absent."[61]

On the morning of the fight, Flynn relaxed at the Montezuma while Johnson spent the morning on a drive. "He has let no day pass since his machines arrived here without

During their 1912 title fight, champion Jack Johnson (right) winked, grinned and talked to those ringside — all the while outclassing challenger Jim Flynn (photograph courtesy of O'Malley Family/Annie Leonard).

adding a few miles at least to his automobile experiences," wrote the dailies. "He whirled into town at the end of his ride today and was on hand for some time to the admiring groups on the hotel porches. Clad in light colored clothing the champion looked gigantic as he moved among men of ordinary stature."[62]

It was also noted that Johnson insisted on being paid the full amount owed him — $31,000 — before entering the ring.

Flynn remained optimistic when he made it into town, telling the media: "I am going to be champion of the world about 2 o'clock this afternoon. I have worked for two years to this end and I am sure that I will restore the world's heavyweight championship to the white race. Two years ago today the little old ball of fate dropped into the black hole. This afternoon it is going to drop into the white hole and this is no idle buncombe."[63]

Johnson dispelled the notion that he was a lesser fighter now than when he beat Jeffries two years before in Reno. "All this talk of my two years' rest having slowed me up is nonsense," he said, predicting a victory in "fifteen rounds, no more, perhaps less" for the scheduled 45-round bout — the longest in New Mexico history.[64]

The weather was perfect, clear skies with a light, cool breeze, as fans started filing into the arena two hours before the 2 P.M. start time, while carpenters were still hustling to finish last-minute work, tacking down white canvas over the ring floor and wrapping the corner posts with padding. While several hundred unpaid fans were, reportedly, able to sneak their way in, double canvas walls stood ten feet high to discourage gate crashers. At ten minutes to first bell — still no sign of either fighter — the Las Vegas silver cornet band began to play. Yet, there remained a "complete absence of yelling or signs or other enthusiasm,"[65] even from the 200 Pueblo fans in white rooter hats clumped together to cheer on Flynn.

At 2:04, ring announcer Tommy Cannon of Oklahoma City entered the ring. He saluted the estimated 200 women in the audience, then reminded the fans to mind their manners when shouting comments during the fight. To kill time, an exhibition between youngsters was staged — 58-pound Kenneth Day, of Colorado Springs, going four one-minute rounds with his brother Freddie.

Cannon recognized notables and officials at ringside, which numbered far fewer than those at Reno two years prior: Texas great white hope Cass Tarver, who was there to challenge the winner; referee Ed Smith; timekeeper Otto Floto, of Denver; and representatives from the two principals, Al Tearney of Flynn's camp and Tom Flannigan from Johnson's.

With still no sight of the fighters, Cannon called out challenges that had arrived by wire: an offer for Johnson to fight Joe Jeanette for $20,000 had arrived from New York City; Paris was offering $30,000 for the same fight; white hope Al Palzer had wired to say he'd posted a $5,000 forfeit to fight the winner; yet another white hoper, Luther McCarty, wanted Flynn in New York, win or lose; and Bill McClain, manager for Sam McVey, was introduced, hoping to arrange a battle with the victor.

At 2:27, Johnson made his way to the ring, wearing the same striped bathrobe he wore at Reno when he'd defeated Jeffries. Promoter Curley, Flynn and his seconds, followed.

"He spent much of his time sauntering about the ring, greeting friends"[66] — that is, until he spied Johnson's wife, Etta, sitting at ringside. Flynn approached.

"Ain't you pulling for me, Mrs. Johnson?" he asked but Etta merely smiled, saying nothing. Some reports had Flynn suggesting to Etta that she cheer for someone her own color.

The principals donned their gloves and announcer Cannon announced their weights — 196 pounds for "the fighting fireman of Pueblo" and 219 pounds for Johnson, "champion heavyweight of the world."[67]

The ring was cleared at 2:48 P.M. and referee Smith called the two together for a quick rules meeting. At 2:49, the bell rang. Flynn approached Johnson, his hand outstretched.

"Will you shake hands, Jack?"

"No," was the champion's answer, and the fight was on.

Smiling constantly through the fight, Johnson avoided Flynn's clumsy rushes, peppering him with jabs and rights that not only jolted the challenger early, but opened up a deep gash under the Puebloan's left eye.

"As Flynn rushed, Johnson simply grasped him about the shoulders and held him at bay, all the while grinning like an ape," went the round-by-round report over the wire. Johnson toyed with Flynn, landing uppercuts to the jaw while maintaining conversation. "The champion early indicated it was to be a battle of words as well as blows, time and again exchanging the usual repartee with the spectators."[68]

By the end of the second, Flynn was bleeding from the mouth, as well as from his eye cut sustained in the first. "Flynn spat blood in a stream," when Johnson opened up with a volley in the third. The challenger's only success came by cutting short a "witty remark of Johnson's by twice hooking his right to the jaw."[69]

Flynn continued rushing in the fourth — and Johnson continued catching the challenger coming in. Indulging Flynn, Johnson slapped his stomach, inviting Flynn to take a shot. The challenger drew a rare cheer from the crowd when he was able to land a left to Johnson's jaw, but he ended the round with his face covered with blood.

Johnson stuck his stomach out throughout the fifth, inviting Flynn to punch him. Time again, Flynn would fall into the same trap, rushing in while Johnson peppered him with hard lefts and rights before tying up.

"I can't fight while he's holding me," Flynn complained to the referee while Johnson continued to hold a running conversation with both his wife and cornermen.

The head-butting began in the sixth, as Flynn increased his complaints to the referee. Meanwhile, Johnson continued to bash Flynn's mug.

In the seventh, frustrated by the champ's ability to smother him, Flynn launched his head skyward at Johnson. "Flynn's feet were both off the floor time and again with the energy he put into his bounds," went the round-by-round. "Some times he seemed to leap

Rare photograph of the 1912 world heavyweight title fight between Jack Johnson and Jim Flynn as it was being stopped by Capt. Fred Fornoff of the New Mexico Mounted Police. It was later questioned why Fornoff had stopped the fight in the ninth — the same round as the bet he'd placed earlier in the day (photograph courtesy of O'Malley Family/Annie Leonard).

two feet into the air in frantic plunges at the elusive black jaw above him. Referee Smith forced Flynn back toward his corner half a dozen times."[70]

"Stop that butting," Ref Smith would shake his finger at Flynn. "Stop it or I will disqualify you."

"The nigger's holding me," Flynn would roar back. "He's holding me all the time. He's holding me like this," and he offered to illustrate on the referee. Smith evaded the blood-smeared arms held toward him and waved the men together again. Johnson objected and, when the fight continued, he unleashed a volley on Flynn that staggered the challenger. The seventh ended with the referee warning Flynn to cease his head-butting or risk disqualification.[71]

In the eighth, Flynn tried three more times to butt — and he was warned an equal number of times by the ref, who clearly did not want to stop the fight on a foul. "The round was very much like its predecessors, with Johnson uppercutting and Flynn butting viciously, at the same time losing a world of blood. Flynn was helpless in the champion's hands and for the tenth time in this round was warned, the referee adding, 'Once more and I'll disqualify you.'"[72]

Johnson continued to smile, antagonizing Flynn and calling him a "billy goat." The challenger kept fouling, until Johnson turned to Smith. "Mr. Referee, when are you going to give me this fight on a foul?"[73] he asked, just as Governor McDonald's representative, Captain Fred Fornoff of the New Mexico Mounted Police, jumped into the ring with his deputies to declare that the bout was no longer a boxing contest, but a brutal exhibition.

"We will have no more fighting of this kind,"[74] Fornoff said to Smith.

With the fight "officially" over, referee Smith, "after puzzling over matters a few seconds,"[75] announced Johnson the winner. "There was not a cheer during the fight and the crowd accepted the referee's action with apparent relief. It was the general opinion that Flynn was eager to be disqualified."[76]

"At the time the captain stopped the fight neither man was hurt in the slightest degree," wrote Otto Floto. "That Referee Smith was perfectly able to handle the situation and the butting in of the state's official was either a desire to get into the picture or as inexperience."[77] What Floto mentioned next has been overlooked in Johnson-Flynn reports: "Personally, we think Captain Fornoff a splendid fellow, but it will take more than few lines from his friends to explain to me how it came to pass that all the officials under him had tickets on Johnson to win in the NINTH ROUND. Perhaps it is merely an incident, however."[78]

The *Optic* not only blamed Fornoff and the governor, but Flynn for his poor showing and unsportsmanlike behavior, promoter Curley for false promises, and Albuquerque media for criticizing the fight at the expense of Las Vegas businesses and citizens.

Despite dominating Flynn, Johnson was still condemned in his victory for not knocking out Flynn. The damage to Flynn was obvious, but at least one reporter — well-respected W. W. Naughton who wrote for the Hearst syndication — noted that Johnson was no longer smiling by the time the fight was stopped. "Johnson was a somewhat bedraggled champion," he wrote. "His stamina had been affected by the constant pegging of gloves against his stomach and it was noticed that he no longer maintained the grin which he wore in the preceding rounds."[79]

Immediately after the fight, Johnson, his face unmarked, collected his bets and briefly addressed the crowd at the fight headquarters:

I hardly think I was given proper treatment during the fight. Anyone with half an eye could see I was taking all the fight out of Flynn with my straight lefts and uppercuts and he was not hurting me a bit. I was handling him carefully, just as I did when I fought him before, and just as I did when I boxed Mr. Jeffries at Reno. Flynn is a foul fighter, but he had the sympathy of the crowd as the under dog has when opposed to a champion. I am sure I could have knocked Flynn out in a few more rounds if he had continued to fight fairly instead of acting like a billy goat. However, I have retained the championship and will always be ready to box any man who is considered a suitable opponent.[80]

With that, Johnson left for his camp where he packed up for Chicago.

Facing the fiscal damage and negative press, Las Vegas promoters were optimistic. In fact, one week after Johnson-Flynn, Charles O'Malley was already talking about bringing back Johnson to face Al Palzer, another great white hope.

The *Morning Journal* remained skeptical: "O'Malley says he'd like to get back the money he lost on the Flynn fight ... however, there are many who believe that the possibility of another 'championship' contest being staged in Las Vegas, or New Mexico, is too remote to be seriously considered. In the first place it would hardly draw a corporal's guard in attendance, the recent fistic fiasco ruining whatever chances the merits of the coming bout might have to commend in the sport loving world."[81]

The *El Paso Times* also had something to say: "Las Vegas? Sure, must have heard of it somewhere. Well, that place is 'coming back.' Not one whit daunted by having once howled about the most dismally dreary failure in pugilistic history, they are looking for another fight.... Right here let it be said that this fight, it if is ever held, will be a fight and will so far eclipse the Flynn thing that the painful memory will simply lay down and die."[82]

Fortunately for Las Vegas, Johnson vs. Palzer had little chance of happening.

Johnson's fight in New Mexico would be the last time he'd fight on U.S. soil as a champion. Fighting as blatantly dirty as Flynn was the U.S. government that eventually forced the champion out of the country. In 1913, Johnson was convicted by an all-white jury for violating the Mann Act, an obscure law making it a violation to transport women across state lines for immoral purposes. Skipping bail, Johnson left the country and lived in exile for the next seven years, during which he lost his championship in 1915 to Jess Willard in Havana, Cuba, on what was promoter Curley's last big boxing card. When the penniless, beltless Johnson surrendered to federal agents in 1920, he was taken to the U.S. penitentiary at Fort Leavenworth to serve a year-long sentence.

Nearly 100 years later, there have been several attempts to grant Johnson a posthumous pardon but, to date, none have transpired.

After his final attempt at a world championship, Flynn, $6,000 richer after July 4, fought for another 13 years against rated contenders. In February 1917, he became the only man to knock out future world champion Jack Dempsey, but was stopped early in the rematch. Locally, Flynn would not return to New Mexico, but his name lived on when two local pugs borrowed his moniker over the next two decades.

As for Las Vegas and the sport of boxing? The Meadow City might not have had another world championship since the 1912 Johnson-Flynn fiasco, but the town was certainly not down for the count when it came to boxing.

8. The First Golden Age, 1912–1916

"I love the game, that's why I keep at it. There's no money in it, but I'm always happy when I've got a good fight booked. You never heard of me buying any city blocks with money I made from the fight game, did you?"
—Mark Levy, in *Santa Fe New Mexican*, 1915[1]

The assertion that fistic events have never properly been staged in Albuquerque is raw.
—*Albuquerque Morning Journal*, 1914[2]

The 1912 World's Heavyweight Championship may be the single most significant fight to ever land in New Mexico, but it contributed very little to boosting the local boxing scene once it was over. That was in the hands of several promoters and the fists of local pugilists who emerged from the coal mines, ranches and small towns. In other words, boxing in New Mexico was doing just fine without the Johnson-Flynn fight, thank you. In fact, boxing might have done *better* if the fiasco associated with that fight had not taken place in the 47th state.

But if Johnson-Flynn accomplished anything, it ensured that prizefighting had new laws that not only stamped it as legal, but somewhat regulated it. For the next four years, it was full steam ahead for a sport that would see its first golden age in New Mexico.

In Las Vegas, "King" O'Malley could be credited with snagging the attention of Jack Curley for the world's heavyweight championship, but it was Mark Levy who became the biggest influence of the era. As one of just a handful of boxing promoters over the next century who carried their respective eras with consistent, quality shows, Levy would quickly become known as the "Father of the Fight Game" and, decades later, the "*God*father of the Fight Game."

Levy joined his brother Jake in New Mexico during 1911 to get into the clothing business. Jake, who'd sold his hotel business on Coney Island in New York to come out west in 1900, was also a known sportsmen and gambler who raced thoroughbreds. Over the next two decades, he would become a fixture in Santa Fe rings as a referee. With Jake's help, Mark became established as the president of the local order of The Fraternal Order of Eagles.

As president, part of Levy's job was to provide entertainment for the Eagles' monthly meetings. In addition to musical and acrobatic acts, Levy staged at least half a dozen "debates" or "exhibitions" with local glove artists — all for the purpose of private-membership entertainment. When statehood deemed the masquerades as unnecessary, Levy wasted no time making himself the *de facto* boxing promoter by forming the New Mexico Athletic Club.

During 1912, Levy promoted all 20 shows held in Albuquerque — the highest number of shows ever staged in a single year by a single promoter in state history. During the next few years, Levy would throw more than 50 cards, most of them at the Elks' Opera House, in downtown Albuquerque. The first show there by Levy, on Jan. 26, 1912, brought but 300 people — but, by the end of the year, Levy was able to pack the Elks' Opera House to capacity at 1,200 fans, approximately 10 percent of the city's population at the time.

Levy experimented and Levy borrowed, visiting fight centers on both coasts where he picked up winning formulas. The key, Levy knew, was in developing local talent, producing hometown draws and pitting them against increasingly tougher opposition. Prelims were almost always all-local, and those who started at the four-rounders worked their way up the ladder until they were main eventers. The formula has virtually remained the same for a hundred years.

"Use what you got" became key and, in New Mexico, lightweights were the golden division.

In his debut show at the Elks,' Levy paired up two New Mexicans for state lightweight honors — Luis Gonzales, of Silver City, and Clarence "Soldier" Hunt, an ex-soldier from Fort Wingate. With the win going to Gonzales, the callouts poured in and a virtual round robin that lasted several years was launched. Gonzales was defeated by Gallup's Eddie Gregory, who drew with Hunt before Louie Newman put him on the chopping block. With Levy masterminding Newman's return to New Mexico, the former Las Vegas favorite cleaned up the local scene before Dallas "Ironman" Stanley Yoakum became the man to beat. Adding spice to the lightweight wars were John "Lefty" Floyd, Raton's Ev Winters, Memphis transplant "Congo Kid," Roswell's Johnny Connolly, Santa Fe's Mike Baca and Old Town's Jack Torres, who was soon on his way to the top of the local heap.

During the next few years, anyone attending a Levy-promoted card could also expect to see regulars like Al Smaulding, formerly of Clayton; Leo Luna, who fought under the ring name "Young Herrera" in honor of Mexico's first great boxer, Aurelio Herrera; Lee Brazos, the "Cheyenne Kid"; Belen's Clyde "Kid" Day; Boots Wecker, a.k.a. "Young" Canole; "Barber" Robinson; the Carson brothers, Benny and Jack; "Young" Brito, the "Pride of Barelas"; Tommy "Kid" Gilfeather; "Young" Barney Kurtz; Santiago Montoya, who would be one of two "Young Jim Flynn" boxers to come out of Albuquerque; John "Kid" Anaya, from Trinidad, Colorado; Young Patsy Kline; Espiridion Guevarra, who would be the first of two "Insurrecto Kid" boxers; Manuel "Young" Chavez; and Manuel "Kid" Stern, who would give the city one of its first major crosstown rival matches, against Jack Torres.

Several long-running veterans would get their starts in this era, as well. Silver City-born Timo Sanchez, who would be known as "Dynamite Tommy," would fight in three decades and Santa Fe's Esteban "Demon" Rivera would box until the late '20s. (Fighting longer than all of them, ironically, would be a fighter in the modern era — Johnny Tapia — who would span 23 years, fighting in *four* decades.) Another long-running veteran was youngster Andy Sanchez, who fought twice on Levy's cards in 1912, then moved to the West Coast where, fighting as "Jack Burns," he spent the next 13 years fighting somewhere between 60 and 100 times in four- and six-rounders.[3]

Letting the locals duke it out, Levy watched the cream rise to the top — names like Jack Torres, and Perfecto Romero, who fought under "Young Joe Rivers." Torres grew to be Levy's top box-office draw — outside of Benny Chavez, that is — while Rivers' career would be cut short long before he peaked.

Levy knew just when to up the ante for the local boys. While some locals opted to venture out on their own, most of the time when a fighter peaked locally Levy brought in the bigger guns from the West Coast, Colorado or Texas to test the goods. Yoakum, who would go on to fight several big names, might have been the most popular of visiting fighters, but the list includes Coloradoans Harry Riede, the "Aspen Whirlwind," Pete Jensen, "The Battling Dane," Charlie "The Fighting Newsboy" Pierson and Bob York; "The Salt Lake City Bearcat" Vic Hanson; El Paso battlers Kid Payo, Spider Moffatt and Battling Chico; West Coast top-notchers Harry Atwood, Johnny "Kid" Williams, Tommy Ryan, Walter "Roundhouse Kid" Stanton and Fred "Kid" George; Midwesterners Pierce Matthews, Jeff "The Fighting Ghost" Clarke and Jack "The Kewanee Tiger" Herrick; and East Coasters "Battling" Frank Mantell, Jack Mitchell and Eddie Marino.

Some out-of-towners made their homes in the developing fight town, as Harry (Kid) Schaefer, from Cheyenne, Wyo., did, becoming as local as anyone else. Other times, the big names were a one-hit attempt at a big gate, as was the case with Johnny Dundee in 1913.

Hoping to put Albuquerque on the pugilistic map with a fight that would eclipse the Johnson-Flynn fiasco exactly one year before, Levy arranged for a real world-class match-up that would make the eastern cities forget about the 1912 fizzle. Considered one of the greatest featherweights of all time, Sicilian-born Giuseppe Carrora—Johnny Dundee to the boxing world—fought an amazing 330 professional bouts between 1910 and 1932, winning world titles at feather and junior lightweight. At the time he fought in Albuquerque, on July 4, 1913, the "Scotch Wop" was considered the No. 1 contender to World Featherweight Champion Johnny Kilbane, based on the 20-round draw the two had fought in Vernon, California, earlier in the year.[4]

The man in the opposite corner was no slouch, either. Tommy Dixon, of Kansas City, might not have been a champion—but he fought 'em all. Prior to fighting Dundee, Dixon had fought a 10-round draw with former champ Monte Attell, three draws with champ Kilbane and had gone the distance with everyone from Joe Rivers to Tommy Sullivan.

The fighters arrived the third week of June to promote their Albuquerque showdown with public workouts. The city and press reacted favorably, noting skills never seen before, especially by Dundee. "The cleverness and the quickness of the New Yorker was little short of astonishing,"[5] reporters praised. "Beyond taking a run in the county and eating a few plates of spaghetti," the "little Italian" had no need to do but little labor, but he obliged the local fighters by sparring and showing them "just where to cop an opponent on the jaw."[6]

The timing was important because that same afternoon there would be a Santa Fe to Albuquerque motor car race and the winning driver was expected to cross the finish line five blocks away from the Armory, at Second and Central, shortly after 4 P.M. A loud whistle in the center of town alerted everyone when the first car reached Bernalillo, 18 miles north and roughly 38 minutes away.

It had been several years since the Armory had hosted a boxing event and Levy wanted to re-introduce the sport in grand style. Instead of bringing the old ring used at the Elks', which was ground level, Levy had a new one built—24 feet square and three feet off the floor. Levy also promised that spectators would receive round-by-round bulletins from the world lightweight championship between Joe Rivers and Willie Ritchie in San Francisco that day, in addition to the day's baseball scores.

With Governor McDonald having capped a ten-round limit on prize fights the year before—an unofficial law no one was willing to challenge—Levy made up the difference with locally significant fights. El Paso's Kid Payo fought a draw with Los Angeles top-notcher Kid Williams, while Santa Fe's Mike Baca and Albuquerque's Young Joe Rivers copped wins. In the main, Dundee floored Dixon three times en route to a decision win that impressed the crowd.

Receiving national attention, the fight was supposed to make ring history with a crowd that would fill the 3,000-seat capacity at the Armory, but all Levy got were 900 fans willing to buy tickets ranging from $1 general admission to $5 ringside. "The card certainly deserved a much better patronage," wrote the *Morning Journal*. "Levy took a bath."[7] Foreseeing a profit, Levy had agreed to pay twice as much rent, $50 instead of the usual $25 charged by the Elks'. But two days before the fight, the management upped the price to $250.

Levy didn't give up, at least not right away. Three weeks later, he was back at the Elks' Opera House with an all-local card. While Denver became the premiere fight center for the Southwest, Levy slowly built up Albuquerque — and he found his cash cow in Benny Chavez.

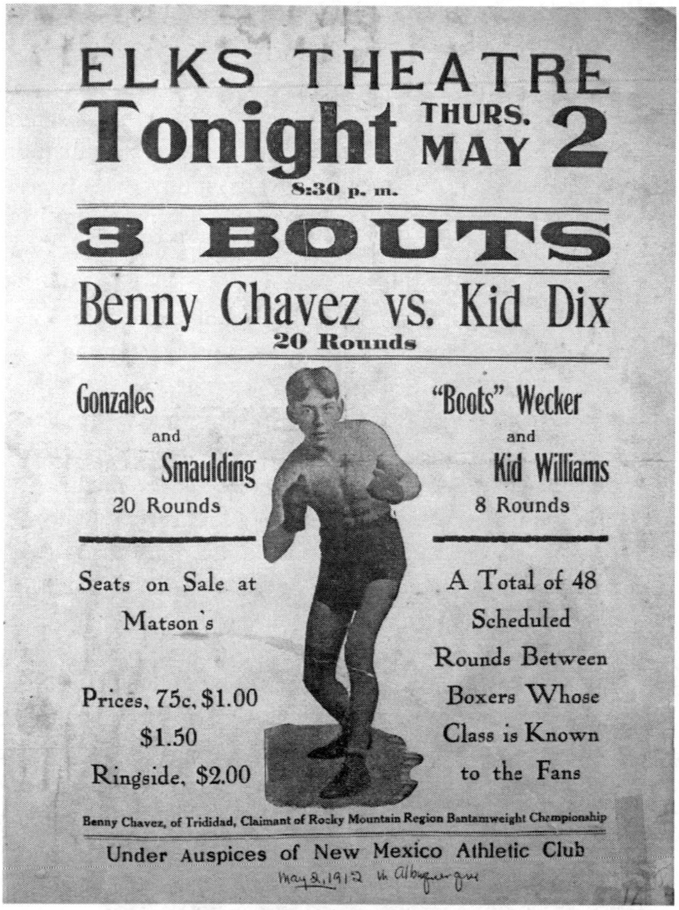

In May 1912, Levy reintroduced the Wagon Mound-born Chavez to Albuquerque.

ELKS THEATRE
Tonight THURS. MAY 2
8:30 p. m.

3 BOUTS
Benny Chavez vs. Kid Dix
20 Rounds

Gonzales
and
Smaulding
20 Rounds

"Boots" Wecker
and
Kid Williams
8 Rounds

Seats on Sale at Matson's

A Total of 48 Scheduled Rounds Between Boxers Whose Class is Known to the Fans

Prices, 75c, $1.00
$1.50
Ringside, $2.00

Benny Chavez, of Trididad, Claimant of Rocky Mountain Region Bantamweight Championship

Under Auspices of New Mexico Athletic Club

Benny Chavez's first fight in a major New Mexican city — Albuquerque — was on May 2, 1912, on a card held at the Elks' Opera House. Though the crowd was disappointing, by the end of the year, Benny was a box-office smash every time he showed up in New Mexico. Against unheralded Kid Dix, of New York, Benny scored a third-round knockout.

Before knocking out late substitute Kid Dix, before a small crowd at the Elks', the "Trinidad Whirlwind" fought just once in his home state, on an obscure card in Clayton in 1911. Already panned as the next great bantam and the Southwestern hope for a contender in Colorado, Levy aimed to do the same thing in New Mexico. One week after his initial bout, Chavez was matched up at the Elks' again, with Harry Riede, a bona fide southwestern name against whom Chavez won a 20-round decision for the Rocky Mountain bantamweight title.

It was Levy's biggest crowd yet — nearly as many people showed up for that as would show up for Dundee-Dixon a year later. While Chavez headlined Las Vegas and several shows in Colorado, he returned under Levy in October for the first capacity crowd at the Elks' — 1,200. Three more sold-out shows in early 1913 followed, at which time Levy lost his box-office draw to other promoters and locales. Levy worked on Torres, whose reputation was now building.

It was ironic that the biggest upset in 1913 would end up on a rival promoter's card — and the switch in allegiance did not win over fans for Chavez in Albuquerque. On Feb. 20, Chavez' soaring rise was stopped short with a shocking knockout loss to West Coast veteran Battling Chico.

Chavez fought one more time for Levy, in January 1914, but the crowd did not compare to his success in the previous two years. By then, Chavez hardly needed New Mexico — he was on his way to a shot at the world championship. Levy had other fighters and rivalries to build, but no one could compare with Chavez's drawing power — and big name fights, as seen with Dundee-Dixon, would eventually bankrupt Levy, who'd lost $1,000 on that fight.

Unsatisfied with the waning support of local fans and having learned the hard way about fighters' loyalty, Levy threw up his hands in December 1914, signing over the New Mexico Athletic Club to Fred Winsor and Charles G. Wilfong.

With 20 years experience in the game, Winsor had arrived in the city as manager of Fred "Kid" George. Wilfong had arrived from Pennsylvania seeking fortune in the New Mexico oil fields and by forming a public utility company. The New Mexico Athletic Club turned into the Cactus Athletic Club and, after several disappointing cards, the crowds declined.

Levy went to Santa Fe, had better luck there with a handful of cards, but what took two years to play out in Albuquerque, took but half a year. By the middle of 1914, Levy left New Mexico for Brooklyn — but it would not be the last New Mexico would hear of him.

After Winsor gave up, Denver promoter Jack Kanner tried his hand during 1916, bringing back Yoakum, who drew 1,000 by fighting Denver's Frankie Murphy during the Cattlemen's Convention, but it proved to be a one-hit wonder. Yoakum's former rival, Louis Newman, tried his hand, as well, during 1916, staging a Memorial Day show with Torres and Benny Cordova, who would make his first hometown appearance after two years of fighting in Mexico and Texas, but just 600 showed up.

Surrounding towns around Albuquerque — Belen, Magdalena and Socorro — contributed to the scene with less than a dozen shows during 1912 to 1916, but the interest was waning and a war was approaching. The fight count in Albuquerque went from 20 in '12 and 22 in '13 to just 13 in '14. Years 1915 and 1916 had just four shows apiece — by then, World War I hammered home the final nail in the boxing coffin.

The Great Fight North

> Las Vegas? Sure, must have heard of it somewhere. Well, that place is "coming back."
> Not one whit daunted by having once howled about the most dismally dreary failure
> in pugilistic history, they are looking for another fight.
> — El Paso Morning Times, 1912[8]

Charles O'Malley was not the kind of man who gave up.

While the world was shaking its head over the Jack Johnson–Jim Flynn fiasco on July 4, 1912, O'Malley waited out the year, then announced that boxing would return to the Meadow City, "having recovered from the black eye it got on the Fourth of last July."[9] Taking a page from the Levy book on boxing, O'Malley formed the Las Vegas Athletic Club, which put on the majority of the 18 shows in Las Vegas during the next four years.

The year before, O'Malley had planted the seeds, not waiting for the outcome of Johnson-Flynn to define local boxing in his hometown. On May 25, 1912, O'Malley secured the services of Benny Chavez to headline a show at the Duncan Opera House, where he knocked out well-respected veteran Kid Williams. The standing-room-only crowd was proof that the town would — and could — support boxing, but O'Malley had to wait for the town's resentment over Johnson-Flynn to subside.

In March 1913, O'Malley brought back Chavez, who destroyed overmatched Oklahoman Kid Hite, before a crowd of approximately 400. "The attendance showed that it will not be difficult to awaken the sleeping boxing enthusiasm in Las Vegas," wrote the *Optic*.[10]

Three straight capacity crowds at the Opera House proved the newspaper right. In May and June, Las Vegas-born Louis Newman returned home for the first time in seven years, winning back-to-back decisions. Claiming the Southwest lightweight championship, Newman was forced to prove it against Dallas slugger Stanley Yoakum, against whom the once-local kid could only get a draw.

Attendances suffered in August, when O'Malley announced he would challenge the governor's unlawful decree on a ten-round limit, with a 20-round main event. When a small crowd showed up to watch Yoakum fight another out-of-towner, the fight was reduced to 10 (it ended by TKO in the seventh) and the prelims were called off. Taking another long break from the game, O'Malley "left the city this morning for the mountains where he will forget all about the fighting game with men and go after a fish, which is a far more profitable vocation."[11]

While O'Malley was "out fishing," local entrepreneurs Vincente Montoya and Nick Cordova tried to fill the gap with all-local shows. When Santa Fe lightweight Mike Baca failed to capture interest in Vegas, they, too, took a break. Meanwhile, yet a third promoter tried his hand by pitting lightweight Jose Sotero "Young" Duran, who was making waves in both Las Vegas and Raton, against Mora's main fighter, Pepe Gallegos. The crowd was an improvement enough for O'Malley to stage a return in February 1914.

With O'Malley alternating shows with Montoya and Cordova, Young Duran became the local draw — and O'Malley capitalized on New Year's Day 1915 by bringing back Chavez to take him on. The fight, at the Las Vegas Armory, was a dud, for not only was Duran brutally outclassed, but the poor heat at the venue discouraged attendance.

Without a local hero to draw a crowd, the scene dwindled with only sporadic success. Yoakum drew a near-capacity crowd at the Opera House in July but better fighters from Santa Fe and Albuquerque kept the Las Vegas pugs from building reputations while out-of-towners failed to attract. The following year was worse. By 1916, former Southwestern hopeful Newman had retired and Chavez had his sights on bigger prey than the city could offer.

Mora and Springer staged several shows, Pepe Gallegos the main attraction. Young Duran managed to draw in Springer. Further north, Cimarron, Ute Park and Taos were one-hit wonders.

In Raton, at the state line, it was a different story. Boxing at the "Gate City" was frequent, once every few months, on average. Not only did Raton have proven lightweight Ev Winters, but it also had Duran, who'd left Las Vegas after 1913 due to an ugly street fight that had fans turning against him.

Certainly one of the busiest fighters of his day, Duran bounced around from Albuquerque to Santa Fe to Las Vegas — wherever he could land a fight. He fought Mike Baca five times (0–5), Albuquerque's Benny Carson four times (1-2-1), and even braved Chavez, lasting seven before the inevitable KO. Duran wasn't the only local who fell to Chavez — Raton's Eddie "Kid" Leech fell before his fists twice, once in Raton, another time in Trinidad, Colorado.

Though Raton promoters traded pugs with Trinidad (like Otis "Kid" Bruce), Winters remained their biggest draw. In October 1912, a sold-out crowd of 600 (in a town of approximately 5,000) at the Aerodome Theatre watched Winters draw with top-notcher Frankie White, of Chicago. The fight was so good, they did it again on Thanksgiving—another draw—and on Feb. 1, 1913, at which time Winters was able to land his sleep-producing haymaker. Despite the loss, White stayed for a time in Raton, headlining several shows.

The biggest fight of the era was the last-known appearance of Raton's best prizefighter, Winters, who took on Stanley Yoakum, on Sept. 30, 1915, at the Rex Theatre. In a clash of throwback sluggers, Winters was pummeled bad enough to retire—permanently—at the onset of round five.

While Raton's Ray Kinney and Elizabethtown's Joe Lowry kept the local scene interesting in 1915, on cards held at Leason Hall under J. W. Eldredge, Raton's interest in boxing faded, though it would resurface in later years.

It was Santa Fe that surprised the most. Because of the obvious anti-prizefight sentiment permeating the *New Mexican*, not many would've given the Capital City much of a chance to cultivate entertainment less high-brow than art and theater. But from 1912 to 1916, several promoters again, with Albuquerque's Levy at the lead, provided the city with a show every few months—every *other* month in 1914.

Unlike Las Vegas, Santa Fe thrived because the *fighters* thrived. While many of those featured in Albuquerque also fought in Santa Fe, it was a lineup of locally-brewed boxers that packed the Elks' Opera House downtown. Santa Fe rode the wave of pre-fight hype prior to Johnson-Flynn, with Levy's Santa Fe Athletic Club producing four cards that were merely extensions of Albuquerque lineups. It took nearly another year for Levy to return and, by then, there were local Santa Feans to use in the prelims.

One local was Mike Baca, the "Pride of Santa Fe," who headlined more fights in the state's capital than any other fighter. On Labor Day 1913, Baca gave his hometown its biggest local card of the era when he defeated Young Duran at the Elks' for state lightweight honors. The two rematched three weeks later, with Baca winning again.

In the curtain raiser of the first Baca-Duran bill, another fighter—Esteban Rivera, who'd soon be known in Santa Fe as "Demon" Rivera—made his debut, either knocking out, or getting knocked out by, his brother.[12] By the end of the year, he, too, would be a regular installment on Santa Fe shows.

With cards promoted by Levy, Baca's manager, William Gregg, and Daniel C. Ortiz, who also managed the local minor league baseball team, crowds of 300 to 500 packed the Elks'. Baca's brother Perfecto and Albuquerque's Jack Torres added to the lineup.

The highlight of the era was the 1916 rematch between Baca and Roswell's Johnny Connolly. The two would fight a total of six times between 1915 and 1920. Four bouts between Demon Rivera and Perfecto Baca also defined the era in Santa Fe.

White Hopes Rise, White Hopes Fall in Clovis

> Dull summer. Not more than six white hopes have been showing up per week.
> — El Paso Morning Times, 1912[13]

> The crowd cried out its disapproval of the match, calling Tarver "baby boxer." They met in the center of the ring, Tarver smiling his ready smile at such a trifle of work ahead. Willie [sic] sprang from the floor, landing a terrific right smash to Tarver's

head, who began to listen to the birdies sing and from which sleep he did not come out of for some time. Willie placed his hat on his head, told the fans he was delayed getting there as he stopped at one of the lunch rooms across the street to order a steak and it would be ready by the time he got this little job over, so he would have to rush on over and partake of his evening meal while the followers of Tarver tried to bring him back to the land of lantern-glow.

— Clovis Evening News Journal, 1913[14]

It's ironic that the town that launched one of the biggest anti-prizefight crusades of 1912 would jump on the boxing bandwagon by preaching the need for great white hopes. Preachers of another sort, hoping to stanch the Johnson-Flynn fight, banded together to form a campaign that caught on like wildfire throughout New Mexico — and all the impetus they needed was to be found in a brutal fight shown before a capacity crowd at the Lyceum Club in Clovis.

Raton's Ev Winters, unable to stay clear of controversy no matter where he was fighting, was matched against Oklahoma's Benny Pappan, whose regional claim to fame was being, reportedly, "the only full-blooded Indian in the ring today."[15] The fight was more of a slaughter, and although there were certainly more brutal mismatches before and after this one, it gave the town's religious leaders what they needed to protest the evils of prizefighting.

"The moral sensibility of Clovis has been shocked and the Christian citizenship humiliated by the recent Winters-Pappan so-called boxing bout," said a spokesman for the newly formed "Ministerial Alliance of Clovis"[16] that would petition Governor McDonald and provide inspiration for other towns to form similar groups of protest.

Other than provide comic relief during the first state legislative session, the protests over prizefighting did little to stem the tide, with both Johnson-Flynn and the feisty fight scene in Clovis. Just three months after the Winters-Pappan match, another attempt was made to continue the scene in Clovis, and it's only worth a mention because it appears to be the first mixed martial arts card in New Mexico history.

The *Clovis News* called it a farce, saying it was "either a frame-up or lacked the proper kind of material to make it popular." Pitting the "Jiu Jitsu science against the American slugging method," Japanese George Kogo quickly put pugilist Frank Piper to sleep with a choke hold. "The Jap immediately arose from his victory; but it was several minutes before the crowd could understand that the bout was over.... Again the Jap proved himself the better man by settling his bills while the white man left on the early train, unceremoniously leaving his debts behind."[17] The unpopular match momentarily stemmed the tide, but boxing was back in full force by the summer.

"Fireman" Jim Flynn's attempt to wrest the world heavyweight championship from Jack Johnson might've been a joke to boxing fans, but White America wasn't about to give up on a search for a great white hope. "While Texas takes no special pride in having given to the world the present holder of the championship title in pugilism," wrote the *Dallas Morning News*, "it will be peculiarly gratifying and singularly appropriate if there should come forth from this state a white man who will wrest the honor from the Ethiopian race and reclaim it for the whites."[18]

In the Southwest, that white man was believed to be 20-year-old, 6'6", 250-pound cowboy Cass Tarver, from little known Anson, Texas. Prior to 1912, Tarver had been built up by fighting no-namers in his backyard. One month after Flynn failed against Johnson, Tarver signed to fight for the first time out of his Texas — in Clovis, on August 29, 1912. Justified in picking unknown Dallas pug Frank Beverly as his opponent, it was explained that the "Anson Giant's" aim was to "achieve national recognition by mopping up all the second raters,"[19] before taking on the big boys.

Despite the match, the hype surrounding the fight throughout New Mexico and Texas made it the biggest fight to ever land in the area. Arriving a week before the fight, Tarver staged the usual public workouts. A special arena was built on South Main Street by promoter E. M. Deam and his Coyote Club to accommodate the crowd of 1,000 that would show up in the town of Clovis, population 3,500, at the time.

The arena might not have held up—two tiers of seats gave way, injuring "masses of humanity with timbers,"[20] though just one was seriously injured—but the fight itself did not disappoint. Beverly was game, but outgunned by Tarver. After being bloodied in the sixth, staggered in the seventh and floored in the eighth, Beverly's corner threw in the sponge before the ninth bell could clang.

"Lookout Jack, he is after your scalp now,"[21] wrote the *Tucumcari News*. Another Tarver bout was immediately arranged for September. Skirting the color line, Tarver's management announced that he was now ready to fight any great white hope in the Southwest. "Denver" Jack Geyer was chosen, at first, but the trial horse who'd fought much better fighters was swapped for a safer bet in Chicago veteran John Wille, who was calling himself the "Destroyer of White Hopes." Really a blown-up middle or light-heavyweight, the 5'8" Wille had fought an estimated 50 times since 1900, against top-notchers like Sam Langford, Philadelphia Jack O'Brien, Jack Root, Marvin Hart and Jack Blackburn. Wille's best win was a 15-round decision over Young Peter Jackson, the year before.

Wille won over the town of nearby Portales, where he trained, while Tarver became the darling of Clovis. Through Wille, Tarver was supposed to reach the next level—but the only level achieved was a horizontal one when Wille shocked the 2,000 people in attendance with a first-round knockout of the "Anson Giant." A defeat was bad enough for the formerly undefeated, great white hype, but Tarver toppled to the canvas three times before the knockout blow—a right to the point of the chin—with the embarrassing time of 1:30.

"Oh well, it won't happen this way always,"[22] Tarver told the reporter of the *Clovis Journal*. He was half-right, for, in Shreveport, Louisiana, two months later, Tarver had fellow white hope Carl Morris on the brink of a knockout when a blow to the groin had the ref awarding the win to Morris. For Clovis, Tarver was out. Morris was not.

By the summer of 1913, boxing promotions in Clovis had been turned over to the Clovis Athletic Club, with F. H. Herbert and J. B. Meacham at the helm. Seeing the success their predecessor had with great white hopes, Morris was booked for mid–July.

Morris arrived a month early to win over the locals, while opponents for the "Sapulpa Giant" bounced around second-rate white hopes until Marty Cutler, of Chicago, was signed the first week of July. To maximize attendance, promoters arranged for "Ladies Day," two days before the fight, "free and to afford the gentler sex an opportunity to see the gladiators work"; gave away free postcards, courtesy of the Clovis Athletic Club, showing Morris "in fighting pose" to send to anyone aspiring to come see the July 16 bout; installed telegraphs, at which an operator would send bulletins between rounds from ringside "for the whole world to watch the big fight as it happened"; offered "special" tickets priced at $1 general, $2 reserved and $4 ringside; and offered reduced rates on the Santa Fe railroad, from all points east and west.[23]

A huge crowd, well beyond the 2,000 that saw Tarver KO'd by Wille in 1912, was expected, and indicated by the 40 out-of-town automobiles counted the year before, compared to the 200 in town for Morris. In an effort to increase that number, an auto parade

10 ROUND BOXING CONTEST

At Clovis, N. M., July 16

CARL MORRIS vs. MARTY CUTLER

of Sapulpa, Oklahoma.   of Chicago, Illinois.

Second Largest Boxing Contest Ever Staged in New Mexico

1000 CHOICE SEATS AT $1.00

Staged in Big Open Air Arena. **Fast Preliminaries---12 Rounds.**
Opening Preliminary at 8:45 Sharp.

Carl Morris needs no advertising. This big fellow is known from coast to coast--- a clean fighter--- a gentleman and destined to be champion of the world in 18 months. This may be your last chance to see the Sapulpa Giant in this part of the country.

Reduced Railroad Rates over Santa Fe from Albuquerque and intermediate points; Pecos and intermediate points; Canadian to Clovis and all intermediate points.

Prices are within reach of all. Get your tickets as there will be no free list.

Marty Cutler is the man who was chief trainer to Jack Johnson for several years. A recognized heavywight the world over. He has fought with Johnson all over the U. S. A., Australia and France. He tips the scales at around 230 pounds. When he clashes with Morris, fight fans will witness the best matched bout between heavyweights ever staged in New Mexico.

If you want the game to thrive, help us make this match a success.

Write, telephone or telegraph for reservations. Address Secretary Clovis Athletic Club.

ADMISSION
$1.00,   Reserved $2.00,   Ringside $4.00

AUSPICES
The Clovis Athletic Club

The July 16, 1913, heavyweight fight between white hopes Carl Morris and Marty Cutler helped to put Clovis, New Mexico, on the pugilistic map. Nearly 2,000 fight-fans showed up to watch Morris batter down Cutler in less than two rounds.

was announced the day before the bout. Though falling short of the expected 4,000, the fight not only matched the attendance of 2,000 of Tarver-Wille, but very nearly its duration. No match for Morris, Cutler was punished through the opening round, nearly done in with an "early stomach blow that put him on the rocks," and went down at the beginning of the second, with a broken nose and bleeding mouth.[24]

Promoter Meacham apologized for the short duration and, crying over a financial loss, promised Clovis that he would see to it that local fighters and those in lighter divisions would be headlined from here on out.

The Clovis Athletic Club made good on their word. One month later, 1,500 fans attended the open-air arena on Main St. to watch Chicago lightweight Earl Sweeney take on John "Kid" Anaya, a New Mexico favorite, with several local fighters stacking the undercard. Clovis regulars, however, lacked the skill level — or opportunity — to take their craft past the club level. Fighters like Dave "Babe" Garner, "Battling" Wilbur Roberts, Peck McGovern, Othei Beck and Omaha transplant Sam "Red" Billingsley had to be content fighting each other, or fighters from Portales, Roswell and West Texas.

Mose Crutch, who wrote an article about Clovis in the '10s, summed it all up by calling Babe Garner "Ol' Reliable": "Whenever a new fighter came to town the scouts would drag Babe out from under some building where he was at work and told him there was a newcomer posing as a fighter. Without training, and fighting in his underwear, Babe blasted the hopes of any number of highly touted fighters."[25]

While Garner and the irregular regulars had let their leather gloves dry out on the back porch, the scene in Clovis died down — but it would re-emerge in full force in the late '20s and '30s as a major fight center in New Mexico.

The Carbon City

> The past few matches have been of such character that considerable interest was being displayed as the matches had been hard ones with no taint of crooked work, but the affair of Tuesday night has put an end for the time being into boxing contests in Gallup.
> — Gallup Herald, 1916[26]

The story of boxing in Gallup is, in part, the story of Peter Kitchen, who located to McKinley County in 1887 after eight years of bouncing around the West. The liquor business in nearby Gibson prompted a move to Gallup where, in 1895, he established Kitchen's Opera House, the state's longest running boxing venue. Though Gallup would not reach its full potential until the 1930s, the stage at Kitchen's set the stage with a flare-up of both fighters and shows from 1912 to 1916. Averaging one show every three to four months, the Opera House solidified itself as the place go to for club fights due west.

After having the unforgettable distinction of throwing the first legal show, between forgettable heavyweights Frank Pantalone and Emmett Kadletz, on Jan. 6, 1912, Gallup improved on quality by staging a 20-round lightweight match between Gibson's William Barday and former soldier Clarence Hunt, with the winner to face top local pug Eddie Gregory the following month.

Gregory was the big name of the day. After the Gallup lightweight scored an upset win over Luis Gonzales for state honors, then drew with respected Denver veteran Harry Riede, on Levy cards in Albuquerque, he became the biggest draw west of the Duke City. Louis Newman's punishing win over Gregory tarnished his reputation, but he continued to headline Gallup shows in his hometown until, by 1916, he was helping Kitchen promote.

Gregory was replaced by Walter "Kid" Oliver, who became Gallup's star in 1913, defeating everyone but Albuquerque's Jack Torres. There was also Barday, of Gibson; bantam "Kid" Willard, who cleaned up until he was up against a veteran; Pete and Joe Corretto, whose rivalry at lightweight with "Young" Fidel Silva, of Gibson, headlined at least two shows; and a youngster named Jack Myrick, who debuted in 1916 and would return after World War I to carve out a local reputation.

As other towns did, Gallup attracted its share of road warriors. San Francisco veteran Tommy Ryan fought in at least two shows in 1912; Denver's Rube Smith was a guest in 1913; and Jack Boyd, of Spokane, fought at least four times in the Carbon City.

The scene came to a screeching halt on Decoration Day, May 30, 1916, however, when a crowd of 300 at Kitchen's showed up to watch white middleweight Happy (Tug) Wilson and black San Francisco veteran John Thomas fight what they thought would be ten rounds of action. Instead, it ended with a near riot and several arrests after the fighters were accused of staging a frame-up.

While Wilson "demonstrated that he knew absolutely nothing about the fighting game," the veteran Thomas "had a hard time keeping far enough away from him so that he could not hit him." The stalling continued in the second, until "Wilson claimed foul before he was even hit, and then it appeared that according to agreement, the smoke fouled and the decision was given to the white faced man."[27] Pandemonium broke loose, "with cat calls, hisses and cries of fake and frame-up."[28]

After the two fighters had divided the spoils at the gate, an angry mob of 200 formed. They found Thomas, "placed a rope around his neck and led him to the town limits and told him to beat it west. He went a short distance and returned, and is now in the city jail charged with being a party to a fake fight."[29] Wilson and promoter Haley Shobe were also arrested and fined $15 in lieu of a 30-day jail sentence for fixing a fight. After evidence had been collected and witnesses came forth, all three were driven out of town. "The result of the disgraceful affair has been such that the boxing game will be dead in Gallup for some time,"[30] read the story in the *Herald*.

It took nearly four years for boxing's return to Gallup.

Mining for Mettle

> *Boxing bouts are the regular thing in every small mining town of New Mexico. They are taking well. The class of fighters going on before the miners is far below that which would be called into action should a club be organized in larger cities.*
> *— El Paso Morning Times, 1916*[31]

The mining boom that started in the 1880s continued well into the second decade of the Twentieth Century, with miners from all over the country flocking to the Southwestern mountains to dig up silver, copper, lead, iron and other precious metals. Boomtowns sprang up around the mines and near the area's leading metropolitan area, Silver City, named after its richest resource. Wherever you found mines, you found brothels, gambling halls, saloons and an overabundance of testosterone-rich miners willing to fight, or watch one. Aided by Central, Fort Bayard, Gibson, Hanover, Hurley, Lordsburg, Mogollon, Pinos Altos and Santa Rita, Silver City was the first to hit the mother lode in the boxing ring.

After a slow start, Silver City averaged at least one show every month in 1913 and 1914, with half again that number occurring in surrounding towns like Mogollon or Santa Rita. By 1915, Silver City was leading the state in fight action and though it slowed somewhat the following year, as trouble on the border distracted available fighters to military camps, activity in the mining towns remained steady during times of war, unlike the rest of the state.

Things were quiet until a grappler from Red Wing, Minn., found himself in the area trying to make a buck. Theodore "Foxy" Miller had toured the rest of the country as a matt artist, but when he got to Silver City, he saw gold, not silver. By 1913, Miller was staging shows, headlining himself in an occasional wrestling bout, with any miners from the camps who had the inclination to climb into the ring after a day's work below ground.

For two years, Foxy Miller built up a scene that remained strong until the '20s. His first show, at the Elks' Opera House, might have only attracted a fair crowd, but by the end of the year, it wasn't uncommon to see a capacity house of 400 shell out 50 cents for a ducat, with women always free when escorted.

The mines produced homegrown scrappers like Gus Flores, Luis Gonzales, his brother Benny, Frank Romero, Jess "The Pinos Altos Cowboy" Light, Lordsburg's "Speedy" Moreno and Santa Rita's Jack Lopez. For the "Defenders of the Faith for the Colored Population of Silver City,"[32] there was "The Rabbit," "Big Smoke" and "Blackie." Blackie mopped the floors and cut hair at the Cottage, a sanatorium for patients with tuberculosis. "Big Smoke" was better known as "Young Jack Johnson," who was really James Green, a soldier stationed at Camp Furlong who would fight some of the biggest names in middleweight around the country after his time in New Mexico.

Silver City also inherited in-state scrappers like Young Willard, originally of Gallup; Albuquerque's Al Smaulding and Harry "Kid" Schaefer; and respected veterans of the fight game like Fred "Kid" George, who was the biggest draw, Bob York, Jack Herrick, Jeff Clarke, "Mexican" Pete Everett and Kid Payo. Due to its proximity to the many army camps, veterans of a different nature found a home in the Silver City ring. Pitting army fighters with miners would become a regular billing in the mining towns.

Unlike attempts in the more "civilized" cities, there was little attempt to pretend the scene was about clean, fancy moves in the ring. If the Wild West still existed anywhere in the state in the first half of the '10s, it was in the mining towns. There was nothing urbane in the following 1915 story:

> Kid George, a light heavyweight prize fighter who is training at Central for a bout with Harry Wallace, a negro pugilist, on June 5, killed a cow with a powerful right arm and fist, on a wager with backers of the negro. The wager was made at the White House bar at Central, and the cow was supplied by James Wiley, of that place. George caught the cow behind the left ear with a straight blow from the shoulder, and the animal dropped as if struck by a sledge hammer. It is reported that since the exhibition, which was witnessed by a large crowd, Wallace's appetite and enthusiasm have been affected.[33]

Foxy Miller carved out a lucrative niche, but what he wanted was to be rich, and he added Deming to his territory. After several years, however, he tired of the game and moved to Arizona to be a pillow-top salesman. By 1916, word in Silver City had it that ol' Foxy *had* gotten rich, by inheriting $150,000 from a rich German uncle, with the only stipulation that he had to be married by Jan. 1, 1917. Miller advertised for a wife and obviously found one, because by 1917 his wife was filing for divorce on the grounds that her husband was a German spy who was, reportedly, imprisoned at Fort Leavenworth for treason. When Miller returned to Silver City later that year, he disputed the story, offering up his presence as proof.

By the time Miller came back to Silver City, the torch of fight promotions had passed. Roswell promoter Fred Sloan had tried his hand, as had Deming's Jack O'Leary, but it wasn't until mining moguls William McKinney and Michigan native Otto Forster teamed up that the scene found steady ringleaders. By 1916, Forster, working solo now, had solidified a formula for Silver City that mirrored Mark Levy's plan for Duke City aspirants.

The first two stars in Silver City had been Luis Gonzales and Gus Flores. After Gonzales' knockout of Soldier Hunt, on Levy's 1912 opener in Albuquerque, the Silver City miner billed as New Mexico's "Native Son" was thought to be the real thing. But back-to-back losses had Gonzales back home and in the mines. Gonzales claimed a broken hand was the reason he'd lost one bout, but nothing could explain his disastrous loss to Al Smaulding. "Gonzales apparently was afraid of his adversary and whenever he received a wallop or two he would go down on his hands and knees and try to quit,"[34] had been the *Albuquerque Journal's* report.

Though called out repeatedly by the state's other lightweights, Gonzales disappeared for the duration of 1912, but resurfaced in the Silver City ring in July 1913, knocking out veteran Bart Gordon. A return match on home turf against Smaulding was next, but instead of proving that the first loss had been a fluke, Gonzales was battered down again and forced to quit in round four.

In September 1913, taking the fight on short notice, Gonzales "retained some of his lost honor,"[35] by knocking out longtime veteran Bob York—but the rematch evened the score. After losing three of his next four bouts, knockouts at the hands of Jack Herrick, Kid Ross and Kid Patrick, Gonzales got the hint and retired.

Another Silver City pug's time was just beginning when Gonzales was winding down. By day, Rafael—"Gus" to those around him—Flores worked as a drugstore clerk at Howell's in Silver City. By night, the aspiring featherweight worked his way up the ranks. Though he never ventured out of southern New Mexico, Flores fought often, especially in 1913 and 1914.

Flores brought an entirely new meaning to the phrase "box office *draw*," for 11 of his known 18 bouts ended in a draw. Flores drew twice with El Paso's Gene Payo, four times with battle-tested "Spider" Moffatt, once with Jack Lopez, and another time with army fighter Larry Strouer.

In 1914, Albuquerque fight manager Louis Benjamin, who piloted Smaulding's career during his peak time, sought to bring Flores to the next level, but the Silver City kid did not want to leave his locale and family. After two fights in 1915, Flores retired, only to resurface briefly in 1919.

Having drawn with Flores in 1915, Santa Rita miner Jack Lopez established himself as a comer in the mining towns. During the next two years, Lopez would carve out a local reputation by becoming the man to beat at lightweight, losing only to Washington veteran Freddie Anderson. Lopez' time would come later in the decade.

Yet another Silver City fighter was just starting to fight when Flores was finishing up in 1915. Only 14 years old at the time, "Young Sanchez"—who would be known from New Mexico to the West Coast in later years as "Dynamite Tommy"—made his debut on a card headlined by Smaulding and Herrick at the Elks' Theater. Over the next several years, Sanchez would become a regular prelim fighter and it wouldn't be until moving to Albuquerque, after World War I, that he'd start to attract a following.

Though Silver City and its surrounding mining camps and towns failed to produce a world beater, between Forster and Miller, several significant fights landed in the area. The April 2, 1915, fight between middleweight veterans Kid George and Jack Kelly might've had the largest crowd in the era, at 800, but it was the March 21, 1914, billing of El Paso's Kid Lee and Battling Mantell, a Brooklyn soldier with the 13th Cavalry, for the Southwestern lightweight championship, that remains on record as the first time three ringside judges were used to score a fight in New Mexico. Typically, the decision rested in the hands of a single referee.

Despite stormy weather, nearly 700 people showed up at the Elks' on Sept. 4, 1916, to watch Albuquerque's Benny Cordova knock out former contender Bud Anderson in round 19 of a 20-rounder. As a work-around to the state's unofficial ten-round limit, Cordova and Anderson were signed to go ten rounds twice for a guaranteed purse of $1,000—the largest payday to date for Silver City.

As Pancho Villa stirred up trouble on the border and America started to brace for inevitable participation in a world war, boxing died down nearly everywhere but army camps and Silver City. For boxing, miners were only beginning.

Pugs of the Pecos Valley

> O. P. Wilson, manager for Higgins, is so sure that this boy is the man to step in Herrick's place in the championship line that he says he will mortgage his hotel in Roswell if necessary to get change to place on his boy. He said last night that he and his Roswell friends have a great advantage over the usual run of men in the fight game, as the Pecos valley has thousands of cattle that need tending and all kinds of hay to cut and Roswell hardware stores have a corner on pitch forks so there is plenty to do at home in the event they have misjudged their man.
>
> — El Paso Morning Times, 1916[36]

There were no shortcuts for Roswell to get into the fight game, but an attempt was made in April 1912 when local entrepreneurs made an attempt to steal the Johnson-Flynn fight from Las Vegas. Representing local businessmen of the Pecos Valley, Otto Baumer telegraphed promoter Jack Curley, offering up Hayne's Park in Roswell or the NMMI's grounds as sites that could hold as many as 20,000 spectators. His deal already made with O'Malley, however, Curley passed. Baumer got off easy. Roswell, however, did not.

Jumping on the boxing bandwagon whether they had a world's championship fight or not, Roswell might've been lucky to have produced the likes of Alfred Higgins and Johnny Connolly, but they had to suffer through the bumps and take their lumps during their first big era of boxing. Though able to produce a show nearly every two months from 1912 to 1914, before losing their key fighters to retirement and the army, the town suffered through several promoters, venues and controversies.

What kept the scene in Roswell together was, in the end, a single fighter, who went by the name "Pride of the Pecos Valley." Ironically, what unraveled the scene was another fighter, this one the "Duke of the Pecos."

Without waiting for Curley's rejection wire, Roswell moved ahead on its own when a couple of local businessmen formed the Empire Athletic Club, staging two shows in the back end of Gross Brothers' Billiard Parlors, which had an maximum occupancy of 250. When nearly 300 crammed into the parlor on Decoration Day 1912, manager Joseph Castledine ("Kid Herrin" in his fighting days, back in Kansas City) knew he was on to something — and some*one*, when local kid Johnny Connolly nearly knocked out crosstown rival Fitz Cravens.

When Castledine tried to duplicate his success on June 8, he was outstaged by the newly-formed Roswell Athletic Club, which used the spacious Armory, with its capacity of 1,400, to hold a show not four days later. Unlike the Empire Athletic Club, this new version earned the support of the local paper by stating there would be no decisions, that betting was discouraged and that the bouts were purely of an athletic nature.

The 500 people who showed up to watch Alf Higgins headline a show of amateurs in three-rounders from the NMMI could only be improved upon by lengthier battles — and that's what O. P. Wilson and V. R. Marichel (who doubled as a fighter when needed) went after in August. A crowd of 1,000 packed the Armory to watch Higgins fight his first ten-rounder.

After three years of fighting, most of the time while enrolled at the NMMI, the "Duke of the Pecos" was on a mission to prove he was the real thing. Denver veteran Jimmy McDon-

Roswell middleweight Alfred Higgins, a.k.a. the "Duke of the Pecos," fought from 1910 to 1915, winning all his hometown fights. But when he stepped up to stiffer competition, he could not make the grade.

ald was a real test for someone who'd only been up against local boys, and Higgins might have been the aggressor, throwing twice as many punches, but a draw was all he could pull off. The successful card paved the way for another Higgins-headlined show in October. This time, Higgins, up against another veteran, Pete Shaugnessy, of Fort Worth, copped the referee's decision.

Calling himself the Southwestern champ, Higgins issued challenges to the top middleweights of the area — which included well-known veterans Herrick, Mitchell and Patrick — to fight in Juarez, El Paso or Roswell. Herrick, the man to beat, licked his chops and quickly accepted the challenge against the unproven Roswell kid. A Fourth of July fight with Herrick was arranged for the Bullring in Juarez, but after a wrist injury, Higgins backed out, then almost immediately announced he was fighting Salt Lake City's Charlie Pierson in Clovis, a fight that appears to have never happened. By the end of July, a return to Roswell was announced for Higgins. The opponent was unheralded Frank Tuggles, a black fighter from Dallas, who went down in six, as expected.

Putting off Herrick, Higgins was headlined for the Armory on Labor Day 1913. This time, the opponent, his toughest to date, would be New Orleans' Johnny "Kid" Patrick. If all went well, Higgins would take a stab at Herrick. The Patrick fight might have ended with a knockout win for Higgins, but the knockout blow that carried more impact was the one received by Roswell. In fact, the fight may be one of the most controversial matches in New Mexico's history.

There were *two* knockout punches, reported the *Roswell Daily Record*: "Patrick scored the first knockout in the opening round, when he put Higgins to sleep with a terrific jab to the jaw. It was about the middle of the round. Higgins scored his knockout in the fourth round, or rather the third round of the second battle."[37]

What happened in between the two knockouts enraged fight fans from around the state. Before Higgins could be counted out by referee J. W. Stockard, a riot in the ring ensued, when Tuggles, Higgins' former opponent, now his sparring partner, leapt into the ring with a bucket of water and a sponge to bring the local favorite back to the land of the living. Patrick, of course, immediately protested, which prompted Tuggles to drop his gear

The September 28, 1913, Southwest Middleweight Championship fight between well-known Jack Herrick, "The Fighting Tiger" of Kewanee, Ill., and Roswell's Al Higgins was staged in Juarez, Mexico. It was supposed to be Higgins' coming-out party, but the youngster was schooled by longtime veteran Herrick, who knocked out the "Duke of the Pecos" in four rounds.

and take a swing at the New Orleans fighter. While Tuggles was fighting bare-knuckled against Patrick, who still had his gloves on, somebody turned off the lights at the Armory.

Minutes or seconds later (depending on the accounts), when the lights came back on, Higgins was standing in his corner ready to fight again while Patrick and Tuggles were on the canvas, wrestling and throwing punches at each other. One fight was stopped and the other — the main event, that is — was called to begin anew.

With Higgins recovered and Patrick in a weakened state from his tussle with Tuggles, the fight resumed. Again, Higgins was floored by Patrick — this time, however, he recovered and came back in the second round to turn the fight around over an exasperated Patrick. In the fourth, Higgins was able to knock out his opponent.

"The incident in question has done more to hurt the boxing game in the state than anything that has yet occurred — not excepting the Flynn-Johnson fiasco at Las Vegas a year ago — is generally admitted,"[38] wrote the *New Mexican*.

Higgins threw up his hands, saying the first knockdown had occurred so close to the end of the round that it had been his intention to stay down until hearing the clang of the bell. He took no responsibility for Tuggles' action. Patrick, on the other hand, was enraged at the hometown robbery, further stating that he'd been fouled by Tuggles when the lights went off and, possibly, hit with a blackjack.

Rather than back out and let things simmer down in Roswell, local promoters Wilson and Marichal sought to capitalize on the drama, immediately billing Tuggles and Patrick to settle their differences in the ring, on Sept. 19, 1913. The fight did not gain any more fans.

"The boxing game in Roswell was given another blow to the solar plexus," wrote the *Daily Record*'s reporter after watching a ten-round fiasco that ended in a draw. More of a wrestling, or hugging, match, the two men avoided contact: "In three rounds not a blow was struck and some of the fans in the audience go so far as to say that the fighters never got their gloves together in those rounds."[39]

"I wish I owned a newspaper," is the way one of the county officials expressed himself this morning. "I'd surely write up this fight game in this city and I'd tell you about some of the rottenness."[40]

Goes without saying, Tuggles was finished in Roswell — but so was Higgins.

Forced to hit the road and hoping to return to his hometown as a coming champ could only be done by beating the top middleweight in the region. And in 1913 that was the "Kewanee Tiger," Jack Herrick, who was headlining shows at the border, the mining towns, and Albuquerque.

Tuggles in tow, Higgins arrived in El Paso two weeks before his Sept. 28 20-round date with the Kewanee Tiger in the Juarez Bullring, billed as the middleweight championship of the Southwest. The "Cowboy fighter" piqued local interest, but to the hard-to-please border fans, hundreds of which showed up to watch him train, "the lad is a puzzle.... He leaves everything to his manager and contents himself with sticking to his work and wandering around the town when not in his room."[41]

"Herrick will have to be made of iron if I do not lay him out for the count,"[42] Higgins told the *El Paso Times*. Most locals got a good laugh out of that one, the prediction prompting very few to lay a bet on the Roswell kid. In the end, Higgins did gain a bit of respect. Boxing scribe Jack Brace ruled him "game enough but doesn't suit the fight game" and "so far out of his class" against a man like Herrick.[43] Before the biggest crowd of his career, Higgins fell before Herrick in four, being staggered in the first, dominated through the second and third, and floored in the fourth. The ref stopped the one-sided fight at 1:05.

Higgins disappeared from both the game and Roswell, moving to Santa Fe where he became a guard at the penitentiary. A year after losing to Herrick, Higgins resurfaced in the Albuquerque ring in October 1914, to fight a ten-round draw with respected veteran Bob York. After another long layoff, he showed up closer to his old hometown, in Lovington, where he ended his career with a win by decisioning Bart Gordon.

By then, Roswell had forgotten Higgins — they were now on the Connolly bandwagon.

Though Roswell had a few other locals who were regulars in the ring — Fitz Cravens, Alf's brother Babe, and Ray Carper — no other fighter would ever become as popular as the "Pride of the Pecos Valley," Johnny Connolly. By the time Higgins was ruled out, Connolly was headlining his hometown, after years of fighting prelims around the state, from Capitan to Carrizozo to Clovis. In October 1913, Connolly knocked out Red Billingsley before his biggest hometown crowd yet.

Though Connolly was recognized as the man to beat for state featherweight honors, Fred Sloan, who'd taken over promoting at the Armory in Roswell, preferred the bigger men like Joe Herrick (brother to Jack), York and Gordon, but, in June 1914, he teased the locals who were clamoring for the hometowner by pitting 200-fight veteran Spider Moffatt with Jack Horan, of New York, the winner to fight Connolly. After Moffat won, Connolly was next, on July 3, 1914, and the two fought for Southwest featherweight honors.

Connolly was given a pat on his back for his draw with a veteran like Moffatt. Inching north in weight, Connolly defeated Oklahoma lightweight Tip Gross next. By 1915, just as Roswell was winding down its fight action, Connolly was matched up with the man who would define his career — Santa Fe's Mike Baca. Their series of fights would define both men's careers while providing New Mexico with seven bouts over eight years. Both Connolly and Baca put their careers on the shelf and headed for the enlistment office as war approached.

Soldiers in the South

> *Deming will be represented in the contest by the well known scrapper Charles Schei-digger, who in other words says: "Leave it to me, boys."*
> — *Deming Herald, 1914*[44]

> *Physical art is gripping the great heart of Columbus sports, recent attendances at the big mills having proved that its hold is gradually approaching the strangling stage.*
> — *El Paso Morning Times, 1916*[45]

If you wanted the best action in the Southwest, the border was the place to be. Outdoing Albuquerque as a fight center, El Paso and Juarez, collectively, boasted a higher caliber of fighter and bigger crowds. Fifty miles north of El Paso, in Las Cruces, the fight scene struggled — but in Deming and Columbus, the scene was also beginning to thrive.

Borrowing El Paso fighters Kid Payo, Kid Steele, Frankie Fowser and Kid Lee, the Moose Club of Las Cruces staged several shows in the summer of 1912, then made an attempt at a world-class attraction in February 1913 when they pitted former world bantamweight champion Frankie Conley against Earl Puryear of New Orleans, now fighting out of El Paso, in a ten-rounder benefit for the local baseball club.

The former champ had not only been secured as (a very brief) director of the El Paso Athletic Club, but was considering a local matchup against rising star Benny Chavez. As of

36—ROUNDS of BOXING—36
LORDSBURG, N. M., JULY 5, 4:30 P. M.
KID GEORGE vs. DICK GILBERT---10 Rounds
of Sacramento   of Denver, Colorado

FRANKIE FOWSER vs. BOB YORK—10 ROUNDS
of El Paso, Texas   of Pueblo, Colorado

and two other good bouts, in the largest arena ever constructed in New Mexico. Under the auspices of Central Athletic Club

ALSTON & LARABEE, Managers

KID GEORGE	GEORGE H. LAWSON, Referee	DICK GILBERT
Kid George has lost 3 fights out of 104 battles		Record
Record	**BALL GAMES----BIG CELEBRATION**	Rube Smith, N. D., 10 R.
Walter Stanton, K. O., 2 R.		Frank Jeffries, K. O., 6 R.
Rufe Williams, won, 4 R.		Joe Borrell, won, 15 R.
Otto Berg, won Dec. 20 R.	Special Rates On All Railroads	Battling Levinsky, won 25 R
Fritz Holland, K. O., 6 R.		Jack Clark, K. O., 4 R.
Frank Mantell, Draw, 20 R.	**COME and ENJOY YOURSELF.**	Glen Coakley, D., 15 R.
Pat Bradley, K. O., 4 R.		Kid George, D.
Brick Burgess, K. O., 13 R.		Won from famous Jack Dillon.
John Thomas, K. O., 6 R.		The men have fought 10 rounds
Jack Kelly, K. O., 6 R.		to a draw.
And 85 other battles.		

Fight poster for July 5, 1915, show in Lordsburg, New Mexico. For the card, an outdoor arena was built to accommodate a crowd of 2,000, though only half of that showed up. Still a big show by New Mexico standards, especially in 1915, the card headlined middleweight veteran Kid George, who drew with Denver pug Dick Gilbert.

early 1913, Conley had already done it all. In 1910, the Italian-born resident of Kenosha, Wis., had knocked out Monte Attell in the 42nd round of a 45-rounder for the world bantamweight title, which he'd lost to Johnny Coulon. With losses to Johnny Dundee, Johnny Kilbane and Joe Rivers, many considered Conley a finished fighter by the time he arrived at the border for a short-lived stay.

Just about everything that could go wrong, did, in Las Cruces.

Puryear was replaced with Kid Lee, who then pulled out on a moment's notice, claiming a broken arm. An unnamed substitute "who was offered and installed by the New Mexicans, was mauled around the ring, and in the second round, the towel was thrown in the ring by his seconds."[46]

Conley did not stick around. Nor did Las Cruces clubs try their hands at boxing for several years. Fight fans in the City of Crosses had to go to the border to get their fight fix.

Or to Deming.

Long before Deming would become famous in New Mexico for its annual Great American Duck Race, it would be known for the 30,000 army troops stationed at Camp Cody, in northwest Deming. And long before there was Camp Cody, which led the area in a wartime boxing explosion in the latter half of the decade, there was Camp Brookes and the 1,000 soldiers stationed there.

In Deming's first known prize fight since the 1890s, the town saw its first legal action on Dec. 13, 1912, when the athletic division of the 18th Cavalry, stationed 32 miles south in Columbus, staged a show at the Crystal Theatre. Leadership and venues went from the

Fight poster for Nov. 30, 1916, show in Deming, New Mexico. The 15-round lightweight showdown between Freddie Anderson of Medford, Oregon, and Bud Hamilton, of Denver, was one of several soldier cards held during the latter half of the 1910s. As other areas saw a decline in boxing action, towns like Deming, Silver City, El Paso and Columbus saw an increase, as soldiers were stationed to the border for training and the Mexican threat.

Crystal to the Comet Theatre, and from military athletic divisions to well-known Foxy Miller, as the numbers of shows progressed. There were three shows in 1913, which increased to 9 in '14 and to 8 the following year.

By the time the U.S. Army was engaged in the hunt for Pancho Villa south of the border in 1916, Deming was shaping up to be a major fight center. Troubles with Villa followed by World War I only solidified the town and military camps as a mecca for boxing in New Mexico. Deming's only competition would be Columbus.

Soldiers with any ring experience were encouraged to get into the ring, but when Miller took over the Crystal Theatre in 1914, he replaced soldier boxers with proven veterans who were drawing in Silver City and El Paso — ol' reliables like Herrick and Patrick, who twice headlined Deming in Feb. 1914. Foxy not only recruited local civilians, like Charles Scheidigger, a Deming electrician, but saw the demand in pitting miner fighters against the army's top boxers. When Silver City's Gus Flores drew with Larry Strouer, who was stationed at Camp Furlong in Columbus, the Crystal Theatre saw its biggest crowd yet, and special trains ran from the mining camps and Columbus to Deming.

Hailing Scheidigger as a coming great white hope, Miller milked his box-office appeal, overmatching him first with well-known veteran Bart Gordon, now with the National Guard in Roswell, whom he shockingly defeated in the summer of 1914 for the New Mexico heavyweight championship. Scheidigger was then pitted against Lordsburg miner Edward Scarborough, whom he KO'd in the early rounds of a ten-rounder. Miller dared the 13th Cavalry to come up with someone to beat Scheidigger. Before they did, the reluctant heavyweight had called it quits.

This was just about the same time that a young soldier made the news in Deming for cutting up a local with a knife during a street fight. Boxer Carl Jones got 60 days in the clink when he attacked Deming's Jack Arnold — and Arnold got the hint that maybe he should learn to fight, which he did. Several months later, the featherweight was slinging leather in the local ring.

By 1915, as trouble at the border became more imminent and Miller returned to Silver City, briefly, before leaving for Arizona, boxing promotions once more returned to the 13th Cavalry's athletic division in Deming, and to several local promoters who all had short runs.

Soldier boxing was on, with guys like Arnold carving out a reputation that would carry him through the war and a long-running prizefighting career throughout Texas in the 1920s. Arnold headlined shows in Deming, taking on local soldiers and border veterans.

Though Arnold sold tickets, the biggest fight in Deming, pre–World War I, was held at the Crystal Theatre between Kid George and John Thomas. Civilian fighters, however, started to lose their purses to experienced soldier boxers as 1916 approached.

In Columbus, it was the same story.

Two shows in 1913 quickly became one a month by 1916, when soldiers who'd been fighters before enlisting, and several who learned how to fight in the camps, became the new draws. Veterans like Johnny "Kid" Williams and Bud Hamilton were replaced with the men in khaki, former fighters "Battling" Frank Mantell, Larry Strouer, Freddie Anderson, Bull Foster and Rufus Williams. Camp, border and even Southwestern championships were billed and fought for, drawing crowds of 1,000 and paving the way for the sport to not only survive during war time, but thrive.

Columbus and Deming prospered when El Paso didn't. Promoters in the hard luck border town were always battling Texas politicos and the state statutes prohibiting prizefighting. When the heat was on, the action shifted across the river to Juarez. During the Mexican

Revolution, that wasn't always an option, however. In 1912, seeking solution and safe haven, El Paso promoters were once again spying that patch of land "located near the end of the electric car line just across the river from the smelter."[47]

Would-be promoters Jimmy Lee and Nick Depeder thought the New Mexican plot of land was the perfect place for a tented arena that would hold 2,500. They signed a three-year lease with the owner of the land, J. Wutherford, named it "Bohemia Heights," and started to construct a bridge for what would be the first card thrown by the newly-formed El Paso Athletic Club. An August 4 date was set for a Jack Herrick-Kid Mitchell fight, then changed to the 3rd to avoid any bible-thumpers moaning about Sunday fights. Battling Nelson and Bobby Waugh were contacted for the club's second show and the *El Paso Morning Times* began to predict the site would quickly become the top fight center in the country.

And that's just about the time Bohemia Heights crashed on the rocks below — well, nine feet below, in the muddy banks of the Rio Grande.

Call it bad timing. Plans for Bohemian Heights were drawn up during the same month, no less, that saw Johnson vs. Flynn. After losing *that* battle, Gov. McDonald was determined to win the next one. "There will be no more prize fights in New Mexico," proclaimed the governor. "I mean that prize fighting in New Mexico is over."[48]

It wasn't of course, but Bohemia Heights was shut down.

"While near scrappers gaily pound each other into pulp and poorly constructed rings break down in Albuquerque, which, the geography says, is in New Mexico, the stern eye of the powers at Santa Fe light on Bohemia Heights and the stern voice says 'Nix,'" argued the *Times*. "All of which may be all right, but why should fights be allowed in one part of the state and not in another?"[49]

El Paso wasn't finished with the slice of New Mexico called "Bohemia Heights," any more than New Mexico was finished with prizefighting. Both would find a way to survive and thrive during the 1910s.

9. Rise of New Mexicans, 1912–1916

Over in Albuquerque Benny Cordova is a local idol and that state also boasts Mike Baca and Jack Torres and the great and only Benny Chavez. It has now come to pass that an Irish or American lad can not stick up his hand and ask for a scrap anywhere in the great southwest unless he finds a Mexican willing to quarrel for a stipulated sum with the compass of a two strand ring 20 feet square. There are some who predict that some day the name of the gent who wears the championship belt may have a name that makes a noise like Mexico.

—*Tucson Daily Citizen*, 1919[1]

Mexican boxers are getting to be a habit nowadays.

- *Los Angeles Times*, 1913[2]

In an era when every hometown paper claimed every new fight card was "the best ever staged in these parts," local fighters were almost always declared to be "of championship timber" just by knocking out the local opposition and, maybe, a journeyman from Denver or Texas.

Sometimes the rivalries were so good, as was seen in the case of Roswell's Johnny Connolly and Santa Fe's Mike Baca, that New Mexicans would fight half a dozen times over the course of years. Other times, a fighter with potential to be a contender, as Albuquerque's Benny Cordova was, would fight that many times against the same foe, but in different states, even countries.

But world beaters, guys of *real* championship timber, were rare. Of New Mexico's original hometown fighters, only one would have the potential to be a champ. Most were merely good enough to carve their name into the annals of state history—but a few had potential to capture the attention of their region, like Louis Newman, Ev Winters and Al Smaulding.

As these old-timers from another era wound down their careers, the scenes around the state quickly groomed youngsters who now had the opportunities to fight as often as they liked, *without* the threat of arrest. Emerging from the border came Cordova, who joined Jack Torres and Perfecto Romero as top names in Albuquerque. They were joined by out-of-towners, like Harry "Kid" Schaefer, now calling New Mexico home, in replacing the old-timers who'd either reached their potential or were slowing down.

Newman's Transition

Now don't faint! That's what O'Malley came near doing this morning, however, when he received a letter from the Spanish-American fighter informing him that he was

155

manager for Yoakum and would be glad to send his boy there for a bout with Boyd. Doubtless Newman, finding he could not manage Yoakum in the ring, decided to do so out of the canvas-covered square. Newman is also manager for Benny Chavez, and is getting to be something of a pugilistic personage from the box office side.
— *Las Vegas Daily Optic,* 1913[3]

Las Vegas-born lightweight Louis Newman was just beginning to peak in his boxing career. Unfortunately for him, so were the other Southwestern lightweights, like Eddie Johnson, of Pueblo, Colorado.

If there's ever been a single "arch-enemy" for New Mexico talent, it was Eddie Johnson. Not that Eddie had it in for his neighbors to the south; there were very few fighters Johnson *wouldn't* fight — from lightweight to middleweight — during his 18-year career. And, especially from New Mexico, there were very few with the skills to beat him.

On Jan. 22, 1912, Newman tried for the second time to be named Southwestern lightweight champ when he went to Johnson's backyard of Pueblo. "In a battle that saw Newman's cleverness over the raw brutality of Johnson, the bigger punch won out." After going down in round one, "it was merely a question of how much punishment the New Mexican could stand." Newman tried to outbox the raw slugger in the second, but barely survived the third. In the fourth, Newman "indicated a design to quit."[4]

While Mark Levy tried to arrange a New Mexico return, Newman took several months off, staying in Denver to fight tough Phil Kearney in May. Another loss resulted, though Newman rebounded with a knockout win over a lesser fighter he'd already defeated. In June, Newman agreed to return to his home state, though Levy did him no favors by setting up a collision course with the No. 1 man at lightweight in the state, Stanley Yoakum.

Prior to meeting Newman, Yoakum had knocked out top Texan Bobby Waugh twice — but a draw with Newman's New Mexican rival Ev Winters had Newman thinking he had a chance. "I know Yoakum is a tough boy with a punch," he told the press, "but that is all he has."[5]

On June 17, the two clashed at the Elks' Opera House. Though barely able to weather Yoakum's mauling, brawling style, by the 20th round, Newman's "assimilation of punishment and his flashes of speed" were enough to warrant a referee's decision of a draw.[6] With Newman displaying two black eyes, both nearly closed, and a left cheek abrasion with Yoakum suffering but a split lower lip, they were signed two days later by Levy to fight a rematch, to take place 11 days after the first one.

The draw made Newman an instant attraction and, after public workouts at the Elks', he told the media that not only had he "held Yoakum too cheap," but the Oklahoma slugger was every bit as good as Eddie Johnson. Yoakum dismissed Newman, saying he'd better be "making hay while the sun shines,"[7] if he wanted any chance to outbox him.

Levy promised the winner a shot against Rudy "Boer" Unholz on the July 3 appetizer card the day before Johnson-Flynn in Las Vegas. A local match-up would not only test Curley's "electric-lighted" arena that evening, but would serve to rev up locals that a "home boy" would be going up against a star lightweight like Unholz,[8] who'd racked up over 100 fights all over the world against the top names.

The odds favored Yoakum, and for good reason. The 20-round rematch saw a brutal display by Yoakum, who "did not bear a mark of the battle. Newman, on the other hand, was badly battered, his left eye being closed and having suffered severely from body punches."[9] Though Newman won over fans with his gameness, the fight was stopped in round 16. Barely able to stand, Newman showed spirit by calling out the winner of the July 3 Yoakum-Unholz match.

Newman stayed on in Albuquerque, headlining an Aug. 16 show against the Levy-groomed Congo Kid. The fight stunk up the place, and Newman had to wait until September for another opportunity, this time against Gallup's Eddie Gregory, whom Newman "used for a chopping block, beating him in every round."[10] Soldier Hunt, one month later, was also outclassed in a distance fight.

Having cleaned up the locals and with Yoakum now in demand for bigger purses outside the state, Newman returned to work in Denver, then picked up the glove game in May 1913 with an unimpressive win over Earl "Kid" Brown. Thereafter, Newman made his return to Las Vegas, for the first time in five years. Promoter O'Malley was careful with his matchmaking, pitting him against Bud Boyd of Saguache, Colorado. A ten-round decision win earned him a match with Harry Schaefer. Though nearly closing his foe's eyes near the end, "it was the Spanish American's boxing skills, and cool head that prevailed." Newman still lacked the "one thing that would make him a topnotcher, a sleep-producing blow."[11]

By now, Yoakum had returned, fresh off a string of victories on the West Coast. Newman, meanwhile, had joined forces with the camp of Benny Chavez and local fans were contemplating a third match against the "Ironman" for this "new and improved" Newman. After a tune-up win in July 1913 in Denver, the match was made with Yoakum for July 24 in Las Vegas. While Newman trained in Trinidad with Chavez, whose career he was now managing, Yoakum slipped into Las Vegas and won the locals over by saying he would end Newman's career.

Newman arrived three days before the fight, saying, "He holds nothing over me in my estimation, and I will show the Las Vegas fans that I can come back strong even with a man who claims a decision over me."[12]

"Yoakum undoubtedly had the better of the argument, practically from the beginning to the end, though his superiority over Newman was so slight that the referee was unable to do other than declare the bout a draw," reported the *Optic*, noting that although Newman objected to the ruling, "it was apparent to the big crowd present that the Las Vegan had been somewhat fortunate in not having been declared the loser."[13]

When Yoakum immediately called for a 15- or 20-round rematch, Newman not only refused but stunned his nemesis by saying he wanted to manage him instead.

The June 17, 1912, 20-round lightweight showdown between Stanley Yoakum, of Dallas, and Las Vegas' Louis Newman was one of the most anticipated fights of New Mexico's first year as a state. The two fought to a draw, though Yoakum won the rematch, 11 days later, with a 16-round knockout.

A Classy Program

ELKS' THEATER

Monday June 17
8:30 P. M.

The Chief Events:

A 20 ROUND BOUT

133 Pounds

Louis Newman
of Denver,

vs.

"Kid' Yoakum
of Dallas.

A 10 Round Bout

128 Pounds

Jimmy Donovan
of San Francisco,

vs.

The Congo Kid
of Memphis, Tenn.

The boys have been matched for their ability to scrap; and it is believed they have been matched evenly in experience, science, weight and gameness.

Auspices New Mexico Athletic Club.
Mark Levy, Director

Prices 75c, $1,
$1.50
Ringside $2

"Look here, Stanley," said Newman. "I'm managing you from now on."

"What!" gasped Yoakum.

"I said I'm managing you from now on, d'ye you hear? I'm going to handle both you and [Benny] Chavez."[14]

Hit cleaner than any punch Newman had ever thrown at him, Yoakum hesitated, shrugged and agreed.

Later, Newman said that if he couldn't decisively beat guys like Yoakum, and if he could not win the lightweight championship, there was no point in fighting any longer. Instead, he would take someone else to the championship. Retiring with a record of 27-4-10, 19 KOs, and 7 no decisions, Las Vegas' first star prizefighter moved into Phase II of his career — as a manager, promoter and matchmaker.

Newman proved a better manager than fighter, guiding Chavez toward a world championship through 1914, before the Southwestern star returned to his original manager, George Joseph. New Mexico fans were outraged with Chavez, but felt better for Newman when he began guiding the career of Jack Torres in 1914, whom many thought would be New Mexico's first world champion.

With Yoakum, Newman piloted his former foe toward a the lightweight championship and came just a fight or two from doing it. In a fight that was still being talked about in Denver 20 years later as one of its all-time greatest wars, Yoakum was KO'd in round 19 of a 20-rounder by one of the era's greatest lightweights, Charlie White, who soon went on to challenge World Lightweight Champion Freddie Welsh the following year.

After breaking with Yoakum and Chavez, and Torres retiring, Newman moved on to Oklahoma City in the early '20s, then Detroit where, in the '30s onward, he was a matchmaker and promoter for the Olympic Arena.

Seasoned Winters

Shafer's punch, as compared with that of Winters, is but as the sound of a feather dropped from a six-story building to the pavement to that of a Colorado snowslide.
— Raton Reporter, 1912[15]

No true sportsman will promote another fight in which Winters is a principal. He has sacrificed the respect of every sportsman and his name should appear hereafter in the same catalogue with the man who amused himself jabbing pins in the flesh of a helpless baby, or the wife beater and animal torturer. Though a white man he is forty-nine shades darker than the native born Ethiopian who runs loose on the hot sands of Central Africa.
—Trinidad Chronicle-News, 1913[16]

There was nothing easy about Everett Winters. Mid-career in 1912, when boxing might have been legal and the offers plenty for a durable lightweight like Winters, the man who had made a career out of outsmarting the law and fighting on the road, had no reason to change now.

The Raton pug could have stayed at home in 1912 to fight the new crop of youngsters who were claiming to be the state's lightweight champion. Instead, the bulk of fights were done the same way Winters had always conducted business — hard, and on the road. It was apparent, from his choice of opposition, that Winters wanted only to maximize his purses and to fight the best lightweights in the region. Before he hit the road in 1912 an offer came that Winters could not resist.

Clovis bragging that local favorite Benny Pappan was the next great lightweight and offering the chance to prove otherwise was too great a temptation for Winters. On his way to Texas for fatter purses, Winters cleaned up in Clovis. Before a capacity crowd at the Lyceum Theatre, Winters, outweighing, outbrawling and outclassing the Oklahoma Indian, needed but four rounds before Pappan had to be "carried from the ring, bleeding from the face and left ear."[17] Winters earned $202 and was on his way to Texas while, behind him, the brutal fight launched a statewide protest of prizefighting by religious groups.

Winters might have stayed longer in Clovis, for there was talk that the former lightweight champion Battling Nelson himself would be willing to come to New Mexico if he could get paid $1,000 up front. With the Lyceum's total gate of $427 for a packed house, there seemed "little probability that a sufficiently tempting purse can be raised to bring Nelson here."[18]

On his way east, Winters drew with Jack Smith in Oklahoma, then headed to Dallas to face the winner of a top-notch showdown between Texas' No. 1 lightweight, Bobby Waugh, and former title challenger Johnny Moran, of New York. When Waugh fell ill for his Mar. 5 showdown with Moran, Winters stepped in on less than a week's notice.

The Raton product was outclassed, losing every round, but went the 15-round distance with Moran, who "beat a constant tattoo on Winters' nose and eyes" with "triphammer regularity."[19] Hoping for another big fight, Winters remained in Dallas and, two weeks later, when a main event fell out at the Yeoman's Club, he was matched up with fellow scrapper Stanley Yoakum. They fought to a ten-round draw.

After landing a fight against Colorado's top lightweight, Eddie Johnson, Winters, now being called "Ol' Reliable" by scribes in Colorado, headed back west, making a pit stop in Oklahoma where Pappan swore he would even the score — this time Winters took him out in three.

A win over Johnson in his backyard of San Juan, Colorado, on March 19, would have put Winters back on track, for Johnson had destroyed Louis Newman earlier that year. Winters was on his way to winning the fight when momentum tilted toward Johnson midway through, and the Puebloan finished strong enough to get the ref's nod.

While promoter Levy sought to bring Winters down to fight a rematch with Yoakum, the Raton veteran stayed at home for a series of fights against Chicago's Frankie White, whom he'd drawn against in 1911. White had also just recently lost to Johnson in Alamosa.

Nearly 600 people showed up at the Aerodome to watch Winters return to Raton, on Oct. 3, 1912. Yet, the "famous hay-maker with the Raton brand upon it" failed to "produce slumber" upon the clever Windy City lad whose body shots nearly had Winters out at the end of ten rounds. The ref ruled a draw and the promoters set up a rematch on Thanksgiving Eve, one month later.[20] Once again, with Winters starting out and White ending strong, their third fight was ruled a draw. A final bout was scheduled for Feb. 1, also in Raton.

This time, there was a definitive ending. "Before the mill it was generally conceded that White was the cleverer of the two — now it is conceded no longer," wrote the *Raton Range*. Winters outgeneraled White, landing two blows for every one, flooring "his man with a flashing right cross, and started him towards his dressing room with a left hook which lifted him off the ropes. The local man came out of the ring with hair unruffled and without even a scratch."[21]

Perhaps sick of fighting on the road, Winters relented to Levy in April, agreeing to fight in Albuquerque for the first time in his career, against Harry Schaefer. "The scrap was everything that critics could demand, but the house was not more than half filled," reported the *Morning Journal*. With Schaefer the aggressor for much of the fight, Winters woke up in the final round with a "whirlwind finish" that not only had Schaefer groggy, but was enough to secure a draw by the referee.[22]

It was later reported that Winters had not only fought with a damaged right hand, sustained days before in training, but had also injured the left paw in the early rounds. As one paper reported, "When Ev arrived Saturday, his hands were so swollen that one might have judged he was wearing the boxing gloves with which he fought."[23]

A rematch was talked about for May, but Winters' injuries kept him out of the ring until August, when he took a fight against former sparring partner Otis Bruce in Trinidad. Meanwhile, Las Vegas promoter Charles O'Malley was setting up a rematch with Yoakum for Aug. 18 — but the fight in Trinidad killed Winters' local appeal for good.

Before the fight, Winters was praised for his condition while Bruce, "the negro boy, is going into the fight of his life. Winters is admired and a favorite because of his cleanly and manly living, and because of it has developed a physique that he should well be proud of. Winters looks anything but like a fighter but when one visits the training quarters and observes his bouts with sparring partners, he is easily recognized as the coming champion of the lightweight class."[24]

After the fight, it was a different story. Not only did Winters lose — he was disqualified, for twice kneeing Bruce in the groin — but he was *arrested* after the fight for his fouls.

> Winters repeatedly used foul tactics throughout the fight. A furore was created at the ringside as Winters' offense grew more flagrant and police interference was necessary to prevent violence from the crowd. After the fight, Winters and his seconds, Rube Smith and M. Donohue, were arrested and lodged in the city jail on a charge of vagrancy.... There is a certain amount of race prejudice exhibited when a colored man meets a white man in the ring and the white man is inclined to want to see a white man win. However, when Winters fouled Bruce in the tenth round and fouled him again in the next, there was not a spectator in the house who saw the foul but began to 'pull' for the colored man.[25]

After being released from jail and booted from Trinidad, Winters found out that his lucrative Las Vegas payday with Yoakum had been nixed. He had been replaced.

It was nearly a year before Winters returned to the ring and, even then, it was probably half-heartedly. Winters lost a ten-rounder in Denver to Danny O'Brien. Yet one year later, on Sept. 30, 1915, Winters was back in the news, telling the *Raton Range* that he was planning to make another go at prizefighting, with an eastern invasion.

Local promoters bought into it, bringing Yoakum back to New Mexico for that long-awaited rematch. The fight closed the book on Winters when the too-seasoned Yoakum forced Winters to quit at the beginning of round five. "During the second round, a blow from Yoakum's pile driver, caught Winters squarely in the physiognomy, breaking the bridge of the nose, rendering the local boy groggy during the fourth. Greater ring experience and superior skill manifested at every stage of the game by the clever Denver boy was clearly apparent to the large audience of fans who were disappointed, but not greatly surprised, at the sudden termination of the fight."[26]

Winters then disappeared from the papers, his fate unknown.

Bootblack State Champ

> *Found: One husky complexion Colorado-maduro, weight 158 pounds, disposition decidedly belligerent, eats 'em alive and likes 'em raw as a steady diet.*
> *—Albuquerque Morning Journal,* 1912[27]

Al Smaulding was both blessed and cursed.

The good news was that during his peak years, 1912 to 1914, New Mexico's leading home-grown middleweight had plenty of opportunities and opponents to fight. The bad news came, fight after fight, with the men Smaulding found himself staring at in the opposite corner.

It was no easy task to call oneself New Mexico's state champion, when the men you had to best had been collected coast to coast and deposited in the growing state. With fight opportunities at the border, the mining towns and Albuquerque, veterans like Jeff Clarke, Kid George and Jack Herrick flocked to the new state — and Smaulding became the local guy to beat.

Never going long without a fight, Smaulding's brawling style made him a favorite with the fans — but his inconsistent performances made it a love-hate relationship.

When Bazz Smaulding relocated his family from Clayton to Albuquerque, the former "Clayton Blacksmith" found a new hometown to fight for, yet he wasn't the first choice for the local promoter to establish as New Mexico's premier middleweight champion.

According to Levy, Smaulding "for some time has been grazing in the fertile fields of Clayton, way up near the Colorado" and had a "positive relish for punishment and an all-consuming desire to get in the squared circle with [Luis] Gonzales."[28] Yet, for reasons unclear, on the night before Smaulding and Gonzales were to fight, Smaulding pulled out and was replaced with Gallup's Eddie Gregory, who scored the upset with a bizarre 21st-round disqualification.

One month later, the 19-year-old blacksmith got his chance to lace on the six-ouncers when, on March 8, he was brought in as opponent for West Coast veteran Jimmie "Sailor" Burke. When Smaulding KO'd his man in two rounds, Levy brought him back to the Elks' Opera House in April to face Pennsylvania miner Jack Mitchell, who'd been fighting his away across the country. Unknown in local fight circles, Mitchell proved too much for the still-learning Smaulding, who found himself in dreamland, stretched out on the canvas and having to be carried to his dressing room after just two rounds of a scheduled 20-rounder.

Despite the loss, the media did not yet rule out Smaulding as a local comer, and when West Coaster Walter "Roundhouse Kid" Stanton came to town for a bout in April, just after the Mitchell loss, he told the *Morning Journal* that he had "volunteered to teach the colored boxer the fine points of the game in return for using him as a punching bag."[29] Smaulding sparred with both principals on the coming card — Stanton and Indiana iron worker Frank Coakley, who assessed the blacksmith, telling the media that all Smaulding lacked was experience. "If he is not overmatched," said Coakley, "I see no reason why he should not be as good as the best ones in his class in a year or so."[30]

Still written off as a has-been or never-will-be, Smaulding was lined up as fodder for Gonzales, one month later at the Elks'. Though "confident that he is the colored boy's master,"[31] the fight wasn't even close. Securing his role as New Mexico's middleweight champion, Smaulding destroyed the Silver City middleweight. "The less said about it, the better," wrote the *Morning Journal*. "Gonzales apparently was afraid of his adversary and whenever he received a wallop or two he would go down on his hands and knees and try to quit."[32]

With no one local to challenge Smaulding, who was inactive for much of the summer, Levy brought in heavy-hitting veteran Charlie "The Fighting Newsboy" Pierson on Sept. 11, who would fight back-to-back draws with the blacksmith. Neither confirming nor negating his legitimacy as a comer beyond New Mexico with the two draws, Smaulding did not impress the locals, clinching too much and tiring in the later rounds. He was considered lucky to walk away with draws.

When baseball hero Bill Pettus, hoping to rekindle his boxing career, arrived in town for a November 1912 match with Tony Caponi, Smaulding provided the sparring. After Pettus repeatedly floored the blacksmith in the gym, Smaulding's reputation took another blow. Knocking out late substitute and much lighter Lee Brazos in his next bout did not convince otherwise.

Fight fallouts and bad opponent choices plagued Smaulding in 1913, who kept busy beating overhyped Kid Dempsey of Texas (KO-2), Kansas City's Buster O'Neill (TKO-5), and unknown Black (or "Battling") Scotty of Phoenix. Not drawing a crowd, Levy was unwilling to spend the money to test Smaulding on a higher caliber opponent, forcing the blacksmith to ride the rails to Silver City, where he would fight off and on for the next couple years.

First up was a rematch with Gonzales on the miner's home turf, in the summer of 1913. Gonzales had blamed a hand injury for the first loss, but the second time around he was only able to survive one more round, throwing up the sponge two minutes into the fourth round after getting floored five times. After more fights fell out in Albuquerque, Smaulding went north to Raton to get a fight, where he disposed of Denver veteran K.O. Brown in two rounds, setting up Smaulding for his best year yet in 1914.

Fighting his toughest opposition, Smaulding fought eight times, yet was only able to score two wins, with five draws and just one loss — but with every fight against the best middleweights in the Southwest.

There was the "Salt Lake Bearcat," Vic Hansen, who'd been fighting since 1907, and had gone 20 rounds to a draw with contender Gunboat Smith. Smaulding drew in ten, though Hansen had been "picked by the wise ones to stop Smaulding inside the limit."[33]

Against slugger Jack Herrick, Smaulding earned back-to-back draws, once again surprising critics and showing himself to be "a beautiful scientific boxer with the agility of a panther." Having "dodged the famous Herrick haymaker" and gone ten rounds "with a man of Herrick's class" was "quite a feather in Smaulding's cap."[34] After the second draw, it was surmised that "a draw decision is all either man will ever be able to get in ten rounds, if they should fight from now until Doomsday, so evenly matched are they. Should it be possible to pull of a twenty round contest, there would be an entirely different story."[35]

After returning to Albuquerque to score a second-round knockout over relative unknown Kid Winterstein, Smaulding returned to Silver City where he faced the toughest opponent of his career, Jeff "The Fighting Ghost" Clarke, of Joplin, Mo. With wins over former title challenger Peter Maher, Joe Jeanette and Luther McCarty, Clarke was "some pumpkin in the fight world."[36] Yet, against Smaulding, the best the veteran could pull off was a surprising draw.

"Smaulding's draw with Clarke, although it was over the short distance route, demonstrates that the Albuquerque boy undoubtedly has class," wrote the *Enterprise*.[37] "Smaulding showed up wonderfully clever and proved himself a capable fighting machine against the onslaught of the greatest fighter who has ever appeared before the Silver City fans and successful stalled off the tornado like rushes of the Ghost for ten rounds. That he could do this against such fast company speaks much for Al's cleverness."[38]

Suddenly popular in Albuquerque, Levy arranged for a rematch 11 days later, during which time Smaulding got married. The rematch was billed and hyped as a make-or-break test to see if Smaulding had championship timber, a hope that had been elevated by draws with Hansen, Herrick and Clarke. Once again, however, the fight resulted in a draw, with "The Ghost" failing to "hold any spooky terror" for Smaulding, "who piled up an early lead and weathered a ninth round body shot that floored him."[39]

For reasons unknown, and just when he'd scored his biggest success, Smaulding was inactive from May to December 1914 — and that's when another top-notcher, Kid George, arrived in Albuquerque. By now, Levy had given up control of the New Mexico Athletic Club to Fred Winsor, who also doubled as manager for the Sacramento middleweight. Smaulding, rusty from most of the year off, was brought in as an opponent, losing his first fight in nearly three years.

The loss was a turning point in his career. "It was the first time an Albuquerque crowd has seen Smaulding go down from a well delivered punch since Mitchell stopped him and that was in an early period of his ring career," reported the *Morning Journal*. Weathering the knockdown, Smaulding was punished but survived to lose a ten-round decision.[40]

After defeating Jack "Kid" Thomas in Socorro two weeks later (actually the ref called it a draw until the booing crowd demanded he give a verdict), Smaulding was back in the Albuquerque ring rematching George, who defeated him again. And then *again*, five months later, in Silver City.

Three straight draws, two with Bob York and one with Harry Wallace, who was returning to New Mexico for the first time since his Las Vegas days in 1908, at least took him out of the loser's circle, but after losing to Herrick in October 1915, back in Silver City, Smaulding was looked upon as a has-been.

Beating unknown Danny Sullivan in Belen, on Feb. 25, 1916, would mark the last time Smaulding would ever score a win. Consecutive draws with veteran Jack Boyd, then a loss in five rounds, all in Socorro, further marred his record. A draw and a loss to John Thomas, both in Gallup, followed. Smaulding's "old time flash"[41] could not be resurrected and, as 1916 came to a close, the blacksmith enlisted in the U.S. Army and retired from the ring.

Actually, Smaulding was far from finished with boxing, but his days as a threat were over.

At Fort Bayard, Smaulding was a boxing instructor for the troops, and it must've given him the confidence he needed to stage a comeback in 1919 against army champion Johnny Sudenberg, who KO'd Smaulding in the seventh. Smaulding retired again, but came back yet again in 1921, after his wife, Rosie, had passed away. After leaving the service, Smaulding hit the road where he became a human punching bag for up-and-comers. Fighting everywhere but New Mexico — from the border to Arizona — Smaulding lost to several big names, including Lee Anderson, Jack Thompson, Jack Taylor and Kid Norfolk.

In an interview in 1958, when Smaulding was 64 years old, he told Jim Lame of the *Albuquerque Journal* that he decided to hang up the gloves after an accident in the railroad shop where he was working. "I dropped a wheel on my foot and broke it," said Smaulding. "After that I could never move around, so I quit."[42] It would be the last time the "Clayton Blacksmith" would be recognized for his achievements in the ring for, in November 1971, Smaulding died from natural causes at the age of 79.

The "Mexican Mist"

> Jack Torres is without a doubt one of the greatest natural fighters the west has ever produced. He has a left that works like a triphammer and lands as accurately as bullets from the rifle of a crack shot. His defense is well-nigh impregnable. He punches hard with either hand and hits like a flash. All of the old-timers who have seen him in action are predicting a great future for him.
>
> — Las Vegas Daily Optic, 1915[43]

Jack Torres welterweight seemed due for the world crown about 10 years ago, but never made the grade.

— *Portland Oregonian,* 1926[44]

They called him the "Mexican Mist" and years after his name disappeared from print, old boxing scribes would maintain that he was the first world-class fighter to come out of Albuquerque. If nothing else, he was the first real boxer out of New Mexico, known for his piston-like jab and blazing right crosses.

Joaquin "Jack" Torres might have been good enough to mix with the best welterweights of his day, but injuries kept him from reaching his peak and challenging Benny Chavez for bragging rights as New Mexico's first real top-notcher. Because Chavez fought most of his career while living in Trinidad, Colorado, Torres, of Old Town ("Old Albuquerque" back in the day), does hold the distinction of being the first big potential fighter raised and groomed at home.

In the modern era, "groomed" sometimes equates to being "coddled." In the 1910s, groomed meant being given opportunities to fight, and that's just what promoter Mark Levy gave him. It wasn't uncommon to be thrown into the deep end, your first or second time at bat, fighting eight- and ten-rounders against a veteran. It was sink or swim — and Torres was one of those who swam.

Moved along by Levy for the first few years before the promoter left town, he was passed on to Louis Newman, who'd retired from the ring to manage the greatest trio of Southwesterners at the time: Chavez, Stanley Yoakum and Torres. Though it was Levy who really discovered him, Newman took the credit, claiming to have found him working in the American Lumber mill in Albuquerque, a "16-year-old stripling of 122 pounds at that time [who] hungered to become a fighter," who would linger around Levy's New Mexico Athletic Club. When Newman saw Torres and Chavez sparring one afternoon, he spotted enough natural talent to "put the gloves on with him himself to teach him a little about boxing."[45]

Far before Newman came into the picture, however, Torres was developed by Levy as far as he could go in New Mexico. After an initial showing as a youngster in 1912, in which Torres destroyed an unknown opponent in just 11 seconds, Levy, believing "Torres is a good enough boxer to deserve a worthy oppo-

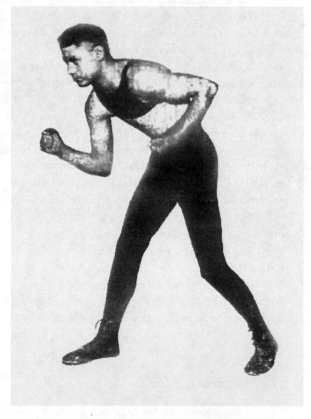

The "Mexican Mist," Jack Torres, of Old Town, Albuquerque, was the first world-class fighter born, raised and groomed in New Mexico. He fought several top contender and had the attention of East Coasters when a series of injuries toppled Torres from contention.

nent,"[46] gave the aspiring pug his chance on New Year's Day when he threw Torres on as an eight-round prelim at the Elks'. It would be the first of ten bouts during 1913 for Torres and by the time the year ended, he was Levy's biggest local draw.

A lightweight at the time, the 17-year-old Torres buzzed through late sub, black fighter Vic Stewart, and then outboxed Tommy Moran, later that month, through four rounds. Against Magdalena's Young Sam Langford, Torres went down in a flash knockdown but got back up to punish his foe for another decision. When Harry Schaefer pulled out of his March showdown with Gallup's Kid Oliver, unable to make 133 pounds, Torres stepped in at the last minute. Oliver's weight was little better than a featherweight, however, and there was "little glory" in the "waltz dream" win for Torres, who danced around Oliver, putting him down four times en route to a sixth-round TKO win.[47]

Levy took Torres to Santa Fe, where he was expected to breeze through Manuel "Kid" Stern in a hyped-up grudge match. Stern's only black mark had been a loss to the more-experienced Schaefer. But, in the biggest local upset of the year, Torres was floored four times before being counted out in the sixth. An immediate rematch was announced for Albuquerque. This time Stern was the expected favorite, having "started the referee crooning the well-known 'ten' litany over the Old Albuquerque lad"[48] in Santa Fe.

It was almost the same result — just with a different winner. Torres, showing "a crouch which gives him an almost impenetrable defense" and a "haymaker right uppercut he can plant to a vital spot any time he wants to,"[49] put Stern on the canvas three times in the fifth and down for the count in the sixth with a right.

Santa Fe sent down undefeated Mike Baca in November 1913, but he was wiped out in just one round. There was no one to stop Torres, at least locally, so Levy lined up St. Louis veteran Pierce Matthews, who'd already headlined two Albuquerque shows, beating Schaefer and Frank Mantell. With five times the number of bouts Torres had, an estimated 50, Matthews had been fighting since 1909. "This bout would determine for Torres whether he has reached the limit of his ascent in the pugilistic game, and will continue in the ranks of preliminary fighters, or whether he will figure in main events hereafter,"[50] it was determined.

On three holiday cards — Thanksgiving, Christmas and New Year's Day 1914 — Torres and Matthews went a total of 23 rounds. At first, Matthews gave Torres trouble, the veteran scoring a flash knockdown and keeping the local kid on the defense for most of the fight. Torres showed enough flash of genius, however, and it was ruled a draw.

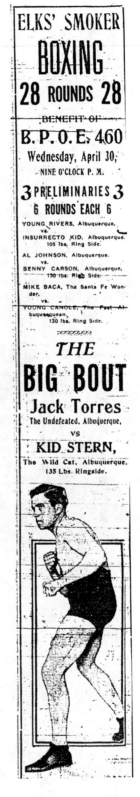

Fight poster for April 30, 1913. Jack Torres vs. Kid Stern was one of the year's biggest upsets in New Mexico. Stern was supposed to be a breeze-through for rising local star Torres, who was rudely KO'd in six rounds. Torres had his vengeance three months later when he paid back Stern with his own KO.

A rematch was arranged for Christmas Day. "I don't see how it is possible for me to lose," Matthews said. "I know Torres is a good boy with a mighty wallop, but he wasn't able to get his wallop in when we fought before, and I don't understand how he can figure to get in this time.... I confidently expect to put him away inside of six rounds."[51]

"I am going to do my fighting in the ring and not in the newspapers," was Torres' reply. "But if I don't drop Matthews.... I will be the most surprised fellow in Albuquerque."[52]

Torres won the rematch, and though he had built himself a lead by outpointing his tiring foe, referee Fat Shearn spoiled the fight by disqualifying Matthews for a low blow most saw as "a clean right to the stomach, [though] one hardly acknowledged by Torres himself."[53]

Matthews demanded a third fight, resulting in a six-round draw on New Year's Day.

It was right about this time that Newman entered the picture, "discovering" Torres and promising to take him to the next level rather than let him flounder as a club fighter in New Mexico. Torres bought the spiel — Newman's well known ring record and piloting both Chavez and Yoakum? How could you go wrong?

"Only a step to the top," said Jack's father, Benito Torres. "Jack doesn't intend to stop where he is now. He is out for the championship."[54]

With Newman calling the shots, the ring-savvy manager tested Torres at first, bringing in Colorado's Harry Riede, who was coming off a decision over Newman's prize lightweight, Yoakum. Showing a chin and with "neither fighter loafing in any round," Torres was on his way to a decision win when the Aspen boy, taking "the major shade of the punishment," was disqualified for repeated low blows.[55]

Satisfied that his new pupil had what it took, Newman pushed on, taking Torres to Gallup, where he scored an easy knockout over Blinkie McDonald, then back to the Duke City for what was supposed to be a "stay-busy" fight against Schaefer. Albuquerque's adopted lightweight from Wyoming proved tougher than expected — and so did the three judges who ruled a draw what the crowd saw as a Torres win.

Working with Levy, Newman arranged for a host of gatekeepers, veterans and journeymen to further test and temper Torres. One fight, in Gallup, was a slaughter — Osage Indian Mitchell, who'd been tossed into the ring against Torres at the insistence of the promoters — but the rest served to prepare Torres for bigger names outside the state.

Torres made 80-bout veteran "Battling Dane" Pete Jensen look clumsy, then journeyed to Denver to fight the co-main on the Yoakum–Charlie White bill at the Stockyards. Though the *Denver Post* saw Torres winning most of the rounds, Torres brought home a draw for his efforts.

Retiring from fighting to manage, Louis Newman sought to bring Albuquerque's Jack Torres to the next level. Newman lined up Denver's toughest to temper Torres.

Now campaigning as a light welterweight, unable to dry out to lightweight, Torres took on El Paso's Frankie Fowser next, in Albuquerque, scoring a clean knockdown and winning a newspaper decision in a bout ruled a no-decision if the two finished the fight on their feet. Edging Fowser convinced Newman that it was time to take his understudy on the road.

Newman arranged for Torres to face his toughest foe yet in Midwestern fighter Bud Logan on Nov. 10, 1914, in his first 15-rounder at St. Joseph, Mo. For the first nine rounds, Torres impressed the locals, "beating Logan all the way." Logan came back in the tenth, slowing Torres, and, one round later, as "Torres came out of his corner, Logan caught him on the jaw with a right swing and the boys went into a clinch. A light body blow finished Torres and he sank to the mat."[56]

Despite the loss, boxing scribe Ham Hamilton of the *St. Joseph Gazette* wrote, "Torres probably made the best impression in local fistic circles of any boxer who ever appeared here. He is fast, clever and a hard hitter. His judgment of distance is marvelous. For the first eight rounds of his bout with Logan he moved so fast that the local boy scarcely was able to lay a glove on him."[57]

It was a huge setback for a kid who claimed he was leaving to conquer the world. With his head bowed, Torres returned to the Southwest. A trio of rematches were set up; all three marked a transition in the "Mexican Mist." On Thanksgiving in Santa Fe, Torres scored a decisive win over a bloodied Schaefer in their rematch; on Dec. 10, he fought Riede again, this time a KO in six instead of a win by DQ; and, on Dec. 30, against Pierson, who'd been on even terms with him in July, he won a solid decision.

Newman renewed his efforts to match Torres outside the state. There was no chance to be a world champ fighting in New Mexico and, besides, their free ticket on Levy's cards had been cashed in since Albuquerque's premier promoter was packing up for Santa Fe and then Brooklyn. Nineteen-fifteen was spent almost entirely on the road — and it was a dynamite year for the kid from the *barrio*.

"Torres has biffed his way to popularity," wrote the *Morning Journal*. "Local fans have seen nearly every chapter of his fight to the top in New Mexico. The boy started as a preliminary fighter ... with a long-range right uppercut that carried stunning force and a jack-knife crouch. Torres has discarded both now. He has learned that his abnormally long reach and quick hitting are his best defense and these carry him through most of his bouts unscathed."[58]

Piloted by Newman and now trained by experienced battler Kid George, Torres returned to Missouri to even the score with Logan. The second time around, Torres proved far too clever for Logan, winning a referee's decision in the Missourian's hometown of St. Joseph. The *Gazette*'s Hamilton poured on the praise:

> While we lament the loss of Bud Logan ... we must give due credit to the swarthy skinned boy from the south. He is about the cleverest boxer who ever appeared in a local ring and he fought a grand battle last night. Only cool-headed ring generalship, unquestionably directed from his corner, saved a repetition of Torres' defeat here in November at the hands of Logan. He fought carefully, uncorking his dazzling speed only when he could hit and get away into a cover. His defensive work was out of the ordinary.... Torres is a boy who is likely to beat any man of his weight in the country, and the chances are he can.... Jack Torres is bound to be heard from.[59]

Torres was on his way "to be heard from" in boxing circles.

Based in Denver all year under Newman, with Yoakum and Chavez, Torres went back and forth from Colorado to Missouri. St. Joseph had him back four more times during the year. Along the way, Torres returned just once to New Mexico, in a rubber match on July 5 in Santa Fe with Kid Schaefer, who vowed that "it won't be Torres dickering for championship contests after the 5th. It'll be your old friend Harry — now just pin that in your bonnet."[60]

In a match billed as the fight of the year and drawing a full house, with "43 women including Santa Fe's most prominent society matrons,"[61] Schaefer learned the hard way against the seasoned Torres, who pumped his jab, cut him in the fifth, then closed his eyes with uppercuts in the seventh. In the eighth round, Schaefer was wobbling so badly, his corner threw in the towel to save him from a knockout.

On the road, against much superior opposition, Torres oftentimes had to settle for the draw in someone else's hometown — as in the case of his bout against Eddie Johnson. *Rocky Mountain News* scribe Abe Pollock, scoring it 11-2-2 in rounds for Torres, called it a fiasco, when they met at the Broadway Emporium in Denver, March 17, 1915:

> From start to finish, Torres outhit, outpunched, outfought Johnson, and at the windup the Puebloan was practically at his mercy. And yet Referee George English called it a draw! ... Maybe he saw it that way, but if he did, he was about the only man in the house outside of perhaps Johnson, who did, for all of the verdicts which I have seen, and some of them in small towns, too, this one stands out as one of the worst yet.... Try as Johnson might, he could not do anything with the eel-like lad from New Mexico, who slipped in and out with lightning speed."[62]

The next day, Pollock wrote, "The Torres-Johnson battle was the chief topic of conversation in fandom yesterday, and many expressed themselves as thoroly [*sic*] disgusted with the way the game has been conducted here lately. Bum decisions, fizzles and frosts, with the fighters ready to quit and run out on the promoters, have been the rule, and because we have no boxing commission."[63] Newman tried for a rematch but it could not be arranged.

Twice, in April, and again in September, Torres drew with Johnny Salvatore, another tough Midwestern battler in his prime. In the first, Torres won all but two rounds, closed his opponent's eye in the sixth and had him groggy in the 12th — yet the hometown ref declared it a draw. The second time, local scribes scored it 7-4-4 in rounds for Torres, yet the ref, once again, saw a draw.

Torres fought Dick Wells, of Cincinnati, Ohio, three times during 1915, all in Colorado — with two decisions and a draw, all 15-rounders. "The Mexican came out of the tussles undamaged, with smiles from ear to ear which decorated his countenance," Pollock reported. "Wells ran along the ropes like a tame lion and then ran up to his master, Torres, who chopped him with a countless number of telling wallops."[64]

In the second bout, Torres outlanded Wells three to one for the decision, but in the third, in Trinidad, the ref's ruling of a draw "caused no murmur of dissent," though popular opinion saw Torres ahead in a conflict of styles. Torres "has a nifty way of side-stepping in an exchange and whipping out a right and left from angles, and he seldom fails to hit the bullseye,"[65] the Trinidad press noted.

Another trilogy was fought with Canadian champion Frank Barrieau. With the Canuck showing a masterful defense, Torres was forced to lead and chase, then settle for draws in the first two encounters. In the third, though, Torres had Barrieau figured out, and he brought home the win.

In Denver, Torres TKO'd the usually-durable Phil Kearney, who "saw more gloves than he has ever watched in his boxing career"[66] before throwing up the sponge in the ninth. In St. Joseph, he had to, once again, settle for the draw though outboxing Johnny "Kid" Alberts by utilizing his piston jab "with a right cross that had Alberts completely puzzled."[67]

By the end of 1915, Torres was known throughout the country. Newman declared that the New Mexican, now a full-fledged welterweight, had his sights on no less than the champ, Jack Britton, or the No. 1, Ted "Kid" Lewis, who would trade places with Britton several times over the years. It wasn't enough, however, to be a threat in the Southwest or the Midwest; if you wanted the champ, you had to fight on the East Coast, and that's just what Newman had in mind.

"Now Newman has another Mexican fighter in his stable, Jack Torres of Albuquerque — and the probabilities are that Torres will be the greatest boxer Newman has ever had," the optimistic *Optic* commented in Las Vegas. "If Torres continues to improve as he has improved in the past for another year or two, Jack Torres will be the welterweight champion of the world. And that statement is no foolish guess."[68]

For a time, Newman came close to landing a bout between Torres and Ted Lewis at the Stockyards, but when that fell through, Newman lined up another campaign on the road. Just 19 years old but "fighting with the polish of an old ring-head,"[69] Torres returned to the Midwest for a string of fights that would hopefully inch him closer to the East Coast and fighting under the bright lights of the Garden in New York.

Through March everything seemed to be going right for Torres. He righted his previous draw with Alberts with a decisive win, scoring two knockdown blows in the final 15th, and kept the rust off by fighting lesser names from Missouri to Memphis.

Then came Art Magirl, on March 6. Fighting since 1910, the Bartlesville, Okla. fighter was a known knockout artist with over 100 bouts. The veteran proved too ringwise for Torres, who lost his first fight in 15 months. Surviving two knockdowns though winning an equal number of rounds, Torres was the second choice for the ref after eight hard rounds.

The setback wasn't enough for Newman to pull back from canceling plans for the eastern seaboard, and a rematch was set up two months later, this time in Colorado Springs. With six weeks to prepare, Torres tore up the gym in preparation, while Newman lined up two additional bouts leading up to the Magirl rematch. On May 5 in Kansas City, Torres fought an eight-round draw with Dick Wells again, Torres now 2-0-2 with him. Remaining in Kansas City, Torres took on Mickey Sheridan just one week before Magirl, in what was yet another unpopular draw. "Kansas City fight bugs probably are getting used to them by this time," reported the *Kansas City Star*. "Time and again the crowd has seen a battler win clearly and yet get only a draw or even suffer the decision given against him. Last night it was the same way. Jack Torres outpointed Chicagoan Mickey Sheridan by a safe margin and yet Johnny Hughes raised both hands."[70]

Frustrated with the draws, Torres entered the ring against Magirl on May 19 outweighed 152 to 142. The pressure was on. Western sporting writers were declaring the winner to be a serious contender for the champ Britton, who'd recently defeated Lewis again. Before a crowd of 1,800, Torres fought a close fight until the fateful ninth round, when a questionable knockdown had the local ref stopping the bout and ruling it a TKO win for Magirl.

Torres came home for two fights following the latest setback, beating Jimmy Connors on a Memorial Day show in Albuquerque and a fifth bout with Dick Wells in Las Vegas — their third draw. Meanwhile, Newman was in touch with promoters in Boston, who were looking to keep Lewis busy if Torres was really serious about that East Coast debut.

Newman declined: "While I fancy [Torres] is good enough to hold his own with any man his weight in the world, right now, still I want him to be a bit more seasoned before giving him the supreme test,"[71] he told the press. Newman also turned down an offer to go 15 rounds with the champ Britton, in a non-title bout in Kansas City, feeling Torres was not yet ready to face the top two welterweights in the world. He was, after all, just 20 years old.

In August, Newman took Torres to Idaho to face Johnny Tillman of St. Paul, Minn. Tillman, 22, was on a meteoric rise to contention, and he handed Torres a 15-round loss. Later, Tillman would go on to get a shot at the welterweight title in 1918, losing to then-champ Lewis.

Newman could not afford another setback, so he brought Torres back to Colorado to get him back on track, beating Johnnie Dunn in Walsenburg with a 15-round decision. Torres also joined the camp of top-notcher Charlie White, who was training for a title shot at Freddie Welsh, as *he* prepared for a September rematch with Mickey Sheridan in St. Paul.

After Torres came back with yet another loss, the scribes started to voice their doubt that he was of championship timber. When Lewis was asked about fighting Torres, he responded with, "The young Mexican has proved to be a great fighter, but he hasn't shown the fighting heart and until he does, there is little prospect that he will get a chance."[72]

Newman put Torres on the shelf for two months, then sent him to Kansas City where he won a decision over young local Hugh Walker. Torres came back to Colorado where he fought Wells for the umpteenth time, but this time the Albuquerque kid was knocked out in four rounds. It was a full minute before Torres could get up and stagger to his corner.

Torres was sent back into action a month later, this time dropping a 12-round decision to Sailor Jerabek, who was losing most of his fights. It looked like curtains for Torres, who appeared to be a spent fighter at 21. There *was* something wrong, but no one was talking — certainly not Newman, who was no longer around.

No longer headlining shows, Torres returned to Kansas City for a New Year's Day show in 1917, on a card headlined by Benny Chavez. He was able to net a much-needed win over journeyman Bert Mullen, who pounded Torres unmercifully for the first three rounds, prompting cries of "Stop it!" from the crowd. But Torres held on and, by the eighth, turned the fight around, stopping Mullen. Torres stayed on in Kansas City where, at the end of the month, he picked up a decision over little-known Paul Roman.

Torres was suddenly his old self—at least that's what the Albuquerque papers were now proclaiming. Torres reached out to Mark Levy, now in New York, who agreed to introduce him to the "fistic circles in the big town."[73] Levy had wanted to take Torres with him when he'd moved back to Brooklyn the year before, but Newman had gotten in the way. "Levy believed then, and evidently still believes that Jack will be a strong card in the ten-round game of Gotham."[74]

Just as soon as Torres' "Eastern invasion" was announced, it was cancelled when a "minor injury" turned into a right-shoulder dislocation that now threatened retirement. Torres tried to nurse his shoulder back to fighting form, taking on rising Portland welterweight Al Sommers five weeks later, but he came home from Wallace, Idaho, with another loss.

In April, Torres tried again, this time with Barrieau, against whom, at his best, he'd fought two draws and a win. The fourth Barrieau fight was over in a round-and-a-half:

Barrieau started off like a whirlwind, landed a right jolt to Torres' jaw which shook the Mexican's whole anatomy, and just for good measure, slammed Torres with rights and lefts all around the ring. Torres, who seemed to have a good punch in his right, tried in vain to connect with some vital point on the Canadian fighter's chin or body. He might have been a dead man for all the progress he made. Barrieau saw that the first punch he had landed had dazed Torres, so he followed up his advantage and sent Torres to his corner bleeding from the mouth and apparently wondering if someone had declared war on all Mexicans…. Returning to the conflict, Torres sparred a bit, and seemed to be just about to start something when a few more well-directed wallops on the head [made] him groggy. A right swing to the jaw sent him to the mat and calmly and deliberately he drifted off into Dreamland. He was assisted from the ring by his seconds.[75]

It was over for the "Mexican Mist." After returning home to Albuquerque, where he was called out several times during the year, Torres was diagnosed with cataracts. His eyesight had been declining since 1916, right about the time he'd started to lose.

Torres helped out Benny Cordova, and, to everyone's surprise, accepted a last-minute fight in October 1917 against the much-heavier and, reportedly, undefeated Young Jack Johnson (James Green) in Silver City. It was his last hurrah, and he returned home with a six-round decision win, nearly knocking out the local favorite.

"The fans were rather dubious when Torres entered the ring, for he was outweighed by 20 or 25 pounds by the negro," wrote the *Silver City Independent*. After Johnson landed his one and only big shot, in the first, Torres went to work. "He mussed up Johnson's face with a left jab that seldom failed to land, and worked on the negro's midsection with a pathetic persistency — pathetic for Johnson. He had Johnson doubled up and hanging on in every clinch and from the fourth round until the end of the sixth, had the heavyweight all but out."[76]

Promoter Otto Floto was so impressed he begged Torres to meet Otto Wallace, but Torres declined — he could barely see. There was talk of yet another comeback during the next year or so, against Mexican Pete Everett, Eddie Johnson or Speedball Hayden, but except for an exhibition with his stablemate Cordova, Torres remained retired.

Though he stayed in the game as a referee through the 1920s, the name "Jack Torres" disappeared from the sports page. In the early 1930s, he relocated to Los Angeles where he died in 1970.

Back in Albuquerque, once in a while someone would bring up the question, "Whatever happened to Jack Torres?" The inevitable response: "Wasn't he supposed to be champion?"

Benny Cordova

> They don't make 'em in these parts good enough to beat Bennie Cordova, however. That fact was made evident in yesterday's bout. The little Mexican has more speed, skill, strength and stamina than any lightweight ever seen in this portion of the state, and his claim that he will some day wear the lightweight crown of the world does not look to be an absurd claim to those who have seen him in action.
> — El Paso Herald, 1915[77]

Abenicio Cordova, who started as "Young Cordova" and finished as "Old Man Benny," will not only go down as one of New Mexico's top lightweights, but the man who produced the state's longest running boxing legacy, spanning six decades.

Benny's own 11-year career tells the tale of an Albuquerque boilermaker who repeatedly tried to break into contention, and a Southwestern champion best known for his epic battles with Texan Bobby Waugh — a top contender worthy of a title shot that never came. Over six years, the two would fight seven times in seven different cities, three states and two countries, totaling 105 rounds. Unlike others who were content to remain in New Mexico as state champions, Cordova had no problem going wherever the fights were — and he became a local favorite every place he fought.

The Cordova family came from the village of Cabezon, a stage stop, farming and sheep-raising community in northern New Mexico between Santa Fe and Fort Wingate. Five years after Benny was born, in 1900, the Cordovas relocated to Albuquerque where Benny's father owned a grocery store and dance hall.

At age 17, Cordova took a job with the railroad and the job took him to the border, where he caught the attention of a local promoter: "Jed English was the man to single him out as a boxer. He made his early reputation in impromptu bouts with kids of his home neighborhood. In the neighborhood championship tilts, all boys boxed barefooted and bareknuckled for 10-cent purses. And it was because Benny was unable one day to beat his man with his dukes that he resorted to kicking his opponent in the shins. Benny broke a toe and lost the bout by disqualification. It was his first lesson on the real rules of the game and he steadily advanced from then on."[78]

Benny Cordova of Albuquerque was one of New Mexico's greatest lightweights. A southwestern champ and a fringe contender, he was best known for his seven fights with highly-rated Bobby Waugh, of Fort Worth, Texas. Over six years, the two would fight seven times in seven different cities, three states and two countries, totaling 105 rounds. Unlike others who were content to remain in New Mexico as state champions, Cordova had no problem going wherever the fights were — and he became a local favorite every place he fought.

Benny told his son, Benny, Jr., that it had been the local Juarez promoter who first convinced him to take his aggression from the streets to the ring — and it was his dislike of a local kid he wanted to fight, that provided initial motivation. "There was a young boxer that tried to scare him," recalled Benny, Jr. "His name was 'Kid Pio,' but one punch and the young boxer was out. My dad was convinced by a gentleman by the name of Benitez that he should become a prize fighter. He fought Kid Pio again and knocked him out with one punch. But as he was down he kept on hitting him and lost the fight. I asked him why he kept hitting him. He said, 'At first I thought we were playing, but when they put [on] the gloves, he hit me hard and I got mad.'"[79]

"Benitez" was R. C. Benitez, one of Juarez's first consistent promoters and "Pio" was actually "Payo," one of three fighting brothers. Gene, or "Young" Payo, was Benny's nemesis, at least at first.

Benitez used Cordova in several battle royals, then graduated him into four-rounders in the latter half of 1913. His first two bouts were against the aforementioned Payo — two draws — and they would fight again the following year, Cordova winning one and losing one, by disqualification, for hitting Payo after knocking him down.

With boxing illegal in El Paso, almost all of Cordova's early fights, as many as 20 of them in 1913 and 1914, were at Juarez's Plaza de Toros, where Mexicans and Texans made up a mixed crowd to watch the fights for 50 cents or a dollar. Winning most, but not all, Cordova took on Payo, Gene Delmont and the original Battling Chico, the latter two of whom would develop into solid fighters over the next decade.

A featherweight at first, Cordova moved up to six-, then 10- and 20-rounders by the summer of 1914. His first big test was against black Albuquerque fighter John "Lefty" Floyd, on Aug. 2, 1914. "[Cordova] is coming to the front rapidly and gives every indication of developing into a good lightweight," reported the *El Paso Times*. "He also is a hard hitter and the negro will have a little on him in this respect, while in all other respects the two are about on a par."[80]

It wasn't much of a contest. Cordova sent the more-experienced Floyd to the canvas five times before the bout was stopped in the second, though he was lucky to get away with the win after fouling his foe twice, hitting him while he was down, when Floyd tried to get up from a knockdown. Though praised for his ferocity, he was criticized for his lack of skills and disdain for rules — but that's what made him a local favorite, too.

"Cordova is a fine two-handed fighter with more cleverness than the fighters of his nationality usually possess," wrote the boxing authority at the border, Hy Schneider. "[Aurelio] Herrera, [Joe] Rivers and [Benny] Chavez were not noted for their cleverness. The local Mexican is a tremendous puncher, another feature of the Mexican fighters.... Cordova has shown instances of lack of ring generalship but the writer puts this down to lack of experience. Certain it is that he has shown more in each succeeding fight."[81]

Schneider was right. Cordova improved dramatically, and his next two headlined bouts in Juarez, against far more experienced Charley Lucca, who'd been fighting since 1905 and had nearly 80 bouts, and Walt Walters, resulted in distance draws — but no fouls.

When the scene temporarily dried up, in early 1915, due to the Mexican Revolution, Cordova moved on, diving into the talent-rich waters of Texas and Louisiana. Fighting in frequent spurts, Cordova rode the rails to San Antonio, Galveston, Dallas and Shreveport, fighting the best lightweights in the region.

Cordova's first stop was San Antonio, where he drew with respected New Orleans lightweight Frankie Russell, who'd racked up three times the number of fights against top names, including a newspaper win over Battling Nelson. "That he was game was proved by the drubbing he received," the locals wrote, noting "that he came back and made the New Orleans Italian hang on for dear life in the closing round which speaks well for Cordova."[82]

After the draw with Russell, Cordova rode a streak of knockout wins before he was matched up against his toughest opponent to date in San Antonio, on May 12. No one expected Cordova to stand up to 50-fight veteran, Australian champion Jack Read, but they were giving him a puncher's chance. "Experience, years of it, won the fight for Read," wrote the *San Antonio Light*. "Benny's seconds held him in leash until the final round for a grandstand finish and a knock-out which, however, was not forthcoming."[83] Needing a knockout to win, Cordova tore into Read, nearly taking him out in the tenth, winning the round but not the fight. Despite the wide margin of points lead, the referee was criticized for giving Read the fight and the police had to stifle a near riot when fans stormed the ring demanding that Cordova be issued a draw.

Read's manager, Bud Burmester, was outraged with Cordova, complaining of repeated fouls, the most blatant of which was in the fifth when Cordova threw Read to the floor. Cordova showed "such a display of tricks of the game, [it] leads me to think that Cordova has had more fights than he is credited with and it is hardly possible for him to learn them in such a short time."[84]

At the time, Cordova had less than 20 bouts — he later attributed his "display of tricks" to learning the fight game at the border.

Despite the loss, and being outgeneraled for most of the fight, San Antonio fans praised him as a coming champ, and he stayed on for several more fights, drawing with Jack Shelton and rematching Russell. In three San Antonio bouts, Cordova and Russell would result in two draws and one no-decision. Cordova had Clarence "Kid" Ligon quitting after five rounds, and earned a draw with top-notcher Tommy Gary, who hit cleaner and won the newspaper vote, though Benny's gameness and ability to absorb punishment swayed the referee to rule it even.

By mid-year, Cordova's Texas invasion was making enough noise to draw attention in Albuquerque. Promoter Levy started talking about bringing Benny home, possibly against Stanley Yoakum. "Cordova, although a Barelas boy, has never fought here," noted the *Morning Journal*. "The San Antonio, Tex. people think he is the coming lightweight champion and their opinion coupled with the showing he has made in scraps there has stirred up local interest and aroused a desire to see him in the ring."[85] It would be nearly another year before that happened.

In the meantime, if Cordova was going to make it in Texas, Cordova knew he had to fight Fort Worth battler Bobby Waugh. By 1915, there were very few fighters in the Southwest that Waugh hadn't fought. Active since 1911 with an estimated 50 bouts, the Fort Worth battler was being touted as a coming champ hoping for a shot at a bona fide contender, if not the champion.

In July, Cordova got his wish to face Waugh, and the two clashed in Shreveport, or rather, Cordova *survived* Waugh, who "made a chopping block of ... the highly touted Mexican lightweight.... Cordova's holding on tactics is all that saved him from a knockout."[86]

Cordova would get another chance — in fact, he would get *six* more, two more in 1915. Six weeks after his boxing lesson with Waugh, Cordova, "anxious to wipe out the stain of defeat," got his rematch. "He will battle with the grim determination that has marked his fights in San Antonio."[87]

It was a much different fight, and despite a "hurricane finish," the man everyone was calling the top Texas lightweight couldn't get more than a draw against the young border battler. Waugh had Cordova's eye bleeding in the fifth and led for several rounds following the injury, but "Benny boxed the best bout he ever has shown here, showing he is improving in the fine points of the game at a rapid rate. He is fast getting out of the habit of letting the other champ lead and score points while he rests on his oars. The Mexican right now can give any lightweight in this vicinity a run for his money."[88]

Despite putting himself on even terms with Waugh, Cordova was passed over when Juarez promoters chose the Fort Worth battler to fight Battling Nelson on the border's biggest battle of the year. In an epic war, Waugh would get the win.

Cordova telegraphed a challenge to the victor — and it was accepted. This time, the promoters of Juarez took heed of the fighter who'd been groomed at the border, and, using the momentum created by Waugh in defeating Nelson, brought back Cordova. In his final bout of 1915, scheduled for Sept. 19, just two weeks after Waugh beat Nelson, Cordova returned to his old haunts at the border to prepare.

This time around, the 133-pounders would go the long route — 20 instead of the 10- and 15-round matches previously fought. Cordova and Waugh arrived a week before, allowing the border towns plenty of time to hype the fight that would see the former homeboy taking on the conqueror of a legend. Though Waugh was a favorite, given his experience and ring generalship, the "husky little Mexican" who'd drawn with Waugh the month before had a better-than-average chance for the upset. "In the opinion of the writer, who saw Cordova's first preliminary fight, the improvement of the Albuquerque boy is little short of a revelation," wrote Bud Rutherford of the *El Paso Times*. "Cordova figures to whip Waugh, as his speed and aggressiveness exceeds that of the Texas champion, while his punching ability is undoubtedly greater," but "Benny was swinging a pair of school books from a strap while the Fort Worth boy was having his first fights."[89]

Fight fans skipped back and cross the border so many times during the week to visit the two camps, that everyone forgot there was a Mexican Revolution going on. In fact, representatives of General Pancho Villa, in occupation of Juarez, assured Americans that they *could* come and go, "with every assurance as to their personal safety and confident that the authorities will afford them every courtesy and protection. In short, visitors to Juarez are as safe there as El Paso."[90]

Promoter Meek of the Juarez Athletic Club spiced up the showdown by promising that he would secure no less than World Lightweight Champion Freddie Welsh to fight the winner and that Juarez would become the fight center of the continent. There was also talk of fighting Joe Rivers in California for a big $3,000 payday. Neither one happened, though.

The fight itself did turn out to be a fight of the ages, of sorts, but not without controversy. The turnout was disappointing — only 1,800 — but only because it poured and poured, from round one to round 20, until the crowd, fighters and canvas were soaked and soggy. The gloves were so wet "they felt as if they weighed a pound before the contest was half over, the punches taking a peculiar flopping effect."[91] The *Times'* Rutherford wrote:

> Whipped by a consistent wind and beaten by an incessant rain, which fell without intermission, Benny Cordova and Bobby Waugh fought like two little battlers in the Juarez arena last night for some sixty minutes to a draw in the opinion of Referee Billy Smith ... and last night that shade can safely be awarded to the dark-skinned little Mexican by virtue of forcing the fight and landing

Ticket stub, Benny Cordova vs. Bobby Waugh III. Of their seven fights, the third one became the most controversial after Waugh declared he'd been threatened by Pancho Villa's forces to let Cordova win. The press wrote otherwise — that Cordova deserved the draw.

the cleaner blows during the latter part of the encounter. Of course, Waugh earned a fair share of the honors, but on the merits of the battle, is only fair to accord a shade to the fast little New Mexican who had his opponent on the defense from the thirteenth on.... The two combatants sparred, slipped, slammed and skidded over the slippery canvas with first one having the advantage and then the other, alternating in leads and the scoring of points.... Any time these two men meet there will be a real fight in store.[92]

Referee Smith — the same Smith who'd fought as "Australian Billy" in the 1890s — ruled it draw, and the crowd did not complain. Rutherford saw it even up until the 13th round when Cordova, bleeding badly, took over, snapping one-twos and weathering the deadly uppercuts thrown by the Texan. Cordova had proven himself a better boxer and a huge improvement over the fouling slugger who'd left the border the year before.

There was no controversy. At least not until Waugh returned to Fort Worth. There, he told the press that a representative of General Villa — Pancho's brother Hipolito, who administered the revenues from gambling and horse racing that helped fund the revolutionaries — had threatened him with death if he whipped Cordova. Therefore, Waugh said, he'd stalled, fearing to open up on his opponent. Later, the story expanded to include that Hipolito Villa had bet heavily on Cordova and did not want to lose. The story became part of the legend that was Waugh and, by the time he passed away, Hipolito had been replaced with Pancho, who'd personally threatened the *gringo* fighter from Texas.

But at the border, there was no mention of Villa or threats — and no controversy mentioned in the newspapers — just a close fight the locals saw as Cordova winning, but barely.

Unbeknownst that he would soon be hearing about Waugh's alibi, Cordova came home to Albuquerque to relax and undergo a nose operation, his sinuses making it difficult to breathe during a fight. Now a celebrity in his hometown, the *Journal* reported, "Benny Cordova, a little broader, a little more 'set' and bearing a few reminiscences of his battles in the way of a slightly cauliflowered ear and a sadly battered nose, is back home. Aside from these minor matters Benny is much the same as ever. He is just as modest as he always was and the laurels he has been winning do not seem to have oppressed his spirit or creased his brow."[93]

Cordova took the rest of the year off, but after reading about Waugh's account of their 20-rounder in Juarez, immediately agreed to fight his nemesis again. The two were scheduled for Jan. 31, 1916, this time in Waugh's hometown of Fort Worth.

Offering no excuses, Cordova came home with a hard-fought 15-round decision loss in a fight Fort Worth scribes said wasn't even close: "Bobby did not let Cordova win a round, although in three stanzas the Mexican got an even break by some extraordinary feats in boxing. Waugh took the other twelve rounds with a big margin to spare.... He stepped in and out of the Mexican's guard at will and on one or two occasions made the brown skinned San Antonio boy appear as a novice. For some time Cordova has been heralded as Waugh's most worthy rival among Texas lightweights, but aside from his ability to assimilate Bobby's heavy drives, the Mexican does not class with the native son."[94]

Cordova moved on to Galveston, where Waugh was right behind him. In March, they fought a fifth time, with Waugh's hometown paper printing, "This will make the 'steenth time that Bobby has met the greaser and in view of the terrible lacing given Benny at their last meeting, it is a big wonder if the Mexican would stand for a return engagement."[95]

Not only did Cordova, the "greaser," "stand" up to Waugh, but referee Torrence actually awarded him the decision after ten tough rounds in the Galveston ring. "The action met with a round of hisses from the big crowd present. [The referee] also received a punch in the jaw from the Fort Worth battler. ... Torrence then announced that he had made a mistake in giving Cordova the fight and called it a draw. The first decision given by Torrence was hasty and ill advised."[96]

It was a new low point for Cordova, but it would only get worse. In his next fight, also in Galveston, he suffered the first knockout loss of his career against Jack Shelton, San Antonio's answer to the Texas championship. One report had Shelton landing a right on the chin; other reports claimed Cordova had been struck while trying to rise from his knees.

Regardless, Cordova had had enough of Texas, for now, and he came home to Albuquerque to fight for the first time in his career. Despite the reputation Cordova had built up on the road against top-notch fighters, he had to settle for second billing to headliner Jack Torres on a Memorial Day card. As a homecoming gift, he was given Lefty Floyd, whom Cordova had already knocked out early on.

This time around, Floyd swore he was in proper condition for "Mistah Cordova." "If you want to hear a hearty laugh, just step up to Floyd and tell him Cordova says he is going to knock him out,"[97] the *Journal* suggested, doing its best to hype the fight. Cordova "went about his slaughter with the mathematical calmness of a vivisectionist. He drove home lefts and rights to Floyd's body almost at will."[98]

Sparring regularly with Torres brought Louis Newman into the picture. The fast-talking manager promised him big things — possibly a fight with Ad Wolgast — if he came up north. In June, Cordova took on tough Joe "The Wop" Flynn in Denver. The fight was going his way until the 11th when Flynn turned it around, winning by a TKO. Less than a month later, Cordova was in Raton, where veteran Walt Walters outpointed him in a 15-rounder.

Calling it quits with Newman, Cordova came home and returned to work as a boilermaker, putting aside thoughts of prizefighting. Until September, that is, when he got an offer he couldn't refuse down in Silver City — a $1,000 purse to be split 75/25 toward the winner. Times were changing — purses were getting lighter and the feel of war was in the air. This might have been seen as his last civilian fight in a while. All Cordova had to do was defeat Bud Anderson, formerly of Tacoma, Wash.

Two years before, Anderson had been heralded as a coming champ, having defeated Leach Cross, Joe Mandot and K. O. Brown. But after an attack of appendicitis, gallstones and a shipyard accident where a co-worker had turned a compressed air-gun on him as a practical joke, Anderson had undergone a series of operations and been forced to retire. Now the former topnotcher was working his way out of the mines of Santa Rita and staging a comeback.

Cordova was the perfect opponent — he was known in the southern half of the state, had drawn with Waugh on two occasions and best of all, he'd lost his last two fights. In a bout advertising a Southwest lightweight championship, Cordova and Anderson went one shy of the scheduled 20. It was a punishing battle for both fighters, "Anderson fighting desperately with his kidney punch and body blows, which made him a winner in his prime," while "Cordova assimilated a world of punishment, mastered Anderson's style of battling along toward the close and finally ended the contest with a right hook to the jaw, which sent Anderson to the canvas for the final count."[99]

Forster tried to arrange a fight between Cordova and Ad Wolgast, but the former champ wanted too much money. Seven-hundred and fifty dollars richer, Cordova came home to his wife and two-year-old son. "Benny has a job that pays him nearly $100/per month and he intends to stick to it until he organizes another bank roll before again taking up the fight game,"[100] wrote the *El Paso Times*.

Four months later, he was heading back down to southern New Mexico, this time having

Benny Cordova's 1917 showdown with soldier champion Tommy O'Toole at the Smelter Arena began a losing streak for the New Mexican lightweight. O'Toole punished Cordova for ten rounds in the outdoor venue in a windy hail storm.

agreed to fight Tommy O'Toole, now the man to beat at the border. Could be that Cordova was underestimating O'Toole, a Fort Bliss soldier boxer with limited prize-fight experience before enlisting. Though undefeated at the border, O'Toole was no Bobby Waugh.

The two were scheduled for ten rounds at the newly-erected Smelter Arena, on the New Mexico side of the Rio Grande. With "his chest well pumped up," Cordova blew into town a week before to train at the Central Café in El Paso with the Payo brothers, telling the press, "I'm anxious to meet this hard hitting soldier from the Pennsy artillery camp, for I think I can still hold my own with most any of them. He's touted as a good boy — just the kind I want to meet. I'm going to do everything I can to beat him and convince the El Paso boxing fans that Cordova is still the king bee in this part of the country."[101]

The fight kicked off a disastrous year of 1917 for Cordova.

The expected crowd of 3,000 was cut in half when a storm pelted the outdoor arena — and O'Toole proceeded to pelt Cordova. "Tommy O'Toole certainly looked like a million dollars yesterday when he crowned Benny Cordova with everything except the water bottle at the Smelter arena,"[102] wrote Chuck Swan of the *El Paso Herald*. "Benny Cordova never had a ghost of a chance," agreed the *Times*. After an even first round, O'Toole gave the veteran a beating and Cordova weathered, both, the weather and the soldier boxer, for ten miserable rounds.

Cordova fought three more times in 1917, losing a 20-round decision to Kid Ligon, whom he'd KO'd two years before, at Silver City in April, though the crowd booed the verdict; a four-round decision in Vernon, California, to Tommy O'Brien that had Cordova coming home early from a West Coast "invasion"; and, in October, a 20-round decision in his sixth fight against Waugh.

Waugh was ever on Cordova's mind and, this time, the stakes were big. In his biggest promotion of the year, promoter Floto was promising the winner a guaranteed match against legend Joe Rivers. Though he'd told the press he'd retired to raise a family and work for the railroad, Cordova could not — and would not — turn down the chance to face Waugh again, not when a win would mean bigger paydays and a chance at a star like Rivers.

Cordova gave it his all — and for the first nine rounds, anyway, gave as good as he got. But Waugh was too seasoned, and in the prime of his life. After Waugh caught Cordova with a left hook to the point of the chin in the ninth, Cordova became little more than a sponge for punishment, showing just a few flashes of his old self. In the 12th, Cordova went down from a body shot and, in the 16th, met the canvas again before being saved by the bell. "Never in a local ring did a boxer take a worse beating,"[103] wrote the *Silver City Enterprise*.

Cordova returned to his trade and family in the Duke City, vowing never to fight again. He'd be as good as his word, at least for two years.

Baca, Connolly and the First Rivalries

The report has been going the rounds that Baca expects to win in jug time with a K. O., but this is taken with a grain of salt in the Connolly camp. Of course, the latter has more at stake in that he is the title holder of the lightweight championship of New Mexico, but on the other hand, that is a crown that Baca has coveted for some time, and he is sure to make a hard effort to wrest it from Connolly.

— *Santa Fe New Mexican*, 1921[104]

Like no other sport, rivalries have fueled, and oftentimes defined, boxing. Where would Muhammad Ali have been without Joe Frazier or George Foreman? Or Joe Louis without Max Schmeling? Boxing in New Mexico was no exception.

In its first prosperous era, rivalries made the era. Benny Cordova would never have proven to be half the fighter he was if Bobby Waugh had not been around to bring out his best. Louis Newman's trilogy with Stanley Yoakum not only peaked the Las Vegas fighter, but prompted him to hang up the gloves to manage not only his former rival, but also Benny Chavez and Jack Torres.

Torres had his own rival, in Harry "Kid" Schaefer, between 1914 and 1915, all in New Mexico, and four bouts against Frank Barrieau, all on the road. Ev Winters fought Frankie White four times upstate, and in Silver City, Gus Flores battled Spider Moffatt as many times. Benny Chavez would have no fewer than four main nemeses, whom he fought as many as six times. In New Mexico, out-of-town middleweights Jack Herrick, Bob York, Kid Thomas and Kid George fought each other so many times that sportswriters lost count.

The fights the locals cared most about, however, were the ones fought on home turf between home fighters — and there were plenty of 'em. Perfecto Romero fought trios with Manuel "Young" Chavez, Young Herrera, Demon Rivera and the original Insurrecto Kid; against Jack Carson, there were no fewer than seven bouts. Rivera fought Young Chavez three times and crosstown rival Perfecto Baca four, maybe five times; Young Duran and Benny Carson stepped to it four times in one year, while Duran and Mike Baca had five wars between 1913 and 1916.

The most grueling and most popular of all state rivalries — at least until the '60s when Flory Olguin and Joey Limas would get into it, and the '90s storybook rivalry between Johnny Tapia and Danny Romero — was the one between Santa Fe's Mike Baca and Johnny Connolly of Roswell. Between 1915 and 1921, the two would face one another a total of nine times, once fighting two days in a row. As individual fighters, Baca and Connolly might not have been able to transcend the state and turn the heads of West or East Coast scribes, but their rivalry defined the state.

In over 100 years of boxing in Roswell, there was never as popular a fighter as "The Pecos Valley Wonder." Born in 1893, John Boyle Connolly arrived in Roswell around 1910 when his family moved from Clare, Iowa. He was enrolled at the New Mexico Military Institute, where he took up the sport of boxing.

At age 19, Connolly was fighting as a pro, whizzing through the locals as the Roswell and eastern New Mexico fight scene burgeoned. Fighting often at home, in Clovis, Capitan and Carrizozo, Connolly quickly established himself as the top featherweight in the lower half of the state when he stopped eastern New Mexico favorite Red Billingsley on Oct. 13, 1913.

In his first big fight, for the mythical Southwest featherweight championship, Connolly, undefeated with fewer than 20 bouts, was pitted against 200-bout West Coast veteran Spider Moffatt in his hometown for a Fourth of July celebration card. Connolly should have been the underdog, but in Roswell, the less-savvy scribes saw a toss-up. "Spider says he is going to whip Johnny and Johnny says he is going to whip Spider — so there you are," ran the *Roswell Record*. "Pick your winner on hunches, intuition or otherwise and may the best boy win. It's a positive certainty that both are going in for victory and blood and it will be a real battle and not resemble in any manner whatever a pink tea social or 'Café Chantant.'"[105]

Though outweighed, the Roswell kid's aggression earned him a draw against the crafty Spider. "The local boy started in like a house-afire and during the opening round landed pretty stiff on his older opponent. Moffatt grew stronger towards the middle of the fight but things were a nip-and-tuck affair until the end."[106]

The fight was so good, a rematch was set up for Lovington, one month later, resulting in yet another draw, this time in eight rounds. The publicity got a boost when the Spider put on exhibitions sparring with his wife.

Connolly moved up to lightweight, then moved on, beating El Paso veteran Dutch Crozier and Oklahoman Tip Gross — his toughest to date. By the middle of 1915, Connolly declared himself New Mexico's lightweight champion. Only problem was, the upper half of the state was declaring a young Santa Fean as champ.

Prior to 1915, lightweight had been the loaded division in New Mexico. But the old-timers — Newman, Winters and Yoakum, namely — had retired or moved on, to be replaced by youngsters. Mike Baca, the "Pride of Santa Fe" was seen as the best of them. His family native New Mexican, Miguel Baca was born the same year as Connolly, 1893, in Santa Fe. He started fighting one year after Connolly, in 1913.

Johnny Connolly

Of Roswell, the lightweight champion of New Mexico, who is to meet Tommy Nelson, of El Paso the Border lightweight champion, in a 10 round go

AT THE ARMORY

THURSDAY JULY 15th.

Auspices of the American Legion

Johnny Connolly took on tough Tommy Nelson in Roswell, July 15, 1920. Besides his nine bouts with Mike Baca, Nelson was one of his more significant wins.

Tempered by tougher locals than those Connolly breezed through, Baca defeated the best feathers, between his hometown and Albuquerque, putting his first rivalry behind him with three wins over scrappy Young Duran. By the end of his first year, Santa Feans thought he was good enough to beat Jack Torres, but after a first round knockout — his first loss — he came home and got back on the saddle. Moving up to lightweight, Baca's only setback in 1914 was a DQ. By the end of the year, with Torres having moved to welterweight who was fighting on the road for bigger stakes, Baca was seen as the leading lightweight. Unless you lived in Roswell, for that's where Baca was headed in the early fall of 1915. For the next year and a half, Connolly and Baca were all about fighting Baca and Connolly. Connolly *only* fought Baca, while the Santa Fean had a few other fights.

Connolly's backers had wanted Baca earlier, but the fight had been turned down. One year later, there was no getting around it, and Baca's team figured the biggest statement that could be made was to fight the Pecos Valley Wonder in his backyard. "This is the contest the fight fans have been wanting to see for two years," stated the *Santa Fe New Mexican*. "The news was hailed with delight."[107]

They met on Sept. 6, 1915, before a packed house at the Roswell Armory, for what would be the first of nine clashes, with a total distance run of 102 rounds. As hyped as it was, between the Santa Fe and Roswell dailies, there was no smack talk between fighters. Connolly gave nothing but respect to Baca, who, in turn, called his foe the classiest fighter he'd ever face.

"While there was action galore, there was little blood and the contest was clean and free of all brutality,"[108] reported the *Roswell Evening News*. With a reach and four-pound weight advantage, Connolly outboxed Baca for the decision.

The rematch was booked for Feb. 31, 1916, this time on Baca's turf, at the Elks' Theater, in a winner-take-all ten-round fight. Though the card was stolen with yet another rivalry match — Demon Rivera vs. Perfecto Romero, "who fought like tiger cubs" for the state featherweight title — Baca showed enough improvement to earn a draw. "The second fight began breezily enough," reported the *New Mexican*, "but before the middle the pugilists seemed to lack steam and their punches resembled polite taps. Connolly's defense work and Baca's violent rushes in the early part of the fight won the approval of fight fans."[109]

Seven months later, Baca was back in Roswell, determined to defeat Connolly, but he came home with a draw — better than a loss, though it left New Mexico without a definitive lightweight champion.

With war on the horizon, opportunities were drying up for professional boxers, but when promoters in Hagerman (between Roswell and Artesia) staged a grand Fourth of July celebration in 1917, Baca and Connolly were not only booked for their fourth engagement — but their *fifth*.

After two fights in two days, ten rounds apiece, on July 3 and 4, a winner — and state champ — was declared. On Tuesday night, the 3rd, the referee opted to rule a draw between the evenly matched lightweights, but one night later, the "Pecos Valley Wonder" was declared winner, for the second time in their five-bout series. "In the seventh Connolly delivered a blow to the heart and Baca was never able to fight after that,"[110] reported the *Roswell Record*.

Connolly took time off, going to Hot Springs (which was later renamed Truth or Consequences) for "treatment, rest and recuperation"[111] — a portent that things were 100 percent with the Roswell fighter's health. Soon after, both Baca and Connolly enlisted in the U.S. Army and their paths took them elsewhere. When the war was over, Baca and Connolly would resume their personal war, in the ring.

Tragedy

Three local lads who bid fair to work their respective ways towards championships in their classes. Young Joe Rivers, bantamweight; Benny Cordova, lightweight; and Jack Torres, welterweight, have all done such uniformly good work that they are right now knocking at the doors of the champions in their classes.

— Santa Fe New Mexican, 1916[112]

A "square" fellow in the ring and out of it, Harry Schaefer had many friends here.... *As a boxer Schaefer was a game lad and popular. But he was never known to fake or loaf it in the ring here.*

— Gallup Independent, 1916[113]

Death rang the final bell in New Mexico's first golden age of boxing.

One fighter had been groomed in the trenches of local prelims; the other had arrived in the new state with experience, but after conquering hometowners had been accepted as one of New Mexico's own. Just as Albuquerque closed the door on boxing, both fighters had been forced to hit the road in order to get a fight. One fighter went to Denver and never came back; the other headed to Gallup but never arrived.

Originally from Cheyenne, Wyo., Harry "Kid" Schaefer — his real name Francis Gentil — had been a full-fledged veteran by the time he got to Albuquerque in 1913. Fighting since 1910 from Wyoming to Chicago, Schaefer found steady employment on Levy-promoted cards in the Duke City as a gatekeeper, of sorts. Matched up against youngsters wanting to prove themselves better-than-club-level and experienced enough to take on any visiting veteran as a main event, Schaefer was always one fight away from becoming a comer himself, but, over time, became *the* man to beat at lightweight.

A draw with Raton's Ev Winters and several wins over John "Kid" Anaya opened eyes, but it was his trilogy with Jack Torres that gave him the most acclaim. A ten-round draw in April 1914 was followed by a decision win in the upset of the year, eight months later. After he scored a big win in Juarez, in which he floored top veteran Bob York eight times en route to a decision win, a rematch with Torres in July 1915 saw him TKO'd in eight — by then, Torres had proved himself in another class, just beyond Schaefer's abilities.

While clamoring for a fourth shot at Albuquerque's rising star and unable to score a fight in his adopted hometown, beyond a four-rounder in January 1916, Schaefer rode the rails west on the Santa Fe No. 9 toward Gallup where a ten-rounder had been arranged against Charles Boyd.

To keep warm, Schaefer found a spot on the engine car between the coal passer and the back of the water tank — a two-foot space that is, alternately, empty, then occupied by coal as the passer slowly releases air. It was there the pugilist's body was found, behind a pile of coal that had slowly crushed the life out of him. Eight dollars and letters from his wife were found in his pockets.

The life and death of Perfecto Romero was even more tragic — only because the demise did not occur on a train, but in the ring.

Perfecto was one of dozens of Romeros who fought out of New Mexico; and one of at least 100 fighters who took some form of the "Joe Rivers" moniker. The original Joe Rivers was Jose Ybarra, a fourth-generation California fighter of Mexican descent who fought from 1910 to 1923. There was also "Arizona Joe Rivers," "California Joe Rivers," "Soldier Joe Rivers," "Gloucester Joe Rivers," a couple of "Mexican Joe" Riverses, "El Paso Joe

Rivers," and even a "Sunny Joe Rivers." Romero was one of dozens of "Young Joe Rivers" who fought in the next three decades.

Long before there were straw-weight and minimum-weight divisions, there were "paper-weights," and that's where you could find the 105-pounder who turned pro on March 28, 1913, on a Levy-promoted card that saw Schaefer hand Manuel "Kid" Stern his first loss, landing an uppercut that "raised Stern off his feet and when he landed he fell in a heap."[114]

Like other paperweights, Romero had the misfortune of having to give up weight against bantamweights, just to get a fight. But he also had the fortune to fight in the South-west where others his own size were readily available. More often than not, though, that meant having to fight the same opponents more than once. Between 1913 and 1916, Romero fought Manuel Chavez, Leo Luna and the original Insurrecto Kid three times apiece, and stepped into the ring against Jack Carson seven times.

After three years of prelim bouts and growing into a bantamweight without a single loss on his record, Romero was ready for a headline fight by 1916. Only problem was, the scene was drying up in the Duke City and the native New Mexican, following in the footsteps of Newman, Chavez and Torres, would first have to make it or break it in Denver.

The first bout in the Mile High City came off without a hitch when he knocked out Charley Snyder in three rounds. Then he was matched with San Francisco's Jack Bratton before the National Athletic Club on Dec. 7, 1916. In a six-round bout at 118, Romero lost for the first time in his career when, with a "clear lead in four of the six rounds, an even break in one and one-half sessions, the referee for some unknown reason decided that a whirlwind finish by Bratton, in the latter half of the final round was sufficient to wipe out all scores."[115]

After local papers complained of the injustice, a rematch was booked for Dec. 18 — Romero's first ten-rounder with a co-main

Perfecto Romero, a.k.a. "Young Joe Rivers," was undefeated in New Mexico when he went to Denver in 1916. After losing a hometown decision to Jack Bratton on Dec. 7, 1916, at the demand of local press he was rematched for Dec. 18. During the fight, he was knocked down four times and, after the stoppage in round six, he soon died from a brain hemorrhage (Courtesy Rosalie Spinello).

billing. The results made front page news of the *Rocky Mountain News*: "FIGHTER IS KILLED AT NATIONAL CLUB BY BLOW ON HEAD."[116]

Unlike in the first bout, Romero had been "taking a severe beating" by Bratton. In the fifth, he went down four times, twice by body shots, twice by head blows. "Apparently ignorant of the rules of the ring which permit a fighter knocked to the floor to take the count of nine, he staggered to his feet, only to be met with another blow before he could collect his senses sufficiently to 'cover.'" Refusing to quit, let alone rest during the minute between rounds, Romero insisted on standing while his corner desperately worked on him. When the bell rang, "he walked half dazed to the center of the ring, where he was met with a blow on the head. He went to the floor but arose with a set smile, apparently unable to find his opponent. Again Bratton hit him, and this time seconds threw the towel into the ring, signifying the end of the encounter."[117] Romero was assisted back to the dressing room where he was given "several kinds" of stimulants. An hour and a half after the bout, "he told his cornermen that he felt fine, then stood up, fell back suddenly and died."[118]

The fight shook up Denver boxing circles and there was an investigation into the fight, but the blows were ruled accidental by a jury. Bratton, who insisted his blows hadn't been that hard, was cleared of any wrongdoing. Though a heart attack was given as cause of death, it was changed to a cerebral hemorrhage.

"No gamer fighter entered the ring than young Romero," wrote the *Albuquerque Journal*. "He loved the game for its own sake, and the size of the purse seemed to matter not half so much to him as the joy of fighting.... His whirlwind style of fighting endeared him to all lovers of a good, hearty scrap. It was never necessary to urge him to get going — the great difficulty that his handlers had was in preventing him from over-exerting himself in the early stages of a contest. He numbered his admirers here by the hundred, and there was no lack of backing for him when it was announced that he would go in the ring. He was never beaten by any boy of his inches and weight, and there is little doubt that had he lived he would have become a fighter of note."[119]

10. Fall and Rise, Fall and Rise — the Saga of Benny Chavez, 1912–1917

Out in the district of the frijoles Chavez is looked upon as the greatest fighting machine ever raised there.

— *Kansas City Post*, 1916[1]

One year into the game, it was obvious that many changes had to be made if Chavez was going to live up to the Southwest's heavy expectations making the transition from comer to contender. There was no shame in losing during your rookie years, even getting KO'd by a fighter like Patsy Brannigan, but the hype that had preceded his growth had his home states, Colorado and New Mexico, demanding nothing less than a remarkable return as Chavez entered his second year of fighting as a pro.

The first fight of 1912 was supposed to spell redemption — a rematch in Dallas against Young Abe Attell, against whom Chavez had admitted carrying when they fought in Trinidad in 1911. This time there was no slacking to cover a bet although, perhaps underestimating Attell's ability and unable to land his wild swings, Chavez came home with a 15-round decision loss after being outjabbed.

After a get-back win in Trinidad, Chavez sought a bigger fight but Colorado promoters were reluctant. Mark Levy of Albuquerque was not, and he offered the Wagon Mound-born bantam a second home. Chavez wanted too much money at first, which did not make him many fans in the city that had been revved up to receive him. When no other fights materialized, Chavez conceded and, for the next year, he bounced back and forth from New Mexico to Colorado, stacking up win after win in a comeback that soon marked him as the Southwest's bantamweight champion on the verge of contention.

Levy headlined Chavez twice in May 1912, first taking out overmatched, unknown Brooklyn foe Kid Dix, who'd been fighting in Kansas City and Denver. The mismatch did not draw, but the next card, one week later, packed it.

In a 20-rounder for the Rocky Mountain bantamweight championship, Chavez was rematched with 17-year-old "Aspen Whirlwind" Harry Riede (a.k.a. "Johnny Murphy"), who'd been chasing his Trinidad nemesis since losing to him the year before. Once again, Chavez poured it on Riede, who "assimilated enough punishment toward the close of the battle to have put out half a dozen fighters."[2]

Reports of the fight enticed Trinidad promoters to stage a third Chavez-Riede fight on the Fourth of July — the same day as the Johnson-Flynn heavyweight championship in Las Vegas and the Rivers-Wolgast lightweight title match in Los Angeles. Before a crowd

of 800, and just a few minutes after the crowd had been informed that Johnson was still the heavyweight champion, Chavez closed the book on Riede, stopping him in the eighth after a bloody battle that saw the Aspen kid battered mercilessly.

In between the Riede bouts, Chavez headlined his first show in Las Vegas, scoring yet another big win, this time over East Coast comer Johnny "Kid" Williams, who made things "extremely interesting" in the early rounds, until "Chavez got his famous right uppercut to Williams' jaw"[3] for three knockdowns and the count. Williams was enough of a name to use twice. In December 1912, Chavez beat him up in Trinidad, this time stopping him two rounds sooner.

Overmatched Max Feeney, of Omaha, and Eddie Leach, of Raton, who was knocked out cold in the 12th, kept Chavez busy, but Tommy Ryan, who dropped a decision to Chavez in October, before yet another sold-out show in Albuquerque, was a hard enough fight to warrant a New Year's Day rematch in 1913. The standing-room-only show watched Chavez outclass Ryan until the ninth when the New Mexican suffered a flash knockdown. Chavez reassured his growing fan base by nearly stopping Ryan at the final bell.

Chavez's only blemish of 1912 was a draw in Walsenburg, Colorado, against Olaf Shonskey, who, outweighing Chavez by 13 pounds, suffered three knockdowns and a beating, but was somehow awarded a draw by a referee. The decision nearly sparked a riot.

The biggest win of the year took place on Labor Day in what was Trinidad's biggest fight to date.

No doubt about it, former world champion Monte Attell — brother to living legend Abe Attell — was the biggest name since Brannigan. Though past his prime,

As depicted in 1912–1913, Benny Chavez just might be the greatest fighter ever to come out of New Mexico. Born in Wagon Mound, New Mexico, Chavez started fighting professionally after his family relocated to Trinidad, Colorado.

Attell was considered, at least in Colorado, to be "just one rung down from the ladder from being where [World Champion Johnny] Coulon is."[4] The top-notch veteran, active since 1902, had been the reigning bantam champ in 1909, until Frankie Conley beat him in '10, during which time his brother Abe had been the featherweight champ. Since losing the title, however, Monte had been reduced to a trial horse, though his experience, 71 bouts in all, and having fought everyone from Johnny Kilbane to Brannigan, made him a big risk for a 19-year-old with just 20 fights.

They were scheduled for 20 rounds,

Ticket stub for Chavez vs. Attell. Headlining Central Park in Trinidad, Colorado, Benny Chavez defeated former World Bantamweight Champion Monte Attell, who lost by disqualification for striking the hometown favorite during the 12th round. Benny was safely ahead on low points by the time of stoppage.

though it would go less than a dozen. Attell's body blows and infighting gave Chavez trouble, but the ex-champ had seen better days. Chavez landed the harder shots, flooring Attell four times and slicing open a cut over the left eye before the 12th round when, having been warned several times prior, the ex-champ was disqualified for a low blow. Most people would remember what came after. After referee Chris Waller held up Chavez's arm, declaring him winner, Attell's manager, David Goorback, struck the referee. The ring was rushed by spectators, officials and cornermen, causing the platform to collapse. Luckily, no one was seriously hurt.

After the Attell fight, Chavez's manager, George Joseph, aggressively called out all Southwest bantams, including El Paso's Kid Payo, former champ Harry Forbes and Brannigan. Chavez was now touted, at least in the Southwest, as a bona fide aspirant for the world's championship.

It was time to leave. At least that was the advice given by Albuquerque promoter Levy, who said Chavez was "wasting his time fighting around the Southwest"[5] and needed to target the West or East Coast if he wanted to attain the next level.

When Chavez showed up in Albuquerque for his rematch with Ryan, it was without his manager Joseph. Things were moving quickly for Chavez and a change in management and training was in the works—as well as a plan to invade the West. Just a couple more fights in Southwest was the plan. It would be one fight too many.

Upset in Albuquerque

> Chavez says the first time they fought, Chico simply paralyzed him by his elegance and too-lofty disdain.
>
> —Los Angeles Times, 1913[6]

Better than a tune-up and more like a stepping stone, Battling Chico was a Los Angeles veteran who'd been fighting since 1910 against the biggest names on both coasts. His reputation was enough to draw more than 100 people when he stepped off the No. 2 train in Albuquerque. The fans knew, when Chico clashed with Benny, Feb. 20, 1913, at the Elks', there was going to be a war. The battle, however, was won before the bell ever clanged.

> Benny was a little desert boy who had never been out of New Mexico in his life. Chico came out from Los Angeles to fight him at Albuquerque.... He was almost stifled by the condescension of the city boy. When they got together to arrange the terms of their first fight, Chavez slouched into the conference with a pair of khaki overalls and a blue shirt open at the throat and a soiled sombrero. Enter the fastidious citified Battling Chico with filmy silk socks like a chorus girl, silk shirt and tailor-made clothes and an air of heavy langor [sic]. Chavez, being a little too heavy for a genuine bantamweight, inquired nervously, "What weight must I make for you?"
>
> Chico waved a contemptuously [sic] hand, "Aw, you can weigh a ton if you want to: I don't care what you weigh. The more you weigh the bigger bump you'll make when you hit."
>
> Chavez gulped, and timidly inquired whom the magnificent young person wanted for referee. "Anybody, anybody," said Chico, indifferently. "Just so he can count ten: that's all I care."
>
> "Count ten?" repeated Chavez, bewildered. "How dy'a mean — ten?"
>
> "Well," said Chico, "that's all he'll have to do. About the second round I'm going to hand you a left hook right there over the liver (jabbing the astonished anatomy of Chavez with his thumb) and all the referee will have to do is count ten over you."[7]

And that's pretty much what happened. Before the biggest crowd Albuquerque had ever seen for a prize fight, 1,200 standing room only, Chavez was knocked out in less than two rounds.

"From the time the first blow in the opening round was struck to the knock-out, Chico was complete master of Chavez at every stage of the game," chronicled the *Morning Journal*. "Chavez landed few if any clean blows while every time Chico led with either right or left, he planted his glove on a vital spot, and when he had Chavez in distress, he followed up on the advantage with the quickness of a flash."[8]

In between the first and second round, Chavez sat in his corner, a worried look on his face, lacking the usual confidence. Then, in the second, "Before the audience knew what had happened, [Chico] had sent the Rocky Mountain champion to the mat with a terrific left uppercut to the stomach and a crashing right cross to the jaw. As Referee George Nash toiled off the seconds, Chavez, rose to his knees, resting on his hands. It was plain that he was a beaten boy. At the count of nine he gamely got up and staggered across the ring, oblivious to everything. Chico whipped his left to Chavez's unprotected jaw and he fell to the canvas for the count, decisively beaten."[9]

Return

> *In Hoc Signo Vinces. Centuries ago the noble crusaders adopted this motto as an inspiration to victory. Last night at the stockyards stadium Benny Chavez, the little Trinidad Mexican, transplanted the fist for the sword and sending his straight left jab to Brannigan's knob, murmured, "By this sign I conquer."*
>
> — Otto Floto, in Denver Post, 1913[10]

"I was out of shape, I'd broken it off with my manager, and I took Chico for a bum slouch," would be Benny's excuses — everything but the intimidation he'd later admit. The road back would be a hard one but, by the end of the year, the Southwest would once again have faith in Benny.

Meanwhile, Chavez had to restore faith in himself.

BATTLING CHICO

CHICO
vs.
CHAVEZ

OPEN AIR BOXING
CONTEST

HAPPENS
TODAY
AT

Traction Park
2:30 p. m. Sharp

BENNIE CHAVEZ

28 ROUNDS OF THE FASTEST
BOXING EVER STAGED
IN THE SOUTHWEST.

Every Bout a Match

5-ROUND SEMI WIND-UP
BETWEEN
KID SCHAFFER
of Cheyenne, Wyoming,
vs.
KID ANAYA
(The Fighting Indian) of
Trinidad, Colo.

TWO EXCITING PRELIMI-
NARIES WILL START
THE SHOW.

"ABSOLUTELY" the best show
of the kind ever witnessed in
this section of the country.

The Ladies Are Especially
Invited

The full equipment of street
cars will be ready to accommodate the crowd at 1:00 o'clock.

Everybody's Going

Those who knew him said despite all his skills in the ring that he was emotionally fragile—Chico had been proof of that. Many expected him to go the way of most successful club fighters who get just a taste of prominence. Benny would either sink back down to fighting at small-town clubhouses year after year, until even the young locals were beating the old man who used to be a somebody ... or he'd rise from the ashes.

With a bit of help, Chavez did just that.

Weaving his way out of his own career into those of his brethren desert pugs wandered Louis Newman. With George Joseph on the outs with Chavez, Newman stepped right into place, persuading Chavez that he could take him to the next level. "See, whatcha need is a couple getback wins, then we go right back at Battling Chico," he told his new charge.

Keeping Chavez busy with a handful of confidence-building wins over lesser opposition, Newman moved Chavez into his Denver home, then ran the fighter back and forth, from Colorado to New Mexico, while he set up the rematch with Battling Chico.

It was a learning experience for Newman, who found out that managing a fighter meant more than wheeling and dealing with promoters in several states, or coddling a damaged psyche—you also had to respect their quirks. Chavez was a superstitious one, as Newman would find out. There's the famous story of the horseshoes.

While doing his early morning road work, Benny would pick up and collect horseshoes—bear in mind the time period—which he would pile in a corner of his room, before marking in a book how many he'd collected. While staying with the Newmans, Chavez came home from the Owl Club where he trained to find his pile of lucky horseshoes missing. "He became rather quiet and sullen," locking himself in his room until his manager returned, late in the evening. Chavez grabbed him as he entered the door, demanding to know where his horseshoes were. Newman asked his mother, who admitted she'd thrown them away, thinking they were junk. Luckily, they were recovered. "Chavez was not satisfied until he had taken them to his room and counted them. He then looked up a book in which he keeps a tally of the number of horse shoes picked up each morning. When he found that the number of the book corresponded with the number of horse shoes he was himself. If he had not found the shoes he would not have slept all night."[11]

With wins over Charles Burns, Young Hite, Kid Leach and Eddie Marino, all but one by knockout, Newman guaranteed Albuquerque promoters that Chavez was ready for Chico again, when they met again

The first fight between Benny Chavez and Battling Chico saw the year's biggest upset when Chico shocked the fans with a stunning knockout of Benny. Four months later, Benny bounced back with a vengeance, outclassing Chico in a ten-rounder.

on Decoration Day, May 30, for the Southwest bantamweight title, before another packed house at the Elks.'

It was a different outcome and Chavez, a completely different fighter. Winning a dominant decision, Chavez gave Chico a "severe lacing. At the close, Chico's right eye was closed and his face was badly battered. In the last round, Chico tried repeatedly for a knockout but Chavez danced out of reach and pecked at the Los Angeles bantam's face with stinging lefts.... The Trinidad youth was too quick and Chico plainly puzzled."[12]

"He's ready for the big boys now," declared Newman, who was already talking about moving up to featherweight, with Chavez having a hard time making the 116-pound bantam limit. A master at hype, Newman knew he had to temper Chavez with hard fights before he could throw him into the ring with a champ or top contender like Eddie Campi, but that didn't stop him from name-dropping. Chavez, said Newman, was ready for the likes of Johnny Dundee (who was headlining Albuquerque on July 4) or the champ, Johnny Coulon, in Trinidad (whose telegram was read from the ring at Chavez's next fight, unofficially agreeing to a match).

Confident that he'd gotten the old Benny back, Newman brought in San Francisco gatekeeper Harry Dell for a Fourth of July card in Trinidad. Dell had been a veteran since 1906 with an estimated 70 wars, and had faced all the top guys. As expected, Chavez administered a "merciless punishment," scoring an eleventh-round knockout that had Dell "dazed and bleeding up against the ropes and staggered forward to receive from his opponent, the blow that brought him to his knees while referee Ike Goldman counted ten."[13]

After a telegram sent by former Chavez conqueror Brannigan was read ringside, Newman went to work on a rematch, which was arranged for Aug. 11 in Denver. A victory over Brannigan would earn Chavez a shot at the champ, even if it wasn't a title fight. After talking with Coulon's camp, a Labor Day match was tentatively arranged, should Benny survive Brannigan.

"It is my one ambition to fight the bantamweight champion," Chavez told the press. "And if I am matched with him I am sure that I can win."[14]

Newman told him to focus on the man before him, Brannigan, and, well, the tune-ups leading up to the rematch. In July, Chavez

A buck fifty was well worth a ringside seat to watch the May 30, 1913, rematch between Benny Chavez and Los Angeles veteran Battling Chico at Albuquerque's Traction Park.

scored an easy knockout over Kid Peppers in Denver and, just ten days before Brannigan, returned to Albuquerque where Battling Chico awaited the rubber match. In their final bout, Chavez scored a second dominating decision though he "failed to master a stiff enough punch to score a knockout, though he tried repeatedly to put over the sleep producer."[15]

Brannigan

> *Chavez is a likeable little chap with a pair of orbs that sparkle like incandescent lights. A splendid little personality that warms up to you and cements a sort of bond of friendly feeling. To our mind he would prove a capital representative as leader of the featherweight brigade.*
>
> — *Denver Post,* 1913[16]

With the chapter on Chico closed, Chavez prepared for Brannigan, who'd not been as far west since the last time he was in Colorado, standing over the local idol as the ref tolled ten. Since beating Chavez in 1911, the Pittsburgh featherweight had fought 28 times, losing but one newspaper decision.

After two years of fighting and solidifying his claim of Southwest bantamweight champion, Benny Chavez became the first bona fide contender from New Mexico. By 1914, he was looking at a title shot against the featherweight champion, Johnny Kilbane.

Rocky Mountain News scribe Abe Pollock, who'd been at the first fight, called the rematch an "18-karat exhibition between two featherweights, who, in my opinion, are among the best in the country."[17] He also predicted a different ending, writing, "When Chavez met Brannigan in a former contest he knew but little of the finer points of the game and was easy to feint into the opening that would permit a boxer like Brannigan to whip over the punch that brings home the bacon. Matters will be different in the coming contest."[18]

Denver Post writers noted not just the physically improved skills, but the mental change in Chavez. "Benny is undaunted ... and leads us to believe that not the slightest fear possesses him regarding the outcome of the conflict. In fact, Chavez would rather discuss the argument now going on between Huerta and the supporters of Madero in Mexico than his coming bout."[19] Usually just smiling and nodding, Benny had plenty to say:

> I've been fighting only a short time; in fact, two years covers the whole of my ring career.... In that time I have met good, bad and indifferent fighters. In that space, I have won and lost battles. Won through determination and experience I gained as I went along, and lost in the beginning through inexperience and lack of knowledge of the ring game. I have been defeated — but I have managed since then to wipe out every defeat scored against me with the possible exception of the Brannigan decision. It is to clear my record of this blot that I insisted on the promoter of the coming bout to secure Brannigan as an opponent. I know I could have had my choice of half a dozen easier boys than Patsy, but the win he holds over me rankles in my mind and I am going to eliminate it — if I can.[20]

Chavez vs. Brannigan II just might be the single best performance of Benny's career. Though scribes in Denver were masters of sports prose, the fight was best summed up by a street urchin running out of the arena and shouting to his friend: "Hey, Skinny, the Mexican lamed the whey out of him!"[21]

"Taking into consideration the fact that the easterner on a previous occasion had knocked Benny out in six rounds, it was astonishing to note the sang-froid manner in which the Colorado fighter went at his task," wrote the *Post*'s Otto Floto. "When we stop and figure that Chavez is still a neophyte and that his best years as well as the major portion of his fighting career still lays [*sic*] before him, his performance last night proved all the more remarkable.... From viewing last nights' [*sic*] performance, everything that Benny Chavez demonstrated in that ring bordered on greatness."[22]

Nearly every round went to Chavez, who mastered the master at every aspect of the game, drawing first blood and delivering the harder shots to win nearly every round. Both local newspapers gave Chavez eight rounds, with one round to Brannigan, and one even. "It was as clean-cut a victory as we have witnessed in many a moon,"[23] wrote Floto. "Kilbane or Coulon will have to look to their laurels, if they ever meet him in a prize ring."[24]

Rise

> I want to go East, West, North and South and meet the best men those sections boast of. I either want to be champion of the world in my class or I want to retire and try my hand at something else. I love to fight— mind I don't mean I love to fight through my animosity I bear an opponent— for believe me, when any of my battles end I shake my adversary's hand and forget any feeling that may have crept into the contest. My love for fighting is born from my desire to achieve; to reach the top of my chosen profession, and not from motives to administer punishment. When I gain that ambition I shall be satisfied and feel repaid for whatever efforts it may have cost to attain the goal.
> — *Benny Chavez, 1913*[25]

Chavez was suddenly in demand. Eastern promoters wanted him to fight Kid Williams in Baltimore, the Midwest wanted Chavez against Milwaukee's Matty McCue, and West Coasters had Eddie Campi willing and waiting.

At the Owl Club where Benny trained, crowds of 200 showed up to watch him train for his next fight, which was three weeks after beating Brannigan. Once again headlining the Stockyards Auditorium, Chavez was up against 24-year-old Frankie Burns, who'd proven good enough to draw with Coulon in his five-year career. In fact, the winner was promised the champ — a familiar tune from the champ's manager.

Burns was tougher than expected, and it took Chavez several rounds to figure his opponent out, trying to "avoid the whipleft [*sic*] left of Burns,"[26] who caught him coming in. Chavez began to find his mark and, forcing the fight, staggered his opponent late. The referee declared it a draw.

Coulon was mentioned again, a possibility for Thanksgiving Day, but Newman wasn't planning on putting Chavez on the shelf in the duration. Former champ Frankie Conley was lined up for October in December and, after making him look like a novice, Chavez announced he was heading for the West Coast.

Deciding to take the rest of the year off and being criticized for it, the champion was out. Give up the belt or defend it, the public cried. Sure, Coulon agreed to fight the No. 1— just as soon as the top challenger could be determined. The East called for Baltimore's Kid Williams while the West cried for Eddie Campi.

The name "Benny Chavez" was also in the mix, so Campi agreed to a November show-down on his turf, with the winner fighting Williams, the winner of *that* battle to face the champion in early 1914. So, Chavez packed up for Los Angeles.

West Coast Invasion: Chavez vs. Campi

I'm a tough Mex.

— *Benny Chavez, 1913*[27]

"The only thing Chavez will take home with him will be a spanking and a few souvenir cards of himself riding ostriches, alligators and such like," was the boast of Eddie Campi's manager, Timothy McGrath.[28]

The champion of the Rocky Mountain region and Southwest knew he was in for a war, and that Frenchman Campi was more than just a "skinny young jabber from up San Fran way."[29]

There was a *reason* Campi was, at least in the western half of the United States, con-sidered the people's bantam champ rather than Johnny Coulon, who refused to put his title at stake. While Chavez had racked up 36 fights fighting throughout the Southwest since 1911, Campi was a five-year veteran with over 50 fights, with just two losses: to Jimmy Fox and Kid Williams, the East's No. 1.

When both Campi's camp and the Los Angeles press declared an easy fight against the desert pug, Chavez and Newman knew they were in deep water — not only from the fighter, but from the papers. If Benny survived the writers, Campi would be a breeze in the ring. Needless to say, the fight was well publicized.

The fight was scheduled for Nov. 4 at the area's top venue — Tom McCarey's outdoor arena in Vernon. McCarey had been responsible for the boxing boom in the Los Angeles area, years before the Olympic Auditorium became the place to go. Near Vernon was a training camp owned by Jack Doyle — simply "Doyle's."

Training with former foe Battling Chico under Earl Mohan, Chavez put in his work at Doyle's, while writers and celebrities swung by to get a glimpse at the "little Mex" many were daring to say had a chance against their unbeatable Campi. Impressed, they were not. He was an easy target for chic city folk and know-it-all sports scribes.

"*This* is the guy who beat Battling Chico?" was the general reaction, at first. "He's slow and clumsy," was how entertainer and female impersonator Julian Eltinge saw Chavez. Granted, no one looked good sparring with Chico; and Benny never looked great in the gym, but saved his best efforts for the fight, where it counted. "I don't think he's all that slow and clumsy," was the opinion of promoter McCarey. "The little fellow did better with Frankie Burns than Eddie Campi did. He is the only boy who has ever beaten Patsy Bran-nigan."[30]

"Battling Chico must've been 'makin' a meal' of bi-chloride of mercury when they fought," wrote a scribe for the *Los Angeles Times*. As for Chavez beating Brannigan? "Must've been the Mexican grub."[31]

> Or the chili "peteens" [piqin] ... if you want to take two or three of them beans into your face, they'd make more excitement inside than Barbary Coast whiskey. I guess about two of them beans in a Mexican would be enough to start a revolution. Just before a fight, while they're waiting in the corner, I bet the seconds pour about a sackful of these here fire seeds down that guy Chavez,

put some turpentine in his coffee and turn him loose. I suggest he gets a couple beans aboard and then lights into them stall-fed guys like [Frankie] Burns and [Patsy] Brannigan and starts a revolution wit' em."[32]

Chavez's chances with Campi? "About as much chance as a man without any arms has to catch a greased pig. That little Mex will think somebody is squirtin' boxin' gloves at him through a hose.... I guess somebody must have hated Chavez when he was a baby and has been savin' this up fer him ever since."[33]

The *Los Angeles Examiner* might've agreed about "Smiling Benny's" chances, but they did note *some* talent: "The lad from Wagon Mound, and he refers with as much pride to the New Mexico cactus point as a New York does his Broadway, is as fast as a youth we used to know under the name of Attell. Also, he is scientific enough for all purposes and as a whole stacks up as a classy member of the clever boxer class. If Benjamin has been over-advertised at all, the puff was at the expense of his hitting powers. It is difficult to see the tortilla teaser in the light of a knockerout."[34]

The *Los Angeles Herald*'s Jay Davidson didn't see the skill, but figured there must be *something* he brought to the ring: "Benny Chavez does not pretend to be a fancy boxer, but he says he is a go-getter when he gets inside the ring. Judging by what he did to Patsy Brannigan, Frankie Burns and Frankie Conley, he has some excuse for his confidence. A boy without class hardly could whip any one of this formidable trio, so it might be wise not to put too much stress upon his failure to come up to expectations in the training camp bouts.... Don't pick a plum before it's ripe."[35]

De Witt Van Court of the *Times* warned that Benny could prove dangerous, with his "champion cauliflower ear" à la George Dixon, but that it was hard to get a line on him in the gym. "Chavez had little to enthuse the fans with his boxing, because he has no particular style, but he is as quick as a flash and can hit a hard blow with either hand and from any angle, and seems to be much better at close quarters than at long range."[36]

Stories of Chavez's meals — beans, tortillas and chile — spiced up the stories, as did an incident in which Doyle's pet bear nearly took off Benny's hand. Chavez had been playing with the bear when it lashed out, trapping the New Mexican's hand in its chain. Luckily, there was no injury.

As reports were printed, the odds were stacked heavily in Campi's corner, but Chavez appeared unfazed. "Hah," he'd exclaim when Campi was mentioned, the reporter exaggerating his Mexican — or *New* Mexican dialect. "I theenk he's an awful little feller but where he go with a me? Noo place. I jes' naturally jab heem in mouth, in nose, in eye, and then lay one on hees chin. I a bad mex. Ask Chico. Chico my friend. I leek heem twice."[37]

"Chavez will have to put up the battle of his life," Campi's trainer, Joe Lewis, stated while Newman showed great concern about Campi's "runaway tactics." "I have known [Chavez] since his kid days," said Newman. "I've seen him grow up, and know every trick of the ring that he has in his makeup, and I have seen Campi in action. I honestly can't see where Campi has any license to stay the limit with him."[38]

The final verdict, two days before the fight, was that Campi was just too clever and dazzling for the "rugged little Mexican boy," and, with neither one an apparent knockout artist, "Tuesday night's card looms up as a battle of speed and cleverness."[39]

Looking past Chavez, Campi was already talking about what he'd do to Kid Williams and then Coulon — or whether the champ was going to duck him. If he did, Campi would sail right past bantam to challenger Johnny Kilbane, the featherweight champion.

When asked about Kilbane, Chavez replied, "Please say fo' me that as queek as I smash little boy Campi all up I take on Kilbane. One, two, three day an' I get up to 122 pounds. Kilbane? Huh! Easy fo' me. I tough guy. Ask Chico."[40]

Campi merely scoffed, threatening to "flattin this greaser out in about five rounds or six rounds — think five — and after that you may sign Kilbane for me."[41]

In the end, the local press had it right.

"It is quite safe to say that Chavez saw more boxing gloves last night than he will during the rest of his life, and each glove was on the end of one of Campi's arms," wrote the *Times*. From the first round until the eighteenth Campi simply smothered Benny with a shower of blows from both hands."[42]

Though winning the crowd over with his aggression, Chavez was not able to press his game until the 18th round, when he crowded Campi, landing hard shots until the 20th and final round. Though winning the fights on points, Campi was hooted by the crowd as he left the ring, though "nobody seemed to know what for, unless it was because he beat Chavez so easily."[43]

The *Times* suggested Chavez take boxing lessons, calling him game and willing, but lacking science. "What good is any puncher's punch to him, if he is unable to land it?" wrote Van Court, adding, "If Benny Chavez's manager is seriously thinking of matching him with Johnny Kilbane, he had better have Benny learn a lot more of the boxing game than he knows now."[44]

It was a loss, but not a devastating one.

"Campi beat me alright," Chavez admitted. "Campi is without doubt the fastest boy I ever saw in my life. He cannot hit hard enough to break an egg, but his speed and cleverness make it so difficult for an opponent to hit him that unless Campi is actually knocked out, he is sure to win."[45]

Chavez chalked up the loss to experience, and said having to dry out to bantamweight had been a mistake. Newman announced they were moving up to featherweight. Campi and Williams could have Coulon — they were now after Kilbane.

The Road to Kilbane

> Bennie Chavez — "our" Benny — has gone and fired Louis Newman as his manager. The two no longer raise anthems of praise to each other. On the contrary, quite the reverse. Each one is looking for a chance to soak the other on the bean with something real hard and blunt.
>
> —*Albuquerque Morning Journal*, 1913[46]

Despite the loss, there were plenty of opportunities to fight in the Southwest for Benny Chavez. He'd been outboxed, but not outclassed. Going 20 rounds with a guy like Campi only to lose a decision did not mean that Chavez was *not* going to make it in the big ring.

Chavez went right back to work — only now, sometime between the Campi fight and his return to Denver, on Dec. 11, 1913, Rocky Mountain's top hope for a champion parted ways with Louis Newman. It did not go over well with fight fans, neither in Denver nor in New Mexico, who saw the contender as biting the hand that fed him. The *Denver Post*'s Otto Floto gave him "the medal for being the prize swellhead of all ring history."[47] The *Albuquerque Journal* wrote, "Until he joined fortunes with the Las Vegas man, Chavez considered himself lucky to get enough money out of his battles to keep up the visible supply of 'ham and eggs' until the next battle came on. During the last six months, or since Newman has been handling him, the Trinidad boy has probably seen more real money that he ever before dreamed there was in the world."[48]

Taking over Chavez's management was Arthur O. Ross, who was now promising Chavez big fights in the East. Ross had handled El Paso welterweight Frankie Fowser, who'd had minor success during an eastern tour before returning to the border.

As if trying to prove he was still championship timber, Chavez took on Jimmy Fox, one of two top-notchers who had a win over Campi, but the best Benny could do was a draw in his hometown. Again, Chavez was outboxed, but his aggression, body attack, harder punches and a clean knockdown in the fifth evened the score.

A draw wasn't good enough, anymore. Suddenly, there was talk of the champ "slipping" ... "not progressing at the pace he followed in the past." Most Denverites thought he'd won the fight with Fox, despite the draw, but they were still sour over the split with Newman. "Chavez has evidently acquired the big head. He has placed himself, in his own opinion, upon a glittering pinnacle called fame, whose real foundation is atmosphere, though he does not appear to realize that he is in danger of a fall."[49]

TKO wins over lesser opposition set up a third fight with Patsy Brannigan in March. This time, Chavez beat him even more convincingly in a 15-rounder.

Shortly thereafter, he got the telegram — featherweight Champion Johnny Kilbane was coming to Denver.

Johnny Kilbane, considered one of the greatest featherweight champions of all time, defended the championship for 11 years. Unfortunately, it was against Kilbane that the first New Mexican received a title shot. On May 29, 1914, top bantamweight contender Benny Chavez of Wagon Mound, New Mexico, stepped into a Denver ring for a shot at Kilbane's laurels. The champ retained his title with a second-round knockout (Library of Congress, Prints & Photographs Division [LC-B2-2366–7]).

A Shot at the Champ

If [Chavez] doesn't develop stage fright [against Kilbane] there will be a raise in the chile con carne market after the battle.
            —Abe Pollock, in *Rocky Mountain News*, 1914[50]

When young Benny Chavez signed articles on May 2, 1914, to fight the featherweight champion of the world on May 29, there weren't too many lining up to bet on him. By fight night, however, the Denver press and public had worked itself into thinking that, just maybe, "Smilin' Benny" had a chance.

Hadn't Kilbane been about Benny's age — 21— when he first fought for a title? And even though he lost, didn't he come back even more determined a year later to win? If Benny lost, there was always next time, wasn't there? Hadn't Chavez come back from that loss to Brannigan, only to dominate the next two fights? Didn't Chavez *always* do better the second, or third time around?

Chavez might be moving up in weight, he might not have Louis Newman in his corner, but when the opportunity came to fight a guy like Kilbane, he couldn't turn it down, not when it landed in his backyard. Not when local promoters were coughing up $5,000 to make it happen — a fifth of that going to the hometown challenger.

"There has never been a Mexican champion," mused the *News'* Abe Pollock. "Joe Rivers and Aurelio Herrera represent the sum total of contenders of that nationality who have fought for the title and both fell short, but Benny says all his Mexican friends are looking for him to win where the others failed, and he intends to put up the battle of his ring career."[51]

Denver hadn't had a world title fight since Colorado's one and only world champion, William J. Rothwell — "Young Corbett II" to the fight world — had defended his laurels on home dirt, back in 1902. In fact, it had been the same belt, the world featherweight title, Corbett had defended, against Kid Broad, at the Coliseum, winning a ten-round decision. Corbett had vacated the belt, and Abe Attell had snatched it up soon after, defending it 14 times before losing it to Kilbane in 1912.

There was a certain poetry in the belt's return to Colorado — should Chavez pull off what would amount to the upset of the year.

Other than fighting on home turf, Chavez was a serious underdog against a champ like Kilbane. There were few fighters on the planet of his caliber — during and *since* the '10s. *The Ring* magazine's Nat Fleischer ranked the future Hall-of-Famer as the No. 5 featherweight of all-time. The man who would hold the title for an amazing 11 years had little to fear from a Southwest fighter who'd been outfoxed by Campi — and at a lower weight. For Kilbane, it was easy money, especially since the only way he could lose his title was if he was knocked out or lost by fouling. Should the fight go the 15-round distance, a "no-decision" would be rendered.

Fear of a knockout? Kilbane had a granite chin; his only loss by stoppage had been a controversial low blow in 1909. No, Benny's only chance was to use all 20 rounds in wearing down a more-experienced ring general like Kilbane, who rarely fought anything over 10 and hadn't gone 20 since a draw with Johnny Dundee the year before.

Born in Cleveland, Ohio, in 1889, Kilbane had started his ring career in 1907. By 1910, he was good enough to challenge Attell for the title. Kilbane lost, but kept at it, fighting everyone from Brannigan to Joe Rivers to Frankie Conley, before rematching Attell in 1912. This time he brought the title home to Cleveland from Vernon, California, and had been the champion since. He was no villain, either, but well-liked by the scribes, even those in Denver, who wrote, "Personally, Kilbane is very quiet, unassuming young fellow who dresses more like a tennis player than a champion boxer and from his actions and conversations, a person who didn't know him would take him for a college student."[52]

Arriving with his wife and daughter, Kilbane was met by a huge crowd when his train arrived. After being checked into the Albany Hotel by matchmaker Johnny Corbett and promoter Al Chears, Kilbane handed over his eight-diamond, 11-karat belt, which was put on display at Lowenham's Jewelry, where an estimated 100 people a day came in to see it.

"I can truthfully say that I never saw a contest which has developed as much genuine interest in every quarter in such a short space of time, as this one has," wrote Pollock, who would also referee the bout. "People who care nothing for boxing contests, and have never been to one in their life, are around listening to the fight dope and have expressed opinions that makes them nothing short of a fight fan, and a great many of these will break the monotony of a five-cent nickel show by loosening up for a ringside seat when the two boys clash at the big stockyards arena."[53]

Chavez trained at the Colorado Athletic Club under Norman Selby, of Kid McCoy fame. "He intends to take Benny in hand and put him wise to the mysteries of the famous cork screw blow which he originated years ago that has won many a battle for him against heavy odds," Pollock entertained his readers. "He will also show his pupil the right shift, which is one of the greatest points a boxer can have and which very few of the present crop know how to use."[54]

In reality, there was not enough time for Chavez to learn new tricks, though he tried "to make up in strength what he is shy of in science. Johnny is liable to have a good, warm session after things get to moving."[55]

With special trains arranged from all points in New Mexico and Colorado, ticket prices were doubled on account of the $5,000 purse, $1 for the cheap seats, $3 ringside. Two days before the fight, both Kilbane and Chavez were weighing 121½, a half-pound under the limit.

On the day of the fight, final comments had Kilbane giving Chavez plenty of respect: "I have not got him underestimated, as his defeat of Patsy Brannigan stands him as a good man and one who will give any boxer in the world trouble. As my title is at stake, I intend to take no chances and will carry the fight to him from the tap of the gong."[56]

A railroad ticket stub from the Denver & Rio Grande Railroad for a special "Kilbane-Chavez Prize Fight Special" line to accommodate fans from Trinidad, Colorado, to Denver. It was one of several additional lines from several points in Colorado and northern New Mexico.

Benny, on the other hand, said, "Now that I have at last seen my ambition fulfilled by getting a crack at the title, I will show my friends that their confidence in my ability has not been misplaced.... Notwithstanding Kilbane's cleverness and reputation, I will start from the call and go after him."[57]

On May 29, 1914, a

crowd of 5,000 packed into the Stockyards Stadium to watch Kilbane make $500 a minute in his three-and-a-half-minute fight against New Mexico's and Colorado's prayer for a world champion.

They sparred for an opening early in the first, before Chavez rushed the champion. Swinging wildly, he missed with a left, then a right, while the champ smiled, showing fancy footwork. Chavez closed the distance, trying to land an uppercut inside, but Kilbane grinned again as the blow whizzed past his face. Kilbane took a step back and started to jab, landing on Chavez. He jabbed again, followed with a clean right. Chavez rushed in, clinched, swinging wildly as the bell signaled the end of the first frame. The challenger walked back to his corner, unhurt but discouraged, having been unable to land a single blow.

Benny's cornermen revved him up, telling him, "He's a stiff! Go in and get 'im!" Which is just what Chavez attempted to do. "His heart popped up into his throat as he left the corner at the bell for the second with the thought that he had a chance to win the featherweight crown."[58]

Chavez rushed the champ again when the bell clanged. Kilbane clinched, smothering Benny's uppercuts. Ref Pollock called for a break. Kilbane swung a right and this time Chavez clinched, missing inside with his right as the champ landed a short left and right. After breaking, "Kilbane stepped in quickly, placing a hard left to the jaw. Chavez went down.... When he arose all his fight was gone and it was merely a question as to how long he could stay."[59]

Clearly hurt, Chavez got back up. "Kilbane again stepped in, this time with a light left and a hard right to the jaw. The effect was the same except that the receiver stayed down for only a few seconds."[60] Yet again, Chavez tried to stand on rubbery legs, "helpless and unable to cover up. Still game, Chavez came up again only to take another hard right that put him under the ropes. Although practically out, he insisted on more, and was again put down along the edge of the ring. Seeing that there was nothing else to do, and wishing to speed matters up a trifle, the champion shot over the final blow, a left to the same old place."[61]

This time, Chavez stayed down a full minute. "The first man to reach him was the champion, who stayed with his fallen opponent until the latter was safely in his corner."[62] Chavez was still dazed when he left the ring, his head bowed.

The press did not pull any punches in their reports of what had turned out to be a mismatch. Not even the *Trinidad Chronicle-News* spared a kind word: "Benny was outclassed and beaten from the tap of the gong until he was lifted out of the ring.... Chavez, a game and clever little fighter, pride of Trinidad, has been temporarily relegated to the discard as a championship aspirant."[63]

Everything from bad management to ineffective training to lousy cornermen was blamed, but, in the end, the simple explanation was that Chavez had been outclassed. He admitted as much, saying he'd expected the champ to box him, leaving him an opportunity to "land a hard one that would win me the championship."[64] Chavez then added:

In all my other fights in which I have ever been knocked groggy, my opponent has stood in one place set for the blow that was to finish me and I could always manage to fall into a clinch. Now even when a fighter waits for you when you are dazed that way, he seems like about ninety and it is hard to get inside the arms of the real boxer that you are fighting instead of one of his eighty-nine shadows. Well, when I started to get up and had crawled to my knees, as I have said, I faced a problem that I had never been up against before. Instead of standing, waiting for me, Johnny Kilbane was dancing all around me like a kid around a May pole, so that instead of ninety Kilbanes

I saw 900. I saw there was no chance to fall into clinch with 900 men, so I took the last one throw that was left to me — a wild swing that might hit the Kilbane out of that regiment in front of me who was of real, live flesh and blood. I didn't, and — I guess you know more about what happened after that than I do. [65]

Chavez begged for another shot at Kilbane, promising to work his way back to the top. It would never happen — though Benny would never stop trying.

Ruin to Return

> Chavez, however, is a most erratic fighter. There have been times when his work has been so mediocre that one would say he had "gone back." He does not always fight up to his class.
>
> — *Trinidad Chronicle News*, 1915[66]

Benny Chavez would never again get a chance at a title, but for the next couple years, at least, he was still considered a contender.

After a get-back win on the Fourth of July in Trinidad, a knockout over Harry Lub, it was time for Chavez to claw his way back up the ladder with the hopes that Kilbane would still be champ when, and if, he got another chance at the belt. (Though talking about moving up to lightweight back in 1914, Kilbane would later change his mind and remain a featherweight with a long-running title reign from 1912 to 1923.)

For the remainder of 1914, Chavez would have but two opponents — Gene Delmont of Memphis and Ritchie Mitchell of Milwaukee, against whom he'd fight five times.

The first Chavez-Delmont fight was hyped as an eliminator for Kilbane, but that was far from official. In April, Delmont had fought an eight-round draw with the champion, which made him a 3–1 favorite over Chavez when they fought in Denver, on July 21.

Benny not only outslugged Delmont, but outboxed him, winning all but one stanza in a 15-rounder. "Chavez had all the old qualifications that caused us not so long ago to predict great things for him," wrote the *Denver Times*. "He was a champion last night. That kind of fighting would have given Kilbane his hands full, and another story might have been written had he assumed it." "Now back on the pugilistic map," Chavez repeated his win over Delmont on Aug. 3, again in Denver. [67]

Mitchell was next. The Milwaukee battler, active since 1912, had an identical record to Chavez but had never gone the 20-round distance. With a reach and height advantage, Mitchell outboxed Chavez, flooring him in the tenth and knocking him through the ropes when the 20th-round bell rang prematurely at 1:45 — but the best he could do in Denver was a draw. Chavez missed repeatedly and was unable to get past Mitchell's left — honest Abe Pollock could only give the homeboy five rounds.

Mitchell rightfully demanded a rematch — this time in *his* hometown of Milwaukee.

Meanwhile, Chavez swapped managers again, leaving Arthur Ross for Fred Winsor, long-time Southwestern fight promoter who made two mistakes, first campaigning Chavez at 122 to 126 when he could, with proper training, still make 118 to 119, and possibly bantamweight; then going to Milwaukee for the Mitchell rematch.

Chavez came home from his first fight in the Midwest with a loss. Chavez might've won the first round, but in the second Mitchell buried his left in Benny's bread basket and he dropped to the canvas where, "groaning with pain and grasping for wind,"[68] he was counted out.

No longer as popular in Denver, Chavez had a tougher time lining up his next fight, so Winsor brought him to Juarez on Nov. 15 for a third bout against Delmont, who'd been fighting there. The locals were thrilled to get someone of Chavez's caliber there — especially after he KO'd Gene Payo in sparring — but they sent him home with a draw.

Chavez did not venture out of the Southwest in 1915, returning to New Mexico on New Year's Day where he beat up overmatched Las Vegan Young Duran in Las Vegas. It would be the last time he would fight in New Mexico as a bona fide contender. The rest of the year was spent in Colorado — and he did not have an easy time of it.

In March, back in Denver, he fought rising local Joe "The Wop" Flynn in what should've been a tune-up. Ahead on the scorecards after 15 rounds of "fighting like wildcats, standing toe to toe,"[69] Chavez protested in the 16th round when Flynn came out, his body and face covered in grease. Instead, ref George English turned to Flynn and raised his arm. The house was in an uproar and Chavez protested, to no avail.

But for two bouts against lesser opposition — both won by knockout — Chavez spent the rest of the year consumed with Matty Smith. No fewer than six times did he face Smith, and, by the time he finished the year, Chavez saw he was at the tail-end of featherweight contention, his name rarely mentioned now.

From Racine, Wisconsin, Smith had been fighting in Denver since late 1914. Having beaten all locals at featherweight, Smith was the logical choice for Chavez, at least in Colorado. Top-shelf fighters — not to mention Kilbane — were passing on Benny now. Smith was not in Chavez's class, and Denverites expected him to give the Racine man a good trimming.

He didn't. Instead, they fought a 15-round draw, Chavez having an edge in boxing but Smith's boring-in tactics evening the score. Six weeks later, they were rematched in Trinidad. This time Chavez fought a safe fight in a "tame affair" that "demonstrated quite clearly that Chavez lacks the force and steam that characterized his work two years ago when he was at his best."[70]

In September they did it again, this time in Pueblo; once again, a 20-round draw. A 15-round draw in nearby Colorado Springs in November, and a points win for Benny in December, at the same location, finished out the year, and the series, with Chavez ahead 2-0-4.

Smith wrote home, citing hometown robberies, dislocated shoulders and dishonest referees, while Coloradoans were unhappy for a different reason. No one thought Benny had lost any of his bouts with Smith, they just thought he was slipping. But there was still hope:

> Chavez, however, is a most erratic fighter. There have been times when his work has been so mediocre that one would say he had "gone back." He does not always fight up to his class ... [But] his career is not yet over. If he exercises horse sense and judgment and keeps in training and in the best physical condition he is ripe for big game.... Adding nothing to him for past performances which were not up to standard, detracting nothing from any contest in which he might have had a hairline favor and speaking fairly, Chavez is still good. Get me — still good.[71]

It was about this time that Louis Newman re-entered the picture.

The Last Run

> *It's only a few years ago folks in these diggings asserted a little Mexican chap from Trinidad, Colorado, would some day be a champion.... He finally came to Denver and all the good things said of him were verified by his performances in the ring. Then*

success became too great a burden for him to bear. He quivered and trembled under the load—at least he imagined he did. He took himself seriously and just when the apex of his ambitions was to be reached he shook his old associations from him and his decline began. He fell from the high perch upon which he roosted until he became only an ordinary boy fighting lightweights in order to get a few dollars, giving away weight to any opponent because financial needs demanded it. Then suddenly he bethought himself, reached out for some of his former staunch friends and said friends came to his assistance.

—Otto Floto, in *Denver Post*, 1916[72]

"We're getting the hell out of Colorado," was the advice of reunited manager Louie Newman. "Kansas City, here we come."

Speaking from experience, Newman had already seen talent wither and die in the Southwest. If you wanted to make it, you got out—it wasn't enough to import the occasional big name who wasn't used to the altitude. More often than not, they'd go back where they came from and complain of a hometown robbery. It was better to go somewhere new, and to stay hungry, not grow complacent in your hometown.

Newman chose Kansas City. Chavez chose Kansas City as well, especially after he met and married a local girl there in early February.

Through March, Chavez would fight his first six fights of 1916 in the budding fight town. Having convinced the local promoters there that his fighter had seen better days—not entirely incorrect—Chavez was, at first, little more than an acid test for Tommy Buck, a fringe contender out of Philadelphia. No longer called a contender but a "crafty, cagey veteran," Chavez easily defeated Buck, then, in a rematch, "treated him to a far more artistic trimming,"[73] replacing poor Tommy as the latest headliner.

Then Kansas City brought in "Louisiana" from Philadelphia. "Louisiana" Joe Riderberg was, at least, a name that could re-launch the Chavez name. Though his claim to fame was a knockdown and newspaper win over Baltimore's Kid Williams (now the champ at bantam, having defeated Campi on his way to Coulon), he'd also fought and beaten several big names. It was just what Chavez needed.

What he didn't need was a draw, which is what Chavez got when they met the first two times, on Jan. 31 and Feb. 14. The fights were good enough to warrant a third bout, on March 9—though, this time, with "each one knocking at the door to Kid Williams' bantam throne room, 3,000 people booed when 'Loosy' got the "peculiar decision."[74] Freeman Alford of the *Kansas City Post* praised Benny, who nearly had his man out several times, and panned Louisiana for his fouling.

Locals were thrilled with the bouts, but beyond a steady paycheck, with Chavez on the short end of a decision, there was little hope that he was going to regain his former glory. But Newman wasn't stupid. "We're targeting Williams now," he told the press. Though it had originally been his idea to move to featherweight, Newman criticized Chavez's attempt to dethrone Kilbane. Williams would've been a better choice—and their current one.

Having defeated two men who'd previously beaten the champ, in non-title affairs, Newman had an argument, despite Benny's loss, which did not hurt him all that much. Denver sat up and took notice again, Floto writing, "There's a transformation in the boy. He is dressed neatly now; he is a little gentleman in all his dealings; he has married a good little girl in Kansas City, and those who knew him a year ago will hardly recognize the same Benny Chavez they knew."[75]

There was, once again, talk of going to the East Coast and fighting top names. Before they could arrange something, Chavez kept busy knocking out Kansas City local Charley Aronson, "the boy with the glass jaw," before heading back to Denver, where Chick Hayes was waiting.

The Indianapolis fighter was not supposed to be in the same league as Chavez, though he'd scored at least one win over a contender, Johnny Ertle, but it took Benny three fights to get a win. The first two, in Denver and Kansas City, were draws and the third was a 20-round decision for Chavez.

Despite the big talk of going East, Chavez spent the remainder of the year on the road, from Ely to Missouri, always returning to Denver, where he could draw a bigger crowd and purse. In Denver, he fought Louisiana one more time, giving him a lacing before winning on a foul in the 14th round.

Sometime between his 15-round draw with Roy Moore in Denver, in late July, and his final bout with Louisiana, Chavez broke ties with Newman again. Once again with Winsor, he joined the camp of Lightweight Champion Freddie Welsh in August for a time, which netted him attention, as did his plentiful wins. With just one loss in the year (the dis-

The Mexican Flash

BENNY CHAVEZ

Will train at the Auditorium, third floor, at 3 o'clock each afternoon, up to and including Saturday, for his bout with "Louisiana" at Kansas City. He will fight Champion Kilbane later.

See this lightning boxer.

Admission, 10 Cents

After losing to Johnny Kilbane in 1914, Benny Chavez continued to fight his way back into contention—and he was successful, though he never received a second chance at a world title. While fighting in Kansas City, Missouri, during 1916, Chavez fought Philadelphia contender Joe Riderberg, a.k.a. "Louisiana," four times, drawing twice, winning once and losing once.

putable one to Louisiana), by November, Williams was talking about bringing Chavez to Baltimore in December—all he had to do was beat an Englishman named Benny McNeil no one knew too much about.

Without Newman at the helm, Chavez had been fighting increasingly obscure opponents, for smaller purses, while write-ups on his once-promising career were becoming slimmer with each fight. Chavez might not ever get a shot at Williams, so he took the chance and accepted the McNeil bout, which was set up for a Thanksgiving card in St. Louis.

"McNeil, who is virtually unknown, stepped in and flattened the sensational fighter who, it is said, has Champion Kid Williams bulldozed," ran the *Associated Press* wire that holiday evening. "After a minute in the fourth round McNeil swung a full right to the jaw and followed with a left. Chavez staggered and crashed to the floor. Throughout the remainder of the round Chavez was either on the floor or just getting up. He fell without being hit. A right to the head ended the bout in the seventh."[76]

When the two rematched in Kansas City on New Year's Day 1917, McNeil knocked out Chavez again, this time in the ninth. "Kansas Citians hailed a new fistic idol last night — Benny McNeil. And in 'ringing in the new,' they watched the fall of an old one — Benny Chavez."[77]

Chavez returned to Denver where he scored back-to-back wins over mediocre foes before losing three straight. He was KO'd in one by Jack Bratton in Denver; KO'd in one by Young Joe Azevedo in Salt Lake City; and KO'd in seven by a guy he'd once knocked out, Young Wright Morgan, before his hometown of Trinidad. After evening the score with Bratton, in Ely, Nev., then losing again by a KO in the first in a rematch with Azevedo, Benny disappeared.

11. Border Battles, Soldier Wars, 1916–1919

Army boxing stars are coming to the front in the southwest.
— *El Paso Herald*, 1916[1]

A fighting heart beat beneath the khaki of every American. Boxing did not put the fighting heart there, but boxing did much to develop the fighting.
— *El Paso Morning Times*, 1919[2]

New Mexico might have had its first golden age after statehood, but by 1916, the possibility of war on two fronts — at the border and overseas — was drying up the state's major fight centers. With Mark Levy having returned to New York and no one able to fill the void he'd left, Albuquerque was finished as a fight town for the time being, while around the state, Las Vegas, Santa Fe, Gallup, Raton and the other leading cities were losing zeal — and men — to war.

In some places, however, boxing not only survived, but thrived. Mix in three major army bases near the border, then throw in the many mining towns of southern New Mexico kept busy during war time with the demand of precious metals, and you had everything in place for what was one of the best-though-short-lived scenarios for pugilism two states and two countries have ever seen — especially during war.

Between the U.S. and Mexico, southern New Mexico and El Paso, soldiers were pitted against soldiers, rookies with enlisted professionals, soldiers with miners, and all of 'em against seasoned ring veterans who'd been punching for pay since 1912. Wartime boxing at the border not only caught on, but would groom a new generation of prizefighters for the following decade.

Fort Wingate, in western New Mexico, had been the first army installation to stage prize fights. With the U.S. Army virtually immune to the territorial ban on boxing, Wingate held a series of shows in 1910. Just as the fort fed off fight-friendly Gallup, so did Fort Bayard, with Silver City and the surrounding mining camps of southeast New Mexico.

Soldiers stationed at Bayard made the rounds to the surrounding camps or headlined shows on base where they were pitted against popular miner-boxers. Bayard regulars like New Yorker Julius Green, San Francisco's Robert Gregory and Kentuckian Paul O'Brien fought each other, or miners Gus Flores and Luis Gonzales, against whom they usually lost. It wasn't until Tommy Atkins laced up that Fort Bayard had a local champ.

By the time Atkins first fought in New Mexico, he already had a reputation from fighting on the West Coast. Between 1914 and 1916, Atkins might not have won all his local fights (in fact, he lost most of his *big* fights), but his trilogy with Juan Horcasitas, a miner from the Chino Copper Mine, made him a local draw.

While Bayard and the mining towns provided a solid fan base through the next several years, it was at Deming and Columbus — and their ties to Fort Bliss in nearby El Paso — that provided the grounds, literally, for a boxing explosion.

The Mexican Revolution had called for several military camps near the border. Since the Battle of Juarez, in 1911, when *insurrectos* had captured the city, Fort Bliss had expanded greatly. As many as 50,000 men, from infantry, cavalry and National Guardsmen, would be stationed there during its peak. With the encouragement of its commanders, Fort Bliss created an athletic division and by 1915 the auxiliary camps of Fort Bliss — Camp Cotton and Camp Steward — were staging soldier vs. soldier boxing. Stringent Texas laws on prizefighting, however, kept the pros from playing; civilian fighters had to fight in New Mexico or on the other side of the Rio Grande in Juarez where, most of the time, the insurrectionists were all too happy to receive the sport — and any payoff money given them by the promoters.

While headquartering in Juarez, General Pancho Villa had not only allowed, but encouraged, boxing to thrive on his side of the border, assuring safe travel for *gringos* willing to cross over to Mexico. In fact, for nearly two months, it looked as if the Jack Johnson–Jess Willard fight of 1915 was going to take place in the Villa-occupied city of Juarez.

While soldiers took up the sport of boxing and with seasoned professionals, now soldiers, from around the country taking the lead, the sport was as common as inter-camp baseball. Things were developing at a rapid pace in New Mexico, as well, at Camp Furlong, right on the border in Columbus, and at Camp Deming, adjacent to Deming, 35 miles to the north. As a whole, boxing was much better received in New Mexico where the sport was legal, and the army camps only added to the action at first, before taking it over.

Since 1904, the National Guard had used the area around the town of Deming for training. In 1914, Camp Brookes, home for a thousand troops at one time, was established due to the hostilities south of the border. By 1916, the area had been christened "Camp Deming," which soon turned into "Camp Cody," named after the famous buffalo hunter, William F. Cody.

During its peak period, 30,000 men would be housed in 6,000 framed tents that had floors, electric lights and coal heaters. In time, Camp Cody would not only build an immense outdoor arena, built specifically for boxing, but also five YMCA buildings, a Knights of Columbus hall and a press to run its own newspaper, the *Trench & Camp*, which ran from October 1917 to December 1918. With the military encouraging sports, inter-camp boxers would compete regularly, with the best of them clashing with Camp Furlong and Fort Bliss fighters, as well as seasoned pros from the mining towns, El Paso and Juarez.

Averaging a show a month through 1919, though doubling the action in 1918, Camp Cody shows flourished during war. But when the Mexican threat was eliminated and the Treaty of Versailles signed, the fights were nixed as the garrisons were emptied.

Soldier vs. soldier fights under the direction of the 13th Cavalry were staged as early as 1912 at Deming's Crystal Theatre. In 1914, it was all about civilian boxers, with occasional Guardsmen getting into the action — the original Insurrecto Kid, Mike Baca and Fitz Cravens all fought while serving — but, by the end of the year, the area was quickly developing a handful of cavalrymen from Camp Deming. While the town had their local favorites — Jack Arnold being the top draw — the camp had Curley Bayless, of Arkansas, and Roy Cogill, of Wyoming, who drew the biggest house in 1916 when he challenged, and lost to, Fort Bliss' Johnny Newton, the U.S. Army's official welterweight champion.

Deming's biggest competition and source for opposition was Columbus' Camp Furlong. Headquarters for the 13th Cavalry and the 24th Infantry, the camp had been staging soldier bouts as early as the Fourth of July 1913, when the winner of a tournament was promised a $30 purse. In 1914, at one of the several theatres in Columbus, soldiers mixed with miners, but it was the ten-round fight for the border patrol's lightweight championship, on Aug. 1, 1914, that drew its biggest pre-war crowd.

New York City prizefighter Larry Strouer, the "Iron Man of the Army," arrived at Columbus a veteran of 40 bouts. Drawing crowds as large as 1,500, Strouer was a human sponge for punishment ("but took it with a smile"[3]) you could never count out because halfway through his 10- or 20-rounder, a late rally could easily win back a fight. Strouer's pair of battles with Joe Kale, his draw with Silver City miner Gus Flores and a hometown "draw" against Fort Bliss champ Johnny Papke made him a local favorite.

Alongside Strouer was his nemesis "Battling" Frank Mantell, a ham-and-egger from Brooklyn who'd originally been assigned to the camp as a boxing instructor for former Belen draw Clyde Day, now fighting for Uncle Sam. Mantell had been fighting in Juarez, but after enlisting in March 1914, he wore the khakis during the war. His trio against Strouer, who first drew, then twice defeated Mantell, provided the blueprint for soldier rival with border championships.

By 1915, most of the bouts in Columbus were soldier-based. One year later, the border town was leading the state with at least a dozen shows, beaten only by Deming one year, through war time. The town itself tripled in size during the war, to about 2,500 residents between 1916 and 1920, while Camp Furlong went from 1,419 troops (1,170 of whom were black soldiers with the 13th and 24th infantry) to 4,109 (3,599 black) in 1920.

In the early months of 1916, boxing along the border — in Deming, Columbus, the mining towns and Fort Bliss — was doing just fine. But Pancho Villa made it better.

Chasing Pancho

> *Being a fighter himself, General Pancho Villa believes all men engaged in the fight game should face fire without any "stalling."*
> — *El Paso Morning Times*, 1913[4]

Feeling betrayed by a government that continued to recognize the leadership of his enemy, President Venustiano Carranza, and spurned by a U.S. merchant who'd stopped supplying him with guns and ammo, General Pancho Villa felt entirely justified in staging a raid on the army garrison stationed at Columbus on the morning of March 9, 1916.

At 4:15 A.M., while most of the garrison and city was asleep, Villa gave the order to open fire. What started as a raid turned into a two-hour battle that left 18 Americans and more than 100 of Villa's own force dead. Six soldiers and two civilians were wounded as well — including boxer James Venner, who survived a bullet to the gut.

Villa's actions simultaneously launched two movements. One was the Punitive Expedition. The other was a pugilistic explosion that the expedition would have upon the area.

Six days after the attack, President Woodrow Wilson ordered General John J. Pershing to capture Villa. Leading 12,000 soldiers, Pershing pushed ahead into Mexico in search of Villa. As a military operation, the expedition was a failure. Border raids continued to occur, during and after the expedition, while Villa was able to evade U.S. troops.

As far as boxing goes, however, the expedition was a hit. During the expedition, which lasted until Feb. 7, 1917, soldiers battled the tedium of camp life by battling one another, resulting in at least a half dozen staged fight cards.

As the expeditionary troops expanded to 12,000, youngsters laced up and trained under seasoned veterans in camp — a list that included 47-year-old Joe (Brock) Blackburn, Bull Foster, Jack Fitzgerald, Fighting Dick Oleson, Deming's Jack Arnold, Kid Carr, Joe Kale, Benny Miller, Young Allen, Jack Mulvaney and Battling Dovitch — all former prizefighters before enlisting.

Two fighters quickly rose to the top of the pugilistic food chain: Whitey Burns, a towhead scrapper with the 16th Cavalry, who claimed the U.S. Army's middleweight title with a win over Jack Fitzgerald while on the Expedition, and Rufus Williams, a ring veteran from San Francisco, of the segregated 10th Cavalry. Williams not only carried a reputation from the West Coast, where he'd battled name fighters like Battling Ortega and Willie Meehan, usually giving up 10 to 30 pounds, but he'd furthered his reputation as a soldier-boxer while stationed in Hawaii and the Philippines.

After a 20-round draw during the Expedition failed to answer the question of superiority, Burns and Williams were matched on Jan. 2, 1917, this time for the U.S. Army welterweight championship — approved by Pershing, himself, who must not have been aware that Johnny Newton at Fort Bliss already held the honors. When "Pershing's mascot"[5] — as Williams became known — was awarded the decision, his name found itself across wire reports printed across the country; by the time he returned to Columbus, he was the biggest draw in New Mexico.

"Army officers arriving from Mexico say the name of Williams is synonymous with victory among the punitive expedition troopers," wrote the *El Paso Morning Times*. "So much so that Major General Pershing is said to be deeply interested in Williams' success, even if folks do call Williams 'cinder colored.'"[6]

Williams, however, would not only emerge as *the* fighter from the Expedition but, equally important, would take a young 24th Infantryman named Thomas Hayden under his wing. The lives and careers of Williams and Hayden would intertwine for years.

With Williams and Burns at the helm, the army fighters returned to their posts at Camp Furlong and Fort Bliss, sparking a new era in local, and soldier, boxing.

Punitive Expedition to Pugilistic Explosion

> *A new tribe of boxers — or the return of some of the old heads who fought here before — is the menu for sport followers of El Paso when the punitive expedition gets into the states from Mexico.*
>
> — *El Paso Morning Times,* 1917[7]

Pancho Villa was still loose in Mexico stirring up trouble and the world news was bleak with The Great War. German Zeppelins were dropping bombs on England. There was civil war in China, rebellion in Ireland, revolution in Russia, Finland and Costa Rica. And it was only a matter of time before President Wilson, who'd resisted thus far, declared the U.S. at war.

But at the border in early 1917, if you were a boxing fan, anyway, life was good.

Further draining New Mexico cities of civilian boxers, National Guard units from Texas, Arizona and New Mexico had been called into service on May 8, 1916, swelling the ranks of both the Expeditionary forces and the garrisons at Deming and Columbus.

In fact, on a Memorial Day boxing card held at the Armory in Albuquerque, May 30, 1916, Major Bernard Ruppe had climbed into the ring during the intermission between the

Cordova-Floyd fight and the Torres-Conners headliner to call for recruits willing to serve at the Mexican border.

One of the youngsters sitting ringside that night was Natividad Juarez, who was so overcome by the major's appeal that he enlisted while the main event was still in progress. The new recruit was assigned to Camp Furlong and it was there that Juarez received his first lesson as a boxer. During his stay, Juarez would not only get into the ring a dozen or so times, but he would pick up the moniker dropped by Espiridion Guevara years ago — "Insurrecto Kid." The second — and last — incarnation of the Insurrecto Kid began his career at 112 pounds, but 17 years later he'd finish it at 130. By then, there weren't too many people who remembered his real name.

Juarez wasn't the only one taking up boxing. Camp commanders everywhere were encouraging soldiers to climb into the ring to brush up their hand-to-hand combat skills. With the return of the Expeditionary champs, the activity only increased.

Larry Strouer was making the transition from fighter to promoter. Now known as the "Midnight Cavalryman," Strouer fought his remaining fights in the ring with a flaring red scarf tied around his hips — a lucky charm that was the gift of a "western cowgirl" whose father, a friend of Strouer's, had been killed on the night Villa raided Columbus.[8] Now a civilian, Strouer revved up the locals fighting in the mining towns and El Paso, then turned to promoting, focusing on expeditionary fighters who were returning to the area as heroes.

It was the only time in New Mexico's history of pugdom that black fighters became regular headliners, though Bob Foster would change some of that in the '70s. Strouer, with co-promoter J. H. Lemire, saw dollar signs in making even bigger heroes out of army soldiers, ignoring all color lines in pitting white vs. black, Furlong vs. Cody and New Mexico vs. Fort Bliss. Despite the Hispanic population, proximity to Mexico, and sudden influx of soldiers to the camps — a healthy sampling of the American melting pot — local black fighters had been no strangers to the boxing scene in New Mexico and El Paso, but those in Columbus would become the men to beat — and to avoid.

Late 1916 to mid–1917 saw three headliners in the New Mexico camps: Bull Foster, Whitey Burns and Rufus Williams, who was, most likely, the most experienced fighter in the area. It wasn't long before he was called "The Old Master."

In the first Punitive-themed shows, 10th Cavalryman and Expedition fighter Bull Foster, the former Texas champ before enlisting, made a statement by defeating long-time Furlong welterweight champ Chuck Kinney, from Chicago. "Swinging like a barn gate and missing," the 12th cavalryman was no match for "the good natured and terrific punching of the 'Bull.'"[9] Foster was able to clean up on the local scene, but he was, in turn, brutalized by Burns during the Expedition and defeated three times by Williams.

As the U.S. Army welter champ, Burns, a "blond-topped 158-pound package of pep,"[10] had been Pershing's pet before Williams, until the famous general turned the boys in khaki back around and headed for home. Uncrowned by Williams, the Scranton, Pennsylvania, native was reassigned to Fort Bliss where he outgrew welterweight, then defeated the best middleweights.

As Williams was reassigned from the 10th Cavalry to the also-segregated 24th Infantry — both units had been part of the original Buffalo Soldiers during the Civil War — his claim to the U.S. Army's welterweight championship was immediately questioned by followers of the man bearing the same title just a few miles away at Fort Bliss: Johnny Newton.

Williams surrendered to the relentless Henry Smith, who would develop into the first black manager and promoter in state history. A former sparring partner of Jack Johnson, Smith would, over the next several years, guide many careers and stage some of the area's biggest fights for the black fighters of the 24th.

Ol' Rufus would be Smith's calling card, and it didn't take him long to drum up drama over the Williams and Newton claims to the same title. Smith offered the Ohio army champ the unheard of amount of $1,000 to fight his "black demon of Columbus," instead of the lighter men he'd been beating up at the nearby Smelter Arena. "The Ohio champion has earned much more than a thousand while boxing here, and the fans need not be surprised if the Buckeye slammer takes on the Columbus darkey,"[11] wrote Hy Schneider of the *El Paso Morning Times* — *the* sports scribe of the time and region.

Fans, however, *were* surprised. Passing on Smith's "roll of greenbacks," Newton's manager, Bill Hull, "refused to entertain a proposition calling for his boy to meet the darkey cyclone."[12] Newton would not cross the color line.

Foster and Burns, however, didn't have a problem — and neither would Bart Gordon, a well-known ring veteran since 1913 pulling National Guard duty at Columbus. Foster, at the order of his manager Vic Fisher, had to whistle a different tune in early March 1917, however, when it was announced that, after losing to Rufus, he would not be fighting a rematch. "As long as Burns is under my management, he will box no negro boy," stated Fisher. "I am content to have him confine his efforts to the realm of the white boxer. Under no condition will I consider having Burns meet a negro. This is final."[13]

Gordon banked on his experience, but Williams punished him for ten rounds on March 3, 1917, for a referee's decision. Six days later, and giving up 35 pounds, the 150-pound Williams took on another veteran in the Columbus ring, "Mexican" Pete Everett. The 42-year-old pioneer, living in Las Vegas, New Mexico, and fighting sporadically throughout the Southwest, Silver City and Juarez, had been fighting since 1894. Earlier fights included a 20-round distance loss to Jack Johnson, and a three-round stoppage loss to James J. Jeffries; recent fights had Everett pulling off a crafty upset win over Kid George and going 1-1-1 in a trio with Silver City's "Big Smoke," Young Jack Johnson.

Against Williams, however, Everett lasted but four rounds. The living legend returned to Las Vegas where he made news again in June. Drunk while dining on a bowl of chile at the Bridge Bar in Vegas, he'd turned to the crowd and yelled, "To hell with the United States government! To hell with the flag and to hell with all the *gringoes* [*sic*] that are here present!" Everett was arrested, fined $100 and sentenced to 100 days in jail.[14]

After stopping Everett, Williams cleaned up at the border, rematching Bull Foster twice and taking on all comers. Only Newton could defeat Williams, it was surmised — and the white version of the U.S. Army's welterweight title was not crossing the color line.

Smelter Shelter, 1916–1917

The setting for these matches is picturesque. Sand hills of New Mexico form a background to the west while, off to the southwest the blue mountains of Mexico show through the film of smelter smoke. There is no roof over the arena and the boxers struggle on the elevated, canvas covered platform in the full glare of the midwinter sun. As the army is the best patron of the arena, the sloping benches surrounding the ring are filled with soldiers in their olive drab service uniforms with a circle of automobiles around the arena, many being occupied by women who drive out to watch the contests. The matchmaker for this unique boxing club is a former National League baseball player and his contests have the sanction of the regimental chaplains as they are clean exhibitions which furnish entertainment for the enlisted men who are off duty.

—Associated Press, 1917[15]

During the Expedition, Johnny Newton made himself the most popular fighter on the border.

The Ohio infantryman had gotten his start in the mitt game on a fluke, climbing into the ring on a dare against the legendary Battling Nelson while the former lightweight champ had passed through his town on a theatrical tour. Nelson spanked the youngster, flooring him seven times, but even in defeat, Newton was hooked.

With a handful of pre-war fights under his belt on the local scene, it wasn't until he'd enlisted that his skills soared. By the time Rufus Williams came home from Old Mexico bearing the same title Newton had won in October by defeating Johnny Simpson, the "level-headed, triple-footed and lynx-eyed peddler of the leathery pillowed jabs and jolts"[16] was also the Southwestern welterweight champ after knocking out tough Floyd Johnson of Camp Deming in Columbus.

It was Newton's next fight, however, that cements his place in New Mexico history.

Due to Texas laws prohibiting prize fights, El Pasoans had staged their big shows across the river in Juarez and their smaller ones under the cover of private-membership clubs — a risky venture, at best. Fort Bliss and surrounding camps had, in recent years, provided new options. But, in late 1916, it was bad enough that Juarez was increasingly becoming a tougher place to stage a fight, but bouts staged on military camps came under fire, prompting Assistant Attorney General Walter Keeling to remind anti-prizefight politicians in Texas that sports and entertainment occurring within the confines of military camps were governed by U.S.—not Texas—laws. Furthermore, boxing, said Keeling, was "part of the athletic and welfare work of the army, for the benefit and entertainment of the enlisted men."[17]

The YMCAs on base, on the other hand, were not likely to pay the top army fighters more than a handout collected from a crowd of soldiers, nor was there a venue on army grounds to handle large crowds, not yet in 1916. Furthermore, military camps were closed to both civilian promoters and boxers, necessitating an alternative that would not only provide a purse but a crowd to pay for it.

On the other hand, the army was not *against* soldiers fighting elsewhere, be it Deming, Columbus or Silver City, though Juarez was off-limits, given the Mexican Revolution.

Once again El Pasoans looked to a patch of land across the Courchesne Bridge over the Rio Grande on New Mexico land. The same plot of land El Paso promoters had christened "Bohemia Heights" in 1912, that had been nipped in the bud by former Governor McDonald, the same plot of land used briefly in the 1890s for a handful of fights during New Mexico's territorial days, became the hope of the border town. This time, with the backing of Uncle Sam and no official law prohibiting its use, it was a go.

A new arena, built in December 1916 to seat 2,000, was financed by Chicago entrepreneur Charles Ford, who spent his winters at the border. Matchmaking, arena management and promotions fell in the lap of the amiable "Sunny" Jim Brown, who had his hands full in the five months that saw nine cards staged at the Smelter Arena.

The open-air arena was always under construction. Though only 600 showed up for the first show, on Dec. 18, 1916, by the middle of January, 2,500 were crammed into the makeshift arena, stretched beyond capacity. New bleachers were hastily added — just one of the endless mending and "improvements" that kept Brown hopping. Having to keep up with attendance was a good thing — weather was not. The glare of the sun was combatted with a sun shade, but heavy winter winds continually tore into the canvas exterior and broke timbers that braced the sun shade, while dust and winds tore into both fighters and spectators, calling for a 15-foot-high board fence and windshield that would "keep away the wind, throw a laugh into the face of the dust, and in general save the clothes of a lot of fans from the cleaners."[18]

The shades and fences helped, but not much could eliminate the transportation problem. Spectators had to either walk a couple of miles or use the busses that Brown had to hire. Free of charge to ticketholders who would spend between $1 and $3 for admission, the busses carted fans back and forth from the Hotel Paso del Norte, in downtown El Paso, a process that brought complaints from fans who did not want to miss opening bouts or spend half the night waiting for a return trip.

Despite the wind, the journey and the dirt, fights at the Smelter were talked about for years by patrons and reporters who remembered its picturesque settings:

> I tried to count the people — I got as far as 1,589 soldiers and then I got dizzy from looking at so much khaki and had to quit. The ticket man said there were about five hundred civilians there with their wives and sweethearts.... There's going to be another prize fight next Sunday at the same place and the ring will be draped in flags, the band will play, there will be a large gathering of pretty women in pretty dresses, and best of all, the favorite of the south — Fred Anderson, of Deming, is going to put up a strong battle against Tommy O'Toole, of Pennsylvania, just to see if he can't carry off the lightweight championship of the south.[19]

Equally important as the locale were the fighters who were transformed into local stars — beginning with the first headliner, Johnny Newton.

Though a less than optimal crowd showed up at the opener to watch Newton duke out a draw with Brooklyn veteran Eddie Duffy, who was crafty enough to box "through the entire bout with his back to the glaring sun,"[20] the Ohio infantryman was drawing a packed house by the end of January. Newton defended his U.S. Army welterweight title by knocking out fellow Fort Bliss soldier Billy Bailey in January 1917, while an octet of soldiers from the Second Ohio band sang "Dixie Doodle."

In his last Smelter — and local — appearance, Newton took seven rounds to stop Hank Vandewaker, who "never once mussed Johnny's pompadour"[21] on Feb. 22. After beating "Vandy," *Times* sports scribe Schneider demanded that Newton step up and fight a real man, and that just *maybe* it was an oversight that promoter Burns "forgot" to read the challenge and $1,000 offer by that "darkey scrapper" of Columbus, Rufus Williams. He wrote, "Such a small matter as that of a thousand fish would not prevent the bout?"[22] Just in time, having "cleaned up" by making a cumulative $1,500 since the fall while stationed at Fort Bliss, Newton's unit was recalled home to the Buckeye State.

Newton might have been the first darling at Fort Bliss and the Smelter, but reluctance to cross the color line and inability to make the welterweight limit had fans turning instead to featherweights.

Border fans thought they had a comer in Philadelphia's Tommy Livingston, who showed he wasn't afraid to venture out from the gates of Fort Bliss when he defeated Denver veteran Kiscus Lubb in Tucumcari, on Oct. 4, 1916, on short notice, no less. But when Livingston crashed to the canvas and was counted out, courtesy of fellow Pennsylvanian Tommy O'Toole, in the second Smelter show on New Year's Eve 1916, they had their next star.

O'Toole proved himself beyond expectations when he not only defeated former border headliner Benny Cordova, but made the "terror of this region ... the little Mexican who has been heralded around here as the best in the game,"[23] look like a rank amateur on Jan. 14,

1917, to win the mythical Southwestern lightweight championship. Moving up from feather to lightweight for the first time, the "snappy little Irishman"[24] gave the man who'd faced Texan terror Bobby Waugh six times, the "lacing of his life,"[25] while sleet and hail whipped the fighters and 1,500 brave spectators at the Smelter.

O'Toole, who would be deemed the "best lightweight boxer who ever laced a glove along the Rio Grande in military boxing exhibitions,"[26] was pitted against another civilian boxer in his next Smelter appearance — Vancouver-born Freddie Anderson, brother to well-known pug Bud and Deming's hope for a southwestern lightweight champion. Hoping to unsaddle the soldier boy before his unit was deployed, Anderson came close, but was unable to spoil O'Toole's last two fights in the area.

In a pair of whirlwind battles — Feb. 4 and Mar. 9, 1917 — O'Toole, fighting well under the lightweight limit of 133 and closer to feather, defeated Anderson, first by a close 20-round majority decision (in the only bout to use three judges at the Smelter) and then by knockout, when he "dropped the complete pause insignia over the roof of the House of Anderson after one minute and 40 seconds of mixing in the sixth round of the second section of the bout."[27] (Twenty-round bouts were prohibited in New Mexico, so promoters staged two 10-round bouts, one immediately following the other.)

Unlike Newton, O'Toole proclaimed himself ready to take on all comers, including Waugh and Otto Wallace, who was penciled in as the next headliner at the Smelter for a shot at the army hero. Before that could happen, the Smelter Arena lost its greatest draw when the Pennsylvania unit returned to Philadelphia.

Promoter Brown had big plans. While Newton and O'Toole had headlined the majority of Smelter cards, other Fort Bliss fighters were on their way up the ladder. There was Ira "Flash" Barend of El Paso, who sought redemption after a KO loss to Livingston; Carter Croshaw, the fighting conductor from Michigan; Philly's "Terrible" Terry Murphy; Johnny Kolopus of Ohio; Battling Cullins; "Pug" Doyle; Texan Carl "Caveman" Carlson, who lived up to his nickname; "Battling" Jack Burke, and Harry "Scogie" Muskopf. In the final Smelter show, on Apr. 25, 1917, Muskopf fought Denver pug Bud Hamilton, enlisted now at Fort Bliss, in an eight-rounder that came close to being nixed last minute due to a very slim crowd. Originally scheduled for 15 rounds, the "Tale of the Final Jab" was reduced to eight when Hamilton refused to fight until a guarantee could be made from a number of ringside "red bloods" who coughed up an agreed-upon purse.[28]

After the Muskopf-Hamilton fight, things fell apart. For one, America had just entered the war; just about the time the arena's financial backer decided it was time to go home to Chicago. Though electric lights had just been installed at the arena, Ford pulled the plug. Weekly boxing shows at Fort Bliss that were easier to attend also chopped away at the Smelter's attendance. One such "smoker" had somehow managed to cram 1,500 people into the tiny YMCA building. Fort Bliss now had designs to build their own arena on site.

The days of the Smelter Arena were over ... for now.

Camp Cody

Have you ever seen one hundred or more men, each with a pair of boxing gloves on his hands, standing in two long lines, going through various prescribed motions? If you haven't, you perhaps will be interested in seeing the workout of the company athletic instructors, in the rear of the division's athletic office, each Wednesday afternoon.

— El Paso Morning Times, 1918[29]

When Deming featherweight Marty Falk was transferred to Fort McPherson, California, in 1918, he lamented about the "slow life" there. "I'm a fighting man," he wrote the boys at the *El Paso Times*. "And I haven't had a chance to put the gloves on since coming here, as there don't seem to be any one willing to box. And, boy, that is just the opposite from the Cody bunch."[30]

How true it was. Though the country was at war, boxing did not skip a beat at the border. Backed by Uncle Sam, fighting in the ring equated to preparing for battle—if you could throw a punch, you could thrust a bayonet in the trenches overseas. That's what champions like Johnny Kilbane, Johnny Dundee, Packey McFarland, 44 athletic directors and 30 boxing instructors were telling soldiers at military installations across the country.

At the border, Fort Bliss, Camp Furlong and Camp Cody only increased ring activity when the U.S. declared war on Germany, on April 6, 1917. Tournaments between divisions and camps were regular affairs, while the top fighters, representing their camps and the U.S. Army, were pitted against the best in the region.

Though there was often a blurred line between prizefighting and boxing, or between professional and amateur bouts, the military stressed clean athletics in the art of self defense. "A number of clever boxers have been developed at the camps," ran the PR from the War Department. "They are not pugs and probably never would make first-class professional pugilists, but that is not the object."[31]

The object was morale, entertainment and preparation for hand-to-hand combat. If any of the three camps were able to maintain this, it was Camp Cody of Deming. With the closing of the Smelter and with Deming sports in hiatus, Camp Cody boxing, under the direction of Lt. Roy Shuster, took over in November 1917.

It was estimated that every company had one or more boxers with previous experience at Cody, which enabled the athletic division to put together a solid team. Under boxing instructor Tommy Connolly, a former sparring partner of Freddie Welsh and a veteran since 1911, along with Billy Koehler, a Minneapolis veteran, a team was assembled. As troops were deployed or moved, the team would see new coaches—bantam Buck Timothy, who'd been tentatively matched against top-notcher Billy Ertle before enlisting, and El Paso's Gene Payo—while the troops tripled in number.

At heavyweight was 6'4" Iowan Ralph Alexander "The Great" of Waterloo, Iowa, a newbie with the gloves but who would go on to be a decent Midwestern heavyweight after the war. Running back and forth from middle to light-heavy was Guy Buckles, of Omaha, Neb., who, from 1907 to 1912, had had moderate success in the Midwest. The middleweight division was covered by Jack "The Cody Slasher" Duarte, of San Francisco, while Cody's top welters were both from Davenport, Iowa: Jack Racer, a ham-and-egger who'd faced top names (usually losing), but had, in 1914, nearly died from injuries sustained in a Wisconsin fight when he lapsed into a coma, and Roy "Bum Steamer" Steuhmer, the "fighting horseshoer" and "fighter who can also box"[32] from the camp of Packey McFarland. At lightweight, there was Nebraska's Jack Barry and Minnesota's Jack "Scientific Kid" Young. When Young was transferred to Fort Bliss, Nebraskans Albert "Kid" Strayer and Roy "Bat" Brennan and Texan Billy Kleck rose to the top. The chosen featherweight was Chicago's Marty Falk, who fought a trilogy with Fort Bliss' Jack Arnold. At bantam, it was up to William "Packey" McFarland, who struggled against Fort Bliss' superior boxers.

Fights were allowed off-base until Camp Cody's athletic board funded a massive outdoor stadium on an old reservoir that had once been used to supply water to El Paso. A 45' × 80' stage, on which sat a ring, was constructed. The stadium would generate some of the biggest crowds ever seen at a boxing match — even by today's standards. It wasn't hard to figure out why, when the board announced that entertainment at Camp Cody Stadium would be free to the troops and visiting civilians. Pep talks by General George Harris and a 150-piece band playing patriotic and ragtime music added to the shows.

Preventing the boxing scene from expanding like the quasi-civilian cards seen in Columbus and at the Smelter Arena, the athletic board banned civilian boxers from fighting on military space. They also did away with lengthy bouts over 10 rounds, limiting the cards to inter-camp and tournament shows against other camps. At the same time, athletic instructors mandated boxing as compulsory for all soldiers, following the pattern set by Fort Bliss.

An estimated crowd of 10,000 spectators showed up to see the first Camp Cody Athletics show on Nov. 17, 1917, that contained but four exhibitions, a speech by the top brass and three wrestling bouts. In the main event, civilian boxers Bobby Waugh and Jack Lopez sparred for three rounds — the rest featured the Camp Cody boxing team.

Even when the board started charging admission (50 cents for soldiers, 75 cents for civilians), then relaxed its ban of civilian fighters, in 1918, several thousand still showed up to watch a ten-rounder between Buckles or Duarte, Racer or Steamer; Bobby Waugh knock out Snipes Fitzpatrick; or the Cody team take on the best from Fort Bliss in a series of four-round tournament bouts.

The highest attendance was reached on Aug 16, 1918, when the numbers approached 12,000 on a card that didn't even feature the best of Cody or Bliss, or a even a civilian boxer draw like Waugh, but rather officers fighting officers of the camp. Five days later "The Stadium" hit those numbers again, though the *Deming Headlight* argued that it was 8,000 while the on-site paper, *Trench & Camp*, insisted on 12,000.

No doubt, the spectator numbers of the era belonged to Camp Cody. But the top fighters of the day were 35 miles south at Camp Furlong.

The 24th's Hour

Physical art is gripping the great heart of Columbus sports, recent attendances at the big mills having proved that its hold is gradually approaching the strangling stage.
— *El Paso Morning Times*, 1916[33]

It's ironic that Camp Cody, almost entirely white, had been named after the famous buffalo hunter while the units that had evolved from the original buffalo soldiers occupied the segregated base of Camp Furlong at Columbus.

When pairing up the fighters, however, the Midwestern ham-and-eggers that made up the Camp Cody team paled in more than color when compared to the so-called "cyclone darkeys" and "cinder-hued demons" of the 24th Infantry. The fighters who rose to the top of Camp Furlong's pot — and there would be more than 4,000 troops in which to cull through — had not had an easy time of prizefighting in pre-war civilian life.

The era of black heavyweight champion Jack Johnson was not kind to black fighters. Though there might've been less of an issue in New Mexico than the bigger fight states, black pugilists were generally ignored by the press and avoided in the ring. When they did get a fight, they were oftentimes outweighed. Until he joined the U. S. Army, Rufus Williams said he'd gotten used to giving up 20 to 30 pounds every time he fought against someone of lighter hue.

The border and mining towns had headlined black fighters since 1912. Al Smaulding and Lefty Floyd of New Mexico had been matched up pretty fairly, as had "Old Smoke" —

BOXING

Event, for Welterweight Championship of the Border

CRYSTAL THEATRE, Columbus, N. M., MONDAY, Sept. 2, 1918

BABY CABELL

BATTLING KID REYES

MAIN EVENT-15 ROUNDS

Battling Kid Reyes
of El Paso, Texas
142 Pounds

VS

Baby Cabell
M. G. Co. 24th Infantry
145 Pounds

This bout will decide the welterweigh championship of the Border. These two boys met on July 4th, last, and put up a real fight from start to finish

SEMI-WINDUP--10 ROUNDS

| IRON JAW GINK PARKER | vs | JOE FORD |
| 130 lbs.   CO. H 24TH INF. | | 136 lbs.   CO. B 24TH INF. |

A grudge fight for the Lightweight Championship of the 24th

A 4-ROUND CURTAIN RAISER

JOE FORD

GINK PARKER

Doors Open at 8:00
First Bout Starts at 8:30

General Admission $0.55:   Reserved $1.10.
Ringside $1.65, Including War Tax

Ladies Patronage Solicited

Secure Your Tickets in Advance

Tickets on Sale at Johnson's Pool Hall, 12th Cavalry and 24th Infantry Exchanges

HENRY DAVIS - - - - MANAGER

Fight poster for Sept. 20, 1918, at the Crystal Theatre in Columbus, New Mexico. It was the first of many boxing shows for Camp Furlong's athletic department. The card pitted Fort Bliss' top welterweight, Battling Kid Reyes, against Camp Furlong's champ, Gene "Babe" Cabell, who was KO'd in 12.

Young Jack Johnson — at Silver City. Any racial tension that "The Fighting Ghost," Jeff Clarke might've brought to Juarez had gone unreported, though, at the same time, he was described as "not a very handsome darkey, but he is 'some powehful fightah.'"[34]

The region was not alone in using black fighters in battle royals seen as comedy numbers ("side splitters"[35] or "corkscrew numbers"[36] that were "more fun than a barrel of monkeys"[37]), though. Battle royals were a regular — had been before the war and would be for years after. For a brief time, however, they were put aside — at least in using young black aspirants, who were usually blindfolded. Silver City promoters might've been stubborn. "There will also be a battle royal as an opener for the afternoon's sport if the necessary number of dusky-hued boys can be located and dragged into the arena,"[38] they announced for a show in 1918. But, by 1917, it wasn't uncommon to hear that "there will be no battle royal, owing to the fact that apparently all of the real, honest-to-goodness colored scrappers in this town have joined the army."[39] That was almost entirely due to the segregated troops at Columbus and their corps of prizefighters.

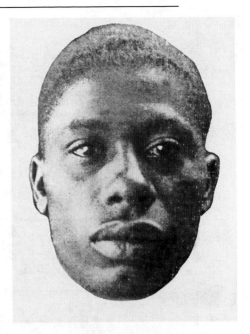

Thomas "Speedball" Hayden carved out a reputation during World War I while stationed with the 24th Infantry in Columbus, New Mexico. Hayden was one of the most successful soldier-boxers during the war, and one of the first main-event black fighters in New Mexico.

There was Gene Cabell, sometimes nicknamed "Babe" or "Baby," and sometimes "Gorilla Baby"; Joe Brock Blackburn, the Bernard Hopkins of his time who, in 1919, was still competitive at 49 years old; Jimmie "Hard-Hitting" Wright, who would develop into the border's welterweight champion; Clarence "Kid" Ross, of Clifton, Ariz., who'd been a regular in Juarez before the war; "Gink" Parker; "Rabbit" Rogers; "Fighting" McDaniels; and the man who would become the most popular fighter of 'em all during the era, "Speedball" Hayden.

The glory of the 24th all started with Rufus Williams, who came back from the Punitive Expedition as a hero as the man to beat, only to find Fort Bliss had snagged his title of U. S. Army welterweight champion for Johnny Newton. The "Black Demon" of Columbus was reduced to the "cinder-colored champion of Mexico"[40] while the "Buckeye Slammer" of Fort Bliss played it safe by drawing the color line long enough to leave the area.

Williams would get plenty of competition during the war, however, when two names emerged to threaten the "Old Master": Johnny Sudenberg from Fort Bliss and another 24th infantryman whom Williams had taken under his wing during the Expedition.

Thomas Hayden, from Indianapolis, Ind., had been a jockey before enlisting, but had been taught the sweet science from Williams during the Expedition. After their return from Old Mexico, it didn't take long for Hayden to make his rise in the local ring. Within six months, border fight fans were talking more about "Speedball" than "Ol' Rufus."

The inevitable showdown between pupil and teacher — champ and challenger — became the biggest fight of the year at the border on Nov. 22, 1917, with a standing-room-only

BOXING CHAMPIONSHIP
CONTEST

CRYSTAL THEATRE
Columbus, N. M.
THURSDAY, NOV. 22, 1917

RUFUS WILLIAMS

155 Pounds, "The Old Master"   Middle Weight Champion U. S. Army

vs

THOMAS HAYDEN

145 Pounds. "Speed Ball"   Welter Weight Champion of the 24th Infantry

RUFUS WILLIAMS, (the Old Master) needs no introduction to the sport-loving public, being the undisputed champion of the whole U. S. Army, having successfully defended his title in the Philippine Islands, Hawiian Islands, in Old Mexico with General Pershing's Expedition, and also here on the border. Williams has not lost a decision in the last four years.

"SPEED-BALL" HAYDEN, the Welter-Weight Champion of the 24th Infantry. A young boxer, but has shown more class than any boxer on the border, having won all his bouts with such ease he is better known as Knock-um Dead Hayden. He carries a knock-out punch in either hand, as his record shows his last 7 fights were all won by a knock-out inside of the limit, and it is conceded by the majority who have seen him in action that any man he can hit, he can beat. He will be a worthy opponent for Rufus Williams.

Curtain Raiser
A Grand Battle Royal
Between Five Huskie Battlers
Of the Rough and Ready, Slam-Bang, Go-As-You-Please Style

General Admission $1.00.   Reserved Seats $1.50.   Ringside $2.00
All Seats Reserved and Numbered

Doors Open at 7 o'clock. Bout Starts at 8 p. m. Tickets on Sale at Johnson & Howard Pool Hall and 12th Cavalry Exchange

Come Early to Avoid the Rush and Secure a Good Seat

Grand Ball After Boxing Contest   **Everybody Welcome**

Union Labor

HENRY DAVIS, Promoter

The fight of the year at the border during 1917 was the showdown between student and master: "The Ol' Master," Rufus Williams, and rising star of the 24th Infantry, undefeated Thomas "Speedball" Hayden. After they clashed, on Nov. 22, 1917, at the Crystal Theater in Columbus, it was the beginning of a new era for soldier boxing, with the Speedball at the forefront.

crowd of 1,200 packed into the Crystal Theatre of Columbus, with special trains scheduled from El Paso, Deming and Silver City. Williams, who'd been fighting for seven years, had not lost a fight since 1916 while Hayden, though undefeated, was still a rookie.

Speedball was in trouble early, going down twice in the first and punished thoroughly by his former mentor in the second. He was "practically dragged back to his corner when the bell rang, dead on his feet," but came out "like a bearcat in the third," to turn the fight around. By the 11th round, Williams was staggering across the ring. "A shot to the body had Williams tottering, than crashing to the canvas. Grinning, Williams made the count, barely surviving the remainder of the round. Rufus was out and he seemed to know it—but the smile still remained. The gong sounded for the twelfth round and Williams, game to the core, tried to rise, but tottered weakly.... Referee Dick Monohan showed Hayden's right arm skyward as token of victory—and a new champion was made."[41]

By December 1917, Johnny Sudenberg, the latest golden-haired child of Fort Bliss, was the natural challenger—and he *wasn't* drawing color lines. Sudenberg already had a reputation that preceded his vic-

Hoping for a chance to face the area's premier welter and middleweight, Speedball Hayden, Clarence "Kid" Ross, of the 24th Infantry in Columbus, and Hock Bones, a veteran from Memphis, were scheduled to go 15 at the Crystal Theatre in Columbus. In an upset, Ross won the decision on a fight that was cut short two rounds when two of the judges, who were also army officers, ended the fight early to allow soldiers to make the 11 P.M. check. Writer Jack London was the third judge.

tories at Fort Bliss. A ring veteran since 1913 and having fought on both coasts, Sudenberg had fought three fights in Nevada against future world heavyweight champion Jack Dempsey. Giving up weight to the "Manassa Mauler," Sudenberg had drawn twice before losing by a knockout. In one of the bouts, however, Sudenberg had floored Dempsey a total of nine times.

Speedball and Sudenberg were matched for 15 rounds on Christmas Day 1917 for Hayden's official U.S. Army middleweight title he'd won from Rufus, at Columbus' Crystal Theatre. Before a record crowd of 1,400, the fight would barely go a round. It was a thriller while it lasted, with Sudenberg going down for a seven-count but, in the final minute, after landing his first solid blow—a left hook—Sudenberg followed up with a blow that strayed south of the border. Worse: After Hayden sank to the canvas, Sudenberg, in his eagerness, struck his foe while down. No one blamed Sudenberg for intentional fouling, but the fight was given to Hayden, who retained his title.

During 1918, as the war raged on overseas, Hayden went undefeated, fighting five times. Memphis battler Hock Bones was brought in, first, to defend his mythical "World Colored Middleweight Championship" against Clarence Ross, in January, only to lose it to Hayden, who not only moved up in weight, but floored the champ twice while battering his "face to a jelly" in their one-sided 15-rounder.[42]

Hayden defended again in May, granting Ol' Rufus a rematch but winning by a third-round knockout in a controversial fight that had Hayden actually choking him out against the ropes. "Whether or not this mode of fighting is in accordance with the rules the writer can't say," wrote the *Columbus Courier*. "The decision was very unpopular, and such tactics will certainly cause the ban to be placed on fighting in Columbus for all time to come if ever allowed to happen again."[43] Hayden and Williams would fight several more times over the years — the best Rufus would do was a draw, in 1919.

The inevitable, much-demanded Hayden-Sudenberg rematch took place on May 30, 1918. This time Speedball left home turf to fight in El Paso, before a crowd of 2,500 — the capacity at the Fort Bliss Punch Bowl. Hayden, weighing in the same as Sudenberg, at 158, but in full uniform, outclassed the 7th Cavalry hopeful for a referee's decision, though he was unable to score the knockout.

Having defeated the major players, Hayden fell into inactivity while other 24th fighters rose to the forefront. Kid Ross became a worthy challenger for Hayden when he beat Hock Bones on a card that had writer Jack London sitting ringside, on Aug. 26, 1918. When the press demanded a Hayden-Ross showdown for the middleweight championship of the Army and border, it was lined up for September, then continually pushed back due to an outbreak of influenza that had not only hit the camps but all of New Mexico.

By the time Hayden and Ross got into the ring, on Nov. 16, 1918, it had become the main event of a card celebrating the end of the war. Before a crowd of 3,500 at the newly-constructed outdoor arena at Camp Furlong, "Ross put up the gamest battle of his career ... but was not quite ready for the champion Speedball," who landed the "dreamland kayo" at 2:45 of the 20th, final round.[44]

The end of the war signaled the

BOXING!

AT THE

Remodeled 24th Inf. Arena

Thanksgiving Afternoon

Hardhitting Wright vs. Gorrillo Jones---20 Rounds
Clarence Kid Ross vs. Speedball Hayden---15 Rounds
Battltng Dudley vs. Babe Cabell---8 Rounds
Wilfred Smith vs. William Thompson---4 Rounds

47---Rounds of Fighting---47

24TH INFANTRY BAND

Gates Open 1:30; Prices $1, $2, $3

The Nov. 16, 1918, showdown between Speedball Hayden and Clarence "Kid" Ross had been on-and-off for two months due to an outbreak of influenza in the fall of 1918. When it finally happened on November 16, 1918, it was without the Hardhitting Wright–Gorilla Jones fight. Hayden and Gorilla Jones would meet several times over the years.

beginning of the end of regimental boxing at the border, but the battles at Columbus continued due to the Mexican threat still posed by Pancho Villa. In fact, as most camps downsized or shut down, Camp Furlong's troops — and boxing — only increased.

In 1919, the 24th's Athletic Board took over the sport, cutting out civilian promoters and moving most fights on-base from Columbus' downtown theaters, and reducing prices by half: 10 cents for soldiers, 25 cents for civilians. The crowds continued to pour into the outdoor arena.

The war was over, but soldier boxing was not.

Silver City, 1917–1918

> *Boxing bouts are the regular thing in every small mining town of New Mexico. They are taking well.*
> — *El Paso Morning Times*, 1916[45]

With the explosion of soldier boxing during the war, old-school civilian prizefighting was kept alive by Otto Forster in the mining towns. While the military pushed "clean sports" for the advancement of athletics, hard-working miners and bigger name pugs *not* associated with Uncle Sam found a welcome spot in dingy theaters and clubs of Silver City. It kept ol' reliables — like Otto Wallace, Bobby Waugh and Benny Cordova — on the payroll while providing opportunities for aspiring miners who had an inkling to lace on the Levinsons.

Though groomed in the last holdout of traditional prizefighting during the war, miner-boxers did not have it easy. Athletic boards ignored the local civilians, though Forster did not hesitate to sign a miner to fight a soldier boxer on one of his shows. More often than not, it meant a New Mexican was up against someone with more experience.

During the war and final years of the Mexican Revolution, when the careers of Luis Gonzales and Gus Flores had played out, Santa Rita's Jack Lopez sought to fight his way out of the mines. In the late '10s, that meant clearing out the local threats, then stepping up to every visiting veteran and soldier close to his weight.

For a part-time fighter like Lopez, that meant an up-and-down career. Lopez wasn't quite as ring savvy as Washington lightweight Freddie Anderson in 1915, but another year-and-a-half of campaigning improved enough to even the score. At Deming in 1917, Lopez convinced his hometown crowd that miners made better fighters than soldiers when he "made such a monkey out of ["Caveman"] Carlson that he quit cold in the middle of the third round."[46] But, in the toughest fight of his life, at the peak of his career, Lopez was sadly outclassed, though game enough to go 17 rounds against top-notch veteran Otto Wallace, in Silver City. Though he usually had the best of Camp Cody soldiers, Lopez lost by a 13th-round TKO to Fort Bliss' Scientific Kid Young in 1919. After Camp Furlong's Baby Cabell took him out in four rounds in 1921, the Lopez name faded from print.

Veterans like Mexican Pete Everett, Kid George and the Anderson brothers, Bud and Freddie, found homes for a time in the mining towns. Bud Anderson, of Vancouver, Wash., had been a contender several years earlier, having faced the likes of Leach Cross and beaten Joe Mandot before giving up the game on advice from his physician.

After working in the mines of Santa Rita, Anderson tried to stage a comeback in New Mexico at the tail-end of 1916, at the Elks' Theater in Silver City, but Benny Cordova was there to spoil it with a 19th-round knockout. He tried a couple more times, against lesser names, but, by then, most of the attention was on his younger brother Freddie, also a lightweight, who'd made a name for himself by beating Lopez. It was enough for the duo to get out of the mines and to Deming, where Freddie fought back-to-back classics in 1916 with Hamilton. In 1917 at the Smelter Arena, Tommy O'Toole first edged him in a close 20-rounder, then knocked him out in 16 for Southwestern lightweight honors.

The biggest fights of the era, at least in the interest of the mining towns, involved Texas lightweight Bobby Waugh — Cordova's career nemesis. Waugh headlined Silver City no fewer than four times in 1917, the last of which rates as one of New Mexico's most significant fights.

Waugh needed six rounds to TKO San Francisco's Buzz Hughes in July and 14 rounds to stop Australia's Jack Read in September. Then, in an eliminator, the winner to face legend Joe Rivers, Waugh had to settle for a 20-round decision in his seventh fight with Cordova, in late October.

Waugh vs. Rivers — the year's capper — was slated for Oct. 17, at the Elks' Theater, where promoter Forster was criticized for holding such a big fight on such a small stage where 600 filled the space, and for nearly tripling the price of tickets, ranging from $3 to $5. Regardless, the bout was rightfully hyped as the "biggest fight in the history of Silver City."[47]

The future Hall-of-Famer, whose name had been borrowed countless times in the Southwest alone, was considered the uncrowned champion from his legendary fight with Ad Wolgast, on July 4, 1912, which saw a double knockout in round 13. (Referee Jack Welch, who turned down the Johnson-Flynn bout in Las Vegas held on the same day, for the lightweight bout, awarded Wolgast the win since he'd started to rise before the completion of the double ten-count.) Rivers, whose real name was Jose Ybarra, had also challenged Willie Ritchie for the lightweight title in 1913 and fought everyone, including Freddie Welsh, Johnny Dundee and Leach Cross.

In fact, Rivers was an easy favorite over Waugh. Ironically, the Texas champ had twice as many fights as Rivers and had gone the 20-round route frequently, while Rivers had not done so in years.

In the end, both the fight and Rivers proved a disappointment. Waugh was on his way to giving Rivers a "severe beating and had the Californian in a bad way," when Rivers, already repeatedly warned for fouling, "used his left knee"[48] to stop Waugh during one of his rushes. The blatant foul resulted in Rivers' disqualification and a booing crowd.

Jack Lopez, of Santa Rita, New Mexico, was one of the most popular mining fighters during the four-year era during World War I and the Mexican Revolution.

Waugh received $465 for his big win while Rivers had been guaranteed $1,000, win, lose or draw. "One thing certain," ran the Independent. "Rivers never will be asked to fight in a Silver City ring again." Waugh, on the other hand, continued to return to both Silver City and Deming through 1919, in bouts against Otto Wallace and Eddie Johnson.

Finales at the Border

> *He's a machine gun operator in Uncle Sam's army but heavy artillery in the roped arena.*
>
> —*Albuquerque Morning Journal, 1916*[49]

In the aftermath of war, America began its first full year of hope in 1919, but life at the border did not change all that much. Pancho Villa was still stirring up trouble in Mexico and that meant army life would continue for soldiers if you were at Fort Bliss or at Camp Furlong—and army life meant boxing.

At Fort Bliss, after countless packed smokers at the on-base YMCA buildings, the "Punch Bowl," also called the "Studorium" after promoter/matchmaker Carl Studor, opened in early 1918, just in time to catch the fast rise of feisty Baltimore featherweight Nick Gundy, who became El Paso's No. 1 fighter. Proclaimed the "Giant Killer" who'd "rather fight than eat,"[50] Gundy won over fans by fighting "Fighting" Dick Olson with a broken arm for a draw. By 1919, he was the border's featherweight champ.

With Gundy at the vanguard, Fort Bliss dominated the lower weights, but it was all about Camp Furlong and the 24th Infantry above featherweight. At welter to middle, the border still belonged to Speedball Hayden, who was still proving to be the best drawing card around.

Challenges were coming from all over the country. Camp Funston thought they had the answer to Hayden when they sent down undefeated Navy Rostan of Chicago, but he went home with a 7th round knockout loss. With fewer and fewer fighters enlisted, the Athletic Board at Columbus knew they were going to have to import a ring veteran—not the soldier type—if they were going to make good on their claims that the Speedball was a claimant to Middleweight Champion Mike O'Dowd.

A Silver City promoter tried to cajole Jack Torres out of retirement, but he was finished. Bobby Waugh was game but, at lightweight, giving up 20 pounds to fight Hayden was not taken seriously. Finally, they decided on Pueblo's Eddie Johnson—the same guy who'd, once upon a time, defeated Louis Newman and gone the distance with former champ Young Corbett II. Fighting since 1905 with over 100 bouts, the grizzled pug would help legitimize Hayden's claim in the real prizefight ring, not just the soldier's arena.

The two met in Silver City on April 1, 1919, and despite outweighing Johnson 155 to 147, all the youth and speed in the world couldn't help the Speedball. In the biggest upset of the year at the border, Hayden suffered his first loss. Though making it through all 20 rounds, Hayden was floored six times by the gritty ring general from Pueblo. "It was no surmise that Wednesday was a dark gloomy day in Columbus,"[51] wrote the *Enterprise*.

Claiming he'd been out of shape, Hayden demanded a rematch. A month later, at Columbus, Hayden bounced back with a surprising second-round knockout over Oakland veteran Jimmy Duffy, then six weeks later, in June, rematched Johnson, who demanded neutral ground at Fort Bliss' Studorium. The week before, Johnson had fought Waugh in a 20-rounder at Silver City; he was used to fighting on everyone else's home turf, but against Hayden, he refused to go to Columbus.

This time around, it was a different story, with Hayden coolly outboxing Johnson for the 20-round decision before 2,800 at the Punch Bowl. The old Speedball was back — but things were quickly changing at the border.

Deming's fight scene was quickly declining. The troops had been demobilized and Camp Cody had, overnight, become a ghost town. Everything but the hospital had been taken down — it would be used as a tuberculosis sanatorium for soldiers until ownership was transferred to the local Chamber of Commerce in 1922, who would sell it to the Sisters of Notre Dame a year later. As the camp depopulated, the outdoor Stadium was put to use by Arthur Holmgrem, who would manage Gundy through the '20s. The former featherweight was now struggling with on-the-road fights, his reign ending when 24th Infantry featherweight Rabbit Rogers had scored the upset knockout. After Holmgrem came W. W. Wilcox, who pitted miner-boxers with the remaining soldiers, before the entire Deming scene dried up.

When the Mexican Revolution ended in 1920, Juarez was back as a fight center. Fort Bliss would continue the game through the '20s and, at Columbus, the wars raged on — for a short while, anyway.

First there came the official military order from Fort Sam Houston that boxing was no longer being deemed "as being so valuable to the command as other athletic training in which a large number participate. Such contests are, however, of general interest to the command. To avoid any tendency to commercialize athletics in the array admissions will not be charged to any athletic contests."[52]

With the war over, boxing was no longer being used to train or keep the troops in shape. Fight cards were no longer looked upon as morale-building entertainment. Without charging patrons, big cards — on a consistent basis, anyway — were no longer a possibility.

Columbus pushed forward, charging steeper admissions to offer bigger purses to fighters, not just the proverbial collection-plate offering from the gate. The city attracted tougher fighters — and not just the soldiers who wanted to prove they were the best in the camp. For a fighter like Hayden, who'd been groomed under the protection of the generals and considered a camp mascot, life was about to get a lot harder.

Even with his surprising loss to Johnson, Hayden had not given up his goal of becoming a top-notcher and, in late 1919, Hayden was honorably discharged from the army to pursue a career in the ring. In Phoenix, Hayden fought his old mentor Williams but could do no better than a draw, then a decision. After another disappointing draw in Columbus against El Paso veteran Frankie Fowser, Hayden left for San Francisco, fighting a series of four-rounders that did little for his rep, then returned to Silver City where he scored an 11th-round TKO over old nemesis Johnson. Declaring himself ready for everyone, Hayden was matched up tough in Columbus against black legend Gorilla Jones.

While Hayden was fighting in California, Jones had moved in at the border, establishing himself as the big draw in Juarez, now fully immersed in the post–Pancho fight scene. When Hayden returned, in late 1920, he found his followers fewer in number and himself, an underdog with the bookies, against Gorilla.

They would fight three times in the next five months. By a fluke, Hayden beat Jones in their first match, by DQ; the second time, on Christmas Day, also at Columbus, the former 24th star was destroyed in nine rounds. The loss sealed Hayden's fate — border fans now preferred to see local stars like the Payo brothers, Fort Worth's "Dandy" Dick Griffin at Bliss, or cross the river to see future world champion Tiger Flowers, who would soon enter the picture by destroying Jones.

Hayden hit the road, decisioning Jones at Phoenix in 1921. Then, after a series of draws, from Casper, Wyoming, to Albuquerque and Juarez, his reputation and draw started to fade. He attempted a comeback at the border in early 1922, fighting Jones a fourth time, but this time Gorilla floored Hayden an embarrassing 12 times before knocking him out in the ninth. Like other former 24th fighters, Hayden returned to the road, sometimes winning, sometimes losing.

Back at the border, the name "Speedball" was filed away, as quickly forgotten as the brief but furious era of soldier boxing that had consumed the area before, during and after the war. Fights at Columbus came to a halt (the last one being Hayden's loss to Kid Brown in 1922) while Fort Bayard continued off-and-on through the mid–'20s. Fort Bliss carried on bouts through the '30s, however, finally phasing out pro boxing for military amateur bouts. Eventually, that, too, disappeared.

Without their military umbrella, black fighters at the border declined in number. Homegrown hopefuls — a list that included Jose Rivers, Mike Vasquez, Tony Herrera and Babe Colima — battled their way up the ladder while those once famous with the 24th Infantry, or at Fort Bliss, scattered to the four winds, fighting here and there before succumbing to a similar fate met by their helmsman, Hayden. It wouldn't be the former army stars — the Haydens or the Sudenbergs, the O'Tooles or the Cabells — who would make it post-war, post–Revolution, but a new breed of fighting man, at least in New Mexico.

12. Veterans of the Ring,
Veterans of the War, 1918–1922

The war may have made the world or at least that part of it bossed by Uncle Sam—
safe for boxing as well as for democracy.
—*Albuquerque Morning Journal*, 1918[1]

Private Manuel Chavez was in the right place at the right time, the third week of March 1919. After completing his tour of duty at Camp Wheeler in Georgia, Chavez took the Santa Fe rail back home to Albuquerque where he learned the Albuquerque Chamber of Commerce and the newly-formed Duke City Athletic Club were throwing a fight card the following evening for the New Mexico Cattle and Horse Growers Association.

Nothing like the fights—Chavez had fought before the war as a prelim boxer when Mark Levy was running the show in the Duke City. *And* he'd fought in the army. Recently, too.

While making the rounds in town, it didn't take Chavez long to find out that former Fort Bliss star Jack "Scientific Kid" Young was unable to make Saturday night's main event against Battling Sampson, another former El Paso soldier. It took even less time for Chavez to convince the somewhat desperate promoters he was in the pink of condition and ready to step in against Sampson.

In front of a packed house of 2,000 fight-starved fans in a town of little more than 15,000 that hadn't seen action since before the war, Chavez became an overnight favorite by knocking out Sampson in round three of a scheduled eight-rounder. In a prelim, two veterans who'd been crippled in the war—"Sailor" Green and "Soldier" Brown—went four rounds to a draw, "hopping about the ring on their single legs, dealing each other yeoman blows, as if there was a personal feud between them,"[2] earning exactly $84 in coins thrown by spectators.

The fight scene in Albuquerque had a new beginning.

"What is the United States going to do about boxing when our soldiers return from the war?"[3] was the question Robert Edgren put forth in *The New York Evening World*, in early 1919. Edgren estimated that those who'd taken up boxing during the war numbered in the millions. He predicted a major revival.

It was especially true in New Mexico, on the verge of a second golden era in peace time. Motor cars were on the rise. The speed limit did not exceed 30 m.p.h. and occasionally you saw a Hudson or a Maxwell, but mainly there were Model T's. No one had a radio, but the band in the downtown plaza on Sunday afternoons continually played "I'm Always Chasing Rainbows." Chewing gum was still five cents, a chicken dinner at the

226

Albuquerque Pullman Café would set you back 85 cents and admission to the fights was $1.

After the initial success on March 26, 1919, J. R. T. Herrera and P. Palladini of the Duke City Athletic Club went to work on a second show for May 2, giving Chavez another headliner. Expecting (and getting) a smaller crowd, they held the card at Herald Hall. Chavez KO'd Battling Kruse of San Antonio, Tex., while another war veteran, Magdaleno "Sailor" Gonzales, beat up Kruse's younger brother.

Though they had new soldier-boxers to build on, promoters — control passing to Louis Benjamin — brought back the names that had made the sport before the war: Benny and Benny. Cordova and Chavez, that is. Cordova returned to the ring in late May and Chavez in September — though the crowd nearly rioted and two were arrested when San Francisco's Jack Douglas was given a decision over the former contender.

Boxing was back, and so was the controversy that came with it.

When wrestler George Pineau took over promoting in 1920, he added wrestling to the menu — a template that would continue for decades, especially in the '30s. Pineau was more concerned about giving himself a spot on his cards, though, and control passed over to John

Victory Boxing
Contest
TONIGHT
MAIN EVENT—TEN ROUNDS
LIGHTWEIGHTS
YOUNG CHAVEZ vs.
Albuquerque, New Mexico
BATTLING KRUSE
San Antonio, Texas

Semi-Windup—Ten Rounds
WILDCAT GONZALEZ vs.
Champion U. S. S. Maine
YOUNG WILLARD
El Paso, Texas
FEATHERWEIGHTS

Two Fast Preliminaries Between Local Talent
These Boys Have All Returned from Serving Our Country and Have Good Reputations.
General Admission, $1.00   Ringside, $1.50
HERALD HALL
One-half Block North from Central Avenue on Third
DUKE CITY ATHLETIC CLUB

"Victory Boxing" marked a return to the sport after World War I. Manuel "Young" Chavez became an overnight star when he stepped off the train, post-deployment, and into the ring earlier in the year. By May 2, 1919, the night of Chavez's bout against Battling Kruse, the veteran soldier was just what the public was looking for to lead a local return to the sport.

Flaska, who was the first one to fill the Armory. Three thousand people showed up to watch Benny Cordova draw with Denver's Carl Mackey — that's one out of every five people in the Albuquerque area. Though promoting in the early '20s, Flaska, a Cleveland fighter in the early '10s, was better remembered as New Mexico's longest running referee. Though briefly returning to the promotion game in the '30s, Flaska was the third man in the ring well into the '50s.

With the two Bennies headlining the bigger shows, Sailor Gonzalez made a fast rise alongside Manuel Chavez, though he was able to retain top billing longer. Chavez, somewhat lucky in his first two headliners, soon lost to the imports and was reduced to preliminary bouts on later cards.

While Albuquerque was able to revitalize boxing, Santa Fe had a rougher time of it. In the summer of 1918, Governor Washington Lindsay, citing "assault and battery," shut down the promotion of a card headlining local favorite Mike Baca and Mexican Pete Everett. The mounted police received orders "to cooperate with the sheriff of Santa Fe county," and the bout was prevented.[4]

Baca resurfaced after the war in the former mining town of Cerrillos in May 1919 — the first show there since the 1890s — then returned to the Capital City for a Fourth of July card at the Elks' Theater, where he solidified his place as state lightweight champion in the first New Mexico title fight since 1916. Santa Fe, however, was slow to warm up to boxing's return, forcing Baca to ride the rails to the many other returning fight centers in the state.

Clayton was one of the first towns to wake up after the war, seeing almost as much action as it had in the territorial days, with a streak of bi-monthly shows. After (re)forming the Clayton Athletic Club, promoter Jack Lucero launched a series of prize fights not in the Mission Theatre of downtown Clayton, but in the *basement* of the theatre. Before long, they were able to move upstairs.

Bantamweight Raphael Chavez was the top local draw, along with Snorty Sherwood, who'd learned to fight during the war while stationed at Mare Island, California. With Claytonites paving the way, the Athletic Club was soon bringing in the stars of the day: Walter Caldwell of Springer, who ended Sherwood's hopes for a career with a knockout blow, and Benny Chavez, during the former contender's final campaign.

Any doubt that boxing was back was dispelled during the Fourth of July 1919, for no less than eight cities staged shows, including Clayton, Clovis, Columbus, Gallup, Santa Fe, Silver City, Springer and Taos. Though action popped up in Hot Springs, Taos, Carlsbad, even Hurley, where "the pipe fitting demon"[5] Frank Hager fought two men in one night, the bigger towns that had run the sport before the war were once again doing business after the war.

Like Gallup. In March 1919, fights returned to Kitchen's Opera House downtown, where local stars Joe Corretto, Freddie Baxter and Jack Myrick drew the fans. Bigger name fighters included both Bennies, Chavez and Cordova.

Though once KO'd by Baxter, Myrick became the slightly bigger name, especially after he fought a draw with Albuquerque's Sailor Gonzales on a card headlining Benny Chavez. Hoping that the former contender was old enough — safe enough — for the young and hungry Myrick, Gallup coughed up a big enough purse to bring Chavez to them on Nov. 7, 1919. It was Myrick's peak performance when he was able to wrangle a draw from the hometown ref. "His entry into the fighting game marks a new epoch in the history of the game in this city and vicinity,"[6] wrote the *Carbon City News*.

Without a chance to exploit his newfound greatness, Myrick took off, enlisting in the Navy where he fought a fair number of fights while stationed at the Great Lakes Training School in Illinois. Myrick married a Chicago gal and when he returned to Gallup, he fought a couple more times before quietly retiring. Myrick then refereed and promoted through the '30s.

Action in Clovis re-emerged in July 1919, with locals Tommy Morrison and Frank Dice in the starring roles, at least until promoters were able to wrangle Johnny Connolly and Mike Baca to battle for the umpteenth time. Connolly, recently discharged from the Army when he fought Baca in Clovis, on Aug. 2, was also responsible for the wave of shows in his hometown through 1921.

Also backing up their hometown boy was the small town of Springer. Headlining their first show since 1915, the town gave rise to the most popular fighter in the early 1920s — Sgt. Walter Caldwell. As the soldier-boxer rose through the ranks, headlining around the state, the familiar pre-war names would play out what they had left in their respective gas tanks.

Old Names Return

> *Rivera is peeved at the newspapers. He claims that he has been wronged in being called a Mexican.*
>
> — *Duluth News Tribune,* 1921[7]

Perfecto Romero and Harry Schaefer were dead. Louis Newman, Ev Winters and Al Smaulding were ancient history in 1919. Jack Torres was finished. With the two Bennies at the front of a post-war revival comeback, several other New Mexicans dusted off the rust and declared that their earlier days hadn't been their best.

Santa Fe's Demon Rivera returned in 1919 for the second half of his career, losing to Insurrecto Kid in a ten-rounder before relocating to Colorado where he stayed busy for

Earliest known photograph of Timo Sanchez (second from left), circa. 1915 in Silver City, New Mexico. Timo's on-and-off career spanned three decades, from Silver City to Albuquerque to Santa Fe (courtesy of Benny Sanchez).

the next two years fighting their best bantams and feathers. Rivera fought Pueblo's Mike Pagano in five draws and one win, went 1–1 with Joe "The Wop" Flynn, then beat Joe "Awful" Coffee. Finished in Colorado, the Demon trekked through Wyoming and Montana, becoming the first New Mexican to fight in Minnesota, before coming home in 1922 a much better fighter. Back in Santa Fe, Rivera became a sort of gatekeeper for prospective young-sters.

In the second of four comebacks, "Dynamite Tommy" would return for a time. When Timo Sanchez had first appeared in the ring, lacing on a pair of four-ouncers sparingly stuffed with horsehair back in 1915, he'd been a 105-pound 16-year-old. As the son of a Baptist minister, he'd been on the move his entire life — from Alamosa, Col-

orado, where he was born, then to Las Vegas, Santa Fe, Alcalde, Alam-ogordo and Silver City. Now, with his own family, Sanchez was in Albuquerque and, at age 19, had not added a single pound to his minuscule frame. Sanchez fought sparingly in 1919 and in the early '20s — he would not peak until later in the decade when sports scribes became so impressed with the fleaweight's punching power, they started using the "Dynamite" moniker.

Santiago Montoya — Young Jim Flynn — was another youngster from before the war. Fighting young, as Sanchez had, and losing most, Flynn returned to the professional ring after serving at Camp Omaha, Nebraska, during the war. Working his way up from prelims, the Albu-querque welter was main event mate-rial by 1922, and fought consistently for a time. After three bouts with Cyclone Williams, and a bad loss to Ralph Pena, going down eight times before a six-round stoppage, Flynn tapered off, though he would resur-face from time to time.

Timo Sanchez, a.k.a. "Dynamite Tommy," might've been the greatest flyweight ever produced in New Mexico, until Danny Romero, but he was cursed during his era by being too small and light. Timo fought from 100 to 110 pounds, forcing him to regularly give up weight — whether it was in New Mexico or on the West Coast (courtesy of Benny Sanchez).

There was no better revival in post-war New Mexico than the rivalry created by their two star lightweights — Johnny Connolly of Roswell and Mike Baca of Santa Fe. Between the two, they re-created the glory of a state championship.

Rivalry Renewal: Connolly vs. Baca

Their repeated encounters have given each a ring knowledge of the other which practically precludes any possibility of a knockout except one from a chance blow. Each knows the other's style and tactics.

— Clovis Journal, 1919[8]

Shortly after Mike Baca and Johnny Connolly fought their fourth and fifth bouts, back to back on July 3 and 4, 1917, in the unlikely place of Hagerman, New Mexico, the two laid aside their gloves to enlist.

Baca served as a National Guardsman during World War I, though even while enlisted, he tried to keep sharp by fighting veteran Mexican Pete Everett in a bout that had the governor intervening. Connolly, on the other hand, entered officers' training camp in Fort Leon, in Springs, Texas, in August 1917, and, as a first lieutenant, was assigned to the 34th Division stationed in France shortly before the war came to an end. After the war, Connolly returned to Roswell's New Mexico Military Institute as a boxing instructor.

As soon as the war and boxing promotions permitted, in May 1919, Baca was back in the ring, shaking off the rust against Alfredo Martinez in Cerrillos. After Albuquerque's Manuel Chavez called him out for state lightweight honors, Baca declared himself champion with a six-round knockout in Santa Fe, on July 2, 1919.

Not so quickly, said the pugilist pundits. Have you forgotten your old nemesis, Señor Connolly?

The challenge went south to Roswell where it was immediately accepted. There were no tune-ups for Connolly, who agreed to battle Baca a sixth time for the New Mexico state lightweight championship in Santa Fe. Just as soon as it was announced, however, it was cancelled when Connolly fell ill — but Santa Fe fight fans went from disappointed to angry when they found out, after the fact, that the bout had been moved to Clovis, where promoters stole the fight with an offer of a bigger purse. While the *Santa Fe New Mexican*

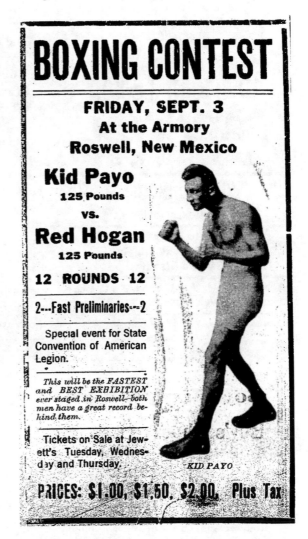

BOXING CONTEST

FRIDAY, SEPT. 3
At the Armory
Roswell, New Mexico

Kid Payo
125 Pounds

vs.

Red Hogan
125 Pounds

12 ROUNDS 12

2---Fast Preliminaries---2

Special event for State Convention of American Legion.

This will be the FASTEST and BEST EXHIBITION ever staged in Roswell—both men have a great record behind them.

Tickets on Sale at Jewett's Tuesday, Wednesday and Thursday.

KID PAYO

PRICES: $1.00, $1.50, $2.00, Plus Tax

One of the few Roswell cards in the early '20s that did *not* feature Johnny Connolly. Then again, Connolly had pulled out with an injury. On September 3, 1920, at the Armory in Roswell, El Paso veteran Kid Payo won a decision over Red Hogan.

reported Connolly's illness, the *Roswell Daily Record* printed, on Aug. 7, that Connolly was away, "visiting friends"[9] in Clovis and that the fight had been cancelled.

On Aug. 6 at the Elks' Auditorium in Clovis before a crowd of 1,000, Connolly defeated Baca for the third time, making it an even three draws and three defeats for the frustrated Santa Fean.

It wasn't easy, though. The "Pride of the Pecos Valley" was recently "discharged from the army and had not had the usual amount of training ... had two teeth knocked out and showed other facial disfigurement."[10] Though Connolly led the fighting, Baca finished in better shape. "Popular sentiment would credit Baca with a shade the better of the fighting, and the contention is that the bout should have been a draw," was the verdict of the *Clovis Journal*. "It is stated that the referee penalized Baca for butting and rough work with his shoulders."[11]

Connolly vs. Baca VII also landed in Clovis when the lightweights were at it again a month later, on Labor Day. The "fight was one that brought the audience to its feet in a frenzy. Conley [*sic*] is a range fighter who spars well for openings. Baca's bewildering speed, cool head and propensity to dodge Conley's attack has won for the boy from Santa Fe, many followers."[12]

It was another draw. Two more showdowns would occur, but in the meantime, Baca and Connolly went their separate ways. Connolly fought four times and Baca just once, before the eighth bout. Baca outpointed 24th Infantryman Eddie Swanson in Albuquerque while Connolly was matched up in Carlsbad with another name from his past, Dutch Crozier, whom he'd beaten in 1915.

The former Army boxer now had twice the experience of Connolly, and was able to net the win when the Roswell fighter was DQ'd in the sixth. In a close fight many saw as a draw, Connolly won his next bout with Crozier. With two more wins — over Jack Gorman in Dexter, and a first-round KO over Tommie Rouse in Roswell (Rouse was unable to continue after Connolly landed two blows propelling him through the ropes, so that he hit his head on a board and the brick wall) — Connolly was ready for Baca again.

With Santa Fe struggling to start up their post-war scene, the eighth showdown landed on Connolly's turf at the capacity-filled Armory in Roswell on May 8, 1920. This time, they fought their first 15-rounder and the extra three rounds prompted the Roswell referee to award Connolly his fourth win over Baca. They would meet one more time.

Again, they fought separate opponents, Baca knocking out unknown Johnny Wilson in Albuquerque before taking a long layoff. Connolly

American Legion

CARNIVAL

MAY 5, 6, 7, 8,

30   BIG ATTRACTIONS   30

For Your Entertainment

Areoplane Flights Daily
Big Fireworks Display
Street Dancing

Army Jazz Orchestra from Ft. Bliss
Roswell Juvenile Band

John Connolly of Roswell VS. **Mike Baca of Santa Fe** **15 ROUNDS** 2 preliminaries **ARMORY, May 7**	**A Mysterious Magician** Will present a novel Entertainment of slight of hand, surprises & illusions **MACK and SMITH** **Comedy Acrobats**
MERRY GO ROUND and numerous other high class attractions	**JOHNNY SHAWNER** **The Slack Wire Artist**

Confetti Peddlers and Hot Dog Artists will all be here.   **Come and Enjoy Yourself**

HELP US Build A Home

This Carnival is being staged solely by the Charles M.
deBremond Post of The American Legion.

The greatest rivalry New Mexico has ever produced was between lightweights Johnny Connolly, of Roswell, and Mike Baca, of Santa Fe. Between 1915 and 1921, the two fought nine times, Connolly winning four, drawing four and losing once. This fight poster depicts their eighth showdown, on May 9, 1920, in Roswell.

defeated former Fort Bliss star Tommy Nelson in Roswell and then he, too, took time off for a long winter in Hot Springs where he was, again, fighting some sort of unreported illness.

By March 1921, Connolly was back. He joined Nick Sollito's stable at Fort Bliss for a time, anxious to take his career to the next level, and was subsequently matched against his toughest opponent to date, Freddie Hill. The Fort Worth battler had a far more impressive resume than that of Connolly. With a draw over Bobby Waugh, two knockouts over Billy Kleck, a decision over Otto Wallace

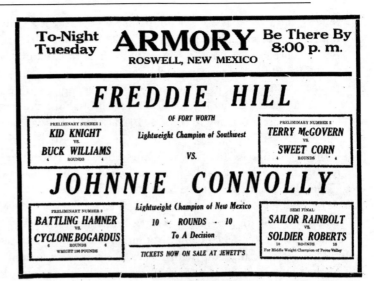

To-Night Tuesday **ARMORY** **Be There By 8:00 p.m.**
ROSWELL, NEW MEXICO

FREDDIE HILL
OF FORT WORTH
Lightweight Champion of Southwest

PRELIMINARY NUMBER 1		PRELIMINARY NUMBER 2
KID KNIGHT	VS.	**TERRY McGOVERN**
BUCK WILLIAMS		**SWEET CORN**
4 ROUNDS 4		4 ROUNDS 4

VS.

JOHNNIE CONNOLLY
Lightweight Champion of New Mexico

PRELIMINARY NUMBER 3		SEMI FINAL
BATTLING HAMNER	10 - ROUNDS - 10	**SAILOR RAINBOLT**
CYCLONE BOGARDUS	To A Decision	**SOLDIER ROBERTS**
6 ROUNDS 6		10 ROUNDS 10
WEIGHT 190 POUNDS		For Middle Weight Champion of Pecos Valley

TICKETS NOW ON SALE AT JEWETT'S

Though he was mainly known for his nine bouts against Mike Baca, the biggest fight of Johnny Connolly's career was his 1921 showdown with Freddie Hill, for the Southwest lightweight championship. Though game and in the fight, Connolly dropped a ten-round decision to the more-experienced Hill.

and a draw with Gene Delmont, Hill was a heavy favorite when the two fought on April 19 in Roswell for the Southwestern lightweight championship. Taking no chances with a hometown referee, Hill demanded two additional judges to render a verdict.

Clearly outmatched, Connolly was in trouble in the seventh, but was able to avoid a knockout loss. The local star "put up a game fight all the way though and in the eight and ninth rounds showed his great pluck and determination by carrying the fight to Hill and while he landed frequently his blows never seemed to worry the Texas fighter to any great extent."[13]

Connolly returned to train in El Paso, hoping to make a name for himself at the border. Throwing his hat in the ring as a challenger for any lightweight, from Dal Hawkins to Mike Vasquez, he kept busy with a draw in Lubbock against Joe Denton before Hawkins agreed to meet Connolly at Fort Bayard. As the fight neared, Hawkins pulled out of the fight. In his place came—who else?—Mike Baca.

On July 18, 1921, Baca and Connolly fought their ninth—and final—bout in a 15-rounder. Unlike all previous encounters, this one was on true neutral ground and, despite Baca's never having beaten Connolly, there was some heavy money on the Santa Fean:

> The wise ones are picking Connolly to win, but Baca has improved wonderfully in the past few months, it is said, and is likely to upset the dope as well as the Roswell title holder. One Albuquerque fan, who has seen both train, is out with a little side bet of $500 even money, that Connolly don't last 10 rounds or a two to one bet that Baca wins the fight. To date he has had no takers, although it is rumored that a few Fort Bayard men, who have seen Connolly training, will cover the bet this week.[14]

Several hundred people showed up to see Connolly and Baca spar two nights before the bout and the promoters, the Fort Bayard Athletic Association, even installed lights for the evening event, which was a first for the camp. An estimated 2,000 showed up to watch the 15-round war that saw Connolly lose for the first time against Baca. Avoiding Connolly's punches, Baca was able to bore in and rack up rounds with his infighting. The *Roswell Daily Record* scored nine rounds for Baca, with three to Connolly, and three even.

Connolly asked for a rematch — a tenth and final bout — and while Baca agreed, it was not ever going to happen, for Roswell's greatest fighter never fought again.

Illness kept Connolly out of the ring throughout the remainder of 1921. For a time, it looked like he was going to recover. In May 1922, he was back in the gym and planning to fight in Texas. Soon after, he dabbled in local politics, running for county treasurer, but before he could see the campaign through, he was admitted to the hospital in June for, reportedly, stomach trouble. It was much more than that: on October 20, 1922, John Boyle Connolly passed away from a battle with typhoid fever.

Having finally secured his long-awaited post as the New Mexico lightweight champion, Baca fought on for a couple of years, achieving notoriety beyond his rivalry with Connolly. The Santa Fean fought a couple of times in Colorado, then returned home where there was talk of a classic matchup with former Southwestern champ Benny Cordova. They were booked to go at it on Sept. 5, 1921, at the Rialto in Santa Fe but, on the night of the fight, the physician refused to let an ailing Cordova fight. The packed house was emptied and refunds given.

Four nights later, Baca got his chance to fight for a Southwestern title in Albuquerque when he took on Arizona's Billy Alger. Though he won, it would go down as one of the worst hometown decisions in state history. "Alger won almost every round,"[15] wrote the *Albuquerque Evening Herald*, noting that the referee, Steve Marcos, had also been the promoter. While the Albuquerque Boxing Commission revoked Marcos' license, sports scribes from El Paso to Arizona raked Baca over the coals, demanding that he fight Alger again, or a *real* Southwest champion, like Freddie Hill, who'd defeated Connolly.

Baca kept a low profile for the rest of the year, but by December, local promoters tried again to match him up with Cordova. Once again, the bout was nixed when the Albuquerque veteran was deemed out of shape, or past his prime.

The lightly-regarded "Southwest lightweight champ" got his chance to prove he deserved his title on Jan. 17, 1922, when, at the Santa Fe Armory, Baca was pitted against tough Denverite Frank Herrera — but trading a black eye for a bloody nose, Baca could do no better than a draw. In July, they rematched, but the fight was so bad that referee Captain Ed Safford, having to break up their relentless clinching, declared it a no-decision rather than a draw.

Without Connolly, Baca couldn't win. And like Connolly, he was destined to be a state champion who could not rise to the next level.

Baca fought but once in 1923, a win by DQ over Denver's Jack Doyle. Though he continually talked about rematching Billy Alger — sports scribes called it "legitimizing his title"— he never did. In 1924, Baca staged a last-ditch comeback and, for a time, there was talk of fighting Eddie Mack, the new rising star, though it did not materialize. What did, were back-to-back draws with Colorado's lightweight champion Bobby Moore, the second of which saw the "Mike of old" in the "fight of his life."[16]

By now, Baca had been fighting for 11 years. There was talk of Mexico City and a third Moore fight, but it did not happen. When Kansas comer Jimmy Lanning waltzed into his hometown in May 1924 to outclass Baca, giving him a "severe lacing" and leaving his face "beaten to a bloody pulp," Baca was praised for his gameness and going the 12-round limit. In the final rounds, Baca's cornermen, "on the verge of tears," begged him not to go back out for more punishment, but Mike said, "The only way you can get me out is to carry me out after I'm knocked out."[17]

Baca would fight one more time, on July 12, 1924, at El Paso where he'd win by DQ over Battling McPeak, before retiring.

"Old Benny"

> He's coming back, boys: Benny Cordova, Mexican lightweight, one of the best, fastest and cleanest little punchers that ever swished in the thin Texas atmosphere with the padded mitts ... is coming back to the ring game in the southwest and that he hopes that his old-time ring enemy — Bobby Waugh — is the first man the promoters turn 'im loose against.
>
> — El Paso Morning Times, 1919[18]

> It is observed that Benny uses the word "fight" while most boxers say "box."
> — Tucson Daily Citizen, 1920[19]

Unlike Manuel Chavez, who enjoyed a quick basking in the limelight because he'd stepped off the Santa Fe into main event status, Benny Cordova always had lousy timing. By the time he'd decided to fight at home, the scene had died out and the feel of war was in the air.

After World War I, the lightweight who'd carved out his reputation by taking on the best in Texas in the first half of the decade helped ease the Duke City back into boxing in the latter half. "Not averse to picking up a steam hammer to provide *frijoles*,"[20] working as a card-carrying boilermaker during the war, Cordova decided it was time to make a return.

In 1919, *two* Cordovas made their return to the ring. Benny's brother Solomon, a flyweight barely 110 pounds who fought under the "Young Nelson" tag, launched a short career at the border when El Paso's Battling Chico II took him under his wing. After three draws, two of them against Timo Sanchez, Solomon slipped away from the ring.

Not so older brother Benny. Though past his prime, he was irked by his showing against Tommy O'Toole at the Smelter in 1917 and his last loss to Bobby Waugh. He had plenty left in his tank and was damn well going to show Albuquerque what he was made of. Again, his timing was lousy. After contacting promoters and former manager R. C. Benetiz at the border, about making a return there and how about calling on Waugh, he was told to hang tight. "Benny is under the impression that the Border is open and that all the favorite Mexican sports are in full sway in Juarez," wrote the El Paso Times. "Such, however, is not the case and, until the passport nails are jerked, the pastimes will have to rest a bit easy. The tull, however, cannot very last for all time, Benny."[21]

Impatiently waiting for Albuquerque to wake up after the war, Cordova decided to "invade" the West Coast, but it proved as short-lived as his younger brother's career. After a couple four-round no-decision bouts, Benny came back. He was a 15- and 20-round fighter. What could you possibly accomplish in just four rounds?

After those first post–World War I, military-themed shows had the sport re-launched, local promoters turned to the old-timers, so Benny got his chance on May 30, 1919. Showing "all his old-time jazz,"[22] he KO'd Memphis lightweight Bert Coxhill, a former sparring partner for Freddie Welsh now training at Cordova's old haunts in El Paso.

The fight set up a big Labor Day card headlining Cordova against tough Carl Mackey (a.k.a. "Billy Mack"). The 22-year-old Denver fighter was deemed the Rocky Mountain champion after defeating the likes of Stanley Yoakum, Joe "The Wop" Flynn and the best in Texas. It was a tough fight for Cordova, who was not quite expecting the body attack Mackey brought to the ring on Sept. 1 at the Armory, before their first capacity crowd, breaking the record for the highest Albuquerque crowd.

Mackey took the fight to the veteran. "The local boy seemed to be unable to devise an effective defense against the blow and there wasn't a round in which Carl's mighty left didn't crash into his stomach," went the morning paper. But "Benny never upheld his reputation for ruggedness and gameness. He took the punishment unwincingly and occasionally smiled over his opponent's shoulder at some friend he saw in the crowd of spectators, although fighting usually appears to be serious business to Benny. He seldom smiles in the ring."[23]

Down but not out, and as popular as ever in the Duke City, Cordova hit the road in 1920, fighting back and forth from Albuquerque to Arizona and Texas, where he decisioned Jerry Dalton. Taking the Insurrecto Kid under his wing — a youngster Cordova boasted he could go "forty rounds without a drink of water or a drop of moonshine"[24] — he fought a draw with, then knocked out, Al McManus between Miami, Arizona, and Gallup, then came home to outbox Benny Garcia before a crowd of 1,200 at the Armory, on March 16, 1920.

Two losses in April followed, to Earl "Young" France in Tucson, and Otto Wallace in San Antone.

"Nursing his bruised left hand and cussing the five ounce gloves they use over in New Mexico,"[25] Cordova had to postpone the France bout, and when it happened, on April 9, he never got a chance to test out his sore paws. "I chased France all over the ring," Cordova complained. "I will admit that France can beat me in a foot race. He sure is a fast bird on his feet."[26]

Three weeks later, Cordova weathered the storm of fast Wallace, losing again. A San Antonio reporter wrote, "How a human could stand up and take terrific wallops to the head, face, jaw and body, sent in by that battering ram, Otto Wallace, and not even sag a leg is almost beyond comprehension." Bruised and panting after being declared the winner, Wallace praised his foe, saying, "That man, Benny Cordova, is the toughest fighter I ever met. He can take more punishment and come back better than nine-tenths of the lightweights in the ring today."[27]

On a Fourth of July card back home, Cordova was on the giving end of the punishment when he decisioned San Antonio's Bobby Green in a 12-rounder. The win set up a rematch with Mackey, on Aug. 3, 1920. This time, the Armory was standing-room-only — packed beyond capacity with an estimated crowd of 3,200 that, again, broke the record for highest Albuquerque fight attendance. Relatives of "Old Benny" recalled the fight in the 1990s:

> He shadow-boxed as he skipped and danced through the uproar. And Benny's fans, grown men who would otherwise, in normal situations, have shown some restraint, stood on their chairs in a mostly futile effort to catch an early glimpse of the gladiator. It was a grand spectacle. "Go get 'em, Benny!" they yelled. "Knock out the *gringo!*" Without a doubt, it was Benny's crowd. But Mackey was a tiger and the crowd only teased him. As he made his way into the ring, someone yelled, "Hey, *gringo!* This time, they're gonna carry you outta here!"[28]

Mackey won the first half of their 12-rounder by outjabbing Cordova, but in the seventh, the hometown favorite had his foe bleeding from the nose and a cut over his eye. Boring in and forcing the fight, Cordova fought his way back to a draw. One man was so distraught that Cordova had not won that he threw a chunk of ice at the referee.

Cordova made the same mistakes in a September bout in Ray, Ariz., when he allowed Tommy Carter to build up such an early lead that the late charges made by Benny could not sway the referee. He came home with another loss, keeping a low profile until the following year, though keeping the rust off by fighting three times during a carnival in November against overmatched opponents.

Cordova was not destined for a world championship — the losses were proof of that — but he still had something to prove. And he wanted one more shot at Waugh. After knocking out Akron journeyman Eddie McGuire in February 1921, he got his chance, when a seventh Cordova-Waugh war was lined up for March 30.

"For years Benny and Bobby have been battling — so long, in fact, that they've become intimate friends," wrote the *New Mexican*. "The Albuquerque battler calls his dearest rival — in the trick language of Bill Shakespeare — by the abbreviation of 'Bob' and asks, 'How is the family?' when they meet.... But when the gong rings they fight."[29]

This was just what Albuquerque needed — an old-fashioned scrap between *real* fighters, not those fancy dancers that were appearing in the ring having learned to "box" instead of "fight" while enlisted. The *Tucson Daily Citizen* said it best:

> Benny and Waugh are pugilistic twins after a fashion. They really belong to the old school of fighters — the school that produced fighters and not financiers and fancy steppers. Both possess what is called in the pugilistic parlance the "fighting heart" and when they meet they always give the ringsiders the impression they're trying to prove Old Man Darwin's theory — or somebody else's — about the survival of the fittest."[30]

In his eighth and final fight against Waugh, the only one to take place in Albuquerque, Cordova did not lose. Nor did he win. Neither did the crowd get what they wanted for "both boxers showed skill as dodgers and flashes of science but the bout was one which could not be called fast. Clinches were frequent and the boxers did not rush the bout usually delaying after each clinch before mixing. At times the fans wondered if the boxers were afraid of each other. Throughout the entire bout each boxer appeared as though he was playing for an opening, wishing the other would strike first."[31]

The reality was that both fighters were slowing down. Unbeknownst to the less-than-expected crowd at Barelas Hall, both Cordova and Waugh were having health problems, after having been through a decade of wars in the ring. "One look at Benny's battered features convinces even a novice of his ability in taking punishment," wrote the *Citizen*. "He has all the earmarks of the rugged battler — and others that don't decorate his receiving apparatus. He carries more scars than a champion pit bull — because he isn't one of the boys who held that a tin ear is a sign of inefficiency."[32]

Fighting longer than he should have, Cordova continued. He was on the road in Ohio from April to May, collecting purses and winning all but one bout against seasoned Midwest lightweights. May saw Cordova back in San Antone, where he paid back Tommy Carter for a previous loss in controversial fashion, mauling and brawling his opponent in a foulfest. Carter demanded a rematch and got one. On July 7 at Fort Bliss, he not only paid Cordova back but stopped the Albuquerque veteran in 11 rounds. As the 15-round bout wore on, Cordova weakened, then found himself on the receiving end of such punishment that the crowd demanded a stoppage in the 10th when a punch flattened Benny. He rose, dazed, and was barely able to stumble back to his corner when the bell rang. In between rounds, Cordova's corner threw in the towel.

Cordova was through — or, he should have been.

Back in Albuquerque, promoters wanted a Mike Baca-Cordova showdown, but the fight was nixed on the day it was to happen when a physician refused to let Benny lace up, declaring the veteran "unfit to enter the ring.... By going into the ring Cordova would have risked being killed outright. The doctor told him this, but he insisted upon fighting anyhow until the promoters flatly announced he could not go on."[33]

Though ill from August to October, Cordova was well enough to promote his own show in November, and then stage a return in December. Declaring himself "recovered," Cordova proved it by fighting Trinidad veteran Frank Herrera to a 15-round draw.

In January 1922, Cordova did the same thing he'd always done: he hit the road. From Colorado to Texas and Louisiana, Benny tried to repeat his greatest year — 1915 — by blazing through familiar ground in New Orleans, Galveston and San Antonio. The Waughs and Wallaces and Hendersons of the past had been replaced with guys like Bobby Green and Kid Goldie — younger, faster and in better health than Cordova, who still managed to come back home in the summer with more wins than losses. At home, Cordova fought a draw with Johnny "Kid" Mex and then announced his retirement.

In December 1923, Cordova announced his *un*retirement, fighting Southwest comer Dal Hawkins to a 12-round draw. It would be his last New Mexico fight — but not his last fight. Six months later, he reappeared in Tijuana, Mexico, where he lost an eight-round decision. This time, he retired for good.

Unlike the other Benny — Chavez, of course — this one remained part of the fight scene. "Old Man Benny" had finished his career, but his four fighting sons were growing up fast.

Benny's Last Hurrah

> Benny Chavez, the idol of devotees of boxing when the game was in its heyday here,
> who packed more houses in Albuquerque, than any other glove slinger, is coming back
> after several years of absence from the local ring.
> —*Albuquerque Morning Journal*, 1919[34]

Like many others did when war was declared, Benny Chavez disappeared from the ring into the U.S. Army. Enlisting while at Ely, Nevada, Chavez was transferred to Camp Kearny, California, and it was expected that he would see action in France sometime in 1918.

Chavez didn't see France, but he did see a bit of ring action while an enlisted man, losing a six-rounder in Salt Lake City to local featherweight Andy "Kid" Davis. "Way too rusty to defeat the 'farmer boy,'"[35] Chavez stayed out of the ring for the remainder of the year.

After the war, Chavez resumed his boxing career — it was the only thing he knew how to do — showing up in Excelsior, Missouri, where he won and drew with fringe contenders, then lost to higher-ranked Memphis Pal Moore. Chavez wasn't fooling anyone. After 89 fights since 1911, though but 26 years old, Chavez's championship days were over and he was called a glutton for punishment, especially against Moore, who had him wincing every time he was clobbered in the bread basket.

Chavez took another break and, with fellow boxer Frankie Burns, left the ring for the harvest fields of Napoleon, Missouri, where he planned to work for 50 cents an hour. Farm work was short-lived. After just a couple months, Chavez reunited with old-time manager George Joseph, of Trinidad, who was announcing Benny's grand return.

Chavez returned where he had started — in Colorado and New Mexico. Chavez took on the role of a stepping stone for youngsters, losing in Denver, then winning in Walsenburg, before getting booked in Albuquerque on Sept. 8, 1919, against Jack "Spike" Douglas, a ham-and-egger from San Francisco.

It had been three years since Chavez had been to the Duke City, but promoter Louis Benjamin knew his name alone would pack the house and hasten boxing's post-war return to the city. He was right — but no one walked out of the Armory that night satisfied, especially Chavez, who was not given the decision in the very first fight in state history that saw three judges (not two, with the ref) scoring at ringside.

"Chavez was not beaten," manager Joseph complained, noting that his fighter nearly had Douglas out in the final round. "We want a rematch! Give us 15 rounds — or 20 — but not 10."[36]

A 15-round rematch was booked for two weeks later. In between fights, Douglas enjoyed his success over the former contender. Erroneously billed as "the boy who knocked out Benny Chavez,"[37] he secured two fights in Arizona, which he won. Upon his return he encountered a steaming Benny. Claiming he had no control over what the Arizona papers printed, Douglas promised he would "make it so," this time around. "Jack is my pie and I'm going to do the cutting," Chavez told the papers, while Joseph challenged Douglas to a bet —100 "berries" that he couldn't "whip his boy" again.[38]

For the rematch, the three-judge panel was dropped for one good referee, Tony Ortiz, whom was agreed on by both parties. With an increase in attendance — an estimated 2,000 — Benny showed flashes of his high-energy, old-time self, dominating Douglas through 15 rounds for the win.

Back on the map, at least in the Southwest, Chavez hit the road, first going to Arizona, where he lost to highly-touted Ralph Lincoln, then defeated former Fort Bliss star Nick Gundy, having to chase his opponent around the ring in the later rounds. In November, he was in Gallup, drawing with local favorite Jack Myrick for a purse of $250, then finished the year with a third match against Douglas, this time in Clayton, having to settle for a 12-round draw.

Chavez fought six times in 1920, all in northern New Mexico and southern Colorado, evenly splitting his wins, draws and losses, 2-2-2. He finished the year in his hometown of Trinidad, where he was knocked out in five rounds by Young Sol, whom *he'd* knocked out just two months before, and "thereby consigned the latter to the has-been class."[39]

There wasn't much left in Chavez's tank. At best, he was called a "foxy old veteran" or "crafty." In general, it was seen that "Chavez seems to have slackened up but little since the days when he was boiling them over as fast as they came up. Benny has been up and down like an elevator the past two years but he retains much of his erstwhile stuff and is capable of making it unpleasant for any boy of his weight."[40]

More bad luck followed. Somewhere along the way, Benny separated from his wife, whom he'd married in 1917. And following the loss to Sol, Benny's brother Andronica, a bar owner, was shot and killed in a fight.

Benny retired again. One year later, Chavez *un*retired. The former title challenger would make his last stand in Albuquerque.

In what would be his 104th fight, Chavez was matched against former soldier-boxer Sailor Gonzalez, on a quick rise and the Duke City's pick for regional featherweight honors, at least in 1921. It was less about whether Gonzalez was made of the right stuff, and more about whether Benny could come back. Not quite answering either question, Chavez let most of the fight slip away before showing "flashes of his old form in the last moments,"[41] and, despite scoring two knockdowns, he lost the 12-round decision to Gonzalez.

The two were rematched five weeks later on a Thanksgiving card, this time at 15 rounds. Once again, in typical Chavez fashion, New Mexico's first contender carried the fight to the speedy youngster, dropping Sailor three times en route to a decision.

A third fight with Young Sol was in the works for early 1922 when Chavez was "advised by his physician not to box until he has had more opportunity to recuperate from his recent illness which has kept him out of the ring for most of the past year."[42] The rumors, of course, were that Chavez was heavily drinking. By the end of February 1922, his health was reported to be improving, though it was expected that he would stay out of the ring for at least a year.

Chavez was finished.

By the summer of 1922, he tried his hand at promoting, managing and training. He guided the early career of Young Dempsey, trained Demon Rivera, even sparred with upcoming fighters, and made ringside appearances, where he was always announced, always cheered for.

In 1924, Benny showed up on a Raton card where he fought an exhibition, and, shortly thereafter, quietly won a comeback fight against an overmatched foe in Aguilar, Colorado.

Then his name disappeared from print. Another "Benny Chavez"—Albuquerque's Solomon Chavez—was now making a name for himself and other than the occasional "Whatever happened to...?" reference, Benny fell on hard times in Trinidad.

By 1932, Benny Chavez would be dead.

New Breed, 1921–1922

Buoyed by a heart of steel and fighting like the marines and doughboys at Chataeu Thierry, Sailor Kramer battled his way to victory.
                                                            — Los Angeles Times, 1918[43]

Post-war prizefighting saw a new breed of fighter in New Mexico. While promoters sought to squeeze dry whatever remained of old-school fighters like the two Bennies, science-based technicians groomed at the expense of Uncle Sam were now the men climbing between the ropes.

Besides Manuel Chavez, who stepped off the Santa Fe rails and into the ring in Albuquerque, there was featherweight Magdaleno "Sailor" Gonzales, who'd learned to fight in the Navy. Gonzales became a regular in May 1919, drawing with Gallup's Jack Myrick and Manny Chavez twice before hitting main event status by the end of the year. Gonzales' four wars with the Insurrecto Kid revved up the postwar crowd, but it was his points win over legend Benny Chavez in 1921 that saw him peak. Gonzales lost the rematch to Benny, but he kept busy in the early-to-mid '20s, sliding down to a prelim fighter again and fighting for the last time in 1927.

Having picked up the "Insurrecto Kid" moniker made famous by Espidiron Guevara earlier in the decade, Natividad Juarez had learned to box while a guardsman at Camp Furlong, in Columbus, reportedly fighting 14 times and losing but once. Staying busy in the ring post-war, Insurrecto became a New Mexican fight card fixture through the '20s and '30s. As the scene was restored, Insurrecto fought Gonzales four times and Kid Anaya six times, before spreading out by adding Texas and Arizona to his route.

In 1921, there was rarely a card in Albuquerque that did *not* have Juarez and Anaya fighting each other. Anaya evened the series in 1922, with two wins, two losses and two draws. As regular as Insurrecto, Anaya fought on and off until 1931.

There was also welterweight Young Jim Flynn — Santiago Montoya — a youngster from the Levy days who returned from the war in 1919 as a regular. Montoya dominated his peers but struggled against more experienced imports, fighting through the '20s and staging a return in the '30s.

Albuquerque wasn't the only place cultivating the new breed of boxer and headlining fighters with the all-too-familiar "Sailor" and "Soldier" monikers that would disappear as the '20s wore on. In Roswell, there was "Soldier" Lester Atkins, "Sailor" Fox and "Sailor" Lillard Rainbolt, who'd fought as a youngster earlier in the decade. Rainbolt came back from the Navy to fight a series of prelims from 1919 to 1921.

In Las Cruces, black featherweight Leo Bradley, who'd learned to box at Fort Bliss, became their first real hometowner. While enlisted, Bradley could not get past Columbus' "Rabbit" Rogers, but, post-war, headlined several small shows in 'Cruces from 1920 to 1923. His biggest fight was against the heavy-hitting Mike Vasquez, who knocked him out; and his high point, a KO over El Paso's Jack Kane in 1923.

From Raton came Ray Kinney, who was one of a dozen fighters named "Young Wallace" in the 1920s. *This* Young Wallace had been born in Colorado Springs but had grown up in Raton before the war. Kinney enlisted in the Navy where he fought as many as 40 times on the West Coast, becoming the Pacific Fleet's welter and middleweight champion. After the war, he came home to take up the professional game, heading Raton's resurgence in the early '20s. After he was utterly destroyed by Eddie Johnson in 1922, Kinney slowed down and called it a day.

The busiest World War I veteran of all from New Mexico was Frank Kremis, who would end his career without fighting a single time in his home state. Born in Springer in 1898, Kremis did not fight until he was in the Navy. While stationed at Mare Island in California, Kremis, fighting as "Sailor Kramer," became a West Coast regular, fighting at least 70 times.

Almost all of Kremis' bouts were four-rounders and his busiest year was 1920, during which the ex-sailor climbed through the ropes 17 times. Most notable were his wars with Danny Kramer, who became a title challenger in 1925 when he was TKO'd in nine rounds by World Featherweight Champion Louis Kaplan at Madison Square Garden. Kramer and Kremis/Kramer fought four times in 1919 and twice in 1922, finishing their string of popular wars at 2-2-2. Ten years after, Los Angeles scribes still recalled at least one of the Kramer-Kramer battles: "Possibly the most fiercely contested battle that ever thrilled Southland bugs was that between Danny Kramer and Sailor Kramer at the Hollywood Stadium. It was a ring classic and will never pass into boxing oblivion."[44]

Though his ring exploits were unknown in his home state, Kremis was not only the busiest post-war former soldier-boxer, but the most traveled, having fought from coast to coast, and in Australia. By 1923, Kramer had tapered down his activity and, with just a couple fights in 1925, retired.

Springer later reclaimed its connection to Kremis, who eventually returned to New Mexico.

Ironically, it was that same small town that lays claim to New Mexico's greatest soldier-boxer of the era. Post-war, no one had the impact than did the kid from Springer, Walter Caldwell.

The Long and Rangy Kid from Springer

Caldwell is a mighty good boy.... He looks like a comer to me and right now is good enough to give any of them a real fight. He's fast and hits mighty hard, and he can take them, too. Best of all, he's got a fighting heart. He's got to be put down and out completely before he is stopped.

— Jack Dempsey, 1921[45]

If Jack Torres and the two Bennies were the state's answer to the 1910s, then Walter Caldwell from the small town of Springer was the first attempt at a world beater for the '20s.

The 6'4", 160-pounder with a reach of 75 inches was the closest thing to a middleweight contender the state has ever had. And though he came up short at the top level, Caldwell's close contender coup might be less remembered than a friendship with the great Jack Dempsey. While fighting on the West Coast in the early '20s, Caldwell had the opportunity to spar with the heavyweight champ, who knocked him out. Two years later, when Caldwell was at his peak, Dempsey expressed an interest in managing the Springer middleweight, but, after a streak of bad luck, nothing ever came of it.

Like Kremis, also from Springer and born the same year, 1898, Caldwell did not lace up until the war, after having signed up for the New Mexico National Guard in 1917. By April, he was already a noted boxer in Company G, before getting shipped off to Camp Kearney in California, then La Guerche, France. While a sergeant with the 115th Military Police in France, Caldwell sowed the seeds of his popularity when several of his letters home were printed in the *Colfax County Stockman*.

It's unknown how many bouts Caldwell participated in while enlisted. Whether it was "a few" to "a great number," Caldwell felt comfortable enough to launch a professional career when he came home in 1919. Headlining a Fourth of July card, Caldwell was pitted against Coloradoan Kid Sandoval, "who declared he'd knock Caldwell out in the third round, but the tables were reversed on him as he found in his opponent a human scientific whirlwind with cyclone blows."[46]

With his brother Ray acting as manager, Caldwell got the attention of Clayton promoters, who booked him for August for the "inauguration of the fight game there"[47] against local favorite Jack "Snorty" Sherwood, a former Marines fighter. Giving up 30 pounds, Caldwell not only knocked out Snorty, but the near-heavyweight did not regain consciousness for an hour-and-a-half and would never fight again.

Back at the Pastime Theater in Springer on Labor Day, Caldwell was given a test against former Fort Bliss boxer Jack Fitzgerald. Though Caldwell dropped his opponent in the first, the more experienced Fitzgerald turned the fight around to earn a draw.

"After showing the home folks what he learned in the way of handling his fists, [Caldwell] is touted in the neighborhood of Springer an upcoming champ,"[48] wrote Caldwell's hometown paper. Albuquerque promoter Louie Benjamin agreed. Any rookie who was good enough to draw with Fitzgerald, who called Walter "a soldier and a tough bird,"[49] was good enough to headline New Mexico's premier fight town.

It wouldn't be easy, warned Benjamin, who offered Caldwell his biggest purse yet — and his biggest opponent in well-known veteran Fred "Kid" George, who'd been headlining fight cards in the Southwest for a decade now. It was a giant step for a youngster, especially in a 15-rounder. The Kid, "who must have gotten his youthful appellation before he attained his present register,"[50] was a heavy favorite. The *Albuquerque Morning Journal* argued for

Caldwell, however, stating, "Shortage of experience is not usually counted as a favoring factor in the prize ring, but when it has the support of a wallop of the kind that Caldwell carries around in his shoulders it's likely to prove an asset as it is to prove a disability."[51]

The classic battle of youth vs. experience produced the thriller of the year. Not only did Caldwell produce enough stamina to go the distance, not only did he outbox, outpunch and outgeneral George, but, the end did not lack drama. The *Journal* called it "the most thrilling finish ever staged in a Duke City ring." The shot to the chin "hurled George bodily out of the ring and dropped him prostrate in the laps of ringsiders. The blow, although terrific, failed to put George away for the count, and he gamely crawled back into the ring. His stay there was ephemeral however. Another 42-centimeter right made a target of his chin and once more projected him bodily over the ropes. This time when George fell — outside the ring — he did not rise until the referee had counted the ten seconds necessary to make Caldwell the winner by the K.O. route."[52]

Caldwell won over the crowd and, overnight, became New Mexico's No. 1 draw.

Walter Caldwell, of Springer, New Mexico, became the leading soldier-boxer following World War I. The hard-hitting middleweight might have made the big time had he not been rushed by manager Tom Jones in the early '20s (courtesy of Gary Allison/Caldwell Family).

The kid from Springer had no problem staying busy and picking up a fat purse. In November, he returned to Clayton for a $500 guarantee, to fight former Canadian Army champ "Speedy" Sparks, who was calling him yellow for postponing an October fight after Caldwell had opted for George. Going down six times before the sleep-producing eighth round, Sparks was no match for Caldwell. A shot to the solar plexus and an uppercut right to the jaw and it was "Now I lay me down to sleep" for Sparks, who "went down like a glass doll."[53]

George, meanwhile, was demanding a rematch — and if Caldwell was half the man he was, he'd meet him on the veteran's home turf, in Bisbee, Ariz. Caldwell did just that and, on Nov. 21, 1919, defeated George a second time. Though going down in the third from a shot to the jaw, the veteran who'd been fighting since 1908 avoided a knockout loss, then announced his retirement (which would not last). Pulling a Louie Newman, who retired after his last fight with Stanley Yoakum to manage his former nemesis, George announced that if you can't beat 'em, join 'em — he'd be managing the youngster from here on out. "No more fighting for me," he told the press. "I have a middleweight of class in Caldwell and he will make good."[54]

George guided Caldwell through April 1920 before they broke. With his connections limited to the Southwest and West Coast, George tried to land Speedball Hayden's former nemesis, Rufus Williams, but that did not happen. Instead, Caldwell opened up 1920 with another show in Albuquerque against "Denver" Jack O'Brien. After going down seven times before the fourth, O'Brien told his corner, "I can't, that guy hits too hard,"[55] and the fight was stopped in the fourth.

While training on the West Coast, Springer middleweight Walter Caldwell (right) was a sparring partner for World Heavyweight Champion Jack Dempsey (left). Though it wasn't publicized when it happened, he was also knocked out by the champ during sparring (courtesy of Gary Allison/Caldwell Family).

Caldwell was now the hottest ticket in the Southwest. He wasn't in demand just in New Mexico — Arizona and El Paso wanted him. He was a fighter "of the genuine type,"[56] not just in the ring; a kid groomed by Uncle Sam, who'd seen action overseas and was now making good.

George announced that Caldwell would be staging a West Coast invasion and, along the way, he knocked out Philadelphia journeyman Jack Rooney with a left hook, showing he wasn't a one-trick pony with just a right hand. The plan was to go west, conquer, then slingshot to the east in pursuit of the title held by Mike O'Dowd.

California laws restricted boxing to four-rounders, which was not exactly Caldwell's forte. In his first bout, he nearly had Rex Morris out on his feet, but had to settle for a decision. It was enough to catch the attention of local scribes:

Walter Caldwell who hails from Albuquerque — the place where we get off and walk around the block and send postcards home and watch the tourists snap-shooting the Injuns and all that ... made a wreck out of one Rex Morris.... Caldwell is so tall that he had to lean over to keep the ring light from hitting him on the head. For four rounds he hammered the game Morris all over the place. Rex probably will have to get up early this morning and order a new nose. Caldwell is a greenhorn, but he has all the makings of a real fighter. He was just a bit over-anxious or he would have stopped Rex.[57]

In between back-to-back draws with Cliff Jordan, on Jan. 30 and Feb. 27, the *Los Angeles Times* called the 21-year-old Caldwell "still green, but can hit and box fairly well for a youngster."[58]

Somewhat frustrated, having expected to bowl over Los Angeles with his power, Caldwell told Albuquerque press that the "coast is hard place for a new man, because he has to send every man the K.O. route before he is ever recognized."[59] Caldwell returned to Albuquerque for a lengthier fight, only to knock out veteran Jack Taylor in four with a left hook, then went back to Vernon.

Walter Caldwell (right) and his manager, former foe Fred "Kid" George (left). Kid George couldn't beat former soldier Caldwell, so he offered to manage him instead. Caldwell was the most popular of the veterans returning to New Mexico after World War I to stage a boxing career.

Kid George had lined up an April 27 bout with Edward Kruvosky — a San Francisco veteran of 100 bouts and the Pacific Coast light-heavyweight champion. Outweighed by 20 pounds — 165 to Kruvosky's 185 — Caldwell was a big underdog, the "wise ones" picking the "old-timer who knows every trick of the game" to win.[60]

The wise ones were right. Though "foxy Kruvosky" weathered Caldwell's "cartwheel rights" in the second, he counter-punched the youngster, introducing the New Mexican to the canvas for the first time in the third. Drawing "the cork copiously" right on the "beezer," Kruvosky copped the win and Caldwell was a "well-beaten mortal when the gong sounded."[61]

Caldwell's first defeat was blamed on George, for throwing the kid in with a cagey fox like Kruvosky, and a much heavier one at that. He was "still too 'green' for an old-timer like Kayo Kruvosky," wrote H.M. Walker, sports editor of the *Los Angeles Examiner*.[62]

George was out — and Tom Jones was in. Dubbed the "Maker of Pugilistic Champions," Jones' specialty was finding unknowns, or underdogs, and making top-notchers out of them, then saying "I told you so." He'd managed Jess Willard going into the world heavyweight championship, defeating Jack Johnson in 1915 at Havana, Cuba, as well as Ad Wolgast and Billy Papke. After splitting ways with middleweight contender Bryan Downey, Jones was looking for new blood — and vengeance against Downey — so in May, he signed Caldwell, bringing him to the Midwest where his ties were strongest.

Jones' motives were clear to everyone but Caldwell, and he wasn't any easier on Caldwell than George had been. First, Jones matched up Caldwell with tough Jimmy Delaney in Omaha, Neb., then he threw him into deep water to fight Downey.

Against Delaney, on June 16, 1920, in Omaha, Neb., Caldwell held his own, drawing in ten hard-fought rounds. That was saying a lot about Caldwell, for the much more experienced Delaney had recently defeated Johnny Sudenberg, former border champion, and would, in 1923 and 1924, give future champ Gene Tunney a run for his money.

"Caldwell had a horrible wallop, that he threw into Mr. Delaney's face many times,

Despite a loss to future world champion Bryan Downey in 1920, Walter Caldwell was ever on the verge of contention in the middleweight division (Courtesy of Gary Allison/Caldwell Family).

but the St. Paul kid was hard as nails and could not even be fazed," reported the *Omaha World-Herald.* "In the eighth round Caldwell staged a battle that, if he had kept it up, would have won the fight for him either by decision or by the K.O. route. Caldwell showed much lack of experience, but he looks like the making of a good fighter, and after a few more months under the management of Tom Jones some big things can be expected of him."[63]

Rather than hone Caldwell and desperate for payback, Jones arranged for the Springer lad to fight Downey in his hometown of Columbus, Ohio, on a Fourth of July card.

Jones had groomed Downey from 1916 to his current contender status before splitting in December 1919 on unfriendly terms. Downey's "coincidental" signing of another tough middleweight in Caldwell was transparent to local press. "I would be foolish, indeed, if were I to bring him to Columbus to meet Downey unless I thought he could win," Jones told the *Columbus Dispatch.* "A defeat would make me out as a poor judge of boxers and their worth. It would also give the Downeys a chance to crow, and this time I want to be the man to laugh."[64]

A win over Downey would put Caldwell on the fast track and into contention. For a rookie with just 14 professional bouts, it was a change from the long, slow road Benny Chavez had to endure. But it was not to be, for Caldwell was knocked out in the third round.

Downey would go on to fight for the World Middleweight Championship in 1921 against Johnny Wilson, who would retain the title on a foul. The Cleveland Boxing Commission, however, would later nullify the referee's decision and award the title to Downey, who'd floored Wilson three times before the stoppage. When they rematched later in the year, a 12-round draw did not settle the matters and Downey fought on as the "Ohio Middleweight Champion," since no other state honored the title.

After losing to Downey, Caldwell returned to New Mexico, offering no alibis for the defeat and admitting Downey was the better man. Though there was talk of Australia, Texas and Arizona, Caldwell's next two bouts were at home. In Las Vegas, on Aug. 25, 1920, Caldwell beat up overmatched Jack Roth in four, then rematched Jack Rooney in Albuquerque, on Sept. 10.

Rooney claimed to have been suffering from an ulcerated tooth when Caldwell had KO'd him earlier in the year. Plus, he'd overestimated the "clod-hopper from New Mexico, who trained on buttermilk and ran over the sand hills for exercise," taking for "granted that Caldwell was a farmer."[65] This time around, Rooney was knocked out a round later — in the second.

Still under Jones, Caldwell relocated his training camp to Fort Bliss through the end of the year while a fight in Dallas was secured against Jack Reeves for Dec. 15. Reeves had been a very active fighter since 1919, mainly in California's four-round game where he had a draw and a win over Caldwell's former foe, Kruvosky. Reeves' wins over name fighters Frank Barrieau and Spud Murphy made him a favorite in Dallas.

If the experience didn't overmatch Caldwell, Reeves' reach, height and weight did. Still, giving up at least ten pounds, Caldwell came close to the upset win when he scored a knockdown in the first. Reeves recovered and, by the sixth, had a stream of blood flowing down the left side of Caldwell's face after a brow cut opened up. The infighting did Caldwell in and, unable to keep a distance, he crumpled to the floor in the seventh.

Returning to El Paso, with his second loss now, Caldwell told Hy Schneider of the *El Paso Times* that George had done a better job than the world-famous Jones. Reuniting with George, Caldwell started over, beginning with a hometown fight on Feb. 26, 1921, in Springer.

Strictly a Southwest fighter in 1921, Caldwell had his busiest year, though it was far from a successful one — and mistakes in management *continued* to be made. After three stay-at-home bouts, between Springer and Raton, Caldwell TKO'd ill-matched "Hambone" Rodriguez, then drew with and decisioned Young Wallace in back-to-back bouts. A third fight with Wallace and a bout against Eddie Johnson were nixed, however, when George erred in lining up Gorilla Jones for Caldwell on March 19 in Columbus.

In an era when most white fighters were drawing the color line, Caldwell did not have a problem risking his career against the dangerous Jones, who'd practically finished Speedball Hayden. After just a couple of rounds, Kid George figured there was no need for Caldwell to go out on a stretcher — he tossed in the sponge.

Caldwell trekked north for the next five fights, looping back and forth from Raton to Denver and Colorado Springs, once again firing Kid George. This time, former opponent

Jack Rooney took over. In Raton, Caldwell KO'd lightly-regarded Bud Clancy, of Detroit, in one. Then, on the Fourth of July, also in Raton, he faced veteran George Shade who replaced New York City's Eddie O'Hare (who would soon face Gene Tunney, then die in an auto accident).

A 100-bout veteran from Vallejo, California, Shade was supposed to be a tough fight — and it was — but an at-home win. Instead, it ended in a 15-round draw. At first, the ref declared the bout in favor of Caldwell but "the roar of [protest] that swept up the stage when the decision was announced caused a hasty revision of that thought."[66]

New Mexico's faith in Caldwell began to falter, even after he knocked out St. Paul veteran Billy Emke in one round, on July 20 in Colorado Springs, for, right after, he was pitted against Colorado's top middleweight, George Manley.

Once again, Caldwell had swapped pilots. J. C. Carlton, a fire chief of Raton, was now managing him, at least temporarily, and the decision was rendered to campaign solely in Colorado, and to target Manley. "I am going to win because I have to,"[67] said Caldwell, before entering the Denver ring on Aug. 12.

The fight itself was "slow and uninteresting," at least according to scribe Abe Pollock, with "Manley dancing out of way and Caldwell missing shot after shot." Caldwell "missed at least fifty times with his much-touted right" though Manley wasn't any better — he "seemed to be afraid of his opponent and fought a cool, careful battle, being satisfied by boxing his opponent."[68] Agreeing with the referee's decision to give Manley the bout, Pollock gave Caldwell one round, Manley five and had nine even.

Despite the loss, Caldwell got another chance to face a topnotcher in Battling Ortega just 12 days later in Colorado Springs, with the winner to take on St. Paul contender Mike Gibbons on Labor Day. Caldwell came close to knocking out Ortega in the opening round but the San Francisco veteran "came back and pursued Caldwell all over the ring, landing rights and lefts to the body. At the end of the second round, Caldwell's manager announced that his boxer would be unable to continue. A hard left to the stomach in the middle of the round put an end to whatever chance the New Mexico boxer might have had to win."[69]

Hoping to end the year on the upswing and erase at least one of his losses, Caldwell was rematched with his least dangerous conqueror, Gorilla Jones, on Oct. 6, on home turf in Raton. With plenty of time to prepare this time around, Caldwell "took and gave punishment ... but was able to pile up enough points for the win" and "put his mitt brand on the Gorilla's ear in their little affair."[70]

Caldwell and Jones renewed their "feud of old standing" on Nov. 3, 1921, and, after a year's absence, the middleweight hopeful returned to Albuquerque where he discovered he was still popular. After a month of "roughing it in the mountains near Springer,"[71] Caldwell kept his edge, but could not repeat his success against Jones, having to settle for a draw.

Caldwell was a non-entity during 1922. The press still talked about him, but he was no Benny Chavez. There were too many doubts.

Caldwell disappeared to Hawaii for four months, though he became the first New Mexican to ever fight there when he destroyed Honolulu's only claim to boxing, Faatola Tuffale, in a single round. A crowd of 1,200 at the Yuraku-Kwan Theater was "dumbfounded by the kaleidoscopic rapidity with which their idol was shattered by a rapid succession of haymakers to the jaw and temples of their hero. With glazed eyes, a pitiful stare, Tuffale ruled under the terrible onslaught of his conqueror and, retaining only a semblance of his fighting instinct, was mercifully spared the finishing blow which the towering catlike New Mexican stood ready to deliver."[72] The victory earned Caldwell a carved walking stick and plenty of popularity in Hawaii, but in the States it did little for his waning reputation.

Caldwell returned to the four-round game in California between April and August, winning two, losing one and drawing once, then tried to fight Denver's Henry Pross, a bout that was cancelled three times — twice for inclement weather and once for a lack of audience. Caldwell took the rest of the year off.

In 1923, the Springer middleweight launched a final serious campaign, assuring Raton promoters that he'd intended to remain a Southwest fighter. Things had changed for Caldwell, who had plans to marry his Springer sweetheart. By now, the realization had set in that true contention was beyond his reach, but he could, at least, carve out a niche as the Southwest champion. That meant defeating Manley, Dick Dundee and Andy Palmer, both of Arizona, or Tiger Flowers, who was headlining Juarez after blowing out Gorilla Jones.

Keenest on Caldwell's mind was Manley, and on March 15 in Raton he defeated his former conqueror, albeit by DQ when an accidental blow landed low. One month later, they were rematched. This time, Caldwell earned the decision, aggressively outboxing Manley and regaining a bit of local prestige.

In May, he headlined Albuquerque for the last time, taking on Arizona's Dick Dundee. Caldwell had punching power, height and reach on his side; Dundee had defense and speed. Though praise was saved for the lower weight fighters on the card, namely Young Benny Chavez and Dynamite Tommy Sanchez, Caldwell outpowered Dundee in a somewhat slow fight, winning a majority decision.

The kid from Springer was possibly back on track. That was the general consensus, that is, until Denver's Tommy Commiskey, expected to be a walkover on a June card in Raton, shocked local fans with a fourth-round knockout of Caldwell. Sealing his fate as a has-been was a fourth fight with Manley on Aug. 12, 1923, in Denver, from which he returned on the short end of a 12-round decision.

No one heard from Caldwell through the winter of 1923–1924, but he resurfaced in Vernon, California, hoping to rekindle his career. After a win, then a third round knockout loss, Caldwell quietly retired.

13. In Search of a Champion, 1922–1925

"Ladies are reserving seats by phone," says George Ringling, which has been unheard of here in previous boxing contests, "but why shouldn't they? They do it in California, New York and nearly every other section of the country, and if a boxing contest is all right for the husbands to see and appreciate, why not for the wife, mother, sister or daughter."

—Albuquerque Morning Journal, 1923[1]

Having recovered from war and armed with a new breed of fighting men, boxing was alive and well in New Mexico in the early 1920s. The only thing missing was a big name to rally behind and solidify the sport. Benny Chavez was done, Benny Cordova wasn't too far behind, and the only thing faster than Walter Caldwell's rise had been his fall. By 1924, the scene was faltering again. The fight-a-month average maintained by the Duke City started to slow. Leading the way meant legitimizing the sport—and attempts were made on several levels.

One of the stabs at legitimacy meant forming a boxing commission. The idea was nothing new. In an editorial printed in 1912, three weeks after the Jack Johnson–Jim Flynn fight, the *Santa Fe New Mexican* proposed the need for an authoritative body that would answer to the public while sanctioning and licensing athletes, promoters and ring officials. The commission would "insure good, clean and evenly matched fights" while standing "for a square deal."[2]

Nearly a decade later, the first boxing commission wouldn't come out of the capital. It wouldn't even come out of New Mexico's leading fight town, Albuquerque, but rather Clayton, of all places, population 2,100, during March 1920.

It was all about being "on the square" for the "sport loving" people of Clayton who were "averse to being hoodwinked out of their coin by a bunch of four-flushers who only want to grab their coin and get out." Fans had been ripped off plenty, so to insure that it would no longer occur, a "Boxing Commission has been appointed here who will hereafter attend the matches, and they are determined that if there is any show of frame-ups or faking the fighters will receive none of the gate money, and therefore will have to devise other ways of getting their meal tickets besides fleecing the gentle public."[3]

By the end of summer that same year, Albuquerque's city commissioners, spurred on by several unsatisfying fights, held a meeting to propose a new ordinance that would "keep out the 'ham' and 'egg' fighters and the 'once-in-a-while' promoters," requiring a leap up from the $10 promoter's license to $100. Nothing came of it, but the threats of such a steep fee kept local promoters from staging anything approaching the "hoodwink" level.[4]

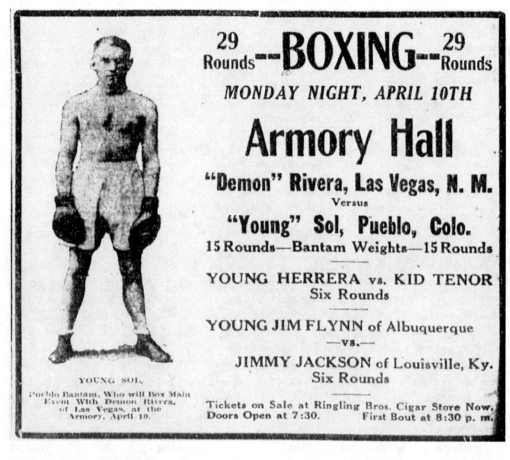

29 Rounds --BOXING-- 29 Rounds

MONDAY NIGHT, APRIL 10TH

Armory Hall

"Demon" Rivera, Las Vegas, N. M.

Versus

"Young" Sol, Pueblo, Colo.

15 Rounds—Bantam Weights—15 Rounds

YOUNG HERRERA vs. KID TENOR
Six Rounds

YOUNG JIM FLYNN of Albuquerque
—vs.—
JIMMY JACKSON of Louisville, Ky.
Six Rounds

YOUNG SOL.
Pueblo Bantam, Who will Box Main
Event With Demon Rivera,
of Las Vegas, at the
Armory, April 10.

Tickets on Sale at Ringling Bros. Cigar Store Now.
Doors Open at 7:30.   First Bout at 8:30 p. m.

Long-time veteran from Santa Fe, Demon Rivera proved his stuff on April 10, 1922, when he took on Pueblo, Colorado's Young Sol in a 15-rounder at the Armory in Albuquerque.

That is, until Sept. 9, 1921, when Mike Baca received an early Christmas present in the form of the Southwest lightweight championship when he "defeated" Billy Alger, thanks to referee *and* promoter Steve Marcos. The city revoked Marcos' license and started flexing their muscle, forming the Albuquerque Boxing Commission, which became a live entity on Sept. 14, 1921. Though the ABC's influence would end at the city's limits, boxing fans could now rest assured that fake fights, poorly matched bouts and bad decisions would find no home in the Duke City.

The new commission immediately started flexing its muscle.

The first card under the watchful eye of the ABC occurred at the Armory on Oct. 17, 1921. The show, promoted by Dan Padilla and the Duke City Athletic Club, brought in 1,000 fans who watched Sailor Gonzales upset Benny Chavez for a decision—without controversy.

In November, Battling Ortega was told by the ABC to disappear from the Duke City after a bad performance against John "Kid" Candelaria. One month later, Toby Montoya lost his purse because the commission thought he could've beaten the count in a third-round knockdown by Young Herrera—and then Herrera, in turn, was barred from the ring six months later when he "grew tired in the third and laid down,"[5] never mind that his opponent, "One Round" Martinez, outweighed him by 20 pounds.

Though fighters and promoters complained that the commission was being too trivial, no one complained in February 1923 when the commish got tough following a fight with black legend Sam Langford and a white fighter whose name was given as "Australian" Tom McCarty, but who was really an El Paso pug named Joe Daley, also a sparring partner of "The Boston Tar Baby's."

> The first round opened at twenty minutes to ten. Before he climbed into the ring, Sam remarked that he was going to catch the ten minutes after ten train to El Paso. He had world's [sic] of time. In the first round the fighting was even because there wasn't any. McCarty easily had the lead in interpretive dancing. Sam didn't dare hit him. He had agreed to let the "ham-and-egger" stay a round. In the early moments of the second, he cuffed McCarty and shoved him over on his neck. The referee counted a decade. McCarty lifted his head at nine and stretched out again at ten. Then he got up and went for the seconds and referee — but he stayed away from the Tar Baby, who was climbing through the ropes and making for the ten-ten train.[6]

The ABC went into a frenzy, barring both fighters from Albuquerque and forging a new set of rules — in short, borrowing most of the New York commission's rules — that would go into effect on the next fight card. There would be no more "'go-as-you-please' affairs." Boxers would have to "earn their money" if they didn't want to be barred permanently. Rabbit killers, kidney punches and pivot blows were forbidden, and fighters scoring a knockdown would no longer be able to stand over their opponent waiting to "smash him as soon as he was cleared of the floor." Finally, not that it had been an issue either, white vs. black fighters would be "absolutely taboo for the future."[7]

While the race decree would soon be ignored, the ABC did not waste time showing they were serious. In April, Young Benny Chavez and Cyclone Williams were disqualified for kidney punches. In June, the ABC cancelled exhibitions and fights with youngsters under age 16 and, in October, they said no more fights would be allowed on Wednesday nights, because the Armory was too close to a church that held meetings that night of the week. Eventually, the ABC relaxed after promoters complained they were choking the life out of the fight scene.

Though they flirted with the idea in 1923, it took Santa Fe eight years to form their own commission. Clovis took nine.

In April 1929, the Santa Fe Boxing Commission was formed but when the members failed to do their job eight months later, after Cleveland heavyweight Andy Moran "sent over a hard right uppercut and missed,"[8] causing Chihuahua Kid Brown to fake a knockout, Santa Fe's mayor, James McConvery, suspended boxing in the city for six months.

While promoters complained about commissions (an ongoing battle even today), they argued that legitimacy in the fight world could only come about by raising a local boy made of championship timber, or by bringing in big name fighters — it was the Mark Levy model of thinking, and it was easier said than done.

Though guys like Stanley Yoakum, Harry Schaefer and Kid George had been well received in the past, hadn't anyone learned from the Johnson-Flynn fight? Or the Johnny Dundee–Tommy Dixon fiasco that attracted but 900 fans? And even when a big leaguer like Langford had attracted 1,100, hadn't controversy followed?

Big names would lend legitimacy, was the argument.

Other fight centers could sway World Heavyweight Champion Jack Dempsey to guest referee, stage an exhibition, or just sit ringside at a fight. Not so in New Mexico, not even when the champ spent three weeks in 1923 hunting in the Sangre de Cristo mountains. "New Mexico is home to me,"[9] the Manassa Mauler told the *New Mexican*, reminiscing about his boyhood days when he would peddle fruit from Taos. The press ran endless articles about Dempsey's hunting adventures, his next and last fight, and his run-ins with the Game Warden's Office, who demanded to know if the champ was going to hunt deer with his three wolfhounds, stag hound and bull dog, or if bear and mountain lion were his targets. Meanwhile, all invitations to attend smokers thrown in his honor, or to attend a fight, went unanswered.

Even Roswell had better luck the year before when World Lightweight Champion Benny Leonard stopped over at the expense of the local Elks chapter to stage an exhibition on a local boxing show. When Santa Fe promoter Daniel C. Ortiz wired a request to stay an extra day to do the same in Santa Fe, Leonard apologized, saying he had to get a move on to Los Angeles.

If the scene was going to survive the '20s, a new name would have to emerge. Chavez and Cordova had packed in 2,000 to 3,000; Caldwell, over 1,000. The state needed its own champion, a new star, whether he was borrowed or produced. Or both.

New Mexico was waiting for Eddie Mack.

Home Cooked

> The boxing card will hold many thrills. Nothing but local talent will be shown, but oh boy! What talent!
> — *Roswell Daily Record,* 1924[10]

By mid-decade of the 1920s every town had their hometown hero.

Proving there was life after Caldwell, Springer produced welterweight Frankie "Young" Zamora. Headlining hometown cards and shows in Wagon Mound, Dawson and Raton, Zamora blazed through the locals, winning most by knockout, peaking with a first-round stoppage over highly-touted El Pasoan Walter Garrett, then disappeared until the late '20s, when he staged a comeback.

Farther north, at the state line in Raton, Louis "KO" Pino fought the first half of his career, through the mid–'20s, going from a prelim on Caldwell shows to main event status, before crossing over into Colorado where there were more opportunities. Pino would return later in the decade.

In Santa Fe, while Mike Baca was winding down his career, the Pacheco brothers had arrived. Henry "Kid" Pacheco took over Baca's reign as the Ancient City's "Native Son"; he was aided by his younger brother, Manuel "Young" Pacheco. A third brother, Joe, would follow.

After fighting 34 times in the Marines (where he was either 33–1 or 21-1-12, depending on the source), and copping honors as champion of the Hawaiian Islands, then fighting the pro game for several bouts while stationed at Mare Island (where one of the wins was a KO over Gene Delmont, an old foe of Benny Chavez's), Henry came home in 1923. Sporting a "wicked hula in either mitt,"[11] Pacheco became a regular on Santa Fe, Albuquerque and, occasionally, Fort Bliss shows.

After mopping the floor with Albuquerque's Manny Chavez, Kid Pacheco cleaned up locally, boxing through the decade as a stay-at-home fighter, losing but a few times while calling himself the Southwest bantamweight champ, at least for a while. Henry's brother Manuel climbed into the ring a year after his older brother, finding a regular spot on Santa

Fe shows, though he was unable to achieve as much prestige. In his first five years, Young Pacheco went unbeaten, and he fought well into the '30s, while Henry's last bout was in 1930.

Neither Pacheco attained the notoriety that shadowed "Young" Benny Chavez, who was called everything from "The Bad Boy of Boxing" to "The Spanish Flash."

Before there was Johnny Tapia and after there was (the original) Benny Chavez, there was Solomon Chavez, who hoped the name would rub off when he started fighting at the border while enlisted. There was no relation to the original Benny, but he had a brother and a cousin who boxed, and a son as well. Solomon's cousin was *Tony* Chavez, who would be a top name in the '30s and early '40s on the West Coast; his brother was Joe, and his son, yet another Solomon. Confused? Consider a four-round curtain raiser on a card held Sept. 7, 1925, in Albuquerque when a "Joe Chavez" fought "Kid Chavez," with Joe being the original Benny Chavez's brother, and Kid Chavez, the brother of *Young* Benny, being Solomon Chavez.

Young Benny — Solomon, that is — was born in 1905 at Socorro and raised in Albuquerque. First lacing on the leather while at Fort Bliss, Young Benny did not raise many eyebrows during his early years, neither at the border nor in his hometown, to which he returned to fight in late 1922. Chavez lost and drew nearly as often as he won while fighting at Forts Bayard and Bliss, or his most frequent haunt, across the river in Juarez. As a regular, Chavez was tempered in four-rounders, usually losing against the likes of Jose Rivers or Young Gonzalez and written about as being overanxious and unpredictable, yet exciting. With 22 bouts under his belt, the bantamweight from the border came home only to get disqualified in one of his early hometown bouts for excessive kidney and rabbit punches ("What are those?" the Juarez-groomed pug asked the referee afterward).

Solomon "Young Benny" Chavez (right) very early in his career, probably while at Fort Bliss in the early '20s. Man at the left is unknown.

Drawing with, then beating "Barber" Sandoval, and pitting his sheer aggression against Kid Pacheco's classy boxing skills for a draw raised eyebrows. A KO over "One Round" Martinez, a draw with former border conqueror Pete Loya and a decision win over Pacheco in the rematch elevated him to local favorite by 1924.

Controversy and raw deals made Chavez even more popular.

There was a controversial split decision to Telesfor Baca in October 1924, in a bout that would "have rendered a stretch of the imagination to the breaking point to have given Baca a draw,"[12] let alone the win. Fist fights broke out in the crowd and the police rushed in to quell a riot in the making. Following the Baca bout, Chavez lost in Santa Fe to their hometown pride, Kid Pacheco, for whom the rounds had been decreased to two-and-a-half minutes to accommodate the local fave's injured hand. Then, in a rematch with Baca, that had Chavez going "through his usual procedure of giving Kid Baca a sound thrashing,"[13] he had to settle for a draw.

Inconsistency was the name of the game for Chavez. Though he was often "home-towned" in his hometown, other times he would lose his temper in the ring, getting into a shouting match with a referee or judge, and his weight would show the variation of his training, fluctuating between 115 and 126.

Yet, he was good — "Kid's got potential," the scribes would say—and he had no problem taking on the best Southwestern fighters of his division, whether it was in Arizona, Colorado or New Mexico. Though losing to Benny "Kid" Carter and Benny Silva on the road, he was good enough to beat Jackie Sanders and draw with Pinkie Uriquidi, the "Juarez Jumping Jack."

After losing another fight by DQ in Albuquerque, on July 2, 1925, in a fight that saw Chavez flooring his foe from body shots, he made plans to leave. Unable to secure a single main event in his hometown, passed over for a shot at rising star Eddie Mack, and sick of all the bad decisions, Chavez, now a 50-bout veteran, left New Mexico in 1926.

New Mexico had not seen the last of Solomon Chavez. Neither had Nick "Kid" Mortio, who'd managed to outslick the aggressive Duke City pug.

A product of the Fort Bliss ring game, but otherwise born and bred in New Mexico, Nick Manti would develop into one of the flashiest, speediest cuties ever to grace a Southwest ring. Manti was better known as "Kid Mortio," and almost always followed up with the "San Marcial Flash," "Santa Rosa Flash" or "Fort Bliss Flash," depending upon whether you wanted to refer to his hometown, place of birth or his military post.

For the most part, Mortio was San Marcial's claim-to-fame. Though the small railroad town, 30 miles south of Socorro, would later be known for its near-destruction in 1929, when the Rio Grande flooded and put the town under as much as six feet of water, in the early to mid–'20s it was known for Mortio.

While stationed at Fort Bliss in 1920, Mortio's natural athleticism caught the attention of Jim Erwin, the famed matchmaker of the Punch Bowl, during a basketball game. Erwin approached the 18-year-old "frail kid, hardly weighing over 110 pounds," who told the matchmaker, "I've never put on a boxing glove in my life — never even *seen* a boxing match." Erwin talked him into giving it a try, then taught him the basics and threw him into his first rounder against the more-experienced Battling Chico II on Mar. 10, 1920. Held "in a downpour of hail and rain in the old open air arena," the fight was declared a draw and the local legend of Kid Mortio had begun.[14]

Mortio trained, ate and lived boxing. It wasn't long before he was stamped the Army's southern department bantamweight champ. The *El Paso Times*' Hy Schneider would soon call him the "fastest boy afoot in the southwest,"[15] though he was criticized for lack of punching power and for occasionally outrunning his opponents. For border fans, who preferred the raw clash of sluggers, Mortio's sprint and zip wins might have showed him "up as a marvel, but as a prize fight it was decidedly to the Roquefort."[16]

After two years of fighting fours and sixers and eight-rounders, losing but a few, Mortio was ready for main events. The man to beat at the border was El Paso's Jose Rivers, and in 1922 *the* big fights being talked about on both sides of the Rio Grande were Mortio-Rivers I, II, III and IV.

While Mortio was a "speed king," Rivers had the perfect remedy with his "poisonous straight wallop from either side."[17] In their first two matches, both held at Fort Bliss, Mortio became the first man to beat the "unbeatable" Rivers. "Mortio [was] too slick for Rivers," in the first bout that had the El Paso slugger claiming a "bum paw." Calling Mortio a coward by his hit-and-run methods, Mortio indulged his crosstown nemesis the rematch and six weeks later,

> [Mortio] made a human punching bag of Rivers for five rounds, hammered him unmercifully, floored Rivers three times, once reached down and lifted Rivers to his feet, indicating clearly that he refused to permit Rivers to quit. Mortio deliberately cut Rivers' mouth and nose, made a target of his eye and battered his face until referee Jimmy Kramer mercifully stopped the match. Rivers had gone down for the third time in the sixth round. Kramer awarded the fight to Mortio after 1 minute and 55 seconds of the sixth had passed.[18]

Of his 200-plus bouts, this one-sided win over Rivers stands out as Mortio's single best performance. In 1922, the twin wins over Rivers gave the San Marcial Flash his peak marquee, as well — just as fights III and IV toppled him from his lofty perch.

Just one month after slaughtering Rivers, Mortio's zip was zapped by a bout-ending shot to the solar plexus, courtesy of Rabbit Rogers of the 24th Infantry in Columbus. Seeking to get back on top, Mortio agreed to fight Rivers a third time, in front of a pro–Mexican crowd at the Garden Arena in Juarez, where fights were notoriously unsportsmanlike. This time, Rivers was allowed to maul and brawl Mortio, in a much smaller ring, as well. Throwing low blows, backhands, elbows, rabbit punches and with much shoving, Rivers battered Mortio while the referee looked away with each foul. The Flash was knocked or shoved down a total of six times before the ref stopped the fight in the fourth.

Mortio demanded a rematch and one week later, again in Juarez, Rivers pocketed his bag of tricks and scored a clean knockout in a bout that said the El Pasoan was at his best, while Mortio was at his worst.

Though still a popular fighter for his bouts with Rivers, as well as holding four wins and two draws with Mexican favorite Pete Loya, Mortio, like Young Benny had done, decided it was time to branch out and fight in New Mexico. Mortio's resume still made him one of the top featherweights in the Southwest.

Mortio, Chavez and the Pachecos were not the only ones heating up the scene in central New Mexico.

In Albuquerque, a youngster named Alfonso Valencia, fighting under the moniker "Young Pancho Villa" was beginning what would be one of the longest running careers while another Valencia — Louie "Red" Valencia — flirted with the sport in Bernalillo, launching what would end up being *the* longest career in promotions.

In Albuquerque there was also George "Kid Marchi, the "Fighting Chef," who'd come from Maryland and had fought in Colorado before relocating to New Mexico. There was "Barber" Sandoval — Teodosio to his family — who was ounce found guilty of assault and battery when he grabbed a local attorney he was sore at and cussed at him in public.

Timo Sanchez was on the shelf during most of the early '20s, but in 1923, he staged a one-year return, his most notable win being a dynamite fifth-round knockout over rising Coloradoan Young Jack Dempsey, who was under the care of one Benny Chavez of Trinidad.

While familiar names like Insurrecto Kid and Demon Rivera were "gimmes" on any fight-card, and "Sailor" Gonzalez and "Sailor" Jack sought to make the transition from soldier-boxing to gritty prizefighting, a pair of unrelated Martinez featherweights, "One Round" from the Duke City and Freddie from Santa Fe, and a pair of Romeros, Joe and "Red," assured the growing fight town that the game was now owned, and forevermore *would* be owned, by the brown-skinned locals.

From the North and South

> *Joe the Wop has sent a red hot challenge.... The Wop is one of the speed boys of the bantamweight division in the west and it is said that he has been looking around for more worlds to conquer.*
>
> —*Albuquerque Morning Journal*, 1922[19]

As New Mexico's second golden age of boxing began to heat up, then simmer, talent from surrounding states was tossed into the pot. By the time Eddie Mack made his appearance—*re*appearance, actually—in the Land of Enchantment, the caldron would boil over, prepping ring fans for a feast of fights through the latter half of the 1920s.

They came from the south, north and east—Coloradoans, Texans, Mexicans—bearing names like "Big Chief," "Broken Tooth," "Dandy" and yet another "Joe Rivers," looking for paydays, looking to expand their Southwest conquest, and looking for Mack.

At the border, most of the soldiers were gone and the out-of-towners that had pervaded the earlier scene had been replaced by locals who now had developed into real fighters. Rivalry between Fort Bliss' Punch Bowl and Juarez had created claimants for a host of Southwest titles.

The pioneers of prizefighting in El Paso—the Payo brothers, Cip and Gene—were winding down their own careers. After a historic 33-fight draw with Jimmy Fitten in Mexico City, on Jan. 21, 1922, Kid Payo decided to hang up the gloves to become the area's de facto referee over the next two decades while his younger brother Gene gave up the gloves after losing in his hometown to Texan comer "Dandy" Dick Griffin. Meanwhile, another Payo—Angelo— was on the rise.

Old blood was replaced with new, and at bantam to feather, the names were many. Pete "Broken Tooth" Loya and Pinky Uriquidi, the "Mexican Jumping Bean of Juarez," became the first Mexicans from the southern side of the border to make good. After beating each other up in several bouts, they moved up the ladder and headed north.

There had always been too many boxers known as "Joe Rivers," but in the early '20s, at the border, the only one anyone cared about was the Chihuahua-born fighter residing in El Paso, who was not be confused with the "Mexican" Joe Rivers, who was fighting in Texas, or any one of a handful of "Young Joe" Riverses who'd popped up all over the country. This "Joe Rivers" soon tired of the confusion, as well, and in 1923 announced that from here on out, he was simply "Jose Rivers."

Beginning his career at the age of 14 in 1920, Rivers was undefeated until he was outsped, then TKO'd by Kid Mortio. After turning the tables on his rival, Rivers became *the* man to beat at the border. Commonly referred to as the "Mexican Midget Mantler" or the "Pocket Edition of Jack Dempsey," Rivers, too, looked northwards to Albuquerque after cleaning out the border.

He was preceded by "Big Chief" Mike Vasquez. The El Paso featherweight who, as a youngster, had attended Albuquerque's Indian School, blazed through his first two years of fights at the border, occasionally fighting at Fort Bayard and throughout southern New Mexico — the most notable of which was in 1920 at Carrizozo, where he knocked out the locally-touted "Kid" Aaron Lee before a crowd of 1,500.

Vasquez gave Albuquerque a taste of his power in September 1922, when he defended his claim as Southwestern featherweight champion, knocking out Philly fighter Johnny Romaine. After campaigning throughout the Pacific Coast, Texas and Mexico, he returned to Albuquerque in 1924 the veteran of nearly 100 battles now, to draw with, then defeat, Harry Bramer and decision Dick Griffin. After losing to near-contender Johnny McCoy, Vasquez left for Texas in 1926, but would return later in the decade when the timing was right.

Also with ties to the state was Richard Lawrence Griffin, better known as "Dandy" Dick Griffin, who was born in Albuquerque but raised in Leadville, Colorado. Griffin's family relocated to Fort Worth, Texas, where he learned to fight. Griffin started fighting in 1915 and would have close to 200 bouts before he retired in 1926, nearly blind (later he *would* lose his sight). There probably wasn't a city Griffin did *not* fight in while touring coast to coast, and he would often return to the border, especially in the early '20s when he ruled the bantamweight roost. Griffin won over the border by uncrowning El Paso's long-time favorite Kid Payo, then followed up by beating up younger brother Gene. He fought in New Mexico but once — beating George Spencer in Roswell, on May 9, 1921 — though bigger cities never stopped trying to bill him. Though looking like a real contender early in the decade, Griffin would defeat two world champions (Joe Lynch and Pete Herman) and a third "uncrowned" champ, Pal Moore, by fighting every name bantam. Mortio lost to Griffin — though Vasquez passed his acid test, defeating him in 1925 at the Punch Bowl, though that was long after Griffin had peaked.

Though retiring in 1926, Griffin was far from done with both the border and New Mexico. He would reappear early in the '30s, with a bigger bang than he'd ever achieved by fighting.

Vasquez and Rivers became the main threats from the south. Colorado supplied the rest.

If New Mexico staged an

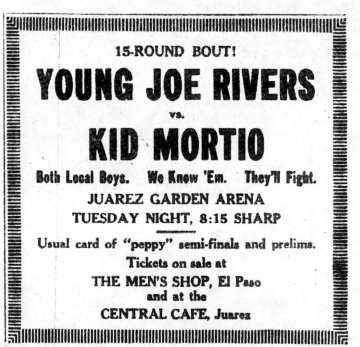

15-ROUND BOUT!

YOUNG JOE RIVERS

vs.

KID MORTIO

Both Local Boys.   We Know 'Em.   They'll Fight.

JUAREZ GARDEN ARENA
TUESDAY NIGHT, 8:15 SHARP

———

Usual card of "peppy" semi-finals and prelims.

Tickets on sale at
THE MEN'S SHOP, El Paso
and at the
CENTRAL CAFE, Juarez

During the '20s, many boxers were were known as "Young Joe Rivers," but the one that mattered in New Mexico, or at the border, was Jose Rivera, who later went by his real name. His four wars with San Marcial speedster Nick "Kid" Mortio, in 1922, were the talk of El Paso that year. They went 2–2 in '22.

estimated 500 fight cards during the 1920s, Colorado can most likely brag triple the number. Denver was the state's boxing hub, but towns throughout the state holding regular action included Canon City, Colorado Springs, Durango, Leadville, Pueblo and Trinidad. It was a solid era for Colorado — and it would only get better.

Canon City claimed Sidney "Kid" Belt; Colorado Springs sprung Don "Terror" Long; Dolores sent Cowboy Padgett, the "stinging cow-puncher"; Pueblo still had the ever-rugged Eddie Johnson, while bringing up youngsters Joe "Awful" Coffee, Joe "The Wop" Flynn and Joe "The Wop" Kelly, Johnny Kid Mex and Young Sol; and post–Chavez Trinidad had Frank Herrera and Boney Gagliardi. From Denver came Harry Bramer and Wyoming import Nobe Cervantes.

The greatest fighter from Colorado would come from Alamosa, however — and that man wouldn't become so much a threat to New Mexico as the biggest draw they had ever seen.

The Alamosa Flash

> An effort is being made to sign up the "Mexican Kid," who is said to be fast and clever. Several poor bouts had almost killed interest of boxing fans ... but Eddie Mack revived that interest with his fast, clean fighting. When he fights again, he will be sure of a capacity house.
> — Santa Fe New Mexican, 1922[20]

> Eddie isn't only a slam-bang performer, he's a clever boxer with a haymaker, or two of 'em — one in each mitt.
> — Santa Fe New Mexican, 1922[21]

For boxing, the greatest thing about the '20s was Eddie Mack.

For boxers, the worst thing about the decade was Eddie Mack.

Under the decade of Mack, boxing not only survived but flourished, allowing dozens of other locals more opportunities to fight than they would've otherwise had. On the other hand, if you were a featherweight or — later — a lightweight, you couldn't possibly compete, or beat, Mack, though it did not stop several from trying. Mack transcended the hometown hero — and in two states.

Before there was the great Eddie Mack, there was Pedro Christostomo Quintana. Mr. and Mrs. Efren Quintana preferred that their son go to school to be an attorney. Pedro agreed. Seeing no reason why he couldn't do both, the young high school student came up with an alias and proceeded to become one of the best mitt slingers — quite possibly *the* best — New Mexico has ever produced.

Though born in the small town of Pojoaque, 15 miles north of Santa Fe, on Nov. 2, 1906, Pedro grew up in Alamosa, Colorado, just a couple of miles from Manassa, home to the great Jack Dempsey. It was while attending Alamosa High School that Quintana slipped away to Denver at the start of 1922 to enter an amateur boxing tournament at the Denver Athletic Club. So that his parents wouldn't find out, Pedro assumed the alias of "Eddie Mack."

Pedro wasn't the first Eddie Mack — and he wouldn't be the last. In boxing alone, there were, or would be, nearly three dozen Eddie Macks. There was a Connecticut flyweight named Eddie Mack as far back as the 1890s; an Eddie Mack out of Denver in the '10s; a Stamford, Conn., fighter in the '20s who later promoted; even a heavyweight Eddie Mack from Pennsylvania in the 1980s. None of these Macks, however, would parallel the success of the "Alamosa Flash."

As a gangly, 15-year-old bantamweight fighting for the M & O Cigar Boxing Club, Mack was a stand-out in the tourney, earning praise as a "crack entry" and described as a "first-class little ring general — cool, fast and with a stiff punch."[22] Mack beat his first three opponents but, unable to keep his weight down to the 116-pound limit, was disqualified at the finals.

Mack did what everyone did back then — he turned pro. Four weeks after the tournament, on Feb. 21, 1922, the 15-year-old high school student trekked north to Fort Collins to fight a six-rounder with Abe Tobin, a ham-and-egg veteran who'd been fighting off and on for ten years. In round five, Tobin succumbed to youth and Mack had his first pro win.

During the next four months, mainly in Creede and Denver, Mack breezed his way through the competition, his only speed bumps being the Newly brothers, "Kid" and "Young." Though Mack knocked both of them out, the hard-hitting Newlys each scored a knockdown.

After 11 fights — all wins, eight by knockout — Mack was looking to expand his horizons and return to New Mexico, where he still had relatives. Eddie used his brother's connections.

Bernie Quintana would also earn a reputation with his fists, fighting under the marquee of his brother as "Bernie Mack," but it was as a top-notch baseball player that he was best known. During 1922, Quintana was a leading batsman for the Albuquerque Grays — a team managed by Daniel C. Ortiz, who was also the leading boxing promoter in Santa Fe.

Putting Bernie's brother Eddie on his July 12, 1922, show, headlining Mike Baca and Trinidad's Frank Herrera at the Rialto Theater, was the best favor he ever did. Actually, it wasn't much of a favor but more of a sink-or-swim six-rounder against Albuquerque knockout artist "One Round" Martinez. Undefeated since 1920, One Round lasted but two against Mack, who fought "coolly as a veteran of a hundred battles, pecking ... with his left and ducking the Duke City boy's haymakers. With the ease of a born athlete, Eddie shot his left across before the first was more than a minute old and 'One Round' dropped to the floor with a thud."[23] Martinez survived the first, only to go down two more times before being counted out.

The 15-year-old kid was such a hit, they brought him back in October to face Demon Rivera, the Santa Fe veteran with over 100 fights, in what would be Mack's first 12-rounder. In 1922, Rivera was the most experienced veteran in the state, having fought through the Midwest and Colorado, and in frequent 20-rounders, when Mack had never been past five. Furthermore, Rivera had only been stopped once — his pro debut in 1913. Needless to say, Rivera was a heavy favorite to cop the Southwest bantamweight title at stake. When Mack showed up at public workouts, before crowds of 200 at a time, the odds were temporarily reversed, until Rivera showed up, his cauliflower ears and flattened beezer convincing fight bugs that the kid had little chance against the rugged veteran.

The war and slugging that ensued in the 11 rounds it lasted made Mack-Rivera the fight of the year in Santa Fe. After two even rounds, "Mack took the lead and from then on was credited with every heat. Demon was plainly outclassed, but didn't flinch, didn't foul and kept doggedly boring in, trying to score with one of his haymakers until, completely exhausted, he couldn't stand on his feet any longer. At the finish a vigorous shove would topple him over." Rivera's experience, blocking and ducking made a difficult target, but by the tenth Mack was getting to him. Despite four earlier knockdowns, Rivera had hitherto scorned the ref's counts, prompting Eddie to look over at his brother Bernie as if to say, "This is the toughest bird I've ever met."

In the 11th, however, Demon weakened and Mack sent him through the ropes with a right to the jaw. Rivera was dazed, but refused to quit. "Mack helped him through the ropes and stood with one arm around his shoulders in a faked clinch until he recovered somewhat. Still, Demon refused to quit and Mack, as if reluctant to hit him again, shoved him over. This time, when the referee began to count, the sponge flew into the ring and the fight was over."[24]

Santa Fe had a new draw and the Southwestern sky was the limit for securing Mack's next opponent. At bantamweight to feather, there were many to pick from. While promoter Ortiz looked around for the next challenge, Mack returned to high school in Alamosa, finding time to defeat another respected veteran in Colorado, Sidney "Kid" Belt.

By the time Mack was able to return to Santa Fe, Ortiz had lined up Nick Mortio, from the border. Having KO'd "One Round" and the Demon, Mack was expected to win, but Mortio's speed and experience — 50 bouts and wins over Jose Rivers — had the sold-out crowd of 1,000 expecting a close fight on the night of Feb. 23, 1923.

It was one flash against the other — the "Alamosa Flash" vs. the "San Marcial Flash" — but after just two rounds and change, Mortio was looking more like a "Flash" in the pan. "Only for a brief two minutes in the first round did Mortio show any flashiness — then [he was] chiefly on the defensive.... Dancing about the ring and dodging as though worked by a string, Mortio was grinning broadly with confidence; while a look of seriousness began to settle on Mack's fighting mug. Then, like a bolt out of a clear sky, the fight was as good as finished." A big right from Mack dropped Mortio, "as though hit by a brick" and he "made a perfect landing on the back of his koko."[25]

It was the first of 13 knockdowns. Mortio would go down once in the first, six times in the second and six times in the third before his seconds sailed in the towel — and the "San Marcial Flash" would hold the record for the number of knockdowns endured in a single fight well into the '30s.

Mack returned to Colorado to finish his junior year of high school, promising to return during a break in March. Back home, he kept busy with local fights throughout southern Colorado, beating Belt again, among others, but he was ready to resume bigger opponents and bigger paydays.

Now Albuquerque wanted in on the action. Promoters Dan Padilla and Capt. John F. Harn, who were competing with each other, could offer Mack a fatter purse in the bigger city.

A tougher chin was demanded for the high school prodigy, now 16 and a full-fledged featherweight. The man to beat was Jose Rivers of El Paso, the Southwest featherweight champion. Though the "logical contender" for Rivers' laurels, Mack "politely" declined, citing the importance of keeping his grades up in high school. No one was too sure how to react — a prizefighter had never declined a fight before based on *studying*. On the other hand, what 16-year-old kid had ever mowed through his first 19 opponents — grown men and veterans — the way Mack had? "Does Mack fear Rivers?" became the question, from El Paso to Denver. Has "Mack learned Jose packs dynamite in both fins as well as being a fast boxer?"[26]

There were other issues at stake. A purse of $160 had been offered Mack, but he stood to make more than that if the gate amounted to the expected $1,500 — probably *much* more than that. There was also the rumor that, having inked a deal with Santa Fe promoter

Ortiz, Mack had no intention of coming to Albuquerque. Whatever the case, Mack was panned by the fans, who painted him green *and* yellow. Mack merely shrugged, stayed in school and fought locally in Colorado.

At first, promoter Capt. Harn, Padilla's crosstown competitor, took a stand about Mack fighting in Albuquerque. Sure, Mack was just the man to give the scene its much-needed shot in the arm, but it was Rivers or nobody, Harn said, and for good reason. The city boxing scene had redemption on its mind, having just survived the Sam Langford fiasco. Instead of touting Mack, Harn sent for Rivers to fight someone else in Albuquerque. With Mack dodging Rivers, it made the El Pasoan a much more popular fighter when he fought at the Armory, on April 23, 1923. Defending his Southwestern title, he destroyed over-matched Pete McCarthy, of St. Louis, in three rounds — and that only made the fans want a Mack showdown even more.

Meanwhile, Mack was talking with Ortiz about coming back to Santa Fe, which brought even more criticism from the Duke City. Rivers called him a coward, but said he would fight him in Albuquerque or El Paso, where there was more money to be made, but never in Santa Fe. Mack was loyal, though, and had worked out a quasi managerial deal with Ortiz. Ortiz, however, saw value in expanding, and worked out his own deal with Padilla; the two agreed to co-promote Mack's debut in the Duke City.

Suddenly, writers in Albuquerque started to backtrack and apologize for calling Mack yellow. He was no coward, they wrote, just a "clean young man who sticks to his word"[27] with a fine sense of business.

The Mack-Rivers showdown was set for Memorial Day, May 30, at the Barelas Baseball Park, 15 rounds for Rivers' Southwest featherweight title, and it looked to be the biggest battle New Mexico had staged since Johnson-Flynn. After Mack sprained his ankle in a high school baseball game, the fight was moved to the Armory, on June 19. While other names clamored to fight the winner — Pete Loya, Dick Griffin, and Kid Pacheco yelling the loudest — over 1,000 tickets were pre-sold before the fight was cancelled again. This time, it was Rivers, with an ulcerated tooth. "The cost and trouble of three things are underestimated," wrote the *Journal*. "Sending a boy to college, overhauling an auto and getting Rivers and Mack together in the ring."[28]

While Albuquerque didn't get *the* fight, they got *a* fight with Mack, when Padilla and Ortiz got together to book the youngster at the Armory for mid- or late July. While Mack relocated to Santa Fe to train, negotiations with Rivers were concluded — then nixed yet again. Rivers was unable to quit his daytime job driving an ice wagon, to train for Mack. Promoters, fans and Mack, alike, threw up their hands. Midwesterner Al Dale was chosen to fight Mack.

Crowds of 350 showed up to watch the boy wonder spar against the likes of Dynamite Tommy, Young Pancho Villa and Kid Anaya, while scribes pondered Eddie's chances of exceeding the accomplishments of Benny Chavez. "He is New Mexico's best bid for honors in the featherweight division since the original Benny Chavez mounted to within reaching distance of the pinnacle of that class," wrote the *Journal*. "Those who have seen Mack in action predict a great future for him, while some even say he has a great chance to go even further than Chavez did."[29]

On July 20, youth won out over experience and the ham-and-egger from Kansas City was down twice before being counted out in the sixth round.

"Who's next for Mack?" became the most talked about sports topic in Albuquerque and Santa Fe. No longer trying to make the impossible Rivers fight, Ortiz lined up all comers. Mack floored former foe Kid Newly eight times before knocking him out cold in the third at Santa Fe, on Aug. 14. It took several minutes to revive Newly and "Mack appeared worried and slapped Newly on the back in relief when he opened his eyes."[30]

When the fans demanded someone tougher, Joe "Awful" Coffee was brought down from Colorado, to face Mack on Aug. 22 in Albuquerque. Born Joseph Rutkofsky in Minsk, Russia, the Pueblo pug, who'd started fighting in his early teens around 1917, was given his nickname by a Denver sportswriter for reasons no one knew. Though Mack towered over the 5'1" Puebloan, the stocky Coffee, "muscular as the village smithy,"[31] was unbeaten in two years.

Coffee fought Mack the only way he knew how: close the gap and hammer away. Mack indulged Coffee the slugfest but the ref wasn't willing to let slide the several low blows leveled by the shorter man and "Awful" was DQ'd in the fifth. Citing injustice, Coffee demanded a rematch and got one for Labor Day, also in Albuquerque. The gate had been large enough and the fight pleasing enough to warrant the next fight. This time, the fight went the distance, Mack battering and chopping his way to a win, though he was unable to put the rugged Coffee down more than once. In the end, "Awful" Coffee took an awful beating but couldn't be spilled.

By now, New Mexicans were calling for Rivers again, but by the time he was able to commit to a fight, Mack was back in school, juggling studies and training, and refusing to drop out or take time off studying for the sake of the sweet science. Now a senior, Mack wrote Ortiz, saying he could afford the time off in December for a Rivers showdown, but he would not commit to a Thanksgiving fight due to high school football where he was — what else? — the quarterback and team captain.

In the fall and early winter, fights in New Mexico went on without Mack. In his absence, the scene still had momentum, for the first time in years. Using Mack as the carrot, Rivers came back to headline an Albuquerque show in November, knocking out Cleveland's Battling Richie. Mack challenged the winner and Rivers accepted.

This time, it was on — Ortiz and Padilla lined up a card for the Christmas season. The exact date, promised promoter Ortiz, would be soon announced, when Mack could figure out time away from school. Doubling as a sports scribe for the *New Mexican*, Ortiz explained:

> Many people think all Mack has to do to fight Rivers is to board the train in the morning in Alamosa, make connections in Antonito, and then here, and get in Albuquerque early in the evening, exchange blows with Mr. Rivers, ride back to Santa Fe, take the D & R. G. W., get into Alamosa and go to school the next day.... Mr. Mack when he meets the famous Mr. Rivers will have to do some training, and that isn't easy when you are in your senior year in school, as Mack is, with all his mind in trigonometry, chemistry, Latin, French, Spanish, etc., and with his little spare time employed in being captain and helping coach his high school football team which is making a good record.[32]

The fight was lined up for the Armory for Dec. 27, 1923, and it was the most anticipated New Mexican fight since the Benny Chavez–Battling Chico rematch in 1913, with fans more evenly divided on the outcome. If it went the distance, Mack was expected to win, with his science and footwork. If the fight ended early, it would be because of Rivers' slugging and boring-in style. At age 17 and with just 22 bouts, Mack was the much less experienced; Rivers was four years older and had nearly five times the fights. But Mack had beaten solid veterans before and the fight was even money — unless you were betting on yet another postponement or cancellation. Fans and scribes were amazed when the fight went on as planned.

Padilla and Ortiz expected the biggest house Albuquerque had ever seen and the best fight seen in New Mexico in 1923 — they got both. The Armory packed in 3,250 people who came to watch a war, and they got one.

After an first even round, Mack staggered Rivers in the second and battered his nose in the third. The El Pasoan came back in the fourth and fifth, going to Mack's body, edging those frames. In the sixth, the fight was in Mack's pocket. Circling Rivers, who stood in the center of the ring, Mack poured "an incessant volume of jabs and pokes to the El Pasoan's face," until Rivers' nose "looked like a piece of hamburger."[33]

Rivers was groggy in the sixth and punished in the seventh. "Mack was smiling, Joe was serious and bloody,"[34] wrote the *Journal*'s scribe. Despite the awful punishment, Rivers landed his best punch in the ninth — a right that rocked Mack back. Mack returned fire, trying to land a knockout punch on the practically helpless Rivers, who would not give in.

"Jose Rivers did not quit," noted the *Journal*. "He sat in his corner totally blind after taking a terrific beating in the tenth. His second had to throw the towel in, although Jose wanted to fight anyway."[35] Rivers' left eye was closed, his right was a bloody mess — and Mack was without a scratch; his "hair was hardly mussed up."[36]

The Southwest had a new featherweight champion and the era of Eddie Mack — and New Mexico's second Golden Age of boxing — had officially begun.

14. The House That Mack Built, 1925–1928

Another championship flower is growing in the fistic gardens in San Luis Valley, birthplace of Jack Dempsey, king of the heavies. This flower happens to be a featherweight and is known to the ring as Eddie Mack. He is a youngster, still going to high school, and his real name, Pete Quintana, indicates he is either Spanish or Mexican.
— *Associated Press*, 1924[1]

No doubt about it, Albuquerque's Dan Padilla and Santa Fe's Daniel Ortiz were the main boxing players in the '20s. Securely latched on to Eddie Mack, they were assured that fans would pack the Armory, Rialto or Elks'—wherever Mack was headlining. If they had chosen to duke it out for bragging rights to New Mexico's latest and greatest, it's not likely they would have succeeded, either.

They were not strangers to one another. Both had origins in baseball: Ortiz had skippered the Santa Fe Grays and Padilla piloted the Albuquerque Browns and the Albuquerque Grays. Padilla had actually managed the Albuquerque team in the days when Bill Pettus had been hopping back and forth between the two sports, back in 1911. In 1920, Padilla staged an exhibition with Benny Cordova before a game with the Grays and Gibson Miners. One year later, he became Albuquerque's primary promoter, through 1924.

Ortiz, the man who really discovered Mack, promoted from 1922 through the end of decade, in both Santa Fe, his hometown, and Albuquerque. After the sport came close to tanking, Ortiz was credited with saving it; there was even talk of making him the official promoter in Albuquerque and Santa Fe, denying others who sought licenses.

There *were* others, however.

After World War I, local posts of the American Legion became major backers of fights. The Legion, formed in 1919 by World War I veterans, immediately began hosting shows around the state — including Albuquerque, Clayton, Fort Bayard, Gallup, Roswell and Silver City — and they would continue to do so through the late 1950s. Sometimes the Legion teamed up with local promoters or organizations, but approximately 250 cards, 150 of them between 1919 and 1932, would be conducted under the Legion banner.

The Veterans of Foreign Wars was another staunch supporter of boxing, beginning in the early '20s. For years, the VFW and American Legion put on shows as the Fort Bayard Athletic Association, right about the time Columbus and Deming pulled the plug on prizefighting. In 1922, the VFW tried to jump start the Albuquerque scene, to no avail. There were also numerous posts of the Moose Lodge, Knights of Columbus, Elks Lodge and the New Mexico National Guard staging shows through the '20s and beyond.

Shortly after Ortiz and Padilla paved the way for a scene by introducing Mack, George

Ringling got in on the action. Ringling owned a cigar store in downtown Albuquerque but it was his "powerful lungs and silver tone"[2] voice as the de facto ring announcer that originally had everyone's attention. Ringling's "Let it go!" was an early frontrunner for Michael Buffer's "Let's get ready to Rumble!" at least in the Duke City. Ringling promoted with the Legion 1925–1926, worked solo 1927–1928, then came back with the Legion in the early '30s.

When the Albuquerque Boxing Commission called for a get-tough policy on promoters and fights, Capt. John F. Harn of the National Guard was elected to "control the destinies of the local fight world."[3] What he couldn't control was Mack, so his reign was brief and limited to 1923.

Ortiz and Padilla kept a tight rein on the big fights, but as Mack got too big for New Mexico and started fighting out of town, other promoters moved in. Johnny Giannini threw shows in Albuquerque during 1927, until he was accused of fight fixing in 1929.

Twenty-three-year-old Louie "Red" Valencia began his 45-year career in 1926. He stayed away from Albuquerque, throwing shows in Bernalillo until 1928 when Giannini fell from grace. Valencia wasn't limited to promoting but also managed fighters, worked corners and served as an official.

Outside of the two core fight centers, the Kitchen's Opera House in Gallup had a healthy scene in the early '20s, under Tom Danforth and the Gallup Athletic Club. Later, Guido Zecca and the American Legion would become the driving force, from the late '20s through the '30s. In Raton, the Shuler Auditorium was the home for boxing, under promoters Case and J. W. Eldredge.

Columbus and Fort Bayard continued their combination soldier and pro cards in the early '20s but as camps were broken down and fighters discharged, the scene dwindled away. Cloudcroft, however, had a streak of fights between 1922 and 1924, limiting the action to three-round soldier bouts throwing leather in the Red Cross tent for meager purses and the glory of calling themselves camp champs.

As soldier boxing disappeared, small-town prizefighting reappeared, from San Marcial to Las Vegas to Clayton. Almost always, a scene was built around a name. San Marcial had Nick Mortio, who headlined a dozen shows between '24 and '26. At Gallup it was all about Jack Myrick and the Insurrecto Kid, though promoters occasionally imported a regional star like Jose Rivers, Young Benny Chavez or Winslow's Young Garduno. Jimmy Thais was the top local draw for a time, and several amateur bouts were staged with youngsters who would define western New Mexico in the next decade. Madrid held fights to benefit their baseball team; Clovis geared up in 1928 for what would be a long run of shows through the '30s; and Roswell, recovering from the death of Johnny Connolly, would return to action in the mid '20s, though they struggled to find another star like the one they'd had.

The next decade would be all about the smaller towns and their hometown heroes. However, this decade, for the most part, belonged to Eddie Mack.

Student of the Game

> *Eddie Mack is New Mexico's leading contender for featherweight honors — as well as being the most managed boxer in the game according to rumor, report and claim, but one of the least managed according to his own statements.*
>
> — *Albuquerque Morning Journal,* 1923[4]

To the rest of the country, being a so-called "Southwest champion" meant very little in the scheme of things. For those in New Mexico, Colorado, El Paso and parts of Arizona, it meant someone from the desert or the Rocky Mountains had a chance to fight the big boys of either coast.

Benny Chavez had come close, a decade past. Eddie Mack was a sure thing as a coming champ.

Mack was but 17 years old, and it was a bit premature for scribes to start talking about the big leaguers. Just days after dethroning Rivers for Southwestern featherweight honors, Mack was being mentioned in the same sentence as Johnny Dundee. The chance of landing a lucky one against such a star, wrote the *Journal*, "would well be worth taking a good beating for."[5] No one reminded the nameless scribe that it was *that* sort of logic that sent an ill-prepared Benny Chavez in against world champion Johnny Kilbane in 1914.

What saved the senior of Alamosa High School was that *Eddie Mack* was primarily managing Eddie Mack, and it was books before bouts for the aspiring prizefighter.

Mack went back to Alamosa and was busy with mid-year exams until February 1924, while Ortiz cooked up a long list of credible opponents.

All the while in high school and, later, college, Eddie Mack became not only the first New Mexican to fight a current world champion, but the first to beat one.

Life without Mack went on between Albuquerque and Santa Fe. Mike Baca and Henry Pacheco graced the Capital City's ring while Mike Vasquez of El Paso came to Albuquerque to fight former Mack foe Kid Belt. Before the fight, everyone was screaming for Mack-Vasquez. After the fight, a slow but sure win for Vasquez, it was a different story, never mind "Big Chief's" big talk about going "fifteen rounds or forty"[6] with Mack.

The fans wanted Harry Bramer, of Denver, to fight Mack, but the strongest candidate Ortiz would, or could, secure was Wildcat Monte. The Amarillo fighter would go on to become one of the busiest fighters of all time, entering the ring over 300 times between 1923 and 1937. In 1924 alone, he would tally up 38 fights, and, in subsequent years, come close to that. When he fought Mack, "The Golden Sandstorm" was young, reportedly undefeated (he had a few losses no one in the press knew about) and was equal to Mack in height, reach and, almost, age, being one year older.

The two were booked for the Rialto Theater in Santa Fe for Feb. 12, 1924. Monte arrived four days early to spar with locals Demon Rivera, Kid Pacheco and Freddie Martinez, convincing crowds of 200 that his style would give Mack fits. The demand for Mack had grown so much that tickets were double the usual: $2 for the floor, $2.50 ringside. Seven hundred filled the seats and aisles beyond capacity, until they "could not have squeezed in another with a shoe horn."[7]

It wasn't even close. Monte "proved a flash in the pan and just for a few seconds in the opening frame" did he give "Eddie a run for the mazuma."[8] Then Mack went to work, dropping the Wildcat once in the first, twice in the second and five times in the third before the sponge went tumbling into the ring.

At ringside, a challenge was read by Bramer, who'd decisioned Joe "Awful" Coffee (that night in Colorado), Don "Terror" Long, Frankie Monroe, Jose Rivers and Mike Vasquez. Ortiz wanted Bramer next, but weight disagreements pushed the fight back until June. In the meantime, Joe "The Wop" Kelly of Pueblo was lined up for Mar. 4, again in Santa Fe.

Kelly danced around the ring "smiling like a tooth-paste 'ad'" and staying out of Mack's reach until the sixth when Eddie judged "him ripe for picking," flooring him four times before giving him "a one-way ticket to the Land of Wynken, Blynken & Nod."[9]

After a tune-up in his hometown of Alamosa — a first for Mack — in which he KO'd George Henderson in one, Bramer was secured for Santa Fe on June 12.

Bramer went far enough back to have lost in 1916 to New Mexico's *first* candidate for a world champion, Benny Chavez. With close to 200 fights and a solid veteran for nine years, Bramer was dangerous, but not unbeatable. Any real threat Bramer posed for Mack had been dismissed when Vasquez had put Bramer on the canvas twice en route to a clear-cut decision in March. Sure, the balding 25-year-old had faced two world champs — Pete Herman and Joe Lynch — but he'd been knocked out plenty of times. Then again, Mack *was* only 17, with but 25 bouts. And Bramer *was* displaying an eerie confidence, even offering up his purse to charity if he lost. He called Mack a "scaredy-cat," and bragged that he would not only be the kid's master, but would "drop Mack for the ten-count as sure as water rolls off a duck's back."[10] According to Bramer, Mack's stellar rise was too good to be true. The smack talk had such an impact on the pre-fight hype in Santa Fe that promoter Ortiz moved it from the Crystal Theatre's maximum capacity of 700 to the Armory's 1,100, where a special four-foot platform was built to elevate the ring — a first for the Capital City.

Breaking records for a Santa Fe attendance, it was standing room only for the sold-out crowd that shelled out $1.25 for the cheap seats upstairs, $2.25 for main and $3 for a ringside view — and there probably wasn't a single soul in the house who wasn't shocked, other than Bramer.

And maybe Benny Chavez, who was sitting at ringside that night. Almost an exact decade earlier, a veteran named Battling Chico had wandered into town, gotten his goat and scored the biggest upset of the decade in New Mexico. You can bet Benny knew just what Mack was going through when the older veteran methodically took the kid apart, taking Eddie's jabs and straight rights, then "retaliating with ripping lefts and rights to the short ribs"[11] at range.

Though he was able to score a flash knockdown in the third, Mack was increasingly outgeneraled through the fight. At the end of round five, Eddie's older brother Bernie offered the wrong advice: "Hey! you're giving the guy too much respect! Snap that jab and move! When he drops his left, put him on his butt!"[12]

As round six opened, Mack went after Bramer, who stood his ground, center-ring, exchanging heavily. The crowd was on its feet, roaring for Mack to turn the fight around. Eddie tried to reverse the momentum, but couldn't. With less than 60 seconds on the clock, Mack landed a bone-crushing hook to Bramer's temple but the veteran not only took it, but returned a "terrific right to the solar plexus"[13] that had Mack out on his feet when the bell rang.

Bernie leapt through the ropes, assisting his brother to the stool. Eddie's legs wobbled like Jell-O and he never would've made it back to his corner without help. "It's over," he mumbled. Bernie put his ear closer to Eddie's swollen lips to hear what he was whispering: "I've had it. That's it." Bernie couldn't believe it. "What are you saying? You've never quit anything in your life!"[14] Eddie said nothing. His face hurt too much to try and talk. He slouched on his stool, a beaten man. The next day's write-up would say he threw in the towel himself.

With the city in shock, Mack had lost his first fight, and the Southwest featherweight title, to a better man — and he would be the first one to say it. "The defeat will do me good," he told the *Journal*, offering no excuses for the loss. "I'll just have to work harder from now on."[15] Which is exactly what he did.

Mack did not leap right back into a rematch with Bramer but returned to Colorado for his next two bouts. While playing basketball for Alamosa High, Mack defeated Kid Belt again, in nearby Pagosa Springs, then took on Coffee a third time, this time in Denver, on July 21.

Mack returned to Albuquerque on Aug. 18, hoping to fight Vasquez, who'd just returned from a successful campaign in Mexico. When Vasquez got sick, they had to settle for Young Billy Papke, a veteran from Sacramento, California, who'd been campaigning in Colorado. Now coached by Tony Boggie, Johnny Kilbane's former trainer, Mack blew through Papke who, up to the sixth round, took what Eddie had to offer quite serenely, "smiling most of the time and chewing gum placidly." But in the seventh, Papke "walked to his corner, holding his stomach and refusing to continue the fight."[16]

It was enough to convince New Mexico that Mack was back. Avoiding bigger fights, Mack kept busy with three straight knockouts, needing seven to take care of Kid Sullivan in Durango, on Sept. 12, three to stop Tinnie Minnick in Santa Fe, three days later, and two to floor Billie Fisher in Walsenburg, on Nov. 27.

While New Mexico waited for the Mack-Bramer rematch, Rivers came up from El Paso in September to defeat Mack's conqueror with a disqualification win that nearly sparked a riot at Santa Fe's Rialto. In the Rivers-Bramer rematch, held in Albuquerque a month later, a 12-round draw was the verdict. The public didn't want a third — they wanted Mack back in the ring with Bramer, so much so that the Albuquerque Boxing Commission decided they'd deny Eddie a license to fight in their city, unless it was against Bramer ... though they would settle for Don "Terror" Long or Vasquez.

Mack promised an aggressive campaign for 1925, but that included the books as well as boxing. After pressure by the press, Mack relented, taking the "Long" shot, but further rankling the Albuquerque crowd by doing so in Denver, and only in a three-rounder, with the winner going on to fight Bramer, location to be determined. With his studies, it was all he had time for, he said.

Long, who'd long been accusing the 18-year-old of ducking him, was not happy settling for a three-rounder. Long, too, was a schoolboy and, while attending Denver University as a dental student, had been able to beat Bramer in two out of three fights.

In what was really an appetizer of a fight, Mack proved too clever, at least in a three-rounder, and got the unanimous nod. After a tune-up in Walsenburg, three weeks later, knocking out poor overmatched Kid Sullivan a second time, Mack declared he was ready to face the man who'd beaten him the year before.

Both New Mexico and Denver promoters were miffed that Mack chose his hometown of Alamosa for the site of the rematch. By now, Mack was no longer obligated to Santa Fe's Ortiz — and, after two fights in Denver, was building up a following there. Bramer wasn't stupid: He agreed to fight Mack in his backyard, but if the fight went the distance, and both men were on their feet, it would be ruled a draw.

Which is exactly what happened on Feb. 19, 1925, before a capacity crowd at the Alamosa Elks' Hall. The first few rounds were even, but from the fourth on, "Mack kept gaining with each round, and when the bout ended Bramer was all in but his shoe strings ... it was Mack all the way. He gave Bramer a neat trimming."[17]

Despite the draw, Mack was back atop the featherweight heap again and New Mexico promoters were thrilled because not only had the rematch, at least on paper, settled nothing, but a third fight was quickly lined up for Albuquerque.

It was another capacity crowd that crammed the venue on Mar. 5, 1925, to watch an honest-to-goodness grudge match. Neither fighter had been satisfied with the draw in Alamosa. Mack said he'd had the best of the contest, while Bramer begged to differ. The third fight, both vowed, would determine the best featherweight in the Southwest.

There was little doubt who the slightly better boxer was, the night Mack evened the score with Denver's "sly old fox." But it was far from satisfactory to the fans and scribes, who deemed the fight "nip and tuck" and its outcome "queer business."[18]

Mack was off to a rotten start in the first when he injured his right hand. Unable to load up on punches, he boxed and moved. In the fourth round, the fight was stopped when Mack claimed he'd received a low blow. Referee Johnny Flaska, who did not see a foul, referred the matter to the physician, who said if he'd been fouled, it was not "seriously enough to detect it." Mack was given 20 minutes to recover and the fight continued. "After coming out the second time, Mack played more of a long range game and had better success with it, finding Bramer frequently with a jab that made points but did little damage." Then, in the ninth round, Bramer landed a stray shot that had the referee disqualifying him for the low blow.[19]

There would be two more Mack-Bramer bouts to settle the grudge.

Game of the Student

Mack is now recognized as a top-notcher in the pugilistic world and he is closer to the world's champion than any other New Mexico boy since the days of the Original Benny Chavez and the whole west is pulling for him to reach that coveted goal.
— *Santa Fe New Mexican,* 1925[20]

It might've been good P.R. for boxing to have a bookworm as its biggest box-office draw, but fight fans throughout New Mexico breathed a sigh of relief on the morning of June 14, 1925, when the *Albuquerque Morning Journal* ran the headline "EDDIE MACK TO DEVOTE ENTIRE TIME TO BOXING"[21] in its sports section.

The West's most promising fighter had graduated from Alamosa High School, with honors too, all while compiling a boxing record of 35-1-1, with 25 KOs.

The offers poured in. Would Mack come to Chicago? Would he go to Mexico City to fight Jose Rivers? How about headlining Denver's Stockyard Stadium? Newcomers to the Southwest, Sammy Sandow and "Fighting" Nobe Cervantes, were calling him out — how about facing *them*?

Mack's first fight as a high school graduate was against Cervantes, on a card that landed in Santa Fe on June 25, 1925.

Fighting since 1921 up and down the Pacific Coast and in the Southwest, Cervantes (a.k.a. Nobe Ayala) was neither a tune-up nor an aged veteran on his last leg. The youngster was coming off an upset knockout over top contender Lou Paluso in Salt Lake City. Though losing the rematch with Paluso, Cervantes also had wins over Jack Doyle and Abe Mishkind — he was a "real human fighting machine," a "great crowd pleaser" and "made of pig-iron."[22]

More worrisome than the trunk-full of news clippings he showed the boys at the *Santa Fe New Mexican* were his claims that although Mack "is a great little fellow ... awkward and clever,"[23] this "high voltage clouter" would "make the Alamosa boy wish he were back in the high school taking his final 'exams or doing something easy." "Just watch me get Eddie's goat," he said.[24]

Fighting for his old honors, the Southwest featherweight championship, Mack weighed in at a lean 123 while Cervantes came in seven pounds heavier.

"The Terrible Mexican" lived up to his reputation and boasts — but Mack had reached a new level. "Can Eddie take it?" had been the question on everyone's minds. "He answered last night to the satisfaction of every man and woman in that frenzied crowd," ran the local report.

Weathering a near knockout in the third round, Mack showed his stuff by coming back to outbox the "tough hombre," who, bleeding and drained, was nearly stopped in the final round. Mack "put up his greatest fight and gained more glory" with a wide margin decision win than "if he had disposed of Nobe in a round."[25]

The fight was so rough on Mack that he backed out of fighting the winner of the Rivers-Sandow fight in El Paso on June 29 (in which Sandow KO'd Rivers) — but *not* rough enough for him to back out of a fourth fight with Harry Bramer, on July 4 in Durango.

Fighting with the aches and pains of his war with Cervantes, in an outdoor arena during a downpour of rain before 3,000 soggy spectators, Mack was "master of the situation" in all but one round and gave Bramer "a neat trimming" for his one and only newspaper decision.[26]

There was no longer a question who the top man in the Southwest was.

No longer restrained by high school studies, football or basketball, Mack branched out into new territory, accepting an offer to fight tough Pete Loya at the Bullring in Juarez. Loya had drawn with Long and had beaten both Pal Moore and Vasquez, but was considered in the same league as Mack. Entering the ring wearing a big red football sweater with the Alamosa "A" embroidered on it, Mack sought to outbox the "windmill style of boxing" presented by Loya. That worked until "Loya upset Mack's air of confidence," sending over a right cross that floored Mack for a flash knockdown. For the most part, putting aside his superior skills, Mack slugged it out with Loya in a fight most saw him winning, only for the referee to rule it a draw.[27]

"I'll fight anywhere in the United States, but no more fights in Juarez for me," said Mack. "I beat Loya all right, but I guess it's a good thing I didn't get the decision as I believe the crowd would have beaten up both the referee and me if he'd given me the fight. I was lucky to get out of there with my life."[28]

Mack fought one more time during the summer, knocking out Missouri journeyman Carl Stewart in the fifth on a card held on Aug. 21 in Santa Fe. Then he broke the news that although he was not giving up his dreams of becoming a world champion, he was enrolling at Regis College the following month and that studies would, once again, become his priority.

Fight promoters who wanted to book Mack, fight fans who wanted to see the Southwestern champ become a bona fide contender, and other fighters who demanded a shot at the youngster, were frustrated and irked. But Mack continued to fight through the rest of

1925, racking up six more wins, against lesser opposition, as he turned 19, closing the year with a record of 42-1-2, 28 KOs.

In Walsenburg on Sept. 10, Mack cruised his way to a decision over long-time veteran "Dixie Cyclone" Jackie Sanders, of South Carolina. Oct. 2 saw Mack back in Denver, in his fifth and final bout with Bramer, a third-round decision. One month later, Mack rematched Sanders, this time flooring him several times en route to a 12-round decision. On Dec. 11, it was East Coast veteran Eddie Ford who lost, by a second-round TKO, in Denver. Four days later, on Dec. 15, Mack returned to Santa Fe where former Juarez foe Pete Loya was waiting for him. This time, there was no controversial draw but a definitive "whupping," Mack taking him out with a shot to the breadbasket in just six minutes of action. Mack finished the year a week before Christmas, with another three-rounder in Denver, this time beating local veteran Joe "King" Leopold.

As 1926 opened up, there were more names than ever dickering for a shot at Mack. Albuquerque was practically boycotting Mack until he faced Vasquez, and top local scribe Dan Burrows was writing, "Until the Vasquez-Mack fight is off their minds, Duke City devotees of the padded knuckle game will be restless and a bit skeptical about any other card that may be offered them."[29]

In February, Mack faced Frankie Garcia, a borderline contender from Memphis who'd beaten Bramer three years prior, though he would, later that year, defeat soon-to-be light-weight champion Sammy Mandell. Garcia was seen as Mack's toughest opponent to date.

Mack and Garcia fought the three-round game first, in Denver, resulting in a close but well-earned decision. Then they were booked for Santa Fe, 11 days later, where Mack "met with a check, though not a reverse, in his rapid climb up the ladder of fistic fame." Both fighters kept a fast pace, from start to finish, and twice they had to be separated by the ref at the bell. "Not a single knock-down was scored, not a drop of gore was shed, but the crowd was in a frenzy of excitement from beginning to end, yelling, standing on seats and throwing hats into the air. There wasn't a second's cessation of action." Garcia showed an uncanny ability to dodge Mack's hypnotizing left jabs and Mack showed the ring generalship to avoid Garcia's powerhouse right. The draw decision rendered by referee S. J. Mollands was a popular one.[30]

Mack and Garcia would meet again, two years later. In the meantime, Mack went north,

Not many knew who Pedro Christostomo Quintana was, but say "Eddie Mack" and fight folks, coast to coast, would say he was the "Uncrowned Junior Lightweight World Champion" between 1929 and 1930. Mack defeated reigning champ Tod Morgan twice, and drew once, during Morgan's reign, in non-title bouts.

back to Regis, while Garcia trekked south to fight Sandow, who proved the superior fighter, further strengthening the demand for Mack-Sandow.

The college freshman stayed close to home for most of the year, however, keeping busy in Denver in limited four-rounders, with two jaunts to Santa Fe where his old friend Ortiz took care of him in 12-rounders. Between March and May, Mack's only setback was a four-round draw with veteran Jack Kane, whom he'd previously beaten. Without a single knock-out, Mack also outpointed Roy Sutherland, Bud Hamilton and rising young scrapper Young King Tut (his first loss). Fighting increasingly heavier and with less and less time to train, Mack postponed bigger fights, feeling fatigued from pre-law studies.

In his first 12-rounder in months, Mack was rematched in Santa Fe with Don Long on May 17, 1926. Though he outpointed Long, who followed him around "like a bull terrier," Mack showed only flashes of his slam-bang style and was exhausted at the end, "on the verge of collapse."[31] After the fight, Mack said he would not fight again until school was out — and he stuck to his plan, disappearing into his textbooks during the summer.

The Southwest had never seen anything like it. Here was a kid who had all the potential in the world to make it to the top, and he was battling tests and studies instead of big name fighters. Despite the occasional newsprint backslap, the scribes started to voice their demand for Mack to quit playing around and fight someone — Vasquez, Sandow, anyone. Prizefighting was not a part-time occupation.

Mack met the demand halfway on Labor Day, returning to Santa Fe to face Nobe Cervantes again, and it was case in point for the scribes, when all Mack could pull off was a 12-round draw against the man he'd once boxed circles around.

Still, Mack didn't cave, but returned to Regis, though he fought a series of four-rounders through October, all in Denver, adding three wins and a draw to finish the year with a record of 51-1-5, 28 KOs and one newspaper decision, just before turning 20.

The draw was a notable one, being against high-ranking featherweight contender Red Chapman. In fact, Chapman had been dubbed the unofficial world champion, having beaten Johnny Dundee, and with the official champ, Kid Kaplan, refusing to fight him before retiring. Local press exaggerated the significance of the fight, naming Mack as the second New Mexican to face a world champ, which wasn't entirely true — but drawing with a highly-ranked (and future world title challenger), even in a four-rounder, was nothing to sneeze at.

Mack took off the winter, ignoring the promoters' pleas, then returned to the ring for a tune-up four-rounder in Denver, on Feb. 4. Four days later, he was back at Santa Fe's Rialto, in a 12-rounder, the place packed to its rafters. The opponent wasn't what the fans wanted, but if the same Mack who'd struggled with Long and Cervantes in his last local bouts showed up, a prizefighter preoccupied with the "pupilism" instead of pugilism, Billy Mansweller, of Fort Collins, Colorado, was going to give him hell.

"The fight was a give-and-take affair, with Mansweller doing most of the taking," however, and was "Eddie's all the way." Mansweller "fell victim to Mack's scientific fists," crumpling to the canvas after a right and left in the eighth round. Mansweller's handlers had to work a full minute, after lugging him back to his corner, before they could revive their fighter.[32]

Then it was back to Regis.

In between studies, Mack kept sharp in four- and six-rounders on local shows in Denver, staying unbeaten against overmatched fighters and racking up six wins, three by knock-out, before stepping up to a ten-rounder with Chicago's Don Davis, on May 12, 1927, only to come away with a disappointing draw. Though not at his best, he was still able to get the attention of another brainy boxer, none other than World Heavyweight Champion Gene Tunney, who invited him to join his stable on the East Coast. Mack passed, wanting to finish up at Regis before committing himself 100 percent to the sport.

Mack, now more of a lightweight than a featherweight, upped his training enough to clearly outbox Cervantes on May 19 in Pueblo, then took two months off before returning to Santa Fe for the first time in a year for a stay-busy fight with old-timer Charles "Dutch" Crozier on July 22 — the same Crozier who, in an era past, had fought Johnny Connolly. Recently, Crozier had proved wily enough to go the distance with Jose Rivers in Gallup. Against Mack, he lasted but two rounds.

Enough was enough, was the general sentiment amid promoters in three cities. Management at the Stockyards Stadium in Denver tempted Mack with a non-title fight against World Lightweight Champion Sammy Mandell in August, but after that fell through, Mack turned to New Mexico: Ortiz in Santa Fe and George Ringling in Albuquerque, who were both holding him to a statement telegrammed back in January: "There's nothing I'd like better than to fight Mike Vasquez."[33]

The fight was on for August, though Ringling and Ortiz had to duke it out for promotional rights. Delays and postponements moved what the papers were calling an "eternal jinx" from Sept. 2 to Sept. 16, and from Albuquerque to Santa Fe, where a construction crew revamped the Rialto, adding 200 spots.

"I'll show you why Eddie Mack has been dodging me for the last four years,"[34] Vasquez boasted.

Given Mack's preoccupation with college, the fight was thought to be even money. Both fighters had met and beaten the same guys — and Vasquez had twice as many fights on his resume as Mack. As expected, the fight was a classic war.

"There are 1,000 sore throats in Santa Fe today," wrote the *New Mexican*, after a back-and-forth battle that put Mack and Vasquez through "the killing pace of 12 heats.... When Eddie landed his best haymakers he failed to change even Mike's set expression. The El Pasoan made good his rep for toughness. A punch in the *frijole* basket that sunk up to the elbow meant no more to him than a plate of enchiladas assimilated through the regular route." The crowd was split — as was the referee, who ruled it a draw that "seemed to strike the right spot in the house."[35]

A rematch wasn't in the cards, but it wasn't for lack of trying. It just never happened.

Mack spent the remainder of the year back home, where things went from bad to worse. Against tough Tony Caponi at the Stockyards Stadium in Denver, on Oct. 7, Mack was on his way to putting on a clinic, giving "Tony a boxing lesson he will not soon forget," when a shot went low, with less than a minute left on the clock in a 10-rounder. Caponi played up the dramatics, saying he was not able to continue, and the referee gave him the fight.

While Ringling worked a miracle to set up a big Mack vs. Sandow fight at the Armory for late October, Mack was derailed with an inflammation of the kidneys. Sandow settled for Juarez slugger Jose "Bulldog" Gonzalez and, before 2,800 fans at the Armory, they fought a draw the newspapers had Sandow winning.

Though sick, Mack was well enough to rematch Caponi at home, on Nov. 3 in Alamosa, easily outboxing him through ten rounds to finish off his year. But after the fight, Mack was nearly knocked out — for good — with a kidney infection. Mack would be out of the ring until April 1928, as many doubted he would be the same fighter.

King of the Rockies

Mack can come back after a bad start and give his opponent plenty of trouble. Mack showed that he has the real goods and is of big league caliber and with a little more experience will probably get a shot at the world' championship. He is still young and has a lot of time.

— *Santa Fe New Mexican*, 1928[36]

After the longest layoff of his career and having defeated a life-threatening illness, Mack was ready to battle his way back to the top of the Southwest heap. Little did he know that 1928 would be his toughest year yet — though one that would inadvertently pave the way to a world champion.

In Mack's absence, and with his fight against the "Regis College Flash" cancelled in the fall of 1927, Sammy Sandow solidified his claim to the Southwest lightweight — *and* junior lightweight — championships. The Cincinnati battler, fighting since 1915, had faced five world champions and, after relocating to the border in 1926, had beaten everyone from Mike Vasquez to Frankie Garcia and Jose Rivers. The man Sandow really wanted was Mack. "Sandow has been after Eddie's scalp for years and he'd rather fight Eddie Mack than eat,"[37] penned the *New Mexican*.

Again, given Mack's lack of commitment while attending college, Sandow was deemed the favorite by the dopesters. More experienced and having faced tougher fighters, Sandow, unlike Mack, had not been sidelined by a recent illness — or by schoolwork.

Santa Fe and Daniel Ortiz landed the fight, leaving Albuquerque sports fans scratching their heads why a natural like Mack-Sandow wouldn't headline a city that could hold a bigger crowd and subsequent larger purse. But Mack was loyal to Ortiz, though he did throw the Duke City a bone four days before the big fight when he shook off the rust, knocking out set-up opponent Mexican Marcel Zavala in one round, on a card promoted by newcomer Louie "Red" Valencia at the Crystal Theater.

Four nights later, Sandow fought for the last time.

Mack made the long-awaited showdown, which Santa Feans were convinced would be battle of the year, look like a sparring session. Winning all but one round, Mack piled up the points "with his short jabs that shook Sandow up considerably." In the only round Mack lost, Sandow scored a knockdown with "a smart crack to the left ribs."[38] In all other frames, "Eddie boxed and danced around the game old veteran from Texas, punching hard when he wanted to punch and drawing his punches when he felt like it." As the fight came to a close, "Sammy tired fast, but hung on gamely until the final bell."[39]

Mack was off to a great start in 1928, but things would get rough.

Ten days after schooling Sandow, Mack picked up a win in Pueblo against his old foe, Joe Coffee. Then he was matched up against a big-leaguer in Denver on May 15.

Despite 75 pro fights and his reputation as the untouchable "King of the Rockies," Mack was a 2–1 underdog against Sid Terris, New York City's "Ghetto Ghost," all for good reason. Terris was a ring genius with unparalleled speed and considered the top lightweight in the world, after Champion Sammy Mandell and No. 1 Contender Jimmy McLarnin. The year before, Terris had fought a draw with Mandell but, in his last fight, held at Madison Square Garden, he'd been knocked out in one round by McLarnin. Mack felt the time was ripe to fight him — at least that was the advice of Philadelphia's Max "Boo Boo" Hoff, who took on the role of Mack's manager for the fight.

The time wasn't right, however. Terris had Mack on the verge of a knockout in the first. Groggy, Mack survived, giving as good as he got in the second and third. But in the fourth, Terris took over, outclassing Mack down the stretch for a clear-cut decision.

It was a loss, but not a bad one, according to Denver scribes who reasoned that if Mack hadn't gotten careless in the first, he might've earned a draw, which would naturally place the local hopeful as a bona fide contender. Plus, there was also the difference in weight to consider; Terris was a full-fledged lightweight while Mack was barely above feather. On the bright side, Mack had earned his biggest purse to date—$1,743 (Terris got $1,900)—and had fought before his biggest crowd yet, with 4,500 packing the Stockyards.

Hoff, who would later be exposed as a mobster and bootlegger, tried to convince Mack to come east with him, but he declined, shaking hands with local entrepreneur Joe Roth instead. Roth would remain with Mack for the duration of his career.

"Got to keep you busy," was Roth's advice, who worked out a return to Santa Fe with R. W. Morton—Ortiz's replacement as the city's chief promoter—on June 19. "They got this newcomer who wants a shot at you. They call him the 'Human Windmill,' but he's more like the 'Human Wind*bag*.'"[40]

The newcomer was Eddie Murdock and no one knew too much about the Oklahoman pug who'd been calling for Mack's scalp since the moment he arrived in New Mexico. Little did anyone know what a big part of the local scene this *other* Eddie would become for the next 12 years, or that the original Eddie would have the surprise of his life on June 19, 1928.

Debuting in 1925, Murdock fought throughout Oklahoma and Texas an estimated 50 times, many of them losses, before making his debut in New Mexico on May 8, as a relative unknown. After an unrevealing, three-round, no-contest bout with Manuel Pacheco, he was thrown to the wolves against Mike Vasquez, 10 days later. Before Murdock came along, fans had been clamoring once again for Mack-Vasquez II, but after Murdock outgeneraled the rugged border battler, all anyone could talk about was Mack-Murdock. And that suited the Oklahoman Eddie just fine, for he'd come for Mack's head and his title.

Once again, the Rialto was standing-room-only on the night Eddie met Eddie in the ring—only the fight didn't go off as planned, either by result, or on time, at 9:30 P.M. Right before his expected walk to the ring, Murdock demanded to be paid up front—$500 in his estimation—or he'd refuse to fight. After a lengthy shouting match between promoter Morton and Murdock, which was eventually joined by referee Johnny Flaska, Santa Fe Mayor McConvery and Eddie Mack's cornermen, a near-bribe was shelled out to Murdock, who, 90 minutes later, walked out to the ring before a booing crowd of outraged fight fans. Forced to lighten his purse $100 to make the fight happen, Mack followed and, at 11 P.M., the fight was underway.

Mack, usually a slow starter, relied on a quick left jab to take the first two rounds. But as Murdock warmed up, Mack found out the hard way that he was "unable to solve the weird windmill fighting tactics of the blonde Oklahoma slugger and the latter soon had Mack groggy and bleeding from the eye."[41]

Some say Mack had lost a lot of nervous energy while waiting for, then negotiating with Murdock. Others cite the torn canvas as the spoiler for Mack, "a fighter who relies on keen footwork," but whatever the reason was that night, over a thousand stunned spectators sat watching Murdock sweep the last eight rounds, battering the local favorite with a barrage of body punches. Murdock's "ripping jolts to Eddie's kitchenette won him the edict. The Regis college boy was seen frequently hitching his black shorts higher and higher as jolting wallops plunged into him amidships.... Mack made a gallant attempt to off-set the Oklahoman's lead in the 12th, but his onslaught was futile; Murdock already had the bacon in the Frigidaire."[42]

Mack wanted a rematch — immediately — but it wouldn't happen until September. Mack had — what else? — school work waiting for him. The two would rematch in two months. With Mack's nose in his books, Murdock kept sharp, further convincing the fans that his win over Mack was in no way accidental.

On Aug. 2, Murdock headlined a Valencia card at the Armory in Albuquerque, where he fought a disappointing 12-round draw with Rivers. Though the *Journal* thought Murdock had won, the fans weren't sold on the Oklahoman just yet, calling the win over Mack a fluke. Less than three weeks later, Murdock returned to Santa Fe where an over-capacity crowd of 1,500, somehow cramming into the Rialto, watched him defend Mack's former title over Los Angeles veteran Frankie Monroe, who was one fight away from a title shot at World Junior Lightweight Champion Tod Morgan. It was no easy win for Murdock, who put on a "best ever" performance, showing "a far greater degree of aggressiveness and the fury of a Cro-Magnon stone-hatchet thrower." Murdock fought with a bleeding brow and was floored in the eighth, yet won on sheer aggression in a fight that saw referee Herb Davy forcibly separate the fighters after the final bell rang.[43]

New Mexico's newest darling further got Mack's goat when he purchased a pink Chrysler convertible on which was painted "Southwest Junior Lightweight Champion." "The Oklahoma windmill is proud of his crown," reported the *New Mexican*, and "doesn't want to go to the expense of having it removed."[44]

Mack kept a low profile over the summer, but showed up in Denver one week before his rematch with Murdock to decision lightly-regarded Eddie Anderson in a safe, slow and dull fight, while the other Eddie, just five days before the showdown, was in Juarez, defeating hometown favorite Rivers.

Finally landing a big Mack fight, promoter Ringling saw the biggest crowd of the year file through the turnstiles of the Armory on Sept. 18, 1928. Before 3,100 fans and with another big chunk of the area's 16,000 population listening in on KGGM radio, Mack took back his title.

It was more like the *old* Mack that showed up to win all but one round — the ninth — flooring the other Eddie in round eight. Showing a bit of staleness, and having made the mistake of fighting three times in nine days, Murdock had no answer for Mack's improved foot work and defense.

It was almost time to bid *adios*, Mack said afterward. The loss to Terris earlier in the year might have been a loss on paper, but it had paid off by getting the attention of East Coast promoters. Mack trekked east, but before he could net a single bout he had to make a U-turn back home for school and an ailing mother. After finishing out the year, he said, the East Coast would be a priority. In the meantime, Mack would stay busy, stay sharp.

Ringling re-booked him for Oct. 17 against a Los Angeles veteran who was coming home to fight for the first time in three years. Minus the "Young" portion of his moniker, Solomon "Benny" Chavez had returned, supposedly a new fighter. All the improvement in the world, however, was not likely to upset the natural skills possessed by Mack — or so they thought.

It was a fluke loss for Mack, but a loss, and a setback, nevertheless. After an even first round, Chavez stepped on the gas and was "carrying the fight to Mack, who was not behind in dealing blows, however." Mack threw a shot to the bread basket — he never meant for it to stray low. "Chavez was coming in fast, and met the blow before it had risen above the waistline. The blow doubled him up, but several minutes later, he was able to spring lightly from the ring." In the interim, the referee disqualified Mack, setting off a chorus of boos.[45]

It was Mack's third loss that year, and fifth overall. Determined to put it, and Albuquerque, at least for now, behind him, Mack finished the year with three more wins: a TKO over overmatched Al Corbett in Denver, on Oct. 26; a decision over overmatched Manuel Sena in Cheyenne, Wyoming, on Nov. 12; and, two days later, a significant win over highly-rated lightweight Mickey Cohen in Denver.

In New Mexico, the battles raged on, with Chavez, Murdock and Rivers all calling out Mack for rematches, but all of them were ignored. By December, Mack was targeting much bigger game — like Tod Morgan. Eddie Mack and the junior lightweight champion of the world were on a collision course one week into the new year.

15. The Uncrowned Champion, 1929–1930

It's my chance and I'm going to grab it.

— *Eddie Mack,* 1929[1]

Tod Morgan was one of the era's busiest fighters, even as a champion. The only problem was that he was notorious for keeping his world junior lightweight championship belt safely out of harm's way whenever he took a fight. The brains, many said, was manager Frank Churchill, a shrewd businessman who knew how to squeeze every possible nickel out of an ounce of risk.

Morgan, whose real name was Bert Pilkington, came out of Seattle and had amassed 70 bouts before getting a shot at a world championship—a relatively new one, at that.

The golden era of boxing can be defined by distinctive world champions in eight original weight divisions, unlike the modern era that sees a diluted version of the sport with 17 weight classes and four brands of sanctioning bodies doling out titles like vending machines. Nowadays, more than 50 fighters walk around claiming to be a world champion.

It was all about the original eight divisions back in the day, though, in the 1920s, as the 130-pound division reigned for a time. Created in 1920 for top-notch fighters trapped between featherweight and lightweight—126 to 135 pounds—the division was seen as a somewhat synthetic one, the farther one got from New York, where it was created. That is, until Morgan, the biggest name in the Northwest, made a name for himself fighting, *occasionally* defending his belt, on the West Coast.

Hall-of-Famer Johnny Dundee, who'd once fought in Albuquerque, back in 1913, was the first 130-pound champion, hanging onto the championship from 1921 to 1924, except for a brief time when it changed hands with Jack Bernstein in 1923. Steve "Kid" Sullivan picked up the belt in 1924 and, in his third attempt, in 1925, Mike Ballerino captured the title with a 10th-round TKO at the Olympic Auditorium in Los Angeles. Morgan snagged it later in the year.

Before losing the title, years later, Morgan would defend it nearly a dozen times. But against Mack, on Jan. 8, 1929, the belt was not at stake. Mack was little more than an in-between fight for a busy champion who'd just defended his belt eight days before in Milwaukee, against contender Joey Sangor. Mack was a keep-busy sparring session and a fat purse on Morgan's way to the West Coast, where he saw the majority of action. On ten days' notice, Mack was offered the fight of his life, to step into the ring with a world champion for a non-title, ten-round bout.

Mack was on the cusp of big things. With a record of 70-5-7, 35 KOs and the one

Because he'd been limited to the Southwest—mainly Colorado and New Mexico—reigning World Junior Lightweight Champion Tod Morgan (left) may have underestimated Eddie Mack (right) when Mack defeated him in Denver in January 1929. Morgan secured a draw in the rematch, but lost again, later in the year, to Mack.

newspaper win, he was no longer the new kid on the block. But Rocky Mountain or Southwestern champs, 100 bouts or 10, were regularly dismissed as greenhorns unable to cope with the science behind veterans on either coast. It was time for the 23-year-old collegian to see just how far he could get in the prize ring.

The plan was to graduate from Regis College in June, with a pre-law degree in philosophy, then dedicate himself fully to boxing—music to the ears of New Mexico and Colorado railbirds—before returning to school and a career in law. But Morgan, ten days or not, was a fight he could not refuse. A win for Mack would mean a "certainty that Mack would be in position to break into the big league after camping on the outskirts for many years."[2]

Behind their local hero, Denver geared up for the largest crowd in years, hoping for 7,000 at the City Auditorium, while Mack went into intense training, what little preparation he could do in ten days, that is, sparring with Chuck Heffner and drawing crowds of 400 at the Windsor Gymnasium.

Denver braced—maybe even hoped—for a villain, but two hours after stepping off the train, on Jan. 4, 1929, Morgan, "clean-cut and fine appearing ... with a smile which [was] characteristic of the little mite of fighting flesh," was all too likeable. *And* full of respect for Mack. "Unless rumors are wrong, I'll have to go at a fast clip to defeat Mack," he told the press. "I've never seen your Denver boy box, and I don't know what I'm up against. But I have heard a great many complementary [*sic*] remarks and I certainly am not going to take any unnecessary chances."[3]

The press did not have much go to on with Morgan. Local know-it-all Abe Pollock had only seen Morgan fight once, and he'd been losing against Stanislaus Loayza before winning on a DQ. He had a right hand, though, and could throw a mean uppercut. Based on his record, his status as champion and, after watching him in the gym with Johnny McCoy, Morgan was made a heavy four-to-one favorite, though Mack's physical advantages could not be ignored. The local kid had reach, height and solid jab in his corner. The champ was expected to bore his way in, land the harder punches and go to the body.

Mack was given a better chance to score the upset than Benny Chavez had 15 years before in the same city, against Johnny Kilbane. "I feel fine and I think I have a good chance to win,"[4] Mack stated two days before the fight.

On the night before the big fight, both Mack and Morgan took light jogs. Mack "applied himself to his books, displaying a calm hardly expected on the eve of a fight which means so much to him."[5] Morgan, on the other hand, attended a basketball game. Mack might've been calm, but local fans and scribes were concerned. The *Rocky Mountain News'* Curley Grieve wrote:

> Mack is undecided as to his future. He doesn't know whether to continue with his fighting or to drop it altogether and devote time to his studies and other enterprises he has in mind. Eddie, of course, is no dumbbell. He is an excellent student. And he keeps going at the rate of 16 hours every day. For instance, besides training and fighting and studying and attending classes, he instructs in Spanish; teaches the youthful members of the Young America League how to use jab and hook and does considerable writing on the side. Outside of that, Eddie leads a calm and peaceful life. Beneath his gruff and hardy ways, Eddie has a rather sensitive disposition. He has no profound affection for the fight game other than as a means of paying his school bills and socking away a nice bank account. For that reason he would desert the game in a minute providing it held no future for him. To Mack then, the Morgan fight may be a turning point to his career. In the event he should get knocked out, in all probability he would gracefully retire from the scene with the words "goodbye and God bless you."

As it turned out, Grieve had little reason to worry.[6]

Mack vs. Morgan I

> *If Denver wants a world champion prize fighter, he is within its grasp.*
> — *Rocky Mountain News,* 1929[7]

"MACK SOCKS OUT VICTORY OVER CHAMPION MORGAN."[8]

Those who weren't numbered among the 5,000 who paid between $1 and $3 to attend Denver's City Auditorium on the night of Jan. 8, 1929, awoke to that headline the morning after Mack became a local superstar.

After years of flirting with the big leagues, of juggling studies and sweet science, New Mexico-born, Colorado-groomed Eddie Mack became an overnight contender, by scoring one of the biggest victories in either state's boxing history.

The fight was technical at first, "a series of brilliant exchanges" that "increased in frequency and viciousness as the bout progressed. Mack was like a thorobred [*sic*] going to the post for the first time. He was a bit unsteady. But Morgan, used to crowds and used to fighting clever, darting opponents, was as much at home as if he were seated before a fireplace eating peanuts."[9]

As the fight wore on, Mack forgot about the stakes, and the crowd, and while weathering the occasional overhand right or left uppercut that landed by the champ, "the fleet form of Mack was here and there, with a left snapping to Morgan's mouth and a right chop finding its mark on the champion's jaw."[10]

Clearly the master at infighting, Morgan chased, pressing Mack and tattooing his body, but, more often than not, Mack was not there but jabbing and dancing away, landing rights and left hooks upstairs. By the seventh, it was Mack "who was fighting as a champion ... clipping the champ with a hard right and beating Morgan to the punch."[11] The champ had the edge in the eight, a draw, at best, in the ninth, but Mack closed the show and finished strong, convincing the two judges and referee to award him the unanimous decision.

Grieve of the *News* and Poss Parsons, of the *Denver Post*, agreed with the verdict, as did Mack and his pilot, Joe Roth, but both Morgan and his manager Churchill hollered hometown.

"What does a fighter have to do to win in Denver?" Morgan cried after the fight. "I chased Mack 40 miles and if I ever won a fight in my life I won last night." Churchill elaborated, calling it a "raw decision" and claiming Mack should've been disqualified for low blows in the middle rounds — blows that might've been borderline, but when the fight was stopped by the referee, Morgan had dismissed the alleged fouls.[12]

Both Churchill and Morgan would later admit they'd lost. In the meantime, the press hammered the pair, the *News* printing that a lesson in "serenity in face of defeat"[58] was due, and that if they really wanted to make things right, rematch Mack — this time for the title.

Mack, $1,700 richer in his biggest payday, had deserved the win *and* a shot at the title.

Overnight Contender

> *What's a title these days?*
>
> — *Eddie Mack, 1929*[14]

Better than being called an overnight contender was the title of "uncrowned champion."

Both parties wanted a rematch, but Denver wanted a title fight out of it. "Sure, we can do that," Churchill bargained. "But you boys are gonna have to cough up a guarantee of 25,000 bones."

Guaranteeing Morgan $25,000 when the original bout hadn't exceeded $15,000 was not a sound proposition for promoters of the Stockyards. And even then, Mack would have to fight for virtually nothing. After the respective camps went back and forth, a rematch was set for April 24, 1929, at the Stockyards — but, once again, Morgan would leave his belt at home.

Keeping up his studies at Regis, Mack did not let rust gather in the three months between, but rather stepped into the ring six days after beating the world champion. Big risks were out, though, to the dismay of Southwestern top-notchers who'd chased Mack through the decade. The kid was beyond the cactus league now.

In Cheyenne, Wyoming, Mack beat up on Mexican Manuel Sena. On Feb. 1, it was Tommy McCoy's turn to take the toll, at Fort Collins. One week later, Bobby Bridges gazed up at the lights of the Rialto in Santa Fe while a record-breaking 1,500 stood on chairs and crammed the aisles to watch a sixth-round count. "When do we begin to fight?"[15] the Indianapolis opponent queried as his seconds tried to revive him.

Morgan, meanwhile, had been able to get another interested party to cough up the guarantee for a shot at his title. Just three weeks before the Mack rematch, Morgan defended against Santiago Zorrilla at the Olympic Auditorium, winning by a decision.

While studying for finals, Mack stayed at home in March and April to prepare for Morgan. Without the title at stake, fighters could weigh in over the 130-pound limit. Mack had been 134½ in the first fight while Morgan had been 129. In the second, Mack expected to be 132, and Morgan the same, though, just say the word, Roth was saying, put that title at stake and his fighter would have little difficulty making 130.

The press was mainly concerned that Mack would overtrain, or that studying for finals would have a negative effect on giving his all. Mack dismissed the thought, carefully regulating gym and school work. He also shrugged off questions of motivation, in not getting a shot at Morgan's belt.

"What's a title these days?" Mack answered. "Take the welterweight championship of Joe Dundee. He wears it in a fashion, but nobody believes he's the best welter of the day. He can't flaunt his title at will; he must keep it safely locked up. And when Dundee enters the ring, he doesn't cause his opponents to cower in a corner. No, sir; they meet him halfway across the ring. And that's exactly the way I feel."[16]

Scribe Curley Grieve predicted a different Mack in the rematch, one who would not lack confidence and fight "like a young colt facing the starting line for the first race of his life,"[17] stating that the now-contender was at a crossroads. "Shall he make fighting his business or continue with his schooling and turn his energy into different channels?" Grieve pondered aloud. The rematch with Morgan would be the turning point, choosing between a career in law or "the more rugged pastime of scrambling ears,"[18] as well as resorting to reigning over the Rocky Mountains when he could be battling under the bright lights at the Olympic Auditorium or Madison Square Garden.

Odds were called even. More apt to talk about studies, Mack shrugged his shoulders when asked about the outcome. The champ was equally noncommittal, saying, "All in a day's work," and preferring to chat about his photography hobby. Joe Waterman, replacing Morgan's manager Frank Churchill, and Roth, Mack's pilot, were the only ones committing their boys to a win.[19]

By fight night, Morgan was talking about going for the knockout and his next handful of opponents. Mack kept quiet, preferring his gloves to do the talking at City Auditorium.

Mack vs. Morgan II

The topic of the hour around the corners, in the pool rooms and restaurants is Eddie Mack. Not particularly because Mack gained a draw decision with Tod Morgan, junior lightweight champion of the world, which at least proved he was equal if not superior to the champion. But rather because he changed his style to meet the popular fancy of the mob.... Mack has proved one of the cleverest men in the ring and as speedy as any that has been seen in this section in some time. But he did not show the aggression and savageness the mob likes in its heroes until Tuesday night. When Mack rushed from his corner in the fourth round of the fight I sat in blank amazement. And for a fraction of a minute so did the 3,000 spectators. They had not seen or expected such a Mack.

They were perturbed and startled. Can this be Eddie? They were saying to themselves.
But it was no one else. And almost in unison every spectator involuntarily burst forth
in a cheer that rocked the house.

— Rocky Mountain News, 1929[20]

Halfway into the ten-round rematch, it looked as if Eddie Mack was not only going to win, but also send Morgan to the canvas and the 3,000 roaring fans home early.

After weathering two tough opening rounds, Mack, "usually a calm, deliberate fighter ... cast aside his lamb's clothing last night and for the first time in his life became a veritable tornado," wrote Curley Grieve. Mack "battered and slashed, ripped and tore the champion from ring to post. He chased him as a tiger stalks his prey, and pounced upon him with all the savage fury of a wild animal."[21]

Bombarding the champion with a newfound fury, Mack showed his hunger — but he also was fighting a fight Morgan was good at. In the sixth, Morgan slugged back and laying into Mack's body, the hometown favorite went back to boxing on the outside. Round seven saw Mack meet Morgan in the center of the ring, where he pounded the champion's ribs and swiveled his head with rights to the chin. Morgan backed away, through the eighth, then came back at close quarters. The ninth was all Morgan, who hooked to Mack's chin and pounded his midsection. Mack clinched, then, in the final round, had the edge in a virtual slugfest in the pocket. Both were still landing when the bell clanged finality.

Both local papers thought Mack had edged the fight. The judges failed to agree, while the referee ruled it even, resulting in a split draw. Neither fighter bore the scars of the battle, nor did they voice a complaint. "Fine. Great," said Mack. "But they can't say 'home town decision' to *that*." Morgan was less intense. "Was it a good fight?" Morgan asked the press at ringside, who nodded their assent. Smiling, Morgan remarked, "I'm sure glad."[22]

The champion, however, landed his biggest blow *after* the fight, declaring that he would be defending the title Mack had been denied a shot at, on May 6 in Los Angeles, against contender Baby Sal Sorio.

West Coast Invasion, 1929

It is beginning to trickle into local experts' cocos that the Denver dynamiter, who hung it good and proper on Tod Morgan, is a scrapper that has brought a message to the aspiring bozos of his weight in Los Angeles. He has a paralyzing poke in each paw and has a neat little way of applying the grace stroke whenever Manager Joe Roth shoots the nod.

— Los Angeles Times, 1929[23]

Barring unforeseen losses, Joe Roth's plan was to keep his contender Mack busy while he finished up his degree at Regis College — then strike due west for Los Angeles where he could force Morgan to put up his title and where promoters had deep enough pockets to guarantee a title shot.

Mack graduated on May 25. A week before he finished with exams, Mack entered the ring in Denver to outbox top-rated Los Angeles veteran Frankie Garcia in a ten-rounder. Two days before graduation, he went south to Santa Fe to fight El Paso's Bobby Neal, who was sliced and diced in nine rounds before his corner saved him from further bloodshed.

With a mid–July departure date for Los Angeles, and a July 16 date already booked at

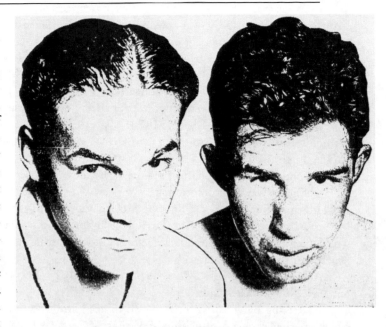

Eddie Mack (right) was the first New Mexican to stage a successful "West Coast Invasion." After beating world champ Tod Morgan in Denver, Mack headed west in order to secure a title shot with Morgan. Mack defeated several big names in Los Angeles, including one fight with Baby Sal Sorio (pictured left), but could not get his title fight.

the Olympic Auditorium, Mack returned to Santa Fe for an *adios* card on July 1. Garcia was the opponent again. The former contender had once defeated champs, and though out of Mack's league now, promoter Jimmy Dooley knew it mattered less about the opponent and more about fans getting a last-chance glimpse of the Southwestern star destined for greatness. It was for that reason that Dooley booked the outdoor venue of Sierra Vista Park. He expected a crowd of 5,000 but got only half of that — still breaking Santa Fe records by an additional 1,000 — for, on the day of the fight, it poured. Both the weather and the fight were disappointing, however. While the fight was a vicious one for nearly five rounds, Garcia was disqualified for a low blow.

Mack packed up and headed west, arriving in Los Angeles on July 6.

Despite telling the press that he was going to concentrate on boxing now, Mack was considering enrolling at Loyola University in Chicago for a degree in law. The next one, two or three fights would decide for him.

Between July and September, Mack fought four times — and for the first time in New Mexico history, a fighter justified the term "West Coast invasion."

Mack walked right into the top spot at the Olympic Auditorium to take on Baby Sal Sorio, who'd just lost to Tod Morgan at Wrigley Field, where the biggest fights in the area were held. Twelve thousand had shown up to watch the champ weather a third-round knockdown to decision Sorio down the stretch. Originally from San Bernadino, Baby Sal — Gaspar Soria at home — was strictly a West Coast fighter; he had been since 1925 and would be until 1935.

Mack trained at the Manhattan Gymnasium, all the while keeping an eye on Morgan, who kept busy at the Olympic Auditorium by taking on the fast-rising Goldie Hess in another over-the-weight bout. When Hess won, becoming, like Mack, another uncrowned champion, promoter Hayden "Wad" Wadhams of the Olympic immediately started talking about the winner of Mack-Sorio fighting Hess. If Mack won, fighting Hess would be a battle of uncrowned champs, with the winner the logical choice for a real title fight against Morgan.

Mack kept quiet, and focused, but Baby Sal, looking past the Rocky Mountain import, was already talking to the press about fighting Goldie. And the press was already talking about the slugfest the fans could expect when Sorio and Hess met in the ring.

Needless to say, no one was giving the youngster from Colorado and New Mexico a chance. Beat Baby Sal? He was considered one of the hardest hitters in the City of Angels and was, reportedly, knocking out one sparring partner a day. But then the reporters saw the new kid in the gym, and they started to think about their common opponents. Both Sorio and Mack had fought Morgan and Mickey Cohen. Mack had decisioned Cohen, while Sal had knocked him out in four. Against Morgan, both had fought draws with the champ in non-title affairs—though Mack had the one win, as well.

Joe Waterman, who'd been Morgan's late substitute manager in April when Frank Churchill hadn't been able to make it to Denver, wasn't all that convinced that it would be Baby Sal fighting Hess. He called Mack "one of the smartest fighters he ever saw pull on a glove,"[24] and admitted that he'd scored the recent draw with Morgan a shade in favor of Mack.

The press warmed up to Mack, as they would continue to do for as long as he fought in California. Not only would he appeal to the fast-growing Hispanic fan base in Los Angeles, but Mack was a well-spoken, intelligent fighter from a small town—22 miles from the world-famous home of legend Jack Dempsey—who'd fought his way through college at the expense of his pugilistic career.

And Mack could fight. *That*, he proved on July 16, 1929, when he not only beat Baby Sal Sorio, but knocked him out.

"Battering Baby Sal with a one-two to head and body through the first three rounds, Mack smashed the hard-punching Mexican to the canvas in the fourth, but the bell, sounding at the count of six, saved Sal," went the recap in the *Los Angeles Times*. "Mack's jarring right hook again found its target a few seconds after the fifth opened, and the San Bernardino boxer was counted out."[25]

Mack had arrived in Los Angeles.

Mack vs. Hess was supposed to be next but promoter Wadhams still figured Sorio-Hess would make a better fight, stylewise. Shelving the showdown he'd already bragged about to the press, Wadhams brought in slugger "Doc" Snell to fight Mack in two weeks. If Snell KO'd Mack, he could move on to Sorio-Hess.

Meanwhile, Roth was at work, pursuing the champion. He told the press that Mack would remain in Los Angeles long enough to get his well-earned shot at the champion. Churchill ignored Roth, however, telling the media that Morgan was recovering from broken ribs suffered in his fight with Hess.

Mack focused on Snell while the press promised the Southwesterner that he was in for an even harder time than they'd expected he'd have with Baby Sal. William McEachern, a former drug store clerk from Tacoma who fought as "Doc Snell," would be making a long-awaited return to Los Angeles, where he'd given the fans several bloody wars, including an upset of future Hall-of-Famer Jimmy McLarnin.

Never mind that Snell was a crowd-pleasing slugger who'd never been counted out, the wise ones made Mack the favorite. "Eddie is the lad that lullabied Baby Sal into peaceful slumbers at the Olympic several weeks ago and he confidently expects to croon the same number to Snell with a few variations, if necessary," the *Times* wrote.[26]

This time, the press got it right. On a card co-headlined by an exhibition with Max Schmeling, who would become world champion in 1930, and with Jack Dempsey sitting ringside, Mack scored his second straight knockout. "Snell won the opening frame by forcing the fighting," but in the next, "Mack did a bit of forcing on his own hook.... In the third round, the college boy from Denver beat down Snell's guard with a terrific body attack and then planted a stiff right to the chin to finish the fight. The bout ended after one minute and twenty-four seconds of the third round."[27]

The press, the fans and Wadhams were now talking Goldie Hess. But Roth and Mack wanted Morgan, and negotiations went back and forth until, finally, Roth offered up $40,000 for a fight at Wrigley Field. If Morgan won, he'd keep all of the gate receipts; if Mack won, the ex-champ would get a $40,000 guarantee. Churchill continued to stall, then finally agreed on one condition: Mack was to first fight Hess in September. The winner would get Morgan later that month, or in October.

Mack was torn. Considering law school at Loyola for the fall, Mack had hoped the summer would be all the time he needed to get an answer from Morgan. Weighing school and prizefighting, Mack figured he'd come too far to turn back now to pass on fighting for the world championship. The press loved him. In Los Angeles, "the little college dandy" was praised, for anyone coming "here literally unsung" to "knock off boys who have been local favorites in such convincing fashion as the Denverite in his two local starts is a hero."[28]

But it was his dual drive for a college degree and career outside the ring that had writers — not just sports writers — commending Mack. From L.A. to Syracuse, stories on Mack were published, and in much greater detail than the passing mentions given him in his two home states. "Giving and taking swats for money is only one of a number of things Eddie does," wrote Lee Shippey in the society column of the *Times*. "He is punching his way to higher education. He is perhaps the only pugilist in these parts who holds a college degree."[29]

Mack's degree in philosophy from Regis, his athletic coaching, diet instruction, fiction writing and plans for future coaching and a degree in law were noted. The *Syracuse Herald* took it a step farther, opening up a lengthy piece on Mack: "Many boxers are boys who threw aside education to scramble ears. But now comes a boxer of championship possibilities who casts overboard his fistic aspirations for an education.... This 22-year-old student boxer does not fall into that class known as 'palookas.' Eddie never has desired fame or fortune — in the prize ring. He wants to be an educated man and he is using his fighting ability only as a means to that end."[30]

When September rolled around, however, it wasn't the books that Mack was studying — it was one Goldie Hess, since Mack vs. Hess was turning out to be a hot box office ticket. Wadhams was already talking about a packed house of 10,000.

Despite Golden Goldie's winning streak, with wins over Morgan and West Coast topnotchers, Mack was a slight favorite. The 20-year-old Ocean Park veteran of 70 bouts was not concerned — he'd been on the short end of his last four bouts, but managed to pull off the "W." "Some call him lucky," wrote the *Times*. "Some call him plucky. But he wins just the same."[31]

Not this time, however. The standing-room-only Olympic Auditorium was beyond packed with 10,400 screaming fans who got to watch "two little bulldogs" in the fight of the year that ended with referee Billy Burke raising "the hands of the boy from Colorado."[32]

Winning eight of the ten rounds, Mack nearly came undone in the end. Outpointed by Mack's "stabbing left," Hess "kept surging to the attack, flinging punches with drunken abandon," hoping to find a chink in Mack's armor. Surviving a left hook to the chin that "would have floored him but for the protecting strands," Hess "charged in like a little tiger," trying for a desperate knockout in the final frames. But Mack had "piled up the points. He fought a game and heady fight and richly deserved the decision."[33]

Mack's reward *should* have been the title shot against Morgan, as all parties had agreed. Only, just days before the fight, Mack received a punch he didn't see coming, that stung him harder than any of the bombs thrown by Hess on Sept. 17: Morgan had accepted terms to fight high-ranking Benny Bass for a guaranteed $35,000 in Philadelphia by the end of the year.

What everyone had been warning Mack and Roth about was proving to be true. Morgan would *never* put his belt up against someone who'd beaten him in an over-the-weight bout, guarantee or no guarantee. Mack was crushed, but Roth had seen this coming. He couldn't wait for Morgan. Eddie had to go after bigger prey.

Mack would be going to Chicago, after all. But it wouldn't be books at Loyola that he'd be battling — it'd be a monster named Tony Canzoneri.

Mack vs. Canzoneri

> *The crowd was hoping that perhaps somewhere a mistake had been made; that the Denver boy would somehow get back in the fighting and win. As the account of the lucky blow that stopped the Denver lad was read, the crowd realized that Mack had been beaten by luck and not a better man, and cheered for the boy who was the king of the local squared ring.*
>
> — *Albuquerque Journal*, 1929[34]

Unable to secure a world title fight at 130 pounds, Eddie Mack moved up to lightweight and took on future Hall-of-Famer Tony Canzoneri in 1929. Despite Mack fighting on a twisted ankle, the fight was on equal terms until the fateful eighth round when Mack slipped and was hammered while going down, losing by TKO. Mack is pictured above with long-time manager Joe Roth (right).

If the junior lightweight championship of the world was going to be denied the uncrowned champion, Mack would set his sights on the *lightweight* championship.

In 1929, fighting World Lightweight Champion Sammy Mandell meant going through the No. 1 Contender, Chicago's Tony Canzoneri, whom Mack would fight just ten days after his war with Goldie Hess.

Just 21 with 74 bouts compiled while primarily campaigning on the East Coast since 1925, Canzoneri was destined for big things. In 1929, he'd already fought for the world bantamweight title twice — drawing, then losing a decision to champion Bud Taylor, in 1927, before moving up to featherweight to become its champion for a year. Then, skipping junior lightweight for 135, Canzoneri lost a split decision to champion Mandell the month before fighting Mack.

Having defeated legends and the best in the game, Mack was a tune-up on his journey to another title shot. Canzoneri, on the other hand, a 7-to-5 favorite, was Mack's ticket to Mandell — a champion known to take on all comers, *unlike* Morgan. Mack had nothing to lose, long shot or no long shot.

Fighting in front of what would be the second largest crowd of his career — 11,242 — at the Chicago Stadium, Mack was more than game. In fact, according to *Chicago Tribune* scribe Walter Eckersall, Mack "might have won the decision" — if he had not sprained his ankle in round one. And if "The Smiling Little New York Italian" had not finished him in the eighth.[35]

> The first round was about even. Both scored with straight lefts to the face and connected with right crosses and swings to the jaw. Fifteen seconds before the close of the round Eddie sprained his ankle coming out of a clinch. Canzoneri won the second round by a wide margin. Mack was in pain, but he fought back gamely while retreating. The third round was about even and Mack took the fourth by clever use of his left hand. The next three rounds were a standoff. At the start of the eighth round Canzoneri tore in. He finally connected with a left swing and Mack took a nine count. After getting to his feet he notified Referee Collins he was unable to continue.[36]

Eckersall and United Press International gave different endings. Eckersall had Mack informing referee Phil Collins that he was unable to continue while UPI called it a stoppage, Collins stopping the fight because Mack was groggy and in no state to continue. Official time was 1:22 of the eighth.

Mack's "bad luck" was a prevailing factor, however, from the sprained ankle in round one to the punch that first floored Eddie in the eighth: "Mack had at least an even break with the New Yorker when he went down, and Canzoneri can consider himself mighty lucky that he won. If ever a fighter went into a lucky punch, Mack did. Canzoneri started a left hook from the floor and Mack, in attempting to evade it, slipped slightly, but enough to throw him off balance. The punch landed flush on Eddie's jaw."[37]

In Albuquerque, the "lucky punch" was a prominent feature of the altered wire report. "Mack had been beaten by luck and not a better man," the *Journal* ran. Regardless, the home crowd "cheered for the boy who was the king of the local squared ring."[38]

Mack vs. Morgan III

> *Pedro Quintana — they call him Eddie Mack, for short — today stands out as a fighter who twice has defeated a champion, with no crown to show for his efforts.*
> — *Santa Fe New Mexican*, 1929[39]

> *His real name is Pedro Quintana, and his people came with Cortez in shining armor to the conquest. Afterwards the Spanish soldiers of his family tree came north on the long and dreadful expeditions over the dread Jornada del Muerto to Santa Fe and Taos with Onate and De Vargas. Eddie was born on the edge of a little Indian pueblo near Santa Fe. He whacks athletes in various points of their anatomy as a means of making a living, but his heart is out in the open country where the white light of the New Mexican sun shines down upon the serene adobes.*
> — *Los Angeles Times*, 1929[40]

In hindsight, targeting the lightweight champion of the world might have been a mistake, for Mack, who was weighing 132 in over-the-weight fights. It was back to the drawing board, once again targeting Tod Morgan, whose fight with Benny Bass had been delayed until the end of 1929.

In need of a pick-me-up win, Mack returned to Denver where he took on former threat Jose Rivers of El Paso in a ten-rounder. What was once the match-up of the year in the Southwest was now a tuner for Mack when, on Oct. 4, 1929, he landed "a picture-perfect right cross to the point of Rivers' jaw, forcing his old foe to execute a "backward dive parallel with the floor, his feet doubled up" before falling as "a crumpled mass upon the canvas."[41]

Mack might not have secured his rightful title shot, but whatever progress he'd made in Los Angeles, even his loss with Canzoneri, was plainly visible back home. Manager Roth was arranging Mack's return to the Olympic Auditorium to fight Bobby Fernandez when Mack's collarbone was injured while sparring. The setback also nixed a return match with Canzoneri at Madison Square Garden.

On a much-needed break, Mack spent time at home, then drove down to New Mexico to visit family and friends. Mack had gone from local hero to legend now. The *Albuquerque Journal* reported: "The fighter spent several hours Monday evening in Ringling's cigar store talking with Patsy Vigil, Johnny Flaska, George Ringling and other old friends, while dozens of youths tiptoed up to the outside of the little office, peered through with admiring glances and whispered, 'That's him.'"[42]

In early November, Wadhams wired Roth to fight the winner of Goldie Hess-Gaston Charles, but by the time he got there, he was offered up another chance at Tod Morgan.

Mack vs. Morgan III would, once again, be an over-the-weight, non-title affair, but the good news was that Morgan planned to fight Benny Bass in Philadelphia on Dec. 27 in what would be his final title defense — win, lose, or draw. The pressure was getting to Morgan, the writers theorized, and he would be moving up to lightweight to target Mandell. If the title went vacant, Mack had a good chance of getting his shot — and if it ended up in Bass' hands, Roth assured him that a trip to Philly could be arranged.

L.A. press cooked up the third fight as a grudge match, the champ seeking revenge for an earlier defeat with Mack, irked that he'd been denied a shot at the belt not once, not twice, but three times now. The press also wrote that Mack was wasting time, "but the fans are with him, this biggest find of the year in Los Angeles."[43]

Mack trained as if the title *did* depend on it, and came in so close to the junior lightweight limit that he was forced to drink water to come in *over*weight. Regardless, Mack was a favorite over Morgan.

On the night of Nov. 27, 1929, before 10,000 at the Olympic, Mack did it again. It wasn't the most exciting fight ever seen at the Olympic and the referee had to prompt the two to fight midway through it, but Mack tore into the champion in the second half. Bloodying Morgan's mouth and nose in the fifth, Mack hammered the champ "into complete submission in the dying moments of the tenth," on his way to a clear-cut decision.[44]

With his moral victory, Mack reinjured his collarbone. The primary damage occurred in the second round, but he was further injured when the ref had yanked it upward in token of victory when the scores were announced.

Mack took time off, finishing the year the same way he started it — as an uncrowned champion, a top contender, and not an inch closer to a title shot.

Before Morgan left for Philadelphia, Roth wrote Tom Donahue, president of the National Boxing Association, about Mack's claim to Morgan's crown, citing his wins over Morgan and his offer of a lucrative guarantee that was ignored in lieu of Bass' offer in Philadelphia. The NBA was slow in acting and, on Dec. 27, Morgan followed through with his plans to defend against Bass, gaining a $35,000 purse but losing his title in relatively quick fashion.

After nearly taking out Bass at the end of the first, Morgan was staggered with a left hook, then dropped for the count of nine with a right in the second. The champ staggered back up but Bass sent him down for the count — and for the title.

Mack Coast to Coast, 1930

Eddie Mack, Regis college boy, who made good in the mitt-flinging business, sets his famous one-two punch to real music. Eddie headlines the Olympic fistic program Tuesday when he collides with Maurice Holtzer, his sixth opponent in Los Angeles. The Frenchman claims that Eddie will be listening to the "birdies" sing instead of the cadence of his own one-two punch.

— Los Angeles Times, 1930[45]

One more year, then law school, was Mack's plan. If a title fight came, it came. If it didn't, Mack would become an attorney — well, he would become an attorney, regardless.

As the new decade opened, Mack was No. 3 at junior lightweight, with Al Singer and Sammy Fuller ahead of him under the new champ, Benny Bass. *The Ring* magazine had him at No. 2.

After six weeks spent between Alamosa and a family ranch in Espanola, his collarbone injury apparently healed, Mack returned to Los Angeles for a Feb. 4, 1930, bout with fellow contender Joey Sangor.

For local fans, it was a battle between the two biggest draws of 1929, with the winner to fight Cecil Payne. Sangor, who promised to take care of Mack with his potent left hook, had "retired" the year before, but stock market losses had destroyed his savings, forcing the old warhorse to return.

Right before Mack had beaten Morgan the first time, Sangor had fought for Morgan's bauble in his hometown of Milwaukee, losing a decision. The 50-bout, freckle-faced fighter first made an impact in 1928, when he became the first one to defeat Sammy Dorfman at Madison Square Garden. He'd also knocked out Baby Sal Sorio and Bud Taylor in '28, Santiago Zorilla in '29, and, like Mack, had lost to Canzoneri, also in '29.

The crowd expected a back-and-forth bloodbath, with Mack a winner by decision. Instead, Mack destroyed Sangor in five rounds in a one-sided fight. In the locker room after the fight, Mack would break down in tears for destroying Sangor the way he had. Sangor would fight one more time, then retire for good.

Returning to Albuquerque on Feb. 12, 1930, for the first time in three years, Mack beat up upstate New York ham-and-egger Johnny "Kid" Blair before 1,600 in a bout that the *Los Angeles Times* did not even bother to mention.

With a shot at lightweight champ Mandell the carrot, Mack, looking for his sixth straight win in Los Angeles, was pitted next against full-fledged French lightweight Maurice Holtzer, on Feb. 25. Unbeaten in four bouts on the West Coast, Holtzer's rushing style, crouch defense and deceptive hitting made an interesting match-up, but Mack was favored to win. That he did, but barely. Though Mack piled up the rounds, he tired in the late stanzas. Holtzer didn't. When Mack was announced the winner, he was booed for the first time at the Olympic.

Two weeks later, on March 11, promoter Wadhams sought to get Mack back in the good graces of the fans by rematching him with Goldie Hess at the Olympic. Hess had been moaning for a year for the return bout and, with both fighting as lightweights, he was confident he'd even the score. After Mack's poor showing against Holtzer, the fans were on Hess' side. The referee was on Mack's, however, and weathering a couple of near knockdowns when Hess connected with big left hooks, Mack outboxed the Ocean Park idol to net a clear-cut decision.

After fighting big name after big name, however, Mack was still no closer to getting a shot at a title, either 130 or 135. Roth reasoned they might have better luck on the other coast, so, with a series of fights in the Southwest, Mack worked his way to New York.

In Phoenix, on Mar. 14, Mack outclassed veteran lightweight Sailor Fay Kosky. Three days later, in Juarez, where Mack vowed never to fight again after his "hometown draw" of 1925 with Pete Loya, who, coincidentally, reffed this bout, he floored Los Angeles journeyman Joe Pimenthal four times before the fatal second-round count.

In April, Mack was back in Denver for two fights, the first of which was against Gaston Charles, the "Boy Bomber" of France, who was a human punching bag for the stars. When the *Rocky Mountain News* printed that Charles hadn't exactly "set the world on fire,"[46] they weren't kidding. For the past two years, he'd faced the best names in the sport — but had gone virtually winless. Against Mack, on April 3, he soaked up a pasting for ten rounds.

Then, two weeks later, unhappy with his controversial win earlier in the year, Mack rematched the Frenchman Holtzer. For the first time since initially fighting Morgan, the uncrowned champ was up against a name contender on home turf. It was a *bon voyage* card, for Roth planned to take Mack and Eddie Murdock — who'd joined his stable — on an eastern invasion. Before 3,500 at the Stockyards arena, Mack won a close but "rather uninteresting"[47] decision over Holtzer, who stayed in his crouch and bore in, but seldom opened up.

The Eddie Mack *adios* tour hit Santa Fe next, on May 6, where an overmatched Johnny Simpson was knocked out in three rounds before 1,800 at a greatly-expanded Rialto Theatre. With all three of Roth's boys on the card — Mack, Murdock and middleweight George Manley — it was billed as the "biggest boxing card" ever for Santa Fe. As star power went, maybe it rated highly, but with the less-than-stellar opposition and a whopping $2 price for general admission, the card failed to produce a masterpiece. The *New Mexican* wrote, "A race between an automobile and a plow horse isn't so interesting."[48]

On that sour note, Mack headed east with but half a plan. A rematch with Canzoneri fell through and Roth was talking to Chicago promoters about meeting the winner of the Sammy Mandell–Al Singer title fight, but, if it happened, it would not be until the fall, at earliest. In the interim, Mack had to impress East Coasters, all the while continuing to win against name fighters.

On June 23, Mack debuted in New York, knocking out Brooklyn trial horse Joey Abrams at Woodhaven's Dexter Park, before 4,000. Abrams was floored three times and had a badly cut ear when the ref stopped the bout in round ten. A month later, at Ebbets Field in Brooklyn, and fighting for the first time in years as a co-feature, Mack had to stay "busy throughout the entire fray with an endless bombardment of lefts and rights"[49] to outpoint late sub Ray Rivera in a ten-rounder.

Finally landing a name fighter on a major card, Mack signed to fight Sammy Dorfman on Aug. 7 at the Polo Grounds. The good news? Mack would get to fight before the biggest attendance of his career, at 38,360. The bad news was that Mack was just a ten-round undercard bout prior to the main event that saw Kid Berg defeat Kid Chocolate. Like Mack, Dorfman, a Jewish New York boxer, had been a leading contender at junior lightweight but never got a title shot; he'd also lost to Canzoneri. Against Mack, Dorfman was good enough to pull off a draw in a fight that barely received a mention.

Mack was disappointed but still determined. Not so, Roth, who was disgusted with the Big Apple. "You have be 'in' with the right crowd in New York or you can't get a fight," he said. "Then after you get a match, you must give this fellow 5 per cent, that one 10, and toss out a hundred here and fifty there for getting you the bout. When you're all through, you've lost money."[50]

It wasn't as if the fighters were any better, Roth complained, naming Morgan, Doc Snell, Hess, Wildcat Carter and, of course, Mack, better fighters than the so-called contenders in New York. And fight the big shots? They were more elusive than Morgan had been.

Speaking of Morgan, the dethroned champion was back home in Seattle fighting the six-round game popular there. When the new rankings came out for the lightweight division — Mack No. 3 behind Berg and Canzoneri — Morgan figured he could use Mack to maneuver a shot at the lightweight champion, now Al Singer, so he called on Mack to visit him on *his* turf, for once.

Mack accepted and the two fought for the fourth — and last — time, on Aug. 29, 1930, at Seattle's Ice Arena. "The fight wasn't a nice one," reported the *Seattle Times*. "The two lightweights snarled, heeled and sometimes even hit low, but they battled all the way." Morgan won the first four rounds, but Mack "came charging across the ring at him," in the fifth, scoring a knockdown. After six, the referee and two judges scored it for Morgan.[51]

Now that he had "failed" in Gotham and lost to Morgan, there was talk of Mack slipping. Albuquerque promoters offered him Benny Chavez, but Mack wasn't taking the bait, not for a light purse, anyway, even though Roth had lost all bargaining power after the loss to Morgan.

World Lightweight Champion Al Singer wasn't looking at Morgan, however. He was looking at the man who just lost to him — Mack. Scoring perhaps the only trump he'd ever pull on Morgan, Mack was the one who got the call from Singer.

It wouldn't be a title fight — what else was new in the world of Eddie Mack? — but it was going to have to do, as Mack set out for Chicago.

Mack vs. Singer

Mack is a boxer but he can hit hard enough to keep pace with the champion.
— Chicago Tribune, 1930[52]

The newly-crowned lightweight champion of the world, Abraham "Al" Singer, the "Battling Bronco of the Bronx," was a relative newcomer to the sport, having turned professional in 1927. In July, his meteoric rise had earned him a title shot against Sammy Mandell, whom he'd knocked out in 1:46 for the title. One fight later, Singer was the one on the canvas when top contender Jimmy McLarnin scored the KO in three. Unfortunately for McLarnin, it was a non-title fight.

Singer was beatable, all right, and Mack knew it. Only problem was, even if Mack was the one with his arm raised on Oct. 14, he wasn't likely to get a rematch for Singer's belt — not before Tony Canzoneri had his shot. Deemed a tune-up for Canzoneri, Singer needed to show the world that *he* was the champ ... only he didn't want to put his belt on the line to do so — and that's where Mack entered the picture.

Though Singer was favored to win, based on knockout power, Mack's boxing skills were expected to give the champion trouble, when the two headlined Chicago Stadium before 9,500 people. They were wrong.

Mack fought the wrong fight, but neither fighter was particularly impressive. "Many of the crowd went away puzzled how Singer won the title," reported the *Tribune*. As for Mack? He "apparently was awed by Singer's reputation, and particularly by the champion's left hook, the blow which toppled Mandell from the throne. Mack was so impressed with Singer's appearance that he fought the major portion of the ten rounds in retreat. Infrequently, he stood his ground, and then only momentarily, ever ready to clinch."[53]

Singer leapt from a crouch, both feet off the canvas, hoping to land his hook on Mack, who traveled backward, evading any knockout blow. It was a dirty fight, as much as an unimpressive one, Mack butting Singer in the second to open up a deep gash over the champ's left eye and Singer repeatedly throwing low blows. Singer was given the edge in most rounds, for the unanimous decision.

With back-to-back losses, Mack's stock plunged. Looking for a get-back win, Mack went to the border to headline a card at the Smelter Arena, where another lightweight contender — El Paso's Tony Herrera — reigned supreme. Though talk of a Mack-Herrera showdown was flirted with, it wasn't Herrera that Mack had come for, but aged veteran Battling Chico II, on Nov. 13, 1930.

On the eve that saw Tony Canzoneri destroy Al Singer in just 1:06 at Madison Square Garden for the world lightweight championship, Mack was toying with, then knocking out Chico before a mere 750 fans, for a meaningless fourth-round knockout.

Mack returned to Los Angeles where he was still popular, agreeing to take on top-ten contender Cecil Payne at the Olympic Auditorium, Nov. 25. Giving his usual spiel, promoter Wadhams was dangling the Canzoneri carrot.

The Louisville fighter was the best of a new crop of lightweights on the West Coast, completely unorthodox, who fought with his hands down yet was able to hit you from every conceivable — and inconceivable — angle. Mack, on the other hand, "fights out of a book. He's a preacher and a dreamer. Payne fights by instinct. He attended the college of hard knocks."[54]

In a fast and furious scrap, "Payne piled up a lead in the first few rounds," but, "unleashing a two-fisted attack in the ninth round, Mack battered Payne into the ropes and it looked like he might win, but Payne came back with a flourish in the final round to hold the young Denver college boy on even terms."[55] It was ruled a draw.

In what would be his first fight in San Bernadino, and last fight in California, Mack closed off the year on Dec. 2, 1930, with a ten-round decision over up-and-coming Los Angeles prospect Herman Ritterhouse. After seven close rounds and fighting with a shoulder injury, Mack pulled ahead at the end for a much-needed win.

The shoulder injury was worse than originally thought, requiring surgery. After the operation, in Denver, Mack recuperated and geared up for 1931 — a year he hoped would put him in the ring with the new champ, Canzoneri.

16. Mackless New Mexico, 1929–1930

Boxing is the greatest game in the world because it is the only one which makes a fellow think rapidly…. In the ring, you can't watch anything but the eyes of your opponent. While you're in action, nobody can help you but yourself.

—Eddie Mack, 1929[1]

The night that Eddie Mack defeated a world champion to become an overnight contender was the night the collective fight scenes in Albuquerque and Santa Fe started to wane. Mack had been the impetus, maybe even the soul, that had driven the sport since 1923. If the major fights hadn't headlined Mack, then they had billed his many current, past and future nemeses.

When Mike Vasquez, Harry Bramer and Jose Rivers all headlined shows while they waited for, or in between their showdowns with Mack, the biggest non–Mack fight was held on Oct. 25, 1927, when Sammy Sandow of El Paso fought a draw with Jose "Bulldog" Gonzalez before 2,800 at the Armory. Even then, Mack had been first choice, but had pulled out sick. The fight was so good that the Bulldog was brought back to fight Rivers in November, but it was Jose's turn to get sick, and he was replaced with ol' reliable Battling Chico II. When Rivers *could* make it, a month later, he lost to Gonzalez.

Not all big fights of the '20s were with or about Mack — just the majority of them.

Santa Fe still had Henry "Kid" Pacheco, who fought throughout northern New Mexico. Las Cruces brought in El Paso's answer to the lightweight division, the "El Paso High School Ghost," Tony Herrera, and, in southern towns, also from El Paso, was Rosy Rosales.

By 1928, two new names and a returning one showed up to challenge — or replace — Mack, who would make his make-or-break break for the West Coast in 1929. From Oklahoma came Eddie Murdock while another southern gent, Dave Jackson, arrived from Little Rock, Arkansas. Also, returning after three years of club fighting in Los Angeles was an older "Young" Benny Chavez.

After Eddie made the big time, the other Eddie, the "other" Benny and Dave kept things cooking in the final two frames of the 1920s, in New Mexico's largest two cities. Murdock and Jackson banged it out five times in '29; Murdock and Chavez fought four, with crowds just a hair shy of Mack level. "Bulldog" Gonzales and Vasquez were thrown into the mix, as well. Though they had local homeboys of their own, Gallup, Roswell, Clovis, and even Taos borrowed Murdock, Jackson and Chavez.

Toward the tail-end of '29, Santa Fe was weaned off of bigger cards, sticking strictly to club shows, though R. W. Morton, promoter of the first Murdock-Mack fight, made a stab at headlining heavyweights. Pairing up black fighters Chihuahua Kid Brown and long-time veteran Aaron Brown, better known as "The Dixie Kid," known for two KO losses to Sam Langford, Morton built an outdoor arena at the south end of Santa Fe that didn't last long. It was one of the early casualties of the Great Depression. The boxing card failed, as well.

Santa Fe went back to the age-old formula of cooking up locals on low budget smokers, the promoters occasionally reaching into their pockets for a better 10-round main event, like the Nov. 18, 1929, showdown between long-time favorite Kid Pacheco and Babe Colima, an El Paso youngster on a fast rise. Pacheco, Colima and several others kept the sport alive.

Dynamite Tommy Returns

> *No boy that has started out from here deserves a better fate than does Tommy. Inability to find opponents around his 105 pounds has been a severe handicap to him. But Tommy hasn't prevented that fact from letting him [sic] drop onto most of the fight cards in this vicinity. To do so he has spotted poundage right and left. Such a stunt may prove disastrously [sic] for a small boy.*
>
> — *New Mexico State Tribune,* 1927[2]

Timo Sanchez — "Dynamite Tommy" in the roped arena — welcomed challenges. Since 1914, the 105-pound package of TNT had made a career of giving up weight, height and plenty of reach to land a fight. Now, as 1926 was coming to a close, he was adding two more disadvantages to the list while staging a comeback: age and time off.

A month away from turning 28, and with over three years of accumulated ring rust, Sanchez wanted back, so promoter Red Valencia gave him a spot against youngster Mickey Morgan — not the toughest, not the easiest. Shortly before the fight, Morgan pulled out

Tommy Sanchez (squatting) with his sparmates outside a boxing gym in Albuquerque, during the late '20s. The other fighters are unknown except for the tallest guy in the back — most likely, that is Eddie Murdock (Courtesy of Benny Sanchez).

Pint-sized Tommy Sanchez gave the West Coast a shot, but was consistently matched up against much bigger opponents. Pictured back row, left to right: Mrs. Hoover, Tommy Sanchez, Micky Young, Mrs. Hussy, George Hussy, Mr. Jones, Mr. Freeman, and an unidentified woman. Seated, front row: George Swartz, Spike Robinson, wrestling champion Bull Montana, Heavyweight World Champion Jack Dempsey, Lightweight World Champion Mushy Callahan and "The Kid" (courtesy of Benny Sanchez).

and was replaced with North Dakota's K.O. Dempsey, who claimed he'd never been defeated. Spotting his sub 15 pounds, Tommy KO'd K.O. in five. The pint-sized kid, who was no longer a kid, but with dynamite in his gloves, was back. More or less.

Promoter Daniel Ortiz had a hell of a time finding an opponent for the well-liked Sanchez, so on Feb. 8, 1927, he threw the paperweight in with another bantamweight, George "Kid" Marchi, as the co-main on the Mack-Billy Mansweller card in Santa Fe. This time, unable to "detonate" against his bigger, more explosive opponent, Dynamite Tommy didn't do so well, when Marchi "hammered [his] facial features ... until an expert butcher couldn't have distinguished it from well-ground hamburger steak."[3]

Tommy was thinking about sticking his gloves back on the peg over his workbench in the garage, when K.O. Dempsey started calling him out again, calling his loss a fluke. *Why not?* Tommy thought. Shortly before his death, in 1996, Sanchez recalled the scene backstage, while he was putting on his ring togs.[4]

"Whatcha lookin' at?" Tommy had noticed Jose Rivers, who was headlining the card, staring at him while he slipped his feet into a pair of old work boots he wore in the ring.

In a decade of fighting and more than 100 fights, at least half on the other side of the border, Rivers had never seen foot garb like Tommy's. "What the hell is that, Tommy?" he asked.

"Aw, Joe, these boots are all I got," Tommy was embarrassed. "I can't afford anything better. But I'll be okay, I'm used to these old things."

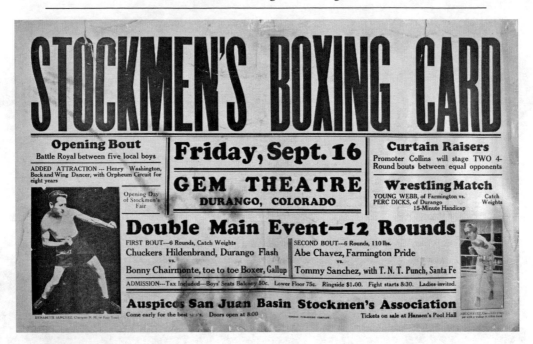

Rising New Mexican star Abie Chavez was opponentless for his fight on September 16, 1932 — that is, until Timo "Dynamite Tommy" Sanchez came out of retirement to take on the pint-sized warrior. In a battle of flyweights — two of the best ever produced in New Mexico — it was youth over experience, with Abie stopping Dynamite Tommy in round three.

Rivers shook his head, then went to his duffle bag, reached in and pulled out a pair of boxing shoes. "These *zapatos* ain't much," he handed them to Tommy. "They ain't been waxed up in a long, long time. They're just taking up valuable space in my gear bag. Here Tommy, you can have 'em."

Despite the difference in weight — Rivers was a lightweight, Tommy a minimum weight (or would've been had there been such a class back in the '20s) — the shoes fit, and Tommy showed his appreciation by knocking out his opponent not once, but *twice* that night.

"K.O." Dempsey sure lived up to his name that night. Shortly after the opening round, Tommy let loose with a right to the jaw that floored Dempsey. He was resting on one knee, trying to decide if he was able to get up, when referee Johnny Flaska counted to ten. The crowd booed and the ring was cleared, but backstage Dempsey demanded another chance — so promoter George Ringling, anxious to appease the crowd, brought the pair back out for a second co-main. This time, Sanchez knocked Dempsey flat in a minute-and-a-half and he was unable to get to his feet in time.

After another prelim bout, on July 4, a decision over Young Kid Mex of Juarez, Sanchez announced he was ready for the big leagues and went to Chicago during the summer of 1927. But the Windy City had an even harder time in finding someone as light as Sanchez who, in peak form, could tip the beam in double digits.

Sanchez retired, then unretired yet again when, in 1928, he headed to California with his brother, who was participating in the Pyle Bunion Derby — a transcontinental foot race. The West Coast, at least, had more opportunity, and Sanchez fought off and on for six months, winning more bouts than he lost, but was almost always outweighed, by as much as 25 pounds.

"They said I could've been great," said Sanchez. "But there was no one my size to be great against. That's the way it goes, I guess."[5]

Under the management of George Hussey, Sanchez made another attempt in Reno, Nevada, during 1929, but lack of opponents had the same result. Tommy came home, retired from the ring, then moved to Santa Fe to manage a furniture store. Yet three years later, he came out of retirement one last time — to face one of the greatest fighters of the era, Abie Chavez.

At this time, though still sparring occasionally, Sanchez kept busy managing the affairs of Frankie Cantou and Andy Carrillo. With Cantou already on the card against Chuckers Hildebrand, the Durango, Colorado, promoters were in need of an opponent to face Chavez. Tommy was ready to wire the matchmaker he would have to look elsewhere when he thought, "Why not try it yourself, Tommy?"

Which is what he did. "I fought for nearly 17 years and now am only 31," Dynamite Tommy told the *Durango Herald*. "I never let myself get in poor condition and am working out daily now. I'll be in good shape by the 16th and am anxious to see how I go. If my works seems satisfactory to me, I may keep on boxing. If not, I'll quit."[6]

Though only 10 pounds heavier, Chavez was too good — too young — for Tommy, who was knocked out in three. This time, he stayed retired.

The Boxer's Butcher Shop

> *After the first of the year Pacheco is going east to take on the best in the country in his class and he does not intend to have a defeat registered against him before leaving.*
> — *Santa Fe New Mexican*, 1929[7]

One of the few New Mexicans who was good enough to fight the lighter, younger incarnation of Eddie Mack, but who never did, was Henry "Kid" Pacheco — but maybe that was a good thing. It was certainly the plan of Daniel Ortiz, not so much to protect Pacheco, but to build him up well before throwing him in with a comer like Mack, who soon drifted north to a heavier weight division, anyway.

It never did happen, and though Henry and his kid brother Manuel became the biggest hometown draws in Santa Fe during the 1920s, "Kid" had to play second fiddle to Mack and "Young" Manuel, second favorite to his older brother. The Pachecos were stay-at-home favorites during the '20s, never fighting farther than a day's ride from the Capital City where they resided and worked as butchers.

Fighter-turned-promoter-then-manager Johnny Duran tried to take Kid Pacheco to the next level in 1925, but, against his toughest opponent to date, Johnny McCoy, who was one of the Southwest's top bantams, the Santa Fean lost a decision.

Locally, and at bantam, Pacheco had no peer in New Mexico, though he was upset by Barber Sandoval in his sole bout of the year in 1927. Pacheco fought sporadically in '28 — two wins and a draw against locals — but had his busiest year in 1929, a year in which Mack was *least* busy in New Mexico.

The Pacheco that had thrilled his hometown in the early '20s as a former Navy champion showed flashes of his former self when he staged a comeback to pay back Trinidad fighter Joe Perez, who fought as "Little Jack Dempsey" under the management of the Original Benny Chavez. Perez had defeated the Kid's brother, but Henry evened the score against the Pacheco clan.

Also that year, Pacheco was able to call himself the Southwest bantam champ when he twice defeated Arizona claimant Joe Lucero in bouts held at home. Pacheco's sole loss in '29 was to rising star Babe Colima, who ruined his year when he was DQ'd for low blows on Nov. 18, 1929. It also spoiled Pacheco's plans to go east.

After an eight-round draw with Joe Martinez, a.k.a. "Young Jack Dempsey" (not to be confused with the "K.O." Dempsey who fought Dynamite Tommy in 1927, or the "Little Jack Dempsey" that Pacheco fought in '29), Pacheco gave up the sport.

With his older brother retired, Manuel Pacheco's activity increased and he stepped up to a new breed of fighters on the rise in the early '30s. He remained a prelim fighter, just as a third brother, Joe, followed suit.

Benny's Return, Rise and Demise

> Benny Chavez, the bad boy of the boxing game is back in Gallup after a term in the 'jugabo' and is anxious to make good.
> — *Gallup Independent*, 1931[8]

By the '30s, you could say that Eddie Mack was the only New Mexican who'd ever successfully launched a so-called "West Coast Invasion." But there were several who didn't fare too badly — Solomon "Young Benny" Chavez was one.

When Chavez headed west from New Mexico, in 1925, he'd been a decent club fighter whose hometown promoters never had the decency to give him a main event fight. The indignant Solomon vowed to come back as a threat to anyone near his weight in the Southwest — which is exactly what he did.

Dropping the "Young" from his moniker and fighting as "Benny Chavez," which brought up recollection of the original Benny, who'd sought success there in the early '10s, Solomon won most of his fights in L.A. area, mainly in the four- to six-round range, and fighting at least two ten-round co-mains on bigger shows staged at Wrigley Field. He was a regular on Olympic Auditorium cards or the smaller Hollywood venue, and became a local favorite with his gutsy fighting, fast feet and hefty wallop.

Eventually, he hooked up with Eddie Sears, who managed World Welterweight Champion Mushy Callahan and, in 1927, fought at Chicago's Wrigley Field, the champ beating Spug Meyers and Benny losing a decision to Joe Salas.

Reports of Chavez's progress were occasionally noted in the Albuquerque papers and, by mid–1927, he'd drawn enough interest for promoters to consider bringing him back home to fight, possibly against Jose Rivers. Then, if he won, they'd see what he could do with Mack. Nothing came of it and Chavez stayed in Los Angeles for another year, fighting everyone from "Bolo Boy" Elias Contreras, whom he decisioned, to Danny Kramer.

What drew more attention than his occasional significant win was the story of Benny's death, reported on Oct. 18, 1928. On the night of the 17th, Chavez had been stabbed at a party and, a day later, died from the wounds. Two days after "dying," however, Chavez climbed into the ring at the Olympic Auditorium to win a six-round decision over Joe Nieto.

Alive and well, Benny dismissed the erroneous reporting and used the publicity, at least in New Mexico, to call out the mighty Mack. In October 1928, he got his chance.

Chavez was hyped as a big leaguer now, having fought the L.A. circuit for three years. The local papers boasted he'd lost but one bout. On Oct. 17, 1928, Mack entered the Albuquerque ring for the first time as a main eventer. If his hometown had been shocked to read about his death earlier in the month, they were equally stunned to hear the news the next morning.

Chavez carried the fight to Mack in the early rounds and was just getting his timing down when a low blow from Mack floored him. Just like that, Chavez had scored one of the biggest upsets of the year. Eddie Murdock had previously beaten Mack but, unlike other South-westerners who were lucky enough to cop the "W" over the "Alamosa Flash," Chavez would be the only one who was not avenged.

The win was seen as hap-penstance — until Nov. 20, 1928, that is, when Mack conqueror met Mack conqueror at Albu-querque's Armory. In a 12-round lightweight bout against Mur-dock, Chavez slugged his way to a crowd-thrilling draw. The fight was so heated at the end that the referee and cornermen had to settle the two pugs down.

It would be the first of a classic New Mexico series of grudge fights with Murdock.

Solomon "Young Benny" Chavez (far right), shown here with his family, made a name for himself in Los Angeles but came back to Albuquerque for local bragging rights later on in the '20s.

Disgusted with the outcome, and with the referee, who was criticized for letting Mur-dock get away with several low blows, Chavez returned to California where news of his win over Mack had preceded him. In San Francisco, Chavez received his biggest West Coast opportunity, fighting the co-main on the Tod Morgan–Santiago Zorilla title fight on Dec. 2, 1928, against highly-touted Ignacio Fernandez, who would, a couple years later, knock out future World Lightweight Champ Al Singer.

Proving he was no fluke fighter, Chavez piled up a lead in the early rounds but the Filipino evened up the score with a couple of closing rallies for what many considered a gift draw for the local favorite, Fernandez. Before Chavez could gain momentum and cap-italize on what many deemed a hometown robbery for a rematch, he was paired with Ray Ravani, who'd beaten him earlier in the year. This time, on Dec. 28, 1928, in San Francisco, Chavez was KO'd in two.

Chavez's rep took another hit on Feb. 5, 1929, when he lost to Sailor Fay Kosky in

Fresno. Fed up with the West Coast, Solomon packed up and came home where a rematch with Murdock was prime on his mind. Looking to get a lucky break and another main event, Chavez called out Santa Fe's Kid Pacheco and Dave Jackson, who was residing in the Capital City now, but neither one wanted to tangle with Chavez.

Murdock did, though. The two were booked for May 24, 1929, at the Armory and, yet again, Chavez was at the raw end of controversy.

Shortly before the fight, weight had become an issue. Chavez, still able to make featherweight, had had no trouble giving up a few pounds to fight Murdock, a solid lightweight. In fact, Murdock had come in *over* 135 and lost his forfeit the first time around. In the rematch, both fighters agreed on 135 — only Murdock came in a whopping 141 while Chavez was ten pounds lighter, at 131.

Like the first one had been, this fight was a blistering war, in action and in temperature, despite promoter Joe Danneck's promise that the stifling heat in the Armory would be combated by electric fans he'd been the first to install. Danneck had also hired 17-year-old Vivian Jones to sing the national anthem and popular songs like "I'll Be with You in the Apple Blossom Time," before and in between bouts — Jones would later go on to play Ethel Mertz on the *I Love Lucy* television show.

With the Oklahoma Windmill standing at range, unleashing chopping lefts and rights every time Chavez bore in, the judges gave the majority of rounds and the decision to Murdock.

Discouraged, Chavez stayed at home this time instead of returning to Los Angeles. In July, local promoter J. S. Carlisle took over Benny's affairs, promising to make a champ of the man who'd defeated Mack who, by now, had defeated champ Tod Morgan. All the big names, from the border to Denver, were called out on behalf of Chavez. Criticized for his lack of training in the past, Chavez committed himself at the camp in San Ysidro in what he deemed his comeback campaign.

Working with promoter Danneck, Carlisle set up Chavez at the Armory on Aug. 30 to face Chicago journeyman Paul Allen, who was taken out in less than two rounds before a light crowd of 600. Bragging about his new and improved fighter, Carlisle told the press he was going west again — just as soon as he cleaned house in New Mexico, which meant Murdock again.

On Sept. 24, 1929, Chavez and Murdock fought again, and there was something to Carlisle's flimflam. "It was a different Benny Chavez than was ever seen in Albuquerque before," the *Journal* reported. "Murdock learned this and paid well for the lesson. Like a brown panther, with arm muscles like steel bands and a torso as resistive as a cast iron drum, Benny tore in to redeem himself,"[9] nearly knocking out Murdock in the tenth on his way to a solid decision.

After a set-up fight in Willard — against a guy named "Rattlesnake Jack," no one had ever heard of — Chavez was rematched with Murdock for the fourth time, on the one-and-only card ever promoted by Simmons Carlisle, on Oct. 17, 1929, at the Armory. "I'm going to surprise this egg Chavez when I get him in the ring again," Murdock told the *Journal*. "I'll make him think his name is mud."[10]

There was plenty of mud to go around after the fight, for it would go down as one of the most controversial matches in New Mexico history.

It was scored a draw but the papers agreed that Murdock won the fight. "The unsinkable came back with vengeance," wrote the *New Mexican*, attributing seven rounds to Murdock, one to Chavez and four even, while the *Journal* attributed eight to Murdock, who "pounded, cuffed and pummeled" Chavez in what they deemed a "slaughter."[11] On the official score-board, the judges disagreed, one ruling it a draw, the other choosing Murdock; referee Flaska deemed it even.

As controversial as the scoring was, what came after nearly killed boxing in Albu-querque. Murdock spilled the beans, telling cops that he'd been offered a nice chunk of change to take a dive against Chavez, by promoter Carlisle.

"Frame-up!" "Sell-out!" the fans immediately yelled, while Mayor Clyde Tingley called for three heads to roll — Murdock's, Chavez's *and* Carlisle's — immediately banning the unholy trio from ring activities within city limits. Carlisle claimed he was innocent, of course, claiming he was being framed by jealous promoters and their cohorts. Chavez merely shrugged, saying he knew *nada*. But Murdock sang to the police.[12]

Murdock swore he'd been offered $250 to lose and he'd agreed, however, planning to double cross Carlisle in the ring by beating Chavez fair and square. Carlisle's license to pro-mote was revoked and a Nov. 5 card headlining Chavez was cancelled, by order of the mayor.

While an investigation revealed even more conflicting statements from others who were allegedly involved, the sport itself took the biggest hit. Reporters, editors and fans began to question the legitimacy of past fights, credibility of officials and whether the city would be better off without the sport.

In the end, Carlisle never promoted again in Albuquerque, Benny Chavez never fought again in his hometown, and it took city officials several years before they allowed Murdock to fight in another Duke City ring.

Amid the controversy, Chavez crept out of town to Denver to fight top-rated Mickey Cohen on Oct. 25. "Chavez, who was shouting his prowess to the world a few weeks ago, failed to show much except a willingness to take punches,"[13] the *Rocky Mountain News* wrote.

With their local reputations shot and unable to fight at home, Carlisle took Chavez and Dave Jackson, of the same stable, on a tour of the Pacific but they never quite made it that far. Finding a welcome mat in Gallup, Chavez fought in December, knocking out little-regarded Arizonian Buster Grant in what would be the first of many fights at Carbon City.

A fight in Phoenix against respected Joey Sangor fell through and Chavez struggled in a 12-rounder against Philadelphia veteran Buck Fleming, winning but showing just a few flashes of his old-time self while injuring his thumb. He spent the next several months of 1930 inactive.

Chavez had a host of personal problems, but the biggest one was his drinking. There were reports of an attack on his sister-in-law for making appearances in court on behalf of Benny's wife, who was looking to file a divorce. There were threats with a revolver.

"Maybe his manager is not getting enough action for his protégé,"[14] mused the *Gallup Herald* in February 1930, shortly before Chavez went to court for coming home drunk and assaulting his wife, then ordering her out of the house. Chavez testified that he was not drunk — he didn't have a dime to buy a drink, having spent all the money he'd earned from his last fight on groceries and rent.

The episodes continued. Chavez spent more time in the drunk tank than he did in the gym, and was arrested more than once. Adding to the domestic disputes was a charge of mugging a black man of his watch and $4.

By now, Carlisle had given up on Chavez while Sam Gold, manager for Buddy Serino, tried to clean up the bottle-battling boxer. With the help of Serino, Chavez was seen around town doing road work and in the gym, gearing up for a final campaign and trying to put his legal troubles behind him.

Unable to fight at home for the previous year's controversy with Murdock, Chavez returned to the ring in Gallup, where, despite his reputation, he was well liked. In the summer, he fought three times — a TKO over a set-up, and two draws with tougher opposition — while his wife, Dolores, filed for divorce.

Called the "bad boy of boxing," Young Benny Chavez was the frontrunner for Johnny Tapia. Chavez was arrested often — all the while maintaining a reputation as a solid threat to any boxer from feather to lightweight.

Having proved Chavez could achieve fitness again, promoter Ringling took the risk and, after convincing the boxing commission that the fighter should be cleared of his suspension, announced that Eddie Mack might be coming back to Albuquerque for a fight and was open to a rematch. Before Mack could commit, Benny fell off the wagon and was arrested for more small-time robbery. This time he landed in the clinker and that's where he stayed throughout the remainder of 1930.

Out and about in the early parts of 1931, Chavez went back to Gallup where promoter Guido Zecca promised the "bad boy of the boxing game" a fight, but only if he could remain "firm in his determination to exile John Barleycorn and work faithfully."[15] Benny promised, Guido delivered and, on March 10, he staged a comeback at Kitchen's Opera House, scoring a win over an unknown opponent — the details are sketchy.

What is *not* sketchy is the fight that occurred on March 25, 1931, at Kitchen's. In what would be his final bout, Chavez was up against Julio Chiaramonte, a 16-year-old prodigy and Gallup's best kept secret. It was a classic battle of veteran vs. youngster, boxer vs. puncher, and "bad boy" vs. the All-American kid. Despite lousy weather, Kitchen's was packed.

"Julio was plainly nervous during the first four rounds, but after that, was the aggressor throughout," went the report in the *Independent*. Using whatever he had left, Chavez fought a torrid war, and "knew he had been through a fight after going ten rounds with the prodigy."[16] While the referee gave the fight to Chavez, two judges overruled, scoring it even, making it a majority draw.

Chavez returned to Albuquerque, where he heard Mack was planning to soon fight. He was. "Just so it isn't Chavez,"[17] Mack told the press. Unable to land a lucrative payday fighting Mack, or to land a fight in his hometown, with just a possibility of fighting April 19 on a Bernalillo smoker, Chavez ultimately lost his battle with booze. "When Benny was drunk there was no telling what he'd do,"[18] a fellow boxer would later say about Solomon Chavez.

On the night of April 17, close to midnight, Don Candelaria was awakened by someone trying to kick in his back door. According to police reports, Candelaria loaded a 16-gauge shotgun and went to investigate, only to find his friend Solomon "Benny" Chavez, who'd been at his house earlier in the evening, intoxicated. When told to go away, Chavez became abusive, cursing Candelaria and ripping the screen door from the hinges. "He turned back and made a grab for his rear pocket," Candelaria told police. "I thought he was pulling a gun, and [I] fired, aiming down to avoid wounding him seriously."[19]

Chavez was rushed to St. Joseph Hospital where he died 3:10 A.M., April 18, 1931, at the age of 28.

Flash and Flood

So I agreed to go on with him and I boxed six rounds, got thirty-five dollars for it. Never saw so many gloves in my life.
— *Louis L'Amour about Kid Mortio, 1981*[20]

"The San Marcial Flash" might've been bounced up and down to the canvas when he entered the ring against Eddie Mack on Feb. 13, 1923, but he was far from being a finished fighter. At the time, Nick "Kid" Mortio had around 50 bouts — he would have more than three times that number before he retired in the early '30s.

After his unlucky 13 knockdowns at the hands of the high school prodigy, Mortio, with his tail between his legs, returned to the border where he won all but one of the remaining bouts of the year, with a highlight 10-round decision over Pete Loya in Juarez. In 1924, Mortio returned north for several fights, drawing, then losing, to Loya, and outpointing a young "Young" Benny Chavez in his hometown of San Marcial.

Before San Marcial went under six feet under during the Rio Grande flood in 1929, Mortio was more popular than the Harvey House in the thriving agricultural and railroad town. At least half a dozen fight cards were staged at San Marcial, all billing Mortio, who outhustled Kid Pacheco, Insurrecto Kid, twice, and Pinky Uriquidi. His only loss at home was a decision to Jackie Sanders, in 1925.

Mortio never did stray too far from home, preferring to fight around his home state, at the border, and in Gallup, leaving the state only to fight across the state line in El Paso or Trinidad, or across the river in Juarez. He won the majority of his fights and his speed and defense prevented him from taking too many beatings. Several times during the '20s, he was considered the bantamweight and featherweight champion of New Mexico and his fighting weight did not stray but a few pounds north in more than a decade of fighting.

As the '20s wore on, the Flash did lose a bit of zip. When his sister married lightweight Tony Herrera, Mortio became part of the team as the El Pasoan rose to contention while living in Chicago. When Herrera's career declined, Mortio returned to New Mexico, going from the "San Marcial Flash" to the "Clovis Flash" and, finally, to the "Santa Rosa Flash."

While working for the railroad, Mortio fought sporadically before retiring in 1930, returning in '31, re-retiring again, and, after outhustling upcoming Santa Fean Andy Carrillo, quitting for good in 1932. Mortio was one of the founding trainers in Clovis' long-running amateur program. He also worked with another fast-moving fighter in the '30s, "Speedy" Ryan of Melrose, and tried his hand at promoting, as well.

After the '30s, Mortio's name disappeared from print, but decades later he was remembered by, of all people, western fiction writer Louis L'Amour, who'd dabbled in prizefighting during the '30s. While traveling through New Mexico, L'Amour passed through what was probably Santa Rosa, where Mortio was fighting an exhibition in the main event. Short on cash, he tracked down the promoter, who told him that Mortio's opponent had pulled out. Despite the weight difference — L'Amour was a middleweight — the future author went the rounds for a $35 payday.

The Human Windmill, the Bald Eagle

Eddie is not regarded as a great boxer on the coast. He is called a great fighter, however.

—Albuquerque Journal, 1930[21]

Murdock has an attitude that is trifle puzzling. In his conversation you gather nothing but that he is glad the fracas is going to take place. The time seems to be of no consequence.

—Santa Fe New Mexican, 1928[22]

Eddie Murdock rolled out of Oklahoma like a tumbleweed with the strength of a hurricane — and New Mexico wasn't quite ready for a character like the "Human Windmill."

His sandy-colored hair, what little there was of it, was always glistening with Brylcream or Wildroot. He had a dimple in his chin, rosy cheeks, steel-blue eyes, and drove a bright yellow Oldsmobile convertible, after trading in his Chrysler.

"There was always a blonde in the car," fellow fighter George "Kid" Marchi remembered in the '90s. "He flaunted flashy women, wore fashionable clothes and had gold teeth. But he could *fight*."[23] Everyone, from Eddie Mack to Jose Rivers to Benny Chavez, found *that* out — the hard way.

Only 19 at the time when he rolled into dusty Albuquerque in 1928, looking for new regions to conquer, or pick up a payday, Murdock was still a veteran of nearly 50 bouts. His brags of never haven taken the count and the sports scribes claiming he had but a few losses were bunk — Murdock had come in second place on nearly a third of his early bouts in the West and Midwest. Back in the golden era of boxing, losing 10 to 20 bouts was what you called "receiving an education."

The farthest thing from a knockout king — there'd be fewer than 20 knockouts by the time he retired in 1940, with around 200 bouts — Murdock fought furiously, hence the nickname "Human Windmill." In the Mack-dominated era, Murdock would not only be remembered as one of Eddie's chief rivals, but, a year later, his primary stablemate, under manager Joe Roth, who brought him to the West Coast to become a legit contender.

Starting as a bantamweight in 1925 and finishing up as a chunky middleweight, the 5'7" Murdock would fight five world champions — six if you count the "uncrowned" one, Mack, of course. But, in New Mexico, he was best remembered for his several rivalries in his pre-contender days, beginning with Mack.

Murdock might've been falsely hyped as an Oklahoma "sensation" by overzealous Santa

Fe promoters, but he proved it when thrown to the wolves on May 18, 1928, against Mike Vasquez. Edging the aggressive El Pasoan, Murdock scored one of the year's biggest upsets. Looking for a bigger payday, Murdock said he'd come seeking Eddie Mack's scalp.

"Eddie vs. Eddie" was lined up for June 19 and instead of shutting up the outspoken Oklahoman, the textbook fighter that was Mack could not figure out Murdock's unorthodox, often freakish, style. Losing his Rocky Mountain lightweight belt to Murdock, who would have his title stenciled on his Chrysler, Mack was hopelessly outpointed in the year's biggest shocker.

Murdock had made it clear he'd come for the glory and the green — and not for fan appreciation, though he got plenty of that over time, anyway. He made *that* clear when he refused to fight Mack until he'd been paid in full, causing a 90-minute delay. Mack had to dig into his own purse for $100 to ensure Murdock's willingness to fight. After the fight, Mack would lose even more when it was Murdock who headlined a string of shows in which the other Eddie would've otherwise been the star.

Milking the attention and paychecks, Murdock took on Rivers in back-to-back bouts. Though he was seen to give Rivers a trimming in both fights, the first resulted in an 11th-round no-decision when Rivers fell out of the ring and was unable to continue. The second was a disputed draw. Two straight wins against Los Angeles veteran Frankie Monroe followed, one in Santa Fe, the other in Juarez, which set up a showdown at Fort Bliss with Rivers on enemy turf.

Murdock returned to his new home of Albuquerque with the win over Rivers and his Southwestern championship secured, just in time to rematch Mack — his third bout in nine days. This time, the fighting schoolboy had studied up and had answers, for he floored the Oklahoman enigma en route to a clear-cut decision to snag his title back.

Despite the setback, all in all, it was a whirlwind year for the "Wind-

BOXING CONTEST
TONIGHT
AT STRAND THEATRE

Under Auspices of 🏅 American Legion

Preliminaries Start at 8:30 P. M. Sharp

Main Event 12 Rounds
Eddie Murdock   vs.   Bus Montes
Albuquerque   135 lbs   El Paso

Semi-Final 8 Rounds
Insurrecto Kid   vs.   Battling Chico
Gallup   125 lbs   Albuquerque

Special Event
Tony Montoya   vs.   Julio Chiaramonte
Two Gallup Terrors in a Return Engagement

Eddie Murdock
Albuquerque, N. M.

Bus Montes
El Paso, Texas

Two Other Good Preliminaries!!

General Admission $1.00   Reserved $1.50
Ringside $2.00

Tickets on Sale: Smith Cigar Store   Strand Theatre
K & M Drug Store   Banner Drug Store

Banned in Albuquerque after being accused of throwing a fight, Eddie Murdock joined former nemesis Eddie Mack in California, where he upset the odds and became a bona fide welterweight contender. Murdock always sought a return to New Mexico, though, and before Albuquerque had him back, he fought in Gallup. On Oct. 11, 1929, the "Bald Eagle" TKO'd "Buzzy" Bus Montes at the Strand Theatre.

mill," who fought 23 times in 1928, ending the year with a 12-round draw with returning Solomon "Benny" Chavez, and two more bouts at the border with Rivers (a draw and second win).

The following year, Murdock fought 15 times, all throughout New Mexico — and six were against Dave Jackson, a series that only increased in intensity. The *New Mexican* wrote, "If this Murdock-Jackson affair is to be definitely settled at any time, the indications are that the two fellows will have to go out behind someone's barn and fight it out."[24] Murdock came out ahead, with three wins, a DQ loss and two draws.

It wasn't just the fighting, though, that saw Murdock's name frequently in print. Maybe not as troublesome as Solomon Chavez, Murdock had his share of run-ins. He was sued by a local car dealership for not making payments on the Olds convertible he'd traded in his Chrysler for. He was arrested for driving his car over a city lawn, and when in court, asked permission to go home to get the $10 fine; when he didn't return, he was arrested again, only to break a window in an attempted escape that landed him in solitary confinement for a time.

Murdock was always getting in trouble, whether he was at fault or not. In December 1928, Murdock was arrested for bank robbery in another state, and the cops grabbed him coming off the train from fighting in El Paso. It was *Paul* Murdock they were looking for, not Eddie, however, so he was released. There were the charges of assault and battery in November 1929, fight fixing a month later (see the previous chapter), and, in 1930, he was arrested for stealing $4,000 worth of jewelry from the wife of his manager, who immediately dumped Murdock. The charges were dropped when a truck driver discovered the missing goods on the side of a highway and Roth went back to managing the unmanageable Murdock.

One year later, this time in Gallup, Murdock, by now rated one of the best welters in the country, was arrested yet again, for drunkenness and resisting arrest. After Murdock testified that, sure he was drunk and surly, but the officer had smacked him with his gun butt. He was charged a minimal fine of $65 and released. Eddie headed back to the gym to train for a fight the following week.

Murdock might've been content to just fight in New Mexico — he was a resident for nearly ten years — but it was his uncanny ability to get in trouble that forced the "Bald Eagle," as he was called in 1929, to leave his Albuquerque nest to soar westward.

After 17 hair-raising fights in New Mexico in 1929, Murdock ended the year with a rematch with crosstown nemesis Benny Chavez, against whom he was 0-1-1. Their fight, on Oct. 17, 1929, resulted in a draw that was more controversial in nature than just the scoring. After Murdock ratted out the promoter about agreeing to lose the fight — then double-crossed him by winning (at least on *his* and the local paper's scorecards), he was barred from future fighting in the Duke City.

He was eventually reinstated in Albuquerque but that wasn't until 1934. With the carpet yanked out from beneath him, he was encouraged to join Eddie Mack's camp — which was the smartest thing Murdock ever did.

On the West Coast, Murdock rivaled Mack's success, scoring the biggest win of his career on Nov. 15, 1929, when he pulled off a major Los Angeles upset by beating highly-rated contender Joe Glick in a decision. After two more significant wins, over "Cowboy" Charlie Cobb on Dec. 13, and Tommy Cello on the 27th, Murdock found himself a rated contender hot on the trail of World Welterweight Champion Mushy Callahan.

In 1930, Murdock fought coast to coast, oftentimes on the same card as stablemate

Mack. He shocked San Francisco fans on Jan. 3, 1930, by not only beating name fighter Willie Siegel, but knocking him out with his first punch. It took ten minutes for Siegel to leave the ring.

Back-to-back draws in San Francisco with contender Frankie Stetson followed — the winner had been promised a shot at Callahan, which never came, though Murdock would remain in contention until 1934.

During 1930, Murdock fought 19 times, almost always against credible opponents. On April 1, he decisioned former champ Jimmy Goodrich at Denver and in New York City, on Aug. 7, lost a hard-fought decision to top contender Baby Joe Gans. Yet, for all the name fights and basking in contender status, Murdock never stopped trying to get back to Albuquerque, though Santa Fe welcomed him back in May, where he knocked out "Knockout" Mike Ortega.

"Tell George Ringling that the only guarantee I want is one round trip ticket from Denver and my hotel bill,"[25] he wrote a friend in August 1930. Mayor Tingley and the Albuquerque Boxing Commission gave him a big fat denial.

Murdock became a regular West Coast fighter in 1931 and 1932, frequenting the Hollywood and San Diego venues, and occasionally returning to Oklahoma or Gallup. On Jan. 26, Murdock lost a decision to World Welterweight Champion Tommy Freeman in Oklahoma City, but that was the only bout he lost that year.

Just when he began to drop from the ratings and when the press was calling him past his prime, Murdock scored his biggest win on Dec. 30, 1932, when he pulled an Eddie Mack by outpointing World Welterweight Champion Jackie Fields in a ten-rounder at San Diego. Outweighed by nine pounds, the 143-pound Murdock floored the champion in round one. Fields came back in the next two rounds, but Murdock, fighting from a crouch that puzzled the champ, once again became the "Human Windmill," upsetting the oddsmakers by decision.

Hot on the trail of a rematch in a title affair, Murdock was avoided through 1933 by Fields, but he managed to fight 27 times, mainly in California, losing but three times. No one could knock him out, that is, until former champ Gorilla Jones, on Oct. 27, 1933, and even then, Murdock weathered six knockdowns and ten rounds.

In 1934, Murdock finally did begin to slow down, and leaving the Coast, fought throughout Texas, Nevada and Washington, where he was KO'd by future middleweight champion Freddie Steele. After milking his worth as a contender, then a former contender, Murdock, bald, paunchy and still a threat to most fighters, eventually found his way back to New Mexico — and Albuquerque.

17. End of an Era, 1931–1932

Some call it madness, others say it's just wrestling. And wrestling is either a sport in which the skill and strength, plus a couple streaks of meanness are pitted against each other, or else it's just a throwback to the dark ages when men were men and able to prove it depending on the viewpoint.

— *Las Vegas Daily Optic*, 1933[1]

Albuquerque wasn't going to wait on the return of Eddie Mack to keep the scene going in 1931. The occasional Mack headliner wasn't going to keep fans happy and, even if it did, the old local challengers were gone. The early 1930s was a period of transformation. Chavez was dead, Murdock was on the West Coast and both, Rivers and Vasquez, were retired. It was a different game now, with new blood on the rise. Most of the new blood, though at least in the Duke City, pertained to a different sport than boxing.

In much the same way that modern aficionados snub their nose at mixed martial arts and the Ultimate Fighting Championship, boxing purists had to step aside in the early '30s to watch the rise of wrestling or "rasslin'." Though somewhat popular in the '10s, the sport blew up in the '30s and, in some areas, threatened to eclipse the sweet science. Flourishing first in Albuquerque, matmen like Francisco Aguayo, Bull Montana, Otis Klingman, Vic Mull, Swede Larson, Walter "Sneeze" Achiu, Yaqui Joe and Mike London grappled and groaned on the canvas, packing in the crowds from the Duke City to Santa Fe, Gallup to Clovis.

There were new boxers on the rise, too — like Buddy Serino in Albuquerque, Jimmy Ortiz in Santa Fe, and Frankie Cantou in Wagon Mound — but, at least at first, they had to be content with fighting at low-budget smokers or sharing the bill with wrestling.

Promoter Jack Fisher of Albuquerque switched over to wrestling as his bread and butter, but he also deserves credit for keeping boxing alive by staging hybrid cards. Fisher staged more than 50 such shows between 1931 and '32, on which one, two, or sometimes three boxing bouts were staged as appetizers for a Francisco Aguayo or Otis Klingman to drop kick, hammerlock or pin his opponent in the main event.

Always looking for ways to cut back on expenses, no-frills promoters rarely paid the local boxers more than $20 for a six-rounder, but Fisher kept the Depression-hurting crowds coming back for more with 75-cent tickets. Another thing he did was to build his own arena. In the fall of '31, Fisher leased the vacant Viaduct Garage at the corner of 2nd and Coal streets, at the overpass, or viaduct. He cleaned it up, painted it in and out, and then put in a ring and bleacher seating. At first the place was loosely dubbed "The Garden of Grapplers," but eventually Jack renamed it "Viaduct Arena."

Hybrid cards caught on around the state, so the reduction in boxing caused fighters to travel more. In Santa Fe, however, where talent was rich, the fight scene actually increased.

310

Big shows were a thing of the past, however — unless Eddie Mack could return. And, in 1931, Mack had to first play out his hopes of fighting for a world title.

Mack's Last Attack

Don't let any of your friends kid up Eddie in trying to make another comeback. It just can't be done. They never come back, and that goes in your case.
—*Abe Pollock,* 1932[2]

After two years of hard campaigning in the big leagues and no closer to a title shot than he'd been at the start, 114-bout veteran lightweight contender Eddie Mack was not only frustrated, but also on the verge of hanging up the gloves. What he wanted was to return to school.

"Give it one more shot," was the advice of manager Joe Roth, so Mack complied.

It took four months to recover from his shoulder surgery — an injury sustained late in 1930 — but, by mid–April, Mack was ready to relaunch his career. Benny Bass was waiting for him in Philadelphia.

In 1929, after snubbing Mack, denying him a title fight when he'd been beaten twice in one year by him, World Junior Lightweight Champion Tod Morgan had given Bass the title shot. The title had changed hands. Since then, Bass had played Morgan's game in fighting frequently, yet *in*frequently putting his title on the line.

It was a game Mack found annoyingly familiar, though he'd moved up to lightweight hoping things would be different. The May 4, 1930, bout between Mack and Bass was same ol', same ol' for Mack — an over-the-weight, non-title affair with Bass' belt safely kept on the mantel. For Mack, it was just another fight with a big name that would line up other big name fights on the East Coast and, possibly, a title shot down the line.

Mack had spent most of the year already on the shelf recovering from an injury — he would spend the *rest* of the year recovering from another one, for what resulted was the worst loss in his career.

"Mack, clever young Spaniard whose fists earned the money to give him a college education, loomed tall and lanky beside the chunky Philadelphian," went the reportage in the *Philadelphia Inquirer.* "He tried to outbox the champion in the opening rounds, but Bass bored in with both hands and sent heavy shots to the head and body."[3]

By the end of the second, Mack was groggy. He continued counter-punching and jabbing away at the fast-rushing Bass, but near the end of the third, "Bass shifted his attack and shot rights and lefts to the jaw. A right hook caught Mack on the button and sent him sprawling."[4] Mack tried to get up but his cornermen and other ringsiders, upon seeing the result of Bass' whopping right, yelled at him to stay down. Mack was counted out with just a few seconds left in the round; his lower jaw had been fractured.

In a way it was a case of "be careful what you wish for," because Mack made the best of his nine-month hiatus to earn a law degree from St. Louis University.

When he wasn't hitting the books, Mack spent time with relatives in Colorado and New Mexico, refereed several fights and worked with locals Frankie Cantou and Jimmy Ortiz in Santa Fe. Mack was also the manager of a jazz band that toured the Southwest; the George Morrison 11-Piece Jazz Band made their first appearance in Santa Fe in June 1931. While in Alamosa, Mack also made headlines when he rushed into a burning house to rescue a four-year-old girl who'd fallen asleep in her seat.

For all the excitement, Mack was ready for one last attempt in the ring when 1932 rolled around. At best, it was a half-hearted effort, for Mack's "farewell tour" took him back to the Southwest, where he began; a serious return would've landed Mack on either coast.

New Mexico wasn't complaining though — what wasn't necessarily good for Mack was good for a state that was combating a pugilistic decline. Mack fought sixteen times between Feb. 16 and October 11, 1932: seven times in Colorado, twice in Portland and the remainder in New Mexico. He would go eight bouts before a loss.

Mack started out with two safe veterans in Colorado, decisioning Pete Pacheco in Denver, then knocking out Portland journeyman Leonard Boskovitch in Pueblo. A match against human punching bag Jack Kane, on Mar. 11 in Santa Fe, compelled *Denver Post* sports editor to telegraph his concern that "Kane was not a fit opponent,"[5] and an easy fifth-round stoppage proved it.

Four days later, Mack returned to Albuquerque to knock out Frankie Fink of Dallas, another ham-and-egger, though manager Roth assured the press that Mack would "need several more warm up fights before he steps back into the ring with top notchers"[6] and, ultimately, Tony Canzoneri, now the world lightweight champion.

Mack's "bum of the week" tour concluded in Gallup. Fighting for the first time there, Mack found an easy target with Chicago warhorse Buck Fielding, who lasted five rounds. A month later, Las Vegas was graced by the former contender, who blasted away overmatched Phil Paynter, of Missouri, in less than two rounds. Two weeks later, it was Milwaukee's Joey Klein's turn to hit the floor in an early knockout when Mack returned to Gallup. Back in Alamosa, the following month, Mack fought for the last time in his hometown, knocking out another tomato can in three.

After eight set-ups, Roth took Mack to Portland for his first challenge.

Ah Wing Lee, alias Jimmy Lee or the "Chinese Lullaby," was coming off his first acid test, a decision over former Mack foe Goldie Hess, and was moving quickly up the lightweight ladder. Lee hadn't lost a fight in 1932 yet.

Due to his experience, Mack was the considerable favorite when he stepped off the plane to fight Lee on June 7, but the crafty Chinaman's southpaw stance gave him fits. Mack was down twice in the second round from lefts to the stomach but he came back strong in the later rounds only to lose the six-round decision. Two weeks later, Mack returned for a rematch. Mack insisted on two more rounds, but the best he could get was a draw.

Mack was slipping. Two months later, Mack fought for the last time in Albuquerque, taking on his old enemy Goldie Hess, who was now far past his prime. Before 1,200 fans at Hopewell Field, Mack failed to win his third fight against the bulldog gatekeeper and had to settle for a majority draw, the ref calling it for Mack and two judges seeing it even.

Ten days later, it was "so long" to Santa Fe, when Mack knocked out lightly-regarded Jack Keenan of Los Angeles before a sold-out crowd at the Rialto. Instead of giving the local scene a boost, "the bout was similar to other fiascos staged in recent years, which have done much to kill the fight game in Santa Fe.... Keenan went down for the count once before the alleged kayo, apparently from nothing more than a slap on the wrist. Boos and catcalls from the audience however brought him to his feet. For the haymaker Mack used a left-handed push which upset Keenan, and the Los Angeles whirlwind took a siesta through the referee's count."[7] Afterward, Keenan was suspended by the local boxing commission while Mack was warned — he would have to guarantee ability of all his future opponents.

One more soup can in Trinidad, on Sept. 5, and Mack stepped up to contender Mickey

Cohen in Denver at the City Auditorium, on Sept. 14. The kid Mack had beaten several years back was now on his way up the ladder while Mack, 26 and fighting nine years now, was on the way down. It was a slam-bang grudge match and though the fans and press had Mack winning, the judges and ref awarded Cohen the win.

"Eddie Mack isn't the master he was two years ago," wrote George Burns of the *Rocky Mountain News*. "He's slower and not quite so alert in his ringmanship, but he still had enough of the old form to jab Cohen off balance as he came in, enough spirit to close in with Cohen and make him like it."[8]

Two weeks later, Wing Lee was cajoled into fighting on Mack's turf in his first ten-rounder, and first fight off the coast. This time, "Mack was Lee's master thruout and gave the Portland lad a sound beating,"[9] taking the clear decision. The shocker was the poor attendance, only 400. Neither Mack, nor the boxing game, apparently had it anymore in the Mile High City.

Promoters tried one more time with Mack — actually *Mack* tried one more time with Mack, but both came up short. On Oct. 11, Mack, coming in at a career heaviest 139, fought a rubber match with Cohen and while the attendance was more than double, the outcome was unexpected.

After a slow first round, Cohen started to force the fighting. Mack retaliated in the second, jabbing and landing his right, but "the rally was short-lived, for the fourth round was all Cohen. Mickey got his right to the body working again and made Eddie hang on. It was the beginning of the end as far as Mack was concerned for he hung on at every opportunity." Cohen had Mack groggy in the fifth, and, in the sixth, "within a minute and a half, Mack was helpless and taking a terrific beating when the towel was tossed."[10]

When the scribes started to write him as a has-been, Mack realized he'd been putting off the inevitable. After 131 bouts, ten years of fighting and a record of 109–12–12, 56 knock-outs and one newspaper win, Eddie Mack retired, ending an era in New Mexico.

The In-Between Breed

> *What's happened to the old-time fighter who used to make a beeline for the first saloon whenever he got paid for a night's work in the ring?*
>
> — *El Paso Times*, 1930[11]

Eddie Mack might have had to settle for his "uncrowned champion" title, but he laid a lot of groundwork that was put to use for decades. Not only did he show the heretofore-disregarded Southwest champions that they stood a chance of making it in bigger fight centers and breaking into top contention, but he proved that local fighters didn't have to stick to the mold to which prizefighters had been cast.

If you wanted to fight, you could fight — but it didn't have to consume your life. You could even go to school.

Which is exactly what ninth-generation Santa Fean Jimmy Ortiz sought to do when he started boxing professionally in 1928. Born the same year that Johnson-Flynn came to Vegas, and Benny Chavez to Albuquerque, Ortiz was in the gym as early as 1924 at the age of 12, helping out Nick Mortio prepare for his big fight against fast-rising Mack. On the night Mack fought his war of a draw with Mike Vasquez in Santa Fe, on Sept. 27, 1927, a 15-year-old by the name of "Young Ortiz" made his debut for a handful of change, going four with "One Round" Martinez for a draw. Jimmy had started his career.

Boxing through high school as a prelim fighter, Ortiz didn't headline until 1931 when he capped a local show, fighting a 10-round draw with crosstown rival Andy "Gump" Carrillo. They would fight six times and while Ortiz could beat everyone else in the lightweight division in New Mexico, Carrillo had his number, scoring four wins with two draws over him.

Maybe it was the talent, it might also have been the college degree Ortiz was pursuing outside the ring, but Mack took him under his wing in 1932. Ortiz had trouble against Babe Colima in 1932, losing a decision in Santa Fe, and might have had a bit of help in bouts with Louis Pena and Benny Ayers. Ortiz won a referee's decision over Pena, though many say the referee had something to do with it — none other than Mack. Pena asked for a rematch and didn't get one, calling the bout a "rather shady shade."[12] And in 1932, Clovis' Ayers was ahead on the cards when the referee — Mack again — stopped the bout on a cut, giving the TKO win to Ortiz.

Well-liked and certainly good to beat almost all other locals at lightweight, Ortiz never did rise past state prominence. After he lost a ten-rounder to Babe Colima in the summer of 1932, Mack took him to the West Coast, but the trip didn't quite make "invasion" status. Ortiz fought for another year on the home front, occasionally in the San Luis Valley, and his biggest fight was for the Southwest lightweight championship on July 21, when he faced Mickey Cohen of Denver. A rated contender, Cohen had just retired Mack, who was promoting the Santa Fe show.

"Mack helped out a lot and he thought maybe I could beat Cohen," Ortiz remembered in the 1990s. "Eddie couldn't work my corner, so Dave Jackson did — but Cohen still beat me. Cohen and I had sparred a few years before and I'd dropped him, but he begged to differ, saying he'd slipped."[13]

Cohen was of another class and he "showered" Ortiz "with a rain of gloves," winning a lopsided decision. "Ortiz, who has been making monkey of New Mexico scrappers, was not experienced enough for the wily Cohen," the *New Mexican* reported. "He kept backing into corners where Cohen belted away at him round after round."[14]

Ortiz fought one more time after that, then devoted his time to continuing his education.

Ortiz's chief nemesis was another Santa Fean, Andres Carrillo, who was born in 1911.

In the ring he was known as Andy "Gump," no doubt after the popular comic strip "The Gumps," by Sidney Smith, that ran from 1917 to 1959. The Gumps were odd, somewhat chinless characters and while Andy might have had a resemblance, his lack of chin did not extend to the ring — at least not until his final bout in 1933, though that was up against a fighter of contender timber.

Fighting flyweight to lightweight, Gump thumped his way through 20 or so bouts as a regular and occasional headliner throughout northern New Mexico. His six-bout series with Ortiz was one of the most popular rivalries of the era, and he came out ahead with four wins and two draws.

Ortiz might have gotten Mack to mentor him, but Carrillo had Dynamite Tommy. Under Tommy's guidance, Gump was recognized as the best lightweight in the state during 1930 and 1931, remaining undefeated until his last two bouts. Despite his rise and promise, the end came quickly.

On Dec. 15, 1931, Carrillo was matched against comebacking Nick Mortio, who "bashed him with a left hook to the shoulder. Carrillo went down clutching his shoulder, got up immediately, then dropped to a knee as Mortio came in,"[15] apparently quitting.

After disappearing for nearly a year, Carrillo sought redemption in 1933 when he took on the much-touted Tony Chavez. Gump was fodder for the coming kid who'd made it good on the West Coast before making a debut in his hometown of Albuquerque. Coming in poor condition, Carrillo still appeared the more clever of the two, until Chavez dumped Gump on the canvas. Showing heart he'd been criticized for lacking the year before against Mortio, Carrillo got back up, only to head back down for two more knockdowns. The *Journal* criticized Carrillo as a "scared boy looking for a soft place to flop."[16]

This time when Carrillo retired, he stayed retired.

Adopted by Santa Feans in the late '20s and early '30s was "Gentleman" Dave Jackson, who blew in from Little Rock, Arkansas, and walked right into main event billing. Unlike his notorious nemesis Eddie Murdock, Jackson did not drink or smoke, and he was always polite, hence his nickname. He was also one of the first New Mexico stars who could claim a top-level amateur record, having fought, reportedly, 60 times, winning his class at the AAU Western Regionals one year before turning pro.

Reporters doubted he was the 60–5 guy he claimed he was (he actually had a handful of losses in the 15 or so bouts he had while fighting through Pennsylvania, Texas and Arkansas), but he was veteran enough to give any New Mexican trouble.

Jackson came through Roswell in the winter of 1928, beating veteran Charlie Cobb, before landing in the state capital where he made his home for the next two years. During that time, Jackson fought every top local but Mack, and he was an instant hit when he stepped into his first 12-rounder to fight Jose Rivers on even terms.

During the next couple of years, he'd fight Rivers three times — two draws and one win. He'd also fight Murdock six times in the most popular rivalry in New Mexico history involving New Mexicans who weren't really New Mexicans. Against the "Bald Eagle," Jackson won once, lost three times and drew twice, all with crowds that were nearly Mack-like in proportion.

Jackson's most famous line was during his one win over Murdock on Jan. 5, 1929, the first time they fought. After being declared winner by disqualification, Jackson, wincing and clearly in pain from a low blow rendered by Murdock, was being carried out of the ring when he turned to the judges and loudly groaned, "I'll go on and fight if you'll carry me back to the ring."[17]

Jackson became a well-known boxing instructor at St. Michael's in Santa Fe, during the early days of amateur boxing. While a resident, he was also joined by younger brothers Harry "Stonewall" Jackson, a bantamweight who fought prelims and co-mains nearly every time Dave did, and Ralph, who only fought as an amateur.

In 1930, Jackson left New Mexico for the West Coast, but didn't have quite the same success. He resurfaced for a time in 1931, winning in Portales, after four straight losses on the road. Jackson retired from fighting, but limited his time in the ring to reffing and training fighters through the '30s.

One of the most popular Santa Fe sluggers was "The Battling Chef," George "Kid" Marchi, who wasn't quite known for his fancy dancing, having "never mastered the Charleston, not for gladiatorial purposes, anyhow."[18] Marchi fought from 1924 to 1933 but, though he would later claim his record was 50-5-2, fewer than 20 of his bouts are known.

Born in Italy, Marchi came to the U.S. with his parents, who first settled in Salida, Colorado, before relocating to Santa Fe in 1922. Two years later, Marchi was swinging with the best of them in the ring, and he went undefeated in prelims until 1927. His first big test was against the diminutive Dynamite Tommy and Marchi got his first headliner by battering the veteran in an eight-rounder. Marchi got his first loss, via 12-round decision, against Barber Sandoval in a smoker held in Bernalillo.

Marchi upset the odds in 1928 by defeating the unbeatable Colima, but thereafter, tapered down his career. In 1931, he tried to come back, against tough Frankie Cantou, but the chef was cooked in six.

"Often my pay for a fight was nothing more than a robe or a pair of boxing shoes,"[44] Marchi remembered of his career half a century later. "My wife didn't want me to do it — but I did. Every time I fought, she went to church to light candles. My father didn't want me to do it neither."

Marchi's father was a stonecutter and, while living in Salida, carved two lions that, to this day, guard the entrance to Alpine Park.

If Santa Fe had Jimmy, Andy, Dave and Georgie, Albuquerque had "Buddy," "Barber" and "Cotton."

Zelphie Henry Serino — "Buddy" to his buds and ringsters — was a Duke City favorite in the late '20s all the way through the '30s, fighting mainly in his home state with an occasional jaunt to Colorado.

Buddy was born in New Orleans in 1908 but after his Palermo, Italy-born father died, in 1917, his mother moved to Albuquerque to raise her two sons and daughter. While his mother slaved away working days as a housemaid at the historic Alvarado Hotel, then evenings and nights as a nurse taking care of TB patients, Serino lived in the orphanage. In the eighth grade, Serino went to work, delivering groceries, washing dishes and, eventually, boxing.

In 1926, Buddy made an ill-fated debut, losing by knockout to a tough young black fighter, Julius Greer. A year later, he tried again, this time *winning* by KO. Serino became a regular on prelims, fighting between Albuquerque and Santa Fe steadily from 1929 to 1931, drawing with the likes of Manuel Pacheco and beating Freddie Martinez.

Fighting from lightweight to welter, Buddy was matched up tough, always opposite those no one wanted to fight. The locals avoided black fighters, but the Italian kid never turned down a fight, short notice or not, beating (sometimes drawing with) darker skinned pugs like "Wildcat" Parker and "Hot Shot" Smith.

After years of prelims, winning all but his initial bout (which had been avenged), Serino got a co-headline billing on Jan. 3, 1930, knocking out Benny Ayers of Clovis, who'd been favored to clean up. When Solomon "Benny" Chavez pulled out of a fight in Gallup, two months later, Serino didn't hesitate to step in against tough Phoenix slugger Mike Stankovich for his first main event. Buddy was in the fight until the sixth, when he went down. Still he managed to stay upright, at least for three more rounds.

Serino chalked up the loss to experience and went on another win streak until late 1931 when he lost back-to-back against his toughest opposition to date, Bip Luntzel and Babe Colima. Though able to remain undefeated as he cruised through 1932, claiming the state welterweight title, Serino's activity was sporadic thereafter. After two bouts in '33, Serino retired, then resurfaced for a single fight in '37.

Though later chalking up his bout count closer to 60 than the 30 verified bouts, Serino had several memories of his ring career in the '80s.

Buddy remembered having to live in a freight car near Roswell with his family while training for a bout there. He vividly recalled the night he pulled his punches on an opponent who kept splattering the audience with blood — Buddy was more concerned about his wife and her new yellow dress. He also talked about the time he split his trunks while fighting—Buddy sprinted to the dressing room to change, only to find out he'd lost the fight by forfeit when he returned. Not all the memories were humorous ones, though. Serino brought up occasional fights at Old Town Dance Hall, and getting pinched for petty burglary during 1930—the same week Benny Chavez was arrested.

"My wife and mother didn't like me fighting," Serino said. "I'd come home with my face so beat up they'd hardly recognize me. But I loved to fight."[20]

Every era had a cast of characters, and at the top of this era was "Barber" Sandoval.

There have been many Barbers in boxing—even in the modern era. In the '10s there was a "Barber" Robinson and a "Barber" Johnson. The '20s had "Barber" Sandoval, real name Teodosio, though nobody seemed to recall. Known for being continually out of shape and ill-trained, Barber made fights harder than they had to be. But "entering the ring with a bowl of jelly rippling above the belt line as he did, takes courage,"[21] one scribe aptly put it.

In his first few fights, all in '23, Sandoval was a featherweight. After retiring for four years, he came back a bantam in 1927, wowing everyone with a main event showing and win over Kid Marchi, then an even bigger win over Henry Pacheco. After that, Sandoval did what everyone thought he would do, which is to not train. He was KO'd on Oct. 25, 1927—and that would mark a three-bout losing streak, followed by a retirement that had the local press losing their favorite, all-too-easy target.

Other minor league local favorites included featherweight Frankie "Fidel" La

Born in New Orleans, Zelphie Henry "Buddy" Serino was a Duke City favorite in the '20s and '30s. He once had to race out of the ring due to split trunks. When he climbed back into the ring, he discovered he'd lost by forfeit.

Barba, a regular in the late '20s and early '30s. Named after the Hall-of-Fame flyweight champ, Frankie never fought a main event, but was noted as one of the era's hardest hitters—as attested by Marchi.

The "Battling Blacksmith," Bill Russler, of Santa Fe, never failed to amuse. Like Sandoval, he was famous for coming in out of shape from 1928 to 1934, and even more notorious for getting disqualified—hitting guys when down, hitting low and, in general, "pouring forth the fouls."[22] He had several bouts with Chief Sammy Ortiz, of San Juan Pueblo, another entertainer, and once climbed out of the ring disgusted with the ref who'd cautioned him one too many times for low blows. Another time, against Charlie Tate, he just quit in the middle of the fight, refusing to fight anymore, for reasons no one could comprehend.

Nicholas Escajeda — "Kid Nick" — also achieved regular mentions in the press, but it usually wasn't from fighting, which he did from 1925 to '31. It wasn't that the Santa Fe bantamweight was a bad fighter, it was just that he carried a tune with his soprano voice better than he carried a fight. A blanket weaver by trade, and originally from Mexico, Kid Nick won a regionally noteworthy singing contest in Las Cruces that earned him a trip and audition in Dallas, a verdict he did not cop.

Walter "Cotton" Henley was mainly known for three things: his crosstown wars with long-time veteran Johnny Duran, having the distinction of scoring one of New Mexico's shortest knockouts on record, and for his shock of blond, almost white, hair that gave him his nickname.

After the "Popular Tow Head" clobbered Young Firpo and Romulo Padilla, Barber Sandoval was sent in to put him in his place. Henley beat him, too, so they sent Cotton up to Santa Fe where the more experienced Manuel Pacheco knocked him out. Henley retaliated by knocking out long-time veteran Duran — three times — and drawing with Buddy Serino. Eventually, they had to rematch Henley with Pacheco, who beat him a second time, but you couldn't keep Cotton down for long.

On Oct. 17, 1929, Henley scored the second quickest knockout on record in New Mexico when he took out Phil Metzgar in just 13 seconds. He was never given a chance to fight for any sort of state title, but Henley beat several good fighters in the state, thereafter, from Young Pancho Villa to Clovis' Paul Mathis, who outweighed the Albuquerque lightweight by 11 pounds.

The Battling Bellhop

I'll give you some training advice. You let stimulants alone and take plenty of exercise, especially walking and running, to get into condition.
— *Jack Johnson to Frankie Cantou, 1931*[23]

Nineteen years after he'd outclassed Jim Flynn in Las Vegas, former world heavyweight champion Jack Johnson returned to Santa Fe, New Mexico. True, he was just passing through, on his way to Los Angeles in his Lincoln roadster with Italian parachute jumper Joseph Camoni, but there was more than enough time to veer off the main road for a taste of Lupe Herrera's famous green chile stew at the Royal Café. Reporters caught up to Johnson at the Coronado, where he reminisced about his 1912 fight. He asked about Mark Levy, the old-time promoter, and about the current scene. He was told that two fighters were especially worth mention. One was Eddie Mack — Johnson had "heard 'bout that one" — who was, at the time, recovering from a broken jaw sustained in his fight with Benny Bass.

The other was just a kid, by the name of Frankie Cantou, and if Johnson wanted to meet him that could be arranged. One of the reporters hustled down the street to the El Fidel Hotel, where Frankie worked as a bellhop, and brought him back to meet the former champ. They sat and chatted, Johnson giving him advice on training and what to do when he stepped into the local ring for the first time, later that week.

At the time, Frankie was greener than the chile Johnson was chowing down, but in the next two years he would outshine all but two others in the state, becoming just one of three driving forces that would propel New Mexico boxing into the '30s.

Ironically, the month that saw Johnson beat Flynn in Vegas was the same month in which Cantou was born. Another irony? Cantou was born in Wagon Mound, the same tiny town where the original Benny Chavez had originated.

As a 19-year-old, Cantou turned pro somewhere in Colorado, in a bout rumored to have been a loss, but there are no records to either affirm nor deny. But his New Mexico career began one week after Johnson split for the Coast, when he outclassed Kid Salazar in Santa Fe for a four-round win.

A slick "southpaw with dynamite in his punch,"[24] Cantou breezed through the first few opponents, picking up wins over Kid Marchi, Kid Nick and Tommy Bruno in his first year.

In 1932, the "Battling Bellhop," as he was called then, was being compared with Mack, as far as potential goes. By summer, the body-punching, speedy southpaw earned himself the title of state bantamweight champion by decisioning Severo "Kid" de Baca. He proved his claim by defeating Bruno two more times, veteran Lee Chavez and Leo Leslie.

By now, he'd attracted the attention of Dynamite Tommy, who took him under his wing. Tommy brought him to Gallup on Nov. 10, 1932, to fight hard-hitting Boney Chiaramonte, who was replaced on short notice against long-time Durango veteran Chuckers Hildebrand.

No one could solve Cantou's southpaw style — until another southpaw, this one craftier and more experienced. Against Hildebrand, Cantou suffered his first real loss, by third-round TKO. The bellhop was dropped in the second, for the first time in his career, then again in the third, though it came out later that he'd injured his left paw early on when the two started trading punches.

It was a minor setback, at least according to manager Sanchez, who was already wrangling for a bout against Chato Laredo or Babe Colima at the border. "We're going to the big time," Cantou's manager promised. "We'll clean up at home and hit the road, the way Eddie Mack did it."[25]

Dynamite Tommy knew he had something with Cantou. In the coming years and new era of boxing for New Mexico, he was going to bring it out.

Local Color

> *"Schoolboy," dusky exponent of the art of leather-pushing of the heavyweight variety, well-known here, is in the calaboose at El Paso, charged with assault with homicidal intent on another ebon warrior of the ring who is also well-known here — Chihuahua Brown, no less. The two will be remembered here particularly for one match they put on in a local ring. Schoolboy gave his version of the Highland Fling, while Chihuahua placidly cakewalked after him throughout the bout. The latter will also be remembered for the one real wallop he has given in his career, and that was a near-death blow to the fight game in Santa Fe.*
>
> *— Santa Fe New Mexican, 1931*[26]

After something of a heyday during the war, with the success of the 24th Infantry at Columbus, black fighters in New Mexico went back to being ignored, ridiculed and just plain avoided during much of the 1920s.

Speedball Hayden, Clarence "Kid" Ross and Rufus Williams had raised a new level of legitimacy, which made them all the more likely to be snubbed in New Mexico rings, where local homeboys were looking to make good. In Juarez, the original Gorilla Jones, and then

Tiger Flowers, had given black fighters a regular arena for legitimate pay, never mind the cries of *"Mayate!"* that rained down amid the darker skinned warriors of the prize ring south of the border — a racist remark still heard in present day Mexico.

With the demise of soldier boxing, black veterans had to take their chances on the road while newcomers had to work their way up the ladder, which often meant participating in battle royals. During the war, young blacks had been replaced with soldiers. With the return of traditional prizefighting, the old school battle royals were slow to make a return. In the '20s, New Mexico was still primarily Mexican-American. In Albuquerque, there were but 213 blacks in 1920 and but 600 as late as 1950.

Battle royals with blacks were rare in the '20s, especially in Albuquerque and Santa Fe, where aspiring youngsters were used. On a card in 1922 in the state capital, local kids were used instead of blacks and instead of the traditional battle royal, a "resurrection of 'Sinn Fein'" was staged, arming five combatants with stuffed shillelaghs, instead of padded gloves," and they were "sent into the ring with instructions to test the resistance of one another's domes and facial decorations. The rules? There won't be any — except that the man who keeps to his feet the longest will get the purse."[27] The same went with Albuquerque, when on a sporadic battle royal, five contestants, introduced as "Pete, Repeat, Kate, Suffocate and Firpo,"[28] slugged it out for five or six minutes.

By the mid–'20s, black-based battle royals had returned in the smaller towns, especially in Roswell and Gallup where "black huskies," "black wallopers," "duskies" or "darkies" were hustled into the ring to batter one another senseless while the brown-and white-skinned crowds yucked it up. At one such Roswell melee, in 1933, "colored boys were blindfolded and each carried a bell."[29]

Despite the general hilarity at which promoters tried to keep black prizefighters, serious fighters drifted into the scene to become threats. While they weren't limited to battle royals, they were often pitted against one another and given names that set them apart from the standard nicknames. Instead of "Battling" monikers, black pugs fought under names like "Hambone Johnson," "Chicken Giblet," "Sloppy Jim," "Ace of Spades," "Kid Corn," "Colorado Happy" and "Happy Jones."

Most careers were short-lived, but every once in a while, a black fighter would battle his way past a comically-intended curtain raiser to become a threat — "Hot Shot" Smith and, later in the '30s, Charlie "Black Panther" Tate were both able to do so.

Louisiana-born Henry Bankley got his start in Gallup as a clouting clown bearing the name "Battling Bozo." After a couple years of prelims in Albuquerque, he reappeared in Gallup as "Hot Shot Smith," where he mainly fought other black fighters like Essex Jenkins or Johnny Wright. Eventually, locals got bored of it and they brought in Albuquerque Italian Buddy Serino, who edged Bankley. Nearly as popular for his run-ins with the law and boozing, "Hot Shot" was eventually replaced with the ferocious "Black Panther" during the early '30s.

When a heavier fighter was sought, Chihuahua Kid Brown or Schoolboy Brown would be brought up from the border. Fighting anyone from middle to heavy, Chihuahua fought over 100 times during the '20s and '30s, from Mexico to Atlanta, facing greats like Sam Langford, Gorilla Jones and Tiger Flowers. In New Mexico, he was seen as little better than a buffoon, though half the time his behavior in the ring warranted the reaction, sometimes quitting, always fouling and occasionally dancing. The Schoolboy had a similar reputation in the ring, but was the better showman, prancing and dramatizing his way through the rounds.

Opportunities for black boxers were few, unless a fighter was in eastern New Mexico, where in the late '20s a black promoter named Wayman Gray was stirring up things.

A Rising in the East

> *Ernie Gross has taken leave of absence to condition himself for his argument with Mr. Willis next week. When seen this morning Ernie was armed with a bowie knife, large steel trap and pair of leg irons. When asked why all the equipment, he answered, "I'm out hunting for a 200-pound sparring partner."*
>
> — *Clovis News Journal*, 1929[30]

Since the death of Johnny Connolly, there was little incentive to stage a fight in Roswell. Once in a while, one of the bigger names from the border came up for a show, but it wasn't until October '27 that there was a reason to bring back boxing — his name was Jack Rubio.

Roswell's National Guard post formed the "Battery A Athletic Club," which put on four shows at the tail end of 1927 and a dozen more the following year. Welterweight Rubio carried the initial momentum, mowing down local challengers like Al Taylor, also of Roswell. By the middle of 1928, there was a demand for a real challenger — and that came in the form of "Cowboy" Charlie Cobb.

Rubio was nowhere near Cobb's league, and he had to settle for second best when the Houston veteran arrived. Cobb fought nine times in the area between Roswell and Carlsbad, two-thirds of his bouts being against two men, Rubio and Dave Jackson. Rubio lost all three. The only man to check Cobb was Dave Jackson, who edged him the first time in 1928, but lost the rematch three weeks later. Cobb said his win was pure luck, the result of wearing a pair of bright red trunks his wife had made for his birthday, one day before the fight. Luck was again with him five months later, when Cobb won the rubber match against Jackson, shortly before packing up for the West Coast.

"It won't be long before Charlie's 'ham and egg' days are over,"[31] the Roswell press predicted. Cobb was a big favorite in Los Angeles, where he fought the next eight years, but he never quite made the big time.

Even with the losses to Cobb, Rubio remained popular enough in the area to fight twice on one day. On July 26, 1928, he fought a six-round draw with border battler Kid Mex in San Patrice. Later that evening, 30 miles east in Roswell, he fought the same guy, who won the decision this time. He was also well-liked enough to inspire a "Young Jack Rubio" to take on his name. ("One would believe that 'Young' was a favorite family name down there,"[32] the *Clovis News-Journal* remarked in 1929.) Rubio didn't progress fast enough, however, and by 1930 old rival Al Taylor was getting the best of him.

Parallel to Roswell's success was the scene in Carlsbad, in the hands of black promoter Wayman Gray, who was catering to darker skinned fighters and population — a first for New Mexico, in the private sector, at least.

If you wanted to see light-heavyweights and heavyweights, Carlsbad was the place to be, for Gray regularly used Chihuahua Kid Brown, Schoolboy Brown and Oklahoman Ham Pounder. The press usually marginalized Gray's shows, oftentimes skipping results but announcing the "hot time in the town of Carlsbad ... when all 'cullud folks' of this section" would get what amounted to *their* version of boxing, followed by a "regular old fashioned negro 'hoe-down' in the form of a 'midnight ramble.'"[33]

As Roswell and Carlsbad lost interest in the game, Clovis, Portales and Tucumcari fired up their rings. The scene in Clovis would draw the most attention, for the town of 8,000 staged nearly 40 shows in just three-and-a-half years.

Like Roswell had done, Clovis came together under the creation of a club and the draw of a local fighter. The first Clovis card in nine years fell on Feb. 8, 1928, at the Rex Theatre, and it was a smoker with local bouts with — of all things — a jiu-jitsu match as the main event. It didn't fare so well, but with the creation of the Casino Boxing Club, and steady shows at the Amusement Auditorium under promoters H. C. Hill and Tom Cavender, serious boxing came out of the shadows. Most of the success was due to "The Ghost Man."

Ernie Gross came out of Nebraska to settle in Clovis in the late '20s. He was, primarily, an engineer for the Santa Fe Railroad, and boxing was a sideline hobby as a means of regaining his frail health in high school.

There were many reasons why Ernie was grossly popular. Clovis was a big railroad town and Gross was a big railroad man — he was also, physically, a big man, which, in a state known for featherweights and bantams, got attention. Occasionally called the "Gene Tunney of the Southwest," Gross was well-educated, refined and a gentleman. Plus, he won fights.

Fighting since 1923, Gross had been Nebraska's middleweight champ. The records are missing but Gross admitted to losing a few bouts early on. In New Mexico, he lost but once, and that was to a man who outweighed him by more than 10 pounds. For all practical purposes, Gross was the top middleweight during the late '20s and early '30s. Headlining shows in Clovis, Gallup and Albuquerque, he beat the best from West Texas and didn't have any problem crossing the color line. The only man to beat Gross was Luther Platter, of Borger, Tex. When they fought a forgettable fight before a capacity crowd at the Amusement Auditorium on Apr. 1, 1930, the fight was so bad (a rarity for Gross) that the Clovis paper wrote, "Detectives have been working on the case since the second round gong to discover evidence that would prove a fight had taken place in the arena."[34] Platter, by the way, might've won the fight, but he was blamed for the lack of excitement.

The Ayers brothers, originally from Fort Worth, were also big hits at Roswell, Portales and Clovis, where they'd settled. Tommy, a middleweight, and the oldest, lost most of his fights against bigger punchers like Gross. Benny, fighting at lightweight to welter, was the far more active. He cleaned up throughout the eastern half of New Mexico, especially while under the tutelage of contender Tony Herrera, and his main rival was Paul "Bearcat" Mathis, of Clovis, against whom he was 1-1-2. When outside his safe zone, Benny usually lost; both Buddy Serino and Jimmy Ortiz checked his claims for state lightweight honors.

Benny Ayers' chief nemesis, Mathis, fought entirely in New Mexico from '28 to '31, returning briefly in '34, in what was an up-and-down career. Though he could not get past the top guys in the central part of the state, Mathis's crowd-pleasing, charging, slashing "bearcat" style won over fans.

The real stars of Clovis were West Texans.

Marlin Owens of Anton, Texas, fought his first year in eastern New Mexico and he was the ultimate spoiler, first beating the Bearcat in the local kid's first acid test, then knocking out Melrose favorite Speedy Ryan in 1931. After cleaning house, other outsiders had to be imported to give him a challenge. In a trilogy fought between Clovis and Portales, Owens and Battling Jack Doss, of Lampasas, Texas, who'd lost more than he won, went 1-0-2 in Owens' favor. Owens fought nine times in 1931, but left after Red Foster of Tulsa came in and knocked him out. The Anton battler went on to fight another 100 or more times, almost exclusively in Texas, before shooting himself in the head in 1941, after an unhappy divorce.

Foster became an overnight sensation when he beat Owens, but he arrived on the scene just as boxing was on the decline and wrestling, all the rage.

West Texas sent over Babe Ruth (real name Leonardo Castaneda) of Amarillo, who lived in Clovis for a spell; Jack "J.D." Spann of Plainview, a .500 fighter noted for his two wars with Bearcat (one win apiece) and KO loss to Speedy Ryan; and Bovina's Wallace Leake, who defeated Mathis and Spann, but was KO'd by David Jackson twice, all during 1929. Among the top-shelf New Mexicans making pay in the area, Nick Mortio was the man. He was followed by Speedy Ryan of Melrose and Vaughn's Marvin "Kid" Williams. Try as they could, only a select few locals made it past the prelims, but Louis "Turkey" Bradford, Ray Willis, Carmel Eastham, Luther Creamer and the ever-entertaining Lonnie "K.O." Noland, who was usually on the wrong end of his moniker, made solid undercards.

As the numbers started to dwindle in Clovis, promoter J. L. McDermott packed up and relocated to Portales, 20 miles southwest, for a string of shows during 1931. Eley "Kid" Locke, a junior welterweight who could beat Spann but not span Mathis, was the closest thing to a hometown draw. The locals, at least, had colorful names, like "Tuffy" Smith, "Hog" George and Battling Omar Livingston, whose star moment was the defeat of Eddie Murdock's kid brother Thurman. Livingston also KO'd unlikely fighter "Puss" Dwyer when the Texas pug, "'suffering' from a scratch on his nose, dropped to his knees for the count in the first."[35]

Promoters, fighters and fans trekked back and forth from Roswell, Clovis, Carlsbad and Portales during the late '20s and early '30s, but Tucumcari, farther north, cooked up their own scene during the period, staging a dozen shows between '29 and '30.

Occasionally promoter Ed Shacklett could cajole a Clovis fighter to make the 80-mile trip, but he made do with El Paso fighters like Battling Chico II, who would fight just about anywhere, Vaughn's Kid Williams, and a handful of locals the small town of 4,000 could whip up, like Percy Reid and Kid Arthur.

The biggest find out of Tucumcari's fleeting heyday was a youngster out of Borger, Texas, named Neal "Pug" Grubbs. When the 15-year-old high schooler came to New Mexico, he had but a handful of fights in Pampa, of which he'd won all but one. When Shacklett pitted the kid against 200-bout veteran Battling Chico III, the press jeered — but the baby-faced Grubbs earned a draw in a fight that saw Chico on the canvas. "For a fighter so youthful, Grubbs displayed marked ring generalship," the *Tucumcari News* praised. "But he seemed to be working thruout under a double wrapping of blankets, apparently being held back by his father, who was in his corner, many thinking the father wanted a draw in order to match the boys for a return bout in Borger, where larger attendance can be secured."[36]

In the end, "Papa" Grubbs was blamed for ruining the kid's career. Within a couple fights, he was touted (locally) as the next Eddie Mack as another schoolboy prodigy, but the old man had him matched up tougher than he needed to be. Eventually, Grubbs was taken to Milwaukee where he changed his ring name to "Larry Greb" and fought another 20 times before retiring in 1940.

Without Grubbs or a local with enough potential to make the next level, the crowd diminished until, on Nov. 1, 1929, fewer than 50 souls showed up to watch what would have been a decent scrap, between Marvin Williams and Red Graves of Amarillo, who refused to fight with such a small gate. In the hole on his last two ventures, Shacklett gave up the game — but he, and the sport, would be back later in the '30s.

One other area was beginning to flourish its fisticuffs. In Guadalupe County, Marvin

"Kid" Williams fought out of the small town of Vaughn. Though primarily fighting in Clovis, Williams, a middleweight, had lived in La Junta, Colorado, before Vaughn, where he debuted in a 1929 ten-round bruisefest with Clovis' Ray Williams. Vaughn's hopeful journeyed north, as well, where he fought a trilogy with Springer's Frankie Zamora, but after he was brutally knocked out cold by little-known Oklahoman Eddie Hewett in Clovis during 1930, he disappeared. A year later, Williams gave it another go, but before he could convince locals he was back, the 22-year-old was knifed to death in his hometown after a dance.

The Smelter's Last Hurrah

Boxing fans who motor out to the Smelter arena tonight will see the next world's lightweight champion in action. Fight experts all over the country agree, almost to the man, that Tony Herrera El Paso boy, is the coming champion of the lightweight division.
— *El Paso Times*, 1930[37]

After more than a decade of fights at Fort Bliss' Punch Bowl, the order from above came down hard: No more boxing. No more *professional* boxing, anyway. Sure, soldier boxing could continue at Bliss, but it had to be amateur. No discussion. It was an end of an era for ringsiders who'd been frequenting the famous venue since the days of Johnny Sudenberg, "Dandy" Dick Griffin and Nick Gundy. As of June 1929, the Punch Bowl was taking the count.

Though Juarez continued to stage twice-a-month shows — it would have consistent action for the next 75 years — El Paso had no place to call its own due to Texas' stringent anti-prizefighting laws that were, astonishingly, still in effect.

Equally throwback were the ways local promoters sought to combat the anti-combat laws. As their predecessors had done 20 years before, promoters formed the "El Paso Athletic Club," a private membership organization that would hold local "meetings" once a month or so at the National Guard Armory. The meetings would, of course, feature entertainment in the form of boxing. While civilians and non-members couldn't *possibly* get in, for tickets were not being sold, "membership cards," on the other hand, *were* readily available for anyone looking to "join the club."

The ol' workaround might've worked at the turn of the century, but in 1929, promoters weren't fooling anyone. They were shut down by local politicians before their first "meeting." That's when Albuquerque-born "Dandy" Dick Griffin made his return to the border — and New Mexico.

The irony was not wasted on local ringsters, for Griffin had been one of the first big headliners at the Punch Bowl. Since retiring from the sport that had left him blind in one eye (he would lose sight in his other eye in 1934), Griffin had gone on to be a successful promoter in Fort Worth — where local politicos *did* look the other way when it came to launching fights at "business clubs."

Griffin had been a topnotcher in his day, but as a promoter and a lobbyist hell-bent on overturning the ban on boxing, he'd have far greater impact. Between 1930 and 1931, he would give El Paso a place to watch the fights.

Griffin waltzed into El Paso, had a talk with the boys who owned the El Paso Electric Plant on the other side of the Rio Grande in New Mexico, secured seven lots of land and brought back the old Smelter Arena. The patch of land across the railway's Courchesne

Bridge that had once been called "Bohemia Heights," and used as far back as the 1890s for boxing's asylum to political naysayers in Texas, had its best, and last, period.

Over a 16-month period, Griffin's Smelter Arena would host 29 fight cards, headlining the biggest names in the Southwest and giving the local hopefuls a home. Griffin saw what the Fort Bliss promoters had been slow to realize: the new game at the border was less about bringing in name fighters and more about bringing up local talent who would, in time, *become* those name fighters — like Tony Herrera and Babe Colima.

The first card, staged for June 3, 1930, headlined young Mexican flyweight Chato Laredo, who, on his way up, decisioned veteran Ernie Hood of Pasadena, California. The card also featured a young El Pasoan named Felix Torres, who, fighting as "Babe Colima," would carve out a reputation in Los Angeles before returning as a rising star to headline the border and New Mexico during the '30s. Only 600 showed up for the first Smelter show, but attendance more than doubled on the second card, one week later; then nearly tripled by the fifth.

The second show headlined the "Brown Symphony in Leather," Tony Herrera, who just might be the single greatest fighter to ever come out of El Paso. Herrera was the real thing — a bona fide contender and a former high school prodigy, as Eddie Mack had been.

Born Tony Campbell to a Mexican mother and Scottish father, who relocated from Fort Worth to El Paso after he was born, Herrera changed his name because he didn't want his parents to know he was fighting while attending high school. It soon became impossible to hide for, fighting regularly on Fort Bliss cards as early as 1923, he was wildly popular in his hometown. Herrera defeated solid veterans, including Insurrecto Kid, Demon Rivera and Mike Vasquez, before hitting the big time in California, New York and Chicago.

With just a couple of losses, Herrera was a top lightweight contender when Griffin brought him back to his hometown on June 11, 1930, to face New York journeyman Augie Pisano. "It was like trying to get out of water when you're drowning,"[38] Pisano would say after being KO'd by Herrera in the fourth. Herrera would headline two shows at the Smelter, then return to the outside world where he was campaigning for a very real title shot.

Tony's brother Carlos, or "Spike," was a regular on the Smelter cards, though he later gave it up because he couldn't make a living at the sport. His stints at the Smelter only earned him $10 for a four-rounder.

Fighting more often than Herrera was Colima. Born in Juarez, Colima grew up in El Paso and hit the road early, fighting first on the West Coast. Returning to the border in 1929, Colima headlined Juarez and then three Smelter cards, before heading to Mexico City where he defeated future Hall-of-Famer and world champ Baby Arizmendi. In the coming years, Colima and Arizmendi would fight four times, drawing twice and each winning once.

Other Smelter headliners included World Welterweight Champion Tommy Freeman, who knocked out Roy Stevens in a non-title affair, Ray Kiser of Tulsa, Okla., Jorge Monzon of Monterrey, Mexico, Chick Rains of Dodge City, Kansas, and none other than the uncrowned junior lightweight champion, Eddie Mack. Former world heavyweight champion Jack Dempsey, a personal friend of Griffin's, also came in to guest referee.

Ol' reliables like Pete Loya and Jose Rivers found spots on cards, but local youngsters on both sides of the Rio Grande, a long list that included Jack Rodgers, Joe Perez (a.k.a. "Little Jack Dempsey"), Diego Acuna, Rod Driguez, Toto Lopez, Bobby Fernandez, Billy Chavez, Oscar Iberri, Ox Cowan, Cesar Castillo and "Jumping" Joe Salcido, found a second home to the Juarez Bullring.

There was even a fighter from Smeltertown — the "roly-poly Smelter welter," Porfiro

Vera, who brought in a big crowd from the Spanish-speaking neighborhood. Smeltertown sat in the shadows of the poisonous copper and lead factories that would lead to its ultimate demise in the '70s.

For a time, it looked as if local former football star, heavyweight Ox Cowan, was going to be a force to be reckoned with, but his hyped-up rivalry in 1930 with Juarez scrapper Ramon "Big Boy" Gomez proved otherwise. The two fought twice, and each time Gomez won.

One of Cowan's opponents, however, did go on to bigger things. In his second pro bout, Cowan took on a 6'4" giant named Glenn Strange who grew up near Alamogordo, but was visiting from his current residence of Chicago. Strange was able to put Cowan on his butt in the first round, but was knocked out cold in the second. He would eventually find his way to Hollywood, where he would be best known for his roles in western movies, and as the Frankenstein monster.

The Smelter Arena was not without problems. As weather worsened, the arena was enclosed but the heat was almost always inadequate. Despite 50 cents for the cheap seats, with escorted ladies admitted free to the $1 seats, the Smelter's inconvenient location continued to hamper attendance. As promoters had arranged during wartime, buses ran back and forth from downtown El Paso and they even paved the bridge, but it didn't help the numbers enough to matter. After just 350 showed up to watch champion Freeman fight, Griffin threw up his hands and returned to Fort Worth, leaving the Smelter in the hands of Bobby Burns and the "Texas Boxing Association."

When Burns tried to bring in contender Herbert "Baby" Stribling in April 1931, only 200 showed up, forcing a last-minute cancellation. Stribling offered to fight for nothing, provided the fans would guarantee opponent Kid Allen's purse, but the offer was not accepted.

With the return of Colima and Laredo, Burns was able to increase the numbers enough to keep the arena open through October — but only at the expense of staging an entirely free card that brought in 3,000. Though able to break the 1,000 mark for another fight or two, it dropped back down and, eventually, the arena padlocked its doors for good following Oct. 15, 1931. In later years, the husk that was the Smelter Arena burned to the ground.

Hot and Coal in Carbon City

> "For months, Gallup fans have asked for boxing," he said. "This card is the best that they'll be able to see anywhere. If they want boxing here it is. Attendance at the Friday night ringside will determine whether I can continue boxing or whether the wrestlers draw the crowds.
>
> — Gallup Independent, 1931[39]

From the late '20s through the mid '30s, you could count on Kitchen's Opera House to stage, on the average, one fight card a month, headlining the occasional out-of-town name fighter and a horde of local youngsters from the city's mines and schools.

When the rest of the state had solidified the dominance of peleadors de la raza, the fighters that came up from below ground in Gallup after a hard day's work in the mines were not only mixed, but plentiful. Due to Gallup's exceptionally pure coal and another mining surge, the city's population had gone from 4,000 in 1920 to 6,000 in 1930. Increased coal production brought an influx of immigrants from Britain, China, Greece and Italy — and the hearty return of prizefighting.

Some of the best fighters were Italian. There were so many "battling wops" that "Carbon City" was more like "Carbon*ara* City," that anyone who fought in Gallup would not get a pasting, but a "pasta-ing" — the jokes were many, but, then again, so were the legion of "spaghetti swatters" that pervaded the ring for a good decade.

It was also an Italian who stirred the pot at Kitchen's, and four saucy siblings who served the patrons at the opera house by dishing out defeats to nearly anyone entering the Gallup ring. The promoter was one Guido Zecca, who took over the prizefight scene in 1929 from Tom Danforth, and the four fighting brothers were Tony, Nardine, Julio and Sam Chiaramonte.

Originally from Sicily, the Chiaramontes had found their way to Allison, two miles outside of Gallup, and then to the city itself, to work the mines. When they were old enough to dig, they left school to make money — but whether they were in school or working, they fought.

The oldest fighting brother Tony, 17 at the time, was the first to enter the ring, though his debut, in 1924, did not bode well for the rest of the clan. Fighting as "Battling Chiaramonte," Tony was knocked out by Sailor Riley of Washington. The knockout "proved that the title [of 'Battling'] had been misapplied,"[40] went the local write-up. One week later, however, Tony was redeemed when, minus the "Battling" moniker, he won a 12-round decision over another regular, Tim Herrera.

Tony would not fight again, but younger brothers Leonardo (Nardine), Julio and Sam would. Nardine, just 12 at the time, was next.

"I didn't care that much for boxing," Nardine recalled nearly 80 years later. "I just started doing it because everyone else was doing it. But I didn't like it. My first fights were alley fights — street or school fights. Then me and my brothers, or with the Corretto or Comodoro brothers, we'd do frame-ups on the street. Get the drunks to throw us change. They'd throw dimes and nickels on the ground.... Boxing was all a bunch of kids at first. Tony was the oldest and he just had a couple fights, but he'd train us and other fighters. We'd fight while in school, or fight when we left school to work in the coal mines. We'd work 10, 12 hours and then go fight at night."[41]

Nardine was just 12 years old when he stepped into the ring for the first time before a packed house of 400 at Kitchen's, on March 6, 1925, to fight a three-round draw with Madera Turner. On that same night, Nardine's brother Sam, not even 10 years old, went three with Dominic Corretto, the same age. "They handle a vicious pair of gloves," the *Gallup Herald* reported. "The match was fought on a winner take all basis [but] both contestants joined in a coin scramble for the offerings from the ringside."[42]

Nardine and Sam were thrown on occasional shows and, in 1929, were joined by Julio, who was 14 when he made what should be, for all practical purposes, his pro debut.

Zecca had taken over promotions in Gallup by '29 and instead of looking for out-of-towners to sell sporadic shows, he worked on bringing up locals — and the Chiaramontes were key to his formula. Until the Chiaramontes were a bit more seasoned (still teenagers), Zecca headlined the Insurrecto Kid, who would be the biggest draw early on, Jimmy Thais and Angel Cantu. Black brothers Essex and Max Jenkins were regulars in the late '20s to early '30s, as was "Hot Shot" Smith. Imported headliners ran the gamut from Eddie Murdock, always a favorite in Gallup, to Dave Jackson, Solomon "Benny" Chavez, Battling Chico II and, during his final year of fighting, Eddie Mack.

There were four fighting Chiaramonte brothers from the coal mines of Gallup. Pictured with their high school football team are Sam "Boney" Chiaramonte ("B.C.") and Nardine Chiaramonte ("N.C.").

Zecca knew he had found gold in the city of coal with the Chiaramontes, however. The fans were already familiar with Nardine, now 16, and Sam, 13. They would soon start cheering for the latest addition, Julio.

Sam was the crowd pleaser — and always would be. By 1929, everyone had forgotten his real name and was calling him "Boney." "He was all bones," recalled Nardine. "He'd had tapeworm when he was young and got really skinny, so we started calling him 'Boney.' It caught on."[43]

The youngest Chiaramonte was making $5 a fight by 1930. Of the remaining trio, Boney would fight the most often and the longest — as a pro, anyway. Boney went undefeated in what should be considered his first eight pro bouts, before going up against two power-houses, Abie Chavez and Tony Chavez, who are two of the best-ever boxers produced in the state. Keeping in mind that Boney was, at the time, a mere 15-year-old, he lost a five-round decision to Abie and a sixer to Tony.

In a career of more than 30 bouts that wasn't just limited to Gallup but included the Four Corners area, Arizona and Albuquerque, Boney would lose just two more times, later in the decade, to Colorado state champion Chuckers Hildebrand and New Mexico state champ Charlie "Black Panther" Tate. But he would also score big wins over solid veterans Eddie Caponi, of Colorado, and Babe Colima.

Though not fighting nearly as often, Nardine fought sporadically from 1930 to 1935, remaining undefeated to the end. His best payday was $75 and his biggest wins included decisions over veteran Phil Usquiano and crosstown rival George Avila. ("He was pretty good — but I couldn't knock him out, and only made $20.") Nardine insists, however, that he lost one fight, absent from the records: "I lost to a Spanish fighter in Cortez [Colorado] around 1935," he recalled. "I was stopped in the sixth or the seventh and I didn't train. I remember thinking, 'I better lay down.'"[44]

Julio was the most successful Chiaramonte. Born Aug. 11, 1915, Julio had all the makings of a Mack or a Herrera. The only problem was he was born and raised, then trained to fight, in Gallup. He was lucky to find a regular ring and willing brothers who would spar with him. We'll never know if Julio Chiaramonte had the same potential as Mack, but one thing is evident: he was every bit Eddie's equal in how he used prizefighting to get an education.

They called him the "Fighting Italian" and the "Bounding Basque." Like his brothers, Julio had to go school and work the coal mines, but he juggled all of that, all the while, between 1929 and 1931, becoming the biggest prospect New Mexico never realized it had. As a professional during that period, Julio did not lose a single fight. He fought 22 times as a pro before turning 17, one just after, racking up a 21-0-2 record, while two of those bouts were against the best fighters in the Southwest, one a world-ranked welterweight.

Julio racked up his first five wins in 1929, then fought seven times in 1930 — twice in Arizona, twice in Durango — and as early as February, promoters were considering a match between the 15-year-old slugging sensation and 200-bout veteran Battling Chico II. They changed their minds, but one year later, instead of a cagey-but-quickly-declining warhorse like Chico, they brought in Benny (Solomon) Chavez, who'd defeated the likes of Mack and Murdock. Benny would decide whether Julio would "go to the top in the profession or continue to perform only in local rings."[45]

They were scheduled for a ten-rounder slated for March 25, 1931. Chavez was a slight favorite, based on experience, but Julio was a live underdog, who had youth and power on his side. As an added bonus, Julio's brother Boney would be taking on Benny's cousin, youngster Tony Chavez — a future contender and world title challenger.

After "ten torrid rounds" that had Chavez scoring with hard lefts to the jaw while rushing at the youngster, and Julio boring in, trying to make it a scrap in the pocket, the fight was ruled a popular draw. Two judges saw it as even, but the ref thought Chavez had the edge. There were no knockdowns and scribes from both local papers thought Chiaramonte might've won had he not held back his right hand as often as he did; on the other hand, Chavez was thought to be fighting cautiously, wary of Chiaramonte's big right hand.

A draw for a 16-year-old high school student, against a 100-bout veteran who'd beaten the likes of Mack and Murdock, was a major victory. Julio's future in the pro ranks was assured — that is, if he wanted it. He was not so sure.

Julio kept fighting, scoring a draw many saw him winning, on the Fourth of July 1931 in Durango against former Mack foe Sidney "Kid" Belt, but when he came home, things were different. Julio wanted an education — and he aimed to use boxing to get it.

When Julio's next bout was announced, August 25, 1931, at Kitchen's, promoter Zecca announced that he would not be paying Chiaramonte the usual purse, but turning over the proceeds of his match "to pay tuition to the New Mexico Military Institute at Roswell"[46] in the fall. At NMMI, Chiaramonte was planning to box — as an amateur.

The lines were blurred back in the early '30s, but, generally, if you got paid to fight, you were no longer an amateur. After 21 bouts, Chiaramonte and Zecca were now saying that all previous bouts had *been* amateur, since the earnings applied to tuition and school expenses. Back in 1931, no one questioned it. Playing it safe, Chiaramonte "refused Zecca's offer" of a purse, even if it was turned over to the school, "in order to keep his amateur standing so that he will be eligible to participate in athletics at the Military Institute."[72]

What came to be known as Julio's farewell card, on Aug. 25, 1931, Zecca lined up Albuquerque's Buddy Serino in a ten-rounder, but on the night before, Serino had been knocked out by Louisville warhorse Bip Luntzel. Serino later said that his head was still ringing when he got up for breakfast, so he tracked down the guy who *gave* him the headache, to fill in for him. Zecca, left with little choice, was wired. Luntzel was game—and why not? He'd never heard of this youngster from Gallup; what could a kid in high school do to a veteran like himself? Especially one who was on his way to fight in the amateurs at NMMI? Why, in Luntzel's own youth, he'd been a promising amateur, winning the semi-finals of the AAU tournament in 1925.

Ol' Bip got whipped in less than four rounds. Chiaramonte exploded out of his corner with such ferocity, Luntzel wished he was back in Albuquerque enjoying the spoils from the night before. He was hurt in the second and, in the third, Chiaramonte smashed a "sizzling right into his ribs," then a left upstairs. Luntzel "slumped against the ropes and fell, striking his head. He was completely out." Referee Duffy gave Luntzel a choice of losing by TKO, or losing the round, if he returned to the ring, which he did, but he didn't last long. In the fourth, Chiaramonte floored him with another big left that had the veteran landing "face downward, like a stunned ox."[48]

After 22 professional bouts, Chiaramonte turned amateur and headed to Roswell where he had two goals: get an education and box on the U.S. Olympic team. Having fought and beaten some of the top men in the Southwest, how tough would fellow youngsters be for Julio? The answer was "not very."

Chiaramonte mowed down the opposition in the amateur leagues. Fighting from welterweight to middleweight, and giving up as much as 25 pounds just to get a fight, Julio was unbeatable. In the first box-offs at NMMI, he knocked out light-heavyweight T. W. Jones, who'd held the Institute's boxing belt for the preceding three years.

After a year at NMMI, Julio returned to Gallup the following summer, where Zecca had lined up a homecoming card on

While still in high school, Julio Chiaramonte proved himself one of the state's toughest fighters by drawing with respected veteran Solomon Chavez and defeating contender Eddie Murdock. After 22 fights as a pro, undefeated, Julio decided to fight as an amateur.

As an amateur and pro, Julio Chiaramonte (right) fought 100 times — losing just one disputed amateur decision while striving to qualify for the Olympic Trials in 1936.

Aug. 23, 1932, for the undefeated amateur, who was itching for a challenge after what had been an easy year for him.

No less of a fighter than ranked world contender Eddie Murdock was brought in. Murdock had faced — and beaten — world champions; he'd even beaten Mack. Sticking an amateur in the same ring — well, an amateur who'd had 22 professional bouts before he was 17 — was tantamount to manslaughter. But it sold tickets.

More unfathomable than the match-up was the belief that they could still claim Chiaramonte was amateur, while fighting a 150-fight veteran, a bona fide welterweight contender, at that. But that's just what they did, claiming Julio's "purse" would be used for books and tuition, which it probably was. They got away with it. And 17-year-old Julio Chiaramonte *won*.

Chiaramonte came on so strong that Murdock used every dirty trick in the book to stay on his pins, fouling Julio no less than four times, though in one of the exchanges, both fighters were accused of throwing low. After the fifth, the local referee was on his way to disqualifying Murdock, but Chiaramonte refused to claim a win by DQ and insisted the fight go on.

He might have wished he had taken the win otherwise, because after losing the early frames, Murdock went to work in the sixth, turning the momentum on Julio, who'd been the "aggressor at all times" through the fifth. Taking most of Chiaramonte's punches "on his gloves, on his elbows, and on the top of his bald head.... Murdock opened his attack in the sixth round which all judges gave him. In this round, he punished Chiaramonte considerably." The fight went back and forth through the final frame, every round featuring "heavy slugging and damage on both sides."[49]

The judges were split. All three judges scored the fight six rounds to four, but two gave the edge to the hometown kid, giving Chiaramonte the win by split verdict. Murdock and his team shouted robbery, saying the "Bald Eagle" had won but, at worst, it should've been ruled, "taking into the consideration the home town element, a draw." "One out-of-town fan who attended the fight said it appeared a draw, but he thought 'it was right to give the local boy a decision since he was a good scrapper.'"[50]

After the Murdock win, Chiaramonte returned to Roswell and the amateurs.

Always seeming to get away with controversy — could be, no one read their weekly papers — Gallup had two other fights that escaped attention in the state.

The first was another Murdock fight, this one on Aug. 30, 1929, in which Murdock and Bulldog Gonzales of El Paso fought a foul-filled brawl that had the referee, first, awarding the win by DQ to the Bulldog in the third, claiming Murdock had used illegal kidney blows. Murdock *and* the judges disagreed and an argument ensued, forcing promoter Zecca to dismiss the ref and take over as third man in the ring. "Murdock led continuously until the tenth round when he landed a solid left to the bread basket. Gonzales flopped to the canvas and claimed a foul. Local doctors at the ringside failed to discover evidence of a foul blow and Murdock was declared the victor."[51]

That's when the fun started. The good news was that it was the biggest crowd that had ever packed into Kitchen's — possibly as many as 900, for the gate was $1,200. The bad news was the same: there were 900 people in the opera house when a riot followed the reading of the verdict. Four men wound up in the hospital, "several [ended up] in bed at home," and 20 were locked up in jail. Murdock called the riot "one of the best he had ever seen."[77] The riot started in Gonzales' corner after the fight. "Gonzales seems to have become tired of the sympathies of one of his admirers and called a policeman. The fan resented the interruption and licked the cop. Then the fun started, Eddie states, and knives, two by fours, and fists, were flung in every direction, with abandon."[52]

"Ah, that's Gallup," was the general reaction in the bigger cities.

"Ah, that's Gallup," was probably the same response when — and *if* — anyone found out about the bout that was staged on May 22, 1931. In 1892, Gallup had been the site of the first known female boxing match. Now, Gallup was staging the *second*:

> In the preliminary bout, Miss Faye Wiggins won the decision in the fourth round after the towel had been thrown to Miss Amy Brock, substituting for Amy Byrd. The two girls put on the first exhibition between the fairer sex, with much slugging, awkward blows and minus the customary hair-pulling.[54]

Women's boxing would not enter the picture again until the late 1950s.

The Ring in Four Corners

> It has developed that Farmington has some good boxers in the amateur class and a few who might be entered in attractive events, so it has been decided to hang up an occasional purse for which boxers and wrestlers from neighboring towns and cities may contend.
>
> — *Farmington Republican*, 1929[55]

In the first half of New Mexico's boxing history, the Four Corners area was strangely quiet. The first known show in the region — that anyone knows about, or was recorded — did not occur until 1927 in Farmington, the biggest city in northwest New Mexico. In 1928, there was *nada*. But in 1929, the fistic art had found a new home. Though eight shows were staged that year, it slowed down thereafter, but remained somewhat consistent. As seen in other towns, the explosion — if it could be called that — was due to one promoter and one fighter.

The fighter, just a youngster at the time, was Abie Chavez and the promoter was, or *would* be, his manager, Carl Duorte, who would become the "Father of Farmington Boxing," staging more than 30 shows through the next three decades. Most of the meaningful ones headlined Chavez. But before there was the "Farmington Flash," before Abie was discovered, there was Duorte teaching boxing and running athletics. Before there was Duorte, however, there was a pug named "Pug" Dial, from Aztec, who was something of a fighter in the area.

On the first Farmington show, Pug was pitted against Canadian Dave Mustafa in a four-rounder that was part of an annual carnival and rodeo. Though slated for ten, it was declared a draw in the fourth when a spectator entered the ring and hit Mustafa not once, but twice, on the head with a beer bottle. It wasn't the best way to start a prizefighting scene.

Two years later, another attempt was made, and by now Duorte had made the move to Farmington. This time, Pug was brought back and pitted against Durango's Toots Markle. The Four Corners' New Mexico-Colorado rivalry, which still exists in the pros in the modern era, was born. Dial clocked Markle in the seventh and he was acknowledged as the San Luis Basin welterweight champion.

Working with the local post of the American Legion, Duorte started staging shows, bringing down Durango's Chuckers Hildebrand to headline — he just might be the most popular fighter ever produced there, though Elco Garcia would be a close rival in the 2000s. Duorte got to thinking, "If only there was someone from New Mexico to challenge Chuckers."

Duorte noticed a youngster playing basketball, fast with his feet and his hands. When the game was over, he told the kid to lace on a pair of gloves, and he threw him into the ring. After knocking out the first two kids and starting on the third, Duorte stopped him and told him to show up for training. The kid was 16-year-old, 100-pound Abie Chavez.

On a card held in an outdoor tent at the Green & Eaton Auction Yard in Farmington, on July 20, 1929, that saw Colorado bantam Frankie Mitchell knock out Ignacio, Colorado's Frank Taylor in three, and Hildebrand outslick Farmington's Wesley Hemstreet, Chavez made his debut in the ring as "Kid Abe," outpointing Johnnie Ford of Durango. On this first full fight card, the locals were suddenly smitten with the sport, and they asked for — and received — another one.

Abie fought, and won, again. Hildebrand, Battling Chico II, and even Eddie Murdock were brought in to headline shows, but the prelims were about the local kid, who was getting better with each fight. In 1930, he was good enough to fight six-rounders — and then he was good enough to headline. Still undefeated, Chavez was taken on the road in 1931 to fight in Gallup — and he wasn't matched up easy. "We're going to splatter some spaghetti!" Chavez would say on his way to the Carbon City, where he twice fought Boney Chiaramonte, for a win and a draw.

By the summer of 1932, Chavez, no longer a 100-pound scrawny kid but a solid 115-pound bantamweight, was ready for his first big fight, against veteran Chuckers Hildebrand. Touted as the "Farmington Whirlwind," which would develop into the long-running "Farmington Flash," Chavez was ready to *really* begin his career.

18. Three for One, 1930–1935

Early this morning, several hours before the shafts of oncoming daylight began to streak the eastern sky, Benny Chavez was "counted out" by the Great Referee in the man's ward of Mt. San Rafael hospital.

—*Trinidad Chronicle-News*, 1931[1]

In the first golden age of boxing in New Mexico, the '10s, between 550 and 600 fight cards had been staged in the new state, with at least a third of that number soldier-based. The '20s had seen around 500 shows, thanks to the post-war surge in interest, and the career of Eddie Mack.

The '30s were a different story. Despite the Great Depression and a sharp decline in activity in the two cities that had led the sport in the decade before—Albuquerque and Santa Fe—nearly 700 shows would be staged around the state. Decade tallies wouldn't even achieve triple-digit status for half a century following the '30s.

Thanks to Jack Fisher and his wrestling-boxing hybrid cards, the sport retained a foothold in the Duke City through 1934. But thereafter, with no big names in the state's fight mecca, Albuquerque lost its lead for much of the decade that remained.

It was not an easy time to be a promoter in Albuquerque. The Albuquerque Boxing Commission, expanded to a five-member board, had bumped up the price of doing business, from $25 to $40 per show and a yearly license from $250 to $400. During an era when there was little free money to spend on entertainment, and no big locals to cheer on, the gates suffered. Not even the light-heavyweight champion of the world, "Slapsie" Maxie Rosenbloom, could draw a profitable gate when he headlined Albuquerque on Dec. 20, 1932, under the new rates enforced by the local commish. Promoters Jack Fisher and Marty Fiedler took a bath when just 600 (though 1,000 were reported) showed up at the Armory, producing a $482 gate that fell all too short of expenses. Rosenbloom got $317, Jack Silva $131, while the fans got a dull fight that saw Rosenbloom waltz ten rounds with San Francisco's Silva.

It could be the fans knew they were in store for a set-up fight, for just 19 days before, Rosenbloom and Silva had danced through ten slow rounds in another city. "If that is the way a champion fights, then give us the ham and eggers," wrote the *Journal*'s Deacon Arledge.[2]

Scribes like Arledge also attributed the lack of interest in prizefighting to the shortage of coming champions. The Original Benny Chavez had thrown himself in front of a bus and later died from his injuries, earlier in the year. The *other* Benny Chavez had been shot and killed the year before. And Eddie Mack had retired.

There *were* fighters on the rise. People were talking about three: another Chavez in Los Angeles, originally from New Mexico, was doing well; Wagon Mound—the town that had coughed up the Original Benny—had that Frankie kid; and up in Farmington, they were bragging about a rookie named Abie. The fans surmised that the three would replace the one that had been Mack.

In the meantime, the nation and the world and the state were in the midst of the Great Depression. Who had money to go to the fights?

The answer to that question was "a lot of people," for around the state, boxing was actually on the rise. Gallup had their "battling wops" and a high school kid who was beating up contenders. Las Vegas was showing more life than it had since Jack Johnson and Jim Flynn had been in residence for the one and only world championship fight that New Mexico had ever had. There were "Johnsons" and a "Firpo" fighting in Vegas, with a giant killer named "Tiny" drawing crowds at the Rialto in Santa Fe.

Even Albuquerque wasn't *that* bad off, considering. On Aug. 31, 1933, newly-crowned World Heavyweight Championship Primo Carnera was mobbed at the city's train station by 1,000 people, on his way to the West Coast. "Da Preem" came down the steps of his Pullman and signed autographs, prompting the press to admit that just maybe, boxing wasn't completely dead in the city.

Decline of the Duke City

> *Although there wasn't a single heretofore "big" name on the card there were few dull moments during the evening.*
>
> —*Albuquerque Journal*, 1933[3]

During the early years of the '30s, some said wrestling kept boxing alive. Others argued that the regular four-, six-, sometimes eight-round boxing prelims Jack Fisher—and, later, Johnny Flaska—opened his hybrid cards with kept the fans from growing bored with the groan-and-grunt sport. Whatever the case, crowds that often saw 1,200 to 1,500 continued flocking to the Viaduct and Crystal Theater arenas from '31 to '34. The shows paved the way to bigger promotions at the Armory or at Hopewell Field, keeping a handful of fighters busy and the door open for the next stars of the era.

Fisher had learned his lesson in 1931, for when he tried to boost up the boxing portion on a card, it flopped. For some reason, he believed there would be interest in two Los Angeles "veteran" welterweights, Johnny Ramirez and Benny Larsen, who headlined the Crystal Theater on April 17 that year. Larsen, "who is said to be the more clever boxer of the two, was either exhausted from not having eaten in several days or was deliberately taking a nose dive. At least he was counted out on the canvas in the second round, although Ramirez hadn't hit him hard enough to break an egg."[4] By the time the local commission got around to investigating the pair, who'd been rumored to drive into the city together, they were gone.

At the club level, there was Tommy Bruno, Young Fidel La Barba and Lee Chavez—men who fought each other so often, they must've been entertaining fights for all their continued rematches. Occasionally Buddy Serino got in a fight, when the card expanded its usual fours and sixes. Old warhorse Johnny Duran continued to fight in his third decade while Dudley Sargent made two dozen appearances, from feather to lightweight. Featherweight "Jumbo" Cimino—Vincent, at home—fought a dozen times, as well.

Several years too late for old Dynamite Tommy, flyweights were finally plentiful. Albuquerque had Louie Booth, "Chief" Max Padilla and Red Pais while Belen boasted Herman "Kid" Silva and comebacking Dick Castillo.

There were uncountable "Battling" battlers, a long list that included Battling Perea, Battling Willie Gallegos, Battling Jack Brown and Battling Eddie Burke. There were those named after other fighters, sometimes confusing record keepers and scribes who thought they were getting the real thing; Babe Colima and Dick Griffin had namesakes who were far from the real deal.

There was also Charlie Tate — the "Black Panther" — who was the most successful black fighter to date in New Mexico. Since Al Smaulding in the early '10s, no dark-skinned pug in the state had been able to rise above prelim status and into occasional main events and a state championship. Sure, the odds were often stacked against him — from short notice to having to give up weight — but, for the most part, Tate was able to pull it off.

Fighting from '33 to '37, the Black Panther was the man to beat at welterweight. And he was feared — for good reason. In one single week in October 1933, Tate scored three knockouts. He went unbeaten in his first dozen fights and was popular enough to land 20 bouts during '34. At first, he had to settle for winning the "colored" version of the state welterweight championship, but after Tate beat Boney Chiaramonte there was no denying his claim to state honors, black, white or brown. Until 1935, Murdock was the only one who could beat him, but after Mike Montoya, Jim Perry and George Avila "tamed" the Panther, he was less of a threat and soon left the state for Louisiana.

Promoter Joe Roybal later credited himself for discovering Tate, though the Panther had been active long before finding fights under the Vegas promoter. "He was working in a garage or car wash and as soon as I saw him, I knew he could fight," said Roybal. In the gym, "Tate was a natural."[5]

George "Tiger" LaGrone was another black fighter, not nearly as successful and usually losing, but he was good enough to score an upset win over a fading Murdock in 1938.

In what would be the first offspring to follow in their pop's footsteps, Raoul Cordova took on the "Young Benny" moniker in the '30s with the hopes of carving out a Southwest reputation like "Old Man Benny" had done 20 years before. Success, however, was limited.

Born in 1915, Raoul was in the ring as early as

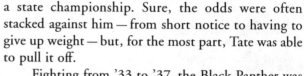

In what would be the first offspring to follow in their pop's footsteps, Raoul Cordova took on the "Young Benny" moniker in the '30s with the hopes of carving out a Southwest reputation like "Old Man Benny" had done 20 years before. Success, however, was limited.

1921, staging exhibitions as a baby fighter on cards at the border, through Texas and at Santa Fe, on which his old man was headlining. On one of the Santa Fe shows, he was joined by "Baby" Chavez, the son of local Manuel Chavez. It wasn't until the end of 1932 that Pops put him in the ring, in a 10-rounder in Belen against long-time veteran Dick Castillo. Cordova netted a draw, but, in January 1933, knocked out warhorse Battling Chico II. Raoul kept busy, occasionally showing "plenty of ability,"[6] but there was none of the flair a world beater like Mack or Chavez had shown early on. In short, Young Benny did fine against most New Mexicans, but could not crack the upper level of feathers and lightweights of the era, such as Tiny Garcia, Babe Colima, Mustang Garcia and Billy Firpo.

The old man didn't make it easy, calling Raoul "Glass Jaw"[7] at home. Occasionally he proved his father wrong, once drawing with Tiny Garcia, drawing with Abie Chavez once (though outweighing him plenty), even stopping "Mustang" at the tail end of his career, in 1939, for the Rocky Mountain lightweight title. In his last bout, in 1940, the old man took him to El Paso where he won a controversial decision over K. O. Barrado, on a card that nearly saw a riot when the verdict was read. The senior Benny also took him back to Texas, where he might not have mowed down the locals as *he* had done, but it inspired several articles who reminisced about the elder Cordova's golden era when

Left and right: Benny Cordova's 11-year career was just the start of a long-running legacy that spanned six decades. Benny's eldest son Raoul, who fought as "Young Benny Cordova," got his start on the road in Mexico and Texas, as a "baby fighter," sparring for the crowds that would watch his father in the main event. In the '30s, Young Benny began his own pro career in New Mexico. His three brothers would follow.

"the 5-year-old Benny would don trunks and tiny gloves and climb into the ring for shadow boxing exhibitions."[8]

If the oldest son of Benny Cordova was unable to make it to the top, Old Man Benny had four more sons to don the gloves in the next few decades.

Albuquerque kept the big shows, and, in the early '30s, they numbered but four — two were promoted by Red Valencia, two by Fisher, and half of them headlined Eddie Mack during his final campaign. The other two flops were the aforementioned Maxie Rosenbloom disaster and an October 1932 Valencia card at the Armory that saw Carl Powell, of Huntsville, Ala., take out Mexico City's Jose Mendez in just one minute, 55 seconds. The knockout "was greeted by boos of the fans, many of whom seemed to think that Senor Jose was 'taking a dive' while the more conservative said that if Jose wasn't laying down, he certainly had a glass jaw."[9]

In February 1933, Eddie Murdock was allowed by the local boxing commission to return after a three-and-a-half-year exile, though only 1,000 showed up at the Armory to watch him outclass San Francisco veteran Petite Mike.

The biggest show of '33 was at Rio Grande Park when Marty Fiedler brought in the big name from up north, Frankie Cantou, to take out Lee Chavez in eight rounds. Though only 1,500 showed up — the same number as a decent wrestling card — the *Journal* wrote that the show, at the very least, provided proof that a promoter didn't have to go outside the state for a main eventer.

Promoters did just that, coming up with the "Big Three": Cantou, Abie Chavez, who'd fought the co-main event on the bill, and Tony Chavez, the Albuquerque-born new star of Los Angeles. Promoters also brought back the somewhat-more-official state championships.

On the next card, one month later, it was Cantou vs. Chavez again, but this time Abie instead of Lee, for the New Mexico state featherweight title, which attracted the biggest post–Mack crowd to date, with 1,800.

There was a buzz again. Abie outpointed Cantou, then went on to challenge Mexican champ Chato Laredo, who'd been cleaning up at the border. It was reminiscent of the early Mack days, when Pete Loya, Mike Vasquez, Kid Mortio and Jose Rivers had trekked north for Southwestern bragging rights. Adding Durango's Chuckers Hildebrand to the equation, the potential for big shows with Chavez and Cantou were multiplied. In 1933, Tony Chavez was lured back to his city of birth, as well, from the City of Angels where he was establishing himself as a coming featherweight. Chavez knocked out Andy "Gump" Carrillo in five on Sept. 8, then returned later in the month to decision Durango's Hildebrand, who'd been giving his namesake Abie such a hard time. Seeing a potential blockbuster showdown in the works, promoter Flaska returned Abie to the city in late October. With the top three state headliners established — Abie, Tony and Frankie — all within a pound or two of fighting one another, 1934 was Albuquerque's last big year of the decade.

Boxing got a much-needed shot in the arm when promoter Mark Levy, "Father of New Mexico Boxing" — now the *grand*father — returned to the city. Levy had started his campaign the year before in Santa Fe, but in '34, he came back home to Albuquerque, digging up his promotional company, the "New Mexico Athletic Club," and seeking to pick up where he left off in 1915. Levy's first return show was Feb. 27, 1934, which headlined Abie Chavez fighting the brother of famed Eddie Murdock, Thurman. Levy brought back Tony Chavez next. After four shows headlining Tony, and three with Abie at top billing, he gave the fans what they'd been clamoring for: Chavez vs. Chavez.

Though it was really a solid featherweight fighting a solid flyweight (who was fighting at bantam, with so few flyweights around), Abie gave Tony hell, winning on the *Journal*'s scorecard, though the judges ruled it for the Albuquerque-born Tony.

The fight was a success — in all aspects but where it counted the most: attendance. Only 700 had shown up at the Armory, where Mack had once packed in crowds of 3,000. Making it in New Mexico wasn't easy, Levy knew, with previous experience. The disappointments continued, when crowds of only 300 and 500 showed up despite dropping ticket prices to just 40 cents for bleachers and $1 for a ringside seat.

Meanwhile, promoter Flaska was bringing in twice the gates with half the purse, with his wrestling and wrestling-boxing hybrids.

First staying tight with a low-budget show headlining Frankie Cantou in September, Levy tried again, digging up old numbers of the Mack-Murdock days. Levy brought back the only Eddie fighting — Murdock — and, in a risky move for the times, pitted him against the Black Panther. Murdock still won, but he came in as a fat middleweight — and it hardly drew more than Chavez-Chavez. Levy held back, thinking less was better, and staged a couple more shows in 1935 with Murdock, who was KO'd by Porfiro Vera. Levy tried several smaller shows though '36, before throwing up his hands and declaring that Albuquerque wasn't quite the fight town everyone gave it credit for.

Just as he'd done 20 years before, Levy returned to Brooklyn. In his absence, Flaska continued the hybrids until those, too, tanked. In the days of the Great Depression, who had money to spare?

What didn't tank were shows promoted with the blaring headline, "FREE BOXING!"

Six shows promoted by A. G. Mader between the summer and fall of 1934 were thrown at Albuquerque's Federal Transient Shelter, located near 1st Street and Tijeras. Mader figured out what to do with the hundreds of boxcar vagrants and drifters coming into the city every month. Many were out-of-work farmers, fleeing from the great drought or the Great Plains on their way to California. In most cases, Albuquerque was a merely a stopover and the Shelter, near the railroad tracks, offered hobo stew, a soft bed and, sometimes, a temporary job. Boxing at the Shelter not only provided entertainment for these distressed hitchhikers, but also enabled the most athletic among them to earn a couple of bucks by volunteering for ring duty. Sure, they were all no-namers, but a fight was a fight, especially when the ducat was free.

On a similar vein, many fight cards were staged at the many Civilian Conservation Corps camps around the state. The work relief camps, which ran from '33 to '42 under President Franklin Roosevelt's New Deal program, were chock full of unemployed, unmarried men between the ages of 18 and 25 — ideal for boxing.

One of those young men from the CCC camps, from Ribera, between Pecos and Las Vegas, was Miguel Tapia. Miguel's first child, Virginia, would be the mother of one of New Mexico's biggest champions — Johnny Tapia. In fact, it was "Grandpa" Miguel who taught Johnny the fundamentals of boxing, and who first brought him to a gym.

After Levy split, Art Woods tried for a time to rejuvenate the scene in 1936, but attendances were too low. Those who'd gotten used to finding spots on hybrid cards either retired or traveled the state to the many other fight centers that took over the scene in the mid-to-late '30s.

Though Tony Chavez returned in 1938 to attract the biggest crowd of the decade — 2,000 fight-starved fans — the boxing scene in Albuquerque, at least for the '30s, was virtually dead. Action went elsewhere. And there was plenty of it.

The Farmington Flash

> *Chavez is one of the few Spanish-American boys to get to the top. He is a sensational, rip-snorting, human buzz-saw when in action, and swings gloves from the first round to the finish.*
>
> —*The Morning Las Vegan,* 1934[10]

> *When Grampa trained me, he'd say, "I'll hit you like Abie Chavez!"*
>
> —*Johnny Tapia,* 2005[11]

Abie Chavez was both blessed and cursed.

Abie's mojo was his ferocity, his chin and his charm. One forgotten sports-writer described him as possessing "brown skin, straight black hair and a row of gleaming teeth that show in a sort of snicker during the heat of a battle."[12] But, like Dynamite Tommy, Abie's jinx was his small stature. First fighting just a hair north of the triple digits, Abie quickly grew into the bantamweight division, but only because he had to, in order to fight. At best, Chavez was a flyweight, so he consistently gave up poundage during his career.

Chavez was also cursed with homesickness and loyalty. During his peak period, Abie had several offers outside the Southwest, but he didn't want to leave New Mexico. He was also fiercely loyal to the man who discovered him while playing basketball in Farmington, Carl Duorte, with whom he would remain his entire career.

Despite the handicaps, Abie is still regarded as one of the best fighters ever produced in New Mexico. With an estimated 70 bouts, he was never stopped, and all of his losses — and most of his wins, for that matter — were against bigger men. He's also the single best fighter to ever come out of northwest New Mexico, where his success had a lasting influence on boxing in the Four Corners area.

Called "Four Corners" for the point at which four states meet — Arizona, Colorado, New Mexico and Utah — the area had produced just a handful of fighters prior to Chavez (and Durango's Chuckers Hildebrand). The majority of the area is rural, rugged and arid land, populated mainly by the native population — Navajo and Ute Mountain — which would go on to produce a steady stream of amateur boxers through the decades, but very few pros. But in over 100 years of state boxing, there's been but 50 or so shows (Durango, Colorado, probably had double or triple that number), and the majority of them headlined Abie or were promoted by his manager, Duorte.

Abie arrived in the area during the '20s, his family being one of the first Hispanic families in Farmington. Born Abran Chavez, on Aug. 5, 1913, he was one of 11 children born to a family 18 miles northeast of Grants in the tiny town of San Mateo, where his father raised and sold sheep.

After his first three years of boxing, Chavez, 18, was ready to step up the action. By 1932, Abie had already "splattered the spaghetti" with the Italian fighters of Gallup. Duorte booked him at bigger fight centers and the kid, now being called the "Farmington Flash," started to build a reputation that, within a year, would have him regarded as one of the top three of the state, sharing the billing with namesake Tony Chavez and Wagon Mound's Frankie Cantou.

After making his debut in the Duke City and having to settle for a draw with long-time veteran Johnny Duran, Abie was ready for his first big test in the summer of '32, being Hildebrand, one of three nemeses who would define Chavez's career. In what was a close

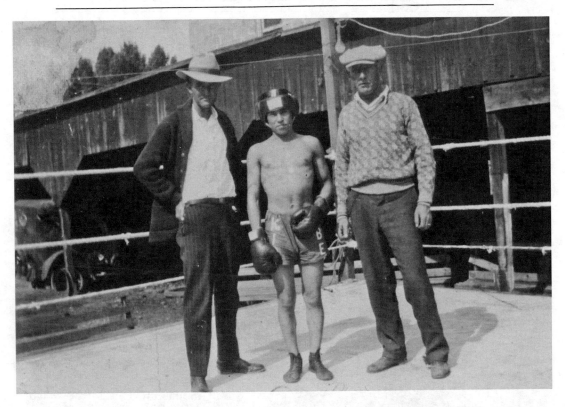

Before he was the "Farmington Flash," flyweight to bantamweight Abie Chavez was "Kid Abe." Abie, one of the top three N.M. fighters of the '30s, is pictured here with manager Carl Duorte (right). The man on the left is unknown.

decision, the more experienced, crafty southpaw handed Abie his first loss in an eight-rounder held in Durango.

Looking for a big win at home, Duorte scoured the state for a name fighter close to Abie's weight — which enticed Dynamite Tommy out of retirement on Sept. 16, 1932, at Farmington's Gem Theater. In what was probably the only fight of his career in which he had a size and weight advantage — Tommy never weighed more than 105 pounds soaking wet — Abie stopped the past-his-prime former favorite in three rounds. On the same dynamite card, Hildebrand defeated Gallup's Boney Chiaramonte and Cantou KO'd a Durango fighter.

Chavez spent the rest of the year moving around, from Durango to Belen to Gallup and back home to Farmington, winning nine of ten bouts and even giving up ten pounds to beat Tommy Bruno, breaking the Albuquerque pug's ribs in the process, for the state bantamweight championship.

By 1933, Abie's rivalry with Hildebrand was a bona fide grudge. After Chuckers returned from training on the West Coast with Speedy Dado, he challenged his Farmington foe to a fight at Durango. Chavez eagerly responded: "I have just read your challenge in the *Herald Democrat*, and don't ever think I will not accept it. I'll fight you outside of Durango, anywhere, any time, from one to twenty rounds, the winner to take all of the purse, with or without gloves."[13] The rematch was set up for Feb. 11, 1933, at the Farmington High School Gym, at 115 pounds.

Hildenbrand promised to send Abie to slumberland before the ten-round limit while Chavez scoffed, promising that "Chuck will hear the birdies sing, even tho it's not springtime yet."[14] Styles make fights and, just six months after the first loss, Chavez hadn't yet polished his buzzsaw panache to make enough of a difference, so he suffered his second loss — but he would get one more shot.

After two more hometown bouts, Duorte took Chavez to the bigger fight centers, which, by the end of the year, had transformed the Farmington Flash into one of the state's biggest draws. Between May and July 1933, he won three bouts with Battling Chico II, despite the aging veteran's weight — with one of those bouts claiming to be for the Southwest featherweight title. There was also a quick jaunt to the West Coast where Chavez was believed to have fought two or three prelims, though the records do not show it. When Abie returned home, he found the boxing community clamoring for a Chavez-Cantou superfight for state bantam laurels. With no one at flyweight to fight, Chavez accepted (coincidentally, there would not be another state flyweight champion until Danny Romero claimed the honors as a 10–0 pro in 1993 — 60 years later).

Cantou had knocked out Lee Chavez in July 1933 for the bantam belt, and was scheduled to defend against Abie in July, which was pushed to Aug. 1, at Albuquerque's Tingley Field, where the biggest post–Mack crowd was expected. The winner would meet Mexican champ Chato Laredo later in the month. Due to the weight advantage, Cantou was the slight favorite, though scribes wrote that the Wagon Mound kid "has a long midriff which Chavez delights in working on."[15] As for the weight difference, Dourte promised that Chavez would have to have "a full meal and a couple of quarts of water under his belt before he can tip the scales at 118 pounds," but that he would "be glad to fight Cantou on a winner-take-all basis and would welcome a side bet of $100."[16]

Fans might have been split, but Abie was eerily positive he had Cantou's number and that his opponent "better start fighting from the bell" or he'd "wind up minus his title and perhaps a few teeth."[17] Cantou followers pointed to their man's crafty left hand, crushing right hook and his southpaw stance — weren't Abie's two

Abie Chavez had all the potential to be a superstar, but chose, instead, to remain a regional champion during the '30s. Abie did not want to leave either his home or his family.

losses to another crafty southpaw? "You can't win," challenged Chavez. "I Cantou," was Cantou's clever counterpunch.[18] A poem even circulated:

> Abie Chavez and Cantou will fight,
> But neither can tell, nor can you,
> If a knockout will be handed to Abie
> Or he'll tie a nice can to Cantou.[19]

Abie's Aug. 1 defeat of Frankie Cantou was the milestone victory marking him "of championship timber." Before 1,800, Chavez landed early, smacking Cantou with the first big punch — a right to the jaw — then went on to floor his foe three times. "For ten rounds he was after the champion like a grim fox terrier and when the final gong sounded there was no doubt that Abie had won the title by a wide margin."[20]

The question was now "How good is Abie Chavez?"[21] Fans were already talking about Chavez giving up even *more* weight to fight Tony Chavez, who agreed to come home from the West Coast, where he was oohing and ahhing folks at the Olympic Auditorium. Not so fast, wrote the scribes — the Aug. 23 bout with Chavez and Chato Laredo would let us know, loud and clear, just how good was Abie.

Laredo was much more experienced than Chavez, and had been a pro since 1925, fighting throughout Mexico, California, Texas and the border. Fifteen-rounders were common for Laredo, who'd faced some of the best fighters in the world. Laredo had a draw and a win over top contender Baby Arizmendi (who would be featherweight champ in '34), a win and three decision losses to Speedy Dado and two decision losses to Midget Wolgast.

"Most people around here believe the Mexican flyweight champion is a little too good for Chavez, but there are others who think Abie can take care of himself with any 115 pounder," wrote the *Journal*. "Abie never backs up, he's tough and he punches hard. He's always in good condition, and he fights just as hard at the end of the bout as at the beginning. Laredo probably will outbox Chavez, but whether he will be able to keep Abie from landing a haymaker is a debatable question."[22]

The answer to the question "How Good?" surprised the skeptics: Abie was *at least* as good as Laredo, for 1,100 at the outdoor venue watched Chavez prove "he could match punches with the major leaguers.... Laredo showed himself the clever boxer with lightning-like punches, but Abie, fighting a heady, cautious battle, landed far the harder blows."[23] The ref, two judges and the local press all had it even, and when the referee announced the verdict, both fighters were cheered.

It was the beginning of another long-running, satisfying rivalry — a six-fight series spanning four years, and every one of them a barnburner.

Promoter Levy jumped on a rematch, offering enough of a purse for the two to fight on Oct. 9, 1933, at St. Michael's Gym. This time around, the "Toy Toreador" from Mexico had the edge. "While Chavez carried the fight to Laredo all the way, the trip availed the Farmington boy very little, as Chato put the leather on him whenever he wished.... Both were trying for a decision by the K. O. route."[24]

The loss did very little to Chavez's draw, for he was booked two more times in Albuquerque to finish out 1933. The opponent lined up was New Orleans' Joey Martin, who'd been fighting on the West Coast. Though he was far from the threat that Laredo presented, Martin stunned the crowd — or, rather, the referee did — at Colombo Hall in Albuquerque, on Oct. 27, when he earned a draw with Abie. The fans, and Abie, demanded a rematch, and got one, one month later. This time, Chavez scored an easy decision.

Looking for new worlds to conquer, and with Albuquerque promoters drawing tighter its purse strings with the advent of 1934, Abie set out for West Texas. In what was billed as a fight for the Southwest bantamweight title in Lubbock, Chavez fought an unfamiliar fighter — but a familiar name — in Thurman Murdock, the younger brother of famed Eddie Murdock who on his way up the ladder, having recently won the Texas bantamweight title. Despite Murdock's reported 140 bouts (they had probably counted the bouts of his amateur career, since Murdock had been an alternate of some sort on the 1932 Olympic team), Chavez was a favorite, and "one of the smoothest little smoothies we've seen."[25]

Chavez scored the unanimous win, then returned two weeks later to knock out veteran Baby Manuel Villa, on Jan. 23, fighting, and stopping, Billy Blunke at Amarillo, just three days before. After headlining Belen for the first time — where Abie had once gone to school and was considered a hometown favorite to the extent that he was sometimes called the "Belen Flash" — Chavez stopped Benny Perez on Feb. 15, 1934. In April, he returned to Belen to knock out journeyman Johnny Stetson in three.

With promoters latching onto the "Murdock" name, Abie was rematched with Thurman on Feb. 27 for his first Albuquerque fight of the year. Murdock started out strong but Chavez came back in the fifth round, knocking his opponent through the ropes. It was his fight from there, and he nearly had Murdock out in the later rounds. Two weeks later, however, he indulged Murdock in a third fight, this time at Clovis where Murdock would attract West Texas fans. Former heavyweight champion Jack Dempsey was the guest referee: "As the diminutive fighters flailed away at each other, the great mauler from Manassa circled the scraping pair like a giant tiger circling two pit cocks."[26] Though Chavez was the aggressor, Murdock had learned enough to counterpunch in a ten-rounder that had Dempsey ruling it even.

It would be the first of three times that Dempsey would referee one of Chavez's fights. "Dempsey wanted to take Dad back east to train and fight," recalled Abie's son, Abie, Jr. "Dad refused for a couple reasons: One, he did not want to leave his loyal trainer behind, and, second, he did not want to leave his family alone. Later on, he told me he regretted his decision."[27]

Chavez fought 17 times in 1934 — and only two were able to defeat him.

The first was Jay Ward of Borger, Texas, who was ripping through the state, undefeated. Fighting Ward in the Texan's backyard, Abie was edged in a decision, but one month later, this time in Albuquerque, Chavez returned the favor.

Albuquerque fans wanted big fights, as far as Abie was concerned — and that meant a rematch with Cantou or a fight with Tony Chavez, who'd just fought a disputed draw with Cantou. There was a third, however, they'd settle for. No one had forgotten the Chavez-Laredo war the year before and a third match was high on the list.

Abie wanted the chance to even the score with Laredo first, so they went at it again on June 19, with Tony Chavez sitting ringside to watch the man he'd next fight. For all the clamoring made by the fans, only 500 of a Depression-weary crowd showed up to see Chavez get his vengeance. "Chavez took plenty of punishment to land the jarring body blows that wore Laredo down to the point where he was almost defenseless during the final rounds,"[28] described the *Journal*. After ten rounds and a majority decision, Chavez was now 1-1-1 with Laredo.

In what was, arguably, the biggest fight of the year, Chavez-Chavez was arranged for the Armory on July 9, 1934, and there was absolutely no reason, reasoned promoter Levy, not to have a sell-out crowd. It was, ultimately, Levy's final straw then, that had him backing out and once again leaving the fight game altogether, when only 700 showed up to see the best featherweight from New Mexico take on the state's best bantam.

Despite the difference in size, it was a clean right to the jaw in round eight landing just "as Abie slipped on the greasy canvas that won the fight for Tony. Abie went down on his face for a no-count and bounced right back up to continue the fight." Abie had won the early rounds with a body attack; Tony took the middle rounds, but Abie finished strong, after the unfortunate knockdown, winning on the *Journal's* scorecard, six to four. The judges and referee, on the other hand, were split, one even and two for Tony, "much to the disgust of the fans," who booed the verdict.[29]

Tony Chavez returned to Los Angeles, where he fought his way up to featherweight and, later, lightweight contention. Abie fought on, mainly in New Mexico, but for a couple attempts over the next two years.

In Gallup, in August 1934, Abie bounced back from the Chavez-Chavez loss by decisioning Baby Azteca, the current Mexican bantamweight champion. After that, it was time to return home to once again face his old nemesis, Chuckers Hildebrand.

Once again, the third time proved a charm and, this time, showing himself at a new level, Abie outclassed his

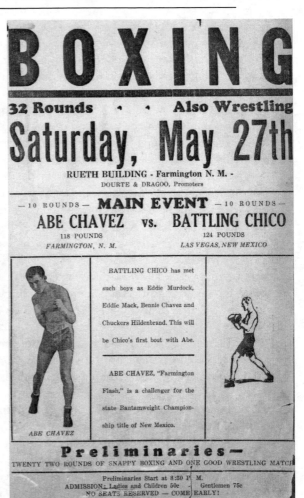

Abie Chavez took on all comers, oftentimes giving up plenty of weight just to fight. In 1933, he fought El Pasoan trial horse Battling Chico II several times, just to stay busy. Chico fought as light as lightweight and as heavy as middleweight; Abie, really a flyweight to bantam, took on bantams to lightweights.

Durango rival, winning eight of the ten rounds. "It was Abe's good generalship in the ring that made the contest as one-sided as it turned out to be," reported the local paper. "Chavez seemed to sense each time that Chuckers was going to try to land one of those terrific blows that have so often put his opponent to sleep, and would duck so that the blow went over his head, and he used the opportunity to get in some telling body blows."[30]

Chavez didn't stop there, but finished off the best year of his career by fighting the much-heavier, taller Babe Colima twice, once in Gallup, the other time in Belen. The two fights were punishing to both fighters and resulted in draws. "He's a tough one,"[31] Abie would say for years. A knockout win over Frankie Hodges in Las Vegas and at least one prelim bout in San Diego, a KO in one over Al Romero, finished off '34.

It was time for New Mexico's top bantam to fly the coop. Before he'd left for the West

Coast, in 1929, Mack had been criticized for hanging around his home states a little too long. The same was now being said for Chavez. He took the advice, but on his first venture out, went in the wrong direction — south. Taking a fourth fight against Laredo was a risky move, having already proved his superiority, but doing so in Laredo's adopted hometown of Juarez was beyond reason.

Once again, mixing his old-style aggression with newly-honed boxing, Abie was on his way to beating Laredo a second time when the Toy Toreador turned the fight around, outslugging, sometimes even outboxing, Chavez to win over the referee and two judges.

Abie's West Coast "invasion" was equally disappointing, mainly as a result of having to give up 10–15 pounds every time he fought. In four-rounders at San Diego and Los Angeles, Chavez came home with as many wins as losses — 2-2-1— then spent the remainder of the year fighting between home, Gallup and Mountainair, beating up locals who were beneath his skill level. Albuquerque was finished as a big fight center for the decade and though the smaller cities were revving up the sport, the purses weren't exactly bulging.

Only one of Abie's opponents — Kid Laredo, not to be confused with *Chato* Laredo — was anything close to a threat, having caught the attention of *The Ring*'s nationwide ratings panel for a time. Against Abie, he was KO'd in two, though the fight was so fierce that "after Laredo took the count, Abie walked over to his corner, and after sitting down, passed out himself."[32]

The next year had even less impact, outside New Mexico, that is. A second knockout over Kid Laredo opened up the year in Farmington. The scene enabled guys like Buzz Manes, Frenchie Ritter and Steve Nahkai, from Farmington, Durango and Shiprock, respectively, in finding regular spots. While the city was enjoying its own prize-fight revival, with frequent cards headlined by Abie, the Farmington Flash was getting a reputation for being a flash in the pan.

In 1936, he fought seven times, remaining undefeated with wins over veterans Leroy Dougan and Trevino Orlando, as well as rising Fort Sumner featherweight Joe Perry. One fight earned him more attention than he wanted: a third-round knockout over what was supposed to be rising bantamweight Kid Lupe Gallinas in Gallup, on July 2, 1936. Turned out, the guy Abie KO'd in three was really Manuel Reyes of El Paso. Promoter Guido Zecca, who was instantly suspicious when Reyes lacked "the mannerisms of an experienced fighter,"[33] demanded to know just who he was. In the end, the brunt of the controversy fell on the El Paso booking agent who'd sent Reyes, and not Zecca or Chavez. With little challenge, Abie took nearly five months off — most of July through November, during which there was talk of invading east or west. But nothing came of it.

On Feb. 3, 1937, in his second hometown of Belen, Chavez evened the score once more with Chato Laredo, though many thought it should've been a draw. One fight later, on May 28, he lost for the first time in Gallup, when New Orleans veteran Henry Moreno edged him down the stretch in a ten-rounder. In the summer, he defeated Orlando again, this time in Dolores, Colorado, then knocked out Las Vegas youngster Frankie Higgins in Farmington on Oct. 3.

Though there was talk of Chavez fighting on the West Coast yet again — some say he did, but no fights were reported — Abie's name faded away during 1938, when he fought just a handful of times. In 1939, Abie fought but once, in Gallup, then decided he'd had enough. Farmington was finished as a fight town and Chavez had missed his chance at the big time.

However, just as Abie started to fade, his former foe, Tony Chavez, was just beginning to shine in Los Angeles.

The Mexican Apache

> *The reason Angelenos underestimate Chavez is that he fought so many preliminaries at the stadium he was almost a part of the fixtures.*
> — *Los Angeles Times,* 1936[34]

One Benny Chavez hadn't been able to do the "West Coast Invasion"—the "younger" version had better luck, though at the club level. Eddie Mack and Eddie Murdock had perfected it during 1929–1931. Due to their problems at getting properly "sized up," Abie Chavez and Dynamite Tommy didn't fare so well. But, in the '30s, showing a gritty persistency, Albuquerque-born Tony Chavez pulled it off.

Cousin to Benny (Solomon) Chavez, Tony was born in 1913 and his first known fight was in 1922 as an amateur on a smoker thrown by Dynamite Tommy for St. Mary's School. It was a rough beginning, getting knocked out in the first, but the youngster showed his fighting spirit by sticking with the sport. Watching cousin Benny fight, then disappear to the West Coast only to return with a bang, left an impression.

Cousin Solomon also gets the credit for bringing his young 18-year-old cousin to Gallup for his first fight. On the March 25, 1931, card headlining Benny's historic draw with Julio Chiaramonte, Tony — actually announced in the ring as "Young Benny"— debuted in the co-main against Julio's brother Boney. "Tony seemed too heavy for Bony and altho the fight lasted the entire six rounds, young Chavez clearly had the edge. He landed cleanly a number of times and scored more frequently than Chiaramonte. However, both boys were willing mixers and it was a good scrap."[35]

It was the beginning of one career — and an end to the other. In another month, Solomon-Benny would be dead from a gunshot wound. Tony would go on to his cousin's old haunting grounds in Los Angeles and, by the time he would finish, 20 years later, he would have an estimated 150 fights while becoming his home state's third contender.

Tony didn't go the way Abie went, cleaning house in city, state, then region, though he returned home several times to break up the monotony of always having to fight endless prelims on the West Coast, during the first stage of his career. After that initial debut in Gallup, Tony kept going west until he got to Los Angeles. By the end of '31, he'd made California his home and connected with promoters in San Diego and Los Angeles for fight opportunities.

Tony Chavez was a cousin to Solomon "Young Benny" Chavez, who'd paved the way for the kid's debut in Gallup in 1931. Chavez left for the West Coast and during the '30s became a bona fide contender.

Tony fought. And fought. And fought. In his first full year of West Coast fights, he climbed into the ring an astounding 22 times — nothing but four-rounders in San Diego, Ventura, Pasadena, Hollywood and Los Angeles venues, including the Olympic Auditorium. Win, lose or draw, Tony was driven to make an impression. Despite seven losses (all decisions), he did. Referred to as the "crack little Mexican from New Mexico," other times as the "Albuquerque Apache" or the "Mexican Apache," the only thing consistent about Tony Chavez was his willingness to fight and the increasingly tougher opposition they threw him in the ring with. There were no easy fights for Chavez — there never really would be, at least not in California.

Nineteen-thirty-three was a repeat of '32, with two differences: occasional six-round bouts and two homecoming bouts in Albuquerque, where the press occasionally noted his progress on the coast. At home, Chavez was cast as not just a prelim kid but a "rising star" on the coast. Besides fanfare, there was another reason; at home, Tony could test his endurance in ten-rounders that were denied prelim fighters in Los Angeles.

Instead of the rare mention in the *Times* or *Daily News*, the Albuquerque press poured it on with Chavez. Was he "anything like the fighter old Solomon 'Benny' Chavez was?" was what everyone wanted to know. A test in the form of Andy "Gump" Carrillo, whose only loss was to veteran speedster Kid Mortio, was set up on Sept. 8 at Colombo Hall for Tony's homecoming. Though flooring Carrillo in the third en route to a fifth-round knockout, Chavez's victory was a hollow one when naysaying scribes said Gump had been out of condition and, besides, Chavez had landed very few clean shots on the "far cleverer" Santa Fean.[36]

With the jury still out for the fans who still missed the drama of Tony's "bad boy" cousin Solomon, another match was booked two weeks later at Tingley Field. This time, Chuckers Hildebrand was brought down from Colorado. The crafty southpaw had just beaten rising New Mexico bantam Abie Chavez and if Tony could beat *him*, well who knew how far he could go.

Chavez had little trouble with the slick veteran southpaw and after flooring Chuckers in the first, and twice in the ninth, landing repeatedly with his straight right, he won a lopsided decision, promoting top local scribe Deacon Arledge to give him the thumbs-up, having "proved himself a fighter of the first water."[37]

Chavez was an overnight star in New Mexico — so he went back to where he *wasn't*, where fighting his way up the ladder was going to net him something more than a state or Southwest championship. Ignoring the locals' cries for a Tony Chavez vs. Abie Chavez match-up, Tony dropped right back into the fight rotation at the Hollywood Legion Stadium. The prospect of being a big fish in the smaller pond of Albuquerque proved tempting, however, as the following year Chavez returned and stayed in the region from March through the summer. "Line 'em up," he told promoters at home.

It was Albuquerque's last big year of the decade, and promoters Flaska and Levy were both pouring what budget they had left into rejuvenating the sport with the best fights they could line up — and the names Tony Chavez, namesake Abie, and Frankie Cantou all factored into the equation of local greatness.

As a warm-up, Chavez, still recognized as the state featherweight champ, took on Henry Jackson of Antonito, reportedly Colorado's champ at feather, but the best he could do was a majority draw in a fight that saw much clinching. Promoter Levy immediately rebooked Chavez and Jackson two weeks later and, this time, the right guy came out ahead with a decision by "battering Jackson goofy"[38] down the stretch. In April, Levy booked Chavez twice. Tony blasted away at overmatched Johnny Gardino for a ten-round decision on April 9, then knocked out Denver's Young Verne Martin in five on an April 25 card that got everyone in trouble, from promoter to fighters.

It was bad enough that the crowd was a slim 300, but they were "treated" to the "cutest bit of punch pulling and slapstick boxing ever displayed in a local ring" before Martin, "so-called Colorado Wildcat, had the grace to take a dive in the fifth round of his track meet with Tony Chavez." The fight was off to such a rotten start that promoter Levy leapt into the ring during the "melee" to beg the boxers to put on a better fight; the local boxing commish was so peeved, they temporarily suspended Levy.[39] Recognizing that the "fans would appreciate seeing another fighter," Levy gave Chavez a "vacation for some time."[40]

While Levy could cook up something better — and he would — Chavez took off for Texas and Colorado for a series of fights. He fought Henry Jackson in two more draws and, at Lubbock, gave up ten pounds in two bouts ending in draws with West Texas featherweight claimant Howard Scott. It wasn't quite the tune-up trip when Chavez came home with one decision loss (to Bobby Calmes) and four draws.

There were to be no more "gimme" fights in Albuquerque, Chavez was notified when he returned. If the top fights couldn't be arranged, there were to be no fights at all. While Levy put together a Chavez-Chavez showdown for July, Tony left for Las Vegas to fight the other big name in New Mexico, Frankie Cantou.

After Chavez had returned to Los Angeles last year, having won the state featherweight title, rising Wagon Mound southpaw Cantou had claimed the championship, based on Tony's absence. On June 6, 1934, the two packed the Armory in Las Vegas to see who the real champ was. It stole a bit of Levy's thunder, for he was vying to make the Chavez-Chavez showdown; but, at the same time, Chavez-Cantou added to its impact, should the Los Angeles comer came back victorious.

Which he did ... and, at the same time, didn't.

Knowing Cantou was a slick southpaw, Chavez closed the distance and went to the body. By the fifth round, Cantou had been chopped down three times, and was unable to continue in the fifth. Problem was, while most of the shots had been borderline, the final blow "appeared low." After ringside physicians examined Cantou, they "declared there was nothing wrong with the Santa Fe fighter. The referee and judges argued almost an hour over what decision should be rendered and finally called the bout a draw."[41]

Many saw it as home cooking in favor of Cantou, but the state featherweight title was still in dispute. All the while, Levy was full speed ahead on a July 9 Chavez-Chavez showdown. Abie had just beaten Chato Laredo and was not only confident in giving up five or six pounds against the "famous" west coaster, but was feisty enough to demand that Tony shave off his bushy beard or he was out. "He hadn't shaved for several weeks, and looked like a member of the House of David," wrote the *Journal*'s Deacon.[42]

Levy did not get the crowd he'd hoped for. Wrestling shows were bringing in over 1,000 and despite Depression-friendly prices of 40 cents for the bleachers only 700 showed up at the Armory to watch Tony win a sizzling though much-disputed decision, on July 9, 1934.

The fans and press thought the much-smaller Abie had clinched the fight, winning six of ten rounds. The first three were Abie's, by virtue of pounding Tony's body. The next three belonged to Tony, who outboxed Abie. The Farmington Flash came back in the seventh by a wide margin and was on his way to taking the eighth when Tony landed a hard right, just as Abie slipped on the canvas, flooring the smaller man. Despite Abie's coming back in the ninth and hitting Tony "five punches for one" in the final stanza, the judges overruled the ref with a majority decision for Tony.[43]

As far as the locals were concerned, Tony Chavez had won by a lucky punch. Even worse? The fans and scribes surmised that three years of fighting on the West Coast didn't necessarily equate to a contender in the works — Abie and Frankie were just as good.

Tony's verdict? Fighting at home wasn't worth the effort — there was too much drama, too much controversy. Chavez returned to Los Angeles and did not come back to fight for nearly four years. In the end, Tony proved his home crowd wrong.

Three days after his bout with Abie, Tony was back in the Hollywood arena, back in the four- and six-round game, finishing the year without a loss, though drawing more often than winning. His dozen bouts at the Hollywood Stadium, where he fought the majority of time, had earned Chavez a whopping total of $455 for the year.

The next year would see a massive upgrade, however. Though there was bad with the good, and he was less busy, with just 11 bouts in all, 1935 saw Chavez finally graduating into the main and co-main stage. It took leaving Los Angeles to do it, too, though it wasn't New Mexico that gave him the clout. In April, Chavez got the offer to fight in Missoula, Montana, against Richie Fontaine, a northwest battler on his way up the ladder and on the verge of contention. When the two fought, on Apr. 20, 1935, Chavez lost a decision and was thus considered safe enough to fight again six days later, this time in Butte, Montana, where Chavez came out ahead with an upset decision.

The win over Fontaine netted him a shot at Portland prospect Frankie Galluci on May 10 in Spokane, Wash., which saw Chavez scoring a technical knockout in the fifth. A knockout over Chicago veteran Mickey Beal followed the very next night. One month later, he was back in Missoula — Fontaine again, who, this time, capped the rubber match with a decision. The mixed bag of wins and losses didn't mark Chavez as an overnight contender, but it did serve to net him a rep as a main eventer capable of going ten-rounders against veterans and fringe contenders.

Chavez bounced back and forth for the rest of the year between Montana and San Francisco. In San Francisco, Chavez picked up wins over easier foes, then was matched up against Richie Fontaine for the fourth time, on Sept. 11, evening the score at two apiece. For the next two bouts it was Fontaine ... and Fontaine, again, the two alternating wins and losses, ending their series of '35 at three apiece. Chavez's back-and-forth struggle with Fontaine marked him as an easy target for ranked featherweight contender Everett Rightmire, who was matched to meet Chavez on Nov. 18, 1935, in Butte, Montana.

Rightmire was Chavez's coming-out party — the equivalent of Mack's initial win over Morgan, back in '29. Rightmire, of Sioux City, Iowa, ranked No. 7 by the National Boxing Association, was next in line to fight World Featherweight Champion Freddie Miller — until the little known, young ham-and-egger Chavez took him out of the running, by knocking him out in the seventh round.

Chavez entered the year 1936 as a featherweight contender and, though fighting but five times, he remained undefeated in what turned out to be his peak year. His new manager, Emmet Ledwith, called out all the top featherweights. When "his boy" had returned home, claimed Ledwith, he discovered "all the feathers giving him the chill." Chavez, he said, "stands ready to meet any featherweight."[44]

After Chavez's first fight of '36, a TKO over Ohio veteran Lloyd Pine in Butte, Mont., he was suddenly a main eventer at the Hollywood arena. This new-and-improved fighter, who'd suddenly developed a knockout punch, was given his first main event in Los Angeles on Apr. 17. "Wiry Tony Chavez, 22-year-old Albuquerque Mexican, who has a trace of Cherokee Indian in his blood stream, will be the happiest fighter in Los Angeles when he climbs into the ring Friday night ... against slugging Mohawk redskin, Pete De Grasse," wrote the *Times*.[45]

Although the Canadian DeGrasse, a veteran of over 200 bouts, had been honed on the East Coast, he was expected to fight Chavez on even terms. But Tony knocked him down in the third en route to a decision. The fight was good enough for a rematch, which was set up for the following month. In the meantime, Chavez took advantage of the attention to hurl out defis, calling out Baby Arizmendi, among other contenders. The press started calling him the "boxing bookworm," when they found out how often he frequented the city's library downtown; they also compared him to his cousin Benny Chavez, though they mistakenly wrote about the wrong Benny — the one who'd challenged Johnny Kilbane for the featherweight title in 1914. The second bout with DeGrasse, on May 22, was another hair-raiser, but Chavez edged the fight in the late rounds, battering DeGrasse bloody.

From the DeGrasse rematch through July, Chavez was eyed by the press when training for Indiana veteran Moon Mullins at Soper's Ranch, as, all the while, his manager yapped on about fighting Arizmendi or high-ranking contender Mike Belloise in New York. Chavez was a 10 to 8 favorite over Mullins, who'd won 18 of 19 bouts in Chicago, and though Ledwith predicted that "'Moon' won't come up for the sixth round,"[46] Chavez was forced to go the distance for the win in what was a less-than-spectacular fight.

The waiting then began. After years and years of endless offers to fight on undercards, Chavez couldn't get a fight to save his life. In August, Arizmendi was outpointed by rising star Henry Armstrong. Neither one wanted to tangle with the "Albuquerque Apache" — at least that's what Chavez's manager was feeding the press. Whether it was true or not, Tony remained inactive until November, when his manager received a telegram from the management of Armstrong for a Dec. 3 fight in St. Louis. Chavez didn't hesitate in accepting the match.

Armstrong would not only go on to be the world featherweight champion, in 1937, but the world lightweight champion *and* the world welterweight champion — at one point holding all three titles simultaneously. "Homicide Hank" is still considered by many to be one of the top two or three fighters of all time. In December 1936, Armstrong's greatness was evident, and Chavez was a hopeless underdog.

For the first seven rounds "that had included toe-to-toe slugging in the fourth and fifth," Armstrong had built up a big lead. But a minute-and-a-half into the eighth round, Armstrong landed a hard-but-low left and "Chavez rolled out of the ring, groaning."[47] The fight was awarded to Chavez.

It was a win by DQ — but still a win. No other New Mexican, past or present, would ever be able to claim a win over a fighter like Armstrong. But it was still seen as a fluke win and a rematch was set up for Jan. 18, 1937, at the Olympic Auditorium.

A crowd of 7,500 — Chavez's biggest audience to date — watched the game 75-fight veteran from Albuquerque fight a future legend. "Winning only one round, the sixth, Chavez forced much of the fighting, but Armstrong kept on the move enough to prevent the New Mexican from getting set before throwing any dynamite. Chavez' handlers tossed in the towel after Armstrong's stinging punches had floored him three times in the ninth and left him out on his feet in the tenth."[48]

It was Chavez's first loss by knockout — then again, there was little shame in losing to man like Armstrong, especially in a fight the *Times* had deemed a "loo-loo,"[49] due to Chavez's gameness.

Now calling *his* loss to Chavez an accident, top contender Everett Rightmire was still smarting from the knockout that had nixed his title fight against World Champ

Freddie Miller. The altitude in Montana was Rightmire's excuse, though the experts weren't buying it. They made Chavez a 10 to 7 favorite at the Legion when the two met on March 5.

It was a risky fight. Losing to Armstrong had not put Chavez's top-ten ranking at risk — but losing to Rightmire could do the job. Proving he belonged in the top-ten featherweights, however, Chavez repeated his original success, tearing into Rightmire who was "covering up at every opportunity"[50] and taking the decision, five rounds to three, with two even.

After a ten-round tune-up against New York journeyman Danny London in April, Chavez made his way to the next level when his manager, Ledwith, was bought out by the esteemed George Parnassus, who took him to New York City for three fights on a four-week mini-invasion. Chavez came back to Los Angeles with two more wins and a draw, outslugging Bronx battler Frankie Terranova, drawing with Frankie Covelli and stopping Govan Rhodes in four. Parnassus had more bouts planned but Chavez's baby had been ill, so he'd left early.

After two months on the shelf, Chavez returned to Butte, Mont., where he knocked out Hubert "Kid" Dennis in four rounds, on Nov. 15, 1937. By now, Parnassus had worked his magic and Chavez was signed to fight Armstrong again, this time on Dec. 6 in Cleveland. Win, lose or draw, Parnassus had also arranged for Chavez to headline the Legion on Dec. 17, in a seventh fight with Fontaine.

With the last three bouts of '37 netting him $1,250 for Dennis, $2,500 vs. Armstrong and $1,100 for Fontaine, Chavez' situation had improved dramatically.

Unfortunately for Chavez, Armstrong, too, had also improved — dramatically. In what would be his third and final bout against the soon-to-be champion, Chavez lasted but 2:04 before a crowd of 12,000 in Cleveland. "The fight was hardly a minute old when Chavez hit the canvas for a count of four. He was up and down seven times before the bout was halted."[51]

Chavez's final fight of '37 was only a slight improvement, meaning he was, at least, not knocked out. In their seventh bout together, it was Fontaine's turn to win, and though the fight at the Legion was close, Fontaine copped the nod.

After another knockout win over Kid Dennis in Butte, Chavez, still ranked at No. 8 among the country's feathers, found the time in March to return home to Albuquerque. The scene in the Duke City had drastically changed and fights were no longer as frequent as they'd been earlier in the decade. But 2,000 showed up at the Armory to see the kid who'd gone to the coast to be a world contender. The scribes and fans who'd criticized Chavez the last time he'd been in town now hailed him as the "Pride of Albuquerque." The victim was rugged-but-overmatched Mexican Willie Davis, who was "too tough to go down" under Chavez's "brilliant brand of fighting."[52]

Parnassus kept Chavez relatively busy in Los Angeles, and he fought five times, mainly at the Legion, and once at the Olympic. A third win over Rightmire occurred on April 22 — this time, Chavez knocked him out in seven — before he was matched against Jimmy Garrison of Kansas City on May 27, 1938, who was taken out in seven rounds.

Now campaigning as a lightweight, Chavez targeted World Champ Lou Ambers, who would lose his title to Armstrong, who, in turn, would also pick up the welterweight title by defeating Barney Ross on May 31, all the while retaining his featherweight title he'd won in late 1937. Armstrong was *that* good.

Back-to-back bouts, on Oct. 7 and Nov. 25, with fringe contender George Hansford finished out 1938 — both were wars that had many questioning whether Chavez was beginning to slip. Hansford was a blast to Chavez's days as a prelim fighter, when he'd dropped two four-rounders to Hansford. In what was their third meet, Chavez lost again. "Those who foolishly established Chavez a ridiculously top-heavy 1-to-2 favorite, sat in pained, anxious silence as they waited impatiently for the tempestuous Tony to get started," wrote Jack Singer of the *Times*. "But Chavez's starter must have jammed. Or else somebody neglected to turn on the ignition."[53]

Chavez offered no alibis, but his right hand was seen in a cast in the following week. Whatever injury he'd sustained did not stop a rematch seven weeks later. With a fourth shot at Armstrong on the line, Chavez looked like he was going to even the score in the "10 rounds of eating around the Maul-berry bush" when Hansford, "storing up his strength for a blistering finish" and "looking like Seabiscuit as he came surging down the stretch," nailed the "scowling Chavez with a flurry of thudding left hooks, right crosses and uppercuts that sent the Mexican reeling into the ropes at the final bell."[54] It was enough for the ref to rule it a draw.

As a featherweight, Chavez had been a rated contender. Now a lightweight, he saw contention slipping further away, especially when he dropped a decision to Fontaine in their eighth bout, on Jan. 13, 1939, at the Legion. Chavez was written off as finished and fodder for high-ranking Georgie Crouch, 11 days later at the Olympic.

"They led the condemned man, Tony Chavez, into the prosecution chamber at the Olympic last night expecting to see Georgie Crouch knock his head off," wrote Braven Dyer of the *Times*. "At the end of 10 furious rounds, Tony was doing the Slambeth Walk down the aisle with the cheers of 5000 fans ringing in his ears. For Referee Abe Roth had just hoisted his hand in token of victory over the sphinx-like Negro who has been hailed as the heir-apparent to the lightweight crown."[55]

Three weeks later, the best Chavez could do was a draw. But three wins followed. Not only did Chavez beat Fontaine (in bout No. 9), but he followed that up with a TKO in the eighth over former featherweight champ Mike Belloise, now past his prime. Three straight losses followed that—Crouch and two decisions to Jimmy Garrison, whom Chavez had TKO'd in '38.

It was up and down with Chavez through the remainder of 1939 and '40. Chavez lost to California Jackie Wilson twice, drew with Garrison again, and scored a handful of wins over less dangerous opponents, even finding time to return to Albuquerque in 1940 for a hometown win.

As World War II started to take fighters away from the ring, Chavez gave up the sport for a different type of fighting—but he would be back.

Newfound Wagon Mound

> *The body of Benny Chavez, who passed away early Monday morning at the local hospital, will be forwarded to Wagon Mound, New Mexico tomorrow for burial. A brother Camelio Chavez lives there. When his body moves in a motor hearse to the New Mexico town it will be covered with flowers sent by the Denver Elks, and a check from McVittie will help defray the cost of the funeral. Some old time friends of Benny Chavez have been raising a purse here also, and all together the veteran of a hundred ferocious ring battles some 15 and 20 years ago; the local boy who fought his way up the top rung of the fistic ladder toward a world's championship, will not lie in a potter's field.*
>
> —*Trinidad News-Chronicle*, 1932[56]

If anyone had forgotten that the origins of the famous — and original — Benny Chavez could be trailed to Wagon Mound, obituaries of New Mexico's first great warrior in early 1932 would serve as a reminder. If not the obits of the daily or weekly Southwestern newspaper, then the active sports section would serve notice that Wagon Mound wasn't yet finished in the ring, for no fewer than three significant fighters came from the tiny town. Covering the majority of weight divisions, there was Frankie Cantou at bantam to feather, Manuel "Billy Firpo" Cruz at lightweight to welter, and Emilio Martinez, middle to lightheavy.

"There were a lot of good fighters who came out of that little town," Lalo Trujillo recalled in the 2000s. In the '30s, Trujillo stepped into the ring 15 times as a prelim fighter. Like Dynamite Tommy, the 110-pound Las Vegan had to give up weight nearly every time. "People have forgotten how good Cantou was — the guy had everything. And Emilio Martinez? He was a big guy and talked a lot, but could back it up. Firpo was another one — he trained with us in Las Vegas, he went all over New Mexico to fight."[57]

Chato Gonzalez, the "Trementina Terror," was one of the early state amateur lightweight champions before terrorizing the welters, fighting from Santa Rosa to Las Vegas in the latter half of the

With Las Vegas gearing up in the '30s for its greatest decade of boxing, there really wasn't a need for the two towns to throw shows of their own, but this was an era of club shows. Wagon Mound had around 18 shows; Springer, nearly the same number; with northern spots like Folsom, Mosquero, Ocate, Roy, Trementina and Watrous adding to the scene. Cantou would be the star of northern New Mexico in the first half of the decade; Firpo and Martinez would steal the scene in the latter half. But there were plenty of other supporting roles to be filled between the stages of Wagon Mound and nearby Springer, which had sprung Walter Caldwell after World War I.

In Wagon Mound, there was Ernie Cordova, a.k.a. "Chief Cardi," game enough for lightweight Tiny Garcia and fast-rising featherweight Larry Cisneros, and who'd once copped a win over Mike Dundee, cousin to former champ Joe of the same name, who'd come in chubby and out of shape; and Solly Garcia, another lightweight who quickly learned his lesson to give the fans more action after "dancing" too long with Springer's Trinidad Cordova — while the crowd shouted, "Kiss me again, honey, I just love it."[58] There was also Willie "Tuffy" Saenz and "Mickey Mouse" — at least that's what they called youngster

Emilio Cantou, brother to Frankie, whose purse would be the coins thrown into the ring for the winner.

Springer had Trinidad Cordova, Chubby Vigil and Moose Maxwell, fighting at light-weight to welter, depending upon what Wagon Mound foe was available. "Cowboy" Willie Roy, "the haymaker artist of the first water" brought the fans from "the picturesque hills of Ocate,"[59] while Roy had "Flashy" Gemez. Trementina might not have any known shows, but they did have Pacifico "Chato" Gonzales, the "Trementina Terror." Gonzales was one of the early state amateur lightweight champions before terrorizing the welters, fighting from Santa Rosa to Las Vegas in the latter half of the '30s.

While Albuquerque and Santa Fe snagged the mega-fights of New Mexico, with Las Vegas taking over as fight center mid-decade for the northern half of the state, Wagon Mound and Springer rarely rose above the smoker level. Maximizing attendances of 300 to 500 at their respective opera houses or the "garage building across the street from the bank"[60] in Wagon Mound, tickets never rose about 50 cents.

Occasionally, there was a title fight, either headlining Cantou, or like the Sept. 2, 1933, state lightweight tilt between Las Vegas' Art Johnson and Santa Fe's Manuel Pacheco that had Eddie Mack cheering from ringside. Most of the fights revolved around residential rivalry — like Wagon Mound vs. Springer rivals, Tuffy Saenz and Kid Miller, or even Raton's Lawrence "Kid" Tusa and Springer's Chubby Vigil, whose long-standing grudge was made famous by their verbal jabs:

> Tusa: "Sure, I'll fight Chubb, but only for old time's sake."
> Chubby: "Tusa's scalp will be just another addition to my string of victories."
> Tusa: "Why not? Chubb is easy money and will only be a 'tune-up' for when I get the 145-pound king of the state, Babe Colima."
> Chubby: "I figure on taking him like Grant took Richmond."[61]

Tusa, by the way, came out ahead when they finally settled the matter, on March 18, 1933, though only after taking a severe beating in the first half of the fight.

For all the local color and success of their smokers, the scene in and around both Wagon Mound and Springer centered around a single name for the early years of the '30s: Frankie Cantou.

After his first two years of fighting, Cantou had suffered just one setback: Chuckers Hildebrand. But under the guidance of pilot Dynamite Tommy, Cantou was being steered toward the big time. Bouncing back from the loss on Nov. 10, 1932, in Gallup, Frankie stayed close to home in the first half of '33, on back-to-back shows in Springer against Colorado bantamweight champion Ernie Lara. With Cantou the New Mexico featherweight champ, the fight was a natural, especially since Cantou had lost an amateur bout to Lara prior to 1931.

It was no easy fight, but Cantou's aggression made the difference when the two first met on Feb. 24, 1933, at the Pastime Theater in Springer. In a rematch held one month later, however, Lara reversed the outcome. Cantou "put up a wonderful fight, meeting every attack and following up with punches that several times put his opponent through the ropes into the laps of ringsiders." As the fight wore on, Cantou faded while Lara retained his freshness and aggression. Despite all the "wonderful" things Cantou was reported to have done, two judges and the ref felt Lara was just a tad bit more "wonderful," giving him the fight unanimously.[62] Dynamite Tommy blamed drying out to bantam for Cantou's lack of steam, and he moved his kid up to featherweight.

Cantou bounced back from his second setback with a first-round knockout over Colorado veteran Mike Gonzales on June 7 in his hometown, and then relocated to Santa Fe to focus on Albuquerque, where the bigger action was. The fans wanted a Frankie-Abie match-up for the state featherweight title, never mind that Abie was the state bantam champ, and they agreed to fight — should Cantou get by Albuquerque hopeful Lee Chavez.

On July 11, Cantou knocked out Lee Chavez in eight for the state featherweight belt before 1,500 at Tingley Field in Albuquerque. Two days later, Cantou vs. Abie Chavez was announced for the 1st of August — by far the most important fight of Cantou's short career. The winner was already lined up to fight Mexican champ Chato Laredo. Training between Santa Fe, Wagon Mound and Albuquerque, where crowds of 500 showed up to watch the two fighters spar, Cantou had the size and power advantage, but Abie was seasoned, with twice as many fights. And he was getting under Frankie's skin, promising that he'd not only "punch Frankie out from underneath his diadem," but would do so "minus a few teeth."[63]

When "Dynamite Tommy" Sanchez retired from the ring, he started training and managing fighters. He was behind the careers of Frankie Cantou and Andres Carrillo during the early '30s (courtesy Benny Sanchez).

Before his biggest crowd to date, 1,800 at Tingley Field, Cantou was bullied by the smaller man, who carried the fight to Frankie in all but one round to snag the championship. "He's still a kid, still learning," was Dynamite Tommy's alibi. "Give him a few more fights, we'll be back on top."[64]

Tommy took Frankie on the road to toughen him up and get his fighting spirit back. In Colorado, Cantou evened the score again with Lara. In West Texas, he knocked out Dick Cody and Jimmy Dundee. Stacking up wins built up the confidence Cantou needed and by March 1934 he was ready again to stage his comeback in New Mexico.

The fans were still talking Abie — but another Chavez was fresh on everyone's mind: Tony Chavez, who was making good on the West Coast. The Albuquerque-born featherweight was on his way home for a series of fights and Dynamite Tommy figured Cantou should get in on the action.

After knocking out Las Vegas prospect Art Johnson in Las Vegas, on March 16, 1934, Cantou was matched up with Tony Chavez for the state featherweight title. Tony hadn't yet fought Abie, but he had defeated Chuckers Hildebrand, who'd defeated both Frankie and Abie. Beating Tony would ease the loss to the other Chavez, as well as secure a rematch for big money.

With nearly triple the number of

fights, Chavez was a favorite by the time the fight landed in Las Vegas on June 6 — a testament that the scene was slipping in the bigger cities. Cantou was banking on his southpaw stance giving Chavez fits, but the Los Angeles veteran shrugged off such questions, pointing to his win over Hildebrand, who'd been a lefty.

Before a packed house of 800 at the Armory in Las Vegas, neither Cantou's nor Chavez's mitt was raised skyward — though the moral victory would go to the Albuquerque featherweight. Cantou went down three times before the fight ended by what was ruled a low blow by Chavez. After an hour of arguing, the two judges and referee ruled it a five-round draw. While a rematch was discussed, Tony went on to fight — and beat, albeit controversially — Abie, before heading back to the coast.

Cantou kept busy, fighting Art Johnson two more times. Some said the Chavez fight was still in his head when he trained for Johnson for their August rematch in Las Vegas; others attest that Cantou just underestimated the tough youngster from Vegas. Whatever the case was, Johnson landed a wallop of a shot in the fifth round that knocked Cantou out cold. Dynamite Tommy called the sleeper punch "lucky" — he also said it was a wake-up call for Cantou. They headed

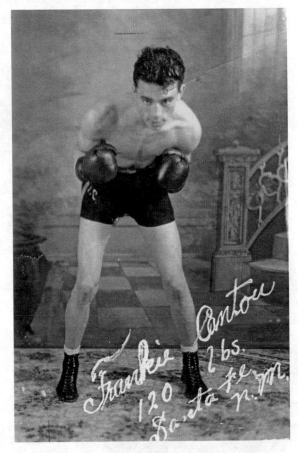

Wagon Mound's Frankie Cantou was well on his way to big things when his life was cut short on October 8, 1934. Cantou was warming up his baby's milk bottle when a container of coal oil exploded. Frankie was severely burned and, two days later, he died from injuries, just 22 years.

back into heavy training and, one month later, on Sept. 19, 1934, Cantou evened the score in Albuquerque by knocking out Johnson in the eighth round. It would be the last time Frankie Cantou would enter a ring.

On Oct. 8, 1934, Cantou was outdoors building a fire at his grandparents' house when a container of coal oil exploded. Frankie was severely burned and, two days later, he died from injuries, just 22 years old.

"He was warming up his baby's milk bottle when it happened," said Frankie's brother Emilio. "He swallowed — inhaled — the flames and we all knew he wasn't going to make it." He added, "It was his dream to be a world champion and he used to tell me that. He never gave it up, even when he got married. It's all he ever wanted to be — a boxer, a champion."[65]

Dynamite Tommy was crushed with the death of his star pupil. "He really had the tools to be something," he'd later say. Tommy read aloud at the funeral: "He took his defeats with a smile and accepted his victories as a step forward.... I have managed several fighters, but none so responsive to the profession as Frankie. His sudden death came as a great shock to all his friends and he will always live in our memories as one of the greatest fighters New Mexico has ever known."[66]

The town of Wagon Mound was so stunned by the loss of their prize champion that it did not notice the slow rise of yet another local. If Cantou was a shaker, Manuel Cruz, better known as "Billy Firpo," was a mover — literally.

Of the 100-plus known Firpo fights, almost all took place in New Mexico. In the '30s, he was the state's busiest fighter — a stay-at-home Tony Chavez — and he was as likely to appear close to home in Las Vegas or Wagon Mound as he was in Silver City, Clovis or Gallup. It's very probable that Firpo never turned down a fight. State, Southwestern and future world champions — he fought them all — and he won most of them, too. In 1934 alone, he fought more than 25 times. In '37, he once fought six times between March 11 and March 25, from Clovis to Springer to Hobbs to Silver City, back to Hobbs, then off to Fort Sumner and Springer. That summer, he also fought three *days* in a row. On July 2, he beat Doc Anderson in Gallup; one night later he was in Estancia, knocking out Benny Garcia in five; on the third night, he was in southern New Mexico fighting an eight-round draw with the future lightweight champion of the world, Verlin "Lew" Jenkins.

Only known photograph of Manuel Cruz, a.k.a. "Billy Firpo," who fought in the '30s out of Wagon Mound, New Mexico. Firpo was the state's busiest fighter. In 1934 alone, he fought more than 25 times. In '37, he fought six times between March 11 and March 25, from Clovis to Springer to Hobbs to Silver City, back to Hobbs, then off to Fort Sumner and Springer.

Firpo traveled so often that all the dates and locations have become as hard to decipher as the hundreds of "Firpos" fighting around the country during boxing's golden age. Cruz was one of dozens of Firpos who'd taken up the modified moniker in honor of Luis Firpo, the "Wild Bull from the Pampas" who'd immortalized himself when he came close to knocking out Jack Dempsey in 1923. Since the original, there'd been "Battling Firpos" all over the map. There was a "Bull Firpo" in North Dakota, a "Charlie Firpo" in Maine, a "T-Bone Firpo" in Phoenix and a Henry "Bald Eagle" Firpo in Louisville. There were Jack and Joe Firpos galore, and more "Kid," "KO" and "Young" Firpos than you knew what to do with. But in New Mexico, there was just Billy Firpo.

Or Billy Cruz. Or Young Cruz. Or whatever combination Manuel Cruz wanted to use. Though he usually went under "Billy Firpo," Cruz would swap out a different moniker if there was an advantage in doing so. For instance, in June 1937 he decided to use his real name to be part of a Las Vegas "amateur" team competing in a class A tournament in Nebraska. In a rarity, he arrived too late to enter.

The "Firpo" name, however, guaranteed action and the kid who slugged at first, and always wore a heart sewn onto his trunks, became so well-liked he was given yet a new nickname: "The Million Dollar Personality Kid."

Born in Wagon Mound in 1918, Firpo's first known fight was on an Espanola card as a 14-year-old amateur. Between '31 and '33, Firpo fought several amateur bouts, including one was against future New Mexican star Larry Cisneros in Taos. Firpo's first pro bout was in

A Night of Real Boxing

MONDAY, APRIL 12, 8:15 Old ELKS Theatre

MAIN EVENT 10 ROUNDS
Verlin Jenkins Vs. **Billy Firpo**
FORT BLISS, TEX.   NEW MEXICO

SEMI-FINAL 6 ROUNDS
JIMMY SHERROD   Vs.   MEXICAN PETE REGAL

SPECIAL 6 ROUNDS
DAVE RIVETTE   Vs.   EDDIE CERDA

PRELIMINARY 4 ROUNDS
FRANKIE ROSE   Vs.   YOUNG JOE LOUIS

GET YOUR RESERVATIONS NOW --- FRANK'S CAFE

ADMISSION
Ringside, **$1.50**; General Admission, **$1.00**   Balcony, **50c**,
All Prices Plus Tax

How good was Wagon Mound's Billy Firpo? Some say he was just a local club fighter, but, at least between 1936 and 1937, he was good enough to draw with Verlin "Lew" Jenkins, who would later evolve into a world champion.

his hometown on April 11, 1933 — a TKO over Donald Anderson. Thanks to Cantou's popularity, there were cards aplenty before Frankie's tragic accident, and Firpo landed frequent spots throughout northern New Mexico, at least six of them in '33 and twice that in '34. Most of the time Firpo won. He fought four times with Albuquerque's Young Benny Cordova (2-1-1) and three times against Las Vegas' Tony Gallegos (0-1-2). Between his early days as a feather, mid-career lightweight bouts, and later years as a welter, there were very few Firpo did *not* fight.

Firpo's knockout of hot Las Vegas prospect Johnny Johnson on an Albuquerque card on Sept. 19, 1934, marked him as a dangerous opponent and a prospect to keep an eye on. After northern New Mexico shows took a hit with the Cantou tragedy, Firpo ventured farther out in 1935, finding a permanent spot on Santa Fe shows. By '36, he was a frequent co-main eventer around the state, usually on shows billing Johnson, Mike Montoya or Tiny Garcia — he was a "young-but-ol' reliable," someone who'd take on anyone, anytime, anywhere, from Raton to Silver City.

By 1937, however, Firpo was headlining many shows of his own. In '37, he lost but once in 20 bouts — a six-rounder taken last minute against Santa Fe's Joe Garcia, whom he'd beaten before. Considered the state's welterweight champion, he helped rejuvenate the Wagon Mound-to-Springer shows, and was often called on to headline in Hobbs and Silver City. But it was in Silver City that he ran into a youngster named Lew.

Though born in Milburn, Texas, in 1916, Lew Jenkins spent several years of his youth in New Mexico while his parents drifted around as fruit pickers. Later on, Jenkins returned to the state while he was enlisted at Fort Bliss. While boxing for extra money, Jenkins took fights in Texas, Arizona and New Mexico. "Dandy" Dick Griffin later claimed to have discovered Jenkins when he wandered into a gym in Dallas looking to make a little beer money, an absolute unknown — but, at least in New Mexico, Jenkins was no stranger in the ring. Jenkins' earliest known fight in New Mexico was on March 5, 1936, when he won a decision over Arizona's Sailor Fay Kosky in Silver City on a card headlined by Jim Perry and Black Panther Tate. Other Jenkins fights in '36 are not known, but he was fairly active in '37.

On April 9, 1937, Jenkins was pitted against Billy Firpo in Silver City in a ten-rounder pitting the respective welter champs of Fort Bliss and New Mexico. "The two sluggers wrestled and fought for the full weary 10-rounds," ran the local report. "Firpo put Jenkins down at least a half dozen times for small counts, but he always came up fighting, and on one occasion he grabbed Firpo, lifted him off his feet and tossed him to the canvas, but Firpo only laughed off the trick and the bout continued to the end of the tenth round, with the judges calling it a draw, although Firpo seemed to get the best of Jenkins in every round."[67]

Firpo would get a second chance to net the win. On July 4, the two fought again in Silver City, but once again, it was ruled a draw after ten rounds. Firpo later insisted he'd beaten Jenkins — both fights were scored as wins in the personal record he kept in his scrapbook.

Jenkins, of course, went on to win the world lightweight title by knocking out Lou Ambers on May 10, 1940, at Madison Square Garden. Firpo never made much of his two draws with Jenkins. He'd had a harder time with some of the regulars fighting in the state, like "Mexican" Pete Regal of Borger, Texas, and ol' Eddie Murdock, who gave Firpo his only losses of 1937. Firpo had twice before fought draws with Regal before losing a decision; against Murdock, a chubby, bald veteran by '37, he got battered in his only really bad loss, going down 11 times but remaining on his feet after 10 rounds.

Firpo bounced back in 1938, securing his state welterweight laurels by beating all challengers, though he was far less active. Then, after an entire career of fighting on the home front, Firpo packed up and hit the road with Questa's rising star, Larry Cisneros, for Michigan where the New Mexico lightweight champ of 1911–1912, Louis Newman, now living in Detroit, had connections. Newman kept both fighters busy in Detroit and Sault St. Marie, and they both came home with more wins than losses.

Back home in the latter half of '39 and through 1940, Firpo picked up where he left off, taking back his state welter crown by beating Johnny Johnson and headlining shows in Vegas, Raton and Wagon Mound. His high point of the year was fighting two draws with Southwest champ Ted "Mustang" Garcia — and a low point was getting KO'd by Belen youngster Benny Valencia.

As World War II approached and the fight scene dried up around the state, Firpo's career was put on hold as he enlisted — but not before taking on regarded welterweight Kid Mexico, on Nov. 24, 1941, in El Paso.

By now, Jenkins was champ. Firpo's "wins" over the now-champ were hyped considerably to push the fight with Mexico. The fight itself, however, did not live up to expectations, when Firpo was stopped in round eight. "Firpo showed nothing whatever to recommend him and spectators left wondering how he possibly could have whipped Lew Jenkins," wrote the *El Paso Times*. Though flooring Mexico in round five, Firpo "went down and up like an elevator," going down four times. "The bell clanged while customers were shouting 'Throw in the towel' and Firpo's chief second was answering in great agitation that he didn't have a towel. Firpo settled the matter by staggering across the ring to hoist Mexico's right in token of 'That's all, boys.'"[68]

For Firpo, that *was* all — at least in the ring. On the battleground, now *that* was another story.

19. The Clouting Caballero, 1930–1939

Found: A good Mexican fighter who has yet to be ballyhooed as another Bert Colima. His name is Emilio Martinez.

— *Los Angeles Times*, 1934[1]

As contenders, Eddie Mack and Tony Chavez fought current and future world champions — men who would later be revered as legends — but going into New Mexico's final golden age of boxing, only one fighter had ever climbed into the ring in a bona fide title scrap, and that was the Original Benny Chavez. Before the '30s would fade away into the '40s and a waiting world war, one other boxer would earn the honor — another Wagon Mounder, Emilio Martinez.

Las Vegas promoter Joe Roybal would later say that Martinez could've been world champion, had he not been such a nut job. "He didn't like to train and when he did, he did so on wine and marijuana," said Roybal.[2]

Martinez *was* a bit unorthodox — but his character outside the ring corresponded to his unconventional striking style. His opponents thought it bad enough that he was a southpaw, but he was oftentimes off-balance, deceptively so, while fighting in a "wide open stance, always seeming to be leaning back from the waist."[3] His punches came from odd angles. Actually, Martinez didn't so much punch as he did *clout*, so much so that they eventually started calling him "The Clouting Caballero."

Just as the Original Benny had been deemed a Trinidad fighter, Martinez was regarded as being from Denver. But it was in Wagon Mound, in 1913, where Emilio Jose was born, then raised. His parents were sugar beet farmers who traveled through northern New Mexico and southern Colorado for work.

It was in New Mexico where Martinez first fought, as well, as a 16-year-old amateur on a card held in Taos, on Feb. 27, 1929, losing a three-rounder to a local kid, Gil Romero. Sometime after that, the Martinez family relocated to Denver where Emilio continued in the amateur ranks. As pro spectators would later find out, watching Martinez fight was never boring. At one amateur bout, he became so enraged when referee Joe Russell stopped the bout to give his opponent, Al Reed, the fight on a foul, that Martinez took a swing at the ref. Emilio's cornermen leapt into the ring to hold their fighter back, but he broke loose and took a second swing as the spectators cheered him on.

A stocky middleweight at age 20, Martinez turned pro in 1932, fighting close to home for the first two years and beating all the locals. Under the management of Denver's Billy Papke, Martinez racked up at least 15 wins, most by knockout, in his first year-and-a-half of fighting, with just one loss — a decision to Hank Kline. By the summer of '33, Martinez was the Colorado middleweight champion, by virtue of defeating Jackie Ray with a ten-round decision.

By 1933, promoters in Wagon Mound and Springer were talking about bringing Martinez back for a homecoming bout, but he had to delay his return for his biggest fight to date on May 17. Before 4,000 at the City Auditorium in Denver, Martinez took on 100-bout veteran Jackie Brady. After 13 years of hard fights, the New York veteran was at the tail-end of his career and was, at best, a welterweight, but his experience posed an acid test for Martinez. After Emilio broke his arm in round one, the test became a matter of survival as Brady toyed with the kid for eight rounds, before Martinez came alive in the last two rounds, knocking Brady down and nearly turning it around. With a bit of home cooking, Brady was lucky to leave Denver with the win, though he had to settle for a split verdict.

After two months nursing his injury, Martinez returned to challenge Jack "Kid" Barger for the Rocky Mountain middleweight championship, in his first pro fight outside Colorado, at Ogden, Utah. By now, Denver scribes were lauding Martinez's potential as a middleweight contender. Barger was a step up from Martinez's competition in Colorado. Fighting since 1927, the Idaho-born fighter had cleaned up regionally, but had been checked in his attempts to storm the East Coast. He predicted a knockout in five rounds over Martinez.

Instead, Barger, who'd never been knocked out before, lasted seven before succumbing to Martinez. Up to the knockout, the fight was a back-and-forth affair, but after the fourth, "it was apparent that one of the two men would kiss the canvas for the ten-count." Martinez floored Barger in the first, but the veteran came back to hold a "slim shade" by the seventh. Martinez, using his "unique attack, ... puzzling Barger with his odd style," clouted his man down with a whopping left.[4] A rematch was set up for the following month, at Ogden again, and this time, Barger had figured Martinez out. Though he was hurt in the fifth, Martinez came back strong and finished ahead in the later rounds to return home with a draw — and his championship intact.

After knocking out respected veteran Henry Firpo in Denver two weeks later, Martinez made his return to New Mexico, headlining Raton on Nov. 15, 1933. Before a capacity crowd at the Shuler Auditorium, Martinez stopped the 200-bout Colorado veteran in round four with a right hook to the jaw.

Nineteen-thirty-four was Martinez's breakout year. Fighting a dozen times, Martinez branched out, fighting from Idaho to Las Vegas, New Mexico, before ending the year in Los Angeles on the verge of contention. Veteran Lou Cozzens was defeated at Idaho in March. In May, at Denver, Martinez battered a battle-scarred George Manley (who'd defeated Walter Caldwell early on) for the Colorado light-heavyweight laurels and, later that month, also in the Mile High City, outslugged and overpowered blown-up welterweight Baby Joe Gans through ten.

By the mid–30s, the color lines were beginning to deteriorate in boxing. Joe Louis was on his way to becoming the world heavyweight champion and the sport was chockfull of black fighters who could no longer be ignored — guys like Henry Armstrong and John Henry Lewis. Fighters inching their way toward contention, especially in the heavier weight classes, no longer had the option to pick and choose according to color. Baby Joe Gans might have had the unfair weight disadvantage, but Emilio's next foe, the famous former middleweight champ Gorilla Jones (not to be confused with the original Gorilla Jones, former nemesis of Speedball Hayden), had years of experience over the Denver hopeful.

The two met on June 18, 1934, at Denver's City Auditorium, before 2,000. Jones' experience and superior defense gave him the advantage in the first half of the fight, but

Martinez waded in, wearing down the ex-champ with aggression and had him in trouble when the final bell rang. Martinez was given the unanimous nod.

By mid–1934, Martinez was making regular visits back home to Las Vegas and Wagon Mound. He fought an exhibition on one show in July, returned to Denver to outpower Leroy Brown on Sept. 7, then fought for the first time in Las Vegas on the 28th.

Touting Martinez as *the* threat to Middleweight Champion Vince Dundee and his opponent Joe Guerrero, as the Mexican champ, promoter Roybal tried to convince the city that the "high class" fight was the most important battle since Johnson-Flynn in 1912. Of course, no one mentioned that Guerrero was losing just as often as winning, on the border. The fight played itself out accordingly, with Martinez needing just ten seconds to knock out Guerrero, who "took a spectacular dive through the ropes." When Martinez "dodged an attempted flying tackle, [Guerrero] knocked himself out to give Martinez the bout in the first few seconds."[5] With his fall to the canvas, Guerrero had given Martinez the record for scoring the state's quickest knockout, dethroning Cotton Henley, with his 13-second KO.

In Colorado, or anywhere else, for that matter, no one paid too much atten-

Emilio Martinez, the "Clouting Caballero," was yet another Wagon Mound–born fighter. In the late '30s, Martinez became a bona fide light-heavyweight contender. Las Vegas promoter Joe Roybal would later say that Emilio Martinez could have been world champion had he not been such a nut job. "He didn't like to train and when he did, he did so on wine and marijuana," said Roybal.

tion to the mismatch, and Martinez started to talk about heading for either coast where bigger purses and better fighters waited. Sometime before December, Martinez was rumored to have outpointed both former champ "Slapsie" Maxie Rosenbloom and Gorilla Jones, in a rematch, but neither fight has ever been confirmed. A win over Rosenbloom would've been the welcome mat of contention for Martinez — and he was still knocking on the door when he planned for a West Coast invasion in the winter of 1934.

Keeping busy in Denver, Martinez first lost, then regained, his state middle and light-heavyweight titles in two ten-round, dual-title fights with Chuck Heffner. Then he left for Los Angeles, where things did not go as planned.

Maybe it was all the praise Martinez received upon his arrival that had him underestimating the man he was up against. Bill Potts of the *Times* wrote that he was the replacement for Bert Colima, that "Emilio is considered one of the best Mexican fighters of modern times. Yet nobody outside of his own home town has given him much of a tumble."[6]

But a "tumble" is what Martinez got, against West Coast regular Leo "K.O." Kelly, when he made his Los Angeles debut on Dec. 11, 1934, at the Olympic Auditorium. Martinez went down twice in the first and twice in the third, before the referee stopped the bout at 2:21.

With his tail between his legs, Martinez slinked back to Colorado, where local promoters pooled together their resources to entice Kelly into a rematch on Emilio's turf. Kelly obliged and this time Martinez came out ahead — but barely. "Colorado's alleged clouting caballero shot one bolt of lightning and then sprinkled," wrote Phil Hewett of the *Rocky Mountain News*. In the second, Kelly had Martinez "knocked out" but "after putting him on the floor twice, stood back flat-footed and allowed Emilio to recover."[7] Martinez came back strong to cop the win.

The win came too late to impress West Coast scribes, but the loss to Kelly — and *near* loss — made him a safe bet for No. 1 contender John Henry Lewis.

By now, Coloradoans were beginning to lose faith in the Clouting Caballero. Instead of fighting at light-heavyweight, he was being told to go back down to middleweight — he was weighing in a run or two away from 160, anyway. What was the point in fighting heavy? Especially against a beast like Lewis. Sure, Martinez would have the hometown advantage, when they clashed on March 13, 1935, before 3,000 fans at the City Auditorium, but the top contender had close to 50 bouts (Martinez had around 36) over the biggest names in the sport.

As expected, Martinez, weighing 166 to Lewis' 173, lost — but it was a scorcher that screamed rematch, with Lewis edging the win by virtue of a "rabbit foot in his hip pocket." "Both fighters were close to exhaustion near the finish but even so, they turned the last two rounds into the best of the fight, with furious punching trades against the ropes," wrote old school scribe Abe Pollock. "Martinez started those long, looping lefts of his in the third and thru that round and the fourth he had the colored boy rubbing his rabbit foot." Lewis turned it around thereafter, getting "Martinez in trouble with a vicious attack in the Denver man's corner, but Martinez snapped back with a renewal of his body punishment that tired the negro." The crowd hooted the decision but two judges and the ref scored the close decision to Lewis.[8]

Martinez would get another chance at Lewis — actually, he would get *three* more chances.

The expected telegrams from the bigger fight centers never arrived in Denver, at least not in 1935, and Emilio stayed in the Southwest for the year, winning all but one of his remaining bouts (a decision to Milwaukee's Tait Littman in Denver) while regaining his state light-heavyweight title. He also fought in New Mexico twice.

In April, Emilio came home for a bit of recreation in the form of a stay-busy fight against an overmatched welterweight. Before a capacity crowd at the Armory in Las Vegas, Martinez enjoyed a 10-pound weight advantage over Billy McDonald, of Amarillo. "The Negro could take it, which he did from gong to gong and until the call for the seventh stanza he was still grinning, grimacing and grimly asking for more," wrote the *Optic*. "The bout was a crowd pleaser — the crowd wanted to see Emilio in action — but it combined comedy, slugging, alley-fighting and the human punching bag act."[9] Though McDonald's corner threw in the towel no fewer than five times, the referee kicked it out an equal number of times as the Amarillo fighter was down a total of 17 times — the record, by the way, in New Mexico.

Martinez returned to Las Vegas in December, and another packed Armory crowd watched their champion hopeful slaughter Reno veteran Tiger "Kid" Carter in five rounds.

In another Vegas stinker — Martinez did not have one serious fight in New Mexico — Emilio "grunted and slapped, pushed and laughed and then took another poke at one dark skinned lad from Nevada"[10] before the referee halted the "*matanza*."[11]

While Martinez had been putzing around in Colorado and New Mexico, John Henry Lewis had gone from No. 1 contender to world champ. On Oct. 31, 1935, Lewis dethroned Bob Olin in St. Louis, then went on to fight six non-title fights, losing but once, to Maxie Rosenbloom in a controversial fight marred with low blows.

Emilio Martinez was non-title opponent number seven. After a less-than-impressive year fighting in Wyoming, Colorado and New Mexico, the Southwestern light-heavyweight champion couldn't possibly give Lewis the fight he'd dished out the year before. But he did.

Now managed by Denver's Denos Pappas, Martinez scored one of the biggest upsets of the year on Jan. 29, 1936, before a disappointing crowd at Denver's City Auditorium. Beefing up to 176 with the light-heavy champ at 181, Martinez "fought one of the greatest fights of his career. He outboxed the champion, had the chocolate Adonis missing from the opening bell to the finish; and justly won.... Lewis' showing probably was not disappointing [as much] as Martinez' display was surprising."[12]

Bothered by Martinez's southpaw stance and an irritating, pawing right jab, Lewis was a sucker for Emilio's clouting left hand. Making Lewis miss, Martinez counted cleanly with the left, clearly winning five of the ten rounds. Pollock gave Lewis two rounds, with three even. "It wasn't a hometown decision although Lewis said afterwards he thought he won. He said Martinez was slower than he was the last time they met."[13]

At a chubby 176, Martinez *was* slower, but now as a light-heavyweight contender, it was where the money was. Having defeated the champion and prompting fans to recall the days of Eddie Mack, seven years before, Martinez hit the road, on a mission to force Lewis to give him a rubber match — this time, with the title at stake.

Martinez did not live up to expectations heaped upon him during the rest of 1936. After a draw in Spokane on March 6 with Red Bruce, Martinez dropped two straight bouts, to contender Allen Matthews in St. Louis.

Lewis had gone to defend his title in March, while plowing through opposition in non-title bouts. His alibi for the loss to Martinez was that it had been a hometown decision.

"Is that so?" Martinez questioned the press when he arrived in St. Louis for his bout with Matthews. "Did Lewis really say that? Why, I beat him every step of the way and he knows it. Toward the end of the fight he was tottering. However, all I want is a chance at him for the title. That's the reason I'm here. I didn't ask the promoters how much I would get for the match with Matthews. All I know is they told me they can get Lewis for a bout with me here and that's what I'm after."[14]

"Who ever heard of Matthews?" Martinez bragged about beating the contender, then had to eat his words when he was outpointed. A rematch was set up for the following month, also in St. Louis, with five rounds added on, making it a 15-rounder. The winner was supposed to be the No. 1 challenger for Lewis but, again, the outcome was the same — a second loss for Martinez, albeit by split decision.

Martinez stayed on in St. Louis, bouncing back with a decision over trial horse Izzy Singer on May 22. Then he returned to the coast where Pappas sold him off to well-known Los Angeles manager Suey Welch, for $2,000. "I think I made a good buy when I bought Martinez's contract," Welch told the press. "Anybody who can beat Lewis — the hard-punching Negro — at such a price is a bargain."[15]

Welch ate his words after lining up top ten contender Johnny "Bandit" Romero in San Diego, whom Martinez had beaten the year before. The San Diego "Bandit" stole Emilio's thunder by scoring a tenth-round TKO. In a desperate attempt to regain his crumbling composure, Martinez was ushered back into the Olympic Auditorium a month later as a short-ender against highly-touted Carmen Barth — who was, at least, a bona fide middleweight contender. The Cleveland Italian continued his winning streak on the Coast while Martinez dropped his second straight bout. It got worse: On November 25, 1936, Martinez traveled to Pittsburgh where he lost yet again, this time to "New England Cyclone" and light-heavy contender Al Gainer.

The only thing consistent about Martinez seemed to be his inconsistency. The Rocky Mountain's hope for a champ had minor success on February 26, 1937, when he at least fought a draw in a rematch with Romero. But one fight later, on March 31, in San Francisco, he dropped a ten-rounder to Michigan contender Marty Simmons.

Though 24, Martinez was seen by most as finished — and that could be why Lewis, still the champ in May 1937, decided to use Martinez on his endless quest for non-title opponents. Once again in St. Louis, on May 4, Martinez, a career-heavy 177, fought the champ for the third time and, this time, it wasn't even close. Martinez was game but Lewis "thought he was punching a bag, not a human being, as he grounded out a one-sided victory." The champ "poured volley after volley of lefts and rights into the head, ribs and back of the game southpaw, as he crouched, glove-covered face, trying to hide the vital points."[16]

Martinez continued to slip — as evident by making three New Mexico appearances in 1937. After losing to Allen Matthews again in June, Martinez returned to Las Vegas in August where he plodded through a close decision over Los Angeles veteran Lowell Sporland, getting into brushes with both the referee and promoter Roybal. In August, he knocked out Cyclone Lynch in Walsenburg, Colorado, adding the Colorado heavyweight title to his collection, then went to Santa Fe in September for back-to-back fights, one week apart. On Sept. 3, Martinez, now a sloppy 183, sleepwalked through a decision over Tiger Jack Wright in a fight that saw very little action and a lot of missing. One week later, Martinez scored his third win over journeyman Sporland, this time stopping him in the tenth. Just before the fight, Joe Roybal — who was not promoting the show — climbed into the ring to announce an upcoming show in Las Vegas headlining a fighter that "Emilio refused to fight." Martinez dove for Roybal and "it took half a dozen ringsiders to separate them."[17] It would be Martinez's final appearance in a New Mexico ring.

The Clouting Caballero continued to slip, losing to the "Alabama Kid" Clarence Reeves in Denver (the very fighter Roybal had goaded Martinez with) by a ninth-round TKO, on Sept. 30, 1937, before a period of inactivity. After a comeback bout in Hot Springs, Ark., he was brought in as the beat-up guy for champion Lewis in what would be their fourth fight.

The champ was under fire for not defending his title so Martinez was brought in as a non-threatening "contender," sparking a wave of controversy that had the New York State Athletic Commission refusing to recognize the 15-rounder held on April 25, 1938 in Minneapolis, Minn., as a title fight. The rest of the world considered the world light-heavyweight title to be at stake. Come late July, Lewis would be stripped of the championship.

In the meantime, Wagon Mound-born Emilio Martinez was going to fight for a world title, becoming the second New Mexican to do so. Unfortunately, Martinez was also at the most vulnerable stage of his career — and well past his prime, by the experts' opinion. Martinez came in at 174 and the champion just under 175, for what was to be the first world title fight in Minnesota in 50 years. It was nothing like the first two fights — and more like the third Martinez-Lewis fight, only shorter.

Martincz lasted but four rounds. Using a straight right, Lewis staggered Martinez early, keeping him on the defensive until a shot to the point of the jaw put the challenger flat on his back, 54 seconds into the fourth.

This time, Martinez was finished. He returned to Colorado, won a couple bouts, lost another, before fighting for the last time on Jan. 7, 1939, in the obscure town of Minturn, Colorado, where he beat former opponent Cyclone Lynch in a defense of his coveted Colorado belt. Later on in the year, the Colorado boxing commission stripped Martinez of his state belt and he was never heard from again, at least in the ring.

20. The Big Scene Goes "Small," 1935–1940

While many boxing events of late years stalling, hugging and driving has been the order of the day, none was seen last night. The one expression heard from the lips of every fan as they left the Rialto was "the boys fought." Santa Fe has always been a good fight town and a few more bouts of the caliber of those last night will make the Ancient City the best showing place in the entire Southwest.

— *Santa Fe New Mexican,* 1937[1]

Staging nearly 700 of the estimated 2,400 fight cards held in New Mexico from 1868 to the present, Albuquerque has always been New Mexico's fight center. Running neck and neck for distant second place are three cities: Gallup, Las Vegas and Santa Fe, all with respective totals somewhere between 150 and 200.

The activity in the Capital — or Ancient — City, as it was called, has always been sporadic. Mike Baca had helped along the sport in his city in the '10s and early '20s. Riding the wave of success that was Eddie Mack, the Pachecos had followed. When Mack called it quits, the era of big fights was over, but a core group of fighters who had been and still *were* being developed, enabled the scene to continue in spurts through most of the '30s.

After Mack's last showing in Santa Fe, in August 1932, local promoters — a list that included former prizefighter Jockey Hamilton, Charles Closson, M. L. Evans and Mack himself — all tried their hands at establishing the next big headliner. No single fighter was going to fit into Mack's shoes but, at the same time, Santa Fe had more collective talent than it had ever had — ever *would* have again.

Promoter Evans was convinced Andy "Gump" Carrillo could make the next hurdle, but when he lost to fading "Flash," Nick Mortio, then was battered down by Tony Chavez in his next fight the following year, Gump was dumped.

After retiring from the ring, Mack moved to Santa Fe where he promoted a few shows headlining El Paso welterweight Babe Colima. The city warmed up to the man no one could beat, that is, until Eddie's old foe, Eddie Murdock, who was still a threat at welter having just defeated former champ Jackie Fields, pulled off the upset on April 4, 1933, by outclassing Colima with an eighth-round knockout.

With sold-out crowds in his first three shows, Mack staged another, this time using Santa Fe youngster Jimmy Ortiz, whom he'd taken under his wing. Hoping he'd clear the hurdle that effectively blocked almost all local club fighters, Mack pitted his former conqueror, Mickey Cohen, against the kid, which turned out to be a bad idea, or a premature move, for Ortiz was outclassed and beaten.

When Mack retired from promoting, and Ortiz, after one more bout, from fighting, the city geared up for the next phase of fisticuffs when the "Father of New Mexico Boxing," Mark Levy, made a return. Levy had left the state in 1915, missing two generations of ring action, but in August 1933 he picked up where he left off, or tried to. Levy's first show back pitted Abie Chavez with Chato Laredo in a much-demanded rematch, with an all-local undercard. St. Michael's Gym was packed as the *New Mexican* wrote that "the fight game seems to have another firm hold on the city."[2] But the following card was such a disaster that Levy packed up and left for Albuquerque where he gave the city its last good year of the decade, before slim Depression-hit crowds had him throwing up his hands.

Nineteen-thirty-four was a drought year, but several promoters, most notably Joe Roybal, who was looking to expand operations from Las Vegas, attempted to "exhume and resuscitate the cauliflower industry."[3] Roybal's shows were less than spectacular, because he sought to push his stable of Las Vegas fighters on Santa Feans who, of course, preferred fighters from their own city. When the Santa Fe Police Department took over, later in the year, the locals were back on, with lightweight Tiny Garcia on a fast rise.

Again, the scene took a hit in 1936. "The manly art of leather pushing seems to be not only dead, but buried, too,"[4] reported the *New Mexican* in March. Some shows were cancelled due to slim crowds. Having learned his lesson the year before, Roybal came through in April, staging the city's biggest show in years, Tiny Garcia vs. Johnny Johnson for the Rocky Mountain lightweight title. After another Garcia-headlined show, Roybal was ousted from the capital by returning Daniel Ortiz, who treated the city to two more big cards at the Rialto, Tiny as the headliner.

Chick Montoya and Roybal produced three shows in 1937, one with Garcia, two others with Emilio Martinez. Thereafter, the scene tanked, with just one more show, in 1938. It would be nearly a decade before professional boxing returned to Santa Fe.

While the sweet science teetered and tottered, youngsters of the Ancient City kept busy, either with at-home bouts or by hitting the road to the many fight centers in operation around the state. There were the Garcias — Tiny and brother Joe, Simon Gonzales, a.k.a. "Babe Montana," Eppie Montoya and Dave Romero. There was also a young hopeful with a familiar name: "Young" Mike Baca.

There were more than enough Bacas out there during the '20s and '30s. There was Las Vegas' Severo de Baca, who was sometimes "Kid Baca," sometimes "Young Baca," and more often than not "Bad News" Baca. Clovis had a Kid Baca, Belen had a Fidel Baca and Albuquerque, Johnny and Dave Baca. Telesfor Baca was San Antonio's (New Mexico) hopeful, while Lee Baca, of Denver, a protégé of Mack's, was one of Colorado's top lightweights. But in Santa Fe, there was only

Martiniano "Tiny" Garcia was the top Santa Fe fighter during the mid to late '30s. As a New Mexican lightweight champ, his only loss at home was to Las Vegas' Johnny Johnson.

one Baca, well, until there were two — Mike Baca and his offspring "Young" Mike Baca, who wasn't a Mike at all, but a Felipe.

Like Benny Cordova's eldest, Felipe Baca had a similar introduction to the world of prizefighting, staging exhibitions and "baby fights" on cards headlined by the old man. Born in 1918, Felipe was in the ring before a crowded arena at the age of five, and fighting for pay at the tender age of 13 in '31. Like Young Benny (Cordova), also a feather to lightweight, Young Mike did not quite pan out the way everyone had hoped. Like Cordova, Baca swept through his early crosstown rivals, winning fours and sixers through the latter half of '31, through '33 — before being thrown to the wolves in the form of Durango's Chuckers Hildebrand. Even though it was a loss by knockout, there wasn't too much shame in losing to a veteran like Hildebrand — especially at the age of 15. Baca had been easy pickings for Hildebrand, who "quickly slugged the Baca youth into helplessness."[5]

Young Mike got back on track, beating Belen's Dick Castillo, the Johnson brothers in Vegas, and other Santa Feans, while fans between his city and Albuquerque clamored for a "Son vs. Son" showdown — Young Mike vs. Young Benny Cordova. As if to prove his superiority, Baca was matched with Omaha's Frankie Hodges, who was training out of Las Vegas under Roybal. Hodges had slaughtered Cordova, no less than three times; against Baca, best he could do was a draw.

Just as the original showdown, between the senior Cordova and Baca, had never happened, neither did the one with their offspring. The opportunity came and went in 1935, when an out-of-shape Cordova pulled out of an August match.

Young Mike continued to improve, but he was battered down in three when he sought to step up again, on Oct. 26, 1935, against Trinidad's Baby Jack Johnson. He was taken on the road, through Arizona, where he won most of his matches, then returned, showing vast improvement. But when he sought to dethrone the state lightweight champ, Tiny Garcia, in a crosstown rival match, on Apr. 23, 1937, he was stopped in four. Baca went down five times before Pops threw in the towel. It wasn't long after that when Young Mike gave it up.

Santa Fe had sought greatness in Young Mike, but it was Tiny Garcia who came closest in the '30s to being the real thing.

"Tiny" was, of course, short for Martiniano, born 1912 in Jaralas, New Mexico, though his family relocated to Fort Collins, Colorado, in the '20s. In the early '30s the Garcias moved to New Mexico at Santa Fe, right about the time Jimmy Ortiz was finishing up, in 1934. Tiny became a regular on local shows, his boring-in style, quick hands and punching power moving more than one scribe to call him a "pocket-sized Dempsey."

"He's willing to mix it and he's likely to win,"[6] Clovis referee Doyle Owenby said of Tiny, while fighter Jim Perry said of him, "I saw Tiny Garcia fight one time ... and he kept coming in, even after he had both eyes shut."[7]

In between the slow years in Santa Fe, Garcia became a regular on Vegas cards, fighting the Johnson brothers, defeating Arthur but having trouble with Johnny in six bouts, between '34 and '35, winning once, losing twice and drawing twice. As the New Mexico lightweight champ, his only loss was to Johnny.

When Tiny ventured out of state, as he did on May 4, 1936, to fight the ninth ranked lightweight in the world, Hubert "Kid" Dennis, whom Tony Chavez would later beat twice, he was stopped in the tenth round after a game effort.

As his 50-bout career wore on, Garcia's rivalries would switch from the Johnsons to Young Benny Cordova (a win and a draw), Ted "Mustang" Garcia (a loss and a draw) and

Joe Perry (two wins and a loss). Tiny also lost to rising Questa battler Larry Cisneros later on, in 1938.

Tiny's brother Joe, slightly heavier at 140, also fought during the '30s, and he had a rougher time of it. He lost the majority of his fights in his first two years, but improved drastically in '37 and '38 — enough to score draws with Billy Firpo, Art Johnson and rising Coloradoan Young Joe Louis (Jack Chase). In his last known bout, Joe lost by TKO to Mustang Garcia, the premier lightweight, after Tiny had been ousted.

Mustang's home, for a time in the '30s, was Las Vegas.

Viva Las Vegas

> *Roland (One-round) Gutierrez facetiously referred to in yesterday's write-up of the Colima-Miller bout as a "pool-room bouncer," is anything but that type of fighter, the Optic is glad to announce. The husky, young left hander is a former high school boy who was compelled to quit school to help support dependent relatives since the death of his father, the late G. M. Gutierrez, and is in reality a clean cut, hard-working boy with a real ambition to became a contender in the local ring cards. He told the Optic today that he had but a few days of fight training before the bout Thursday with Roybal which was his first appearance in a local ring and he knew but little of the rules. Gutierrez is a husky middleweight and may be able to overcome his present awkwardness with more training. He particularly resented the "pool-room" tag because, he says, he spends but little time in such places.*
>
> — *Las Vegas Daily Optic*, 1932[8]

Las Vegas had the distinction — and the curse — of being the site of the famous Jack Johnson–Jim Flynn fight of 1912, but it had largely been excluded from the era of Eddie Mack. Mack had fought there just once, in '32, and that was just about the time the city was gearing up to be a major fight center for the decade.

It was largely due to one man, Joe Roybal, who kept the shows consistent in the '30s with nearly 70 shows. With Albuquerque on the decline and Santa Fe lacking consistency, Vegas became the magnet, drawing some of the Southwest's biggest names, including Ted "Mustang" Garcia, Babe Colima and Emilio Martinez. Roybal's all-star local stable included the Johnson brothers, Mike Montoya, Charlie Tate, Frankie Higgins and Tony Gallegos. Not only did Roybal hit the road with the fighters he managed, but he was always looking to promote in other areas. Besides Vegas, he threw shows in Santa Fe, Santa Rosa and Estancia.

Roybal was quite the character, as tight with his purse as he was loose with his fists and tongue. On a card in Estancia in 1937, Roybal was accused of staging a frame-up with fighter Jimmy De Mandell (who "was hitting the floor too hard and too often to be framed"[9]) by an Estancia businessman — so he knocked him out. Another time, minutes before he was scheduled to fight, Emilio Martinez was provoked into charging him when he leapt into the ring on another promoter's card in Santa Fe to announce an upcoming show with a headliner Martinez refused to fight. A near-riot ensued.

Roybal boxed in high school and, after one pro fight, figured it was easier taking shots as a promoter than as a fighter. He did fight a couple more times, even did an exhibition with Eddie Mack who was guest refereeing one of his shows, but went into full-time promoting by 1934.

At the time, boxing was just getting by in Las Vegas, with no steady promoters. The Las Vegas Fire Department, Herman Speiss and the local post of the VFW had all tried cul-

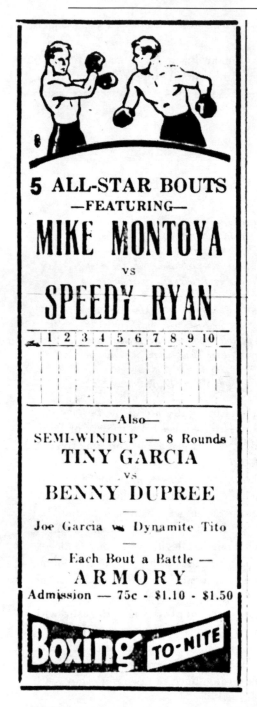

5 ALL-STAR BOUTS
—FEATURING—
MIKE MONTOYA
vs
SPEEDY RYAN

| | 1 | 2 | 3 | 4 | 5 | 6 | 7 | 8 | 9 | 10 | |

—Also—
SEMI-WINDUP — 8 Rounds
TINY GARCIA
vs
BENNY DUPREE
—
Joe Garcia vs Dynamite Tito
—
— Each Bout a Battle —
ARMORY
Admission — 75c - $1.10 - $1.50

Boxing TO-NITE

New Mexico's top two middleweights, Espanola-born Mike Montoya and Melrose's Speedy Ryan, clashed twice in 1935 for local bragging rights. Montoya had power, Ryan had speed. On May 17, 1935, in Las Vegas, they drew in 10 rounds; two months later Montoya edged Ryan.

tivating the scene, without luck. After his first big show, on April 18, 1934, had the Armory "packed from rafter to floor"[10] to watch the "Black Panther" upset Babe Colima, it was full speed ahead for Roybal.

Prior to 1934, it was all about Jimmy Ortiz and Frankie Cantou. When the former retired and the latter died, Colima was a regular headliner — a dozen times in Vegas alone from '32 to '39. The Black Panther headlined six shows while Ted "Mustang" Garcia was top billing for eight.

Espanola-born Mike Montoya, fighting out of La Veta, Colorado, came along and defeated Tate, headlining eight shows that included two hair-raising, winner-take-all bouts with Melrose's Speedy Ryan.

Top contender Emilio Martinez was probably the most popular from 1935 on, as he worked his way up to a title shot — everyone wanted to see the New Mexican native gone good, though almost all of his opponents were tomato cans.

Out-of-towners like Eddie Trujillo (Caponi), of Denver, Al Rivers from Nebraska, Jack Chase (Young Joe Louis) from Colorado, and Ray "Showboat" McQuillan from Idaho graced the Vegas ring. From around the state came the Perry brothers, Abie and Tony Chavez. Prelim regulars included Severo de Baca, Jimmy Pancher, Dawson's "Dynamite" Tito Maez, Frankie "Tuffy" Kavanaugh, Sec "Sunshine" Herrera, "Boots" Lucero, the Gallegos brothers — Tony and Frankie (Higgins), Midget Valentino, and Lalo Trujillo, with Frankie "Panchito" Montoya doing the occasional baby fight curtain raiser as "Baby Pancho." Montoya's time would come in the '40s.

Occasionally you had a name who swapped out monikers faster than Roybal swapped out last minute opponents. Bill Woolery, a college student at Montezuma College, was an intermittent mittslinger who fought enough times to use up his *noms de guerre*, "Bob Brady," "Buck Brady," Billy Woolery," or any combination thereof. He was far from the best, but no one would ever forget a fight in 1934 when he showed up "wearing one wool sock and one tennis shoe."[11] Despite the lack of footwear, he stole the show with a 45-second knockout of Albuquerque's Shanghai Kid.

As the decade wore on, the headliners disappeared and amateur boxing shows brought the number of pros down. In hybrid wrestling shows, Roybal kept the pro game alive for a time, but eventually that, too, faded with the new decade.

For a time, the city was alive with the sport. As Las Vegas reached its peak, in 1935, boxing was about crafty southpaw Johnny Johnson. Like Santa Fe's Tiny Garcia, his chief nemesis in New Mexico, Johnson bordered on being a great fighter, but could not make the next level — but he was one of the most popular. Johnny's mother was Spanish and his father was an immigrant from Sweden who'd come to New Mexico to farm, giving Johnson blond hair and dark brown eyes.

Johnson turned pro in 1932 while still in high school, and became a regular on northern shows. He was the only New Mexican to have an edge over Tiny Garcia, coming out ahead with two wins, two draws and a loss, over six bouts. By 1935, he was the accepted state and Rocky Mountain lightweight champ, which went to Tiny when he ventured out of state.

One of the biggest names in Vegas, New Mexico, in the late '30s was Native American boxer "Mustang" Garcia, who was not only big in New Mexico, but in South Dakota, where he was born, Colorado, Texas and Arizona. Garcia was the son of a Mexican mother and a Crow Native-American father, though he was generally billed as a Blackfoot Indian because his first manager thought it would look better in print than Crow.

The Ring recognized Johnson as a prospect and he proved his mettle on the road, drawing, then beating Eddie Caponi in 1935, defeating Babe Colima in Juarez, then Richie Proo in Pueblo, before running into the wall that was ranked contender Hubert "Kid" Dennis. In 1936, Johnson beat Colima two more times but then lost as many times to Jack Chase, both times by decision in Walsenburg, Colorado. After a quick tour in Los Angeles, where he was piloted briefly by Charlie Hobman, Johnson came home and fought periodically through 1938 before hanging it up with close to 100 bouts.

Johnny's younger brother Art, "The Las Vegas Fighting Schoolboy," stayed closer to home. Art could beat almost everybody at feather in New Mexico but had the misfortune of fighting during Frankie Cantou's rise. Even so, after losing two bouts by knockout to Frankie, Art became the one and only person to knock Cantou out. He also shared opponents with his brother, sometimes even subbing for one another. He fought Tiny Garcia three times early on, winning, losing, and drawing, and Young Mike Baca, who had his number, several times. Fighting only half as often as Johnny, Art gave it up in 1937.

The biggest name in Vegas in the late '30s just may have been the most successful Native American boxer during the era — if not the world, then certainly the Southwest. Ted "Mustang" Garcia was not only big in New Mexico, but in South Dakota, where he was born, Colorado, Texas and Arizona. Garcia was the son of a Mexican mother and a Crow Native-American father, though he was generally billed as a Blackfoot Indian because his first manager thought it would look better in print than Crow. Fighting from featherweight to welter, from 1934 to 1950, Garcia accrued nearly 200 bouts, peaking in the '30s. By the time World War II put his career on hiatus, Garcia had been the featherweight champ of the Dakotas, the lightweight champ of Colorado and New Mexico, and the Rocky Mountain lightweight champ. Like Billy Firpo, Mustang galloped his way around the Southwest, fighting everyone on any sort of notice. For example, in 1941, *The Ring* reported:

> The wild hardhitting Mustang, Indian lightweight fighting out of Galveston, set some sort of an endurance record when he subbed on 24 hours' notice, drove from Galveston to New Orleans (400 miles) and arriving a few hours before fight time, took the measure of Russell Gonzales, classy Filipino battler. Garcia immediately drove back to Corpus Christi, Texas, (600 miles) arriving there only two hours before his scheduled fight and went on to blast out an eight-round knockout victory over the very capable Joe Mendoza.[12]

Mustang first fought in New Mexico in 1937, upsetting Tiny Garcia, though it was a draw in the rematch. After campaigning in Texas — much the way Benny Cordova had done in the '10s — Garcia came back to Las Vegas, terrorizing the lightweights. By 1940, either Mustang's speed had declined enough or the locals were improving, enabling Billy Firpo, Larry Cisneros and Tiny to, at least, draw with the Crow veteran.

While Vegas adopted fighters like Mustang and Fort Sumner's pair of Perrys, and after the Johnson brothers were slowing, another name solidified itself to the Meadow City.

The name "Gallegos" had been around long before the '30s. From Mora to Silver City, there were many Gallegos boxers all over the state. The first Gallegos in a Las Vegas ring was Mora's Pepe Gallegos, who was a regular at the Duncan Opera House in the '10s. Kid Raymundo Gallegos fought in Albuquerque in the '20s and Albert Gallegos fought briefly out of Las Vegas in 1926. The late '30s would see Ralph, or "Sabu," another Gallegos, this one from Chama, who would be one of the state's first amateur stars.

It was an era of brothers, for Fort

Tony Gallegos was a Las Vegas fighter in the '30s who was good enough to TKO granite-chinned Billy Firpo.

Sumner had Jim and Joe Perry, Santa Fe had Tiny and Joe Garcia (they'd also had the Pachecos in the '20s), and Vegas had two sets, Johnny and Art Johnson, then Tony and Frankie Gallegos.

The oldest, Tony, a featherweight at first, made his debut on an Albuquerque card in 1932, then fought occasionally through 1935, staging a brief comeback in '37. Tony was good enough to draw with Firpo — then became one of the rare ones who actually TKO'd him.

Tony's brother Frankie had an odd career. Fighting under his mother's maiden name, Higgins (there'd been plenty of fighting Higginses, as well), Frankie was one of the state's first amateur notables, all the while maintaining a stop-and-go professional career. Though his early bouts in 1934 might or might not be construed as amateur, against fellow youngsters Tiny Timmie Duran, Young Maestas and Lalo Trujillo, his October 1935 showdown with Young Benny Cordova was a definite payday for Higgins, who TKO'd the Albuquerque hopeful.

But after his first series of fights, Higgins did as Julio Chiaramonte did in 1932, when he "turned amateur," entering Clovis' first-ever Amateur Athletic Union (AAU) New Mexico-Texas Golden Gloves Tournament in February 1937. Higgins was one of several former pros in the tourney. Shortly after the meet, Frankie was scheduled to turn pro (for the second time), but he decided to stay amateur, at least for another month, when he found a spot on a Springer card on Mar. 11, 1937, knocking out Ernie Cordova of Wagon Mound.

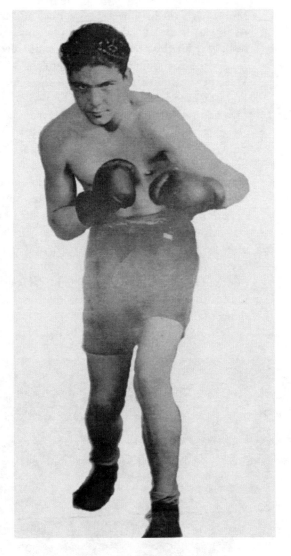

Talent in Las Vegas, New Mexico was deep. Amateur star Frankie Higgins (Gallegos) was one of several who fought in the city. Higgins began a legacy that continues today in the state. His grandson, Shaun Gallegos, became a state champion and fought several big names in the sport.

As a pro, Higgins fought on. He was no match for Abie Chavez, who stopped him in six on Oct. 2, 1937, in Farmington, but Higgins was a cut above the average lightweight. He improved, too, when Mustang Garcia took him on the road in 1938.

Neither Gallegos made main event billing, even in their hometown, but the competition was at its peak. If Mustang Garcia, Johnny Johnson or Emilio Martinez wasn't headlining Roybal's bill, there were two more names making things even more difficult for a hometown boy trying to make the grade.

If the "Clouting Caballero" had decided to herd sheep instead of sling leather, Mike

Montoya might have been the premier middleweight in the two states in which he resided. As it was, he was good enough to be considered the best New Mexico fighter of 1935 — a peak year for the decade — and the state's premier middleweight.

Mike got around. He was born in Espanola but later on lived in both Taos and La Veta, in southern Colorado, where he remained in the latter half of his 80-bout career. Fighting everywhere throughout his two home states, and from Reno to Los Angeles, Montoya had two distinct phases of his career.

Early on, he fought throughout New Mexico. During Raton's last series of consistent shows, Montoya was the biggest name at the New Mexico-Colorado state line, when he first lost to, then beat, Red Foster in two wars that were talked about for years. In 1933, after moving to La Veta, he was a Colorado campaigner. After lasting five frames with former champ Tommy Freeman, at Hot Springs, Arkansas, in 1934, Montoya returned to his original state in '35 to clean up in his peak period.

Montoya lost to Emilio Martinez, but beat his brother at least twice. In New Mexico, only Eddie Murdock could beat Montoya, and even then, by a split decision — but Mike evened the score in the rematch, becoming one of the elite who could brag about knocking out the former welterweight contender. He also knocked out the Black Panther, a win which made him popular. Fast movers, like Melrose's Speedy Ryan, gave him trouble — the fancy dancer held Montoya to a draw before snagging his state middleweight belt by decision.

In 1936, Montoya started to fade. He went 1–2 for the state light-heavy belt with Jim Perry, and dropped three bouts, two by knockout, to Young Joe Louis for Colorado's middleweight title. In '37, there are five known bouts — all losses. Montoya's last year saw more losses than wins and he retired soon after a Sept. 4 loss to Joe Aguilar in a final bid for his old title, the Colorado middleweight strap.

In the mid to late '30s Larry Cisneros carved out a local reputation in the northern part of the state. Larry's time would come after World War II when he would rise to contention on the West Coast during the '40s.

During the entire era, one would hear about the oddball fights happening in Questa, Taos or Folsom. They would almost always center around one name, a featherweight or lightweight who was zipping around northern New Mexico and southern Colorado fighting anyone — a kid with the last name "Cisneros."

There had been a Cisneros or two in the past. One was Jose "Cyclone" Cisneros, who'd headlined a rare Questa card in 1922 when he defeated Charlie Mossman for the New Mexico light-heavyweight title. Two months later, the Cyclone defended against Taos' Joe McAllister on a card whose results are not known.

Right about the same time the lower two-thirds of the state started to hear about this kid, Laureano, or Larry, there reappeared his uncle, old-timer Alex, who'd been campaigning in Colorado for years. Alex reappeared on a Springer card in May 1937, only to lose to Mexican Pete Regal. Alex was past his prime, but look out for the kid, he warned promoters — the kid "had it."

Born on Sept. 17, 1917, Larry's earliest known fight was as a 15-year-old amateur in 1932, when he defeated Young Firpo (probably Billy). According to Larry, he was 17-0-1 as an amateur, and a winner at the AAU Western Regionals in 1936, before turning pro.

Larry Cisneros fought a quiet campaign in the late '30s, fighting through his uncle's old haunts in southern Colorado and throughout the northern portion of New Mexico, on cards held in places where there were few — or no — scribes to report the action.

In the next decade, he would make famous the mining town of Questa, in the heart of the Sangre de Cristo Mountains north of Taos, as they would have Los Angelenos calling him "The Rock of Questa" or "The Rock of New Mexico." In this era, he was, more often than not, the "Questa Bull," and he stampeded through what competition was left in the decade's last two years before World War II put the quietus on the sport.

Cisneros outpointed Tiny Garcia twice in '38, defeated Pete Regal, who'd KO'd Uncle Alex, twice, and cleaned up in Colorado by beating Smokey Kansas, Moose Maxwell and Bobby Valdez. Just when the scene started to die in New Mexico, Cisneros kept busy by heading to the Midwest, with buddy Billy Firpo, for several fights arranged by old-timer Louis Newman. Upon his return, Cisneros beat Chief Cardi in Questa, and Mustang Garcia in San Luis, Colorado, proving he was ready for the next level, with just over 40 bouts under his belt.

Instead, Cisneros got clobbered by the approaching world war — but his tale does not end there. Cisneros not only fought during the coming conflict, but became the next big boxing star from New Mexico during the next decade. But *that* is a tale for the next book.

Forged in the Heat of Kitchen's

> *"It's great being in school," he says. "You see, I'm mighty lucky to be there. There are ten in our family and they all work but me. Our home is at Gallup, N. M. and it's a coal mining town. My dad's a coal miner and so are all my brothers. I'm the lucky one in the family. I never worked in the coal mines except around the edges, sort of, when I was a kid. I've always gone to school. In a big family like ours there always has to be one who goes to school, and I'm the fellow."*
> —Julio Chiaramonte in the *Gallup Independent*, 1936[13]

With a win over ranked welterweight contender Eddie Murdock and a draw with battle-tested Benny Chavez, once a conqueror of Eddie Mack, 16-year-old high school student Julio Chiaramonte had proved himself to be the greatest pro to ever come out of Gallup. That had never been his goal. What Julio wanted was to be the best *amateur* to ever come out of the state, by fighting his way to the Olympics.

Chiaramonte's past — a shoe box full of clippings that included his draw with Chavez and the story on Benny's death — was left under his bed in Gallup when Julio left for Roswell and the New Mexico Military Institute in the fall of '31. When he arrived, the first thing he did was find the NMMI boxing coach, Capt. C. M. Woodbury, who informed him that training would not begin until after football season. Julio pushed to get into the gym and

Woodbury relented, agreeing to work the kid out, maybe show him a thing or two by sparring.

Woodbury knew very little about Julio's past, but after getting banged around by a mere tenth-grader, he knew this year's boxing team had a gem. Life in Roswell was far different than a miner's existence in Gallup — and the fight scene was clean, collegiate athletics, not the gritty, smoke-filled house of rowdy, drunk fight fans that Chiaramonte had been developed in at Kitchen's. Woodbury was equally ignorant of Julio's pro career. As far as he knew, the kid was a promising athlete and there was no need to rush him into competing on the intercollegiate level. As the cadet boxing team began formal training, however, Chiaramonte ran out of sparring partners as the Institute's intramural tournament approached.

By now, the 141-pound light welterweight had grown into middleweight. Though hyped as an upcoming "epic," when Chiaramonte defeated Tom Jones, who'd been the school's middleweight champ for three straight years, it was hardly an effort for someone who'd stepped ten rounds with a bruiser like Benny Chavez. Jones was on the run, but Julio caught up with him in the second, clobbering him down for a spot on the varsity team.

A few weeks later, NMMI hosted a dual meet with Texas Tech, that saw Chiaramonte opponentless, with his rival out on an injury. The heavyweights, too, were unmatched as NMMI was unable to fill the slot. With the meet about to end with a 2–2 draw, Chiaramonte begged the coach to have him fill in at heavy, never mind the 20-pound weight disadvantage — Julio had come from Gallup, where 15-year-olds were thrown in the ring with men in their prime having over 100 bouts. Against his better judgment, the coach gave in. "Okay Chiaramonte, go get your gloves on. But if that guy hits you just one time, I'm stopping the bout. D'ya hear me? Hit and move." Chiaramonte didn't hit and move, he stood and fought, knocking his guy out in round two. Needless to say, Julio was undefeated his first year.

The summer break in 1932 saw Julio's 10-round scorching split-decision win over Murdock — a fight that, by some miracle, never got back to the administration office at NMMI, for when Julio returned to Roswell, he picked up where he left off.

Not only was Julio the captain of the boxing team, but he was also a starting guard on the junior college football team for four years — a team that was good enough to beat varsity teams at the University of New Mexico (UNM) and New Mexico College of Agriculture and Mechanic Arts (which would, in 1960, be renamed New Mexico State University.) In his final year at NMMI, Chiaramonte was captain of both teams.

In four years of boxing at NMMI, Julio lost but a single fight, and he even found time, during the summer of 1934, to fight two more times as "pro" whose purse was either forfeited, or used for books and tuition. On June 28, 1934, he KO'd Emir Jarvis in Holbrook, Ariz., and, one week later, he TKO'd veteran Battling Kelly in what would be his final pro bout, and last bout, altogether, in his hometown of Gallup.

Through all the amateur bouts — and occasional pro ones — Julio never swayed from his goal of making the U.S. Olympic team. In 1936, just before his 21st birthday and during his final year at the NMMI, he and Ralph "Sabu" Gallegos, from UNM, were invited to the AAU Southern Regionals at New Orleans — a gateway tourney for the Olympics. Winners would advance to the semifinals at Cleveland and the winners would box at Boston to determine the Olympic team to go to Berlin.

Both Chiaramonte and Gallegos won their opening bouts, by knockout. Julio defeated his next two opponents by decision, winning at finals and becoming the only boxer on the team who was not from Louisiana. Gallegos had lost at finals by decision, but since winners and runners-up both qualified, the two were on for Cleveland. There, on opening night,

Chiaramonte lost the only fight of his career, amateur *and* professional, when Chicago's Paul Frazier narrowly outpointed him. Trainer Woodbury, who'd accompanied the athletes, called it a "close, beautiful fight but the Negro's long reach was too much."[14] Gallegos would go all the way to the Trials in Boston before losing.

After graduating from NMMI, Chiaramonte went on to the University of Santa Clara. On the football team, under legendary coach Buck Shaw, Chiaramonte played center, though he was never a starter on the team that went undefeated, in back-to-back seasons beating Louisiana State University at the Sugar Bowl Classic at New Orleans. Julio liked football, but boxing remained his first love. He continued to box at Santa Clara, becoming a two-time Pacific Coast Intercollegiate champion. In fact, he was so overwhelming in the college ranks that several of his bouts were won by forfeit.

By his own estimation, Chiaramonte fought exactly 101 bouts — losing just the one amateur bout, in Cleveland, before hanging up the gloves in 1938.

Without their star fighter for most of the decade, Gallup still managed to cook up a healthy fight scene at Kitchen's. There were still the other Chiaramontes — and plenty of name fighters looking for spots on cards when Albuquerque and Santa Fe dried up.

For a time, Sam — "Boney" — left Gallup, to enroll at St. Michael's in Santa Fe, but he was called back to Gallup where he worked the mines and continued prizefighting. Nardine, too, was a cadet for a time at NMMI, but also had to go back to the mines in Gallup when his father got sick. "Dad gave me $400 to quit school and come back home," recalled Nardine. "Tony was running the show at home, but they begged me to come back — so I did."[15]

Nardine fought infrequently, but Boney became the biggest local draw in Gallup. He was good enough to knock out Babe Colima while the El Paso veteran was still in his prime, in '33, and, for a time, there was talk of a West Coast campaign under manager J. W. Laird, but nothing materialized. Boney fought his toughest bout against Denver's "Joltin'" Joe Jaramillo, winning the fight but admitting that he'd fought in a daze from the sixth round on, going down three times. Jaramillo lost two teeth: "The dentist who attended Jaramillo said the teeth were broken off so that the stumps remained in his jaw, and the inside of his lips required several stitches."[16] Against top Arizona fighter Buck "K.O." Simpson, Boney fought five times, losing most; he also had trouble with the Black Panther, who'd hit Boney the "hardest he'd ever been hit."[17] By 1936, Boney slowed down, too, fighting just once that year, and once the following year. After taking three years off, he resurfaced in 1940 to fight again but, by then, the pro boxing scene was dead and buried in Gallup.

Even without the Chiaramontes, promoter Guido Zecca managed to keep the scene hopping through most of the '30s — a decade that saw more than 80 fights, almost all at Kitchen's. During slow periods, Zecca kept boxing alive with hybrid wrestling shows, but almost always managed to return the fans' demand for the sweet science.

Another slow period occurred during 1933 and 1934, during a miners' strike. With the Opera House designated as the headquarters for the striking miners, fights were delayed. When they resumed in March 1934, differences between Zecca and Peter Kitchen's son Alex ("Iky") saw a temporary split in promotions. Zecca teamed up with the American Legion at their hall while Kitchen resumed action at the Opera House. On Aug. 9, 1934, Zecca and the Legion headlined Abie Chavez, who outpointed Baby Azteca; one night later at Kitchen's, Boney Chiaramonte lost to Black Panther Tate.

Georgie Avila was nearly as popular as the Chiaramontes, also starting while in high school as a football star at Sacred Heart. After his first couple of years in the prelims, he was ready for the big leagues of New Mexico by '35, and leapt into ten-rounders, fighting mainly at home but moving around from Arizona to Las Vegas and Santa Fe. In his first ten-rounder, Avila drew with the Black Panther, then Boney, before losing to Nardine Chiaramonte. Johnny Johnson and Buck Simpson also proved too good at first, but as he developed, he eventually beat both Tate and Johnson.

One of Avila's most memorable bouts occurred on Feb. 8, 1935, in a ten-round war with Simpson on a Zecca card at Legion Hall. The ref ruled a draw and, after the crowd booed the decision, the promoter announced that there would be an 11th round to declare the winner. Avila found out about that while he was in his dressing room and he refused to come out for another frame, giving Simpson the "W." It wouldn't be the first time Avila got jobbed; that summer in Santa Fe, Georgie fought Johnny Johnson for the Rocky Mountain lightweight title, and was awarded the decision by two judges and a referee. But the city's athletic commission reversed the decision because Avila had been floored twice during the bout. Johnson retained his title.

The regulars at Kitchen's — and the Legion Hall, for the nine months it was used — were not limited to the "battling wops" of Carbon City. Regular names on the billing included Max and Essex Jenkins, Johnny Estrada, Joey "One Punch" Yurcic, Johnny Herrera, "Gaga" Espinosa, Max Small of Grants, and Ralph Coal, "the fighting baker of Carman's Bakery."[18] So close to the Navajo reservation, Native-American fighters were also more likely to fight in Gallup than anywhere else in the state. There was Navajo Bat Nelson of Fort Defiance, Ariz., Chief Terrapin from the Navajo Rez, Steve Nahkai of Shiprock and Navajo Jerry King. Out-of-towners frequenting Gallup included Burl Merrill of Ramah, Ariz., Battling Chico II of El Paso, and Young Joe Louis (Jack Chase) of Walsenburg, Colorado, who KO'd an aging Eddie Murdock in 1936. Mike Montoya, Murdock, Tate and Simpson were favorite headliners, but Abie Chavez was popular enough to fight in Gallup 13 times, headlining no fewer than nine shows.

Another local favorite, long-time veteran Natividad Juarez, known to sports fans as the Insurrecto Kid (version 2, if you want to be technical), staged a comeback in the early '30s, but in 1933 was shot and killed while entering the house of his ex-wife in Gallup. His killer, Pete Talamonte, got less than ten years in the state prison.

If the death of Insurrecto was a low point, the July 3, 1935, war between Murdock and Montoya might be its high point. Before the second largest attendance of 1,000, Murdock won by split decision at an outdoor arena built to accommodate the crowd. By 1937, when Murdock returned to fight Simpson, just 200 showed up at Kitchen's — by then, the scene was failing. It would be the last pro card until 1939 — a year that saw Gallup's first amateur boxing tournament.

Amateur boxing, under the 20/20 Club, took over and, after two more shows, one in 1940 and the other in '41, pro boxing was gone. The show in '40 was Kitchen's last show. When top Native American heavyweight Junior Munsell landed his knockout punch at 2:35 of round one, on Sept. 25, 1941, on Paul Wyatt, of Oklahoma City, it would be the last professional punch ever thrown in a Gallup boxing ring.

Big-Time Boxing in Small-Town New Mexico

> *It is up to the fans as to whether the game will continue.... Fighters may fight and promoters may promote but they can do nothing without the fans.*
> — *El Paso Times*, 1931[19]

More than they ever had before, the smaller towns of New Mexico came alive during the '30s, as if to take up the slack when Albuquerque, then Santa Fe, slowed down. Surrounding the Duke City, the railroad town of Belen, 34 miles south, Bernalillo, 10 miles north, the ranching town of Estancia, 40 miles east, and Mountainair, 67 miles southeast in the Manzano Mountains, all took advantage of Albuquerque's waning interest to stage shows.

Belen was primarily known for its Harvey House. In the '30s, it was a second home for Abie Chavez, a place to go for the occasional prize fight, and a developing ground for a handful of local battlers.

Belen was the site for a rare black heavyweight fight, between Leroy Haynes, the "second" Dixie Kid (the first being Aaron Brown, who'd fought much earlier), and Chihuahua Kid Brown, from the border, who didn't have much to offer, having come off a failed suicide attempt while doing 75 days in the Santa Fe County Jail. Haynes would go on to make it in California — to the extent that a black fighter *could* make it — and would score two knockouts over former champ Primo Carnera in 1936. It was a repeat fight from a Santa Fe bout in 1929, in which Brown had TKO'd Haynes in the tenth round. Prior to that, Haynes had fought on a couple of Red Valencia's shows in Bernalillo.

The American Legion's post in Belen got on the bandwagon, bringing in Kid Mortio to headline, but by '32, several homeboys were coming along. Former fighter Dick Castillo was in the midst of a comeback, but there was also Herman "Kid" Silva, Fidel Baca, Spec Patterson, Phil Esquiro, Pee Wee Barrera and Benny Garcia, who was Belen's busiest battler. Belen's top name was Abie Chavez, who would headline nine shows between 1932 and '38.

There was also the "Belen Bomber." Second to Abie was Benny Valencia who, just a kid at the time, made a pro debut in 1934, then wrote the fight off as an amateur bout, to dive into the developing amateur scene. Benny fought amateur through the '30s as a welterweight, and was one of the early Golden Gloves champions. In 1937, he was a runner-up in the AAU Nationals. After his successful amateur career, Valencia would re-invent himself as a pro fighter in the '40s — and then again in the '50s.

When the New Mexico Central Railway made its headquarters at Estancia, the agriculture-based county seat of Torrance County, it put an end to the town's isolation. Over 40 fight cards between 1934 and 1939 ensured a stream of visitors from Albuquerque

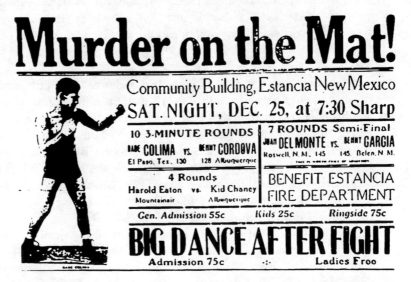

Murder on the Mat!

Community Building, Estancia New Mexico
SAT. NIGHT, DEC. 25, at 7:30 Sharp

10 3-MINUTE ROUNDS	7 ROUNDS Semi-Final
BABE COLIMA vs. BENNY CORDOVA El Paso, Tex. 130 128 Albuquerque	JUAN DELMONTE vs. BENNY GARCIA Roswell, N.M. 145 145 Belen, N.M.
4 Rounds Harold Eaton vs. Kid Chaney Mountainair Albuquerque	BENEFIT ESTANCIA FIRE DEPARTMENT

Gen. Admission 55c   Kids 25c   Ringside 75c

BIG DANCE AFTER FIGHT
Admission 75c   -:-   Ladies Free

After Albuquerque saw a decline in boxing in the late '30s, Estancia picked up the momentum with a series of shows. One of its biggest cards, pitting Babe Colima with Young Benny Cordova, occurred on Christmas Day 1937.

and the surrounding countryside. Peaking with nearly a show a month between '36 and '38, the town gave New Mexico big leaguers a place to fight while bringing up a few of their own locals. Mountainous Mountainair, not nearly as busy being isolated in the Manzanos, offered yet another alternative, with a handful of shows during Estancia's peak period; Bernalillo, to the north, dusted off its ring with a handful of fights as the decade came to a close.

Estancia's first stab at the sport was a flop, with unskilled locals battering away at one another over a two-day Fourth of July celebration in 1933 and the only veteran on the card promoted by C. W. Grant, was K. O. Sanchez of Albuquerque, who beat up his sparring partner "Frisco."

The next three shows, in late summer and through the fall, were better. With Pete Lucero matchmaking for the Estancia Fire Dept. at the Rainbow Garden "arena," middleweight Don Anderson, from nearby Willard, established himself as the local draw on cards that added wrestling and amateur boxing. Lucero was bold enough to stage a 15-round heavyweight bout between locals who'd never gone beyond a couple of rounds, but spectators were pleasantly surprised to watch Estancia's George "Kingfish" Fontaine go at least 11 frames before even-less-known Nick Schmidt from Mountainair knocked him through the ropes onto the floor, then try to stumble back into the ring as his seconds hurled in the towel.

When the weather got warm again, in '34, cards were held south of the Star Theatre in a big open field or at the Community Building. With admission as low as 20 and 45 cents, shows were frequently benefits for the local baseball clubs, and they almost always concluded with dances afterward. Bigger guns were brought in to fight the local star, Anderson. After Jim Perry knocked him out in three, they returned to feeding Anderson the local weekend warriors.

Fighting often enough, some of the locals got pretty good, at least by New Mexico standards. Mountainair's Tommy Richardson became good enough to beat Santa Fe's Joe Garcia. Estancia had Tommy Tindell, whose "he-man scraps"[20] with Richardson were fan favorites, Johnny Imboden and Johnny Del Monte, who was originally from Roswell. Moriarty had Benny West; Barton had Kenneth Parker; and Cedarville had Pete McCloud.

Though 1935 was slow, with just two Anderson-billed cards, the next year opened the floodgates, with ten bouts, then 11 in '37. By now, Albuquerque was a ghost town for boxing and Santa Fe was drifting that way, as well, so the shows in Estancia began to feature bigger names from around the state. Even Anderson's hometown of Willard staged a couple of shows. Mike Montoya, Jim and Joe Perry, Young Benny Cordova and Bobby Vinson, a Dallas pug who'd moved to Santa Fe, all got regular billing. While the Estancia Fire Dept. continued to be the main promoter, Santa Fe's Daniel Ortiz came down to throw two shows, as well. By 1937, the main impetus of the shows in Estancia was Anderson, or, more likely, those who'd beaten him, like Jim Perry and Montoya.

Though the scene began to slow in frequency, but grow in scope, in 1938, the biggest show of the area's era was held on Jan. 29, 1938, when the local fire department headlined "Double Main! Double Action! Boxing!" with two state title fights that saw Tiny Garcia defend his lightweight belt against Joe Perry and Billy Firpo knock out local Juan Del Monte to retain his welterweight strap. Three amateur bouts were held, too, and the sole pro prelim saw Estancia's "Kid Sheepherder" Tracy knock out Albert "Kid Pumpkin" Carbajal from the CCC camp outside Albuquerque. Tickets were 50 cents and Eddie Mack was guest referee for the National Foundation of Infantile Paralysis benefit. A capacity crowd of 500 showed up.

Assured that a house of 500 could make money and bring the bigger name fighters, the Estancia Fire Dept. brought down Murdock in April to test local Pete McCloud, who was, at least, game enough to go eight rounds. The old grizzled veteran, paunchy and bald by now, was a hit and he came back for two more shows. By the end of the

Double Main! - Double Action!

≡ BOXING! ≡

Estancia, January 29, 1938, 7:30 p.m. Sharp

10 ROUNDS

Tiney GARCIA vs. **Joe PERRY**

133, Santa Fe   Both Boys claim the Lightweight Title so they are in for a Real Fight   137, Ft. Sumner

10 ROUNDS

Billy FIRPO vs. **Juan DEL MONTE**

145, Wagon Mound   These boys are fighting for the Welterweight Title of New Mexico   142, Roswell

6 ROUNDS | *3 3-Round Curtain Raisers*

Kid Sheepherder Tracy   vs.   Kid Pumpkin Carabajal | EDDIE MACK, Referee
132, Estancia. Can Tracy take him?   CCC, 130, Albuquerque |

Benefit of National Foundation for Infantile Paralysis.   Help the Crippled Children of the State and Nation
GENERAL ADMISSION 50c   **RINGSIDE $1.00**   **KIDS 25c**

DANCE after the Fights = Come One, Come All

Perhaps the biggest show to land in Estancia was the Jan. 29, 1938, card, with dual state title fights. In one, Tiny Garcia edged Joe Perry for lightweight honors; at welter, Billy Firpo knocked out local hopeful Juan Del Monte, in three rounds.

year, however, the shows lost their luster and the local paper wrote that the latest card was a "fizzle" and that it looked as if "the fight game is taboo in Estancia, for the time being, anyway."[21] Another promoter tried a couple more shows in '39 and '40, but the crowd was no longer there.

Willard star Don Anderson did move on and had marginal success. He might not have able to beat the Mike Montoyas and Jim Perrys of the state, but after enrolling at UNM, where he boxed at the amateur collegiate level despite his 20 or so pro bouts, Anderson improved enough to go the distance with his former conqueror, Perry.

The Perry brothers, Jim and Joe, were from Fort Sumner, where, between '33 and '37, there was another scene brewing. Every one of the 15 or so fight cards staged at Fort Sumner headlined one or both of the Perrys. It's also no accident that the promoter was, more often than not, Joseph Jerry Perry, father to the two prides of Fort Sumner.

The town was known for the military fort of the same name that had imprisoned Navajo and Mescalero Apache Indians in the 1860s. It was also the site of Lucien Maxwell's famous house, where Billy the Kid was shot and killed by Sheriff Pat Garrett. In the '30s, it was all about Jim and Joe Perry and their fists.

Born in 1916, Jim was the older and heavier, fighting from middleweight to light-heavy. Joe, born three years later, in 1919, fought at feather to lightweight. Jim, also called "The Fighting Blacksmith," started in '33 and ended in '37. His fights garnered more attention, at first — physically bigger fighters always did — but Joe, fighting from '33 to '39, fought far more often, since there were four times the number of opponents available.

Both of their debuts occurred at the Granada Theater in downtown Fort Sumner, when a large crowd gathered to watch the first fight card known to be staged there. It might have been the first show, but there had been fighters from Fort Sumner before, like Earnie Rose in 1930 and "Whirlwind" Kelly in 1932. Unlike the one- or two-hit wonders that preceded them, the Perrys would forevermore be the only successful fighters to come out of Fort Sumner. On their debuts, a crowd between 200 and 300 (in a town of 1,000) showed up to watch Jim clobber the "Texaco Rambler" in 40 seconds and Joe outhustle Vernon Baker.

Jim and Joe had parallel climbs to the top of the New Mexico — and nearly Southwest — heap.

Seventeen-year-old Jim cleaned up the east end of the state first, beating Tucumcari's Percy Reid and Melrose's Speedy Ryan. The middleweight moved over to West Texas in 1934, losing just one bout and fighting a trilogy with Pampa's Joe Vernon (two draws and a KO in seven), before returning to New Mexico where he was undefeated through the year, winning the state light-heavy title by July.

Jim was virtually unbeaten against New Mexicans during his career, but for one split-decision loss to hard-hitting Mike Montoya, who was, at the time, the Southwest middleweight champ. The loss was avenged in '36 and Perry reclaimed his belt, only to lose again to Montoya, two months later. The two fought five times, continually swapping the state middleweight and light-heavyweight belts.

In what was probably his most significant fight, Jim lost to long-time veteran George Manley in Colorado Springs, which served notice that Perry would probably not be getting past New Mexico's club level. In 1937, Perry fought a trilogy with Eddie Cerda, a New York Puerto Rican who'd relocated to the state — all within a week's time, coming out ahead with a win and two draws. After losing to Babe Orgovan of Arizona, in Silver City, Jim retired with an estimated 40 bouts and just a handful of losses.

The younger Joe Perry had more like 60 fights, and had a slower climb to the top in New Mexico. Fighting locals for the first couple of years, during which he was still in high school, Joe wasn't really challenged until 1935. Thereafter, he fought Young Benny Cordova twice, for a win and a draw, then became the state featherweight champion in 1936. When Joe moved up to lightweight, he hit the wall that was Tiny Garcia. Though he was able to score one win in their trilogy, he dropped two decisions.

Joe had less success out of state, and his worst loss was a knockout to Babe Colima in Juarez, though he evened the score on home turf later in the year. Joe also lost to Abie Chavez in Belen in '36, and fought a handful of prelims in California during 1937 with marginal success. In 1939, Joe moved to Florida where he fought a couple more times before hanging up the gloves.

During the Perry period, several other Fort Sumner battlers donned the leather to populate J. J. Perry's hometown shows. There was scrappy lightweight Dick Vick, and his two kid brothers, Horace "Hoss" and "Baby" Vick. Horace would go on to win the James J. Braddock Trophy (the equivalent of "Best Fighter") in Clovis' first regional amateur meet in 1937. Other colorfully named pugsters included Humpty Anderson, Sock Pickel and Woodrow Martin.

Though they were hearty travelers, Fort Sumner's pair of Perrys found a welcome spot east of their town in Melrose, Clovis and Hobbs, just as often as they did in Estancia or Las Vegas, for boxing was alive and well at the eastern centers during the '30s. Peaking in 1936 with a show a month, Clovis had around 20 shows between '33 and '37. Melrose and Hobbs each had a handful, centered around their hometown hopefuls.

After the earlier era dominated by Ernie Gross, Bearcat Mathis and Marlin Owens, the Clovis scene came to a complete halt in 1935. After nearly two years of inactivity, "the rising roar for the kill sounded once more"[22] when co-promoters Joe Brown and Floyd Parker brought back a capacity crowd of 611 fans on Apr. 20, 1936, at the Jungleland Arena, formerly known as Amusement Auditorium, then the Skating Rink building, to watch Melrose's Speedy Ryan pummel the 12-year, battle-scarred, Fort Worth veteran Duke Trammel through ten rounds. The East New Mexico vs. West Texas rivalry was on again.

The Disabled American Veterans took over promotion but passed it on to Paul Moffett, with smaller shows, at first, that built up local favorites like Ray Love, Valguene Dixon and Ben Woolsey, with added amateur bouts as prelims. The pro game had a lot to compete with — not just wrestling but amateur boxing, which was growing faster than pro boxing had ever done in the eastern portion of the state.

Fort Sumner's Jim Perry, Clovis' own Earl "Tiger" Smith and out-of-towners like Billy McDonald of Amarillo, Texas, or Kid Mitchell of Hot Springs, Ark., were the main headliners on Moffett's shows. Unlike other areas in the state, black fighters — like Smith, McDonald and Mitchell, as well as Chihuahua Kid Brown and Albuquerque's Tiger LaGrone — found regular spots on Clovis shows.

In '36, Moffett brought back Pug Grubbs, former ring prodigy from Borger, Texas, and his war with Babe Colima might have been the fight of the year, but only a small crowd could attest to it. Grubbs KO'd Colima, though the El Paso veteran probably would have done better had he not fought Joe Perry the night before in Fort Sumner.

It was a case of too many shows in too short a period, as Moffett overdid shows with the Perrys and Grubbs, hoping they would catch on. When the crowds started to decrease with each show, Moffett decided to halt all action until the following year. When he sought to rebuild the scene in 1937, with the help of Las Vegas' Joe Roybal, it was too late, as the pro game in Clovis had been replaced by amateur boxing.

Melrose had better luck, but only because the number of shows were far less and they centered around one name, that being Speedy Ryan.

Born in 1912 at Lockney, Texas but raised in Melrose, the fighter who went from "Jimmy" to "Speedy Ryan" was really Bryan B. Queen, son of the county commissioner, and a blacksmith. Though he'd been fighting since 1929, Ryan didn't peak until the mid–'30s, while under the wing of Nick Mortio.

A regular on Clovis, Portales, Fort Sumner and West Texas cards, the "shuffling slugger" of Melrose fought at least 15 times in 1935, and soon rose to claim the state middleweight title. Ryan fought New Mexico's biggest threat to middles, Mike Montoya, three times, winning, losing and drawing. Against Jim Perry, he was 1–1, and, like Perry, he had trouble making the next grade. After beating veteran Duke Trammel in 1936, Ryan took two years off, but staged a comeback in 1938, winning his last two bouts. Then he retired to train amateurs.

North of Clovis in Tucumcari, at the state line separating New Mexico and West Texas, a quick streak of fights transpired late in the decade, in '38, thanks to W. C. "Smokey" Lupkey, who took Percy "Honey Boy" Reid off the shelf, dusted him off and cajoled him back into the ring.

There was one reason for the flurry of activity near Tucumcari — and that was the Conchas Dam. The dam took four years to build and 1938 was its peak year before completion, one year later. The Dam even had its own fighter, with the "Pampa Kid." Though no one seemed to know the West Texan's name, just his hometown, he was a popular fighter on the five shows thrown by Lupkey.

Reid had been the main man in the late '20s and early '30s. After Tucumcari's quick fling with the ring in '29 and '30, "Honey Boy" relocated to Springer where he promoted several shows while continuing to fight. After years of prelims back home, Reid felt ready for the bigger names in 1933. With wins over step-up foes, he challenged Johnny Johnson in 1934. After losing, he retired. Now, along with brother Oscar, Reid was back in 1938, on several shows in Tucumcari — and one at the Conchas Dam, northwest of the city.

After a quick build-up, Reid and the Pampa Kid were slated to fight in an all-local showdown on June 24, 1938, at Dave's Hall. What the outcome was, no one knows, for it was never reported.

Right about the time the dam was finished, Tucumcari bid *adios* to the gloved sport.

Boxing in southern New Mexico would never see another heyday like the era before, during and immediately after World War I. There would be all-too-brief flurries of activity in the '30s, but not enough to sustain a career for a promising prizefighter. Silver City had a scene going in the mid-to-late-'30s — nothing like it had been in the old Otto Floto and Jack Lopez days, but enough to keep the last solid generation of miners occupied.

Those who wanted steady boxing in southern New Mexico had to go to Juarez or El Paso.

In Las Cruces, the lack of action forced two promising boxers to up and leave the area for Chicago in the early '30s. The Mirabal brothers — lightweight Johnny, who fought from '33 to '45, and featherweight Frankie, from '33 to '37 — fought out of the Windy City.

The closest Frankie and Johnny ever came to fighting at home was 1934-'35, when they fought in Juarez. Frankie TKO'd Leroy Dougan when he was home for a visit in '34 and, one year later, Johnny lost a disputed decision to Bobby Fernandez there. Two weeks after that, both Mirabals headlined the just-opened Pan American Arena in Juarez. Johnny, "The Las Cruces Cyclone," decisioned Juarez favorite Chuchu Rubio in the main while Frankie dropped a close one to the more-experienced Manny Candia. On the road, they were regular journeymen on Chicago cards, though Johnny later fought on the West Coast in the latter part of his career, through '38.

In Silver City, it was a different story — but a familiar one. With the breakdown of army camps after the war, the boxing scene in the mining towns had come to a crashing halt in the '20s. Once in a while, Lordsburg, to the far west, would stage a show — in '33 there were six of 'em — but it wasn't until the mid '30s that prizefighting made a solid return in the mining district.

In 1935, Lordsburg had four bouts, Cliff and Central one apiece and Silver City had two, both with low attendance. Most of the shows were the efforts of Reserve's Georgie Stevens, whose son and grandson would carry on the tradition (George Jr. would be a star in the '40s-'50s and grandson Richard, a boxing writer for the *Albuquerque Tribune*). Stevens helped out in Silver City and threw shows in Cliff, Central and Reserve. He also managed Buck Simpson, a frequent headliner.

The action would shift to Central in 1936, with the infamous Brown Derby hosting a half dozen shows. Silver City would have three that year, then have its peak period of the decade in '37-'38, with a show every six weeks or so.

In Lordsburg, Ralph Smith and George Walser staged shows at the "Palador Pavilion," which was nothing more than an erected tent outside the Railroad Club. The burst of activity in Lordsburg was not about mining, but about the construction of the Lordsburg Municipal Airport, the state's first, and also a stop on Charles Lindbergh's "Spirit of St. Louis" tour. The airport added close to 3,000 new residents to the city, turning the railroad town into an aviation town. Most of the Lordsburg fights were smoker level, with CCC camp fighters taking on miners. Former favorite Jack Lopez occasionally reffed a bout or two — in 1933, he even staged a one-night comeback, beating an unknown. Being so close to Arizona, most of the headliners came from there: Buck Simpson, Babe Orgovon, Bob Ford, Art and Jimmy Wakefield, Gene Lovett and Kid Valdon, who'd been fighting in New Mexico as early as 1919.

In Central, the shows were piloted by Louis Suchoff at the popular Brown Derby, which almost always saw a capacity crowd of 300 on Sunday afternoon shows with 55 cent tickets. All the same headliners who fought in Lordsburg or Silver City came to Central, though it had a few of their own locals, like lightweight Al Gonzales.

Besides Stevens' shows, Harry Franks would bring boxing back to the Elks' Theatre in Silver City. Billy Firpo was a regular in the mining town, as was future world champ Lew Jenkins — the two would fight two draws — but it was local featherweight Albert Pena who was the most popular. Former amateur star from the NMMI Harold Bibo (who insisted he was fighting as an amateur), Lordsburg's Art Wakefield, "Cesto the Cuban Kid" and Silver City's Marion York replaced the names of the past everyone had forgotten, like Gus Flores and Jack Lopez.

Stevens brought in shows that saw Jim Perry battle Black Panther Tate, Jenkins' first known New Mexico fight, and curtain raisers with "baby fighter" Georgie Stevens, Jr., picking up the coins after shadowboxing. After securing the sport's return, Stevens moved around, from Reserve to Cliff, while in Silver City, A. C. Cox and Frank took over. Colima, the Perrys, Firpo and Arizona fighters like Moe Hammonds, Buck Simpson and Digger Smith were regulars. When Firpo fought Jenkins in 1937, tickets were 50 cents for the balcony, $1 for the main floor and $1.50 ringside.

Falling prey to the sport of wrestling, that everyone insisted was still a "trend," Cox and Frank switched over to boxing, then did combination cards that kept everyone happy. By the time they attempted to return to old-school prizefighting in March 1938, half of the fighters were refusing pay so they could compete in the first annual Silver City Golden Gloves tournament a week later.

The writing was on the wall. Cox and Frank staged pro-am shows, then finally did away with pros, altogether. Silver City wasn't the only place in New Mexico where this was happening, though.

Demise of Pros, Rise of Amateurs

> *They're signing up! What is believed to be an American first night enrollment record for a city the population of Clovis was set last night when aspiring amateur fighting men of hereabouts swarmed into the chamber of commerce office to register for free training and for a chance to fight for the glory of their city and state against the "enemy" in the Lions' club gigantic A.A.U. New Mexico–Texas championship amateur boxing tournament on the Armory battle front here the nights of Feb. 15, 16 and 17.*
> — *Clovis News Journal*, 1937[23]

Amateur boxing wasn't exactly new to New Mexico; it just hadn't been popular. Getting into the ring for free wasn't anyone's idea of a good time. But as it caught on around the country with AAU and Golden Gloves tournaments during the '30s, the fever hit.

Though the NMMI was the first organization to stage regular shows — it had been doing so since its inception — Santa Fe had staged the first tournament in 1925, with close to 100 youngsters from around the capital entering. The directors of the tourney, Tony Turelli and Leslie Showers, would continue staging AAU meets for 20 years.

"Wholesome athletics" was the goal as the state's first boxing clubs formed in the capital, and then in Albuquerque. St. Michael's had a team; Manuel Pacheco formed the "Cavalry Club," while his brother Henry organized the "West Side Club." Lucio Baca, brother to Mike, had the "East Side Club." St. Michael's College kept the clubs active.

In 1929, boxing came to UNM and Coach Ray Johnson conducted intramural bouts. Over the next few years, the Lobo team could claim some of the best mittmen in the country.

A period of transition ensued, in which many pros decided they'd be better off fighting in the amateur ranks first — like Julio Chiaramonte, who fought the best pros out there, then went on to box in at least 70 amateur bouts in college. He wasn't alone, either. Though tournament rules would later forbid those who'd earlier fought for pay, early in the decade the lines were blurred, or overlooked, as several boxers leapt back and forth. St. Mike's heavyweight Jerry Castro, who was knocked out by Chihuahua Kid Brown on an Espanola card in 1930, "being an amateur, could not take his $5 [purse], but his manager took it to defray actual expenses."[24] At a St. Mike's tournament in 1931, Santa Fe's Vivian Griego, who won the bantam division, was noted as having "fought in prelims to professional bouts on and off for five or six years."[25]

Clovis followed Santa Fe by forming clubs in 1931. Before their first tournament, they held a series of highly publicized training classes conducted by Nick Mortio for amateur prospects. Portales followed in 1931, as, finally, did Albuquerque. "Albuquerque boys will be asking Santa Claus for a pair of boxing gloves for Christmas,"[26] the *Journal* noted in December 1931 when the first state AAU-rules tournament under the Knights of Columbus was announced for 1932. Other than shorter rounds and bigger gloves, there wasn't too much to differentiate between pro and amateur at the time — this was decades before headgear was used.

From collegiate to local and state tournaments, amateur boxing caught on.

By 1935, the UNM team was good enough to capture the Border Conference Boxing Championships held at UNM's Carlisle Gym, with four Lobos — Bob Lane, Ralph "Sabu" Gallegos, Nelson Tydings and Harold Bibo — winning titles. One year later, Gallegos went all the way to the Olympic Trials, where he was eliminated in the quarterfinals. UNM continued to have a dynamite team, but, ironically, the school dropped the boxing program in 1939. (Ten years later, however, they would bring it back and Georgie Stevens — son of the promoter — would be the school star.)

In '37, the Albuquerque Indian School kicked into high gear with an outstanding team that included 104-pound Frankie Yazza from the Navajo reservation — "Chief Flying Fists" to his fans — and flyweight Quinton Thompson, who surpassed Gallegos and Chiaramonte as an amateur by advancing all the way to the AAU National Semifinals in Boston in 1937 before losing on points to Cincinnati's Fred Pope.

That same year, Clovis held its first AAU "Golden Gloves" tournament — though it would only be called that in name. Officially, Golden Gloves did not sanction a tournament in New Mexico for another 12 years. For the first time, promoters warned that "any athlete whose record is not free from taints of professionalism will be barred from participating."[27] Despite the strict rules, there were at least six former pros in the tourney. Nearly 200 boxers from New Mexico and West Texas signed up for three nights of fighting that saw crowds of 2,000 to 2,500 in attendance.

Crowds of 3,000 showed up at UNM to watch the AAU Southwestern tournament in March 1937. Eddie Mack refereed most of the championship bouts that finished with a team that included Santa Fe's Harold Banks, Las Vegas' Frankie Higgins, Chama's Ralph Gallegos, Belen's Benny Valencia and Albuquerque's Quinton Thompson.

Whether it was the 20/20 Club, the Disabled American Veterans, St. Mike's, NMMI or UNM, at Las Vegas, Gallup, Raton or Silver City, amateur boxing was on fire. Clubs formed and smokers were held monthly around the state.

In Roswell, a kid named Jack Quarry came from Texas looking for work as a farm laborer. On Saturday nights, he'd lace up the gloves and, on amateur shows in Hagerman, usually found a willing opponent in Raymond Analla. In the 1980s, neither Raymond nor Jack remembered much about the fights, other than they were "wham-bam" affairs and they happened more than a few times. Both Quarry and Analla would go on to raise important fighters. Raymond would father seven sons who would win 17 New Mexico Golden Gloves state championships between them. Quarry? All three sons would fight in the pro game. Two Quarrys — Jerry and Mike — would end up sharing the ring with the likes of Joe Frazier, Muhammad Ali and Bob Foster.

By the end of the decade, the pro game had been replaced by the amateurs.

What little pro boxing remained in the state was knocked out by the call to war. Trading their gloves in for rifles, New Mexico's last golden era boxers left their state to fight overseas.

Finales

Early this morning, several hours before the shafts of oncoming daylight began to streak the eastern sky, Benny Chavez was "counted out" by the Great Referee in the man's ward of Mt. San Rafael hospital. And when the final stroke of "10" was tolled by Him, the greatest boxer developed in Trinidad or southern Colorado passed on to Valhalla.
—Trinidad Chronicle News, 1932[1]

Benny Chavez

No one heard from, or about, (the Original) Benny Chavez, once he faded from the boxing scene in the early-to-mid-'20s. That is, until 1932.

Benny kept a big fat tome of a scrapbook during his career. On December 27, 1931, for the first time in over a decade, he added something to it. On the front cover, he wrote, "In case something happen [*sic*] give this book to D. M. Bashore."[2]

D. M. Bashore — actually it was "Beshoar" — was Benny's doctor, as all would soon find out.

Less than a month later, the sporting world was shocked to hear that Benny had hurled himself in front of a bus on Commercial St. in downtown Trinidad, Colorado. Benny was crushed, but somehow survived. He was rushed to Mt. San Rafael Hospital in critical condition, yet was conscious enough to express regret that he had not died. His local paper reported, "Today a vast number of people who knew him in the days of his proudest laurels in the roped arena — when he fought like a tiger are wondering whether the faint spark of life will flicker back to fullness or become extinct. Benny Chavez, the 'fighting demon' is too weak now to fight back at the grim specter that hovers by his bed."[3]

Chavez survived the night. In the next two days, stories of his physical decline and hard luck, penniless life went to print. Then, on Jan. 21, Benny summoned up the strength for a second suicide attempt. He tried to strangle himself with the bell cord that summoned the nurse, who arrived just in time to halt the attempt. Yet, nine days later, on Feb. 2, 1932, Benny passed away from his injuries. The fight community in Denver and Trinidad raised the funds for his burial, which took place in his place of birth, Wagon Mound, New Mexico. He was 39 years old.

Eddie Mack

After hanging up the gloves, the uncrowned champion and former junior lightweight and lightweight contender Eddie Mack moved to Santa Fe, where he was married. After working as a campaign manager for Elfego Baca, who was running for office of district attorney, Mack got into the insurance business. Soon after, he became an investigator for the district attorney's office in Santa Fe.

Mack remained in the boxing business for a while, by refereeing, promoting and managing; in 1933 he even started talking about a comeback, but that was short-lived. Mack took a couple fighters under his wing, namely Jimmy Ortiz, Eddie Trujillo, Lee Baca and heavyweight Matt Rhoades, but they never really made it out of the Southwest. After 1936, Mack drifted away from the fight scene, and he last guest refereed in 1945, not long before his death.

The final bell for Mack would toll on August 17, 1946, some 14 years after his ring career had ended.

Last photograph of the original Benny Chavez, in his casket. Benny's tale did not end on a happy note.

The day before he died, Mack had received a phone call from promoter Red Valencia to referee on his next card in Albuquerque. After the two men chatted for several minutes, Mack reached for his hat and headed out the door in a hurry. Eddie was investigating a case in Chama and would have to drive 93 miles to get there. It was late in the evening when he finished his investigation, possibly as late as 11 P.M., when he left Chama for home. By now, his son and daughter were fast asleep but Eddie knew that his wife, Lyle, would be waiting up as she always did. Mack was almost home when he fell asleep at the wheel. His car skidded off the road and flipped over three miles north of the Pojoaque Bridge, just walking distance from where he was born.

A number of people have speculated that Mack was the victim of foul play, stemming from his work with the D.A.'s office. The rumors were discounted in later years by Eddie's son, Eddie Mack Quintana, Jr., who passed away in 2008.

One of Eddie's pallbearers was former nemesis Harry Bramer, who became one of his best friends after they'd both quit the ring.

Thirty years later, in 1976, Eddie's brother Bernie — "Bernie Mack" in the ring — would also die in a car crash while suffering a heart attack near Mora, New Mexico.

Benny Cordova

"Old Man" Benny Cordova passed away on April 2, 1956, at the age of 61. After fighting, he worked for the railroad and farmed, as well. Benny also trained his four sons to fight.

Raoul "Young Benny" Cordova, who finished boxing in 1940, died on Nov. 17, 1978. After fighting, he worked as a machinist and engineer for the railroad. He also refereed from 1943 to 1959, and worked the last boxing show ever held at the Albuquerque Armory, on March 9, 1957.

Both Benny and Raoul showed the effects of their careers, after they'd retired. "There was damage, for sure," Benny's son Meliton explained. "His nose, face and ears were beat up and he slurred. He'd had a hard life and looked older than his age."[4]

After the '30s, Benny's remaining three sons, Benny Jr., Armando and Meliton, all boxed.

Bobby Waugh

Benny Cordova's chief nemesis, Fort Worth's Bobby Waugh, passed away from a lung ailment in 1936 at the age of 43. Always a contender, but never a title challenger, Waugh "woke up one day and realized he was an 'old man,' so far as fighting was concerned, that the crown had passed from Wolgast to Ritchie, to Welsh, to Leonard, while he was fiddling around in Dixie rings."[5] His last fight — his 167th, give or take 50 or 100, was in 1923. His later years were also spent in the sports arena — but instead of a main event fighter, Waugh was a popcorn and candy vendor.

Eddie Murdock

The "Oklahoma Windmill" and "Bald Eagle," Eddie Murdock, who fought five world champions and was a rated welterweight contender, relocated to Huntington Park, California, after his fighting days were over. Murdock married, raised a family, and worked as a welder before he died in 1957, the same way his former stablemate and nemesis Eddie Mack had — in an automobile accident. Murdock was age 50.

Dynamite Tommy

Timo Sanchez, "Dynamite Tommy" to ringsters, passed away from natural causes on Oct. 2, 1996, at the age of 97. After the death of his fighter Frankie Cantou, Dynamite drifted away from the sport, at least until the '50s and '60s when he returned to promoting. He was a financial backer to his brother-in-law, none other than Louis "Red" Valencia.

Al Smaulding

The "Clayton Blacksmith," one of New Mexico's earliest middleweight champions, passed away in November 1971 at the age of 79 in Albuquerque, where he'd resided after fighting as a journeyman in the early '20s.

Mike Baca

"The Pride of Santa Fe," whose brothers and sons all fought, lived in his hometown his entire life and passed away at the age of 71 on March 20, 1965. Mike's oldest son, Felipe, who fought under "Young Mike Baca," died in 1978. As Old Man Benny had done, "Old Man" Mike trained his sons to fight. After Felipe was finishing up his career, Mike Baca, Jr., was just beginning.

Speedball Hayden

After fighting through the '20s on the road and declining to the level of journeyman, Thomas Hayden, "Speedball" to his many followers during the 24th Infantry's heyday at Columbus, finished his career in Casper, Wyoming. His last known fight was on Sept. 2, 1932, when he was TKO'd in seven rounds by a local club fighter, Kid Barger. Hayden lived in Wyoming through the '30s, then returned to his home town of Indianapolis, where he died in 1962.

Walter Caldwell

After Walter Caldwell of Springer retired from the game, he left New Mexico for Los Angeles to be a police officer. Unbeknownst to his New Mexico fans, he was not finished with boxing. In 1927, Walter tried to stage a comeback. He fought twice, winning one by KO while the other fight had an unknown result, then retired again. In 1930, he tried again, but was TKO'd in the fourth. This time, he stayed away from the ring to concentrate on his career and family. Caldwell passed away from natural causes in 1964.

Dandy Dick Griffin

The Albuquerque-born Fort Worth battler, who went on to be a top-notch bantamweight before promoting in Texas and New Mexico, passed away on Nov. 30, 1950, at the age of 52. In between promotions, Griffin and wife Jackie lobbied in Austin, Texas, to get the state to overrule the law prohibiting prizefighting — and in 1933, they were successful. Griffin had retired from fighting when one of his eyes was infected by rosin while fighting the co-main on the Jack Dempsey-Georges Carpentier card in 1921; the injury ultimately resulted in total blindness by 1934.

Tony Herrera

"The Brown Symphony in Leather," El Paso's hope for a world lightweight champion in the '30s, fought on for a few years after his chances at a title fight faded away. After retiring in 1936, with a record of 76–26–4, 21 KOs, Herrera returned to El Paso where he trained several fighters, including Jesse Fonseca, Mike Adame and Manny Ortega. As boxing declined in the city, Herrera took a job with the parks and recreation department and was eventually forgotten. By 1970, his health and mental facilities deteriorated, so he ended up in a nursing home where he eventually died.

Nick Kid Mortio

Nick Manti, the "San Marcial Flash" who fought as "Kid Mortio," is believed to have passed away in Texas sometime in the early 2000s.

The Pachecos

Henry "Kid" Pacheco, oldest of the Pacheco fighting brothers, died on October 25, 1958, at the age of 58. Manuel "Young" Pacheco was 80 when he passed on Sept. 3, 1987.

Buddy Serino

After calling it quits in 1937, Buddy Serino went to work as a ceramic tile setter, as the lost art of terrazzo became his passion. Much of Buddy's terrazzo work while working for the New Mexico Marble and Tile Co. in the '30s and '40s still remains in historic downtown Albuquerque. Serino worked for 23 years with the company, and passed away in 1990.

Jimmy Ortiz

After hanging up the gloves, Jimmy Ortiz continued his education and, in August 1940, received his B.A. from Texas State University. He went on to get an M.A. from Colorado University but also studied at Georgetown University, Catholic University, University of New Mexico, Teachers College and the University of Southern California. During most of his professional life, he was a school teacher and he retired in 1973 to teach at Isleta Pueblo. Jimmy died at the age of 86 on Nov. 19, 1998, in Santa Fe.

The Chiaramontes

During Gallup's last golden era of boxing, the Chiaramonte family went into business with the Chiaramonte Coal Mine. After World War II, when mining activity decreased in Gallup, the family opened the Chiaramonte Hotel and Chiaramonte Cocktail Lounge downtown. Eventually, they sold the business and relocated to Farmington — there are no more Chiaramontes in Gallup.

Julio was a war hero, earning Bronze and Silver Stars. After the war, he got his master's degree at UNM and became a career counselor, first at the Albuquerque Indian School, then at the Technical Vocational Institute, until retiring in 1980. On Feb. 10, 1982, he passed away from a heart attack, at the age of 67.

Julio was the only one who enlisted during the war — Tony, Nardine, and Sam (Boney) were all needed in the coal mines. Nardine passed away in Farmington at the age of 96, on May 26, 2010. His post-fight, post-coal-mining career consisted of working for El Paso Natural Gas Co. Boney became a railroad engineer for the Winslow-Gallup line after fighting and mining. According to his brother Nardine, he was a "hell-raiser" for most of his life, but settled down somewhat to raise daughters who also became railroad engineers. Eventually, his family moved to Arizona and he passed away on March 10, 2005. Tony died young, just 37 years old, in 1949 after a two-year illness.

Abie Chavez

The "Farmington Flash" retired from boxing in 1939, but in 1944 he staged a comeback in Spokane, Wash., where he lost a ten-round decision to Joey Dolan. "Before he tried for a comeback, my mother had been wearing his boxing shoes when she milked the cow," recalled Abie, Jr. "And they still had a little fertilizer on them when he left for Spokane."[6]

Abie returned to a career as a plasterer, at least for another year when he revisited the ring again, to fight Juarez's Sonny Gomez, who'd been headlining Albuquerque in the city's attempt to resurrect boxing. On Sept. 22, 1945, with the famous Eddie Mack guest refereeing, Abie, just a couple pounds north of his original peak weight, at 119, decisioned the 122-pound Gomez, then retired for good.

In the '50s, Abie dabbled in fight promotions and reffed a bit. He also taught his son, Abie Jr., to fight. After a long struggle with alcohol in his final years, Abie passed away on Feb. 12, 1970, when his house caught on fire in an explosion. Shortly before his death, he told his family, "I'm fighting my greatest fight and I'm going to win. I'm betting on myself, even if no one else is."[7]

Following his death, the "Abe Chavez Memorial Trophy" became an annual award to the best boxer competing in the Four Corners Regional Golden Gloves competition — though it is no longer practiced.

Tony Chavez

The Albuquerque-born, Los Angeles-headlining contender enlisted in the U.S. Navy during World War II and, three and a half years later, staged a comeback. He made a living as a past-his-prime opponent from 1946 to 1951, losing much more often than winning at the tail-end. Not much is known about Tony's post-ring life, except that he passed away in 1997.

Billy Firpo

Manuel Cruz, the man known as "Billy Firpo," of Wagon Mound, might not have attained greatness in the ring — but he did on the battlefield. The man who once (some say twice) whipped the great Lew Jenkins went on to become a war hero during World War II.

Cruz was in the initial wave of paratroopers in the invasion of Sicily on July 19, 1943, and he spent seven days there behind enemy lines before being shot by a sniper in the right foot. Patching up his own wound, he fought on. After taking Sicily, the Allies launched an attack on Italy's mainland. Cruz's outfit was ordered to make a jump near the city of Naples, an area defended by highly trained German troops. Again, Billy spent several days behind enemy lines. This time he was wounded in the right knee by German machine gun fire. Again, Cruz went on.

In June 1944, Cruz was part of the Allies' D-Day invasion of Normandy and, this time, he spent more than 30 days in enemy territory. As a paratrooper, Cruz made one more jump during war, parachuting behind German lines in Holland. He was there for 14 days before being hit by a German mortar shell — the explosion ripped away most of his jaw. When the Germans found him, nearly unconscious and covered in blood, they gave him first aid, but then left him there. "I guess they thought I was too far gone and would be too much trouble," Cruz later told the *Las Vegas Optic*. "So they didn't take me prisoner."[8]

Somehow, Cruz, then 26, survived, before he was eventually picked up by American troops and treated in hospitals in Belgium, France, England and, eventually, San Francisco. He was decorated with the Presidential Citation, British Citation, four Silver Star awards and a Purple Heart with three clusters.

Though he came home a decorated war hero, Cruz was too damaged to take up boxing again. Life back in Wagon Mound did not go well for the veteran of the ring and war, who became a heavy drinker. In 1951, Cruz was charged with the second-degree murder of his babysitter and handyman. Cruz died nine years later.

Emilio Martinez

After his ring career was over, life for the "Clouting Caballero" fell into a downward spiral. In February 1939, he was committed to the Colorado State Hospital for the Insane for six months.

Martinez enlisted during World War II, but his whereabouts thereafter have remained something of a mystery, though by 1943 he was living in Los Angeles as a shipyard worker. On Aug. 10, 1943, Martinez went off the deep end — when he tried to call his wife, from whom he was separated, the pay phone's static was so bad he "ripped the receiver from the drug store phone booth, slugged and kicked a customer and went home to play his guitar."[9] The police were called to investigate, after someone called to complain about his cacophonous guitar solo. Just as the cops arrived, Martinez came crashing through the front door, instrument in hand. Thinking the guitar was a gun, the police shot the former prizefighter.

Martinez survived but his final years remain a mystery. Promoter Joe Roybal later said he'd last seen Emilio in 1978 "on Skid Row, the corner of 5th and Alameda,"[10] in Los Angeles. A death certificate on Nov. 20, 1978, confirms his death, at the age of 66.

Ted "Mustang" Garcia

The former Rocky Mountain lightweight champ and star of New Mexico boxing through the late '30s, enlisted during World War II, then resumed his career afterward, fighting as late as 1950. He passed away on March 11, 2008, at the age of 91.

Ralph "Sabu" Gallegos

A four-time Border Conference amateur star and 1936 U. S. Olympic Games alternate, Ralph "Sabu" Gallegos was rumored to have fought one pro fight on a card in his hometown of Chama, New Mexico, before retiring from boxing.

Tony and Frank Gallegos

After fighting in the '30s, Las Vegas boxer Tony V. Gallegos moved to California with his family, where he worked in the Marin County shipyards as a foreman, then returned to

New Mexico where he worked 29 years for the federal government in Los Alamos and Albuquerque. He passed away from natural causes on June 18, 2001, at the age of 83.

Frankie (Higgins) Gallegos passed away on Jan. 11, 1997, in Las Vegas. Frankie's son Frank, Jr., would be a well-known coach for years; *his* son, Shaun, was an amateur standout and a well-known pro during the 2000s. Following in his grandfather and uncle's footsteps, Shaun would capture the state lightweight title and fight several name fighters.

Glossary

Across the River   Term used in El Paso, Texas, referring to the action on the other side of the Rio Grande, in Juarez, Mexico.

Ancient City   Santa Fe.

Bring home the bacon   Bring home a win. First used by the famous Joe Gans.

Bugs   Fans.

Capital City   Santa Fe.

Carbon City   Gallup, also called "Little Pittsburgh" and "Coal City."

Chuco   El Paso, also known as "Pass City."

Claret   A bloody nose.

Coal City   Gallup, also called "Little Pittsburgh," "Carbon City" and "Indian City."

Combination   A traveling prizefight exhibition.

Comer   A boxer with promise.

Curtain raiser   Opening bout on a fight card.

Defi   A challenge.

Dopesters, the dope   "Those in the Know," i.e., the fight experts.

Duke City   Albuquerque

The Fancy   Fight followers in the bareknuckle and early gloved days.

Fancy Dan   Or "fancy dancer," a flashy boxer who moves more than fights.

Finish fight or fight-to-the-finish   A fight unlimited in the number of rounds, completed only when one of the competitors is knocked out or unable to continue.

Frame   A round. "Stanzas" was also used frequently by fight scribes.

Frame-up or frame   A bogus or fixed fight.

"Godfather of the Fight Game"   More often than not, refers to Mark Levy, who established the game in the '10s, then returned to promoting in the '30s.

The Gong   The bell.

Hang the KO sign on   Knock out.

Have a shade   An advantage or edge over.

Haymaker   Not so much a Hail Mary, but a wallop of a punch.

Hummer   A damn good fight.

In the pink   In top condition.

In trim   See "In the pink."

Indian sign   If it happens once, it's an accident. If it happens again it may be a coincidence. But if it happens a third time, it's neither an accident nor coincidence, but a habit. In boxing they call it the "Indian Sign." To Native Americans, an Indian sign is either a blessing or a curse, which has come to describe the strange power an inferior fighter may exert over a more talented rival. It has come to mean one fighter has another one's number.

Jockey scrapper   Term used on the border for lower-weight fighters, influenced by the great popularity of the Juarez horse races in the '10s.

Levinsons   Gloves manufactured by Sol Levinson, which were the "Everlast" or "Reyes" in boxing's golden period.

London Prize Rules   The 29 London Prize Ring Rules were originally drafted in 1838 and revised in 1853. Fights under the London rules were typically bareknuckle, not using gloves. They were superseded by the Marquess of Queensberry rules.

Marquess of Queensberry rules   Code of rules that most directly governs modern boxing. Though penned in the 1860s, the Queensberry rules weren't widely accepted until the 1890s when they replaced the London Prize Rules.

Meadow City   Las Vegas, N.M.

Mill   A prize fight.

Pass City   El Paso, also known as "Chuco."

Pecos Town   Roswell.

Preliminary   In terms of a fight card, a four- or six-rounder, preceding the main or co-main event.

Pug   Short for "pugilist."

Pugilist   A prizefighter or boxer.

Punch Bowl   The Fort Bliss arena in El Paso.

Purse   The stakes, or payday, for a fighter.

Queensbury Rules   See Marquess of Queensberry rules.

Rabbit punch   An illegal punch delivered to the back of the neck. The term is derived from the blow used to kill a rabbit. Earlier, they were also known as "rabbit killers."

Rasslin'   Wrestling, also referred to as the "groan and grunt game."

Scrappers   Fighters.

Semi-final; semi-windup   What is today called a co-main event.

Set-to   A boxing bout or match.

Smoker   Originally, an informal gathering for entertainment or discussion. In boxing, this term evolved to mean, first, a fight card held under the jurisdiction of a private club and, later, a small, local show, often unregulated.

Throw up the sponge   Surrendering; used before "throwing in the towel."

Timber   As in "championship timber," the stuff of champions.

To the scratch; Toe the scratch   The real or imaginary line etched into the ground.

Topnotcher   A fighter of contender status.

Tough   Pug, or scrapper.

Wallop   A big punch.

Winner take all   A type of fight in which the loser gets *nada*.

Chapter Notes

Introduction

1. "'Glove Story' Not Quite Ready for Bestsellerdom," *Albuquerque Journal*, Aug. 20, 1994.

Chapter 1

1. "A Man Killed in a Prize Fight," *Santa Fe New Mexican*, July 16, 1868.
2. "Fight Staged in an Open Field 35 Miles from Albuquerque," *Denver News*, June 28, 1868.
3. *Ibid.*
4. "A Man Killed in a Prize Fight," *Rocky Mountain News*, July 9, 1868.
5. "A Disgusted Pugilist's Wife," *Cleveland Plain Dealer*, Nov. 26, 1867.
6. "Prize Fighting and Things," *Rocky Mountain News*, Aug. 6, 1867.
7. Ibid.
8. "Spirited Battle Between Michael Ryan and Barney Duffey," *Cleveland Plain Dealer*, Nov. 25, 1867.
9. "A Disgusted Pugilist's Wife," *Cleveland Plain Dealer*, Nov. 26, 1867.
10. Ibid.
11. "A Man Killed in a Prize Fight," *Santa Fe New Mexican*, July 16, 1868.
12. "Letter to the Editor," *Rocky Mountain News*, July 24, 1868.
13. "Prize Fighting and Things," *Rocky Mountain News*, Aug. 6, 1867.
14. "Prize Fight," *Santa Fe New Mexican*, July 31, 1868.

Chapter 2

1. "Untitled," *Santa Fe New Mexican*, May 6, 1882.
2. "Around Town," *Santa Fe New Mexican*, July 31, 1872.
3. "Stubborn Prize Fight," *New York Herald*, Dec. 20, 1870. In front of 2,000 spectators, the two punished each other severely, though it was Campbell who was on the short end of it, before being awarded the win by disqualification: "His own father swore he hardly knew him. Blood came from fifty wounds—nose, eyes, cheek and mouth. Disgusting as was his appearance, he still had gameness, and it was a fortunate circumstance that the fight terminated as it did, as in all probability he would have come up to the scratch until he died."
4. "Colorado News Items," *San Francisco Bulletin*, Aug. 31, 1880.
5. "News," *Weekly Register-Call*, Sept. 17, 1880.
6. "Prize Fight Postponed," *Colorado Springs Daily Gazette*, Sept. 22, 1880.
7. "The Prize Fight," *Las Vegas Daily Optic*, Oct. 23, 1880.
8. "General Sporting News," *Cleveland Plain Dealer*, May 18, 1889.
9. "The Prize Ring," *Albuquerque Daily Journal*, Mar. 1, 1882.
10. "No Title," *Santa Fe New Mexican*, May 6, 1882.
11. "A Challenge," *Albuquerque Daily Journal*, Mar. 1, 1882.
12. "A Dallas Prize-Fighter," *Dallas Weekly Herald*, Mar. 16, 1882.
13. "The Pride of Place," *Rocky Mountain News*, Mar. 6, 1882.
14. "Untitled," *Dolores News*, June 10, 1882.
15. "'Six-horse Coach to Silver City—But That Was 38 Years Ago," *Deming Headlight*, July 16, 1920.
16. "Around Town," *Albuquerque Morning Journal*, Oct. 26, 1882.
17. "Sporting News," *Rocky Mountain News*, Nov. 27, 1882. The fight involved lightweights Billy Lynn and James Westley.
18. "News/Opinion," *Las Vegas Daily Gazette*, Mar. 30, 1883.
19. "Rincon Locals," *Rio Grande Republican*, Aug. 25, 1883.
20. "Locallettes," *Las Vegas Daily Gazette*, Jan. 9, 1884.
21. "New Mexico News," *Las Vegas Daily Gazette*, Feb. 19, 1884.
22. "New Mexico News," *Las Vegas Daily Gazette*, Mar. 2, 1884.
23. "New Mexico News," *Las Vegas Daily Gazette*, Mar. 6, 1884.
24. "Locallettes," *Las Vegas Daily Gazette*, Jan. 11, 1884.
25. "Untitled," *Silver City Enterprise*, Mar. 7, 1884.
26. "Untitled," *The Deming Herald* and *Lake Valley Herald*, Mar. 27, 1884.
27. Ibid.
28. "Untitled," *Silver City Enterprise*, Mar. 28, 1884.
29. Anton Mazzanovich, "Details of the Reception Given John L. Sullivan When He Paid Lordsburg a Visit," *Lordsburg Liberal*, Dec. 11, 1931.
30. Anton Mazzanovich, "Details of the Reception Given John L. Sullivan When He Paid Lordsburg a Visit," *Lordsburg Liberal*, Dec. 11, 1931.
31. "Gleanings from Territorial Exchanges," *Rio Grande Republican*, Apr. 17, 1886.
32. "Advertisements," *Las Vegas Daily Optic*, May 6, 1884.
33. "The Prize Fight," *Las Vegas Daily Optic*, May 16, 1884.
34. "A Card," *Las Vegas Daily Optic*, May 17, 1884.
35. "Another Challenge," *Las Vegas Daily Optic*, May 19, 1884.

36. "The Coon Sluggers: Hogan Knocks Smith Out in the Middle of the Sixth Round," *Las Vegas Daily Optic*, May 22, 1884.

37. Ibid.

38. "Another Slugging Match," *Las Vegas Daily Optic*, May 26, 1884.

39. "Untitled," *Las Vegas Daily Optic*, May 29, 1884.

40. Ibid.

41. "Untitled," *Las Vegas Daily Optic*, May 31, 1884.

42. "Untitled," *Las Vegas Daily Optic*, June 2, 1884.

43. "Untitled," *Las Vegas Daily Optic*, June 3, 1884.

44. "Deming Prize Fight," *Silver City Enterprise*, Sept. 19, 1884.

45. Ibid.

46. "The Prize Ring," *The National Police Gazette*, May 24, 1884.

47. "Untitled," *Mesilla Valley Democrat*, Nov. 20, 1888.

48. "New Mexico," *The Daily News*, April 16, 1885.

49. "Gleanings from Territorial Exchanges," *Rio Grande Republican*, Apr. 17, 1886.

50. "Local Laconics," *Albuquerque Morning Democrat*, Aug. 5, 1886.

51. "Local Laconics," *Albuquerque Morning Democrat*, Aug. 8, 1886.

52. "Round About Town," *Santa Fe Daily New Mexican*, Feb. 5, 1887.

53. "Round About Town," *Santa Fe Daily New Mexican*, Feb. 12, 1887.

54. "Legislators Enjoy a Mill," *Rocky Mountain News*, Feb. 17, 1887.

55. "A Hard Bout Between Pitzlin and the Ranchman," *Santa Fe Daily New Mexican*, Feb. 14, 1887.

56. "Among the Athletes," *Rocky Mountain News*, Feb. 7, 1887.

57. "Slugging Match," *Santa Fe New Mexican*, Apr. 26, 1888.

58. "That Knock-out — Santa Fe's Colored Pugilist Does Up the Leadville Man," *Santa Fe New Mexican*, Apr. 28, 1888.

59. "Round About Town," *Santa Fe New Mexican*, May 8, 1888.

60. "Around Town," *Albuquerque Citizen*, July 12, 1889.

61. "Insane Over a Murder," *Las Vegas Daily Optic*, Apr. 25, 1889.

Chapter 3

1. "Untitled," *Santa Fe New Mexican*, Feb. 7, 1891.

2. "Territorial News," *Santa Fe New Mexican*, Aug. 30, 1894.

3. "A Prize Fight on Roller Skates," *National Police Gazette*, March 28, 1885.

4. "Sporting News," *National Police Gazette*, Aug. 17, 1889.

5. "Untitled," *The New York Clipper*, Feb. 1, 1890.

6. "After Welsch," *Albuquerque Morning Democrat*, Aug. 13, 1891.

7. Ibid.

8. "Publication Notices," *Albuquerque Daily Citizen*, April 19, 1898.

9. "Albuquerque Notes," *Santa Fe New Mexican*, June 22, 1898.

10. "Trader at Canyon de Chelly," *The Desert Magazine*, no. 11 (November 1953).

11. "After Welsch," *Albuquerque Morning Democrat*, Aug. 13, 1891.

12. "Sporting News and Notes," *The Milwaukee Journal* (AP), Jan. 29, 1892.

13. "A Brutal Prize Fight," *Philadelphia Inquirer* (AP), Jan. 29, 1892.

14. "Spoiling for a Fight," *Albuquerque Morning Democrat*, May 19, 1892.

15. "Sport," *Gallup Gleaner*, June 4, 1892.

16. "Untitled," *Gallup Gleaner*, Oct. 15, 1892.

17. "New Mexico News," *Santa Fe New Mexican*, July 31, 1894.

18. "Welter Weight Flynn," *Albuquerque Daily Citizen*, July 17, 1894.

19. "Prize Fight at Creede," *Rocky Mountain News*, April 17, 1892.

20. "Untitled," *National Police Gazette*, Dec. 16, 1893.

21. The "Mitchell tactics" refers to the crafty, ringwise style of Charley Mitchell, who fought both John L. Sullivan and James Corbett.

22. "News/Opinion," *Albuquerque Morning Democrat*, Dec. 24, 1893.

23. "Other Topics," *Albuquerque Weekly Citizen*, Mar. 17, 1894.

24. "Untitled," *Albuquerque Morning Democrat*, Apr. 22, 1894.

25. "Flynn Won — Glove Contest in Cerillos Between Flynn and Frazier — The Defeated Outclassed," *Albuquerque Daily Citizen*, Apr. 23, 1894.

26. "A Rattling Tilt — Jim Flynn Knocks Out Frazer at Cerillos in Seventeen Hard Fought Rounds," *Santa Fe New Mexican*, Apr. 23, 1894.

27. "Sporting News," *Las Vegas Daily Optic*, Mar. 21, 1894.

28. "The Coming Big Mill," *Albuquerque Daily Citizen*, June 19, 1894.

29. "The Prize Fight," *Las Vegas Daily Optic*, July 4, 1894.

30. "Welter Weight Flynn," *Albuquerque Daily Citizen*, July 17, 1894.

31. "Local News," *Albuquerque Weekly Citizen*, Sept. 29, 1894.

32. "The Glorious Fourth," *Gallup Gleaner*, July 5, 1895.

33. "Jim Flynn Licked Billy Lewis," *Albuquerque Morning Democrat*, July 6, 1895.

34. "'Swifty' Will Fight," *Arizona Weekly Journal-Miner*, Sept. 28, 1895.

35. "Swifty the Winner," *Arizona Weekly Journal-Miner*, Oct. 2, 1895.

36. "News," *Arizona Weekly Journal-Miner*, Nov. 13, 1895.

37. "Foul Play Denied — Swifty Was Given a Fair Show at Williams," *The Arizona Republican*, Nov. 26, 1895.

38. "Untitled," *Arizona Republic*, Jan. 5, 1898.

39. "Arizona Week by Week," *Republican-Herald*, Nov. 16, 1899.

40. "The Great Fight — An Effort to Have the Corbett-Jackson Mill in the City of the North Pass," *El Paso Daily Times*, Feb. 20, 1894.

41. Elmer M. Million, "History of the Texas Prize Fight Statute," *Texas Law Review*, vol. 17 (1938).

42. "Knocked Out in 2:10," *Dallas Morning News*, June 2, 1890.

43. "Untitled," *Rio Grande Republican*, June 12, 1890.

44. "In Thirty-two Rounds — It Took the Australian Lad 32 Rounds to Knock Out Flahrity," *El Paso Daily Times*, Feb. 20, 1894.

45. "The Fight Today," *El Paso Daily Times*, Feb. 18, 1894.

46. "Thirty Cents Reward, in Chips," *Las Cruces Democrat*, Feb. 21, 1894.

47. "Untitled," *Santa Fe New Mexican*, Feb. 23, 1894.

48. "Billy Lewis Coming," *El Paso Daily Times*, Feb. 21, 1894.

49. "The Prize Ring — Billy Lewis Is Coming at Once to Meet Australian Smith," *El Paso Daily Times*, Feb. 22, 1894.

50. "Untitled," *Albuquerque Morning Democrat*, Mar. 17, 1894.

51. "The Contest," *Albuquerque Daily Citizen*, Mar. 15, 1894.

52. "Smith and Lewis — They Now Say They Will Meet in the Ring on the 18th of March," *El Paso Daily Times*, Mar. 1, 1894.

53. "The Prize Fight — Lewis Knocked Out by Smith at El Paso," *Albuquerque Daily Citizen*, Mar. 19, 1894.

54. "Prize Fighting," *Rio Grande Republican*, Mar. 10, 1893.

55. "The Phenix Prize Ring — A Glove Contest and Scrapping Match Afterward," *Eddy Weekly Current*, June 2, 1893.

56. "Kelly Whips Jeter — Nine Rounds at the Silver King Theatre, Phenix," *Eddy Weekly Current*, June 22, 1893.

57. Ibid.

58. "That Prize Fight," *Eddy County Citizen*, June 27, 1893.

59. "Silver City Siftings," *Santa Fe New Mexican*, June 29, 1893.

60. "Another Match Contemplated," *Eddy Weekly Current*, Jan. 9, 1895.

61. "The Fistic Exhibition," *Roswell Record*, Mar. 22, 1895.

62. Ibid.

63. "Local," *Eddy Weekly Current*, Mar. 27, 1895.

64. "Untitled," *Albuquerque Morning Democrat*, April 14, 1892.

65. "The Prize Fight," *Santa Fe New Mexican*, Jan. 20, 1892.

66. "Glove Contests," *Albuquerque Daily Citizen*, Aug. 17, 1891.

67. "The Prize Fight," *Albuquerque Morning Democrat*, Sept. 18, 1891.

68. Ibid.

69. "Chronic Kicker," *Santa Fe Weekly Sun*, Sept. 19, 1891.

70. Ibid.

71. "After Welsch," *Albuquerque Morning Democrat*, Aug. 13, 1891.

72. "Territorial Tips," *Santa Fe New Mexican*, Nov. 6, 1893.

73. "Welsh Done Up," *Santa Fe New Mexican*, Nov. 10, 1893.

74. "A Prize Fight Arranged," *Albuquerque Morning Democrat*, Jan. 16, 1892.

75. "Glove Contest — McCoy Demonstrates His Ability with the Mittens," *Albuquerque Daily Citizen*, Jan. 21, 1892.

76. "On the Level," *Philadelphia Inquirer*, Jan. 30, 1892.

77. "A Good-sized Kick — The McCoy-Lewis Challenge," *Albuquerque Morning Democrat*, Feb. 9, 1892.

78. "Blood — That Is What it Meant Between Thompson and Wilson Sunday Afternoon," *Albuquerque Morning Democrat*, Feb. 16, 1892.

79. "Now Let McCoy Accept," *Albuquerque Daily Citizen*, Feb. 17, 1892.

80. "He Arrives," *Albuquerque Daily Citizen*, Feb. 24, 1892.

81. "Getting Ready for the Fray," *Albuquerque Morning Democrat*, Mar. 1, 1892.

82. "A Correction," *Albuquerque Daily Citizen*, Mar. 17, 1892.

83. "Declared Off — McCoy Unable to Meet Lewis on Account of Sickness," *Albuquerque Morning Democrat*, Mar. 17, 1892.

84. "Territorial Tips," *Santa Fe New Mexican*, Mar. 17, 1892.

85. "Lively for Sports — The Glove Contests and Wrestling Match Very Interesting," *Albuquerque Daily Citizen*, Mar. 24, 1892.

86. "The Glove Contest," *Albuquerque Morning Democrat*, April 12, 1892.

87. Ibid.

88. "The Prize Fight," *Albuquerque Morning Democrat*, May 12, 1892.

89. "Untitled," *Albuquerque Morning Democrat*, May 14, 1892.

90. "The Prize Ring," *Evening News*, Nov. 27, 1895.

91. "A Private Slugging Match," *Santa Fe New Mexican*, May 25, 1892.

92. E. Meek, "E. Meek Diary," May 27, 1892–Jan. 28, 1983, University of New Mexico, Center for Southwest Research.

93. Ibid.

94. "A Readable Grist," *Santa Fe New Mexican*, Jan. 24, 1895.

95. "A Challenge," *Albuquerque Morning Democrat*, Nov. 28, 1894.

96. "City Chatter," *Albuquerque Morning Democrat*, Nov. 29, 1894.

97. "Collier Said No — And Knocks Out Two Pugs and a Finish Fight," *Albuquerque Morning Democrat*, Dec. 11, 1894.

98. "Biff, Biff, Biff — Dovey Punches Gibson in His Face and Mug, But Fails to Close His Mouth," *Albuquerque Morning Democrat*, Dec. 15, 1894.

99. "Too Modern for the Mossbacks," *Santa Fe New Mexican*, Jan. 28, 1895.

100. "Round About Town," *Santa Fe New Mexican*, Feb. 25, 1895.

101. "Local News," *Albuquerque Morning Democrat*, Feb. 9, 1895.

102. "Now for a Fight," *Albuquerque Morning Democrat*, Feb. 14, 1895.

103. "Untitled," *Albuquerque Morning Democrat*, Feb. 21, 1895.

104. "The Wilson-Dovey Fight," *Albuquerque Morning Democrat*, Feb. 26, 1895.

105. "Their Weights," *Albuquerque Daily Citizen*, Mar. 1, 1895.

106. "Easily Won," *Albuquerque Evening Citizen*, Mar. 4, 1895.

107. "A Draw — The Glove Contest Between Dovey and 'The Spider' Ended in a Draw," *Albuquerque Daily Citizen*, May 25, 1895.

108. "Untitled," *Las Vegas Daily Optic*, May 27, 1895.

109. "Round About Town," *Santa Fe New Mexican*, June 26, 1895.

110. "Round About Town," *Santa Fe New Mexican*, July 4, 1895.

111. "The Fight by Rounds — The Las Vegas Man Stands up for Eight Rounds and Wins Last Night's Glove Contest," *Las Vegas Daily Optic*, July 2, 1895.

112. "Prize Fights Not Wanted," *Albuquerque Morning Journal*, Aug. 3, 1895.

113. Ibid.

Chapter 4

1. "Corbett-Fitzsimmons Fight — A Special Session of the Texas Legislature Called to Pass a Law to Prevent It," *The New York Times*, Sept. 28, 1895.

2. "He Has Called It," Associated Press, Sept. 27, 1895.

3. "Glove Contests — Habeas Corpus Hearing of Relator Jess Clark," *Dallas Morning News*, Sept. 18, 1895.

4. "They Couldn't Fight Here," *Santa Fe New Mexican*, Oct. 15, 1895.

5. "Untitled," *Santa Fe New Mexican*, Oct. 21, 1895.

6. "This Fight a Short One," *New York World*, Dec. 12, 1895.

7. "Sporting World," *Cripple Creek Morning Times*, Dec. 15, 1895.

8. "A Dirty Bit of Business," *Santa Fe New Mexican*, Dec. 31, 1895.

9. "Items of Interest," *Silver City Enterprise*, Jan. 29, 1896.

10. Miguel Antonio Otero, *My Nine Years As Governor of the Territory of New Mexico, 1897–1906* (Santa Fe: Sunstone Press, 2007).

11. "The Prize Fight Law," *Santa Fe New Mexican*, Feb. 6, 1896.

12. "Murray Got His Man," *Rio Grande Republic*, Jan. 17, 1896.

13. "A Contrast," *The Independent*, Jan. 30, 1896.

14. "Murray Got His Man," *Rio Grande Republic*, Jan. 17, 1896.

15. Ibid.

16. "The Champion at Work — Getting in the Pink of Condition for His Fight with Fitzsimmons," *Rio Grande Republican*, Jan. 24, 1896.

17. "From Maher's Quarters — Beings of the Champion and His Party During the Week," *Rio Grande Republican*, Jan. 31, 1896.

18. Ibid.

19. "A Contrast," *The Independent*, Jan. 30, 1896.

20. Ibid.

21. "The Border Pugilists — What Dan Stuart Has to Say to Nay-saying Wagers," *Santa Fe New Mexican*, Feb. 6, 1896.

22. "The Fight Is a Sure Thing," *El Paso Morning Times*, Feb. 9, 1896.

23. "Will they Stop Fight?" *El Paso Morning Times*, Feb. 8, 1896.

24. "Catron Is Suspicious," Associated Press, Feb. 8, 1896.

25. "Catron Wants Credit," Associated Press, Feb. 9, 1896.

26. "Fitz and Maher Will Fight," *Albuquerque Morning Democrat*, Feb. 11, 1896.

27. "The Fights Postponed — Maher's Inflamed Eyes Prevent Him from Fighting Until Monday," *The New York Times*, Feb. 14, 1896.

28. Ibid.

29. "Thornton Replies to Catron," *Santa Fe New Mexican*, Feb. 20, 1896.

30. "Politics and Prize Fighting," *Rocky Mountain News*, Feb. 12, 1896.

31. "Looking for a Duel — Gov. Thornton Calls a Delegate a Liar and a Coward," *Santa Fe New Mexican*, Sept. 12, 1896.

32. "Maher's Eyes Really Sore — At Least the El Paso Correspondents Profess to Believe the Statement," *Santa Fe New Mexican*, Feb. 14, 1896.

33. "Friday Will Suit Maher — He Wants to Fight Then, or Will Give Up His Forfeit Money," *The New York Times*, Feb. 16, 1896.

34. "Disgusted Sports," *Albuquerque Morning Democrat*, Feb. 18, 1896.

35. "Pleasantries of the Pugilists — Still Talking at El Paso," *The New York Times*, Feb. 19, 1896.

36. Ibid.

37. "Off to the Battle Ground — Sports Went by Special Train from El Paso Before Midnight," *The National Police Gazette*, Feb. 29, 1896.

38. "Off to the Battle Ground — Sports Went by Special Train from El Paso Before Midnight," *The National Police Gazette*, Feb. 29, 1896.

39. "Off for the Big Fight — Fitzsimmons, Maher and a Few Spectators Leave El Paso," *The New York Times*, Feb. 21, 1896.

40. "Maher-Fitzsimmons Fight," *Santa Fe New Mexican*, Feb. 21, 1896.

41. "Fitzsimmons Is Champion — He Defeated Maher in Just Ninety-Five Seconds," *The New York Times*, Feb. 29, 1896.

42. "Maher-Fitzsimmons Fight," *Santa Fe New Mexican*, Feb. 21, 1896.

Chapter 5

1. "A Great Session," *Roswell Record*, Feb. 18, 1896.

2. "It Does Seem Inconsistent," *Lincoln News*, Feb. 18, 1896.

3. "Respected the Law," *Albuquerque Morning Democrat*, Feb. 9, 1896.

4. "Athletic Exhibition," *Albuquerque Morning Democrat*, Mar. 1, 1896.

5. "Boxing Contest Tonight at Amador Hall — For a Gymnasium Funds," *Rio Grande Republican*, Apr. 24, 1896.

6. "Local News," *El Paso Herald*, Apr. 25, 1896.

7. "Glances at Our Neighbors," *Denver Evening Post*, May 6, 1897.

8. "Glances at Our Neighbors," *Denver Evening Post*, Aug. 21, 1897.

9. "Untitled," *Santa Fe New Mexican*, June 12, 1899.

10. "A Sparring Exhibition," *Albuquerque Citizen*, Feb. 14, 1900.

11. "Feast of San Geronimo," *Santa Fe New Mexican*, Oct. 6, 1900.

12. "Geronimo Club to Entertain Friends," *Albuquerque Morning Journal*, Feb. 2, 1907.

13. "Cimarron Young Men Organize Athletic Club," *Cimarron News & Press*, Mar. 14, 1907.

14. "Roe Defeated in Boxing Match — An Unexpected Boxing Match Causes Considerable Excitement," *Rio Grande Republican*, Mar. 16, 1906.

15. Ibid.

16. "Untitled," *Rio Grande Republican*, Aug. 17, 1906.

17. "Great Interest in the Indian Boxers," *Albuquerque Morning Journal*, Sept. 8, 1906.

18. "Pujilato — Clayton Retiene El Cinto," *El Fenix*, Aug. 4, 1906.

19. "Butler Got Decision — Interesting Boxing Contest Ended in Four Rounds," *Cimarron News & Press*, May 23, 1907.

20. "G. R. Fitzgerald Gets Cold Feet," *Las Vegas Daily Optic*, Sept. 20, 1907.

21. "Boxing Match Pulled Off — Fifteen Round Go Ends in Fifth," *Cimarron Citizen*, Mar. 4, 1908.

22. Ibid.

23. Ibid.

24. "Had Boxing Contest — Three Five-Round Preliminaries, One Go to the Finish," *Cimarron Citizen*, July 8, 1908.

25. "Geronimo Club in a Lively Entertainment," *Albuquerque Morning Journal*, Feb. 10, 1907.

26. "Entertainment by Geronimo Club," *Albuquerque Morning Journal*, Apr. 21, 1907.

27. "Albuquerque Owes Bob Walker Boxing Money," *Las Vegas Daily Optic*, Oct. 14, 1908.

28. "'Meet Me at Ringside,' Is Salutation of Fans," *Las Vegas Daily Optic*, July 31, 1908.

29. "Fight Promoters to Invade Albuquerque," *Las Vegas Daily Optic*, Aug. 5, 1908.

30. "One Punch Is Enough for Negro Pugilist," *Las Vegas Daily Optic*, Aug. 24, 1907.

31. "Fighters Training for Coming Mill," *Las Vegas Daily Optic*, Sept. 14, 1907.

32. "Struck by Big Brother—Dies," *Las Vegas Daily Optic*, Sept. 18, 1907.

33. "Boxing Bout Has Fatal Ending," *Santa Fe New Mexican*, April 4, 1908.

34. "Fighters Training for Coming Mill," *Las Vegas Daily Optic*, Sept. 14, 1907.

35. "G. R. Fitzgerald Gets Cold Feet," *Las Vegas Daily Optic*, Sept. 20, 1907.

36. "Untitled," *Las Vegas Daily Optic*, Sept. 28, 1907.

37. "Newman Will Take Two Days Rest Before Go," *Las Vegas Daily Optic*, June 25, 1908.

38. "Little Murphy Gets the Decision Over Romero in Ring Bout as Crowd Yells," *Las Vegas Daily Optic*, Aug. 1, 1908.

39. Ibid.

40. Ibid.

41. "Newman and Mapleson Will Meet Labor Day," *Las Vegas Daily Optic*, Aug. 15, 1908.

42. "Angora Goats on Way Across the Continent," *Albuquerque Morning Journal*, July 14, 1908.

43. "Traveling Fighter May Give Exhibition Here," *Las Vegas Daily Optic*, Aug. 21, 1908.

44. "Goat Team Pugilist May Get Matched Here," *Las Vegas Daily Optic*, Aug. 27, 1908.

45. "Ambitious Scrapper Ready to Do Battle," *Albuquerque Morning Journal*, Sept. 15, 1908.

46. "Nothing Doing in the Ring," *Albuquerque Morning Journal*, Sept. 21, 1908.

47. "Walker, Outclassed and with His Finger Dislocated, Fights Gamely," *Las Vegas Daily Optic*, Sept. 23, 1908.

48. "Boxing Bouts May Go More Than 10 Rounds," *Las Vegas Daily Optic*, Sept. 26, 1908.

49. "Walker Sparring with Wallace in Training," *Las Vegas Daily Optic*, Oct. 15, 1908.

50. "Sporting News and Notes," *Las Vegas Daily Optic*, Oct. 16, 1908.

51. "'Alas, Poor Walker, I Knew Him Well,'" *Las Vegas Daily Optic*, Nov. 27, 1908.

52. "Madrid Offers Purse of $400 for Contest," *Las Vegas Daily Optic*, Oct. 29, 1908.

53. "'Alas, Poor Walker, I Knew Him Well,'" *Las Vegas Daily Optic*, Nov. 27, 1908.

54. Ibid.

55. "Pugs Turning Up in Every Town," *Albuquerque Journal*, Sept. 17, 1908.

56. "Denver Man Matched to Fight Kennedy," *Albuquerque Morning Journal*, Dec. 10, 1908.

57. "Kennedy Will Box Pettus," *Albuquerque Morning Journal*, Dec. 22, 1908.

58. "Bill Pettus Puts Kennedy Out in Third," *Albuquerque Morning Journal*, Jan. 20, 1909.

59. "Prize Fighters Are Indicted," *Albuquerque Morning Journal*, Mar. 21, 1909.

60. "Cimarron Has a Candidate for the Ring," *Albuquerque Morning Journal*, Jan. 9, 1909.

61. Ibid.

62. F. Stanley, *The Grant That Maxwell Bought* (Santa Fe: Sunstone Press, 1958).

63. "Untitled," *Cimarron Citizen*, Oct. 27, 1909.

64. Ibid.

65. Stanley, *The Grant That Maxwell Bought*.

66. "Left Handed Reform," *Albuquerque Morning Journal*, July 3, 1910.

67. "Jeffries Will Meet Johnson," *Los Angeles Times*, Mar. 1, 1909.

68. "Clovis Will Make Bid for Fight," *Albuquerque Morning Journal*, June 19, 1910.

69. "Left Handed Reform," *Albuquerque Morning Journal*, July 3, 1910.

70. "Albuquerque Eager for News of Fight," *Albuquerque Morning Journal*, July 4, 1910.

71. Ibid.

72. "Minor City Topics," *Santa Fe New Mexican*, July 5, 1910.

73. "Perpetual Peace for Jeffries Hereafter—The Exchampion Can Now Retire to His Alfalfa Farm for All Time," *Las Vegas Daily Optic*, July 7, 1910.

74. "No Fight Films Go in Roswell Says Mayor," *Albuquerque Morning Journal*, July 9, 1910.

75. "A Closed Incident," *Albuquerque Morning Journal*, July 15, 1910.

76. "Hilton Anxious to Meet Lightweight Fighters," *Albuquerque Morning Journal*, Aug. 19, 1910.

77. "Farrington Tries Out with Big Blacksmith," *Albuquerque Morning Journal*, Jan. 21, 1910.

78. "Johnson-Ketchel Fight Films Are Realistic," *Albuquerque Morning Journal*, Jan. 7, 1910.

79. "Fight Fans Come to Life in Roswell," *Albuquerque Morning Journal*, June 6, 1910.

80. Ibid.

81. "Fight Fans Break Up a Six Round Go," *Albuquerque Morning Journal*, Dec. 27, 1910.

82. "Obar," *Albuquerque Morning Journal*, May 10, 1910.

83. "Nerve of 'Battling' Stops Frenzied Runaway Horse," *Albuquerque Morning Journal*, Aug. 8, 1908.

84. "Battling Nelson May Visit to Vegas," *Las Vegas Daily Optic*, Aug. 6, 1908.

85. "Nerve of 'Battling' Stops Frenzied Runaway Horse," *Albuquerque Morning Journal*, Aug. 8, 1908.

86. Ibid.

87. Ibid.

88. "Battling Nelson Gives Exhibition Here Tonight," *Dallas Morning News*, Feb. 13, 1909.

89. "Battling Nelson Poses as New Mexico Cattle Baron," *Las Vegas Daily Optic*, Aug. 7, 1909.

90. Battling Nelson, *Life, Battles and Career of Battling Nelson* (Hegewisch, Ill., 1908).

91. "Battling Nelson Will Try Hard to Come Back," *Albuquerque Morning Journal*, Mar. 6, 1910.

92. "Battling Nelson Knocked Out by Automobile," *Albuquerque Morning Journal*, Sept 26, 1910.

93. "Confessed Prize Fighter Gets Hour in Jail," *Albuquerque Morning Journal*, Nov. 16, 1911.

94. "Untitled," *McKinley County Republican*, Nov. 17, 1911.

95. "Untitled," *McKinley County Republican*, Feb. 4, 1911.

96. Roger M. Zimmerman, *Stories from Kitchen's Opera House* (Albuquerque, N.M.: Digital 1 Presentations, 2002).

97. "Ev Winters Wins," *Cimarron News*, Mar. 25, 1911.

98. "Confessed Prize Fighter Gets Hour in Jail," *Albuquerque Morning Journal*, Nov. 16, 1911.

99. Ibid.

100. "Building Trades Council Gives Smoker," *Albuquerque Morning Journal*, June 4, 1911.

101. "New Albuquerque Athletic Club," *Albuquerque Morning Journal*, June 8, 1911.

102. "Cherokee Kid and Kid Rhodes in Refined

Sparring at Airdome," *Albuquerque Morning Journal*, June 11, 1911.

103. "Tell Workingmen to Vote for Blue Ballot," *Albuquerque Morning Journal*, Oct. 31, 1911.

104. Ibid.

105. "Clovis Captured by Uncle Sam's Infantrymen," *Albuquerque Morning Journal*, July 16, 1911.

106. "Governor Cruce and the Press — That Prize Fight," *Tulsa World*, June 25, 1911.

Chapter 6

1. "Colorado Boy Rushes Into a Vicious Right Swing," *Rocky Mountain News*, Dec. 26, 1911.

2. "Pettus Will Play with Leland Giants," *Albuquerque Morning Journal*, Mar. 20, 1910.

3. James A. Riley, *The Biographical Encyclopedia of the Negro Baseball Leagues* (New York: Carroll & Graf, 1994).

4. "Would Take Poke at Graham — Pettus of Madrid Accepts Challenge Recently Issued by El Paso Pugilist," *Albuquerque Morning Journal*, Sept. 4, 1908.

5. "Ambitious Scrapper Ready to Do Battle," *Albuquerque Morning Journal*, Sept. 15, 1908.

6. "Madrid Offers Purse of $400 for Contest," *Las Vegas Daily Optic*, Oct. 29, 1908.

7. "Kennedy Will Box Pettus," *Albuquerque Morning Journal*, Dec. 22, 1908.

8. "Bill Pettus Puts Kennedy Out in Third," *Albuquerque Morning Journal*, Jan. 20, 1909.

9. "Pettus in Line for a Big Fight," *Albuquerque Morning Journal*, Mar. 8, 1909.

10. "Bill Pettus Worsts Denver Lad in Eighth Round," *Albuquerque Morning Journal*, June 7, 1909.

11. "Much Interest in Coming Flynn-Pettus Bout," *Las Vegas Daily Optic*, Aug. 28, 1909.

12. Ibid.

13. Ibid.

14. Ibid.

15. "Among the Boxers," *Los Angeles Herald*, Aug. 28, 1909.

16. "Pettus Confident of Making Good Showing," *Albuquerque Morning Journal*, Aug. 31, 1909.

17. "Bill Pettus Goes in Training for Big Match," *Albuquerque Morning Journal*, Sept. 8, 1909.

18. "Easy Money for Bill Pettus Says Roy Corhan," *Albuquerque Morning Journal*, Sept. 19, 1909.

19. "Flynn Gets Decision — Pueblo Fireman Wins Hard-Earned Victory Over Pettus of Albuquerque," *Colorado Springs Gazette*, Sept. 23, 1909.

20. "Bill Pettus Back From Pueblo — Colored Man Who Underwent Severe Grueling at Hands of Jim Flynn Returns to City," *Albuquerque Morning Journal*, Sept. 30, 1909.

21. "Pettus Sparring Partner for Sam Langford — Albuquerque Man Breaking in the Fighting Game on Pacific Coast and Is Fast Learning to Scrap," *Albuquerque Morning Journal*, Feb. 1, 1910.

22. "Pettus Will Play with Leland Giants," *Albuquerque Morning Journal*, Mar. 20, 1910.

23. Ibid.

24. "Bill Pettus Leads World in Batting," *Albuquerque Morning Journal*, Sept. 5, 1910.

25. "Widely Advertised Caponi-Pettus Bout Tame — Chicagoan and Local Boy Fight Ten Slow Rounds to a Draw," *Albuquerque Morning Journal*, Nov. 25, 1912.

26. "Jim Flynn on Way East to Take Rest Cure," *Albuquerque Morning Journal*, Dec. 15, 1912.

27. "Newman Bests 'Texas' in 10-round Contest," *Las Vegas Daily Optic*, July 28, 1908.

28. "Gave Up Linotype to Follow Fight Game, Being the Story of How Louis Newman Gave Up the Keyboard for the Mitts," *Las Vegas Daily Optic,* July 1, 1915.

29. Ibid.

30. "One Punch Is Enough for Negro Pugilist," *Las Vegas Daily Optic*, Aug. 24, 1907.

31. There are inconsistencies in Newman's early fight record, published in 1915, from this time period. Only two of four bouts have been confirmed — and those fights were found to have taken place in 1907, not 1908.

32. "Friends Keep Boxers from Street Battle," *Las Vegas Daily Optic*, June 22, 1908.

33. Ibid.

34. "Newman Bests 'Texas' in 10-Round Contest," *Las Vegas Daily Optic*, July 28, 1908.

35. Ibid.

36. "'Meet Me at Ringside!' Is Slogan of Sports," *Las Vegas Daily Optic*, Sept. 9, 1908.

37. "Lanky Lou Newman Twice Wins Title of Champion in Fight with Mapleson," *Las Vegas Daily Optic,* Sept. 10, 1908.

38. Ibid.

39. "Erlenborn Beats Newman in Six Rounds at D.A.C.," *Rocky Mountain News*, Apr. 16, 1911.

40. "Louis Newman Wins Over Schoel by Decision — Lightning Attack of New Mexico Revelation to Fans Who Had Backed Wyomingite," *Rocky Mountain News*, Sept. 5, 1911.

41. "Winters Wins Laurels," *Cimarron News*, Aug. 5, 1911.

42. "Dane and Winters Battle Tonight at Central Park," *The Chronicle News*, May 29, 1911.

43. "Battling Dane and Ev. Winters Fight 15 Furious Rounds to a Draw," *The Chronicle News* May 31, 1911.

44. Ibid.

45. "Winters Wins Laurels," *Cimarron News*, Aug. 5, 1911.

46. "Gwine [sic] to Bring Home the Chicken," *Cimarron News*, Jan. 7, 1911.

47. "Albuquerque Boxer Recalls Four Bouts with Langford," *Albuquerque Journal*, Feb. 19, 1958.

48. "20-Round Go for Big Smoker by Sports of Cimarron Town," *Albuquerque Morning Journal*, Dec. 30, 1910.

49. "Gwine [sic] to Bring Home the Chicken," *Cimarron News*, Jan. 7, 1911.

50. "Smaulding Easily Winner of the 20-Round Bout — Has Petty Outclassed in Every Way," *Cimarron News*, Jan. 21, 1911.

51. "Boxers Are Ready for Bouts Monday," *Silver City Enterprise*, Mar. 28, 1913.

52. "Boxing Contest at Fort Bayard," *Silver City Enterprise*, May 13, 1910.

53. "Boxing Match Here," *Clovis News*, July 18, 1912.

54. "Fight Fans Have Taken Roswell," *Albuquerque Morning Journal*, June 13, 1910.

55. "Chavez to Tackle Leader of His Class," *The Trinidad Chronicle*, June 12, 1911.

56. "Good Preliminary Bouts to Precede Big Go Friday Night," *The Chronicle News*, May 17, 1911.

57. "Fast Boxers to Meet Here Tonight," *The Trinidad Chronicle*, June 19, 1911.

58. "Chavez Gets Decision Over Harry Reide — Trinidad Featherweight Outpoints Clever Aspen Boy," *The Chronicle News*, Aug. 21, 1911.

59. "Benny Chavez Puts Tom Cody to Sleep," Associated Press, Sept. 22, 1911.

60. Ibid.

61. "Pueblo Boxer No Match for Chavez," *The Chronicle News*, Nov. 4, 1911.

62. "Lub Knocked Out in First Round by Benny Chavez," *The Chronicle News*, Nov. 24, 1911.

63. "Chavez and Attel Battle 10 Rounds to a Draw," *The Chronicle News*, Dec. 8, 1911.

64. "Chavez Supporters Chagrined by Proof of 'Framed Up' Bout," *The Chronicle News*, Dec. 9, 1911.

65. "Chavez-Brannigan Bout Should Prove Best Seen Here," *The Chronicle News*, Dec. 21, 1911.

66. "Chavez Has Chance to Prove Ability," *The Chronicle News*, Dec. 23, 1911.

67. "Brannigan Ready for Chavez Battle — Pittsburg Bantam Surprises Local Fight Fans with His Speed During Training," *Pueblo Chieftain*, Dec. 24, 1911.

68. Ibid.

69. Ibid.

70. "Chavez Knocked Out in Sixty by Patsy Brannigan," *The Chronicle News*, Dec. 26, 1911.

71. Ibid.

72. "Chavez Defeat Not a Disgrace," *The Chronicle News*, Dec. 27, 1911.

73. Ibid.

Chapter 7

1. "The Prize Fight Bill," *Las Cruces Citizen*, Jan. 20, 1912.

2. "Of Brief Duration Was the Boxing Contest at Kitchen's Opera House Saturday Night," *McKinley County Republican*, Jan. 12, 1912.

3. "Big Program Will Be Offered to Sport Fans," *Albuquerque Morning Journal*, Jan. 24, 1912.

4. "Johnson-Flynn Fight Would Disgrace State," *Las Cruces Citizen*, Jan. 20, 1912.

5. "Las Vegas Seeking Fame by Bidding for Prize Fight," *Las Vegas Daily Optic*, Jan. 16, 1912.

6. "The Prize Fight Bill," *Las Cruces Citizen*, Jan. 20, 1912.

7. "Johnson-Flynn Fight Would Disgrace State," *Las Cruces Citizen*, Jan. 20, 1912.

8. "Jack Curley Prefers to Stage Flynn-Johnson Battle in New Mexico," *Albuquerque Morning Journal*, Feb. 9, 1912.

9. "Las Vegas Landed Fight By Going After It," *Albuquerque Morning Journal*, Apr. 23, 1912.

10. "Fight Fans and Ministers at Loggerheads," *Albuquerque Morning Journal*, Feb. 15, 1912.

11. "New Mexico Stands for Decency," *Santa Fe New Mexican*, Feb. 14, 1912.

12. "Curley Partial to Las Vegas," *Albuquerque Morning Journal*, Mar. 2, 1912.

13. "Melrose Mothers' Club on Job," *Albuquerque Morning Journal*, Mar. 11, 1912.

14. "Indians Protest Against Fight Scheduled for Las Vegas," *Albuquerque Morning Journal*, May 12, 1912.

15. "Flynn Is Logical Man to Whip Johnson," *Albuquerque Morning Journal*, Feb. 26, 1912.

16. "Anti Prize Fight Mass Meeting Held Sunday Night," *Clovis News*, Mar. 7, 1912.

17. "Bill in House Permitting 45-Round Bouts," *Albuquerque Morning Journal*, April 10, 1912.

18. State of New Mexico, *Journal of the Senate: Proceedings of the First State Legislature, First Session, March 11th to June 8th, 1912* (Santa Fe: New Mexico Printing Co., 1913).

19. "'Flynn Will Hit Me But Twice,' Says Johnson," *Albuquerque Morning Journal*, June 1, 1912.

20. "The Hub of the World" and "The Eyes of America,

Europe and Australia All on Las Vegas" were stamped on correspondence, postcards and posters.

21. "Twenty Thousand Fans Expected to See Fight," *Albuquerque Morning Journal*, April 22, 1912.

22. "Flynn Given Real Ovation by Las Vegas People," *Albuquerque Morning Journal*, May 10, 1912.

23. "Fear an Unknown Word in Flynn's Training Camp," *Albuquerque Morning Journal*, May 19, 1912.

24. Ibid.

25. "Numerous Fans to Greet Flynn Out Last Night," *Albuquerque Morning Journal*, May 23, 1912.

26. "Flynn Spars Four Rounds with Al Williams," *Albuquerque Morning Journal*, May 24, 1912.

27. "Flynn Calls Bluff of Sheepman Last Night," *Albuquerque Morning Journal*, May 24, 1912.

28. "Williams Loses to Bennie Chavez in 8th Round," *Albuquerque Morning Journal*, May 26, 1912.

29. "Johnson Decides to Do Training in Las Vegas," *Albuquerque Morning Journal*, May 28, 1912.

30. The house, now officially recognized as "The Jack Johnson House," is at 2008 N. Gonzales.

31. "J.A. Johnson to Arrive Here Sunday," *Las Vegas Daily Optic*, May 26, 1912.

32. Ibid.

33. "Flynn Is Mistaken for an Escaped Lunatic," *Albuquerque Morning Journal*, June 3, 1912.

34. Ibid.

35. Ibid.

36. "Jack Johnson in Santa Fe," *Santa Fe New Mexican*, June 7, 1912.

37. "Johnson Willing to Fight Sam Langford," *Weekly Optic and Live Stock Grower*, June 8, 1912.

38. "Jack Johnson in Santa Fe," *Santa Fe New Mexican*, June 7, 1912.

39. "Johnson's Boxing Partners Resent Criticism," *Albuquerque Morning Journal*, June 8, 1912.

40. "Flynn Wants to Be Shot If He Does Not Win Bout," *Weekly Optic and Live Stock Grower*, June 15, 1912.

41. Ibid.

42. Ibid.

43. "Johnson-Flynn Bout Regarded as a Joke," *The New York Times*, June 23, 1912.

44. "Ryan Says Flynn Has No Chance with Johnson," *Albuquerque Morning Journal*, June 18, 1912.

45. "Flynn Is Logical Man to Whip Johnson," *Albuquerque Morning Journal*, Feb. 26, 1912.

46. "Curley Discounts Rumors of Fight Being Stopped," *Albuquerque Morning Journal*, June 19, 1912.

47. "Johnson May Balk If Gate Doesn't Draw Purse," *Albuquerque Morning Journal*, June 27, 1912.

48. "Four Reasons Given by Flynn Why He Should Show Up Well," *Weekly Optic and Live Stock Grower*, June 29, 1912.

49. "Jury to Jolt Jack Johnson Jollily," Associated Press, June 11, 1912.

50. "Johnson Thinks They Are Trying to 'Put One Over' on the Camp," *Weekly Optic and Live Stock Grower*, June 22, 1912.

51. "Jack Johnson Is Not Going to Show Here," *Albuquerque Morning Journal*, June 11, 1912.

52. "Four Reasons Given by Flynn Why He Should Show Up Well," *Weekly Optic and Live Stock Grower*, June 29, 1912.

53. "Fighters Fit for Battle Today at Vegas," *Albuquerque Morning Journal*, July 4, 1912.

54. Ibid.

55. Yoakum and Unholz were promised 50 percent of the gate — which amounted to $2,000 — but after the fight, were handed checks for $228 each, Curley charging them

$500 for "use of the arena." When they complained, Curley's thugs threatened them and the two pugs hightailed it back to Albuquerque rather than stick around to watch the championship fight the next day. Promoter Levy eventually regained what was due the two fighters.

56. "Fighters Fit for Battle Today at Vegas," *Albuquerque Morning Journal*, July 4, 1912.

57. "The Johnson-Flynn Fight," *Albuquerque Morning Journal*, July 5, 1912.

58. "Police Stop Big Fizzle at Vegas," *Santa Fe New Mexican*, July 4, 1912.

59. "Flynn Proves a Miserable Match for Johnson," *Albuquerque Morning Journal*, July 5, 1912.

60. "Fans Unanimous in Condemning Vegas Fiasco," *Albuquerque Morning Journal*, July 5, 1912.

61. "Johnson Wins Fight from Flynn in Ninth Round," Associated Press, July 5, 1912.

62. "Fighters Fit for Battle Today at Vegas," *Albuquerque Morning Journal*, July 4, 1912.

63. "What the Principals Have to Say About Fights," Associated Press, July 4, 1912.

64. Ibid.

65. "Johnson and Flynn Are Fighting It Out," *Salt Lake City Telegram*, July 5, 1912.

66. Ibid.

67. Ibid.

68. "Johnson Wins Fight from Flynn in Ninth Round," Associated Press, July 5, 1912.

69. Ibid.

70. "Flynn Proves a Miserable Match for Johnson," *Albuquerque Morning Journal*, July 5, 1912.

71. Ibid.

72. "Johnson Wins Fight from Flynn in Ninth Round," Associated Press, July 5, 1912.

73. "Decision Goes to Johnson Because of Flynn Butting," *Cleveland Plain Dealer*, July 5, 1912.

74. Ibid.

75. Ibid.

76. "Johnson Wins Fight from Flynn in Ninth Round," Associated Press, July 5, 1912.

77. "Sporting News," *Santa Fe New Mexican*, July 18, 1912.

78. Ibid.

79. "Johnson Is Victor When Flynn Fouls," *Cleveland Plain Dealer*, July 5, 1912.

80. Ibid.

81. "Vegas Willing to Stage Another Big Battle," *Albuquerque Morning Journal*, July 12, 1912.

82. "Boxing Briefs," *El Paso Morning Times*, July 14, 1912.

Chapter 8

1. "Father of Fight Game In State Making Good with Classy Ones," *Santa Fe New Mexican*, Jan. 27, 1915.

2. "Otto Floto Gets Off About As Far Wrong As Even He Could Do," *Albuquerque Morning Journal*, Dec. 21, 1914.

3. Fighting as "Jack Burns," Sanchez actually returned to New Mexico three times to fight: he lost to El Paso's Benny Carson in Gallup, Dec. 15, 1915; drew with Gallup's Freddie Baxter on Aug. 3, 1919; and was KO'd in 5 by the Insurrecto Kid on July 5, 1920, in Albuquerque.

4. It took Dundee 87 fights to get a title fight — and it would take him eight more years to get another one.

5. "Admirers Out to See Dixon and Dundee Train Sunday Proves Record-breaking Day in Point of Attendance," *Albuquerque Morning Journal*, June 30, 1913.

6. "Dixon Will Give Dundee Battle of His Life on Fourth of July," *Albuquerque Morning Journal*, June 24, 1913.

7. "Dundee Is Awarded Decision Over Tommy Dixon," *Albuquerque Morning Journal*, July 5, 1913.

8. "Boxing Briefs," *El Paso Morning Times,* July 14, 1912.

9. "Promoter Comes to Look 'Em Over," *Las Vegas Daily Optic*, May 15, 1912.

10. "Hite No Match for Benny Chaves," *Las Vegas Daily Optic*, Mar. 27, 1913.

11. "Yoakum Has Best of Ladylike Exhibition," *Las Vegas Daily Optic,* Aug. 20, 1913.

12. "Older" Rivera, 95 pounds, was knocked out by "Young" Rivera, 108 pounds.

13. "Boxing Briefs," *El Paso Morning Times*, July 25, 1912.

14. "Old-Time Sports Passed in Review," *Clovis Evening News Journal*, Oct. 19, 1931.

15. "Indian Fighter No Match for White Man at Clovis," *Albuquerque Morning Journal,* Feb. 13, 1912.

16. "Fight Fans and Minsters at Loggerheads," *Albuquerque Morning Journal*, Feb. 15, 1912.

17. "Boxing Bout a Farce," *Clovis News*, May 16, 1912.

18. "Texas May Offer Real White Hope," *Dallas Morning News*, Feb. 12, 1912.

19. "Cass Tarver Signs for Go with Frank Beverly of Dallas," *Fort Worth Star-Telegram*, Aug. 10, 1912.

20. "Anson Giant Wins in Eighth Round," *Clovis Journal*, Aug. 29, 1912.

21. "Cass Tarver Wins," *Tucumcari News*, Aug. 30, 1912.

22. "Big Boy from Texas Gets Knocked Out," *Clovis Journal*, Oct. 3, 1912.

23. "Ladies Day at C.A.C.," *Clovis Journal*, July 11, 1913.

24. "Morris Whips His Man in Second Round," *Clovis Journal*, July 18, 1913.

25. "Old-Time Sports Passed in Review," *Clovis Evening News Journal*, Oct. 19, 1931.

26. "Boxing Contest Ends in Near Riot," *Gallup Herald*, June 3, 1916.

27. "Wilson Wins Over Crooked Route," *Gallup Independent*, June 1, 1916.

28. "Boxing Contest Ends in Near Riot," *Gallup Herald*, June 3, 1916.

29. "Wilson Wins Over Crooked Route," *Gallup Independent*, June 1, 1916.

30. "Boxing Contest Ends in Near Riot," *Gallup Herald*, June 3, 1916.

31. "Boxing Club Needed for Border Cities," *El Paso Morning Times*, May 7, 1916.

32. "Good Boxing Bout in Prospect Feb. 12," *Silver City Enterprise,* Feb. 6, 1914.

33. "Kid George Kills Cow with His Fist," *Santa Fe New Mexican*, May 26, 1915.

34. "Ten Rounds Out of Forty-Eight Are Fought," *Albuquerque Morning Journal*, May 3, 1912.

35. "Gonzales Wins by Knockout," *Silver City Enterprise*, Sept. 19, 1913.

36. "Higgins Attracts," *El Paso Morning Times,* Sept. 24, 1916.

37. "Two Knockouts in Ring Battle," *Roswell Daily Record*, Sept. 3, 1913.

38. "Fighting Game Gets a Black Eye in Roswell," *Santa Fe New Mexican*, Sept. 3, 1913.

39. "Boxing Game Gets Another Bump," *Roswell Daily Record*, Sept. 20, 1913.

40. Ibid.

41. "Each Is Hopeful — Herrick and Higgins Ready," *El Paso Morning Times*, Sept. 26, 1913.

42. Ibid.

43. "Herrick Is Victor," *El Paso Morning Times*, Sept. 29, 1913.

44. "Will Be Exciting Exhibition," *Deming Herald*, Feb. 17, 1914.

45. "Boxing Game Going Good at Columbus," *El Paso Morning Times*, Nov. 5, 1916.

46. "Lee Fails to Meet Frankie Conley," *El Paso Herald*, Feb. 9, 1913.

47. "Jack Herrick, Who Will Meet Kid Mitchell in Big Tent August 4," *El Paso Morning Times,* July 19, 1912.

48. "No More Prize Fighting Says Gov. McDonald," *Deming Headlight*, Aug. 2, 1912.

49. "Boxing Briefs," *El Paso Morning Times*, Aug. 2, 1912.

Chapter 9

1. "Mexicans Gathering Big End of the Money of the Fight Game in the Great Southwest," *Tucson Daily Citizen*, Nov. 11, 1919.

2. "Mexicans May Be Champions," *Los Angeles Times*, Oct. 25, 1913.

3. "O'Malley Says a Resurrection Is Coming," *Las Vegas Daily Optic*, Sept. 19, 1913.

4. "Johnson Defeats Newman Getting Virtual Knockout," *Rocky Mountain News*, Jan. 23, 1912.

5. "Newman Arrives Fit for Bout of Career," *Albuquerque Morning Journal*, June 13, 1912.

6. "Kid Yoakum and Louis Newman Fight Draw," *Albuquerque Morning Journal*, June 18, 1912.

7. "Training Camps of Lightweight Thronged," *Albuquerque Morning Journal*, June 23, 1912.

8. "Lightweights Will Battle Here July 3," *Weekly Optic and Live Stock Grower*, June 28, 1912.

9. "Yoakum Is Given Decision Over Louis Newman," *Albuquerque Morning Journal*, June 29, 1912.

10. "Pierson Fails to Whip Smaulding in Ten Rounds," *Albuquerque Morning Journal*, Sept. 12, 1912.

11. "Newman Wins by Outboxing Harry Shaffer Last Night," *Las Vegas Daily Optic*, June 18, 1913.

12. "Confidence Oozes from Pores of the Rival Boxing Specialists,'" *Las Vegas Daily Optic*, July 24, 1913.

13. "Draw Is Result of Lightweight Bout," *Las Vegas Daily Optic*, July 25, 1913.

14. "Gave Up Linotype to Follow Fight Game," *Las Vegas Daily Optic*, July 1, 1915.

15. "Raton Fans Have Much Confidence in Ev Winters," *Albuquerque Morning Journal*, Apr. 7, 1913.

16. "Winters Is Given Awful Panning by Press," *Albuquerque Morning Journal*, Aug. 8, 1913.

17. "Ev Winters Makes a Good Indian," *Raton Reporter*, Feb. 13, 1912.

18. "Battling Nelson to Meet Winters Here," *Clovis News*, Feb. 22, 1912.

19. "Moran Is Given Decision," *Dallas Morning News*, Mar. 6, 1912.

20. "Winters-White Go Is a Draw," *Raton Range*, Oct. 4, 1912.

21. "Winters Knocks Out Frankie White," *Raton Range*, Feb. 4, 1913.

22. "Kid Shafer Draws with Winters in Classy Bout," *Albuquerque Morning Journal*, Apr. 11, 1913.

23. "Winters Puts Up Game Fight," *Raton Range*, Apr. 15, 1913.

24. "Bruce-Winters Mill Likely to Be Good," *Las Vegas Daily Optic*, Aug. 2, 1913.

25. "Winters Is Given Awful Panning by Press," *Albuquerque Morning Journal*, Aug. 8, 1913.

26. "Yoakum Stops Winters in Four Fast Rounds," *Raton Range*, Oct. 1, 1915.

27. "Hunt's Goat Has Very Suddenly Disappeared," *Albuquerque Morning Journal*, Feb. 2, 1912.

28. Ibid.

29. "Stanton-Coakley Bout One Week from Tonight," *Albuquerque Morning Journal*, Apr. 10, 1912.

30. "Smaulding Should Make Good Fighter Opinion of Coakley," *Albuquerque Morning Journal*, Apr. 17, 1912.

31. "Tonight's Card Is to Be Classiest Ever Seen Here," *Albuquerque Morning Journal*, May 2, 1912.

32. "Ten Rounds Out of Forty-Eight Are Fought," *Albuquerque Morning Journal*, May 3, 1912.

33. "Smaulding Stays 10 Rounds with Vic Hanson," *Albuquerque Morning Journal*, Jan. 2, 1914.

34. "Greatest Boxer Ever Staged in Silver City," *Silver City Enterprise*, Jan. 30, 1914.

35. "Herrick-Smaulding Bout Ends in Another Draw," *Silver City Enterprise*, Feb. 27, 1914.

36. "Fighting Ghost of Joplin to Meet Al Smaulding" *Silver City Enterprise*, Mar. 20, 1914.

37. "Clarke Goes 10 Rounds to Draw with Smaulding," *Albuquerque Morning Journal*, Apr. 2, 1914.

38. "Smaulding Gets a Draw Against Fast Company," *Silver City Enterprise*, Apr. 3, 1914.

39. "'Fighting Ghost' and Smaulding Fight to Draw," *Albuquerque Morning Journal*, Apr. 14, 1914.

40. "George Winner Over Smaulding By Good Margin," *Albuquerque Morning Journal*, Dec. 19, 1914.

41. "Thomas Declared Winner in Fight Saturday Night," *Gallup Independent*, Apr. 20, 1916.

42. "Albuquerque Boxer Recalls Four Bouts with Langford," *Albuquerque Morning Journal*, Feb. 19, 1958.

43. "Gave Up Linotype to Follow Fight Game," *Las Vegas Daily Optic*, July 1, 1915.

44. "Johnson-Flynn Fight Would Disgrace State," *Las Cruces Citizen,* Jan. 20, 1912.

45. "Gave Up Linotype to Follow Fight Game," *Las Vegas Daily Optic*, July 1, 1915.

46. "Preliminaries to Feature Bouts on New Years," *Albuquerque Morning Journal*, Dec. 21, 1912.

47. "Jack Torres Wins from Oliver in Waltz Dream," *Albuquerque Morning Journal*, Mar. 11, 1913.

48. "Stern and Torres Go Battle for Belt Tonight," *Albuquerque Morning Journal*, July 28, 1913.

49. "Jack Torres Wins from Stern by Knockout," *Albuquerque Morning Journal*, July 29, 1913.

50. "Torres Will Meet Matthews Here Next Week," *Albuquerque Morning Journal*, Nov. 20, 1913.

51. "Matthews Says He Will Give K.O. to Torres," *Albuquerque Morning Journal*, Dec. 23, 1913.

52. Ibid.

53. "Torres Presented with Decision by Shearn," *Albuquerque Morning Journal*, Dec. 25, 1913.

54. "Fighters, Trained to a Minute, Both Are Confident of Winning Battle," *Albuquerque Morning Journal*, Mar. 9, 1914.

55. "Torres Is Given Decision Over Riede on Foul," *Albuquerque Morning Journal*, Mar. 10, 1914.

56. "Torres Stopped After Beating Logan 9 Rounds," *Albuquerque Morning Journal*, Nov. 11, 1914.

57. "Torres to Meet Bud Logan Next Week in St. Joe," *Albuquerque Morning Journal*, Jan. 15, 1915.

58. "Jack Torres to Have Chance at Welterweight Championship," *Albuquerque Morning Journal*, Dec. 20, 1914.

59. "Torres Likely to Beat Anyone of His Weight," *Albuquerque Morning Journal*, Jan. 26, 1915.

60. "Well Known Referee Will Officiate in Fight Here," *Santa Fe New Mexican*, June 28, 1915.

61. "Shaeffer Loses in Eighth," *Santa Fe New Mexican*, July 5, 1915.

62. "Torres Wins All the Way But the Best He Gets Is Draw," *Rocky Mountain News*, Mar. 18, 1915.

63. "Kenosha Makes Bid for Gilmore and M'Farland," *Rocky Mountain News*, Mar. 19, 1915.

64. "Torres Wins from Wells," *Rocky Mountain News*, July 31, 1915.

65. "Torres and Wells Battle to Draw at Elks Smoker," *Trinidad Chronicle-News*, Dec. 18, 1915.

66. "Torres Scores Virtual K.O.," *Rocky Mountain News*, May 5, 1915.

67. "Torres Will Lay Claim to World Welter Title," *Albuquerque Morning Journal*, June 21, 1915.

68. "Gave Up Linotype to Follow Fight Game," *Las Vegas Daily Optic*, July 1, 1915.

69. "Torres Going After Welterweight Title," *Las Vegas Daily Optic*, July 14, 1915.

70. "Sport Shrapnel," *Kansas City Star*, May 13, 1916.

71. "Ask Torres to Box Ted Lewis," *El Paso Herald*, May 25, 1915.

72. "Look for a Busy Season — Jack Britton Will Keep Welterweights on the Jump," Associated Press, Sept. 21, 1916.

73. "Levy to Start Jack Torres in New York Ring," *Albuquerque Morning Journal*, Jan. 27, 1917.

74. Ibid.

75. "Harbertson, in Two Straight Falls," *Ogden Examiner*, Apr. 14, 1917.

76. "Waugh Decisively Beats Cordova," *Silver City Independent*, Oct. 30, 1917.

77. "Cordova Beats Sixth Cavalryman," *El Paso Herald*, Apr. 15, 1915.

78. "Benny Cordova," *El Paso Morning Times*, Aug. 1, 1919.

79. From a letter written by Benny Cordova, Jr., to Armando Cordoba, mid–1990s.

80. "Kelly and Gage Ready for Gong," *El Paso Morning Times*, Aug. 1, 1914.

81. "Fans Interested in Coming Contest," *El Paso Morning Times*, Nov. 4, 1914.

82. "Benny Cordova Coming Champ, Says Frank Noel," *Albuquerque Morning Journal*, May 15, 1915.

83. "A Letter From Read's Manager," *San Antonio Light*, May 5, 1915.

84. Ibid.

85. "Young Attell to Battle Cordova or Yoakum Here," *Albuquerque Morning Journal*, July 11, 1915.

86. "Waugh Wins Easy Decision Over Cordova," *Fort Worth Star-Telegram*, July 6, 1915.

87. "Waugh and Cordova Ready for Their Go," *San Antonio Light*, Aug. 17, 1915.

88. "Cordova and Waugh Box to Draw Decision," *San Antonio Light*, Aug. 18, 1915.

89. "Mixing Mexican and Distance Boxer Slow Upon Grind of Training Camp," *El Paso Morning Times*, Sept. 18, 1915.

90. Ibid.

91. "Benny and Bobby Fight to Draw," *El Paso Morning Times*, Sept. 20, 1915.

92. Ibid.

93. "Benny Cordova Home for Rest After Battles," *Albuquerque Morning Journal*, Sept. 30, 1915.

94. "Cordova Is Game But Outclassed by Bobby Waugh," *Fort Worth Star-Telegram*, Feb. 1, 1916.

95. "Kike's Komment," *Fort Worth Star-Telegram*, Mar. 5, 1916.

96. "Waugh Punches Referee After Bad Decision," *Fort Worth Star-Telegram*, Mar. 7, 1916.

97. "Conners Exhibits High Grade Stuff of Ring Battler," *Albuquerque Morning Journal*, May 29, 1916.

98. "Jack Torres Wins on Foul — Cordova Awarded Knockout," *Albuquerque Morning Journal*, May 31, 1916.

99. "Cordova Wins Over Anderson with K.O.," *El Paso Morning Times*, Sept. 5, 1916.

100. "Just Sport for Just Sport Across the Board and Back," *El Paso Morning Times*, Dec. 5, 1916.

101. "Cordova Arrives for Main Go on Jan. 14," *El Paso Morning Times*, Jan. 8, 1917.

102. "Talking it Over — By Chuck Swan," *El Paso Herald*, Jan. 15, 1917.

103. "Waugh Decisively Beats Cordova," *Silver City Independent*, Oct. 30, 1917.

104. "Fight Card for Fort Bayard's Monday Night Show Is Classy," *El Paso Times*, July 17, 1921.

105. "Toss-up Who Wins Friday's Battle," *Roswell Daily Record*, June 29, 1914.

106. "Connolly and Moffatt Draw," *Roswell Daily Record*, July 6, 1914.

107. "Baca-Connolly Fight at Roswell Tickles the Pugilistic Fans," *Santa Fe New Mexican*, Aug. 20, 1915.

108. "Connally [sic] Wins Over Baca," *Roswell Evening News*, Sept. 7, 1915.

109. "Baca and Connelly Get a Draw," *Santa Fe New Mexican*, Feb. 22, 1916.

110. "Connolly Wins from Baca," *Roswell Daily Record*, July 5, 1917.

111. Ibid.

112. "State Wide Interest in Fistic Carnival on Memorial Day," *Santa Fe New Mexican*, May 25, 1916.

113. "Harry Schaefer Meets Terrible Death on Engine," *Gallup Independent*, Feb. 10, 1916.

114. "Kid Shafer Knocks Out Stern in Third Round," *Albuquerque Morning Journal*, Mar. 29, 1913.

115. "Gallant Loses on Foul, Bratton Given Bad Verdict," *Rocky Mountain News*, Dec. 8, 1916.

116. "Fighter is Killed at National Club by Blow on Head," *Rocky Mountain News*, Dec. 19, 1916.

117. Ibid.

118. "Jury Says Blow Killed Fighter," *Rocky Mountain News*, Dec. 20, 1916.

119. "Albuquerque Boy Killed in Prize Fight in Denver," *Albuquerque Morning Journal*, Dec. 19, 1916.

Chapter 10

1. "Crowd Enthusiastic Over Chavez's Great Gym Work," *Kansas City Post*, Jan. 3, 1916.

2. "Chavez Gets Well Earned Decision Over Murphy," *Albuquerque Morning Journal*, May 9, 1912.

3. "Williams Loses to Bennie Chavez in 8th Round," *Albuquerque Morning Journal*, May 26, 1912.

4. "Monte Attel and Chavez Matched for Labor Day," *Trinidad Chronicle-News*, Aug. 13, 1912.

5. "Chavez Is Going to Coast After New Year's Battle," *Albuquerque Morning Journal*, Dec. 15, 1912.

6. "How Chico Got the Goat of Little Benny Chavez," *Los Angeles Times*, Oct. 30, 1913.

7. *Ibid.*

8. "Battling Chico Is Easily Master of Chavez," *Albuquerque Morning Journal*, Feb. 21, 1913.

9. Ibid.

10. "As a Knight of Old, But with Fists For Sword, Chavez Fights to Goal," *Denver Post*, Aug. 12, 1913.

11. "Stray Horse Shoes Chavez' Sole Mascot," *Rocky Mountain News*, Aug. 9, 1913.

12. "Chavez Wins Over Battling Chico Decisively," *Albuquerque Morning Journal*, May 31, 1913.

13. "Chavez Knocks Out Dell in Eleventh; Johnny Coulon Next," *Trinidad Chronicle-News*, July 5, 1913.

14. "Brannigan and Chavez Whirl in Training," *Rocky Mountain News*, Aug. 8, 1913.

15. "Benny Chaves Is Again Winner Over Chico," *Albuquerque Morning Journal*, Aug. 2, 1913.

16. "'Another Colorado Champion' Is Slogan of Little Benny Chavez," *Denver Post*, Aug. 7, 1913.

17. "Tomorrow to Be Crackerjack — Feathers Rank Among Best," *Rocky Mountain News*, Aug. 10, 1913.

18. "Kilbane Only Boxer to Beat Brannigan," *Rocky Mountain News*, Aug. 3, 1913.

19. "'Another Colorado Champion' Is Slogan of Little Benny Chavez," *Denver Post*, Aug. 7, 1913.

20. Ibid.

21. "As a Knight of Old, But with Fists For Sword, Chavez Fights to Goal," *Denver Post*, Aug. 12, 1913.

22. Ibid.

23. Ibid.

24. "Trinidad Boxer Has Promise — Is Aspirant for Heavy Title," *Rocky Mountain News*, Aug. 17, 1913.

25. "'Another Colorado Champion' Is Slogan of Little Benny Chavez," *Denver Post*, Aug. 7, 1913.

26. "Chavez Holds Burns to Draw in Fast Ten-Round Mill," *Rocky Mountain News*, Aug. 30, 1913.

27. "Chavez and Campi Both Doing Some Boasting," *Albuquerque Morning Journal*, Nov. 2, 1913.

28. "Los Angeles Examiner Gives Chavez Publicity," *Albuquerque Morning Journal*, Oct. 24, 1913.

29. Ibid.

30. "'Widow' Looks Upon Chavez," *Los Angeles Times*, Oct. 29, 1913.

31. "Spark Plug M'Closky Hasn't a High Opinion of Benny Chavez as a Boxer," *Los Angeles Times*, Oct. 31, 1913.

32. Ibid.

33. Ibid.

34. "Chavez Tagged as Boxer by Coast Glove Expert," *Albuquerque Morning Journal*, Oct. 31, 1913.

35. "Jay Davidson Says," *Los Angeles Herald*, Nov. 1, 1913.

36. "Van Court Says Chavez Is a Dangerous Boxer," *Los Angeles Times*, Nov. 1, 1913.

37. "Chavez Tagged as Boxer by Coast Glove Expert," *Albuquerque Morning Journal*, Oct. 31, 1913.

38. "Chavez Picked to Beat Campi," Benny Chavez's scrapbook, source and date unknown.

39. "Chavez and Campi Meet Tuesday," *Los Angeles Examiner*, Oct. 31, 1913.

40. "Chavez and Campi Both Doing Some Big Boasting," *Albuquerque Morning Journal*, Nov. 2, 1913.

41. Ibid.

42. "Too Much Class — Chavez Was Bewildered by Cleverness of Campi," *Los Angeles Times*, Nov. 5, 1913.

43. Ibid.

44. "Chavez Will Have to Take Boxing Lessons," *Los Angeles Times*, Nov. 6, 1913.

45. "Chavez Stops Off on His Return to Denver," *Albuquerque Morning Journal*, Nov. 13, 1913.

46. "Benny Chavez and Louis Newman Part Company," *Albuquerque Morning Journal*, Dec. 10, 1913.

47. Ibid.

48. Ibid.

49. "Chavez Slipping But Still Can Come Back," *Las Vegas Daily Optic*, Dec. 14, 1913.

50. "Gilbert Starts Coffee-Grinder for Coming Bout," *Rocky Mountain News*, May 15, 1914.

51. "Chavez Will Give Kilbane Some Job in 15-Round Fight," *Rocky Mountain News*, May 22, 1914.

52. "Kilbane Comes to Denver Friday to Begin Siege," *Rocky Mountain News*, May 20, 1914.

53. "Kilbane-Chavez Battle Has Boxing Fans Buzzing," *Rocky Mountain News*, May 27, 1914.

54. "M'Coy to Train Benny Chavez for Kilbane Battle," *Rocky Mountain News,* May 21, 1914.

55. "Kilbane-Chavez Battle Has Boxing Fans Buzzing," *Rocky Mountain News*, May 27, 1914.

56. "Kilbane and Chavez Clash Tonight," *Rocky Mountain News,* May 29, 1914.

57. Ibid.

58. "Dope is Upset by Chavez and Delmont Bouts," *Denver Times*, July 22, 1914.

59. "Johnny Kilbane Knocks Out Benny Chavez in Two Rounds," *Rocky Mountain News,* May 30, 1914.

60. Ibid.

61. Ibid.

62. Ibid.

63. "Chavez Knocked Out in Second Round by Kilbane," *Trinidad Chronicle News*, May 30, 1914.

64. "Dope Is Upset by Chavez and Delmont Bouts," *Denver Times*, July 22, 1914.

65. Ibid.

66. "Chavez Retains Proud Title of Trinidad Idol," *Trinidad Chronicle News*, Sept. 24, 1915.

67. "Chavez Romps in Front for Nine Rounds and Earns Easy Decision," *Denver Times*, July 22, 1914.

68. "Mitchell Beats Chavez by K.O. in Second Round," *Rocky Mountain News*, Sept. 29, 1914.

69. "Chavez Loses Go for Protesting Unfair Tactics," *Rocky Mountain News*, Mar 5 1915.

70. "Smith and Chavez Battle to a Draw," *Trinidad Chronicle News*, July 6, 1912.

71. "Chavez Retains Proud Title of Trinidad Idol," *Trinidad Chronicle News*, Sept. 24, 1915.

72. "Little Colorado Mexican Renews Good Intentions and Makes Good," *Denver Post*, Mar. 1, 1916.

73. "Kansas City Scribe Lauds Chavez to the Very Skies," *Trinidad Chronicle News*, Jan. 3, 1916.

74. "B. Chavez Won, But Lost — And 'Loosy' Lost, But Won the 15 Round Bout," *Kansas City Post*, Mar. 10, 1916.

75. "Little Colorado Mexican Renews Good Intentions and Makes Good," *Denver Post,* March 4, 1916.

76. "Benny Chavez Given Knockout Punch by Unknown in St. Louis," Associated Press, Nov. 29, 1916.

77. "A New Fistic Idol Born," *Kansas City Star*, Jan. 2, 1917.

Chapter 11

1. Army Fighters Looking for Bouts," *El Paso Herald,* Feb. 22, 1916.

2. "Just Sport for Just Sport Across the Board and Back by Hy Schneider," *El Paso Morning Times*, Sept. 7, 1919.

3. "Strouer Wins from Cale," *Columbus Courier*, July 3, 1914.

4. "Jail Winsor," *El Paso Morning Times*, Nov. 24, 1913.

5. "'Bull' Foster Goes Against R. Williams," *El Paso Morning Times*, Nov. 14, 1916.

6. Ibid.

7. "Sporting Cackle — by Shakes," *El Paso Morning Times*, Jan. 24, 1917

8. "Larry's Red Scarf," *Miami Herald*, June 6, 1918.

9. "Texas Middleweight Defeats Kinney," *El Paso Morning Times*, Oct. 27, 1916.

10. "Burns Earns Decision Over Torrence in 10-Round Tilt at Smelter for Red Cross," *El Paso Morning Times*, Feb. 26, 1917.

11. "$1,000 Purse for Champ Newton," *El Paso Morning Times*, Feb. 14, 1917.

12. "Newton Can't Cross Color Line, Says W. Hull," *El Paso Morning Times*, Feb. 17, 1917.

13. "Burns Draws the Color Line Also," *El Paso Herald*, Mar. 5, 1917.

14. "Boxer, Charged with Insulting U. S. Flag, Gets Stiff Penalty," *Albuquerque Morning Journal*, June 22, 1917.

15. "Soldiers at El Paso Have Boxing Arena in New Mexico," Associated Press, Jan. 27, 1917.

16. "Just Sport for Just Sport Across the Board and Back — by Hy Schneider," *El Paso Morning Times*, Dec. 9, 1916.

17. "Military Camp Bouts Under Jurisdiction Federal Authorities," *El Paso Morning Times,* Nov. 10, 1916.

18. "Enclosed Arena to Insure Comfort for Boxing Fans," *El Paso Morning Times*, Feb. 24, 1917.

19. "Petite Peggy Goes to Prize Fight," *El Paso Morning Times*, Jan. 31, 1917.

20. "Johnny Newton and Eddie Duffy Fight to a Draw," *El Paso Morning Times*, Dec. 19, 1916.

21. "Newton Scores Technical Knockout over 'Vande,'" *El Paso Morning Times*, Feb. 23, 1917.

22. Ibid.

23. "Benny Cordova Signed to Box O'Toole," *El Paso Morning* Times, Jan. 6, 1917.

24. "O'Toole Eager to Battle," *Trench & Camp*, Jan. 8, 1917.

25. "O'Toole Takes Southwestern Crown by Handing Benny Cordova a Beating," *El Paso Morning Times*, Jan. 15, 1917.

26. "Just Sport for Just Sport Across the Board and Back — by Hy Schneider," *El Paso Morning Times*, Mar. 13, 1917.

27. "O'Toole Retains Championship with Knockout," *El Paso Morning Times,* Mar. 10, 1917.

28. "Wednesday Night Bouts at Smelter Will Be Closing Attraction of That Club," *El Paso Morning Times,* Apr. 24, 1917.

29. "Local and Personal," *El Paso Morning Times*, May 17, 1918.

30. "Sport Comment by 'Mack,'" *El Paso Morning Times*, July 19, 1918.

31. "Clean Boxing Is Made Certain in Military Camps," *Albuquerque Morning Journal*, Feb. 20, 1918.

32. "Steuhmer-Duarte Match to Be Stadium February Feature," *Trench & Camp*, Feb. 2, 1918.

33. "Boxing Game Good at Columbus," *El Paso Morning Times*, Nov. 5, 1916.

34. "Jeff Clarke, the Fighting Ghost, Wants Bout," *Albuquerque Morning Journal*, Nov. 22, 1912.

35. "Waugh Victor Over Read at Elks' on Labor Day," *Silver City Enterprise*, Sept. 7, 1917.

36. "Silver City Boxing Show Dated for Next Tuesday," *El Paso Morning Times*, Mar. 28, 1919.

37. "Speedball Hayden Same Old Flash," *El Paso Herald*, Apr. 29, 1921.

38. "Waugh Matched with Wallace," *Deming Herald*, Jan. 11, 1918.

39. "Soldier Fighters Will Stage Fistic Card at Orpheum," *Albuquerque Morning Journal*, Sept. 25, 1917.

40. "Boxing Game Going Good at Columbus," *El Paso Morning Times*, Nov. 5, 1916.

41. "Speedball Hayden Stops Rufus Williams and Wins Middleweight Army Title," *El Paso Morning Times*, Nov. 22, 1917.

42. "Speed-Ball Hayden Wins World Championship from Hock Bones," *Columbus Courier*, Feb. 22, 1918.

43. "Hayden Gets Decision Over Rufus Williams," *Columbus Courier*, May 10, 1918.

44. "Speedball Hayden Knocks Out Ross," *El Paso Morning Times*, Nov. 17, 1918.

45. "Boxing Club Needed for Border Cities," *El Paso Morning Times*, May 7, 1916.

46. "Boxers Fail to Perform," *Deming Herald*, Sept. 7, 1917.

47. "Fans on Tip-Toe for Big Contest," *Silver City Independent*, Nov. 13, 1917.

48. "Bobby Waugh Gets Decision on a Foul," *Silver City Enterprise*, Nov. 16, 1917.

49. "Torrance Has 42 Centimeter Clout in Right," *Albuquerque Morning Journal*, Sept. 25, 1916.

50. "Nick Gundy, 'The Giant Killer,'" *El Paso Herald*, Mar. 9, 1918.

51. "Speedball Hayden Loses to Johnson," *Silver City Enterprise*, April 4, 1919.

52. "Paid Boxing Bouts Disapproved in Order Issues From Southern Commander's Headquarters," *El Paso Morning Times*, Sept. 5, 1919.

Chapter 12

1. "Revival of Boxing Is Likely Result of the World War," *Albuquerque Morning Journal*, Dec. 30, 1918.

2. "Smoker Boxing Card Indicates Comeback Here," *Albuquerque Morning Journal*, Mar. 27, 1919.

3. "Millions of New Boxing Fans Made by War Training," *The New York Evening World*, Jan. 18, 1919.

4. "Prize Fight Prevented," *Pueblo Chieftain*, May 10, 1918.

5. "First Hurley Club Smoker Big Success," *Silver City Enterprise*, Aug. 29, 1919.

6. "Myrick Wins from Champion Chavez," *Carbon City News*, Nov. 8, 1919.

7. "Rivera Looks Good as Fans See Him Work," *Duluth News Tribune*, Dec. 17, 1921.

8. "Prize Fighters in Fast Bouts," *Clovis Journal*, Sept. 4, 1919.

9. "Fight Was Cancelled," *Roswell Daily Record*, Aug. 7, 1919.

10. "Roswell Lightweight Gets Decision Over Mike Baca at Clovis," *Albuquerque Morning Journal*, Aug. 7, 1919.

11. "Tartar Meets Tartar," *Clovis Journal*, Aug. 7, 1919.

12. "Prize Fighters in Fast Bouts," *Clovis Journal*, Sept. 4, 1919.

13. "Hill Wins Bout with Connolly in 10 Rounds," *Roswell Daily Record*, April 20, 1921.

14. "Mike Baca Leaves to Fort Bayard to Meet Connolly Next Monday," *Santa Fe New Mexican*, July 15, 1921.

15. "Decision Handed Baca by Referee at Fight Program," *Albuquerque Evening Herald*, Sept. 10, 1921.

16. "Baca Holds Moore to Dead Heat in Furious Battle," *Santa Fe New Mexican*, May 6, 1924.

17. "Lanning Wins Decision, Gives Baca Severe Lacing," *Santa Fe New Mexican*, May 24, 1924.

18. "Benny Cordova Again After Bout with Waugh," *El Paso Morning Times*, Feb. 8, 1919.

19. "The Squared Circle," *Tucson Daily Citizen*, Jan. 7, 1920.

20. "The Squared Circle," *Tucson Daily Citizen*, April 4, 1920.

21. "Benny Cordova Again After Bout with Waugh," *El Paso Morning Times*, Feb. 8, 1919.

22. "Boxing," *El Paso Morning Times*, July 31, 1919.

23. "Mackey's Tearing Left Makes Him Winner of Bout," *Albuquerque Morning Journal*, Sept. 2, 1919.

24. "The Squared Circle," *Tucson Daily Citizen*, Jan. 11, 1920.

25. "The Squared Circle," *Tucson Daily Citizen*, Mar. 28, 1920.

26. "Benny Cordova Visits Friends in El Paso," *El Paso Times*, April 11, 1920.

27. "Boxing," *El Paso Morning Times*, May 4, 1920.

28. Compiled from interviews with Benny's sons, Raoul and Armando.

29. "The Squared Circle," *Tucson Daily Citizen,* Mar. 28, 1921.

30. Ibid.

31. "Waugh and Cordova Fight is a Draw," *Albuquerque Evening Herald*, Mar. 31, 1921.

32. "The Squared Circle," *Tucson Daily Citizen,* Mar. 28, 1921.

33. "Bout Off When Doctor States Cordova Unfit to Enter Ring," *Santa Fe New Mexican,* Sept. 6, 1921.

34. "Benny Chavez, Old Favorite, to Box for Bankers," *Albuquerque Morning Journal*, Aug. 31, 1919.

35. "Colorado Boxer Shows Well at Times But Outpointed by Local Boy," *Salt Lake City Tribune*, Feb. 26, 1918.

36. "Benny Chavez Is Rematched with Frisco Battler," *Albuquerque Morning Journal*, Sept. 13, 1919.

37. "Big Stake Hangs on Monday Night Bout for Benny Chavez," *Albuquerque Morning Journal*, Sept. 19, 1919.

38. "Benny Chavez Is Rematched with Frisco Battler," *Albuquerque Morning Journal*, Sept. 13, 1919.

39. "Young Sol Kayos Benny Chavez with Clean Knockout in Fifth," *Trinidad Chronicle News*, Sept. 7, 1920.

40. "Boxers Putting in Hard Licks of Training for Labor Day," *Trinidad Chronicle News*, Sept. 2, 1920.

41. "Benny Chavez Wins Decision Over Sailor Gonzales," *Albuquerque Evening Herald*, Nov. 29, 1921.

42. "Boxers Are Set for All-Star Card at Armory," *Albuquerque Morning Journal*, Jan. 18, 1922.

43. "Kramer Wins Vernon Bout," *Los Angeles Times*, Dec. 18, 1918.

44. "Cauliflower Alley Notes," *Los Angeles Times*, Feb. 8, 1931.

45. "Jack Dempsey and Walter Caldwell Renew Old Friendship," *Denver Post*, Aug. 10, 1921.

46. "Caldwell Wins Over Sandoval," *Colfax County Stockman*, July 12, 1919.

47. "Sport Talk," *The Clayton Citizen*, Aug. 21, 1919.

48. "Springer Glove Slinger Is Signed for A. L. Smoker," *Springer Times*, Oct. 9, 1919.

49. "Earl Mohan Arrives from Arizona,"*El Paso Morning Times*, Sept. 4, 1919.

50. "Springer Glove Slinger Is Signed for A. L. Smoker," *Springer Times*, Oct. 9, 1919.

51. "Caldwell Looks Like a Dangerous Opponent for George When They Meet," *Albuquerque Morning Journal*, Oct. 17, 1919.

52. "Caldwell Wins by Knockout in Final Chapter," *Albuquerque Morning Journal*, Oct. 19, 1919.

53. "Caldwell Put the 'Kayo' on Sparks," *The Clayton Citizen*, Nov. 6, 1919.

54. "Kid George Expects to Make Champion of Walter Caldwell," *El Paso Morning Times*, Nov. 27, 1919.

55. "Caldwell Wins Boxing Contest in Fourth Round," *Albuquerque Morning Journal*, Jan. 2, 1920.

56. "New Mexico Middleweight Invades California," *El Paso Morning Times*, Jan. 13, 1920.

57. "The Squared Circle," *Tucson Daily Citizen*, Jan. 23, 1920.

58. "Cliff Has Hard Nut to Crack," *Los Angeles Times*, Jan. 30, 1920.

59. "Caldwell Signs for Boxing Bout in Albuquerque," *Albuquerque Morning Journal*, Feb. 15, 1920.

60. "Double Main Event Tonight," *Los Angeles Times*, Apr. 27, 1920.

61. "Kruvosky Wins by Craftiness," *Los Angeles Times*, Apr. 28, 1920.

62. "Boxing," *El Paso Morning Times*, Apr. 30, 1920.

63. "All of Omaha Fights Are Draws," *Omaha World-Herald*, June 17, 1920.

64. "'Caldwell Will Defeat Downey or I'm One Poor Picker,' Says Jones," *Columbus Dispatch*, July 1, 1920.

65. "Rooney-Green Bout Will Be Held May 17th," *Albuquerque Morning Journal*, Apr. 27, 1920.

66. "Caldwell-Shade Bout Called a Draw," *Raton Range*, July 5, 1921.

67. "Boxing By Hy Schneider," *El Paso Times*, Aug. 11, 1921.

68. "Manley Defeats Caldwell Easily in 12-Round Bout," *Rocky Mountain News*, Aug. 13, 1921.

69. "Caldwell Takes Two Rounds of Pounding by Battling Ortega," Associated Press, Aug. 25, 1921.

70. "Boxing in Juarez This Afternoon," *El Paso Times*, Oct. 9, 1921.

71. "Caldwell Here to Train for Gorilla Jones," *Albuquerque Morning Journal*, Nov. 3, 1921.

72. "Faatola Falls Easy Victim to Caldwell," *Springer Tribune*, Apr. 28, 1922.

Chapter 13

1. "'Knockout King' of Arizona Has Arrived in City," *Albuquerque Morning Journal*, June 15, 1923.

2. "Editorial," *Santa Fe New Mexican*, July 26, 1912.

3. "Jockey Hamilton Puts K.O. on Billy Ashmore," *The Clayton Citizen*, Mar. 11, 1920.

4. "End of Boxing Not Object of New Ordinance," *Albuquerque Morning Journal*, Aug. 7, 1920.

5. "Rivera Awarded Decision Over Sol at Armory," *Albuquerque Morning Journal*, Apr. 11, 1922.

6. "Prize Fight Is Sad Spectacle, Crowd Is Good," *Magee's Independent*, Feb. 16, 1923.

7. "Fighters Fight Fair Else They Will Be Barred," *Albuquerque Morning Journal*, Mar. 1, 1923.

8. "Ghostly Punch Lays Chihuahua Prone on Mat," *Albuquerque Journal*, Dec. 21, 1929.

9. "Dempsey to Hunt Deer, Bear, Lion with Five Huge Dogs," *Santa Fe New Mexican*, Nov. 26, 1923.

10. "Royal Entertainment for Vets Banquet and Smoker," *Roswell Daily Record*, Dec. 31, 1924.

11. "Santa Fe Boy Champion of Ukulele Land," *Santa Fe New Mexican*, Jan. 17, 1923.

12. "Vasquez–Bramer Battle Goes Twelve Fast and Hard Rounds," *Albuquerque Morning Journal*, Oct. 18, 1924.

13. "Vasquez and M'Coy Fight to Draw and Chavez Beats Baca But Judges Think Otherwise," *Albuquerque Morning Journal*, Dec. 5, 1924.

14. "Griffin Trains at Fort, Nick Mortio at San Marcial for Coming Main Event," *El Paso Times*, Oct. 9, 1925.

15. "Joe Rivers Gets Kid Mortio for 10-Round Match on Ft. Bliss Card," *El Paso Times*, Jan. 16, 1922.

16. "Mortio Outruns Kid Buck in 15 Round Sprint in Squared Circle," *El Paso Times*, June 17, 1921.

17. "Mixed Sports Notes," *El Paso Times*, Jan. 20, 1922.

18. "Mortio Beats Young Rivers," *El Paso Times*, Mar. 7, 1922.

19. "Joe the Wop Is After Scalp of Sol or Rivera," *Albuquerque Morning Journal*, Apr. 6, 1922.

20. "Eddie Mack Has Some String of K.O.'s Himself," *Santa Fe New Mexican*, July 11, 1922.

21. Ibid.

22. "D.A.C. Will Wind Up Saturday Night When Amateur Boxers Put On Final Wild Scramble," *Denver Post*, Jan. 28, 1922.

23. "Safford Refuses to Give Decision on Baca-Herrera Fight," *Santa Fe New Mexican*, July 13, 1922.

24. "Mack Wins by Technical K.O. Over Demon in Tough Battle," *Santa Fe New Mexican*, Oct. 3, 1922.

25. "Flash's Seconds Toss Sponge; Mortio Kisses Canvas 13 Times," *Santa Fe New Mexican*, Feb. 14, 1923.

26. "Mack Politely Declines Bout with J. Rivers," *Albuquerque Morning Journal*, Mar. 18, 1923.

27. "Rivers and M'Carthy Are to Clash Tonight in First Title Bout," Apr. 2, 1923.

28. "Jose Rivers Is Off Card June 19," *Albuquerque Morning Journal*, June 8, 1923.

29. "Eddie Mack, New Mexico's Bid for the Featherweight Title," *Albuquerque Morning Journal*, June 11, 1923.

30. "Mack Adds Newly's Name to Growing String of Kayo's," *Santa Fe New Mexican*, Aug. 15, 1923.

31. "Eddie Mack and Joe Coffee to Clash Tonight at the Armory," *Albuquerque Morning Journal*, Aug. 22, 1923.

32. "Sport Dope by Daniel S. Ortiz," *Santa Fe New Mexican*, Nov. 24, 1923.

33. "Mack Sends Rivers Back to Steady Job as Iceman," *Santa Fe New Mexican*, Dec. 28, 1923.

34. "Eddie Mack Beats Game Little Jose Rivers by Technical K.O. After Ten Whirlwind Rounds," *Albuquerque Morning Journal*, Dec. 28, 1924.

35. Ibid.

36. "Mack Sends Rivers Back to Steady Job as Iceman," *Santa Fe New Mexican*, Dec. 28, 1923.

Chapter 14

1. "Dempsey's Home Town Produces Another Star," Associated Press, Feb. 4, 1924.

2. "Many Bouts to Be Staged for Pugdom's Fans," *Albuquerque Morning Journal*, Mar. 20, 1923.

3. "The Alibi Days Have Passed in Fighting Game," *Albuquerque Morning Journal*, Feb. 19, 1923.

4. "Eddie Mack, New Mexico's Bid for the Featherweight Title," *Albuquerque Morning Journal*, June 11, 1923.

5. "Mack May Fight Dundee Here in Spring," *Albuquerque Morning Journal*, Jan. 1, 1924.

6. "Vasquez Eager for a Chance to Battle Mack in Albuquerque," *Albuquerque Morning Journal*, Feb. 10, 1924.

7. "Mack Pulls Wildcat's Claws," *Santa Fe New Mexican*, Feb. 13, 1923.

8. Ibid.

9. "Joe the Wop Takes Snooze in Sixth Round With Mack," *Santa Fe New Mexican*, Mar. 5, 1924.

10. "Expect Bramer to Win Easily — Shower's Dope," *Santa Fe New Mexican*, June 5, 1924.

11. "Mack's Seconds Throw in Towel at End of Fifth," *Albuquerque Morning Journal*, June 13, 1924.

12. From interviews with the Quintana family, 1980s–1990s.

13. "Bramer Wins by Technical Knockout at End of Fifth," *Santa Fe New Mexican*, June 13, 1924.

14. From interviews with the Quintana family, 1980s–1990s.

15. "Rivers Better Than Bramer Is Mack's Belief," *Albuquerque Morning Journal*, June 19, 1924.

16. "Alamosa Flash Forces Papke to Quit in the Seventh After Taking Innumerable Wallops," *Albuquerque Morning Journal*, Aug. 19, 1924.

17. "Mack Handed Bramer Lacing," *Santa Fe New Mexican*, Mar. 2, 1925.

18. "Mack Given Foul Decision Over Bramer in Ninth After Queer Business in Fourth," *Albuquerque Morning Journal*, Mar. 6, 1925.

19. Ibid.

20. "Mack Makes Good Claim to Feather Crown of Southwest," *Santa Fe New Mexican*, Dec. 24, 1925.

21. "Eddie Mack to Devote Entire Time to Boxing," *Albuquerque Morning Journal*, June 14, 1925.

22. "Cervantes Had Trunk Full of Write-ups of His Prowess," *Santa Fe New Mexican*, June 22, 1925.

23. "Nobe Hot Stuff, Lucio's Verdict," *Santa Fe New Mexican*, June 24, 1925.

24. "Will Nobe Turn Out to Be a Rivers or a Bramer?" *Santa Fe New Mexican*, June 25, 1925.

25. "Mack Wins Referee's Verdict," *Santa Fe New Mexican*, June 26, 1925.

26. "Mack Hands Bramer Neat Lacing in Rain," *Santa Fe New Mexican*, July 6, 1925.

27. "Eddie Mack and Pete Loya Draw," *El Paso Times*, Aug. 19, 1925.

28. "Mack Says He Was Lucky to Save His Life," *Albuquerque Morning Journal*, Aug. 13, 1925.

29. "Burrowed Out, by Dan Burrows," *Albuquerque Morning Journal*, Jan. 16, 1926.

30. "Fight 12 Slashing, Slambang Rounds to Popular Draw," *Santa Fe New Mexican*, Feb. 17, 1926.

31. "Mack Gets Referee's Award in Slugging Match With Long," *Santa Fe New Mexican*, May 18, 1926.

32. "Fight Ends With Mansweller Taking Toll of Ten on Canvas," *Santa Fe New Mexican*, Feb. 9, 1927.

33. "Mack Pleased to Meet Mike He Declares," *Albuquerque Journal*, Jan. 20, 1927.

34. "I'll Show Why Eddie Has Been Ducking Him For Last Four Years, Says Vasquez," *Santa Fe New Mexican*, Sept. 16, 1927.

35. "Vasquez Holds Mack to Draw," *Santa Fe New Mexican*, Sept. 17, 1927.

36. "Mack's Showing Against Terris Boosts Stock Up," *Santa Fe New Mexican*, May 17, 1928.

37. "Mack Has Been Dodging Him, Sandow's Idea," *Santa Fe New Mexican*, Apr. 11, 1928.

38. "Mack Winner of Decision Over Sandow," *Santa Fe New Mexican*, Apr. 18, 1928.

39. "Mack Winner of Decision Over Sammy Sandow," *Albuquerque Journal*, Apr. 18, 1928.

40. From interviews with the Quintana family, 1980s–1990s.

41. "Murdock Beats Mack, Takes 10 of 12 Rounds," *Albuquerque Journal*, June 20, 1928.

42. "Murdock Wins, Fight Delayed When Battlers Insist on Pay," *Santa Fe New Mexican*, June 20, 1928.

43. "Murdock Shows Assassin Stuff," *Santa Fe New Mexican*, Aug. 21, 1928.

44. "Murdock Gets Down to Biz," *Santa Fe New Mexican*, Aug. 16, 1928.

45. "Mack's Foul Is Cause of Loss to Ben Chavez," *Albuquerque Journal*, Oct. 18, 1928.

Chapter 15

1. "Morgan and Mack Finish Training," *Rocky Mountain News*, Jan. 7, 1929.

2. "Morgan in Denver Today for Tuesday Go," *Rocky Mountain News*, Jan. 3, 1929.

3. "Morgan's First Workout in Denver Gym," *Rocky Mountain News*, Jan. 5, 1929.

4. "Morgan and Mack Finish Training," *Rocky Mountain News*, Jan. 7, 1929.

5. "Tod Morgan and Eddie Mack Ready for Fistic Clash," *Rocky Mountain News*, Jan. 8, 1929.

6. "As Curley Grieve Sees It — Mack Has Much at Stake, May Retire If Beaten," *Rocky Mountain News*, Jan. 8, 1929.

7. "As Curley Grieve Sees It: Step Forward, Mr. Money Man," *Rocky Mountain News*, Jan. 11, 1929.

8. "Mack Socks Out Victory Over Champion Morgan," *Rocky Mountain News*, Jan. 1929.

9. Ibid.

10. Ibid.

11. Ibid.

12. Ibid.

13. "As Curley Grieve Sees It: Step Forward, Mr. Money Man," *Rocky Mountain News*, Jan. 11, 1929.

14. "Tod Morgan's Crown Casts No Fear," *Rocky Mountain News*, Apr. 19, 1932.

15. "Bridges Easy Job for Mack," *Santa Fe New Mexican*, Feb. 9, 1929.

16. "Tod Morgan's Crown Casts No Fear," *Rocky Mountain News*, Apr. 19, 1932.

17. Ibid.

18. "As Curley Grieve Sees It — Eddie Mack at Crossroads," *Rocky Mountain News*, Apr. 20, 1929.

19. "Mack and Morgan Colllide in Auditorium Tuesday," *Rocky Mountain News*, Apr. 21 1929.

20. "As Curley Grieve Sees It — Mack is Topic of Hour," *Rocky Mountain News*, Apr. 25, 1929.

21. "Morgan and Mack Battle 10 Sensational Rounds to Draw," *Rocky Mountain News*, Apr. 24, 1929.

22. Ibid.

23. "Cauliflower Alley Notes," *Los Angeles Times*, July 28, 1929.

24. "Hess May Face Winner," *Los Angeles Times*, July 11, 1929.

25. "Eddie Mack in Knockout Win," *Los Angeles Times*, July 17, 1929.

26. "Cauliflower Alley Notes," *Los Angeles Times*, July 28, 1929.

27. "Eddie Mack Knocks Out Doc Snell in Third," *Los Angeles Times*, July 31, 1929.

28. "Rabbit Punches by Paul Lowry: A New Ring Hero," *Los Angeles Times*, Aug. 1, 1929.

29. "The Lee Side of L.A. by Lee Shippey," *Los Angeles Times*, Aug. 26, 1929.

30. "Eddie Mack Rates Boxing Second to His Education," *Syracuse Herald*, Sept. 7, 1929.

31. "Goldie Hess to Be Given Acid Test at Hands of Eddie Mack at Olympic Tuesday," *Los Angeles Times*, Sept. 15, 1929.

32. "Mack Whips Hess in Slashing Go at Olympic," *Los Angeles Times*, Sept. 18, 1929.

33. Ibid.

34. "Crowd Cheers Mack in Front of Journal," *Albuquerque Journal*, Sept. 28, 1929.

35. "Canzoneri Stops Eddie Mack in 8th Round," *Chicago Daily Tribune*, Sept. 28, 1929.

36. Ibid.

37. "Tony Canzoneri Defeats Eddie Mack — Denver By Is On Even Terms Most of Fight," *United Press International*, Sept. 28, 1929.

38. "Crowd Cheers Mack in Front of Journal," *Albuquerque Journal*, Sept. 28, 1929.

39. "Mack Defeats World Champ Has No Crown," *Santa Fe New Mexican*, Nov. 27, 1929.

40. "The Lancer by Harry Carr," *Los Angeles Times*, Nov. 28, 1929.

41. "Mack's First Knock-out in a Local Bout," *Santa Fe New Mexican*, Oct. 4, 1929.

42. "Mack Forced to Pass Up Return with Italian," *Albuquerque Journal*, Oct. 15, 1929.

43. "Tod Morgan Seeks Revenge for Previous Defeat in Facing Eddie Mack Tuesday Night," *Los Angeles Times*, Nov. 24, 1929.

44. "Mack Defeats World Champ, Has No Crown," Associated Press, Nov. 27, 1929.

45. "Times His Punches Like a Music Master," *Los Angeles Times*, Feb. 23, 1930.

46. "Three Star Boxers Are Ready to Show Wares on D.A.V. Card," *Rocky Mountain News*, Apr. 2, 1930.

47. "Mack, Murdock Beat Invading Boxers," *Rocky Mountain News*, Apr. 25, 1930.

48. "Mack Given Workout Before a Well-Packed House," *Santa Fe New Mexican*, May 7, 1930.

49. "Brown Is Winner Over Bernasconi," *New York Times*, July 24, 1930.

50. "Roth and Mack Will Shun New York," *Seattle Daily Times*, Aug. 26, 1930.

51. "Morgan Beats Mack; May Do Battle with Singer," *Seattle Daily Times*, Aug. 30, 1930.

52. "Singer Meets Mack Tonight in Nontitle Bout at Stadium," *Chicago Daily Tribune*, Oct. 14, 1930.

53. "Al Singer Whips Eddie Mack in 10 Rounds," *Chicago Daily Tribune*, Oct. 15, 1930.

54. "Payne to Collide Tonight in Olympic Main Event," *Los Angeles Times*, Nov. 25, 1930.

55. "Mack and Payne Box Fast Draw," *Los Angeles Times*, Nov. 26, 1930.

Chapter 16

1. "The Lee Side of L.A. by Lee Shippey," *Los Angeles Times*, Aug. 26, 1929.

2. "Terse Tips by Bert Bliss," *New Mexico State Tribune*, July 2, 1927.

3. "Marchi Makes Punching Bag Out of Dynamite," *Santa Fe New Mexican*, Feb. 9, 1927.

4. Interviews with Timo Sanchez, 1990s.

5. Ibid.

6. "Dynamite Tommy Sanchez Returns to Ring in Bout Next Week with Coloradan," *Durango Herald*, Sept. 9, 1932.

7. "Colima in 50 Battles Without Defeat in Last Two Years," *Santa Fe New Mexican*, Nov. 13, 1929.

8. "Another Card for the Legion," *Gallup Independent*, Feb. 27, 1931.

9. "Chavez Wins the Decision," *Albuquerque Journal*, Sept. 24, 1929."

10. "Murdock Gives Sid Terris Bad Beating in 12," *Albuquerque Journal*, Oct. 5, 1929.

11. "Murdock, Chavez Fight Draw," *Albuquerque Journal*, Oct. 18, 1929."

12. "Carlisle, Fight Promoter, Says He Welcomes Investigation, As Mayor Bars Him, Chavez From Ring," *Albuquerque Journal*, Oct. 19, 1929.

13. "Chavez Takes Decision Over Benny Chavez," *Rocky Mountain News*, Oct. 26.

14. "Sports Comment," *Gallup Herald*, Feb. 24, 1930.

15. "Another Card for the Legion," *Gallup Independent*, Feb. 27, 1931.

16. "Julio and Chavez Go Ends in Draw," *Gallup Independent*, Mar. 27, 1931.

17. "Alamosa Battler Dodges Bout with Gallup Ring Idol," *Gallup Independent*, Apr. 8, 1931.

18. Interviews with Timo Sanchez, 1990s.

19. "Benny Chavez, Boxer, Is Shot While Prowling Around a Home," *Albuquerque Journal*, Apr. 18, 1931.

20. "Interview with Louis L'Amour," TheArmsFamily.com, Sept. 1981.

21. "Murdock Matched with Frankie Stetson," *Albuquerque Journal*, Jan. 8, 1930.

22. "Furious Bout Sure When Two Eddie Clash," *Santa Fe New Mexican*, Sept. 5, 1928.

23. Interviews with George Marchi, 1990s.

24. "Murdock Gets Decision at Judges' Hands," *Santa Fe New Mexican*, Mar. 20, 1929.

25. "Murdock Anxious to Fight Again in Albuquerque," *Albuquerque Journal*, Aug. 18, 1930.

Chapter 17

1. "Local Wrestlers Lose Bouts with Outside Matmen," *Las Vegas Daily Optic*, Aug. 25, 1933.

2. "Around with Abe — By Abe Pollock," *Rocky Mountain News*, Oct. 13, 1932.

3. "Bass Snaps Jaw of Eddie Mack," *Philadelphia Inquirer*, May 5, 1931.

4. Ibid.

5. "Kane Backed by Big Record," *Santa Fe New Mexican*, Mar. 9, 1932.

6. "Mack Seeks Crown," *Albuquerque Journal*, Mar. 14, 1932.

7. "Fast Prelims on Fight Card; Mack Wins Three-Roudn Fiasco," *Santa Fe New Mexican*, Aug. 19, 1932.

8. "Mickey Cohen Wins Unpopular Decision Over Eddie Mack," *Rocky Mountain News*, Sept. 15, 1932.

9. "Eddie Mack Batters Lee to Decision," *Rocky Mountain News*, Sept. 28, 1932

10. "Mickey Cohen Wins by Knockout," *Rocky Mountain News*, Oct. 12, 1932.

11. "New Class of Boxers Being Produced Here," *El Paso Times*, Dec. 24, 1930.

12. "Pena Asks Return Fight with Ortiz," *Raton Range*, Sept. 1, 1931.

13. Interviews with Jimmy Ortiz, 1990s.

14. "Clever Denver Ghetto Ghost Paralyzes Ortiz," *Santa Fe New Mexican*, July 22, 1933.

15. "Two Fighters at Rialto Out Without Being Hit," *Santa Fe New Mexican*, Dec. 16, 1932

16. "Chavez Wins Local Debut with Knockout," *Albuquerque Journal*, Sept. 9, 1933.

17. "Murdock Loses on Foul After Having a Lead," *Albuquerque Journal*, Jan. 5, 1929.

18. "Mack to Say His 'Adios' to Santa Fe with Gloves Tonight," *Santa Fe New Mexican*, May 23, 1929.

19. Interviews with George Marchi, 1980s–1990s.

20. Interviews with Buddy Serino, 1980s.

21. "Terse Tips by Bert Bliss," *New Mexico State Tribune*, Dec. 17, 1927.

22. "Boxing Contest Draws Large Audience," *Wagon Mound Tribune*, May 12, 1933.

23. "Former World Heavyweight Champion Here Last Night," *Santa Fe New Mexican*, July 31, 1931.

24. "Albuquerque Fighters to Show Wares Against Local Champs Here Thursday," *Santa Fe New Mexican*, Nov. 3, 1931.

25. Interviews with Timo Sanchez, 1990s.

26. "Ebon Pugs Who Wouldn't Fight in Ring Here for Money Battle Free on Street," *Santa Fe New Mexican*, Sept. 17, 1931.

27. "Sinn Fein 'Go' on Fistic Card Scheduled for Tuesday Night," *Santa Fe New Mexican*, Jan. 12, 1922.

28. "Athletic Club Gets Sendoff with Bout Card," *Albuquerque Evening Herald*, Sept. 20, 1923.

29. "Fast Ring and Mat Show Seen," *Roswell Morning Democrat*, Aug. 8, 1933.

30. "Among the Railroaders," *Clovis News Journal*, May 6, 1929.

31. "Charlie Cobb Rises Into Championship Status," *Roswell Morning Dispatch*, Jan. 5, 1929.

32. "Unintentional Foul Blow by Mathis Gives Decision to Span," *Clovis News Journal*, Aug. 2 1929.

33. "'Cullud' World Awaits Results of Boxing Bout at Carlsbad," *Roswell Morning Dispatch*, Jan. 17, 1929.

34. "Platter Fails to Open Up and Decision to Gross in a Drab Show," *Clovis News Journal*, Apr. 2, 1930.

35. "Rucker K.O.'D in First Round of Slow Card," *Clovis News Journal*, Aug. 7, 1931.

36. "Chico and Grubbs Fight to a Draw," *Tucumcari News*, Oct. 3, 1929.

37. "Tony Herrera Battles Milton Manguno," *El Paso Times*, Oct. 16, 1930.

38. "Tony Herrera Scores Quick Knockout Over Augie Pisano," *El Paso Times*, June 12, 1930.

39. "Boxers in Trim for Legion Card," *Gallup Independent*, Aug. 13 1931.

40. "A Large Audience Sees Contests," *Gallup Herald*, Feb. 23, 1924.

41. Interviews with the Chiaramontes, 1990s–2000s.

42. "Bobby Pins Guido First Two Falls," *Gallup Herald*, Mar. 7, 1925.

43. Interviews with the Chiaramontes, 1990s–2000s.

44. Ibid.

45. "J. Chiaramonte to Box Benny Chavez," *Gallup Independent*, Mar. 20, 1931.

46. "Zecca Gives Julio Chiaramonte Chance Pay Expenses with Bout," *Gallup Independent*, Aug. 20, 1931.

47. "Julio Chiaramonte Can't Accept Zecca Offer and Keep Standing," *Gallup Independent*, Aug. 24, 1931.

48. "Chiaramonte Wins by K.O. Over Visitor," *Gallup Independent*, Aug. 26, 1931.

49. "Chiaramonte Wins Over Ed Murdock," *Gallup Independent*, Aug. 24, 1932.

50. Ibid.

51. "Prize Fight Ends in Riot," *Gallup Independent*, Aug. 30, 1929.

52. "Riot Was Good While It Was Going — Murdock," *Albuquerque Journal*, Aug. 25, 1929.

53. Ibid.

54. "Sailor Jack Wins Easy Victory in Mat Match Against Masked Marvel," *Gallup Independent*, May 23, 1931.

55. "Developing Fistic Art in Farmington," *Farmington Republican*, Aug. 7, 1929.

Chapter 18

1. "Benny Chavez Was Greatest Boxer in Trinidad," *Trinidad Chronicle-News*, Feb. 8 1932.

2. "Rosenbloom Beats Silva in Uninteresting Bout," *Albuquerque Journal*, Dec. 21, 1932.

3. "Cantou K.O.'s Chavez in Eighth," *Albuquerque Journal*, July 12, 1933.

4. "Boxing Is Flop," *Albuquerque Journal*, Apr. 18, 1931.

5. Interviews with Joe Roybal, 1990s.

6. "Abie Chavez, Martin Fight to Close Draw," *Albuquerque Journal*, Oct. 28, 1933.

7. Interviews with the Cordovas, 1990s–2000s.

8. "Here's the Dope by Albert Reese," *Galveston News*, Jan. 27, 1939.

9. "Powell Knocks Out Mendez in Opening Round," *Albuquerque Journal*, Nov. 1, 1932.

10. "Hodges to Meet Chavez at Armory on December 17," *The Morning Las Vegan*, Dec. 11, 1934.

11. Interviews with Johnny Tapia, 2000s.

12. Interviews with Abic Chavez, Jr., 1990s–200s.

13. "Chavez Accepts Banter," *Durango Herald Democratic*, Jan. 11, 1933.

14. "Hildenbrand Meets Chaves in 10 Round Bout at Farmington," *Durango News*, Feb. 10, 1933.

15. "Santa Fe Boy Wins Mythical State Laurels," *Santa Fe New Mexican*, July 12, 1933.

16. "Cantou Signed for Bout with Abie Chavez," *Albuquerque Journal*, July 13, 1933.

17. "Cantou Is Told He Must Battle to Stay Champ," Abie Chavez's scrapbook, original source unknown, July 1933.

18. Ibid.

19. Ibid.

20. "Chavez Beats Cantou," *Albuquerque Journal*, Aug. 2, 1933.

21. "Acid Test for Abie in Fight with Mexican," *Albuquerque Journal*, Aug. 19, 1933.

22. Ibid.

23. "Chavez, Laredo Fight Furious Bout to a Draw," *Albuquerque Journal*, Aug. 24, 1933.

24. "Laredo Takes Chavez Fast Ten Rounds at St. Mike's," *Santa Fe New Mexican*, Oct. 10, 1933.

25. "Chavez, Murdock Fight for Bantam Title Tonight," *Lubbock Avalanche-Journal*, Jan. 12, 1934.

26. "Abie Chavez and Murdock Battle to Ten Round Draw," *Clovis News-Journal*, Mar. 8, 1934.

27. Interviews with Abie Chavez, Jr, 1990s–2000s.

28. "Abie Chavez Wins By Decision Over Laredo," *Albuquerque Journal*, June 20, 1934.

29. "Tony Wins Disputed Decision," *Albuquerque Journal*, July 10, 1934.

30. "Abe Chavez Is Victor Over Hildenbrand," *Farmington Times Hustler*, Aug. 24, 1934.

31. "Chavez Out to Put Quietus on El Paso Boxer," *Albuquerque Tribune*, Sept. 27, 1934.

32. "Boxing Fans Her See Abe Chavez Score K.O. Over Laredo," *Farmington Times Hustler*, Oct. 4, 1935.

33. "Legion Uncovers Boxer's Identity, Reveal Imposter," *Gallup Independent*, July 3, 1936.

34. "Chavez, Latin Fistic Firecracker, Favored Over Mullins," *Los Angeles Times*, July 3, 1936.

35. "Julio and Chavez Go Ends in Draw," *Gallup Independent*, Mar. 27, 1931.

36. "Chavez Wins Local Debut with Knockout," *Albuquerque Journal*, Sept. 9, 1933.

37. "Tony Chavez Beats Hildebrand," *Albuquerque Journal*, Sept. 27, 1933.

38. "Chavez Beats Jackson with Whirlwind Finish," *Albuquerque Journal*, Mar. 24, 1934.

39. "Martin Dives to Defeat Before Chavez," *Albuquerque Journal*, Apr. 26, 1934.

40. "Promoters of Fights, Wrestling Matches to Be Held Responsible," *Albuquerque Journal*, Apr. 31, 1934.

41. "Tony Chavez and Frankie Cantou in Disputed Draw," *Albuquerque Journal*, June 7, 1934.

42. "Tony Chavez to Shave to Satisfy Foeman for Monday Night," *Albuquerque Journal*, July 7, 1934.

43. "Tony Wins Disputed Decision," *Albuquerque Journal*, July 10, 1934.

44. "The Sports X-Ray by Bob Ray," *Los Angeles Times*, Dec. 16, 1935.

45. "Tony Chavez Gets His Chance," *Los Angeles Times*, Apr. 15, 1936.

46. "Odds Favor Tony Chavez," *Los Angeles Times*, July 2, 1936.

47. "Armstrong Is Loser on Foul in 8th," Associated Press, Dec. 4, 1936.

48. "Armstrong Stops Chavez in Tenth Round at Olympic," *Los Angeles Times*, Jan. 19, 1937.

49. "Rightmire Boxes Chavez in Legion Boxing Feature," *Los Angeles Times*, Feb. 28, 1937.

50. "Chavez Whips Rightmire in Legion Ring," *Los Angeles Times*, Mar. 6, 1937.

51. "Armstrong Stops Chavez in First," *The New York Times*, Dec. 7, 1937.

52. "Chavez Gets Decision Over Davis in Home Town," *Albuquerque Journal*, Mar. 17, 1938.

53. "Hansford Beats Chavez," *Los Angeles Times*, Oct. 8, 1938.

54. "Hansford, Chavez Draw," *Los Angeles Times*, Nov. 26, 1938.

55. "Tony Chavez Captures Decision Over Crouch," *Los Angeles Times*, Jan. 25, 1939.

56. "Old Time Sporting Friends Come to Aid of Benny Chavez," *Trinidad Chronicle News*, Feb. 9, 1932.

57. Interviews with Lalo Trujillo, 2000s.

58. "Ocate Boxing Contest One of the Best," *Wagon Mound Tribune*, Feb. 10, 1933.

59. Ibid.

60. "Big Boxing Contest Is Billed for September Second," *Wagon Mound Tribune*, Aug. 25, 1933.

61. "Another Boxing Contest in Local Arena," *Wagon Mound Tribune*, Mar. 17, 1933.

62. "Full House Enjoys Cantou-Lara Contest," *Wagon Mound Tribune*, Apr. 21, 1933.

63. "Cantou Is Told He Must Battle to Stay Champ," Abie Chavez's scrapbook, original source unknown, July 1933.

64. Interviews with Timo Sanchez, 1990s.

65. Interviews with Emilio Cantou, 2000s.

66. Private papers of the Cantou Family.

67. "Series of Bouts Draw Good Cards," *Silver City Enterprise*, Apr. 16, 1937.

68. "Firpo No Match for Midget Mexico," *El Paso Times*, Nov. 24, 1941.

Chapter 19

1. "New Ring Card Here; Martinez, Conqueror of Gorilla Jones, Manley, on Olympic Bill," *Los Angeles Times*, Nov. 25, 1934.

2. Interviews with Joe Roybal, 1990s.

3. Ibid.

4. "Martinez Stops Kid Barger in Seventh Round," *Ogden Standard*, Aug. 25, 1933.

5. "Martinez Wins Bout at Armory With Guerrero," *The Morning Las Vegan*, Oct. 2, 1934.

6. "New Ring Card Here," *Los Angeles Times*, Nov. 25, 1934.

7. "Martinez Is Winner Over L.A. Fighter," *Rocky Mountain News*, Jan. 22, 1935.

8. "Lewis Wins Close Decision Over Martinez," *Rocky Mountain News*, Mar. 14, 1935.

9. "Knockout Blows Feature Fight on Armory Card," *Las Vegas Daily Optic*, Apr. 23, 1935.

10. "Martinez Wins from Carter Without Much Trouble," *Las Vegas Daily Optic*, Dec. 14, 1935.

11. "Emelio Martinez Derrota a Carter en Cinco Asaltos," *Mora County Star*, Dec. 19 1935.

12. "Colorado Boy Bests Negro in Thriller," *Rocky Mountain News*, Jan. 30, 1936.

13. Ibid.

14. "Never Heard of Matthews," *St. Louis Post-Dispatch*, Mar. 27, 1936.

15. "Barth at 10–7 Over Latin," *Los Angeles Times*, Sept. 3, 1936.

16. "Martinez Outpointed by Lewis," *St. Louis Post-Dispatch*, May 5, 1937.

17. "Emilio Martinez Wins Kayo Over Lowell Sporland," *Santa Fe New Mexican*, Sept. 11, 1937.

Chapter 20

1. "Emilio Martinez Wins Kayo Over Lowell Sporland," *Santa Fe New Mexican*, Sept. 11, 1937.

2. "Laredo Takes Chavez Fast Ten Rounds at St. Mike's," *Santa Fe New Mexican*, Oct. 10, 1933.

3. "Grudge Fight to Headline," *Santa Fe New Mexican*, Nov. 16, 1935.

4. "Commission Halts Lions' Boxing Match," *Santa Fe New Mexican*, Mar. 12, 1936.

5. "Murdock Wins Easily Over Colima," *Santa Fe New Mexican*, Apr. 5, 1933.

6. "2 Good Fight Programs Here Early in Week," *Clovis News Journal*, Oct. 10, 1936.

7. "Grubbs to Fight Garcia at Jungleland Tonight," *Clovis News Journal*, Oct. 13, 1936.

8. "Apologizing for Facetious Name Used for Boxer," *Las Vegas Daily Optic*, Feb. 7 1932.

9. "The Labor Day Boxing," *Estancia News Herald*, Sept. 9, 1937.

10. "Negro Battler Is Winner Over Babe Colima in Fast Go," *Las Vegas Daily Optic*, Apr. 19, 1934.

11. "Tate Is Winner of Fight," *Las Vegas Daily Optic*, May 16, 1934.

12. "News of Texas," *The Ring*, Oct. 1941.

13. "Talk with Julio Chiaramonte Invigorating as Tub of Spinach," *Gallup Independent*, Apr. 11, 1936.

14. "Chiaramonte Loses Decision to Negro," *Gallup Independent*, Apr. 16, 1936.

15. Interviews with Nardine Chiaramonte, 2000s.

16. "Boney Smashes Out Decision After Downed 3 Times by Foe," *Gallup Independent*, Dec. 15, 1936.

17. Interviews with Nardine Chiaramonte, 2000s.

18. "Mull and Waters Tangle Tonight on Aguayo-Clingman Fight Card," *Gallup Independent*, Aug. 4, 1931.

19. "Sport Talkies by Kay Lewis," *El Paso Times*, June 5, 1931.

20. "The Armistice Day Boxing," *Estancia News Herald*, Nov. 10, 1938.

21. "The Fights Saturday Night," *Estancia News Herald*, Sept. 29, 1938.

22. "Capacity Crowd Sees Ryan Decision Trammel," *Clovis News Journal*, Apr. 21, 1936.

23. "Record Enrollment in Boxing," *Clovis News Journal*, Jan. 29, 1937.

24. "Scrapping Saxophonist Kisses Mat," *Santa Fe New Mexican*, Feb. 10, 1930.

25. "Boxing Tournament Opens at St. Michael's Gym," *Santa Fe New Mexican*, Apr. 9, 1931.

26. "Amateur Boxing Tournament Under A.A.U. Rules," *Albuquerque Journal*, Dec. 23, 1931.

27. "Russell to Teach Dempsey's Style of Fighting to Golden Gloves," *Clovis News Journal*, Jan. 17, 1937.

Finales

1. "Benny Chavez Was Greatest Boxer in Trinidad History," *Trinidad News Chronicle*, Feb. 8, 1932.

2. Benny Chavez's scrapbook, Carnegie Library, Trinidad, Colo.

3. "Benny Chavez Survives at Hospital After Plunge in Path of City Bus," *Trinidad Chronicle News*, Jan. 20, 1932.

4. Interviews with Meliton Cordoba, 2000s.

5. "Bobby Waugh, Brilliant Texas Lightweight, Might Have Won Belt, With Capable Manager," *El Paso Times*, Mar. 5, 1923.

6. Interviews with Abie Chavez, Jr., 1990s–2000s.

7. Ibid.

8. "Wagon Mound Boxer Who Was Champ in Ring Comes Back From War Area as Champion in Battle on Germans," *Las Vegas Daily Optic*, January 10, 1945.

9. "Objects to Telephone Service, Shot by Cop," Associated Press, Aug. 10, 1943.

10. Interviews with Joe Roybal, 1990s.

Bibliography

Periodicals

Akron Weekly Pioneer Press (Colorado)
Alamogordo News
Alamosa Journal (Colorado)
Albuquerque Citizen
Albuquerque Evening Herald
Albuquerque Herald
Albuquerque Journal
Albuquerque Morning Democrat
Albuquerque Morning Journal
Albuquerque Tribune
Albuquerque Weekly Citizen
Associated Press
Bayfield Blade
The Belen News
Belen Tribune
The Black Range
Brainerd Daily Dispatch (Minnesota)
Canadian Press
Carbon City News
Carlsbad Argus
Carlsbad Current
Carlsbad Current-Argus Colfax County Stockman
The Carrizozo Outlook
Chicago Defender
Chicago Tribune
The Cimarron Citizen
Cimarron News
Cimarron News & Press
The Clayton Citizen
The Clayton News
Cleveland Plain Dealer
Clovis Journal
Clovis New Mexico Evening News-Journal
Clovis News
Clovis News-Journal
Colorado Springs Daily Gazette
Colorado Transcripts
Columbus Courier
Columbus Daily Courier
Columbus Mirror
Columbus Weekly Courier
Creede Candle
Daily New Mexican

Dallas Morning News
Dallas Weekly Herald
Deming Graphic
Deming Headlight
Deming Herald & Lake Valley Herald
Denver News
Denver Post
Eddy County Citizen
Eddy County News
Eddy Weekly Current
El Fenix
El Paso Herald
El Paso Morning Times
El Paso Times
Ely Record (Nevada)
Estancia News-Herald
Fairplay Flume (Colorado)
Farley Reporter
Farmington Daily Times
Farmington Republican
Farmington Times Hustler
Fort Bayard Athletic Association
Fort Bayard News
Fort Sumner Leader
The Fort Sumner Review
Fort Worth Star-Telegram
Gallup Gleaner
Gallup Herald
Gallup Independent
The Grant Review
Hobbs News-Sun
Lake Valley New Era
Las Cruces Citizen
Las Cruces Daily News
Las Cruces Sun
Las Cruces Sun-News
The Las Vegan
Las Vegas Daily Gazette
Las Vegas Daily Optic
Las Vegas Optic & Livestock Grower
Las Vegas Review Journal
Lordsburg Liberal
Los Alamos Skyliner-News
Los Angeles Citizen-News
Los Angeles Examiner

Los Angeles Mirror
Los Angeles Times
The Lovington Leader
Lubbock Avalanche-Journal
Magee's Independent
McKinley County Republican
The Melrose News
Mora County Patriot
Mora County Star
The Morning Las Vegan
Mountainair Independent
National Police Gazette
Nevada State Journal
The New Mexican
New Mexico State Tribune
New York Clipper
New York Herald
The New York Times
Oakland Tribune
Portales Valley News
Raton Daily Range
Raton Observer
Raton Range
Raton Range and Raton Evening Gazette
Raton Reporter
Raton Weekly Range
Record Journal of Douglas County (Colorado)
Reno Evening Gazette
Reno Gazette-Journal
Ring Magazine
Rio Grande Republican
Rocky Mountain News (Colorado)
Roswell Daily Record
Roswell Evening News
Roswell Morning Dispatch
Roswell Record
Ruidoso News
Sacramento Bee
Sacramento Union
San Antonio Express-News
San Antonio Light
San Francisco Call
Santa Fe Daily New Mexican
Santa Fe New Mexican
Santa Rosa News
Silver City Daily Press
Silver City Daily Press & Independent
Silver City Eagle
Silver City Enterprise
Silver City Independent
Silverton Standard (Colorado)
Socorro Sun
The Southwestern Dispatch
The Spanish-American
The Springer Tribune
The Swastika
Syracuse Herald
Taos Valley News The Taos News

Tiempo
The Trench & Camp
The Trinidad Advertiser (Colorado)
Trinidad Chronicle News (Colorado)
Tucson Daily Citizen
Tucumcari Daily News
Tucumcari News
Tulsa World
Valencia County News Bulletin
Wagon Mound Tribune
Walsenburg Independence (Colorado)
Weekly Ignacio Chieftain (Colorado)
Weekly Register Call (Colorado)
Western Liberal
The Willard Record

Websites

Ancestry.com
Boxrec — Boxrec.com
Cyber Boxing Zone — Cyberboxingzone.com
ESPN — ESPN.com
FightNews — Fightnews.com
Ghost Towns — Ghosttowns.com
Kitchen's Opera House — KitchensOperaHouse.com
New Mexico Boxing — NewMexicoBoxing.com
New Mexico Newspaper Project — http://econtent.
    unm.edu/cdm4/index_NewMexicoNewspapers.
    php
NewspaperArchive.com
WBAN — WomenBoxing.com

Books

Brier, Warren J. The Frightful Punishment: Con Orem
    and Montana's Great Glove Fights of the 1860s. Mis-
    soula: University of Montana Press, 1969.
Dailey, W. R. Henry's Official Western Theatrical
    Guide: 1907–1908. San Francisco: Poster Printers,
    1909.
Donnellon, Matt. The Irish Champion Peter Maher:
    The Untold Story of Ireland's Only World Heavy-
    weight Champion and the Records of the Men He
    Fought. Bloomington: Trafford, 2008.
Gorn, Elliott J. The Manly Art — Bare-Knuckle Prize
    Fighting in America. Ithaca: Cornell University
    Press, 1986.
Isenberg, Michael T. John L. Sullivan and His Amer-
    ica. Urbana: University of Illinois Press, 1994.
Johnson, Jack. My Life and Battles: By Jack Johnson.
    Washington, D.C.: Potomac Books, 2009.
Kent, Graeme. The Great White Hopes: The Quest to
    Defeat Jack Johnson. Stroud: Sutton, 2005.
Lloyd, Alan. The Great Prize Fight. London: Cassell,
    1977.
Mee, Bob. Bare Fists: The History of Bare Knuckle
    Prize Fighting. Woodstock, N.Y.: Overlook Press,
    2001.

Miletech, Leo N. *Dan Stuart's Fistic Carnival.* College Station: Texas A & M University Press, 1994

Nelson, Battling. *Battling Nelson — His Life, Battles and Career.* Hegewisch, Ill., 1908.

Roberts, Randy. *Papa Jack: Jack Johnson and the Era of White Hopes.* New York: Free Press, 1983.

Simmons, Marc. *Albuquerque.* Albuquerque: University of New Mexico Press, 1983.

Stanley, F. *The Grant That Maxwell Bought.* Santa Fe: Sunstone Press, 1958.

State of New Mexico. *Journal of the Senate: Proceedings of the First State Legislature, First Session.* Santa Fe: New Mexico Printing Co., 1913.

Stratton, Porter. *The Territorial Press of New Mexico 1834–1912.* Albuquerque: University of New Mexico Press, 1969.

Ward, Geoffrey C. *Unforgivable Blackness: The Rise and Fall of Jack Johnson.* New York: Vintage, 2006.

Zimmerman, Roger M. *Stories from Kitchen's Opera House.* Albuquerque: Digital 1 Presentations, 2002.

Interviews, Scrapbooks, Clippings and Letters

Frank Chiaramonte, Julio Chiaramonte, Nardine Chiaramonte, Larry Cisneros, John Connolly (relative to Johnny Connolly), Mike Connolly (relative to Johnny Connolly), Meliton Cordoba (Cordova), Armando Cordova (relative to Benny Cordova), Benny Cordova, Jr., Darlene Fajardo (daughter to Buddy Serino), George Marchi, Eddie Mack Quintana, Jr., Joe Roybal, Timo Sanchez, Rosalie Lopez de Spinello (relative to Perfecto Romero), Johnny Tapia, Lalo Trujillo.

Repositories

Bernalillo County Library, Main Branch, Albuquerque

Carnegie Library of Trinidad, Colorado

Center for Southwest Studies at Fort Lewis College, Durango, Colorado

Center for Southwest Research at University of New Mexico, Albuquerque

Library at New Mexico State University, Las Cruces

Lied Library at University of Nevada at Las Vegas

State Records Center and Archives, Santa Fe

University of Texas at El Paso, El Paso

Western New Mexico University Library in Silver City

Zimmerman Library at University of New Mexico, Albuquerque

Index

Numbers in **bold italics** indicate pages with photographs.